A

CLASSIFICATION, ESTIMATION AND PATTERN RECOGNITION

CLASSIFICATION, ESTIMATION AND PATTERN RECOGNITION

TZAY Y. YOUNG
Carnegie-Mellon University

THOMAS W. CALVERT
Simon Fraser University

AMERICAN ELSEVIER PUBLISHING COMPANY, INC.
New York London Amsterdam

AMERICAN ELSEVIER PUBLISHING COMPANY, INC.
52 Vanderbilt Avenue, New York, N.Y. 10017

ELSEVIER PUBLISHING COMPANY
335 Jan Van Galenstraat, P.O. Box 211
Amsterdam, The Netherlands

International Standard Book Number 0-444-00135-2
Library of Congress Card Number 73-1640

Library of Congress Cataloging in Publication Data

Young, Tzay Y 1933-
Classification, estimation, pattern recognition.

Includes bibliographies.
1. Pattern perception. 2. Discriminant analysis.
3. Optical pattern recognition. I. Calvert, Thomas W., joint author. II. Title.
Q327.Y68 621.3819'598 73-1640
ISBN 0-444-00135-2

Manufactured in the United States of America

To Lily and Lorna

Contents

TZAY Y. YOUNG has been a faculty member at Carnegie-Mellon University, Pittsburgh, Pa., since 1964, and is currently an Associate Professor of Electrical Engineering. His experience in the field includes one year as a Member of Technical Staff for Bell Telephone Laboratories, Murray Hill, N.J. A member of IEEE and Sigma Xi, Dr. Young received his B.Sc. in Electrical Engineering from the National Taiwan University, his M.S. in Electrical Engineering from the University of Vermont, and his Ph.D. in Engineering from the Johns Hopkins University. In 1972, he was on sabbatical leave at NASA Goddard Space Flight Center, Greenbelt, Md., working on the processing of radar signals. His research interests include pattern recognition, signal detection and resolution, stochastic estimation algorithms, and computer processing of electrocardiograms.

THOMAS W. CALVERT is Associate Professor of Kinesiology and Computer Science at Simon Fraser University, Burnaby, British Columbia. Before assuming his present post in 1972, Dr. Calvert concurrently held the positions of Associate Professor of Electrical Engineering and Bioengineering, and Chairman of the Biotechnology Program at Carnegie-Mellon University. Between 1960 and 1965, he served successively as lecturer at Western Ontario Institute of Technology, and Instructor of Electrical Engineering at Wayne State University. His industrial experience includes three years as electrical design engineer with an English chemical firm and one year as an instrumentation engineer with Canadair, Ltd., Montreal. Dr. Calvert received his B.Sc. (Eng.) in electrical engineering from University College, London, England, his M.S.E.E. from Wayne State University, and his Ph.D. from Carnegie-Mellon University. He is a member of Sigma Xi, IEEE, AAAS, and the Society for Neuroscience, and is the Associate Editor of the IEEE *Transactions on Computers*, with responsibility for pattern recognition and artificial intelligence.

Preface

This book is primarily intended as a textbook for a graduate course on pattern recognition. Prerequisite to the book is a knowledge of matrices and of the basic concepts of probability and statistics. In many universities, a basic course is offered on random signals and noise, and is often required for graduate students in electrical engineering. The course should be more than sufficient as a prerequisite of this book.

The first six chapters consist of material normally considered as pattern recognition theory. Our emphasis is on the statistical approach with some nonstatistical approaches such as the perceptron discussed in chapter 4. Chapters 7 and 8 deal with applications; one on the computer processing of electrocardiograms and the other on image analysis and character recognition. We hope that by the inclusion of the two applications chapters, we can bridge some of the gaps between the theory and the practice of pattern recognition.

The book probably contains more material than would ordinarily be covered in a one-semester course. For a theoretically oriented class, most of the material in the first six chapters can be covered in a one-semester course, and the two applications chapters may be assigned for reading. For students interested in practical aspects of pattern recognition, the starred sections in the book and most of the material in the chapter on stochastic approximation may be omitted, and the last two chapters should be emphasized. Indeed, the book may be used as a textbook for bioengineering students interested in computer processing of biomedical signals and images. For a two-semester course, it may be necessary to add supplementary material on such topics as recent developments in the linguistic approach, or a more detailed study of image analysis.

It is hoped that the book will be useful as a reference book for research workers. Much of the material in chapters 5, 6, 7, and 8 has never before appeared in book form. The selection of material in these chapters is partly conditioned by the interests of the authors.

The book is based on notes used for a class taught at Carnegie-Mellon University, and we wish to express here our appreciation to the graduate students who suffered through the course.

Tzay Y. Young
Pittsburgh, Pennsylvania

Thomas W. Calvert
Burnaby, British Columbia

1

Introduction

1.1 The Pattern Recognition Problem

Mathematically, pattern recognition is a classification problem. Consider the recognition of characters. We wish to design a system such that a handwritten symbol will be recognized as an "A", a "B", etc. In other words, the machine we design must classify the observed handwritten character into one of 26 classes. The handwritten characters are often ambiguous, and there will be misclassified characters. The major goal in designing a pattern recognition machine is to have a low probability of misclassification.

There are many problems that can be formulated as pattern classification problems. For example, in weather prediction, the weather may be divided into three classes, fair, rain, and possible rain, and the problem is to classify tomorrow's weather into one of these three classes. In the recognition of electrocardiograms, the classes are disease categories plus the class of normal subjects. In binary data transmission, a "one" and a "zero" are represented by signals of amplitudes A_1 and A_0, respectively. The signals are distorted or corrupted by noise when transmitted over communication channels, and the receiver must classify the received signals into "ones" and "zeros." Hence, many of the ideas and principles in pattern recognition may be applied to the design of communication systems and vice versa.

We are interested in pattern recognition by machine. Pattern recognition theory deals with the mathematical aspects common to all pattern recognition problems. To apply the theory to a specific problem, however, requires a thorough understanding of the problem, including its peculiarities and special difficulties.

The input to a pattern recognition machine is a set of N measurements, and the output is the classification. It is convenient to represent the input by an N-dimensional vector $\mathbf{x}$, called a *pattern vector*, with its components

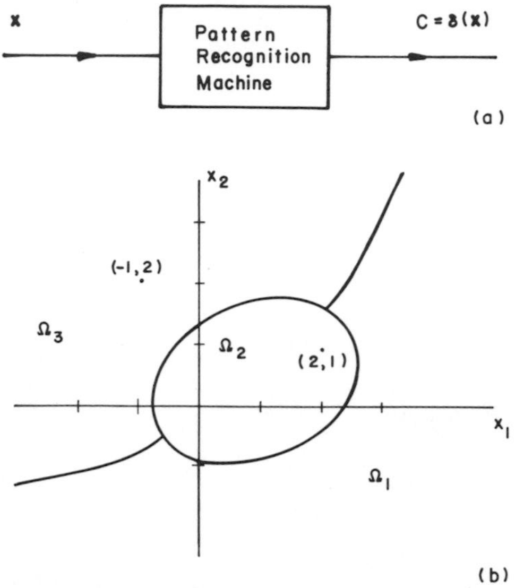

fig. 1.1 Pattern recognition and decision regions.

being the N measurements. The classification at the output depends on the input vector **x**, hence we write

$$C = \delta(\mathbf{x}). \tag{1.1}$$

In other words, the machine must make a decision as to the class to which **x** belongs, and $\delta(\mathbf{x})$ is called a *decision function*. This is shown in figure 1.1(*a*).

Let $\Omega_{\mathbf{x}}$ be the pattern space which is simply the set of all possible values that **x** may assume. For example, let $N = 2$, and assume that the two components of **x**, x_1 and x_2, may be any real number. Then $\Omega_{\mathbf{x}}$ is a two-dimensional Euclidean space as illustrated in figure 1.1(*b*). Suppose there are three classes. A pattern recognition machine will divide $\Omega_{\mathbf{x}}$ into three disjoint *decision regions* Ω_1, Ω_2, and, Ω_3, each corresponding to one class. If a vector $\mathbf{x}^T = [2, 1]$ is observed, $\delta(\mathbf{x}) = C_2$, and **x** is classified as belonging to class 2, since as illustrated in figure 1.1(*b*), **x** falls in the region Ω_2. If the observed pattern vector $\mathbf{x}^T = [-1, 2]$, $\delta(\mathbf{x}) = C_3$ according to the figure. We have used the superscript T in $\mathbf{x}^T$ to denote the transpose of a vector or a matrix.

Thus the design of a pattern recognition machine may be described as finding a rule that divides the pattern space $\Omega_{\mathbf{x}}$ into decision regions. The most important factors that should be considered in the design are the probability of misclassification and the cost of making the classification (i.e., the complexity of the machine and the amount of computation). We note that the decision regions are separated by lines in the two-dimensional case. For the more general case of N-dimensional $\Omega_{\mathbf{x}}$, the decision boundaries are $(N-1)$-dimensional hypersurfaces. The simplest pattern recognition machine uses hyperplanes to separate the decision regions.

The selection of measurements is very important in designing a pattern recognition machine, and is a major factor in its success or failure. There is no general theory on measurement selection because the selection usually depends on the particular pattern recognition problem under consideration. In some problems, the selection of what to measure is fairly simple. In binary data transmission, since the receiver receives signal waveforms, the pattern vector $\mathbf{x}$ simply consists of the amplitudes measured at N different instants. In the recognition of electrocardiograms, we may use either the waveform itself, by taking the values at different instants, or some parameters of the electrocardiogram determined by the experience of physicians. Measurement selection for character recognition is more difficult, and will be discussed in some detail later. Since the values of $\mathbf{x}$ are determined by the measurements, measurement selection defines, in essence, the pattern space $\Omega_{\mathbf{x}}$.

A pattern recognition machine may be divided into two parts, a feature extractor and a classifier, as shown in figure 1.2. The classifier performs the classification, while the feature extractor reduces the dimensionality of input vectors to the classifier. Thus, feature extraction is a linear or nonlinear transformation,

$$\mathbf{y} = \mathcal{T}(\mathbf{x}), \tag{1.2}$$

which transforms a pattern vector $\mathbf{x}$ in the pattern space $\Omega_{\mathbf{x}}$ into a *feature vector* $\mathbf{y}$ in a *feature space* $\Omega_{\mathbf{y}}$. The classifier then classifies $\mathbf{x}$ based on $\mathbf{y}$. Since $\Omega_{\mathbf{y}}$ is of lower dimensionality than $\Omega_{\mathbf{x}}$, the transformation is singular and some information is lost. The feature extractor should reduce the

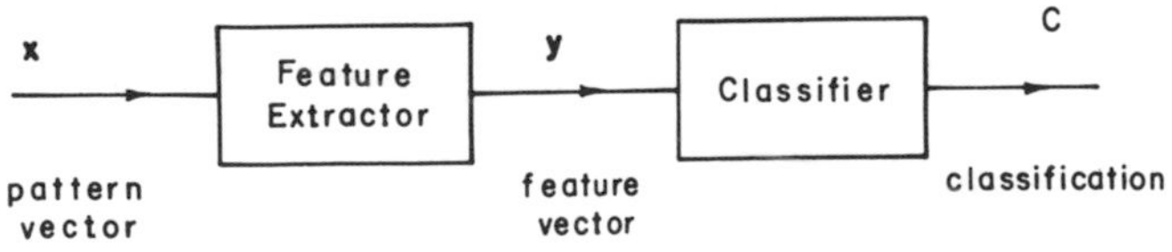

fig. 1.2 Pattern classification and feature extraction.

dimensionality but at the same time maintain a high level of machine performance. A special case of feature extraction is *feature selection* that selects as features a subset of the given measurements.

The division of a pattern recognition machine into feature extractor and classifier is done out of convenience rather than necessity. It is conceivable that the two could be designed in an unified manner using a single performance criterion. When the structure of the machine is very complex and the dimensionality N of the pattern space is high, it is more convenient to design the feature extractor and the classifier separately.

1.2 Pattern Classification and Machine Learning

Pattern vectors may assume various values, and in most interesting pattern recognition problems these values are randomly distributed. A particular pattern vector $\mathbf{x}$ is regarded as a sample of the random vector. To simplify notation, we use $\mathbf{x}$ to denote both the random vector and the sample vector unless we specify otherwise. If the probability distributions of the different classes are known, we may use the statistical theory of classification to design the pattern recognition machine. Such a machine is optimal in terms of probability of misclassification or other related performance criteria.

Usually the probability distributions are unknown or not completely known. Suppose the functional form of the probability distributions is known except for some parameters of the distributions. For example, the pattern vectors may be Gaussian distributed with unknown mean vectors and unknown covariance matrices. Then the general structure of an optimal pattern recognition machine can be determined from the functional form of the distributions. The unknown parameters can be estimated by observing a sequence of random samples, with known or unknown classifications, $\mathbf{x}_1$, $\mathbf{x}_2, \ldots, \mathbf{x}_n$, and letting the machine adapt itself after each observation by modifying its structure continually. As n becomes large, the adaptation leads to a machine of near optimum performance. This is often called machine learning.

The general structure of the machine may be decided by other factors. If we want a machine with simple structure, we may use a linear machine that classifies the pattern vectors using a linear operation. In many cases, the probability distributions are completely unknown, and the general structure must be determined by the subjective judgment of the designer. The designer weighs various factors in deciding the structure, such as the desired performance of the machine, the allowable complexity, and his prior knowledge of the problem, which may or may not be expressed quantitatively.

Once the general structure is decided by the designer, the final form of the machine is determined by the sequence of sample vectors, $\mathbf{x}_1, \mathbf{x}_2, \ldots, \mathbf{x}_n$, which is called the training sequence. The machine modifies its structure automatically without any help from the designer. In a sense, the machine is trained or learns from experience by observing the sequence. This capability of machine learning is the most important and interesting aspect of pattern recognition.

Most schemes of machine learning are recursive. The sample vectors $\mathbf{x}_1, \mathbf{x}_2, \ldots, \mathbf{x}_n$, are observed one at a time, and the machine structure is modified after each observation. They are usually optimal in some sense as n approaches infinity. Thus, a pattern recognition machine operates in two phases, a training or learning phase, and a classification phase. The learning phase should be sufficiently long for the machine to become near optimal.

There are two types of machine learning, supervised and unsupervised. In supervised learning, the classification of each sample of the training sequence, $\mathbf{x}_1, \mathbf{x}_2, \ldots, \mathbf{x}_n$, is known. In other words, during the training phase the machine is told the class to which the sample $\mathbf{x}_i$ belongs, and hence can evaluate its performance at each iteration. This is also called learning with a teacher. In unsupervised learning, or learning without a teacher, the classifications of the training samples are unknown. One approach to unsupervised learning, in fact, is to let the machine classify and learn at the same time. Unsupervised learning is obviously more difficult than supervised learning and would appear impossible at first glance. Investigations in the past decade have shown that properly formulated schemes can give useful results.

1.3 A Pattern Recognition Example

In this section, we use character recognition as an example to illustrate the ideas discussed above. Many fine points of character recognition will be glossed over, since our purpose here is to help our readers to have a better and more concrete understanding of the basic concepts of pattern recognition, rather than of its details. Character recognition will be discussed in some detail in chapter 8.

Consider the handwritten characters shown in figure 1.3(*a*). Each character consists of $15 \times 15 = 225$ black and white squares, and may be represented by a 225-dimensional binary pattern vector $\mathbf{x}$. Let $l = (i - 1) \times 15 + j$; the l-th element of the vector, x_l, equals 0 or 1, depending on whether the square in the i-th row and the j-th column is white or black.

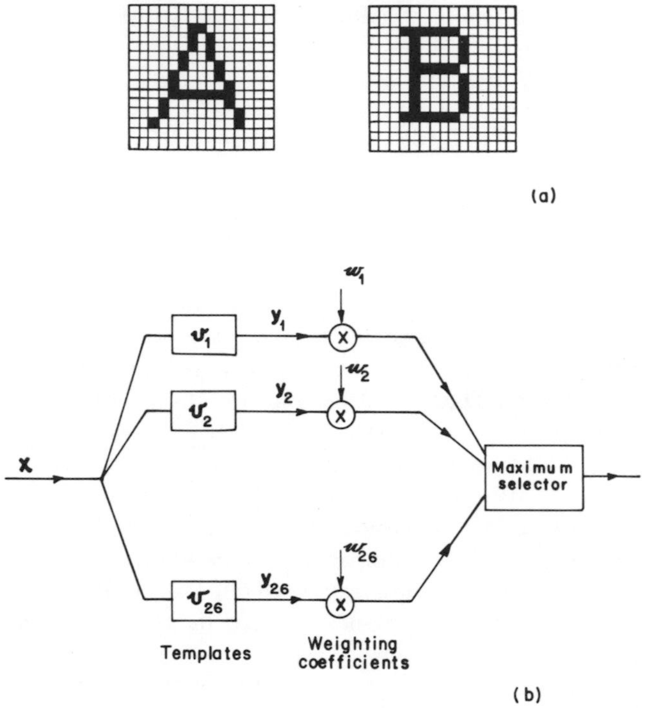

fig. 1.3 Character recognition using template matching.

A commonly used method for character recognition is mask or template matching. A template is simply a standardized letter, and may be represented by a binary vector **v**. The matching of a character **x** to a template **v** is equivalent to taking the product $\mathbf{v}^T\mathbf{x}$. When the two are similar, $\mathbf{v}^T\mathbf{x}$ will have a relatively large value; on the other hand, when they are dissimilar, many of the ones in **x** will be multiplied by zeros in **v** and hence $\mathbf{v}^T\mathbf{x}$ will be small.

Assume that we use one template for each English letter. To match **x** with the 26 templates is equivalent to a linear transformation of **x**,

$$\mathbf{y} = \mathbf{T}\mathbf{x}, \tag{1.3}$$

where **T** is a 26×225 matrix with $\mathbf{T}^T = [\mathbf{v}_1, \mathbf{v}_2, \ldots, \mathbf{v}_{26}]$. Thus, template matching may be regarded as a linear feature extraction scheme. For classification, one may use a simple procedure that assigns the pattern to C_j if y_j has the largest value among the 26 elements of **y**. It is noted that since the 26 templates have different numbers of black squares, each element of $\mathbf{y}$ should be weighted by a weighting coefficient inversely proportional to that number. The block diagram for such a scheme is shown in figure 1.3(*b*). It is interesting to note that the weighting could be included in the linear feature extractor, and the division of the scheme into feature extractor and classifier is, indeed, one of convenience.

There are other ways to specify a pattern vector for character recognition. Fu (1968) uses an 18-dimensional pattern vector, as illustrated in figure 1.4. Each element of $\mathbf{x}$ is a measurement of the distance from the edge of the letter to the edge of the circle along a predetermined path. Note that in this case the values of $\mathbf{x}$ are continuous.

Let us consider for this type of measurement a simple, indeed, naive, classification procedure. Suppose for each class C_k, the mean value $\mathbf{m}_k$ of the pattern vectors is known. When a vector $\mathbf{x}$ is observed, we may calculate the mean-square distances

$$\|\mathbf{x} - \mathbf{m}_k\|^2 = (\mathbf{x} - \mathbf{m}_k)^T(\mathbf{x} - \mathbf{m}_k) \tag{1.4}$$

for all k, and assign $\mathbf{x}$ to C_j if $\|\mathbf{x} - \mathbf{m}_j\|^2$ is minimum. This procedure will perform quite well if the pattern vectors are distributed as in figure 1.5(*a*).

In many cases, the mean values, $\mathbf{m}_k$, are unknown. We may, however, let the machine estimate or learn the mean values from a sequence of training samples with known classifications. Let us assume without loss of generality that the first n samples, $\mathbf{x}_1, \mathbf{x}_2, \ldots, \mathbf{x}_n$, are from C_1. We may then use the sample mean,

$$\boldsymbol{\omega}_1 = \frac{1}{n}\sum_{i=1}^{n} \mathbf{x}_i, \tag{1.5}$$

as an estimate of $\mathbf{m}_1$. Similar estimates can be obtained for other classes. After the training phase, the machine will classify a new observation $\mathbf{x}$ according to (1.4) with $\mathbf{m}_k$ replaced by $\boldsymbol{\omega}_k$.

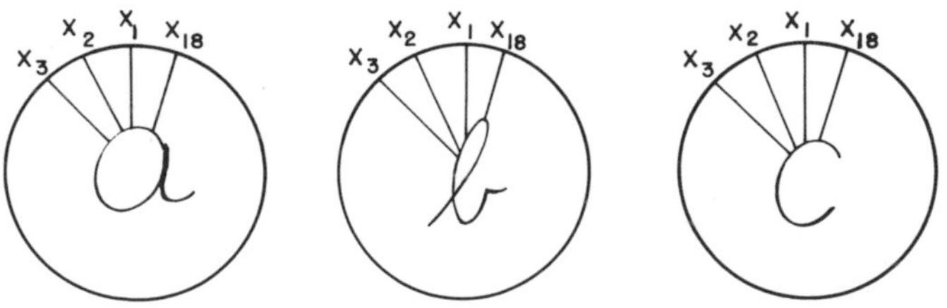

fig. 1.4 Handwritten English letters and measurements (adapted from Fu, 1968).

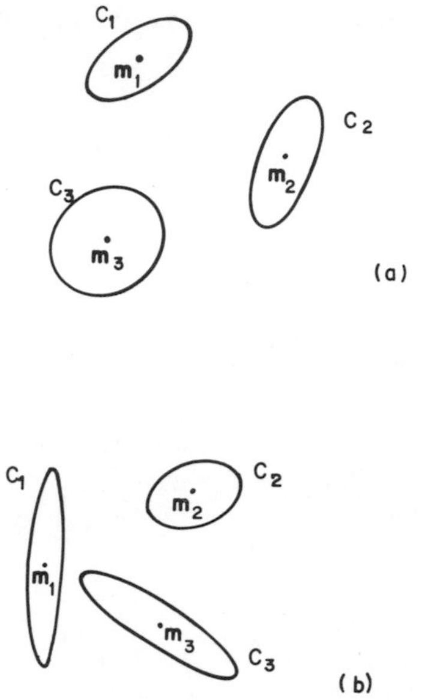

fig. 1.5 Pattern classification using mean values.

It is interesting to note that (1.5) may be written as a recursive equation. Let

$$\omega_1(1) = \mathbf{0}, \quad \omega_1(i+1) = \frac{1}{i}\sum_{l=1}^{i} \mathbf{x}_l .$$

In other words, $\omega_1(i+1)$ is the sample mean based on i samples of C_1. Then,

$$\begin{aligned} \omega_1(i+1) &= \frac{(i-1)}{i}\frac{1}{(i-1)}\sum_{l=1}^{i-1} \mathbf{x}_l + \frac{1}{i}\mathbf{x}_i \\ &= \omega_1(i) + \frac{1}{i}(\mathbf{x}_i - \omega_1(i)). \end{aligned} \tag{1.6}$$

This is in a recursive form, and it is important because the past experience of the machine is summarized in $\omega_1(i)$. The machine adapts itself as each sample arrives, and it is not necessary to store the samples. Since the classifications of the samples are known, this is a supervised learning scheme.

The classification procedure based on (1.4) will not perform well if the pattern vectors are distributed as in figure 1.5(b), where some of the vectors in C_3 are closer to $\mathbf{m}_1$ than to $\mathbf{m}_3$. To remedy this situation, we may weight (1.4) by the inverse of the covariance matrix and use the quadratic form, $(\mathbf{x} - \mathbf{m}_k)^T \mathbf{R}_k^{-1} (\mathbf{x} - \mathbf{m}_k)$. Since like $\mathbf{m}_k$, $\mathbf{R}_k$ is generally unknown, we must use the sample covariance obtained from the training sequence. The computation is more complicated, and we shall not go into details here.

1.4 Organization of the Book

This book consists of eight chapters including the introduction. The next five chapters deal with pattern recognition theory, and the last two chapters treat applications. Some sections and subsections are starred, indicating that they may be omitted in a first reading.

Chapter 2 deals with the classification problem. The probability distribution of pattern vectors of each class is assumed known, and the patterns may be classified optimally by means of hypothesis testing techniques in statistics. The design of an optimal pattern recognition machine depends on the likelihood ratio. In some cases, measurements are costly, and it is desirable to take a small number of measurements during the classification while maintaining a low probability of misclassification. A sequential measurement approach may be used for this purpose.

The next three chapters are concerned with machine learning. Chapter 3 deals primarily with parametric learning, both supervised and unsupervised. The functional form of the probability distributions is known except for some parameters of the distributions. The structure of the pattern recognition machine depends on this functional form, and the machine adapts itself as the parameters are estimated from the training sequence $\mathbf{x}_1$, $\mathbf{x}_2, \ldots,$. The most important learning approach is basically Bayesian. For unsupervised learning, some suboptimal but computationally simple approaches are discussed. Nonparametric approaches that require the storage of all training samples are also presented in this chapter.

After reading chapter 3, the reader may go directly to chapter 4, 5, or 6. In chapter 4, we do not assume any knowledge of probability distributions except the availability of a sequence of training samples with known classifications. Since in this case it is impossible to decide the optimal machine structure, owing to the lack of knowledge of distributions, we choose the simplest structure, a linear machine. A linear machine uses a linear discriminant function $D(\mathbf{x})$. The equation,

$$D(\mathbf{x}) = 0, \tag{1.7}$$

defines a hyperplane that separates the decision regions. This is illustrated

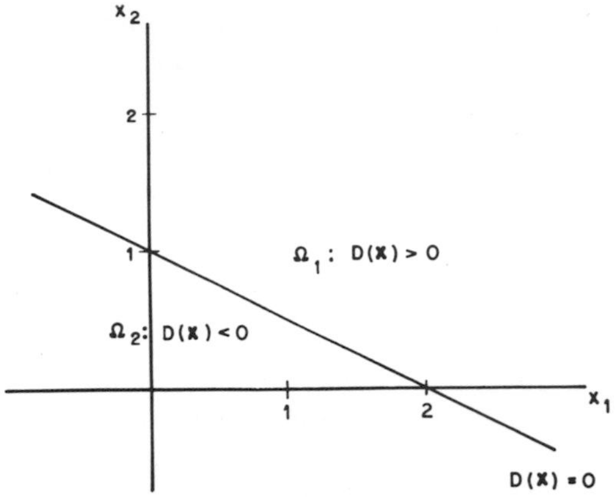

fig. 1.6 A linear discriminant function $D(\mathbf{x}) = x_1 + 2x_2 - 2$.

in figure 1.6. During the classification phase, $\mathbf{x}$ is classified to C_1 or C_2, according to whether or not $D(\mathbf{x}) > 0$, and the structural simplicity in using a linear $D(\mathbf{x})$ is obvious. The training samples allow us to find a linear discrimant function that is optimal in some sense, and recursive algorithms are derived for this purpose. The techniques can easily be generalized to finding quadratic and other nonlinear discriminant functions. Clustering techniques for unsupervised learning are also discussed in this chapter.

The theory of stochastic approximation and its application to pattern recognition are discussed in chapter 5. Stochastic approximation may be regarded as a stochastic equivalent to the gradient method in optimization theory. A stochastic approximation algorithm searches for an optimal solution using random observations which, in our case, are random samples of the training sequence. Algorithms are developed for the estimation of parameters or discriminant functions.

In chapter 6 we discuss the theory of feature extraction. A feature extractor should be designed in such a way that the dimensionality of the feature space is low, and the performance of the machine in terms of error probability is not degraded. The error probability is difficult to evaluate, and other criteria related to error probability are discussed. Linear and nonlinear feature extraction schemes are presented.

Chapter 7 deals with the recognition of electrocardiograms, and chapter 8 is concerned with processing two-dimensional patterns including character recognition. These are two of the most extensively studied pattern recognition problems. Since electrocardiograms and handwritten characters are representatives of one-dimensional and two-dimensional patterns, respectively, some of the techniques developed for them are applicable to other problems. The material also serves the purpose of presenting case studies in the pattern recognition area. It is hoped that by studying special problems, the reader will gain a better perspective and understanding of the theory and practical difficulty of pattern recognition.

References

1. Fu, K. S. 1968. *Sequential Methods in Pattern Recognition and Machine Learning*. Academic Press, New York.
2. Grasselli, A., ed. 1969. *Automatic Interpretation and Classification of Images*. Academic Press, New York.
3. Kanal, L. N., ed. 1968. *Pattern Recognition*. Thompson, Washington, D.C.
4. Meisel, W. S. 1970. *Computer-Oriented Approaches to Pattern Recognition*. Academic Press, New York.
5. Mendel, J. M. and Fu, K. S., eds. 1970. *Adaptive, Learning and Pattern Recognition Systems*. Academic Press, New York.
6. Nilsson, N. J. 1965. *Learning Machines*. McGraw-Hill, New York.
7. Rosenblatt, F. 1961. *Principles of Neurodynamics: Perception and the Theory of Brain Mechanisms*. Spartan Books, Washington, D.C.
8. Rosenfeld, A. 1969. *Picture Processing by Computer*. Academic Press, New York.
9. Sebestyen, G. S. 1962. *Decision-Making Processes in Pattern Recognition*. Macmillan, New York.
10. Tou, J. T. ed. 1967. *Computer and Information Sciences—II*. Academic Press, New York.
11. Tou, J. T. and Wilcox, R. H., eds. 1964. *Computer and Information Sciences*. Spartan Books, Washington, D.C.
12. Watanabe, S., ed. 1969. *Methodologies of Pattern Recognition*. Academic Press, New York.
13. Yovits, M. C., Jacobi, G. T., and Goldstein, G. D., eds. 1962. *Self Organizing Systems 1962*. Spartan Books, Washington, D.C.

2

Statistical Pattern Classification

2.1 Pattern Classification and Hypothesis Testing

The problem of pattern classification may be discussed in the framework of hypothesis testing. Let us consider a simple example. Suppose that we wish to predict a student's success or failure in graduate study based on his GRE (Graduate Record Examination) score. We have two hypotheses—hypothesis H_2, that he will be successful, and hypothesis H_1, that he will fail. Let x be the GRE score, $f_2(x)$ be the conditional probability density of x, given that the student will be successful, and $f_1(x)$ be the conditional density of x, given that he will fail. The density functions $f_1(x)$ and $f_2(x)$ are assumed known from our past experience on this problem. This is a hypothesis testing problem and an obvious decision rule is to accept H_2 and reject H_1 if x is greater than certain threshold value x_0, and accept H_1 and reject H_2 if $x \leqslant x_0$. Note that in this problem it is inevitable that sometimes our prediction will be incorrect, and the best we can do is to choose a decision rule that minimizes the error probability or some related criterion.

For a two-class pattern classification problem, the two hypotheses are H_1, that the pattern vector $\mathbf{x}$ belongs to class C_1, and H_2, that $\mathbf{x}$ belongs to C_2. In statistics, the two hypotheses are often denoted by H_0 and H_1 with H_0 called the null hypothesis and H_1 the alternative hypothesis. We prefer the notation H_1 and H_2 so that the two hypotheses correspond to C_1 and C_2, respectively. When there are more than two classes, H_k is the hypothesis that $\mathbf{x}$ belongs to C_k. A typical example of multiple hypothesis testing is the recognition of English alphabets where $K = 26$.

Throughout this book, we use the convention that in writing a probability density function, say $f(\mathbf{x})$, $\mathbf{x}$ denotes both the random vector and the value it may assume. Thus, $f(\mathbf{x})$ is the probability density of the random vector $\mathbf{x}$, and $f(\boldsymbol{\theta})$ is another density function, the probability density of $\boldsymbol{\theta}$. The functional forms of $f(\mathbf{x})$ and $f(\boldsymbol{\theta})$ are generally not identical.

2.1.1 Bayes classification

Let $\mathbf{x}$ be an N-dimensional pattern vector in the N-dimensional Euclidean space $\Omega_{\mathbf{x}}$, which is called the pattern space. Consider the two-class problem with the hypotheses,

$$\begin{aligned} H_1&: \quad \mathbf{x} \text{ belonging to } C_1, \\ H_2&: \quad \mathbf{x} \text{ belonging to } C_2. \end{aligned} \tag{2.1}$$

Let p be the prior probability that $\mathbf{x}$ belongs to C_1 (i.e., H_1 is true), and

$$\begin{aligned} f_1(\mathbf{x}) &= f(\mathbf{x}|C_1), \\ f_2(\mathbf{x}) &= f(\mathbf{x}|C_2), \end{aligned} \tag{2.2}$$

be the conditional density functions of $\mathbf{x}$ given that $\mathbf{x}$ belongs to C_1 and C_2 respectively. The conditional densities $f_1(\mathbf{x})$ and $f_2(\mathbf{x})$ are often called the *likelihood functions.* The hypothesis testing problem may be interpreted as dividing the pattern space $\Omega_{\mathbf{x}}$ into two disjoint regions, Ω_1 and Ω_2. If the observed sample $\mathbf{x}$ is in Ω_1, we accept the hypothesis H_1 and decide that $\mathbf{x}$ belongs to C_1, and if $\mathbf{x}$ is in Ω_2, we accept H_2. Thus we have a decision function $\delta(\mathbf{x})$ such that $\delta(\mathbf{x}) = C_1$ if $\mathbf{x}$ is in Ω_1 and $\delta(\mathbf{x}) = C_2$ if $\mathbf{x}$ is in Ω_2.

There are obviously many ways to divide $\Omega_{\mathbf{x}}$ into two disjoint regions, and the problem is to find a decision function that is optimal in some sense. We note that in testing the two hypotheses, there are four possible outcomes:

(1) accepting H_1 when H_1 is true;

(2) accepting H_2 when H_1 is true;

(3) accepting H_1 when H_2 is true;

(4) accepting H_2 when H_2 is true.

Two of the four possible outcomes are errors. If we accept H_2 when H_1 is true, i.e., $\delta(\mathbf{x}) = C_2$ when in fact $\mathbf{x}$ belongs to C_1, we commit an *error of the first kind.* On the other hand, if we commit an error by accepting H_1 when H_2 is true, it is an *error of the second kind.* The remaining two possible outcomes are correct decisions. In character recognition, if we wish to distinguish the two classes of handwritten letters "*a*" and "*b*" using a digital computer, and use C_1 and C_2 to denote the classes of "*a*" and "*b*," respectively, the machine commits an error of the first kind when it classifies a pattern vector $\mathbf{x}$ derived from a handwritten letter "*a*" into C_2, the class of "*b*."

Let α be the conditional probability that $\delta(\mathbf{x}) = C_2$ given that H_1 is true, and let β correspond to $\delta(\mathbf{x}) = C_1$ given that H_2 is true. Obviously,

$$\begin{aligned} \alpha &= \int_{\Omega_2} f_1(\mathbf{x})\, d\mathbf{x}, \\ \beta &= \int_{\Omega_1} f_2(\mathbf{x})\, d\mathbf{x}, \end{aligned} \tag{2.3}$$

and α and β are often called, respectively, the probabilities of an error of the first kind and second kind. Given that H_1 is true, the probability of a correct decision is $(1 - \alpha)$, and given that H_2 is true, it is $(1 - \beta)$. We have

$$\begin{aligned} 1 - \alpha &= \int_{\Omega_1} f_1(\mathbf{x})\, dx, \\ 1 - \beta &= \int_{\Omega_2} f_2(\mathbf{x})\, dx. \end{aligned} \tag{2.4}$$

Now if a cost c_1 is assigned to an error of the first kind, and c_2 to an error of the second kind, it is desirable to have a decision rule such that on the average the cost will be as small as possible. Let us denote the average cost per decision by ρ, which is usually called the *risk*. Since the risk involved depends on the prior probability p as well as α and β, we have

$$\begin{aligned} \rho &= c_1 \alpha p + c_2 \beta(1 - p) \\ &= c_1 p \int_{\Omega_2} f_1(\mathbf{x})\, d\mathbf{x} + c_2(1 - p) \int_{\Omega_1} f_2(\mathbf{x})\, d\mathbf{x}. \end{aligned} \tag{2.5}$$

The equation indicates clearly that ρ depends on the decision regions Ω_1 and Ω_2, and a *Bayes classifier* will divide $\Omega_{\mathbf{x}}$ into optimal decision regions in the sense that the risk ρ is minimized.

THEOREM 2.1

Let

$$\Lambda(\mathbf{x}) = \frac{f_2(\mathbf{x})}{f_1(\mathbf{x})} \tag{2.6}$$

be the likelihood ratio, and

$$A = \frac{c_1 p}{c_2(1 - p)}. \tag{2.7}$$

The risk ρ is minimum when the region Ω_1 consists of values of $\mathbf{x}$ for which $\Lambda(\mathbf{x}) \leqslant A$, and the region Ω_2 consists of values of $\mathbf{x}$ for which $\Lambda(\mathbf{x}) > A$.

Proof

Let $\delta(\mathbf{x})$ be the decision function corresponding to the decision rule given above, Ω_1, Ω_2 be the decision regions, and let $\rho(\delta)$ denote the risk. For an arbitrary decision function $\delta'(\mathbf{x})$ with decision regions Ω_1' and Ω_2', the risk is $\rho(\delta')$. Then, according to (2.5), we have

$$\rho(\delta') - \rho(\delta) = c_1 p[\int_{\Omega_2'} f_1(\mathbf{x})\,d\mathbf{x} - \int_{\Omega_2} f_1(\mathbf{x})\,d\mathbf{x}] + c_2(1-p)[\int_{\Omega_1'} f_2(\mathbf{x})\,d\mathbf{x} - \int_{\Omega_1} f_2(\mathbf{x})\,d\mathbf{x}].$$

By examining figure 2.1, we note that the differences between the two regions Ω_2 and Ω_2' are $\Omega_1 \cap \Omega_2'$ and $\Omega_1' \cap \Omega_2$. Hence,

$$\rho(\delta') - \rho(\delta) = c_1 p[\int_{\Omega_1 \cap \Omega_2'} f_1(\mathbf{x})\,d\mathbf{x} - \int_{\Omega_1' \cap \Omega_2} f_1(\mathbf{x})\,d\mathbf{x}] - c_2(1-p)[\int_{\Omega_1 \cap \Omega_2'} f_2(\mathbf{x})\,d\mathbf{x} - \int_{\Omega_1' \cap \Omega_2} f_2(\mathbf{x})\,d\mathbf{x}]. \quad (2.8)$$

Since $c_1 p = c_2(1-p)A$, we obtain

$$\rho(\delta') - \rho(\delta) = c_2(1-p)\{\int_{\Omega_1 \cap \Omega_2'} [Af_1(\mathbf{x}) - f_2(\mathbf{x})]\,d\mathbf{x} + \int_{\Omega_1' \cap \Omega_2} [f_2(\mathbf{x}) - Af_1(\mathbf{x})]\,d\mathbf{x}\}. \quad (2.9)$$

But, according to the assumption of the theorem, when $\mathbf{x}$ is in Ω_1, $\Lambda(\mathbf{x}) \leqslant A$ and

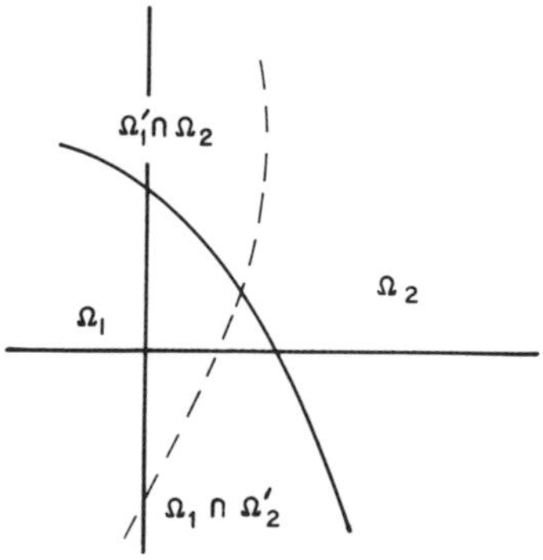

fig. 2.1 The pattern space and decision regions.
——Bayes decision surface,
– – –an arbitrary decision surface that divides the pattern space into Ω_1' and Ω_2'.

$$Af_1(\mathbf{x}) - f_2(\mathbf{x}) \geqslant 0,$$

and when $\mathbf{x}$ is in Ω_2, $\Lambda(\mathbf{x}) > A$ and

$$f_2(\mathbf{x}) - Af_1(\mathbf{x}) > 0.$$

Consequently, the integrands in (2.9) are greater than or equal to zero,

$$\rho(\delta') - \rho(\delta) > 0,$$

and $\rho(\delta)$ is the minimum risk.

The theorem above leads us to a likelihood ratio test. If the likelihood ratio $\Lambda(\mathbf{x}) > A$, we accept H_2, and if $\Lambda(\mathbf{x}) \leqslant A$, we accept H_1. The equation $\Lambda(\mathbf{x}) = A$ defines a *decision surface* that separates the two disjoint decision regions Ω_1 and Ω_2. The costs c_1 and c_2 and the prior probability p have effect on the threshold value A only. Thus the likelihood ratio $\Lambda(\mathbf{x})$ is a fundamental entity for pattern classification, and a Bayes classifier will first calculate $\Lambda(\mathbf{x})$ and then compare it with the threshold value.

It is sometimes more convenient to use the log-likelihood ratio. Since the natural logarithm is a monotonically increasing function, the likelihood ratio test is equivalent to the following decision rule:

$$\begin{aligned} &\text{accept } H_2 \text{ if } \log \Lambda(\mathbf{x}) > \log A, \\ &\text{accept } H_1 \text{ if } \log \Lambda(\mathbf{x}) \leqslant \log A. \end{aligned} \tag{2.10}$$

The minimum risk ρ is called the *Bayes risk*. If $c_1 = c_2 = 1$,

$$\rho = p \int_{\Omega_2} f_1(\mathbf{x})\, d\mathbf{x} + (1 - p) \int_{\Omega_1} f_2(\mathbf{x})\, d\mathbf{x},$$

$$A = \frac{p}{1 - p}.$$

Since in Ω_2, $f_2(\mathbf{x}) > Af_1(\mathbf{x})$, which implies

$$pf_1(\mathbf{x}) < (1 - p) f_2(\mathbf{x}),$$

and likewise in Ω_1,

$$(1 - p) f_2(\mathbf{x}) \leqslant pf_1(\mathbf{x}),$$

the Bayes risk becomes

$$\rho = \int_{\Omega_x} \min[pf_1(\mathbf{x}), (1 - p) f_2(\mathbf{x})]\, d\mathbf{x}, \tag{2.11}$$

which may be called the *Bayes error probability* or *Bayes error rate*.

EXAMPLE 2.1

Let $f_1(x)$ and $f_2(x)$ be one-dimensional Gaussian density functions,

$$\begin{aligned} f_1(x) &= f(x|C_1) = g(x; m_1, r_1), \\ f_2(x) &= f(x|C_2) = g(x; m_2, r_2), \end{aligned} \tag{2.12}$$

where we have used the notation that

$$g(x; m, r) = \frac{1}{\sqrt{2\pi r}} \exp\left[-\frac{(x-m)^2}{2r}\right] \tag{2.13}$$

is the Gaussian density function with mean m and variance r. Then, the likelihood ratio becomes

$$\Lambda(x) = \frac{f_2(x)}{f_1(x)} = \left(\frac{r_1}{r_2}\right)^{1/2} \exp\left[\frac{1}{2r_1}(x-m_1)^2 - \frac{1}{2r_2}(x-m_2)^2\right], \tag{2.14}$$

and when a sample x is observed, the Bayes classifier will calculate $\Lambda(x)$ and compare it with a threshold value $A = c_1 p / c_2(1-p)$.

1 *Equal variance case* Let $r_1 = r_2 = r$ and take the logarithm. We have

$$\log \Lambda(x) = \frac{1}{r}\left[(m_2 - m_1)x - \frac{1}{2}(m_2^2 - m_1^2)\right].$$

Assuming $m_2 > m_1$, we decide that x belongs to C_2 if

$$x > \frac{r \log A}{m_2 - m_1} + \frac{1}{2}(m_2 + m_1); \tag{2.15}$$

otherwise, we decide that x belongs to C_1. The decision regions Ω_1 and Ω_2 are shown in figure 2.2(a).

2 *Equal mean case* In this case, we may assume without loss of generality that $m_1 = m_2 = 0$. We have from (2.14),

$$\log \Lambda(x) = \frac{1}{2} \log \frac{r_1}{r_2} + \frac{1}{2}\left(\frac{1}{r_1} - \frac{1}{r_2}\right)x^2.$$

Assume that $r_2 > r_1$, the Bayes decision rule is then based on the equation

$$x^2 > \frac{2r_1 r_2}{r_2 - r_1}\left(\log A + \frac{1}{2} \log \frac{r_2}{r_1}\right), \tag{2.16}$$

and the decision regions are shown in figure 2.2(b).

2.1.2 Neyman–Pearson Classification

In Bayes classification, the prior probability p and the costs c_1 and c_2 must be known. When we do not have this prior knowledge, we may use the Neyman–Pearson test instead of the Bayes test. We assume that the probability of an error of the first kind α is given, and a Neyman–Pearson classifier will minimize β for the fixed α. In statistics, the fixed α is called the *level of the test*, and $(1 - \beta)$ is called the *power of the test*.

THEOREM 2.2

The Neyman–Pearson classifier that minimizes β for a given value of α is a likelihood ratio test with the threshold A' determined by the equation

$$\int_{A'}^{\infty} h_1(\Lambda)\, d\Lambda = \alpha, \tag{2.17}$$

where $h_1(\Lambda) = h(\Lambda|C_1)$ is the conditional probability of $\Lambda(\mathbf{x})$ given that $\mathbf{x}$ belongs to C_1.

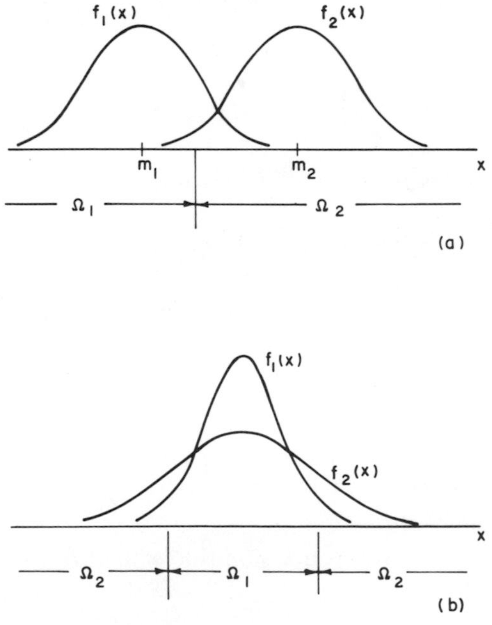

fig. 2.2 One-dimensional Gaussian density functions and decision regions.

Proof

Since α is fixed, we introduce the Lagrange multiplier γ. We wish to minimize

$$\beta + \gamma\alpha = \int_{\Omega_1} f_2(\mathbf{x})\,d\mathbf{x} + \gamma \int_{\Omega_2} f_1(\mathbf{x})\,d\mathbf{x}. \tag{2.18}$$

We note that mathematically (2.18) is quite similar to the Bayes risk,

$$\rho = c_2(1-p)\int_{\Omega_1} f_2(\mathbf{x})\,d\mathbf{x} + c_1 p \int_{\Omega_2} f_1(\mathbf{x})\,d\mathbf{x}, \tag{2.19}$$

and in fact if we let $p = 1/2$, $c_1 = 2\gamma$ and $c_2 = 2$, (2.18) and (2.19) become identical. Hence, by theorem 2.1, the optimal classifier that minimizes (2.18) is the likelihood ratio test $\Lambda(\mathbf{x}) = f_2(\mathbf{x})/f_1(\mathbf{x})$ with the threshold

$$\frac{c_1 p}{c_2(1-p)} = \gamma.$$

The next step is to evaluate the Lagrange multiplier γ by means of the constraint equation

$$\alpha = \int_{\Omega_2} f_1(\mathbf{x})\,d\mathbf{x}. \tag{2.20}$$

We note that $\Lambda(\mathbf{x})$ is a random variable depending on the random vector $\mathbf{x}$, hence we may define a conditional density $h_1(\Lambda) = h(\Lambda|C_1)$. Since $\Lambda(\mathbf{x}) > \gamma$ when $\mathbf{x}$ is in Ω_2 and $\Lambda(\mathbf{x}) \leqslant \gamma$ when $\mathbf{x}$ is in Ω_1, (2.20) may be written as

$$\alpha = \int_{\Omega_2} f_1(\mathbf{x})\,d\mathbf{x} = \int_{\gamma}^{\infty} h_1(\Lambda)\,d\Lambda.$$

Hence the theorem is proved by setting $\gamma = A'$.

Thus the Neyman–Pearson classifier is a likelihood ratio test, which differs from the Bayes classifier only in the manner of evaluating the threshold values. The power of the test may be obtained by

$$1 - \beta = \int_{\Omega_2} f_2(\mathbf{x})\,d\mathbf{x} = \int_{\gamma}^{\infty} h_2(\Lambda)\,d\Lambda, \tag{2.21}$$

where $h_2(\Lambda) = h(\Lambda|C_2)$. The following simple examples illustrate the determination of the threshold and the power of the test.

EXAMPLE 2.2

Let $f_1(x)$ and $f_2(x)$ be two Gaussian density functions with equal variance r and mean values m_1 and m_2 respectively. As shown in example 2.1, the likelihood ratio test is equivalent to that specified in (2.15). Since we wish to use the Neyman–Pearson test, A in (2.15) should be replaced by A'. Assume that $m_2 > m_1$ and let

$$x_0 = \frac{r \log A'}{m_2 - m_1} + \frac{1}{2}(m_2 + m_1).$$

Then the test depends on whether $x > x_0$, and hence instead of $h_1(\Lambda)$ and $h_2(\Lambda)$, we may simply use $f_1(x)$ and $f_2(x)$ in calculating α and β. Thus,

$$\begin{aligned}\alpha &= \int_{x_0}^{\infty} f_1(x)\,dx = \int_{x_0}^{\infty} g(x; m_1, r)\,dx \\ &= \frac{1}{\sqrt{2\pi r}} \int_{x_0}^{\infty} e^{-(x-m_1)^2/2r}\,dx \\ &= 1 - G\left(\frac{x_0 - m_1}{\sqrt{2r}}\right),\end{aligned}$$

where $G(x_0)$ is the normalized Gaussian distribution function

$$G(x_0) = \int_{-\infty}^{x_0} g(x; 0, 1)\,dx. \tag{2.22}$$

The level of the test α may also be expressed in terms of the error function

$$\alpha = \frac{1}{2} - \frac{1}{2}\,\mathrm{erf}\left(\frac{x_0 - m_1}{\sqrt{2r}}\right),$$

where

$$\mathrm{erf}(x_0) = \frac{2}{\sqrt{\pi}} \int_0^{x_0} e^{-x^2}\,dx. \tag{2.23}$$

Since the error function is tabulated in many integral tables, we can find the threshold value x_0 by

$$x_0 = m_1 + \sqrt{2r}\,\mathrm{erf}^{-1}(1 - 2\alpha).$$

The power of the test becomes

$$1 - \beta = \int_{x_0}^{\infty} g(x; m_2, r)\,dx = \frac{1}{2} - \frac{1}{2}\,\mathrm{erf}\left(\frac{x_0 - m_2}{\sqrt{2r}}\right).$$

The calculation of α and $(1 - \beta)$ is represented by the shaded areas in figure 2.3(a). Performance curves relating α, $(1 - \beta)$, and $(m_2 - m_1)/\sqrt{r}$ may be found in many signal detection books.

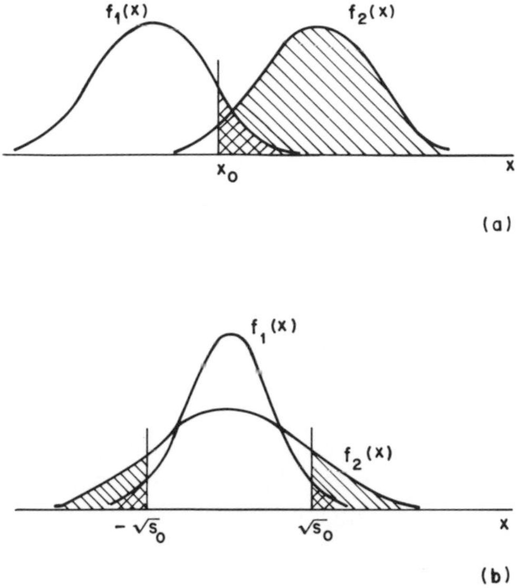

fig. 2.3 The calculation of α and $(1-\beta)$.

EXAMPLE 2.3

Assume that $f_1(x)$ and $f_2(x)$ are Gaussian densities with mean zero and variance r_1 and r_2, $r_1 < r_2$. Let $s = x^2$ and

$$s_0 = \frac{2r_1 r_2}{r_2 - r_1} \log A' + \frac{1}{2} \log \frac{r_2}{r_1}.$$

Then, according to (2.16), the classification is based on s; if $s > s_0$ we accept H_2 and if $s \leqslant s_0$ we accept H_1 (figure 2.3(*b*)). Now

$$\begin{aligned}\alpha &= P\{s > s_0 | x \in C_1\} = P\{|x| > \sqrt{s_0}\ |x \in C_1\} \\ &= \frac{1}{\sqrt{2\pi r_1}} \int_{-\infty}^{-\sqrt{s_0}} e^{-x^2/2r_1}\, dx + \frac{1}{\sqrt{2\pi r_1}} \int_{\sqrt{s_0}}^{\infty} e^{-x^2/2r_1}\, dx \\ &= 1 - \operatorname{erf}\left(\frac{\sqrt{s_0}}{2r_1}\right),\end{aligned}$$

and hence the threshold s_0 is calculated by the relationship

$$s_0 = 2r_1[\mathrm{erf}^{-1}(1 - \alpha)].$$

The power of the test becomes

$$1 - \beta = 1 - \mathrm{erf}\left(\frac{\sqrt{s_0}}{2r_2}\right).$$

Note that in neither example is it necessary to find A'.

2.1.3 *Multiple hypotheses and multiple observations*

The Bayes classification discussed earlier is a binary hypothesis test where we had two hypotheses only. When there are more than two classes, C_k, $k = 1, 2, \ldots, K$, we have a multiple hypothesis test, each hypothesis corresponding to one class. Thus we have

$$H_k\colon \mathbf{x} \text{ belonging to } C_k, \quad k = 1, 2, \ldots, K. \tag{2.24}$$

The problem is to divide the pattern space $\Omega_{\mathbf{x}}$ into K disjoint decision regions, $\Omega_1, \Omega_2, \ldots, \Omega_K$.

Let p_k be the prior probability that $\mathbf{x}$ belongs to C_k, and $f_k(\mathbf{x}) = f(\mathbf{x}|C_k)$ be the conditional density function or the likelihood function. We assume that the costs of an error of different kinds are identical, and set the cost $c = 1$. Then the risk associated with an arbitrary decision function $\delta'(\mathbf{x})$ and decision regions $\Omega'_1, \Omega'_2 \cdots, \Omega'_K$,

$$\rho(\delta') = \sum_{k=1}^{K} \int_{\Omega'_k} [\sum_{l \neq k} p_l f_l(\mathbf{x})]\, d\mathbf{x} \tag{2.25}$$

is in fact the error probability. The Bayes classifier that minimizes ρ will divide $\Omega_{\mathbf{x}}$ into K disjoint regions with each region Ω_j consisting of values of $\mathbf{x}$ such that

$$p_j f_j(\mathbf{x}) \geqslant p_k f_k(\mathbf{x}) \qquad \text{for all } k \neq j. \tag{2.26}$$

To prove the statement above, it is noted that in Ω_j, (2.26) may be written as

$$\sum_{l \neq j} p_l f_l(\mathbf{x}) \leqslant \sum_{l \neq k} p_l f_l(\mathbf{x}) \qquad \text{for all } k \neq j. \tag{2.27}$$

Let $\delta(\mathbf{x})$ be the decision function corresponding to the Bayes classifier, the error probability becomes, according to (2.27),

$$\rho(\delta) = \sum_{j=1}^{K} \int_{\Omega_j} [\sum_{l \neq j} p_l f_l(\mathbf{x})] \, d\mathbf{x} = \int_{\Omega_{\mathbf{x}}} \min_k [\sum_{l \neq k} p_l f_l(\mathbf{x})] \, d\mathbf{x}. \tag{2.28}$$

This equation reduces to (2.11) when $K = 2$. A comparison of (2.25) and (2.28) shows that the Bayes error probability in (2.28) is minimal, since the integrand is minimum for every value of $\mathbf{x}$.

Figure 2.4 illustrates the implementation of the Bayes classifier. When a pattern vector $\mathbf{x}$ is observed, we first calculate the likelihood function $f_k(\mathbf{x})$, multiply it by the prior probability p_k, select the one with the largest value and decide that $\mathbf{x}$ belongs to the class corresponding to the maximum $p_k f_k(\mathbf{x})$. It is interesting to note that by Bayes' rule,

$$p_k f_k(\mathbf{x}) = f(\mathbf{x}|C_k) P(C_k) = P(C_k|\mathbf{x}) f(\mathbf{x}), \tag{2.29}$$

where

$$f(\mathbf{x}) = \sum_{k=1}^{K} p_k f_k(\mathbf{x}) \tag{2.30}$$

is the probability density of $\mathbf{x}$, and is often called a mixture of density functions. It is obvious from (2.29) that comparison of $p_k f_k(\mathbf{x})$ for different k is equivalent to comparing the posterior probability $P(C_k|\mathbf{x})$. Thus, for equal cost, the Bayes classifier is essentially a maximum posterior probability classifier.

Another variation of the basic classification scheme is classification by multiple observations. Assume that a sequence of pattern vectors $\mathbf{x}_1$, $\mathbf{x}_2$, ..., $\mathbf{x}_n$ is observed, and further, all the vectors in the sequence come from the same class, either C_1 or C_2. Thus the two hypotheses are

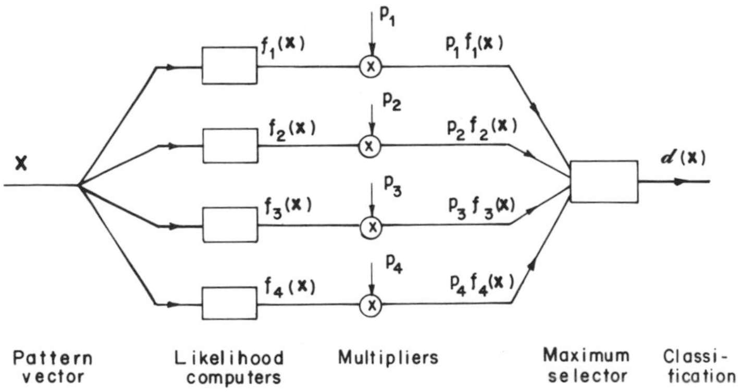

fig. 2.4 Implementation of the Bayes classifier.

$$\begin{aligned} &H_1: \mathbf{x}_i \text{ belonging to } C_1, \ i = 1, 2, \ldots, n, \\ &H_2: \mathbf{x}_i \text{ belonging to } C_2, \ i = 1, 2, \ldots, n. \end{aligned} \tag{2.31}$$

It is obvious that we should use the likelihood ratio test

$$\Lambda_n = \Lambda(\mathbf{x}_1, \mathbf{x}_2, \ldots, \mathbf{x}_n) = \frac{f_2(\mathbf{x}_1, \mathbf{x}_2, \ldots, \mathbf{x}_n)}{f_1(\mathbf{x}_1, \mathbf{x}_2, \ldots, \mathbf{x}_n)}, \tag{2.32}$$

where $f_k(\mathbf{x}_1, \mathbf{x}_2, \ldots, \mathbf{x}_n)$ is the likelihood function of the sequence given that $\mathbf{x}_i \in C_k$, $i = 1, 2, \ldots, n$. Since the samples are observed randomly, it is reasonable to assume that $\mathbf{x}_1, \mathbf{x}_2, \ldots, \mathbf{x}_n$ are independent and identically distributed, i.e.,

$$f_k(\mathbf{x}_1, \mathbf{x}_2, \ldots, \mathbf{x}_n) = \prod_{i=1}^{n} f_k(\mathbf{x}_i), \ k = 1, 2. \tag{2.33}$$

We note that the members of the finite sequence $\mathbf{x}_1, \mathbf{x}_2, \ldots, \mathbf{x}_n$, belong to the same class, either C_1 or C_2. When they belong to C_1, the random samples are all distributed according to $f(\mathbf{x}_i|C_1) = f_1(\mathbf{x}_i)$, and the independence should be in terms of the conditional densities as in (2.33) with $k = 1$. The situation for C_2 is similar, and this type of independence is sometimes called *conditional independence*. We shall use the terms independence and conditional independence interchangeably when there is no risk of confusion.

The likelihood ratio under the above assumption becomes

$$\Lambda_n = \prod_{i=1}^{n} \lambda_i, \tag{2.34}$$

with

$$\lambda_i = \frac{f_2(\mathbf{x}_i)}{f_1(\mathbf{x}_i)}. \tag{2.35}$$

Sometimes it is more convenient to use the log-likelihood ratio,

$$\log \Lambda_n = \sum_{i=1}^{n} \log \lambda_i = \sum_{i=1}^{n} [\log f_2(\mathbf{x}_i) - \log f_1(\mathbf{x}_i)]. \tag{2.36}$$

2.2 Classification of Gaussian Patterns

In this section we assume that each $f_k(\mathbf{x})$ is an N-dimensional Gaussian density function with mean vector $\mathbf{m}_k$ and covariance matrix $\mathbf{R}_k$,

$$f_k(\mathbf{x}) = g(\mathbf{x}; \mathbf{m}_k, \mathbf{R}_k)$$
$$= (2\pi)^{-N/2}|\mathbf{R}_k|^{-1/2}\exp[-\tfrac{1}{2}(\mathbf{x} - \mathbf{m}_k)^T\mathbf{R}_k^{-1}(\mathbf{x} - \mathbf{m}_k)], \qquad (2.37)$$

where $\mathbf{R}_k^{-1}$ exists, $|\mathbf{R}_k|$ is the determinant of the matrix $\mathbf{R}_k$, and the superscript T denotes the transpose of a vector or a matrix.

The Gaussian density function is of particular importance in many areas. It is completely determined by the mean vector and the covariance matrix. In some pattern classification problems, the only knowledge we have is the mean and the covariance. When it is expected that the density function is essentially unimodal, unless there is additional knowledge we might as well approximate the unknown density function by the Gaussian density of the same mean and the same covariance.

2.2.1 Bayes classification of Gaussian patterns

Assuming equal costs, we decide that an observed sample vector $\mathbf{x}$ belongs to C_j if

$$p_j f_j(\mathbf{x}) \geqslant p_k f_k(\mathbf{x}) \qquad \text{for all } k \neq j. \qquad (2.38)$$

Since the logarithm is a monotonically increasing function, let

$$D_k(\mathbf{x}) = \log p_k - \tfrac{1}{2}\log|\mathbf{R}_k| - \tfrac{1}{2}(\mathbf{x} - \mathbf{m}_k)^T\mathbf{R}_k^{-1}(\mathbf{x} - \mathbf{m}_k), \qquad (2.39)$$

and it is obvious from (2.37) and (2.39) that the decision rule in (2.38) is equivalent to

$$D_j(\mathbf{x}) - D_k(\mathbf{x}) \geqslant 0 \qquad \text{for all } k \neq j. \qquad (2.40)$$

We shall call $D_k(\mathbf{x})$, $k = 1, 2 \cdots, K$, *discriminant functions*. It is noted that there are many different ways to choose discriminant functions. For example, $\log D_k(\mathbf{x})$ may also be regarded as a discriminant function since

$$\log D_j(\mathbf{x}) - \log D_k(\mathbf{x}) \geqslant 0 \qquad \text{for all } k \neq j,$$

is obviously equivalent to (2.40). Usually we choose the discriminant function with the simplest form.

The equation,

$$D_j(\mathbf{x}) - D_k(\mathbf{x}) = 0, \qquad (2.41)$$

defines a decision surface. A substitution of $D_j(\mathbf{x})$ and $D_k(\mathbf{x})$ by (2.39) yields

$$\mathbf{x}^T(\mathbf{R}_j^{-1} - \mathbf{R}_k^{-1})\mathbf{x} - 2\mathbf{x}^T(\mathbf{R}_j^{-1}\mathbf{m}_j - \mathbf{R}_k^{-1}\mathbf{m}_k) + \left(\mathbf{m}_j\mathbf{R}_j^{-1}\mathbf{m}_j - \mathbf{m}_k\mathbf{R}_k^{-1}\mathbf{m}_k + \log\left|\frac{\mathbf{R}_j}{\mathbf{R}_k}\right| - 2\log\frac{p_j}{p_k}\right) = 0, \quad (2.42)$$

which defines a quadratic surface. When the matrix $(\mathbf{R}_j^{-1} - \mathbf{R}_k^{-1})$ or its negative is positive definite, the decision surface becomes a hyperellipsoid. If $\mathbf{R}_j^{-1} = \mathbf{R}_k^{-1}$, it reduces to a hyperplane.

When there are only two classes, we define

$$D(\mathbf{x}) = D_1(\mathbf{x}) - D_2(\mathbf{x}), \quad (2.43)$$

and in this case it is customary to call $D(\mathbf{x})$ the discriminant function. The equation $D(\mathbf{x}) = 0$ defines the decision surface. For an observed vector $\mathbf{x}$, if $D(\mathbf{x}) < 0$ we decide $\mathbf{x} \in C_2$, otherwise, $\mathbf{x} \in C_1$.

2.2.2 Equal covariance matrices

Assume two classes with $\mathbf{R}_1 = \mathbf{R}_2 = \mathbf{R}$ and $p_1 = p_2 = 1/2$. Then, according to (2.39) and (2.43),

$$-D(\mathbf{x}) = \mathbf{x}^T\mathbf{R}^{-1}(\mathbf{m}_2 - \mathbf{m}_1) - \frac{1}{2}(\mathbf{m}_2^T\mathbf{R}^{-1}\mathbf{m}_2 - \mathbf{m}_1^T\mathbf{R}^{-1}\mathbf{m}_1). \quad (2.44)$$

$D(\mathbf{x})$ is a linear discriminant function, and the decision surface is a hyperplane. A function of the random vector $\mathbf{x}$ is often called a statistic. If we define a statistic,

$$s = \mathbf{x}^T\mathbf{R}^{-1}(\mathbf{m}_2 - \mathbf{m}_1), \quad (2.45)$$

and let

$$s_0 = \frac{1}{2}(\mathbf{m}_2^T\mathbf{R}^{-1}\mathbf{m}_2 - \mathbf{m}_1^T\mathbf{R}^{-1}\mathbf{m}_1), \quad (2.46)$$

the classification will be based on whether $s < s_0$.

We wish to calculate α, β, and the Bayes error probability ρ. Given that $\mathbf{x} \in C_1$, we have

$$E[s|C_1] = \int_{\Omega_\mathbf{x}} \mathbf{x}^T\mathbf{R}^{-1}(\mathbf{m}_2 - \mathbf{m}_1)f_1(\mathbf{x})\,d\mathbf{x} = \mathbf{m}_1^T\mathbf{R}^{-1}(\mathbf{m}_2 - \mathbf{m}_1),$$

$$E[s^2|C_1] = \int_{\Omega_\mathbf{x}} (\mathbf{m}_2 - \mathbf{m}_1)^T\mathbf{R}^{-1}\mathbf{x}\mathbf{x}^T\mathbf{R}^{-1}(\mathbf{m}_2 - \mathbf{m}_1)f_1(\mathbf{x})\,d\mathbf{x}$$
$$= (\mathbf{m}_2 - \mathbf{m}_1)^T\mathbf{R}^{-1}(\mathbf{R} + \mathbf{m}_1\mathbf{m}_1^T)\mathbf{R}^{-1}(\mathbf{m}_2 - \mathbf{m}_1),$$

where $E[\cdot|\cdot]$ denotes the conditional expectation. The variance is

$$\mathrm{Var}\,[s|C_1] = E[s^2|C_1] - \{E[s|C_1]\}^2 = (\mathbf{m}_2 - \mathbf{m}_1)^T\mathbf{R}^{-1}(\mathbf{m}_2 - \mathbf{m}_1).$$

Similarly,

$$E[s|C_2] = \mathbf{m}_2^T\mathbf{R}^{-1}(\mathbf{m}_2 - \mathbf{m}_1),$$
$$\mathrm{Var}\,[s|C_2] = \mathrm{Var}\,[s|C_1].$$

We may define a measure of separation

$$d^2 = \frac{\{E[s|C_2] - E[s|C_1]\}^2}{\mathrm{Var}\,[s|C_1]} = (\mathbf{m}_2 - \mathbf{m}_1)^T\mathbf{R}^{-1}(\mathbf{m}_2 - \mathbf{m}_1), \qquad (2.47)$$

which is often called the "signal-to-noise ratio" in signal detection theory.

Since s is a linear combination of the components of the Gaussian random vector **x**, it is Gaussian distributed with density function

$$h_1(s) = h(s|C_1) = g(s; \mathbf{m}_1^T\mathbf{R}^{-1}(\mathbf{m}_2 - \mathbf{m}_1), d^2). \qquad (2.48)$$

The probability of an error of the first kind is

$$\alpha = \int_{s_0}^{\infty} h_1(s)\,ds = \frac{1}{2} - \frac{1}{2}\,\mathrm{erf}\left(\frac{s_0 - \mathbf{m}_1^T\mathbf{R}^{-1}(\mathbf{m}_2 - \mathbf{m}_1)}{\sqrt{2}\,d}\right)$$
$$= \frac{1}{2} - \frac{1}{2}\,\mathrm{erf}\left(\frac{d}{\sqrt{8}}\right).$$

It is obvious that with equal costs and $p_1 = p_2 = 1/2$,

$$\rho = \frac{1}{2}(\alpha + \beta) = \alpha = \frac{1}{2} - \frac{1}{2}\,\mathrm{erf}\left(\frac{d}{\sqrt{8}}\right). \qquad (2.49)$$

The Bayes error probability is a monotonically decreasing function of d^2, hence d^2 is a meaningful measure of the separation of the two classes.

A special case of considerable importance is that **R** is an identity matrix. The following example illustrates this case.

EXAMPLE 2.4

Consider a binary communication scheme described below. A message "one" is represented by transmitting a signal $m(t)$, and a message "zero" is represented by transmitting no signal. The received signal is corrupted by additive Gaussian noise $n(t)$. Thus we have at the receiver either $x(t) = m(t) + n(t)$ or $x(t) = n(t)$, and the problem is to decide whether the former or the latter is true. Assuming that observations are made at discrete instants $t_1, t_2, \ldots, t_n$; we may write

$$\mathbf{m}^T = [m(t_1), m(t_2), \ldots, m(t_n)],$$
$$\mathbf{n}^T = [n(t_1), n(t_2), \ldots, n(t_n)],$$
$$\mathbf{x}^T = [x(t_1), x(t_2), \ldots, x(t_n)].$$

The noise at different instants, $n(t_1), n(t_2), \ldots, n(t_n)$, is represented by independent Gaussian random variables with zero mean and unit variance, i.e.,

$$f(\mathbf{n}) = g(\mathbf{n}; \mathbf{0}, \mathbf{I}), \tag{2.50}$$

where **I** is the identity matrix.

The two hypotheses are

$$\begin{aligned} H_1&: \mathbf{x} = \mathbf{n}, \\ H_2&: \mathbf{x} = \mathbf{m} + \mathbf{n}. \end{aligned} \tag{2.51}$$

Clearly, under the hypothesis H_1, $\mathbf{x}$ is distributed in the same way as $\mathbf{n}$. Under H_2, the situation is similar except that the mean value of $\mathbf{x}$ is shifted by the amount $\mathbf{m}$. Hence,

$$f_1(\mathbf{x}) = g(\mathbf{x}; \mathbf{0}, \mathbf{I}),$$
$$f_2(\mathbf{x}) = g(\mathbf{x}; \mathbf{m}, \mathbf{I}),$$

and according to (2.45), we calculate

$$s = \mathbf{x}^T\mathbf{m}, \tag{2.52}$$

and compare it with a certain threshold.

The vector $\mathbf{m}$ in (2.52) represents an operation on the received $\mathbf{x}$, and it also represents the signal waveform. For this reason, it is called the matched filter, matched to the transmitted signal waveform. When $\mathbf{m}_1$ is not zero, $s = \mathbf{x}^T(\mathbf{m}_2 - \mathbf{m}_1)$, and the vector $(\mathbf{m}_2 - \mathbf{m}_1)$ may be regarded as a matched filter. In character recognition, templates are often used for processing data, and templates are essentially matched filters.

2.3 Sequential Classification*

In section 2.1 we discussed briefly classification by multiple observations where a sequence of samples $\mathbf{x}_1, \mathbf{x}_2, \ldots, \mathbf{x}_n$ came from the same class, either C_1 or C_2. The samples are independent and identically distributed, and the likelihood function is

$$\Lambda_n = \frac{f_2(\mathbf{x}_1, \mathbf{x}_2, \ldots, \mathbf{x}_n)}{f_1(\mathbf{x}_1, \mathbf{x}_2, \ldots, \mathbf{x}_n)} = \prod_{i=1}^{n} \frac{f_2(\mathbf{x}_i)}{f_1(\mathbf{x}_i)} = \prod_{i=1}^{n} \lambda_i .$$

The sample size, n, is fixed in this case.

Now suppose that a sequence of pattern vectors $\mathbf{x}_1, \mathbf{x}_2, \ldots$ is observed, one at a time, and the two hypotheses are tested after each observation. In addition to the cost of classification errors, there is also an observation cost. Thus, we may wish to terminate the test after n observations, since additional observations may reduce the error probability only slightly while incurring additional observation cost. Hence, it is desirable to have a procedure that not only tests the two hypotheses at each stage but also permits a decision as to whether or not additional observations should be taken. Such a procedure is called the *sequential probability ratio test*. The termination of the test depends on the previous observations, and hence n, the sample size required in a particular test, is a random variable.

2.3.1 Sequential probability ratio test (SPRT)

The SPRT was introduced and studied extensively by Wald (1947). Let $\mathbf{x}_1, \mathbf{x}_2 \cdots$ be a sequence of sample vectors belonging to the same class, either C_1 or C_2. The samples are mutually independent and identically distributed with either $f_1(\mathbf{x})$ or $f_2(\mathbf{x})$. At the l-th stage, the likelihood ratio is

$$\Lambda_l(\mathbf{x}_1, \mathbf{x}_2, \ldots, \mathbf{x}_l) = \prod_{i=1}^{l} \frac{f_2(\mathbf{x}_i)}{f_1(\mathbf{x}_i)} = \prod_{i=1}^{l} \lambda_i . \tag{2.53}$$

Let A and B be two threshold values, $B < A$. Wald's SPRT uses the following decision rule:

---

* Section may be omitted on first reading.

$$
\begin{aligned}
&\text{if } \Lambda_l \geqslant A, \text{ accept } H_2 \text{ and terminate the test,}\\
&\text{if } \Lambda_l \leqslant B, \text{ accept } H_1 \text{ and terminate the test,}\\
&\text{if } B < \Lambda_l < A,\\
&\qquad\qquad \text{take } (l+1)\text{-th observation and continue the test.}
\end{aligned} \tag{2.54}
$$

Assume that the test is terminated at the n-th stage, then

$$
\begin{aligned}
&B < \Lambda_l < A, l = 1, 2, \ldots, (n-1),\\
&\Lambda_n \leqslant B \quad \text{or} \quad \Lambda_n \geqslant A,
\end{aligned} \tag{2.55}
$$

where n is a random variable.

We wish to derive a relationship between the thresholds, A and B, and the probability of misclassifications. Let $\Omega_{\mathbf{x}}$ be the N-dimensional pattern space, and

$$
\Omega_{\mathbf{x}}^n = \Omega_{\mathbf{x}} \times \Omega_{\mathbf{x}} \cdots \times \Omega_{\mathbf{x}}
$$

be the $n \times N$-dimensional product space. Ω_1^n and Ω_2^n are two decision regions of $\Omega_{\mathbf{x}}^n$ corresponding to accepting H_1 and H_2 respectively. The decision regions are depicted in figure 2.5(a). The probabilities of an error of the first kind and the second kind are denoted by α and β respectively. Now assume that upon the termination at the n-th stage, hypothesis H_2 is accepted. We have

$$
\Lambda_n(\mathbf{x}_1, \mathbf{x}_2, \ldots, \mathbf{x}_n) = \frac{f_2(\mathbf{x}_1, \mathbf{x}_2, \ldots, \mathbf{x}_n)}{f_1(\mathbf{x}_1, \mathbf{x}_2, \ldots, \mathbf{x}_n)} \geqslant A. \tag{2.56}
$$

Figure 2.5(b) shows a typical test result. If instead of Λ_n we had $\Lambda(t) = \Lambda(\mathbf{x}(\tau), 0 \leqslant \tau \leqslant t)$, a continuous function of time, then the test would terminate when $\Lambda(t) = A$ or B. That $\Lambda_n \geqslant A$ in (2.56) is due to the discrete n. But as depicted in figure 2.5(b), since $B < \Lambda_{n-1} < A$, the excess over the boundary, $\Lambda_n - A$ or $B - \Lambda_n$, is usually very small. Thus, under this simplifying assumption, (2.56) becomes, approximately,

$$
\Lambda_n = \frac{f_2(\mathbf{x}_1, \mathbf{x}_2, \ldots, \mathbf{x}_n)}{f_1(\mathbf{x}_1, \mathbf{x}_2, \ldots, \mathbf{x}_n)} = A. \tag{2.57}
$$

Note that the assumption of a small excess over the boundary implies that the nN-vectors in $\Omega_{\mathbf{x}}^n$ will be near the decision surface defined by $\Lambda_n = A$ and cannot penetrate deep into Ω_2^n. Hence, using (2.57), we obtain

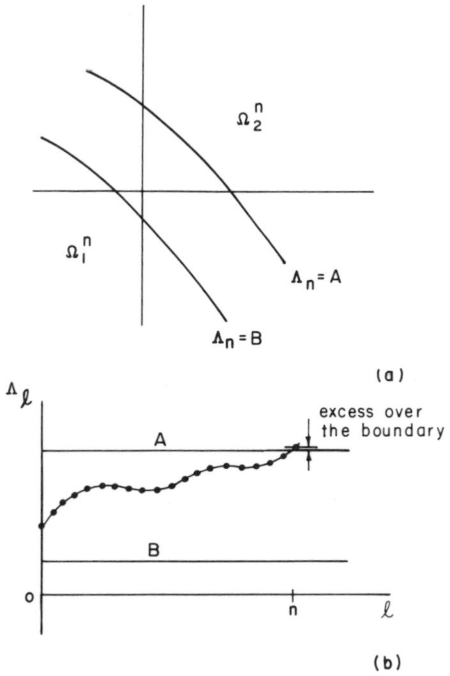

fig. 2.5 Sequential probability ratio test.
(a) Decision regions in $\Omega_{\mathbf{x}}^n$.
(b) A typical test result.

$$\int \cdots \int_{\Omega_2^n} f_2(\mathbf{x}_1, \mathbf{x}_2, \ldots, \mathbf{x}_n)\, d\mathbf{x}_1\, d\mathbf{x}_2 \cdots d\mathbf{x}_n$$
$$= A \int \cdots \int_{\Omega_2^n} f_1(\mathbf{x}_1, \mathbf{x}_2, \ldots, \mathbf{x}_n)\, d\mathbf{x}_1\, d\mathbf{x}_2 \cdots d\mathbf{x}_n. \tag{2.58}$$

The left-hand side of (2.58) is the conditional probability of correctly accepting hypothesis H_2 given that the test terminates at the n-th stage. Let q_n be the probability that it terminates at the n-th stage and consider all possible n. Then,

$$\sum_{n=1}^{\infty} q_n \int \cdots \int_{\Omega_2^n} f_2(\mathbf{x}_1, \mathbf{x}_2, \ldots, \mathbf{x}_n)\, d\mathbf{x}_1\, d\mathbf{x}_2 \cdots, d\mathbf{x}_n = 1 - \beta \tag{2.59}$$

is the probability that H_2 is accepted when H_2 is true. Similarly,

$$\sum_{n=1}^{\infty} q_n \int \cdots \int_{\Omega_2^n} f_1(\mathbf{x}_1, \mathbf{x}_2, \ldots, \mathbf{x}_n)\, d\mathbf{x}_1\, d\mathbf{x}_2 \cdots d\mathbf{x}_n = \alpha, \tag{2.60}$$

is the probability that H_2 is accepted when H_1 is true, or the probability of an error of the first kind. Substituting (2.59) and (2.60) into (2.58) yields

$$(1 - \beta) = A\alpha.$$

Thus, if we specify the allowable α and β, the two thresholds A and B may be determined by

$$A = \frac{1-\beta}{\alpha}, \quad B = \frac{\beta}{1-\alpha}. \tag{2.61}$$

The second equation in (2.61) can be derived in a similar manner. Note that with both α and β less than 1/2, $B < 1 < A$.

Wald and Wolfwitz (1948) showed that SPRT is optimal in the sense that for given α and β there is no other test requiring on the average a smaller number of samples. We do not intend to present the proof; instead we discuss the calculation of the average number of samples.

2.3.2 The average number of samples

Let us consider the log-likelihood ratio

$$\log \Lambda_n = \sum_{i=1}^{n} \log \frac{f_2(\mathbf{x}_i)}{f_1(\mathbf{x}_i)} = \sum_{i=1}^{n} \log \lambda_i . \tag{2.62}$$

Since $\mathbf{x}_i$ is random, log λ_i is a random variable depending on the distribution of $\mathbf{x}_i$. Assuming that H_2 is true, i.e., $\mathbf{x}_i \in C_2$, $i = 1, 2, \ldots$, and noting that the random vectors $\mathbf{x}_i$ are identically distributed, we obtain,

$$E[\log \lambda_i | C_2] = E[\log \lambda | C_2] = \int f_2(\mathbf{x}) \log \frac{f_2(\mathbf{x})}{f_1(\mathbf{x})} dx, \tag{2.63}$$

where the expectation is taken over the density function $f_2(\mathbf{x})$ of C_2. It is noted that since $f_1(\mathbf{x})$ and $f_2(\mathbf{x})$ are known, $E[\log \lambda | C_1]$ and $E[\log \lambda | C_2]$ can be calculated from (2.63).

We have assumed that the test terminates at the n-th stage, or equivalently that n is the number of samples required for the sequential test. Let us define

$$\delta_i = \begin{cases} 1 & \text{if } i \leqslant n, \\ 0 & \text{if } i > n. \end{cases} \tag{2.64}$$

It is obvious that

$$\sum_{i=1}^{\infty} \delta_i = n, \tag{2.65}$$

and

$$\log \Lambda_n = \sum_{i=1}^{n} \log \lambda_i = \sum_{i=1}^{\infty} \delta_i \log \lambda_i . \tag{2.66}$$

Taking conditional expectations,

$$E[\log \Lambda_n | C_2] = \sum_{i=1}^{\infty} E[\delta_i \log \lambda_i | C_2]. \tag{2.67}$$

Let us examine the definition of δ_i and note that (2.64) is equivalent to

$$\delta_i = \begin{cases} 1 & \text{if the test is not terminated up to the } (i-1)\text{-th stage,} \\ 0 & \text{if the test is terminated at or before the } (i-1)\text{-th stage.} \end{cases}$$

Since whether the test is terminated at or before the $(i-1)$-th stage depends on tests at the lst, 2nd, ..., $(i-1)$-th stage, δ_i depends on the samples $\mathbf{x}_1, \mathbf{x}_2, \ldots, \mathbf{x}_{i-1}$ only. On the other hand, $\log \lambda_i$ depends on $\mathbf{x}_i$ only. With $\mathbf{x}_1, \mathbf{x}_2, \ldots, \mathbf{x}_i$ being independent of one another, δ_i is independent of $\log \lambda_i$, and hence by (2.63), (2.65), and (2.67),

$$E[\log \Lambda_n | C_2] = E[\log \lambda | C_2] \sum_{i=1}^{\infty} E[\delta_i | C_2] = E[\log \lambda | C_2] E[n | C_2]. \tag{2.68}$$

Since the test terminates at the n-th stage, if we neglect the excess over the boundary, Λ_n will be either A or B. We note that n is a random variable, and that $\Lambda_n = A$ or B is true for all possible n. Thus, when H_2 is true, the total probability that $\Lambda_n = B$, $n = 1, 2, \ldots$, is the probability of an error of the second kind, β. Similarly, the total probability that $\Lambda_n = A$, $n = 1, 2, \ldots$, given that H_2 is true, is $1 - \beta$. Hence,

$$E[\log \Lambda_n | C_2] = (1-\beta)\log A + \beta \log B. \tag{2.69}$$

A substitution into (2.68) yields

$$E[n | C_2] = \frac{(1-\beta)\log A + \beta \log B}{E[\log \lambda | C_2]}, \tag{2.70}$$

and as mentioned earlier, $E[\log \lambda | C_2]$ may be calculated from (2.63). When H_1 is true, $\mathbf{x}_i$ belongs to C_1, $i = 1, 2, \ldots$, and

$$E[n | C_1] = \frac{\alpha \log A + (1-\alpha)\log B}{E[\log \lambda | C_1]}. \tag{2.71}$$

Let p_1 and p_2 be the prior probability that $\mathbf{x}_i \in C_1$ and C_2 respectively. The average number of samples is

$$E[n] = p_1 E[n|C_1] + p_2 E[n|C_2]. \tag{2.72}$$

2.3.3 *Sequential classification of Gaussian patterns*

Let $\mathbf{x}_1, \mathbf{x}_2, \ldots,$ be a sequence of independent observations belonging to the same class, either C_1 or C_2. The two hypotheses are

$$\begin{aligned} H_1&: \mathbf{x}_i \in C_1, \; i = 1, 2, \ldots, \\ H_2&: \mathbf{x}_i \in C_2, \; i = 1, 2, \ldots. \end{aligned} \tag{2.73}$$

The conditional density functions $f_1(\mathbf{x})$ and $f_2(\mathbf{x})$ are Gaussian densities with equal covariance matrices,

$$\begin{aligned} f_1(\mathbf{x}) &= g(\mathbf{x}; \mathbf{0}, \mathbf{R}), \\ f_2(\mathbf{x}) &= g(\mathbf{x}; \mathbf{m}, \mathbf{R}), \end{aligned} \tag{2.74}$$

and we wish to use the sequential procedure to classify the sequence of observations.

For an SPRT, the two kinds of error probabilities α and β are given. The threshold values for the log-likelihood ratio are

$$\begin{aligned} \log A &= \log \frac{(1-\beta)}{\alpha}, \\ \log B &= \log \frac{\beta}{(1-\alpha)}. \end{aligned} \tag{2.75}$$

Suppose the first sample $\mathbf{x}_1$ is observed, we calculate

$$\begin{aligned} \log \lambda_1 &= \log f_2(\mathbf{x}_1) - \log f_1(\mathbf{x}_1) \\ &= -\frac{1}{2}(\mathbf{x}_1 - \mathbf{m})^T \mathbf{R}^{-1}(\mathbf{x}_1 - \mathbf{m}) + \frac{1}{2}\mathbf{x}_1^T \mathbf{R}^{-1}\mathbf{x}_1 \\ &= \mathbf{x}_1^T \mathbf{R}^{-1}\mathbf{m} - \frac{1}{2}\mathbf{m}^T \mathbf{R}^{-1}\mathbf{m}, \end{aligned} \tag{2.76}$$

and compare it with the threshold values in (2.75). Thus,

$$\text{if } \mathbf{x}_1^T \mathbf{R}^{-1}\mathbf{m} \geqslant \log A + \frac{1}{2}\mathbf{m}^T \mathbf{R}^{-1}\mathbf{m}, \quad \text{accept } H_2,$$

$$\text{if } \mathbf{x}_1^T \mathbf{R}^{-1}\mathbf{m} \leqslant \log B + \frac{1}{2}\mathbf{m}^T \mathbf{R}^{-1}\mathbf{m}, \quad \text{accept } H_1,$$

and if

$$\log B + \frac{1}{2}\mathbf{m}^T\mathbf{R}^{-1}\mathbf{m} < \mathbf{x}_1^T\mathbf{R}^{-1}\mathbf{m} < \log A + \frac{1}{2}\mathbf{m}^T\mathbf{R}^{-1}\mathbf{m},$$

we observe the second sample, calculate

$$\log \lambda_1 + \log \lambda_2 = (\mathbf{x}_1 + \mathbf{x}_2)^T\mathbf{R}^{-1}\mathbf{m} + \mathbf{m}^T\mathbf{R}^{-1}\mathbf{m},$$

and compare it with the same threshold values (2.75).

At the l-th stage, the log-likelihood ratio is

$$\log \Lambda_l = \sum_{i=1}^{l} \log \lambda_i = \sum_{l=1}^{l} \mathbf{x}_i^T\mathbf{R}^{-1}\mathbf{m} - \frac{l}{2}\mathbf{m}^T\mathbf{R}^{-1}\mathbf{m}, \tag{2.77}$$

and we use the following decision rule:

$$\text{if } \sum_{i=1}^{l} \mathbf{x}_i^T\mathbf{R}^{-1}\mathbf{m} \geqslant \log A + \frac{l}{2}\mathbf{m}^T\mathbf{R}^{-1}\mathbf{m}, \quad \text{accept } H_1,$$

$$\text{if } \sum_{i=1}^{l} \mathbf{x}_i^T\mathbf{R}^{-1}\mathbf{m} \leqslant \log B + \frac{l}{2}\mathbf{m}^T\mathbf{R}^{-1}\mathbf{m}, \quad \text{accept } H_2.$$

and if

$$\log B + \frac{l}{2}\mathbf{m}^T\mathbf{R}^{-1}\mathbf{m} < \sum_{i=1}^{l} \mathbf{x}_i^T\mathbf{R}^{-1}\mathbf{m} < \log A + \frac{l}{2}\mathbf{m}^T\mathbf{R}^{-1}\mathbf{m},$$

we take the $(l + 1)$-th observation.

The log-likelihood ratio $\log \lambda$ is a random variable. Let us calculate $E[\log \lambda|C_1]$ and $E[\log \lambda|C_2]$. The expectations are taken over the conditional densities $f_1(\mathbf{x})$ and $f_2(\mathbf{x})$ respectively. Thus, according to (2.63), (2.74), and (2.76),

$$\begin{aligned} E[\log \lambda|C_1] &= E\left[\mathbf{x}^T\mathbf{R}^{-1}\mathbf{m} - \frac{1}{2}\mathbf{m}^T\mathbf{R}^{-1}\mathbf{m}|C_1\right] = -\frac{1}{2}\mathbf{m}^T\mathbf{R}^{-1}\mathbf{m}, \\ E[\log \lambda|C_2] &= E\left[\mathbf{x}^T\mathbf{R}^{-1}\mathbf{m} - \frac{1}{2}\mathbf{m}^T\mathbf{R}^{-1}\mathbf{m}|C_2\right] = \frac{1}{2}\mathbf{m}^T\mathbf{R}^{-1}\mathbf{m}, \end{aligned} \tag{2.78}$$

since $E[\mathbf{x}^T|C_1] = \mathbf{0}^T$ and $E[\mathbf{x}^T|C_2] = \mathbf{m}^T$. Hence, the average numbers of samples for given C_1 and C_2 are

$$\begin{aligned} E[n|C_1] &= -2(\mathbf{m}^T\mathbf{R}^{-1}\mathbf{m})^{-1}\left[\alpha \log \frac{1-\beta}{\alpha} + (1-\alpha)\log \frac{\beta}{1-\alpha}\right], \\ E[n|C_2] &= 2(\mathbf{m}^T\mathbf{R}^{-1}\mathbf{m})^{-1}\left[(1-\beta)\log \frac{1-\beta}{\alpha} + \beta \log \frac{\beta}{1-\alpha}\right]. \end{aligned} \tag{2.79}$$

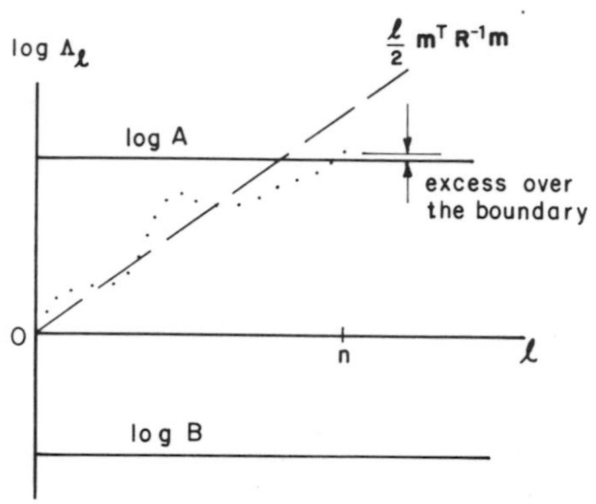

fig. 2.6. Sequential classification of Gaussian patterns.

It is noted that

$$E[\log \Lambda_l|C_1] = lE[\log \lambda|C_1] = -\frac{l}{2}\mathbf{m}^T\mathbf{R}^{-1}\mathbf{m},$$
$$E[\log \Lambda_l|C_2] = lE[\log \lambda|C_2] = \frac{l}{2}\mathbf{m}^T\mathbf{R}^{-1}\mathbf{m}. \tag{2.80}$$

This is rather interesting, since when H_1 is true, the mean value of $\log \Lambda_l$ decreases with l until it eventually crosses the lower threshold $\log B$, and when H_2 is true, it increases and crosses the upper threshold $\log A$. It suggests that the test will eventually terminate. A typical test result is shown in figure 2.6.

It may also be interesting to examine the variances. We have for given C_1 and C_2,

$$\mathrm{Var}[\log \lambda|C_1] = E[\mathbf{m}^T\mathbf{R}^{-1}\mathbf{x}\mathbf{x}^T\mathbf{R}^{-1}\mathbf{m}|C_1] = \mathbf{m}^T\mathbf{R}^{-1}\mathbf{m},$$
$$\mathrm{Var}[\log \lambda|C_2] = E[\mathbf{m}^T\mathbf{R}^{-1}(\mathbf{x}-\mathbf{m})(\mathbf{x}-\mathbf{m})^T\mathbf{R}^{-1}\mathbf{m}|C_2] = \mathbf{m}^T\mathbf{R}^{-1}\mathbf{m}. \tag{2.81}$$

Since $\mathbf{x}_1, \mathbf{x}_2, \ldots,$ are mutually independent, $\log \lambda_1, \log \lambda_2, \ldots,$ are also mutually independent, and

$$\mathrm{Var}[\log \Lambda_l|C_1] = l\,\mathrm{Var}[\log \lambda|C_1] = l\mathbf{m}^T\mathbf{R}^{-1}\mathbf{m},$$
$$\mathrm{Var}[\log \Lambda_l|C_2] = l\,\mathrm{Var}[\log \lambda|C_2] = l\mathbf{m}^T\mathbf{R}^{-1}\mathbf{m}. \tag{2.82}$$

Thus the variances increase with l, and

$$d_l^2 = \frac{\{E[\log \Lambda_l|C_2] - E[\log \Lambda_l|C_1]\}^2}{\mathrm{Var}[\log \Lambda_l|C_1]} = l\mathbf{m}^T\mathbf{R}^{-1}\mathbf{m}, \tag{2.83}$$

may be interpreted as the "signal-to-noise ratio" for l observations as in (2.47). Equation (2.83) indicates that the more observations we take, the better the separation that will be obtained.

2.4 Classification by Sequential Measurements*

In the pattern classification models considered so far, all N measurements (i.e., the N components of the N-vector $\mathbf{x}$) were taken at the same time, and the costs of measurements were not taken into consideration. Let

$$\mathbf{x}^T = [x_1, x_2, \ldots, x_N]. \tag{2.84}$$

When the measurement costs are not negligible and the measurements $x_1, x_2, \ldots, x_N$ may be taken one at a time, we may consider the classification of $\mathbf{x}$ by sequential measurement. The situation is somewhat similar to sequential observation discussed in the previous section. In sequential observation, a sequence of samples is available and the samples are observed one at a time; here we are concerned with one sample only, and the measurements are taken sequentially. The purpose is to obtain a tradeoff between the error of misclassification and the number of measurements.

Sequential measurement was proposed by Fu (1962) and investigated by Fu and his colleagues. It is especially important when the cost of taking a measurement may require elaborate equipment, excessive manpower, or even the interruption of the normal operation, since it takes measurement cost into consideration. In medical diagnosis, if the physician can diagnose the disease category accurately based on a certain test, there is no reason to take another, perhaps costly, test. In this case, the physician may be said to use the sequential measurement procedure.

The SPRT discussed in the last section assumes an infinite sequence; in sequential measurement, N is finite. One possible approach to sequential measurement is to use the truncated Wald SPRT. That is, we use the standard Wald SPRT at the first $(N - 1)$ stages, and if the test has not been terminated then, at the N-th stage we have only two alternatives—accepting either H_1 or H_2. In other words, if necessary, we force the termination of the test at the N-th stage by means of the Bayes or Neyman–Pearson test. The truncated SPRT is not efficient, since in some cases, at least, the decision is largely based on all N measurements, and hence its performance is quite similar to the performance of a test with a fixed number of

* Section may be omitted on first reading.

measurements. To avoid this difficulty, Chien and Fu (1966) suggested a modified SPRT that used time-varying thresholds that approached zero gradually at N, instead of fixed thresholds A and B as in the standard SPRT.

2.4.1 *Modified sequential probability ratio test*

The modified SPRT makes use of time-varying thresholds. Let us define a class of time-varying thresholds for the log-likelihood ratio,

$$\log A(l) = a\left(1 - \frac{l}{N}\right)^{\eta_1},$$
$$\log B(l) = b\left(1 - \frac{l}{N}\right)^{\eta_2}, \tag{2.85}$$
$$l \leqslant N,\ 0 < \eta_1, \eta_2 \leqslant 1,\ b < 0 < a.$$

Typical thresholds are sketched in figure 2.7, and the thresholds of a truncated SPRT are also sketched for purposes of comparison.

At the l-th stage, we calculate the likelihood ratio,

$$\log \Lambda_l(x_1, x_2, \ldots, x_l) = \log \frac{f_2(x_1, x_2, \ldots, x_l)}{f_1(x_1, x_2, \ldots, x_l)}, \tag{2.86}$$

and use a sequential decision rule,

$$\begin{aligned} &\text{if } \log \Lambda_l \geqslant \log A(l), && \text{accept } H_2,\\ &\text{if } \log \Lambda_l \leqslant \log B(l), && \text{accept } H_1,\\ &\text{if } \log B(l) < \log \Lambda_l < \log A(l), && \text{take } (l+1)\text{-th measurement.}\end{aligned} \tag{2.87}$$

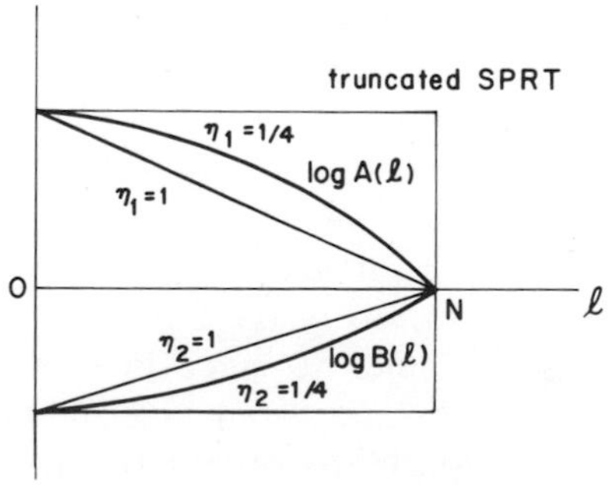

fig. 2.7 Time-varying threshold for modified SPRT (adapted from Chien and Fu, 1966).

The two hypotheses H_1 and H_2 are $\mathbf{x} \in C_1$ and $\mathbf{x} \in C_2$ respectively. The test continues until the log-likelihood ratio crosses one of the two boundaries defined in (2.85).

Let α and β be the probabilities of an error of the first kind and second kind respectively for the modified SPRT, and assume that the test terminates at the n-th stage. We wish to derive a relationship between α, β and $A(l)$, $B(l)$ so that when the allowable error probabilities α and β are given, we may calculate the time-varying thresholds $A(l)$ and $B(l)$. Usually the values of η_1 and η_2 in (2.85) are predetermined, and we simply calculate a and b from α and β. The relationship is more complicated than in the case of a standard SPRT. In order to derive such a relationship, and to determine the average number of samples required, we make the following simplifying assumptions:

(1) $x_1, x_2, \ldots, x_n$ are mutually independent and identically distributed;

(2) the excess over the boundaries is negligible;

(3) α and β are very small, $\alpha, \beta \ll 1$.

Assumption (1) is not very realistic in most sequential measurement problems, and the assumptions are made so as to obtain some tractable, quantitative result.

With assumption (1), the log-likelihood function may be written as

$$\log \Lambda_l = \sum_{j=1}^{l} \log \Lambda_j = \sum_{j=1}^{l} \log \frac{f_2(x_j)}{f_1(x_j)}. \tag{2.88}$$

Since the test terminates at the n-th stage, if we neglect the excess over the boundaries, $\Lambda_n = A(n)$ or $B(n)$. Let

$\alpha_n(A)$, $\alpha_n(B)$ be the probabilities that the log-likelihood ratio crosses the upper and lower bounds, respectively, given that H_1 is true and the test terminates at the n-th stage.

$\beta_n(A)$, $\beta_n(B)$ be the probabilities that the log-likelihood ratio crosses the upper and lower bounds, respectively, given that H_2 is true and the test terminates at the n-th stage.

We note that n is a random variable, and let q_n be the probability that the test terminates at the n-th stage, $n = 1, 2, \ldots, N$. Since we accept H_2 when $\Lambda_n = A(n)$ and accept H_1 when $\Lambda_n = B(n)$, it is clear that $\alpha_n(A)$ and $\beta_n(B)$ correspond to misclassifications, and

$$\begin{aligned} \sum_{n=1}^{N} q_n \alpha_n(A) &= \alpha, \\ \sum_{n=1}^{N} q_n \beta_n(B) &= \beta. \end{aligned} \tag{2.89}$$

Similarly, $\alpha_n(B)$ and $\beta_n(A)$ correspond to correct decisions, and

$$\sum_{n=1}^{N} q_n \alpha_n(B) = 1 - \alpha,$$
$$\sum_{n=1}^{N} q_n \beta_n(A) = 1 - \beta. \tag{2.90}$$

If we let $P(n|C_2, A)$ be the conditional probability of terminating at n, given that H_2 is true and $\Lambda_n = A(n)$, we have

$$P(n|C_2, A) = \frac{q_n \beta_n(A)}{\sum_{j=1}^{N} q_j \beta_j(A)} = \frac{q_n \beta_n(A)}{1-\beta} \tag{2.91}$$

Now similarly to the derivation of (2.58) in the last section, we obtain for $\Lambda_n = A(n)$,

$$\begin{aligned}\int \cdots \int_{\Omega_2^n} f_2(x_1, x_2, \ldots, x_n)\, dx_1\, dx_2 \cdots dx_n \\ = A(n) \int \cdots \int_{\Omega_2^n} f_1(x_1, x_2, \ldots, x_n)\, dx_2 \cdots dx_n,\end{aligned} \tag{2.92}$$

where Ω_2^n is a decision region in the n-space Ω_x^n that corresponds to accepting H_2. By definition, (2.92) is equivalent to

$$\beta_n(A) = A(n)\alpha_n(A). \tag{2.93}$$

We wish to derive a relationship between $A(n)$ and α, β. Using (2.89), (2.90), (2.91), and (2.93), and taking conditional expectation, we obtain

$$\begin{aligned} E[A^{-1}(n)|C_2, A] &= \sum_{n=1}^{N} A^{-1}(n) P(n|C_2, A) = \sum_{n=1}^{N} \frac{\alpha_n(A)}{\beta_n(A)} \frac{q_n \beta_n(A)}{(1-\beta)} \\ &= \frac{1}{1-\beta} \sum_{n=1}^{N} q_n \alpha_n(A) = \frac{\alpha}{1-\beta}. \end{aligned} \tag{2.94}$$

It remains to evaluate the conditional expectation, which is difficult. We must resort to some approximations. By Taylor series expansion, and by neglecting high-order terms,

$$A^{-1}(n) = \exp\left[-a\left(1 - \frac{n}{N}\right)^{\eta_1}\right] \simeq e^{-a}\left[1 + a\eta_1 \frac{n}{N}\right],$$

and

$$E[A^{-1}(n)|C_2, A] = e^{-a}\left\{1 + \frac{a\eta_1}{N} E[n|C_2, A]\right\}. \tag{2.95}$$

Further, since by definition $P(A|C_2) = 1 - \beta$ and $P(B|C_2) = \beta$, and since $\beta \ll 1$,

$$E[n|C_2] = (1 - \beta)E[n|C_2, A] + \beta E[n|C_2, B] \simeq E[n|C_2, A]. \quad (2.96)$$

It follows from (2.94) - (2.96) that with $1 - \beta \simeq 1$,

$$\alpha \simeq e^{-a}\left\{1 + \frac{a\eta_1}{N} E[n|C_2]\right\}, \quad (2.97)$$

and the relationship among α and a and η_1 depends on $E[n|C_2]$.

The evaluation of $E[n|C_2]$ is similar to that described in the last section. Equation (2.68) holds for the modified SPRT, i.e.,

$$E[\log \Lambda_n|C_2] = E[n|C_2]E[\log \lambda|C_2]. \quad (2.98)$$

Because $\log \Lambda_n = \log A(n)$ or $\log B(n)$,

$$\begin{aligned} E[\log \Lambda_n|C_2] &= (1 - \beta)E[\log A(n)|C_2, A] \\ &\quad + \beta E[\log B(n)|C_2, B] \simeq E[\log A(n)|C_2, A]. \end{aligned} \quad (2.99)$$

Again we use Taylor series expansion and neglect the high-order term,

$$\log A(n) = a\left(1 - \frac{n}{N}\right)^{\eta_1} \simeq a\left(1 - \eta_1 \frac{n}{N}\right). \quad (2.100)$$

Combining (2.98), (2.99), and (2.100) yields

$$E[n|C_2] \simeq \frac{a}{E[\log \lambda|C_2] + \eta_1 a/N}. \quad (2.101)$$

A substitution of (2.101) into (2.97) gives us

$$\alpha \simeq e^{-a}\left[1 + \frac{\eta_1 a^2}{NE[\log \lambda|C_2] + \eta_1 a}\right]. \quad (2.102)$$

By a similar derivation,

$$\begin{aligned} E[n|C_1] &\simeq \frac{b}{E[\log \lambda|C_1] + \eta_2 b/N}, \\ \beta &\simeq e^{b}\left[1 - \frac{\eta_2 b^2}{NE[\log \lambda|C_1] + \eta_2 b}\right]. \end{aligned} \quad (2.103)$$

It is interesting to compare the modified SPRT with the standard SPRT. For the standard SPRT with an infinite sequence, we use thresholds $\log A = \log A(0) = a$ and $\log B = \log B(0) = b$, and if α and β are very small, we have, according to (2.70) and (2.61),

$$E[n|C_2] \simeq \frac{a}{E[\log \lambda|C_2]},$$
$$\alpha \simeq \frac{1}{A} = e^{-a}. \tag{2.104}$$

A comparison of $E[n|C_2]$ in (2.101) and (2.104) shows that the modified SPRT requires on the average fewer samples. On the other hand, the error probability α of the modified SPRT is greater than that of the standard SPRT, since the second term in the bracket of (2.102) is positive. This is expected because, as mentioned in the last section, the Wald SPRT is optimal if we assume that an infinite sequence is available.

2.4.2 Pattern classification experiments

Chien and Fu (1966) carried out several pattern classification experiments on a digitial computer using a sequential measurement procedure. The experiments were on recognizing and discriminating two classes of hand-written English letters, *a* and *b*, or three classes of letters, *a*, *b*, and *c*. Sixty samples of each letter were used in the experiments and the samples were collected from different subjects by asking them to write the letters within a two-inch diameter circle. Eighteen measurements were selected for classification (shown in fig. 1.4). Each measurement was the distance from the edge of the letter to the edge of the circle along a predetermined path. The measurements were chosen somewhat arbitrarily with the hope that the probability density function for each class would be Gaussian. Thus it was assumed that

$$f_k(\mathbf{x}) = g(\mathbf{x}; \mathbf{m}_k, \mathbf{R}), \tag{2.105}$$

where $\mathbf{m}_k$ was the N-dimensional mean vector for class C_k and $\mathbf{R}$ the $N \times N$ covariance matrix common to all classes. Both $\mathbf{m}_k$ and $\mathbf{R}$ were estimated from the samples.

For two classes of letters, the log-likelihood ratio at l-th stage is

$$\log \Lambda_l = \mathbf{x}_l^T \mathbf{R}_l^{-1}(\mathbf{m}_{2l} - \mathbf{m}_{1l}) - \frac{1}{2}(\mathbf{m}_{2l} - \mathbf{m}_{1l})^T \mathbf{R}_l^{-1}(\mathbf{m}_{2l} - \mathbf{m}_{1l}),$$

where $\mathbf{x}_l$ and $\mathbf{m}_{kl}$ consist of the first l components of $\mathbf{x}$ and $\mathbf{m}_k$ respectively, and $\mathbf{R}_l$ is the corresponding $l \times l$ minor of the matrix $\mathbf{R}$. We choose $\eta_1 = \eta_2 = 1$, and the thresholds in (2.85) become

$$\log A(l) = a\left(1 - \frac{l}{18}\right),$$

$$\log B(l) = b\left(1 - \frac{l}{18}\right).$$

The values of a and b depend on the error probabilities α and β and on the average number of measurements, as shown in (2.102) and (2.103). The results obtained by Chien and Fu, which are shown in figure 2.8, demonstrate clearly the tradeoff between misclassification errors and the average number of measurements. For comparison purposes, the performance curve is also sketched for recognizing the letters using the standard SPRT. Clearly, for a fixed percentage of misrecognition, the modified SPRT typically requires fewer measurements.

When there are more than two classes, it is necessary to modify the SPRT in another respect. At the l-th stage, we calculate a generalized log-likelihood ratio for each class,

$$\log \Lambda'_{kl} = \log f_k(x_1, x_2, \ldots, x_l) - \frac{1}{K}\sum_{j=1}^{K} \log f_j(x_1, x_2, \ldots, x_l), \tag{2.106}$$

and compare it with a threshold,

$$\log B(l) = b\left(1 - \frac{l}{N}\right), \qquad b < 0. \tag{2.107}$$

The class C_k is dropped from consideration at the l-th stage if

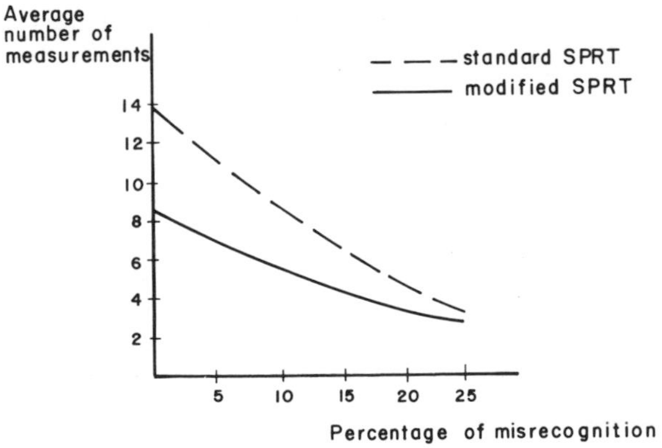

fig. 2.8 Performance curves—recognition of English letters a and b (adapted from Chien and Fu, 1966).

$$\log \Lambda'_{kl} \leqslant \log B(l). \tag{2.108}$$

The test continues until only one class remains that does not satisfy (2.108), and we decide that $\mathbf{x}$ belongs to that class. This is called the generalized sequential probability ratio test (GSPRT). The procedure is applied to the recognition of three classes of handwritten English letters *a*, *b*, and *c*, under the assumption that all three classes are Gaussian distributed as in (2.105). It is found, as in the two-class case, that for a given misclassification error, the modified GSPRT using time-varying thresholds requires a smaller average number of measurements than does the standard GSPRT with constant thresholds.

It is noted that in the Gaussian approximation of $f_k(\mathbf{x})$, the measurements $x_1, x_2, \ldots, x_N$ are correlated and not identically distributed. Thus, although the theoretical derivation is based on the assumption of independence and identical distribution, the experimental results on character recognition demonstrate that the performance of the modified SPRT is as expected, even when assumption (1) is violated.

2.5 Notes and Remarks

Statistical pattern classification is based on the works of many prominent statisticians. Neyman and Pearson (1928, 1933) set forth the basic principles of the theory of hypothesis testing, and Wald (1949) extended the theory to Bayes classification using statistical decision functions. There are many good textbooks on mathematical statistics and decision theory, and the reader is referred to the books by Blackwell and Girshick (1954), Cramér (1946), and Wilks (1962).

A fundamental entity in hypothesis testing is the likelihood ratio $\Lambda(\mathbf{x}) = f_2(\mathbf{x})/f_1(\mathbf{x})$. Whether we use the Bayes test, the Neyman–Pearson test, or, in fact, some other tests, the first step is to calculate the likelihood ratio. The procedures treated in section 2.1 are for simple hypothesis testing. There may be cases when either $f_1(\mathbf{x})$ or $f_2(\mathbf{x})$ is not completely known, but depends on a parameter $\boldsymbol{\theta}$. For example, suppose that the mean value of the pattern vectors of class C_2 is unknown, but we do know its prior density function $f(\boldsymbol{\theta})$. The functional form of the conditional density function of C_2 is known. Thus, we have

$$f_2(\mathbf{x}) = f(\mathbf{x}|C_2) = \int f(\mathbf{x}|\boldsymbol{\theta}, C_2) f(\boldsymbol{\theta})\, d\boldsymbol{\theta} = \int f_2(\mathbf{x}|\boldsymbol{\theta}) f(\boldsymbol{\theta})\, d\boldsymbol{\theta}, \tag{2.109}$$

where both $f_2(\mathbf{x}|\boldsymbol{\theta})$ and $f(\boldsymbol{\theta})$ are known. The likelihood ratio becomes

$$\Lambda(\mathbf{x}) = \frac{f_2(\mathbf{x})}{f_1(\mathbf{x})} = \frac{\int f_2(\mathbf{x}|\boldsymbol{\theta}) f(\boldsymbol{\theta})\, d\boldsymbol{\theta}}{f_1(\mathbf{x})}, \tag{2.110}$$

and such a procedure is called a composite hypothesis testing.

Another variation of the basic hypothesis testing scheme is the compound decision. A sequence of random observations, $\mathbf{x}_1, \mathbf{x}_2, \ldots, \mathbf{x}_n$, is given and, unlike the samples in hypothesis testing by multiple observations (2.31), the samples here may belong to different classes. Thus, $\mathbf{x}_1$ may belong to C_2, $\mathbf{x}_2$ may belong to C_1, $\mathbf{x}_3$ may belong to C_1, etc. We note that for two classes, C_1 and C_2, there are 2^n possibilities, and hence 2^n likelihood functions,

$$\begin{aligned} &f(\mathbf{x}_1, \mathbf{x}_2, \mathbf{x}_3, \ldots, \mathbf{x}_n | C_1, C_1, C_1, \ldots, C_1), \\ &f(\mathbf{x}_1, \mathbf{x}_2, \mathbf{x}_3, \ldots, \mathbf{x}_n | C_2, C_1, C_1, \ldots, C_1), \\ &f(\mathbf{x}_1, \mathbf{x}_2, \mathbf{x}_3, \ldots, \mathbf{x}_n | C_1, C_2, C_1, \ldots, C_1), \\ &\ldots, \\ &f(\mathbf{x}_1, \mathbf{x}_2, \mathbf{x}_3, \ldots, \mathbf{x}_n | C_2, C_2, C_2, \ldots, C_2). \end{aligned} \tag{2.111}$$

This is similar to testing multiple hypotheses, and since there are 2^n hypotheses, the computation is generally quite complicated. If we assume that the prior probabilities of the 2^n sequences of classifications are equal, and that the costs of a misclassified sequence are identical, then according to (2.26), the optimum decision rule is to calculate all 2^n likelihood functions in (2.111), and to select the sequence of classifications that corresponds to the maximum likelihood function. This procedure is called a compound decision.

Two remarks concerning the compound decision are in order. The compound decision procedure can be simplified considerably if $\mathbf{x}_1, \mathbf{x}_2, \ldots, \mathbf{x}_n$ are independent in the sense that

$$f(\mathbf{x}_1, \mathbf{x}_2, \ldots, \mathbf{x}_n) = \prod_{i=1}^{n} f(\mathbf{x}_i), \tag{2.112}$$

where

$$f(\mathbf{x}_i) = p_1 f_1(\mathbf{x}_i) + p_2 f_2(\mathbf{x}_i), \tag{2.113}$$

with p_1, p_2 being the prior probabilities of C_1 and C_2 respectively. The optimal test procedure consists of testing n binary hypotheses and uses one sample at a time. The computation in this case is much simpler than testing the 2^n hypotheses at the same time. In other words, the compound decision procedure is necessary only when $\mathbf{x}_1, \mathbf{x}_2, \ldots, \mathbf{x}_n$ are not independent. The other remark is that in assuming equal cost for different misclassified sequences, it is implicit that the costs for misclassifying one sample, two samples, and n samples are the same. This is not realistic, and we should assign different costs and different prior probabilities to misclassified sequences. Pattern classification by compound decision procedure was proposed by Abend (1966).

Both the Bayes and Neyman–Pearson approaches have been applied successfully to signal detection. Since it is impossible to list all the contributors in this important field, we mention the standard textbooks by Hancock and Wintz (1966), Helstrom (1960), and Van Trees (1968). In pattern recognition, the concept of a decision function was first applied by Chow, in 1957, to character recognition. Chow (1957, 1970) introduced the idea of rejection and used the decision rule that $\delta(\mathbf{x}) = C_j$ if

$$\begin{aligned} p_j f_j(\mathbf{x}) &\geqslant p_k f_k(\mathbf{x}) \qquad \text{for all } k \neq j, \text{ and} \\ p_j f_j(\mathbf{x}) &\geqslant A \sum_{k=1}^{K} p_k f_k(\mathbf{x}), \end{aligned} \tag{2.114}$$

where A was a predetermined threshold value. Otherwise, $\mathbf{x}$ was rejected without being classified. The tradeoff between recognition error and rejection probability was discussed.

Bayes classification of pattern vectors was discussed by Marill and Green (1960), Kanal et al. (1962), and Chu (1965), among others. Chu and Chueh (1967) derived error bounds for Bayes classification. In pattern classification, the pattern vectors of each class are often assumed to be Gaussian distributed, and many important results may be found in the book on multivariate statistical analysis by Anderson (1958). In this chapter we have discussed only briefly the calculation of error probability, mainly because the derivation of a formula for error probability is somewhat complicated even when the pattern vectors are Gaussian distributed (except in the equal covariance case). Fukunaga and Krile (1969) developed a method for calculating the Bayes error rate of Gaussian distributed patterns.

Highleyman (1962) considered the use of linear discriminant functions that defined hyperplanes as decision surfaces. Cooper (1964) investigated the conditions on the probability density functions under which the optimal decision surfaces were hyperplanes, hyperspheres, and hyperquadratics.

The sequential probability ratio test was introduced by Wald in 1947, and its optimal property was shown by Wald and Wolfwitz (1948). The modified SPRT, using time-varying thresholds, was studied by Anderson (1960), Bussgang and Marcus (1964), and Chien and Fu (1966). Fu proposed sequential measurements. In addition to the sequential approach discussed in section 2.4, which followed closely the work by Chien and Fu (1966), dynamic programming (Bellman, 1957) was applied by Fu and Chien (1967), and the rank test (Lehmann, 1953) was used by Fu et al. (1967) for sequential measurement. Readers who are interested in these problems are referred to the authoritative monograph of Fu (1968).

Problems

2.1 Let $\mathbf{x}$ be the pattern vector, $\mathbf{x}^T = [x_1, x_2, \ldots, x_N]$. Consider a two-class pattern classification problem and assume that each component, x_j, is either 1 or 0. Let

$$q_{j1} = P\{x_j = 1|C_1\},$$
$$q_{j2} = P\{x_j = 1|C_2\},$$

and assume that the components $x_1, x_2, \ldots, x_n$ are mutually independent so that

$$P(\mathbf{x}|C_k) = \prod_{j=1}^{N} (q_{jk})^{x_j}(1 - q_{jk})^{1-x_j}, \quad k = 1, 2.$$

Assuming equal costs for the two kinds of errors, and prior probability p, $(1 - p)$, find the discriminant function. Is the decision surface a hyperplane, a hypersphere, or a hyperquadratic?

2.2 Consider the two-class pattern classification problem with C_1, C_2 being Gaussian distributed. The mean vectors $\mathbf{m}_1$ and $\mathbf{m}_2$ and covariance matrices $\mathbf{R}_1$ and $\mathbf{R}_2$ are

(a)

$$\mathbf{m}_1 = \begin{bmatrix} 0 \\ 0 \end{bmatrix}, \quad \mathbf{m}_2 = \begin{bmatrix} 4 \\ 0 \end{bmatrix}, \quad \mathbf{R}_1 = \begin{bmatrix} 1 & 0 \\ 0 & 4 \end{bmatrix}, \quad \mathbf{R}_2 = \begin{bmatrix} 1/4 & 0 \\ 0 & 1 \end{bmatrix}.$$

(b)

$$\mathbf{m}_1 = \begin{bmatrix} 0 \\ 0 \end{bmatrix}, \quad \mathbf{m}_2 = \begin{bmatrix} 4 \\ 0 \end{bmatrix}, \quad \mathbf{R}_1 = \begin{bmatrix} 1 & 0 \\ 0 & 4 \end{bmatrix}, \quad \mathbf{R}_2 = \begin{bmatrix} 1 & 0 \\ 0 & 1 \end{bmatrix}.$$

(c)

$$\mathbf{m}_1 = \begin{bmatrix} 0 \\ 4 \end{bmatrix}, \quad \mathbf{m}_2 = \begin{bmatrix} 4 \\ 0 \end{bmatrix}, \quad \mathbf{R}_1 = \begin{bmatrix} 1 & 0 \\ 0 & 4 \end{bmatrix}, \quad \mathbf{R}_2 = \begin{bmatrix} 4 & 0 \\ 0 & 1 \end{bmatrix}.$$

For each of the above three cases, sketch the decision surfaces and the contour lines for $f_1(\mathbf{x})$ and $f_2(\mathbf{x})$. It is assumed that the prior probability $p = 1/2$ and the costs of the two kinds of errors are identical.

2.3 Let $f_1(\mathbf{x})$ and $f_2(\mathbf{x})$ be Gaussian density functions. Assume equal costs $c_1 = c_2 = 1$ and $p = 1/2$. With

(a)

$$\mathbf{m}_1 = \begin{bmatrix} 0 \\ 0 \end{bmatrix}, \qquad \mathbf{m}_2 = \begin{bmatrix} 1 \\ 1 \end{bmatrix}, \qquad \mathbf{R}_1 = \mathbf{R}_2 = \begin{bmatrix} 1 & 0 \\ 0 & 1/4 \end{bmatrix},$$

(b)

$$\mathbf{m}_1 = \mathbf{m}_2 = \begin{bmatrix} 0 \\ 0 \end{bmatrix}, \qquad \mathbf{R}_1 = \begin{bmatrix} 4 & 0 \\ 0 & 4 \end{bmatrix}, \qquad \mathbf{R}_2 = \begin{bmatrix} 1 & 0 \\ 0 & 1 \end{bmatrix},$$

find the optimum decision rule and determine the error probabilities α and β for each case.

2.4 A random variable x is Gaussian distributed with mean zero and variance r. The random variable is transformed into y by one of the following two transformations

$$y = x^2, \qquad y = x^3.$$

We wish to decide from the observation y which transformation is true. Formulate the hypothesis testing problem and derive the likelihood ratio.

2.5 Consider the multiclass pattern classification problem. The multiple hypotheses are

$$H_k: \quad \mathbf{x} \text{ belonging to } C_k, \qquad k = 1, 2, \ldots, K.$$

Let c_{jk} be the cost of accepting H_j when in fact H_k is true. Derive a Bayes decision rule for this problem.

2.6 Let $f_1(x) = g(x; 0, r)$ and $f_2(x) = g(x; \theta, r)$, where the variance r is assumed known and the mean value θ for $f_2(x)$ is an unknown parameter. Assume that the prior probability density for the random parameter θ is known, $f(\theta) = g(\theta; 1, 1)$. Derive the log-likelihood ratio for this composite hypothesis testing problem, where g denotes a Gaussian density function.

2.7 Let $f_1(x)$ and $f_2(x)$ be Gaussian density functions, $f_1(x) = g(x; 0, 1)$ and $f_2(x) = g(x; 1, 1)$. In deriving the Bayes classifier, it is necessary to know the costs and the prior probability p. Assume that $c_1 = c_2 = 1$, but we are not sure about the prior probability.

(a) Suppose we design the Bayes classifier by assuming $p = 1/4$. However, it turns out that the true prior probability is $p = 3/4$. Calculate the risk involved in this case.

(b) The Bayes risk depends on the prior probability, and we may write $\rho(p)$. There exists a p_0 such that the Bayes risk $\rho(p_0)$ is maximum.

Find p_0 and $\rho(p_0)$ for this problem. When we design the classifier assuming the prior probability p_0, the classifier is called a minimax classifier since we minimize the maximum risk.

(c) If we design the Bayes classifier by assuming p_0, and the actual prior probability is 3/4, what is the risk? Compare the result with that derived in (a).

2.8 Let $x_1, x_2, \ldots$ be a sequence of observed one-dimensional samples belonging either to C_1 or C_2. The two classes are Gaussian distributed with mean zero and variance r_1 and r_2, respectively, $0 < r_1 < r_2$. The samples $x_1, x_2, \ldots$ are mutually independent. Derive a sequential probability ratio test, and sketch the decision boundaries when the test terminates at $n = 1$ and $n = 2$.

2.9 Derive equation (2.103) on the average number of samples, $E[n|C_1]$, and the error probability β. Note that in the definition of the threshold, $b < 0$.

2.10 Let $\mathbf{x}$ be an N-dimensional pattern vector with $N = 10$. The vector $\mathbf{x}$ may come from one of the five possible classes,

$$H_k: \quad \mathbf{x} \text{ belonging to } C_k, \qquad k = 1, 2, \ldots, 5,$$

and given C_k, the conditional probability density is

$$f_k(\mathbf{x}) = g(\mathbf{x}; \mathbf{m}_k, \mathbf{R}).$$

We assume that $\mathbf{m}_k$ and $\mathbf{R}$ are known, and wish to use sequential measurement to classify $\mathbf{x}$. Draw a flow chart and write a detailed computer program for this purpose. Simulate the sequential measurement on a digital computer.

References

1. Abend, K. 1966. Compound decision procedures for pattern recognition. *Proc. NEC* 22:777–780.

2. Anderson, T. W. 1958. *An Introduction to Multivariate Statistical Analysis*. Wiley, New York.

3. ———. 1960. A modification of the sequential probability ratio test to reduce the sample size. *Ann. Math. Stat.* 31:165–197.

4. Bellman, R. 1957. *Dynamic Programming*. Princeton Univ. Press, Princeton, New Jersey.

5. Blackwell, D. and Girshick, M. A. 1954. *Theory of Games and Statistical Decisions*. Wiley, New York.

6. Bussgang, J. J. and Marcus, M. B. 1964. Truncated sequential hypothesis tests. Memo RM-4268-APRA, RAND Corp., Santa Monica, California.

7. Chien, Y. T. and Fu, K. S. 1966. A modified sequential recognition machine using time-varying stopping boundaries. *IEEE Trans. Information Theory* IT-12:206–214.

8. Chow, C. K. 1957. An optimum character recognition system using decision functions. *IRE Trans. Electronic Computers* EC-6:247–253.

9. ———. 1970. On optimum recognition error and reject tradeoff. *IEEE Trans. Information Theory* IT-16:41–46.

10. Chu, J. T. 1965. Optimal decision functions for computer character recognition. *J. Assoc. Computing Machinery* 12:213–226.

11. Chu, J. T. and Chueh, J. C. 1967. Error probability in decision functions for character recognition. *J. Assoc. Computing Machinery* 14:273–280.

12. Cooper, P. W. 1964. Hyperplanes, hyperspheres and hyperquadrics as decision boundaries. In *Computer and Information Sciences*, eds. J. T. Tou and R. H. Wilcox, pp. 111–138. Spartan, Washington, D. C.

13. Cramér, H. 1946. *Mathematical Methods of Statistics*. Princeton Univ. Press, Princeton, New Jersey.

14. Fu, K. S. 1962. A sequential decision model for optimum recognition. *Biological Prototypes and Synthetic Systems*, vol. 1. Plenum, New York.

15. ———. 1968. *Sequential Methods in Pattern Recognition and Machine Learning*. Academic Press, New York.

16. Fu, K. S. and Chien, Y. T. 1967. Sequential recognition using a nonparametric ranking procedure. *IEEE Trans. Information Theory* IT-13:484–492.

17. Fu, K. S., Chien, Y. T., and Cardillo, G. P. 1967. A dynamic programming approach to sequential pattern recognition. *IEEE Trans. Electronic Computers* EC-16:790–803.

18. Fukunaga, K. and Krile, T. F. 1969. Calculation of Bayes recognition error for two multivariate Gaussian distributions. *IEEE Trans. Computers* C-18:220–229.

19. Hancock, J. C. and Wintz, P. A. 1966. *Signal Detection Theory*. McGraw-Hill, New York.

20. Helstrom, C. W. 1960. *Statistical Theory of Signal Detection*. Pergamon, New York.

21. Highleyman, W. H. 1962. Linear decision functions, with applications to pattern recognition. *Proc. IRE* 50:1501–1514.

22. Kanal, L., Slaymaker, F., Smith, D., and Walker, W. 1962. Basic principles of some pattern recognition systems. *Proc. NEC*. 18:279–295.

23. Lehmann, E. L. 1953. The power of rank tests. *Ann. Math. Stat.* 23:23–43.

24. Marill, T. and Green, D. M. 1960. Statistical recognition functions and the design of pattern recognizer. *IRE Trans. Electronic Computers EC-9:472–477.*

25. Neyman, J. and Pearson, E. S. 1928. On the use and interpretation of certain test criteria for purposes of statistical inference. *Biometrika* 20A:Part I, 175–240; Part II, 263–294.

26. ———. 1933. On the problem of the most efficient tests of statistical hypotheses. *Trans. Royal Soc. London*, Series A, 231:289–337.

27. Van Trees, H. L. 1968. *Detection, Estimation, and Modulation Theory*, Part I. Wiley, New York.

28. Wald, A. 1947. *Sequential Analysis*. Wiley, New York.

29. ———. 1949. Statistical decision functions. *Ann. Math. Stat.* 20:165–205.

30. Wald, A. and Wolfwitz, J. 1948. Optimum character of the sequential probability ratio test. *Ann. Math. Stat.* 19:326–339.

31. Wilks, S. S. 1962. *Mathematical Statistics*. Wiley, New York.

3

Estimation Theory and Machine Learning

3.1 Parameter Estimation

In chapter 2 we considered the classification problem where the conditional probability density functions $f_1(\mathbf{x})$ and $f_2(\mathbf{x})$ for given C_1 and C_2, respectively, were assumed completely known. In pattern recognition problems this is often not the case. The pattern recognition machine is presented with a sequence of typical pattern vectors, $\mathbf{x}_1, \mathbf{x}_2, \ldots, \mathbf{x}_n$, classified or unclassified, and the machine must somehow learn to recognize patterns from these samples so that it can classify new pattern vectors as they are observed.

There are several approaches to this problem, and one of the most important is based on classical estimation theory. We assume that the functional form of each of the conditional densities is known, but some of their parameters, such as the mean values and the variances, are unknown. The machine may estimate these parameters from the samples $\mathbf{x}_1, \mathbf{x}_2, \ldots, \mathbf{x}_n$, and use the estimates during the classification phase as if they were true values. In this section we present the basic estimation schemes.

3.1.1 Bayes estimation

Let θ be the unknown parameter whose true value is to be estimated from the random observations $\mathbf{x}_1, \mathbf{x}_2, \ldots, \mathbf{x}_n$. There may be prior knowledge of the unknown parameter, and we assume that this knowledge may be expressed as a prior probability density $f(\theta)$. In other words, we regard the true parameter as a particular value of a random variable θ with known density function $f(\theta)$. Note that in writing $f(\theta)$ we have used the convention that θ denotes both the random variable and the value it may assume.

The probability density function of the random observations $\mathbf{x}_1, \mathbf{x}_2, \ldots, \mathbf{x}_n$ is known, except for the parameter θ, i.e., $f(\mathbf{x}_1, \ldots, \mathbf{x}_n|\theta)$ is known for any given value of θ. We often assume that $\mathbf{x}_1, \mathbf{x}_2, \ldots, \mathbf{x}_n$ for given θ are independent and identically distributed,

$$f(\mathbf{x}_1, \mathbf{x}_2, \ldots, \mathbf{x}_n|\theta) = \prod_{i=1}^{n} f(\mathbf{x}_i|\theta). \tag{3.1}$$

Let $\omega = \omega(\mathbf{x}_1, \mathbf{x}_2, \ldots, \mathbf{x}_n)$ be an estimator for θ based on the samples $\mathbf{x}_1, \mathbf{x}_2, \ldots, \mathbf{x}_n$. Since ω is a function of the random samples, it is obviously a random variable.

We assign for Bayes estimation a *loss function* $l(\omega, \theta)$, which depends on the estimator ω and the true parameter θ. It is reasonable to assume that the loss function depends only on the estimation error $\omega - \theta$,

$$l(\omega, \theta) = l(\omega - \theta). \tag{3.2}$$

Let us define an *average risk* for an estimator ω,

$$\begin{aligned} \rho(\omega) &= E_\theta E[l(\omega - \theta)] \\ &= \int_{\Omega_\theta} \int \cdots \int_{\Omega_{\mathbf{x}}^n} l(\omega - \theta) f(\mathbf{x}_1, \ldots, \mathbf{x}_n, \theta)\, d\mathbf{x}_1 \cdots d\mathbf{x}_n\, d\theta, \end{aligned} \tag{3.3}$$

where $f(\mathbf{x}_1, \ldots, \mathbf{x}_n, \theta)$ is the joint density, Ω_θ is the parameter space, $\Omega_{\mathbf{x}}^n$ is the pattern space, and $\Omega_{\mathbf{x}}^n = \Omega_{\mathbf{x}} \times, \ldots, \times \Omega_{\mathbf{x}}$ is the product space for the n observations. The notation $E_\theta E[\cdot]$ indicates taking expectations first of $\mathbf{x}_1, \ldots, \mathbf{x}_n$ for given θ, and then over the prior density $f(\theta)$. A *Bayes estimator* is the one that minimizes the average risk ρ, and this risk is called the *Bayes risk*.

THEOREM 3.1

The Bayes estimator $\hat{\omega}$ for the quadratic loss function,

$$l(\omega - \theta) = (\omega - \theta)^2, \tag{3.4}$$

is the conditional expectation,

$$\hat{\omega}(\mathbf{x}_1, \ldots, \mathbf{x}_n) = E_\theta[\theta|\mathbf{x}_1, \ldots, \mathbf{x}_n] = \int_{\Omega_\theta} \theta f(\theta|\mathbf{x}_1, \ldots, \mathbf{x}_n)\, d\theta. \tag{3.5}$$

Proof

The average risk $\rho(\omega)$ for the quadratic loss function is

$$\rho(\omega) = \int_{\Omega_\theta} \int \cdots \int_{\Omega_\mathbf{x}^n} (\omega - \theta)^2 f(\mathbf{x}_1, \ldots, \mathbf{x}_n, \theta)\, d\mathbf{x}_1 \cdots d\mathbf{x}_n\, d\theta$$
$$= \int \cdots \int_{\Omega_\mathbf{x}^n} \left[\int_{\Omega_\theta} (\omega - \theta)^2 f(\theta|\mathbf{x}_1, \ldots, \mathbf{x}_n)\, d\theta\right]$$
$$f(\mathbf{x}_1, \ldots, \mathbf{x}_n)\, d\mathbf{x}_1 \cdots d\mathbf{x}_n. \tag{3.6}$$

Since $f(\mathbf{x}_1, \ldots, \mathbf{x}_n)$ is nonnegative, $\rho(\omega)$ is minimum if we minimize

$$\int_{\Omega_\theta} (\omega - \theta)^2 f(\theta|\mathbf{x}_1, \ldots, \mathbf{x}_n)\, d\theta \tag{3.7}$$

for every $\mathbf{x}_1, \ldots, \mathbf{x}_n$. Taking a partial derivative of (3.7) with respect to ω and equating it to zero, we immediately obtain (3.5). Note that the result is a global minimum, since the second ω-derivative of (3.7) equals 2, a positive constant.

We have assumed that $f(\mathbf{x}_1, \ldots, \mathbf{x}_n|\theta)$ and $f(\theta)$ are known. By Bayes' rule,

$$f(\theta|\mathbf{x}_1, \ldots, \mathbf{x}_n) = \frac{f(\mathbf{x}_1, \ldots, \mathbf{x}_n|\theta) f(\theta)}{f(\mathbf{x}_1, \ldots, \mathbf{x}_n)}, \tag{3.8}$$

with

$$f(\mathbf{x}_1, \ldots, \mathbf{x}_n) = \int_{\Omega_\theta} f(\mathbf{x}_1, \ldots, \mathbf{x}_n|\theta) f(\theta)\, d\theta. \tag{3.9}$$

Thus, $f(\theta|\mathbf{x}_1, \ldots, \mathbf{x}_n)$ can be calculated from (3.8) and (3.9) and, in principle, the Bayes estimator for the quadratic loss function can be obtained from (3.5).

As mentioned earlier, an estimator $\omega(\mathbf{x}_1, \ldots, \mathbf{x}_n)$ is a random variable. It is called an *unbiased estimator* if its expectation equals θ,

$$E[\omega] = \int \cdots \int_{\Omega_\mathbf{x}^n} \omega f(\mathbf{x}_1, \ldots, \mathbf{x}_n|\theta)\, d\mathbf{x}_1 \cdots d\mathbf{x}_n = \theta. \tag{3.10}$$

A *bias function* is defined as

$$b(\theta) = E[\omega] - \theta, \tag{3.11}$$

and it is zero for an unbiased estimator. An estimator is called a *consistent estimator* if it converges to the true value θ as n, the number of observations, approaches infinity. Obviously, unbiasedness and consistency are desirable properties.

It is noted that in (3.10) we use the notation $E[\omega]$ instead of $E[\omega|\theta]$ for simplicity. The Bayes estimator in the following example is consistent but biased.

EXAMPLE 3.1

We consider in this example the estimation of the mean of a Gaussian distribution. Let $x_1, x_2, \ldots, x_n$ be a sequence of independent and identically distributed random variables with

$$f(x_1, \ldots, x_n|\theta) = \prod_{i=1}^{n} g(x_i; \theta, r) \tag{3.12}$$

where r is the known variance and θ is the mean value to be estimated. We assume that the prior density of θ is also Gaussian,

$$f(\theta) = g(\theta; 0, \phi_1) \tag{3.13}$$

with zero mean and variance ϕ_1.

We wish to find the Bayes estimator for a quadratic loss function, and must first calculate $f(\theta|x_1, \ldots, x_n)$ according to (3.5). To this end we use (3.12) and (3.13), and write

$$\begin{aligned} f(x_1, \ldots, x_n, \theta) &= f(x_1, \ldots, x_n|\theta) f(\theta) \\ &= (2\pi\phi_1)^{-1/2}(2\pi r)^{-n/2} \exp\left[-\frac{\theta^2}{2\phi_1} - \frac{1}{2r}\sum_{i=1}^{n}(x_i - \theta)^2\right]. \end{aligned}$$

By completing the square for the terms in the exponents, after simple manipulations we obtain,

$$f(x_1, \ldots x_n, \theta) = (2\pi\phi_{n+1})^{-1/2} \exp\left[-\frac{1}{2\phi_{n+1}}\left(\theta - \frac{\phi_{n+1}}{r}\sum_{i=1}^{n} x_i\right)^2\right] h(x_1, \ldots, x_n), \tag{3.14}$$

where

$$\phi_{n+1} = \left(\frac{1}{\phi_1} + \frac{n}{r}\right)^{-1}, \tag{3.15}$$

and $h(x_1, \ldots, x_n)$ is a function depending on $x_1, \ldots, x_n$, but not on θ. For our problem it is not necessary to know the precise expression of $h(x_1, \ldots, x_n)$. Since

$$f(x_1, \ldots, x_n) = \int_{\Omega_\theta} f(x_1, \ldots, x_n, \theta)\, d\theta,$$

if we integrate (3.14) over Ω_θ, we find that, in fact,

$$h(x_1, \ldots, x_n) = f(x_1, \ldots, x_n).$$

Hence, (3.14) implies

$$f(\theta|x_1, \ldots, x_n) = \frac{f(x_1, \ldots, x_n, \theta)}{f(x_1, \ldots, x_n)} = g\left(\theta; \frac{\phi_{n+1}}{r} \sum_{i=1}^{n} x_i, \phi_{n+1}\right). \quad (3.16)$$

This is the posterior probability of θ after observing $x_1, \ldots, x_n$, and it is also Gaussian. A substitution of (3.16) into (3.5) yields the desired Bayes estimator,

$$\hat{\omega}(x_1, \ldots, x_n) = \int_{\Omega_\theta} \theta g\left(\theta; \frac{\phi_{n+1}}{r} \sum_{i=1}^{n} x_i, \phi_{n+1}\right) d\theta = \frac{\phi_{n+1}}{r} \sum_{i=1}^{n} x_i. \quad (3.17)$$

The Bayes estimator may be written recursively. From (3.15) we have

$$\phi_{n+1}^{-1} = \phi_n^{-1} + \frac{1}{r}, \quad (3.18)$$

and if we use the notation,

$$\omega(n+1) = \omega(x_1, \ldots, x_n), \quad (3.19)$$

it is obvious from (3.17) and (3.18) that

$$\hat{\omega}(n+1) = \hat{\omega}(n) + \frac{\phi_{n+1}}{r}(x_n - \hat{\omega}(n)). \quad (3.20)$$

The estimate is a random variable. Taking expectation, we obtain

$$E[\hat{\omega}(n+1)] = \frac{\phi_{n+1}}{r} \sum_{i=1}^{n} E[x_i] = \frac{n\phi_{n+1}}{r}\theta = n\left(n + \frac{r}{\phi_1}\right)^{-1}\theta,$$

which indicates that the estimator is biased. By straightforward manipulation, we have

$$E[(\hat{\omega}(n+1) - \theta)^2] = \phi_{n+1}^2\left(\frac{n}{r} + \frac{\theta^2}{\phi_1^2}\right) = \left(\frac{n}{r} + \frac{\theta^2}{\phi_1^2}\right)\left(\frac{n}{r} + \frac{1}{\phi_1}\right)^{-2},$$

$$E_\theta E[(\hat{\omega}(n+1) - \theta)^2] = \phi_{n+1} = \left(\frac{n}{r} + \frac{1}{\phi_1}\right)^{-1}.$$

As n approaches infinity,

$$\lim_{n\to\infty} E[\hat{\omega}(n+1)] = \theta,$$

$$\lim_{n\to\infty} E[(\hat{\omega}(n+1) - \theta)^2] = 0.$$

Hence the estimator is consistent and asymptotically unbiased.

We have shown in theorem 3.1 that for quadratic loss function, the Bayes estimator is the conditional expectation, $\hat{\omega} = E_\theta[\theta | x_1, \ldots, x_n]$. The result can be generalized. Let us denote $\omega - \theta$ by ω'. If the loss function $l(\omega')$ is symmetric and convex, i.e.,

$$l(\omega') = l(-\omega'),$$
$$l(\lambda\omega_1' + (1-\lambda)\omega_2') \leqslant \lambda l(\omega_1') + (1-\lambda) l(\omega_2'),\ 0 \leqslant \lambda \leqslant 1, \tag{3.21}$$

and if the posterior density $f(\theta | \mathbf{x}_1, \ldots, \mathbf{x}_n)$ is symmetric about its conditional mean, it can be shown that the Bayes estimator is (3.5), the conditional mean. Some of the possible symmetric, convex loss functions are shown in figure 3.1. Thus, (3.5) is applicable for a much wider class of loss functions if the posterior density is symmetric about its conditional mean. We note from (3.16) that for this example the condition is satisfied with the conditional mean being $(\phi_{n+1}/r) \sum x_i$. Hence, the estimator (3.17) is a Bayes estimator for any symmetric, convex loss funtion.

Theorem 3.1 may be extended to the case of multiple unknown parameters. Let $\boldsymbol{\theta}$ be the unknown vector whose components are the unknown parameters. The Bayes estimator that minimizes the quadratic loss function,

$$l(\omega - \boldsymbol{\theta}) = (\omega - \boldsymbol{\theta})^T(\omega - \boldsymbol{\theta}), \tag{3.22}$$

is the conditional expectation

$$\hat{\omega}(\mathbf{x}_1, \ldots, \mathbf{x}_n) = E_{\boldsymbol{\theta}}[\boldsymbol{\theta} | \mathbf{x}_1, \ldots, \mathbf{x}_n] = \int_{\Omega_{\boldsymbol{\theta}}} \boldsymbol{\theta} f(\boldsymbol{\theta} | \mathbf{x}_1, \ldots, \mathbf{x}_n)\, d\boldsymbol{\theta}. \tag{3.23}$$

3.1.2 Maximum likelihood estimation

The Bayes estimator is optimal in terms of the average risk. However, the actual evaluation of (3.5) is usually not simple. Further, the prior density of the unknown parameter $f(\theta)$ is often unknown. It is common in these cases to use the maximum likelihood estimator.

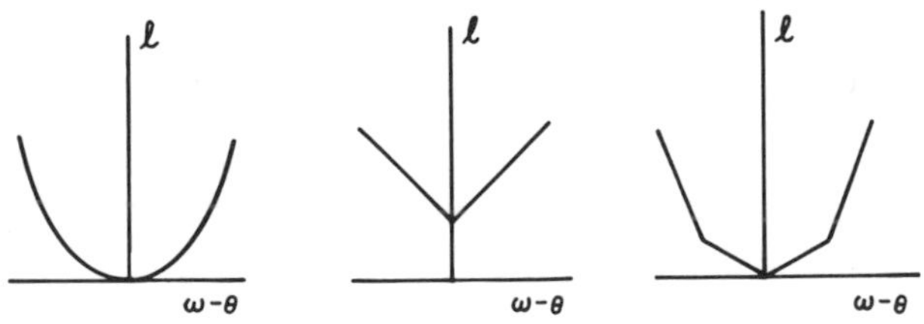

fig. 3.1 Convex, symmetric loss functions.

Let ω be an estimator for the unknown parameter θ, based on the observations $\mathbf{x}_1, \ldots, \mathbf{x}_n$. The conditional density $f(\mathbf{x}_1, \ldots, \mathbf{x}_n|\omega)$ is often called the *likelihood function* of $\mathbf{x}_1, \ldots, \mathbf{x}_n$ for a given estimate ω. Intuitively it seems reasonable to choose as an estimate for θ the value of ω that maximizes $f(\mathbf{x}_1, \ldots, \mathbf{x}_n|\omega)$. Such an estimator is called a maximum likelihood estimator. Since $\log f$ is a monotonically increasing function of f, they have maxima at the same values of ω. Therefore, the maximum likelihood estimator $\tilde{\omega}$ is a solution to the equation

$$\frac{\partial}{\partial \omega} \log f(\mathbf{x}_1, \ldots, \mathbf{x}_n|\omega) = 0, \tag{3.24}$$

if such a solution exists. When $\mathbf{x}_1, \ldots, \mathbf{x}_n$ are conditionally independent,

$$f(\mathbf{x}_1, \ldots, \mathbf{x}_n|\omega) = \prod_{i=1}^{n} f(\mathbf{x}_i|\omega), \tag{3.25}$$

(3.24) may be written as

$$\frac{\partial}{\partial \omega} \sum_{i=1}^{n} \log f(\mathbf{x}_i|\omega) = 0. \tag{3.26}$$

We have introduced the maximum likelihood estimator in a somewhat heuristic manner. It is one of the most important estimators because of its many desirable theoretical properties.

Let

$$V = E[(\omega - \theta)^2] \tag{3.27}$$

be the mean-square estimation error. Note that in (3.27), V is a function of θ, and $E_\theta[V]$ is the average risk of (3.3) with a quadratic loss function. Here we assume that the prior density $f(\theta)$ is unknown, and hence we are interested in V instead of the average risk ρ. An estimator is called an *efficient estimator* if it is unbiased with V equal to the Cramér–Rao lower bound on mean-square estimation error. It is known that if an efficient estimator exists, it is the maximum likelihood estimator. This point will be discussed in some detail in the next section.

The maximum likelihood estimator $\tilde{\omega}(\mathbf{x}_1, \ldots, \mathbf{x}_n)$ is consistent, asymptotically Gaussian, and assymptotically efficient if (see Wilks, 1962):

(1) $(\partial/\partial\theta) f(\mathbf{x}_1, \ldots, \mathbf{x}_n|\theta)$ exists and is absolutely integrable;

(2) the maximum likelihood estimator $\tilde{\omega}$ is unique for $n \geqslant$ some n_o;

(3) $\mathbf{x}_1, \ldots, \mathbf{x}_n$ are independent as defined by (3.25).

When there is more than one unknown parameter, $\boldsymbol{\theta}$ and its estimator $\boldsymbol{\omega}$ are vector-valued. The maximum likelihood estimator $\tilde{\boldsymbol{\omega}}$ can be obtained by solving simultaneously the set of M equations

$$\frac{\partial}{\partial \omega_1} \log f(\mathbf{x}_1, \ldots, \mathbf{x}_n | \boldsymbol{\omega}) = 0,$$

$$\ldots$$

$$\frac{\partial}{\partial \omega_M} \log f(\mathbf{x}_1, \ldots, \mathbf{x}_n | \boldsymbol{\omega}) = 0,$$

where $\omega_1, \ldots, \omega_M$ are the components of the vector $\boldsymbol{\omega}$. The equation may be written as

$$\nabla_{\omega} \log f(\mathbf{x}_1, \ldots, \mathbf{x}_n | \boldsymbol{\omega}) = \mathbf{0}, \tag{3.28}$$

where

$$\nabla_{\omega}^T = \left[\frac{\partial}{\partial \omega_1}, \frac{\partial}{\partial \omega_2}, \ldots, \frac{\partial}{\partial \omega_M} \right]. \tag{3.29}$$

EXAMPLE 3.2

As in example 3.1, we wish to estimate the unknown mean θ from the independent observations $x_1, \ldots, x_n$. The likelihood function is Gaussian,

$$f(x_1, \ldots, x_n | \omega) = \prod_{i=1}^{n} g(x_i; \omega, r). \tag{3.30}$$

However, the prior density $f(\theta)$ is unknown and we use the maximum likelihood estimator to estimate the unknown mean. With

$$\log f(x_1, \ldots, x_n | \omega) = \sum_{i=1}^{n} \left[-\frac{1}{2} \log 2\pi r - \frac{1}{2r} (x_i - \omega)^2 \right],$$

we have

$$\frac{\partial}{\partial \omega} \log f(x_1, \ldots, x_n | \omega) = \frac{1}{r} \sum_{i=1}^{n} (x_i - \omega) = 0, \tag{3.31}$$

and the maximum likelihood estimator is

$$\tilde{\omega} = \frac{1}{n} \sum_{i=1}^{n} x_i. \tag{3.32}$$

In (3.32), $\tilde{\omega}$ is a linear combination of Gaussian random variables, hence $\tilde{\omega}$ is Gaussian distributed with mean and variance given by

$$E[\tilde{\omega}] = \frac{1}{n}\sum_{i=1}^{n} E[x_i] = \theta,$$

$$E[(\tilde{\omega} - \theta)^2] = \frac{1}{n^2}\sum_{i=1}^{n} E[(x_i - \theta)^2] = \frac{r}{n}.$$

Thus $\tilde{\omega}$ is unbiased and consistent. In this example $\tilde{\omega}$ turns out to be the sample mean.

Equation (3.32) may be expressed as a recursive algorithm. Using the notation of (3.19), we have from (3.32),

$$\tilde{\omega}(n+1) = \frac{1}{n}\sum_{i=1}^{n} x_i = \frac{n-1}{n}\left(\frac{1}{n-1}\sum_{i-1}^{n-1} x_i\right) + \frac{1}{n}x_n,$$

hence

$$\tilde{\omega}(n+1) = \tilde{\omega}(n) + \frac{1}{n}(x_n - \tilde{\omega}(n)). \tag{3.33}$$

3.1.3 Convergence concepts

We have introduced the idea of consistency and have said that an estimator is consistent if it converges to the true parameter as n, the number of observations, approaches infinity. Now both the sequence of estimators $\omega(1)$, $\omega(2), \ldots, \omega(n)$ and the unknown parameter θ are random, and we must question what we mean when we say a random sequence converges to a random variable. There are several ways to define the convergence, and the consistency is usually defined in terms of convergence in probability, the weakest form of convergence.

Let $\omega(1), \omega(2), \ldots,$ be a sequence of random variables. The sequence is said to *converge in probability* to the random variable θ if for an arbitrary $\varepsilon > 0$,

$$\lim_{n\to\infty} P\{|\omega(n) - \theta| \geqslant \varepsilon\} = 0. \tag{3.34}$$

The definition is also applicable to the case where θ is a constant instead of a random variable.

Another concept is the mean-square convergence. The sequence is said to *converge in the mean-square sense* if

$$\lim_{n\to\infty} E[(\omega(n) - \theta)^2] = 0. \tag{3.35}$$

The expectation is over the distribution of $\omega(n)$ for given θ. We have demonstrated that the Bayes estimator and the maximum likelihood estimator examples 3.1 and 3.2 satisfy (3.35). The following lemma shows that they are consistent, i.e., they converge to θ in probability.

LEMMA 3.1

Mean-square convergence implies convergence in probability. That is, if the random sequence $\omega(1), \omega(2), \ldots,$ converges to θ in the sense of (3.35), it converges in probability.

Proof

Consider an arbitrary random variable ω with density $f(\omega)$ and denote

$$V = E[(\omega - \theta)^2] = \int_{-\infty}^{\infty} (\omega - \theta)^2 f(\omega)\, d\omega.$$

Since both $f(\omega)$ and $(\omega - \theta)^2$ are nonnegative, we have

$$V \geqslant \int_{|\omega-\theta|\geqslant\varepsilon} (\omega - \theta)^2 f(\omega)\, d\omega \geqslant \varepsilon^2 \int_{|\omega-\theta|\geqslant\varepsilon} f(\omega)\, d\omega.$$

The term at the right-hand side is in fact $\varepsilon^2 P\{|\omega - \theta| \geqslant \varepsilon\}$, hence, for an arbitrary θ,

$$P\{|\omega - \theta| \geqslant \varepsilon\} \leqslant \frac{E[(\omega - \theta)^2]}{\varepsilon^2}, \tag{3.36}$$

which is essentially Chebyshev's inequality.

Now we substitute $\omega(n)$ for ω, and note that if $\omega(n)$ converges in the mean-square sense, the numerator tends to zero as n approaches infinity. Hence, for a fixed ε,

$$\lim_{n\to\infty} P\{|\omega(n) - \theta| \geqslant \varepsilon\} = 0.$$

We say that the sequence $\omega(1), \omega(2), \ldots,$ *converges with probability 1* if

$$\lim_{n\to\infty} P\{|\omega(n+j) - \theta| < \varepsilon,\ j = 0, 1, 2, \ldots, \} = 1. \tag{3.37}$$

Note the difference between (3.34) and (3.37). The former means that for a sufficiently large n only a small percentage of sample sequences will have $|\omega(n) - \theta| \geqslant \varepsilon$. It is possible that many of the sequences having $|\omega(n) - \theta|$

$< \varepsilon$ will have some $\omega(n+j)$ such that $|\omega(n+j) - \theta| \geqslant \varepsilon, j > 0$. Convergence with probability 1, on the other hand requires that a very large percentage of sample sequences will have $|\omega(n+j) - \theta| < \varepsilon, j = 0, 1, 2, \ldots$.

LEMMA 3.2

If the random sequence $\omega(1), \omega(2), \ldots,$ converges with probability 1 to θ, it converges in probability.

Proof

It is obvious that the event $|\omega(n+j) - \theta| < \varepsilon, j = 0, 1, 2, \ldots,$ implies the event $|\omega(n) - \theta| < \varepsilon$, hence,

$$P\{|\omega(n) - \theta| < \varepsilon\} \geqslant P\{|\omega(n+j) - \theta| < \varepsilon,\ j = 0, 1, 2, \ldots\}.$$

Taking limits as $n \to \infty$ and using (3.37), we obtain

$$\lim_{n\to\infty} P\{|\omega(n) - \theta| < \varepsilon\} \geqslant \lim_{n\to\infty} P\{|\omega(n+j) - \theta| < \varepsilon,\ j = 0, 1, 2, \ldots\} = 1.$$

This is obviously equivalent to (3.34), and the sequence converges in probability.

3.2 Cramér–Rao Inequality

Let ω be an estimator for the unknown parameter θ and $f(\mathbf{x}_1, \ldots, \mathbf{x}_n|\theta)$ be the likelihood function for given θ. If $(\partial/\partial\theta) f(\mathbf{x}_1, \ldots, \mathbf{x}_n|\theta)$ exists and is absolutely integrable, the Cramér–Rao inequality is a lower bound on the mean-square error $E[(\omega - \theta)^2]$ for any unbiased estimator. The importance of the bound is obvious since no unbiased estimator can have a mean-square error lower than the one given by the bound.

The following concepts are essential for the derivation of the Cramér–Rao inequality. Since $f(\mathbf{x}_1, \ldots, \mathbf{x}_n|\theta)$ is a conditional density,

$$\int \cdots \int_{\Omega_{\mathbf{x}}^n} f(\mathbf{x}_1, \ldots, \mathbf{x}_n|\theta)\, d\mathbf{x}_1 \cdots d\mathbf{x}_n = 1, \tag{3.38}$$

and

$$\frac{d}{d\theta} \int \cdots \int_{\Omega_{\mathbf{x}}^n} f(\mathbf{x}_1, \ldots, \mathbf{x}_n|\theta)\, d\mathbf{x}_1 \cdots d\mathbf{x}_n = 0. \tag{3.39}$$

If $(\partial/\partial\theta)f(\mathbf{x}_1,\ldots,\mathbf{x}_n|\theta)$ exists and is absolutely integrable, an interchange of the order of differentiation and integration in (3.39) is allowed, and since $(\partial/\partial\theta)f = f(\partial/\partial\theta)\log f$, we obtain

$$\int\cdots\int_{\Omega_{\mathbf{x}}^n}\left[\frac{\partial}{\partial\theta}\log f(\mathbf{x}_1,\ldots,\mathbf{x}_n|\theta)\right]f(\mathbf{x}_1,\ldots,\mathbf{x}_n|\theta)\,d\mathbf{x}_1\cdots d\mathbf{x}_n = 0. \quad (3.40)$$

This equation may be written as

$$E\left[\frac{\partial}{\partial\theta}\log f(\mathbf{x}_1,\ldots,\mathbf{x}_n|\theta)\right] = 0, \quad (3.41)$$

and in statistics, $f(\mathbf{x}_1,\ldots,\mathbf{x}_n|\theta)$ is said to be *regular with respect to its first θ-derivative* if (3.41) holds.

Now let us take derivative of (3.40) with respect to θ. If we assume that both $(\partial/\partial\theta)f(\mathbf{x}_1,\ldots,\mathbf{x}_n|\theta)$ and $(\partial^2/\partial\theta^2)f(\mathbf{x}_1,\ldots,\mathbf{x}_n|\theta)$ exist and are absolutely integrable, we may again interchange the order of differentiation and integration, and obtain

$$\begin{aligned}&\int\cdots\int_{\Omega_{\mathbf{x}}^n}\left[\frac{\partial^2}{\partial\theta^2}\log f(\mathbf{x}_1,\ldots,\mathbf{x}_n|\theta)\right]f(\mathbf{x}_1,\ldots,\mathbf{x}_n|\theta)\,d\mathbf{x}_1\cdots d\mathbf{x}_n\\&\quad+\int\cdots\int_{\Omega_{\mathbf{x}}^n}\left[\frac{\partial}{\partial\theta}\log f(\mathbf{x}_1,\ldots,\mathbf{x}_n|\theta)\right]^2 f(\mathbf{x}_1,\ldots,\mathbf{x}_n|\theta)\,d\mathbf{x}_1\cdots d\mathbf{x}_n\\&\quad= 0,\end{aligned}$$

where again we have used the relationship $(\partial/\partial\theta)f = f(\partial/\partial\theta)\log f$. The equation may be written as

$$E\left[\left(\frac{\partial}{\partial\theta}\log f(\mathbf{x}_1,\ldots,\mathbf{x}_n|\theta)\right)^2\right] = -E\left[\frac{\partial^2}{\partial\theta^2}\log f(\mathbf{x}_1,\ldots,\mathbf{x}_n|\theta)\right], \quad (3.42)$$

and we say that $f(\mathbf{x}_1,\ldots,\mathbf{x}_n|\theta)$ is *regular with respect to its second θ-deriviative* if (3.42) holds. Note that the expectations in (3.41) and (3.42) are with respect to $\mathbf{x}_1,\ldots\mathbf{x}_n$, but not to θ. The entity

$$\sigma_n^2(\theta) = E\left[\left(\frac{\partial}{\partial\theta}\log f(\mathbf{x}_1,\ldots,\mathbf{x}_n|\theta)\right)^2\right], \quad (3.43)$$

is called *Fisher's information.*

3.2.1 Lower bound for unbiased estimators

Let us consider the class of estimators that are unbiased,

$$E[\omega] - \theta = \int \cdots \int_{\Omega_{\mathbf{x}}^n} (\omega - \theta) f(\mathbf{x}_1, \ldots, \mathbf{x}_n | \theta) \, d\mathbf{x}_1 \cdots d\mathbf{x}_n = 0. \quad (3.44)$$

We shall show that the mean-square error in this case is bounded by the inverse of the Fisher information $\sigma_n^2(\theta)$. Note that since the estimators are unbiased, the mean-square error $E[(\omega - \theta)^2]$ is equivalent to the variance of the estimator.

THEOREM 3.2

Let $\omega(\mathbf{x}_1, \ldots, \mathbf{x}_n)$ be an unbiased estimator for θ. If $(\partial/\partial\theta) f(\mathbf{x}_1, \ldots, \mathbf{x}_n|\theta)$ exists and is absolutely integrable, then

$$E[(\omega - \theta)^2] \geqslant \frac{1}{\sigma_n^2(\theta)}. \quad (3.45)$$

The equality holds if and only if

$$\frac{\partial}{\partial\theta} \log f(\mathbf{x}_1, \ldots, \mathbf{x}_n|\theta) = v(\theta)[\omega - \theta], \quad (3.46)$$

where $v(\theta)$ depends possibly on θ but not on $\mathbf{x}_1, \ldots, \mathbf{x}_n$.

Proof

Let us take derivative of (3.44) with respect to θ and note that by assumption the order of differentiation and integration may be interchanged. We obtain immediately

$$\int \cdots \int_{\Omega_{\mathbf{x}}^n} (\omega - \theta) \left[\frac{\partial}{\partial\theta} \log f \right] f \, d\mathbf{x}_1 \cdots d\mathbf{x}_n = 1. \quad (3.47)$$

Applying the Schwartz inequality to (3.47) yields

$$\begin{aligned} 1 &= \left\{ \int \cdots \int_{\Omega_{\mathbf{x}}^n} (\omega - \theta) \left[\frac{\partial}{\partial\theta} \log f \right] f \, d\mathbf{x}_1 \cdots d\mathbf{x}_n \right\}^2 \\ &\leqslant \int \cdots \int_{\Omega_{\mathbf{x}}^n} (\omega - \theta)^2 f \, d\mathbf{x}_1 \cdots d\mathbf{x}_n \\ &\quad \int \cdots \int_{\Omega_{\mathbf{x}}^n} \left[\frac{\partial}{\partial\theta} \log f \right]^2 f \, d\mathbf{x}_1 \cdots d\mathbf{x}_n. \end{aligned} \quad (3.48)$$

A combination of (3.43) and (3.48) gives us (3.45). The Schwartz inequality in (3.48) becomes an equality if and only if (3.46) holds.

An unbiased estimator is called an *efficient estimator* if equality in (3.45) holds. Since $E[(\omega - \theta)^2]$ is the variance for an unbiased estimator, an efficient estimator is a minimum variance estimator among the class of all unbiased estimators.

We have mentioned that if an efficient estimator exists, it is a maximum likelihood estimator. This can be demonstrated by the following argument. Let ω be an efficient estimator and $\tilde{\omega}$ be the maximum likelihood estimator. According to theorem 3.2 and the definition of an efficient estimator,

$$\frac{\partial}{\partial\theta} \log f(\mathbf{x}_1, \ldots, \mathbf{x}_n|\theta)\bigg|_{\theta=\tilde{\omega}} = v(\theta)[\omega - \theta]|_{\theta=\tilde{\omega}}. \tag{3.49}$$

Since (3.46) must be true for any value of θ, in the equation above we simple set $\theta = \tilde{\omega}$. However, at $\tilde{\omega}$ the left-hand side of (3.49) is zero according to the maximum likelihood equation (3.24). Hence,

$$v(\tilde{\omega})[\omega - \tilde{\omega}] = 0.$$

This implies $\tilde{\omega} = \omega$, the efficient estimator, since otherwise $v(\tilde{\omega}) = 0$ would have to be true no matter what the values of the sample sequence $\mathbf{x}_1, \ldots, \mathbf{x}_n$, a trivial result. It should be remarked that the discussion above does not imply that all maximum likelihood estimators are unbiased and efficient, since an efficient estimator may not, in fact, exist.

In theorem 3.2, if we further assume that $(\partial^2/\partial\theta^2)f(\mathbf{x}_1, \ldots, \mathbf{x}_n|\theta)$ exists and is absolutely integrable, the bound (3.45) becomes

$$E[(\omega - \theta)^2] \geqslant \left\{-E\left[\frac{\partial^2}{\partial\theta^2} \log f(\mathbf{x}_1, \ldots, \mathbf{x}_n|\theta)\right]\right\}^{-1}, \tag{3.50}$$

which is sometimes easier to calculate than (3.43). If $\mathbf{x}_1, \ldots, \mathbf{x}_n$ are conditionally independent as defined by (3.1), we may write

$$E[(\omega - \theta)^2] \geqslant \frac{1}{n\sigma^2(\theta)}, \tag{3.51}$$

with

$$\sigma^2(\theta) = E\left[\left(\frac{\partial}{\partial\theta} \log f(\mathbf{x}|\theta)\right)^2\right]. \tag{3.52}$$

EXAMPLE 3.3

We illustrate the application of the Cramér–Rao bound by two simple estimation problems.

(1) Consider the estimation of the mean in example 3.2. The likelihood function is

$$f(x_1, \ldots, x_n|\theta) = \prod_{i=1}^{n} g(x_i; \theta, r).$$

The maximum likelihood estimator is essentially the sample mean,

$$\tilde{\omega}(x_1, \ldots, x_n) = \frac{1}{n} \sum_{i=1}^{n} x_i,$$

and we have shown that it is unbiased, $E[\tilde{\omega}] = \theta$, and

$$E[(\tilde{\omega} - \theta)^2] = \frac{r}{n}.$$

Let us compare it with the Cramér–Rao bound. We have

$$\frac{\partial^2}{\partial\theta^2} \log f(x|\theta) = \frac{\partial^2}{\partial\theta^2}\left[-\frac{1}{2}\log 2\pi r - \frac{1}{2r}(x-\theta)^2\right] = -\frac{1}{r},$$

hence,

$$\sigma_n^2(\theta) = n\sigma^2(\theta) = nE\left[\frac{1}{r}\right] = \frac{n}{r}.$$

Thus, the maximum likelihood estimator in this case is an efficient estimator.

If we compare this result with the Bayes estimator $\hat{\omega}(x_1, \ldots, x_n)$ in example 3.1, we note that

$$E_\theta E[(\hat{\omega} - \theta)^2] = \left(\frac{n}{r} + \frac{1}{\phi_1}\right)^{-1} < \frac{r}{n}.$$

Hence, for the Bayes estimator, $E[(\hat{\omega} - \theta)^2]$ must be less than r/n for some values of θ. This is because $\hat{\omega}$ is a biased estimator, and an efficient estimator is defined in terms of the class of all unbiased estimators only.

(2) Consider the likelihood function,

$$f(x_1, \ldots, x_n|\theta) = \begin{cases} \prod_{i=1}^{n} \exp(\theta - x_i), & x_i \geqslant \theta, \\ 0, & \text{elsewhere.} \end{cases}$$

Suppose we use the following estimation scheme:

$$\omega(x_1, \ldots, x_n) = \hat{x} - \frac{1}{n},$$

where

$$\hat{x} = \min(x_1, \ldots, x_n)$$

denotes the smallest value of the n observed samples. We note that $\hat{x}$ could be any of the n observed values, and further, it implies that the remaining $(n - 1)$ samples must have values greater than or equal to $\hat{x}$. Hence, the probability density $h(\hat{x}|\theta)$ that the smallest value of the n samples is $\hat{x}$ is

$$h(\hat{x}|\theta) = [e^{\theta-\hat{x}} \prod_{x_i \neq \hat{x}} \int_{\hat{x}}^{\infty} e^{\theta - x_i}\, dx_i]n = ne^{n(\theta-\hat{x})}, \quad \hat{x} \geqslant \theta.$$

Hence,

$$E[\omega] = \int_{\theta}^{\infty} \left(\hat{x} - \frac{1}{n}\right) ne^{n(\theta-\hat{x})}\, d\hat{x} = \theta,$$

which is unbiased, and

$$E[(\omega - \theta)^2] = \int_{\theta}^{\infty} \left(\hat{x} - \frac{1}{n}\right)^2 ne^{n(\theta-\hat{x})}\, d\hat{x} - \theta^2 = \frac{1}{n^2}.$$

The estimator is consistent since $E[(\omega - \theta)^2]$ approaches zero as the sample size n approaches infinity.

It is noted that since $x_1, \ldots, x_n$ are independent, $\sigma_n^2(\theta) = n\sigma^2(\theta)$ as in (3.51). Hencc, as n increases, the mean-square error would decrease, but not faster than $1/n$ according to the Cramér–Rao bound. On the other hand, we have shown that it decreases at a rate of $1/n^2$. The apparent contradiction is due to the fact that $f(x|\theta)$ has a discontinuity at θ, hence $\partial f/\partial\theta$ does not exist, and the Cramér–Rao bound is not applicable to this problem.

Theorem 3.2 may be generalized to the case of multiple unknown parameters. Let $\boldsymbol{\omega}(\mathbf{x}_1, \ldots, \mathbf{x}_n)$ be an unbiased estimator for $\boldsymbol{\theta}$ and define a mean-square error matrix

$$\mathbf{V} = E[(\boldsymbol{\omega} - \boldsymbol{\theta})(\boldsymbol{\omega} - \boldsymbol{\theta})^T]. \tag{3.53}$$

If $\nabla_{\boldsymbol{\theta}} f(\mathbf{x}_1, \ldots, \mathbf{x}_n|\boldsymbol{\theta})$ exists, and $|\nabla_{\boldsymbol{\theta}} f(\mathbf{x}_1, \ldots, \mathbf{x}_n|\boldsymbol{\theta})|$ is integrable,

$$\mathbf{V} \geqslant \boldsymbol{\Sigma}^{-1}, \tag{3.54}$$

where the inequality means that $(\mathbf{V} - \mathbf{\Sigma}^{-1})$ is nonnegative definite, and

$$\mathbf{\Sigma} = E[(\nabla_{\boldsymbol{\theta}} \log f(\mathbf{x}_1, \ldots, \mathbf{x}_n | \boldsymbol{\theta}))(\nabla_{\boldsymbol{\theta}} \log f(\mathbf{x}_1, \ldots, \mathbf{x}_n | \boldsymbol{\theta}))^T] \tag{3.55}$$

is commonly called Fisher's information matrix. An efficient estimator may be defined by the equality of (3.54).

Since the nonnegativeness means that $\mathbf{u}^T(\mathbf{V} - \mathbf{\Sigma}^{-1})\mathbf{u} \geqslant 0$ for an arbitrary vector $\mathbf{u}$, if we let $\mathbf{u}$ be a vector with its j-th element $u_j = 1$ and all other elements being zero, we obtain a special case of (3.54),

$$E[(\omega_j - \theta_j)^2] \geqslant (\mathbf{\Sigma}^{-1})_{jj}, \tag{3.56}$$

where ω_j and θ_j are the j-th element of $\boldsymbol{\omega}$ and $\boldsymbol{\theta}$ respectively, and $(\mathbf{\Sigma}^{-1})_{jj}$, is the jj-th element of the matrix $\mathbf{\Sigma}^{-1}$.

3.2.2 Lower bound for biased estimators

Let $\omega(\mathbf{x}_1, \ldots, \mathbf{x}_n)$ be a biased estimator for θ with bias function $b(\theta)$. Then

$$E[\omega] - \theta - b(\theta) =$$
$$\int \cdots \int_{\Omega_{\mathbf{x}}^n} (\omega - \theta - b(\theta)) f(\mathbf{x}_1, \ldots, \mathbf{x}_n | \theta)\, d\mathbf{x}_1 \cdots d\mathbf{x}_n = 0. \tag{3.57}$$

The Cramér–Rao bound in this case depends on $b(\theta)$.

THEOREM 3.3

If $(\partial/\partial\theta) f(\mathbf{x}_1, \ldots, \mathbf{x}_n | \theta)$ exists and is absolutely integrable, the mean-square estimation error satisfies

$$E[(\omega - \theta)^2] \geqslant b^2(\theta) + \frac{1}{\sigma_n^2(\theta)}\left[1 + \frac{db(\theta)}{d\theta}\right]^2. \tag{3.58}$$

The equality holds if and only if

$$\frac{\partial}{\partial\theta} \log f(\mathbf{x}_1, \ldots, \mathbf{x}_n | \theta) = v(\theta)[\omega(\mathbf{x}_1, \ldots, \mathbf{x}_n) - \theta - b(\theta)], \tag{3.59}$$

where $v(\theta)$ possibly depends on θ, but not on $\mathbf{x}_1, \ldots, \mathbf{x}_n$.

Proof

Let us take the derivative of (3.57) and note that we may interchange the order of differentiation and integration. We obtain,

$$\int \cdots \int_{\Omega_{\mathbf{x}}^n} (\omega - \theta - b(\theta))\left[\frac{\partial}{\partial \theta} \log f\right] f d\mathbf{x}_1 \cdots d\mathbf{x}_n = 1 + \frac{db(\theta)}{d\theta}. \quad (3.60)$$

Applying the Schwartz inequality to (3.60) yields

$$\begin{aligned}\left[1 + \frac{db(\theta)}{d\theta}\right]^2 &= \left\{\int \cdots \int_{\Omega_{\mathbf{x}}^n} (\omega - \theta - b(\theta))\left[\frac{\partial}{\partial \theta} \log f\right] f d\mathbf{x}_1 \cdots d\mathbf{x}_n\right\}^2 \\ &\leqslant \int \cdots \int_{\Omega_{\mathbf{x}}^n} (\omega - \theta - b(\theta))^2 f d\mathbf{x}_1 \cdots d\mathbf{x}_n \\ &\quad \int \cdots \int_{\Omega_{\mathbf{x}}^n} \left[\frac{\partial}{\partial \theta} \log f\right]^2 f d\mathbf{x}_1 \cdots d\mathbf{x}_n. \end{aligned} \quad (3.61)$$

Hence,

$$E[(\omega - \theta - b(\theta))^2] \geqslant \frac{1}{\sigma_n^2(\theta)}\left[1 + \frac{db(\theta)}{d\theta}\right]^2. \quad (3.62)$$

Now let us write

$$\begin{aligned} E[(\omega - \theta)^2] &= E[(\omega - \theta - b(\theta) + b(\theta))^2] \\ &= b^2(\theta) + E[(\omega - \theta - b(\theta))^2] + 2b(\theta)E[\omega - \theta - b(\theta)]. \end{aligned} \quad (3.63)$$

The last term is zero by the definition of $b(\theta)$, and therefore, a substitution of $E[(\omega - \theta - b(\theta))^2]$ in (3.62) by (3.63) yields the desired inequality (3.58). Finally, we note that the Schwartz inequality becomes an equality if and only if (3.59) is true.

It is noted that (3.62) is in fact a lower bound on the variance of an estimator with bias $b(\theta)$. When $b(\theta) = 0$, the theorem reduces to theorem 3.2. The application of theorem 3.3 is somewhat limited because in many cases the bias function of the biased estimator is unknown. The values of (3.58) will be different for biased estimators with different bias functions.

3.2.3 Bounds on average mean-square error

If the prior density $f(\theta)$ of the unknown parameter θ is given, the Cramér–Rao inequality may be extended to a lower bound on the average mean-square error, $E_\theta E[(\omega - \theta)^2]$. We discuss briefly here two extensions that are applicable to biased estimators without detailed knowledge of the bias function.

Let $\omega(\mathbf{x}_1, \ldots, \mathbf{x}_n)$ be an estimator for θ, which has a prior density $f(\theta)$. If $(\partial/\partial\theta)[f(\theta)f(\mathbf{x}_1, \ldots, \mathbf{x}_n|\theta)]$ exists and is absolutely integrable in $\Omega_{\mathbf{x}}^n \times \Omega_\theta$, and if the bias function $b(\theta)$ satisfies

$$\lim_{\theta \to \pm\infty} b(\theta)f(\theta) = 0, \tag{3.64}$$

then

$$E_\theta E[(\omega - \theta)^2] \geqslant \left\{E_\theta E\left[\left(\frac{\partial}{\partial\theta}\log f(\theta)f(\mathbf{x}_1, \ldots, \mathbf{x}_n|\theta)\right)^2\right]\right\}^{-1}. \tag{3.65}$$

The proof of the statement is similar to that of theorem 3.2, and is left as an exercise.

Condition (3.64) is easily satisfied since $f(\theta)$ is zero at $\pm\infty$, and it is not necessary to know the detailed form of $b(\theta)$. If $f(\theta)$ is nonzero on an interval $[u_1, u_2]$, and zero elsewhere, e.g., the uniform distribution, (3.65) is not applicable because of the discontinuities of $f(\theta)$ at u_1 and u_2 that violate the condition on $(\partial/\partial\theta)[f(\theta)f(\mathbf{x}_1, \ldots, \mathbf{x}_n|\theta)]$. From another point of view, we note that by considering the interval $[u_1, u_2]$ instead of from $-\infty$ to ∞, we obtain a bound,

$$E_\theta E[(\omega - \theta)^2] \geqslant \left\{E_\theta E\left[\left(\frac{\partial}{\partial\theta}\log f(\theta)f(\mathbf{x}_1, \ldots, \mathbf{x}_n|\theta)\right)^2\right]\right\}^{-1} [1 + f(u_2)b(u_2) - f(u_1)b(u_1)]. \tag{3.66}$$

Since we wish to avoid the discontinuities of $f(\theta)$ at u_1 and u_2, in (3.66) we should use $f(u_1 +)$ and $f(u_2 -)$, which are greater than zero. Hence, bound (3.66) requires the knowledge of the bias function at u_1 and u_2.

Let us assume that $f(\theta)$ is nonzero on the interval $[u_1, u_2]$, and zero elsewhere. A bias-free bound on $E_\theta E[(\omega - \theta)^2]$ may be obtained using the calculus of variations. For an unknown parameter θ with prior density $f(\theta)$, (3.58) of theorem 3.3 implies that

$$E_\theta E[(\omega - \theta)^2] \geqslant \int_{u_1}^{u_2} \left[f(\theta)b^2(\theta) + \frac{f(\theta)}{\sigma_n^2(\theta)}\left(1 + \frac{db(\theta)}{d\theta}\right)^2\right] d\theta. \tag{3.67}$$

To simplify the notation, let $I(\theta, b, \dot{b})$ denote the integrand at the right-hand side of (3.67) with $\dot{b} = db(\theta)/d\theta$. Both $f(\theta)$ and $\sigma_n^2(\theta)$ are nonnegative, hence I and $\int I\,d\theta$ are nonnegative.

We introduce the concept of the most favorable bias function, $\hat{b}(\theta)$, i.e., that bias function that minimizes $\int I\,d\theta$ in (3.67). Obviously, with $b(\theta)$ substituted by $\hat{b}(\theta)$, (3.67) becomes a bound for any estimator. It is known from the theory of the calculus of variations that $\hat{b}(\theta)$ must satisfy the Euler equation (Gelfand and Fomin, 1963, pp. 11-15)

$$\frac{\partial I}{\partial b} - \frac{d}{d\theta}\left(\frac{\partial I}{\partial \dot{b}}\right) = 0,$$

subject to the endpoint conditions

$$\left.\frac{\partial I}{\partial \dot{b}}\right|_{\theta=u_1} = \left.\frac{\partial I}{\partial \dot{b}}\right|_{\theta=u_2} = 0.$$

For our $I(\theta, b, \dot{b})$, the Euler equation is

$$f(\theta)b(\theta) - \frac{d}{d\theta}\left[\frac{f(\theta)}{\sigma_n^2(\theta)}\left(1 + \frac{db(\theta)}{d\theta}\right)\right] = 0, \qquad (3.68)$$

with the endpoint conditions

$$\left.\frac{db(\theta)}{d\theta}\right|_{\theta=u_1} = \left.\frac{db(\theta)}{d\theta}\right|_{\theta=u_2} = -1. \qquad (3.69)$$

It can be shown that $\int I\,d\theta$ is convex, hence the solution $\hat{b}(\theta)$ to (3.68) gives us a global minimum. Thus, for given $f(\theta)$ and $\sigma_n^2(\theta)$, the lower bound may be obtained by first solving the Euler equation (3.68), perhaps numerically on a digital computer, and then substituting the solution into (3.67). A special case where an explicit lower bound can be derived is given as problem 3.5.

There is no guarantee that the solution $\hat{b}(\theta)$ to the Euler equation is truly a bias function of a certain estimator. We simply use it as an intermediary for the derivation of the lower bound.

The application of the calculus of variations requires that the bias function of the estimator is continuously differentiable. If we assume that $(\omega(\partial/\partial\theta)f(\mathbf{x}_1, \ldots, \mathbf{x}_n|\theta))$ exists and is absolutely integrable in $\Omega_{\mathbf{x}}^n$ for $u_1 \leqslant \theta \leqslant u_2$, we obtain by the definition of $b(\theta)$,

$$\frac{db(\theta)}{d\theta} = \int \cdots \int_{\Omega_{\mathbf{x}}^n} \omega(\mathbf{x}_1, \ldots, \mathbf{x}_n) \frac{\partial}{\partial\theta} f(\mathbf{x}_1, \ldots, \mathbf{x}_n|\theta)\,d\mathbf{x}_1 \cdots d\mathbf{x}_n - 1. \qquad (3.70)$$

If we further assume that $(\partial/\partial\theta)f(\mathbf{x}_1 \cdots, \mathbf{x}_n|\theta)$ is continuous for all $\mathbf{x}_1, \ldots, \mathbf{x}_n$ and $u_1 \leqslant \theta \leqslant u_2$, and note that $\omega(\mathbf{x}_1 \cdots, \mathbf{x}_n)$ is independent of θ, we conclude that the integral in (3.70) and hence $db(\theta)/d\theta$ is continuous with respect to θ. Thus, the requirement of continuously differentiable $b(\theta)$ can easily be verified in practice by examining the estimator $\omega(\mathbf{x}_1, \ldots, \mathbf{x}_n)$ and the likelihood function $f(\mathbf{x}_1, \ldots, \mathbf{x}_n|\theta)$.

3.3 Supervised Parametric Learning

A pattern recognition machine operates in two different modes, the training or learning mode, and the classification mode. During the learning mode, the machine observes a sequencc of pattern vectors, $\mathbf{x}_1, \mathbf{x}_2, \ldots,$ and modifies its structure according to the observations. The pattern vectors are usually presented to the machine one at a time, hence the machine must adapt itself in a recursive manner.

For supervised parametric learning, we use a model with the following assumptions.

(1) A sequence of conditionally independent training patterns, $\mathbf{x}_1$, $\mathbf{x}_2 \cdots$, is observed, one pattern at a time. The classification of each training pattern is known.

(2) There are K classes, C_k, $k = 1, 2, \ldots, K$. The probability density function for given C_k is known except for a parameter vector $\boldsymbol{\theta}_k$.

(3) The prior density of the random parameter vector $\boldsymbol{\theta}_k$ is given. It reflects the machine's prior knowledge about $\boldsymbol{\theta}_k$.

Under these assumptions, the machine will estimate the values of $\boldsymbol{\theta}_k$ from the training samples of known classifications. When a new pattern vector, $\mathbf{x}$ of unknown classification is observed, the machine will classify it using the methods described in chapter 2 with the unknown $\boldsymbol{\theta}_k$ substituted by ω_k, the estimate for $\boldsymbol{\theta}_k$ obtained during the training. Thus, we have essentially a parameter estimation problem, and the results of the last two sections are applicable to parametric learning.

The major factor that distinguishes parametric learning from parameter estimation is that the pattern vectors are observed one at a time, hence the estimator must be recursive in nature. Thus, parametric learning is recursive parameter estimation. While mathematically this represents only a slightly different point of view, the point is important in the study of learning machines since each observation may be interpreted as an experience and the machine improves its performance by learning from each experience.

Suppose we wish to estimate $\boldsymbol{\theta}_k$. Obviously the estimation of $\boldsymbol{\theta}_k$ should be based on samples belonging to C_k. Since the classification of each training sample is known, we may select from the sequence of training samples a subsequence that consists of all samples belonging to C_k. To simplify the notation, we drop the subscript k in $\boldsymbol{\theta}_k$. Thus, in this section, $f_k(\boldsymbol{\theta})$ and

$$f_k(\mathbf{x}_1, \ldots, \mathbf{x}_n|\boldsymbol{\theta}) = \prod_{i=1}^{n} f_k(\mathbf{x}_i|\boldsymbol{\theta}) \tag{3.71}$$

are understood to be the prior density and conditional density for class C_k with random parameter $\boldsymbol{\theta}$, and all samples, $\mathbf{x}_1$, $\mathbf{x}_2 \cdots$, belong to class C_k.

3.3.1 *Supervised Bayes learning*

From theorem 3.1, a Bayes estimator with quadratic cost function is

$$\hat{\omega}(\mathbf{x}_1, \ldots, \mathbf{x}_n) = \int_{\Omega_\theta} \boldsymbol{\theta} f_k(\boldsymbol{\theta}|\mathbf{x}_1, \ldots, \mathbf{x}_n)\, d\boldsymbol{\theta}. \tag{3.72}$$

Thus, we must have a recursive method to calculate $f_k(\boldsymbol{\theta}|\mathbf{x}_1, \ldots, \mathbf{x}_n)$.

By Bayes' rule,

$$f_k(\mathbf{x}_1, \boldsymbol{\theta}) = f_k(\boldsymbol{\theta}|\mathbf{x}_1) f_k(\mathbf{x}_1) = f_k(\mathbf{x}_1|\boldsymbol{\theta}) f_k(\boldsymbol{\theta}). \tag{3.73}$$

Noting that

$$f_k(\mathbf{x}_1) = \int_{\Omega_\theta} f_k(\mathbf{x}_1|\boldsymbol{\theta}) f_k(\boldsymbol{\theta})\, d\boldsymbol{\theta}, \tag{3.74}$$

we obtain by (3.73) and (3.74),

$$f_k(\boldsymbol{\theta}|\mathbf{x}_1) = \frac{f_k(\mathbf{x}_1|\boldsymbol{\theta}) f_k(\boldsymbol{\theta})}{\int f_k(\mathbf{x}_1|\boldsymbol{\theta}) f_k(\boldsymbol{\theta})\, d\boldsymbol{\theta}}. \tag{3.75}$$

After observing $\mathbf{x}_1$, $f_k(\mathbf{x}_1|\boldsymbol{\theta})$ is known, and since the prior density $f_k(\boldsymbol{\theta})$ is given, the posterior density $f_k(\boldsymbol{\theta}|\mathbf{x}_1)$ can be calculated by (3.75).

Now suppose we observe a random sample $\mathbf{x}_2$, by Bayes' rule

$$f_k(\boldsymbol{\theta}|\mathbf{x}_1, \mathbf{x}_2) = \frac{f_k(\mathbf{x}_2|\mathbf{x}_1, \boldsymbol{\theta}) f_k(\mathbf{x}_1, \boldsymbol{\theta})}{f_k(\mathbf{x}_1, \mathbf{x}_2)} = \frac{f_k(\mathbf{x}_2|\mathbf{x}_1, \boldsymbol{\theta}) f_k(\boldsymbol{\theta}|\mathbf{x}_1)}{f_k(\mathbf{x}_2|\mathbf{x}_1)}, \tag{3.76}$$

with

$$f_k(\mathbf{x}_2|\mathbf{x}_1) = \int f_k(\mathbf{x}_2|\mathbf{x}_1, \boldsymbol{\theta}) f_k(\boldsymbol{\theta}|\mathbf{x}_1)\, d\boldsymbol{\theta}. \tag{3.77}$$

Since $\mathbf{x}_1$ and $\mathbf{x}_2$ are conditionally independent as defined by (3.71),

$$f_k(\mathbf{x}_2|\mathbf{x}_1, \boldsymbol{\theta}) = \frac{f_k(\mathbf{x}_1, \mathbf{x}_2, \boldsymbol{\theta})}{f_k(\mathbf{x}_1, \boldsymbol{\theta})} = \frac{f_k(\mathbf{x}_1, \mathbf{x}_2|\boldsymbol{\theta})}{f_k(\mathbf{x}_1|\boldsymbol{\theta})} = f_k(\mathbf{x}_2|\boldsymbol{\theta}). \tag{3.78}$$

A substitution of (3.77) and (3.78) into (3.76) yields

$$f_k(\boldsymbol{\theta}|\mathbf{x}_1, \mathbf{x}_2) = \frac{f_k(\mathbf{x}_2|\boldsymbol{\theta}) f_k(\boldsymbol{\theta}|\mathbf{x}_1)}{\int f_k(\mathbf{x}_2|\boldsymbol{\theta}) f_k(\boldsymbol{\theta}|\mathbf{x}_1)\, d\boldsymbol{\theta}}. \tag{3.79}$$

We note that $f_k(\boldsymbol{\theta}|\mathbf{x}_1)$ is the posterior density calculated at the previous stage, but plays the role of prior density in (3.79). It is also interesting to note that (3.77) and (3.78) indicate the dependence of $\mathbf{x}_2$ on $\mathbf{x}_1$ through the common parameter $\boldsymbol{\theta}$.

Generally, at the n-th stage we have

$$f_k(\boldsymbol{\theta}|\mathbf{x}_1, \ldots, \mathbf{x}_n) = \frac{f_k(\mathbf{x}_n|\boldsymbol{\theta}) f_k(\boldsymbol{\theta}|\mathbf{x}_1, \ldots, \mathbf{x}_{n-1})}{\int f_k(\mathbf{x}_n|\boldsymbol{\theta}) f_k(\boldsymbol{\theta}|\mathbf{x}_1, \ldots, \mathbf{x}_{n-1})\, d\boldsymbol{\theta}}. \tag{3.80}$$

This is a recursive formula for the posterior density functions. Since the computations at each stage are similar, the total number of computations increases only linearly with n. At each stage, it is only necessary to store in the machine $f_k(\boldsymbol{\theta}|\mathbf{x}_1, \ldots, \mathbf{x}_n)$ and the known density function $f_k(\mathbf{x}|\boldsymbol{\theta})$. Under some general conditions, $f_k(\boldsymbol{\theta}|\mathbf{x}_1, \ldots, \mathbf{x}_n)$ will approach a narrow spike as n, the number of observations, becomes very large, and the Bayes estimator (3.72) will converge to the true value.

It should be mentioned that generally the posterior density $f_k(\boldsymbol{\theta}|\mathbf{x}_1, \ldots, \mathbf{x}_n)$ is not in a simple functional form, and often can be computed and stored numerically only. Thus it becomes difficult to implement when the dimension of $\boldsymbol{\theta}$ is high. The problem does not arise for some special cases discussed in the following subsections.

3.3.2 Learning the mean vector of a Gaussian distribution

Let us consider the case of learning the mean vector $\boldsymbol{\theta}$ of a Gaussian density with known covariance matrix $\mathbf{R}$,

$$f_k(\mathbf{x}_1, \ldots, \mathbf{x}_n|\boldsymbol{\theta}) = \prod_{i=1}^{n} f_k(\mathbf{x}_i|\boldsymbol{\theta}) = \prod_{i=1}^{n} g(\mathbf{x}_i; \boldsymbol{\theta}, \mathbf{R}), \tag{3.81}$$

where the subscript k denotes class C_k. Assume that the prior density is also Gaussian with mean $\boldsymbol{\omega}(1)$ and covariance $\boldsymbol{\Phi}_1$,

$$f_k(\boldsymbol{\theta}) = g(\boldsymbol{\theta}; \boldsymbol{\omega}(1), \boldsymbol{\Phi}_1). \tag{3.82}$$

By Bayes' rule,

$$f_k(\boldsymbol{\theta}|\mathbf{x}_1) = \frac{f_k(\mathbf{x}_1|\boldsymbol{\theta}) f_k(\boldsymbol{\theta})}{\int f_k(\mathbf{x}_1|\boldsymbol{\theta}) f_k(\boldsymbol{\theta})\, d\boldsymbol{\theta}}. \tag{3.83}$$

We have

$$f_k(\mathbf{x}_1|\boldsymbol{\theta})f_k(\boldsymbol{\theta}) = g(\mathbf{x}_1;\boldsymbol{\theta},\mathbf{R})g(\boldsymbol{\theta};\omega(1),\boldsymbol{\Phi}_1)$$
$$= (2\pi)^{-N}|\mathbf{R}|^{-1/2}|\boldsymbol{\Phi}_1|^{-1/2}\exp[-\tfrac{1}{2}(\mathbf{x}_1-\boldsymbol{\theta})^T\mathbf{R}^{-1}(\mathbf{x}_1-\boldsymbol{\theta})-\tfrac{1}{2}\boldsymbol{\theta}^T\boldsymbol{\Phi}_1^{-1}\boldsymbol{\theta}],$$

where N is the dimensionality of $\mathbf{x}$, and $|\mathbf{R}|$ and $|\boldsymbol{\Phi}_1|$ are the determinants of $\mathbf{R}$ and $\boldsymbol{\Phi}_1$, respectively. By a simple manipulation similar to that in example 3.1, we obtain

$$f_k(\mathbf{x}_1,\boldsymbol{\theta}) = f_k(\mathbf{x}_1|\boldsymbol{\theta})f_k(\boldsymbol{\theta}) = g(\boldsymbol{\theta};\omega(2),\boldsymbol{\Phi}_2)h(\mathbf{x}_1), \tag{3.84}$$

where

$$\begin{aligned}\omega(2) &= \mathbf{R}(\boldsymbol{\Phi}_1+\mathbf{R})^{-1}\omega(1)+\boldsymbol{\Phi}_1(\boldsymbol{\Phi}_1+\mathbf{R})^{-1}\mathbf{x}_1,\\ \boldsymbol{\Phi}_2 &= \mathbf{R}(\boldsymbol{\Phi}_1+\mathbf{R})^{-1}\boldsymbol{\Phi}_1,\end{aligned} \tag{3.85}$$

and $h(\mathbf{x}_1)$ is a function of $\mathbf{x}_1$ only. If we integrate (3.84) with respect to $\boldsymbol{\theta}$, we have

$$f_k(\mathbf{x}_1) = \int f_k(\mathbf{x}_1|\boldsymbol{\theta})f_k(\boldsymbol{\theta})\,d\boldsymbol{\theta} = h(\mathbf{x}_1), \tag{3.86}$$

hence according to (3.83), (3.84), and (3.86), the posterior density is,

$$f_k(\boldsymbol{\theta}|\mathbf{x}_1) = g(\boldsymbol{\theta};\omega(2),\boldsymbol{\Phi}_2). \tag{3.87}$$

The result above may be applied iteratively. Assuming that

$$f_k(\boldsymbol{\theta}|\mathbf{x}_1,\ldots,\mathbf{x}_{n-1}) = g(\boldsymbol{\theta};\omega(n),\boldsymbol{\Phi}_n),$$

we obtain, in a manner similar to that in the derivation of (3.87),

$$f_k(\boldsymbol{\theta}|\mathbf{x}_1,\ldots,\mathbf{x}_n) = g(\boldsymbol{\theta};\omega(n+1),\boldsymbol{\Phi}_{n+1}), \tag{3.88}$$

where

$$\begin{aligned}\omega(n+1) &= \mathbf{R}(\boldsymbol{\Phi}_n+\mathbf{R})^{-1}\omega(n)+\boldsymbol{\Phi}_n(\boldsymbol{\Phi}_n+\mathbf{R})^{-1}\mathbf{x}_n\\ \boldsymbol{\Phi}_{n+1} &= \mathbf{R}(\boldsymbol{\Phi}_n+\mathbf{R})^{-1}\boldsymbol{\Phi}_n.\end{aligned} \tag{3.89}$$

It is easy to verify that (3.89) is equivalent to

$$\begin{aligned}\omega(n+1) &= \frac{1}{n}\mathbf{R}\left(\boldsymbol{\Phi}_1+\frac{1}{n}\mathbf{R}\right)^{-1}\omega(1)+\boldsymbol{\Phi}_1\left(\boldsymbol{\Phi}_1+\frac{1}{n}\mathbf{R}\right)^{-1}\frac{1}{n}\sum_{i=1}^{n}\mathbf{x}_i,\\ \boldsymbol{\Phi}_{n+1} &= \frac{1}{n}\mathbf{R}\left(\boldsymbol{\Phi}_1+\frac{1}{n}\mathbf{R}\right)^{-1}\boldsymbol{\Phi}_1.\end{aligned} \tag{3.90}$$

Hence,

$$\lim_{n\to\infty} \omega(n+1) = \lim_{n\to\infty} \frac{1}{n} \sum_{i=1}^{n} \mathbf{x}_i,$$

$$\lim_{n\to\infty} \mathbf{\Phi}(n+1) = \lim_{n\to\infty} \frac{1}{n}\mathbf{R} = \mathbf{0},$$

and, as $n \to \infty$, $\omega(n+1)$ converges to $\boldsymbol{\theta}$ in the mean-square sense.

The importance of (3.88) is that $f_k(\boldsymbol{\theta})$ and $f_k(\boldsymbol{\theta}|\mathbf{x}_1, \ldots, \mathbf{x}_n)$ are of the same functional form. To emphasize this point, we write

$$\begin{aligned} f_k(\boldsymbol{\theta}) &= g(\boldsymbol{\theta}; \omega(1), \mathbf{\Phi}_1) = v_1(\omega(1), \boldsymbol{\theta}), \\ f_k(\boldsymbol{\theta}|\mathbf{x}_1, \ldots, \mathbf{x}_n) &= g(\boldsymbol{\theta}; \omega(n+1), \mathbf{\Phi}_{n+1}) = v_{n+1}(\omega(n+1), \boldsymbol{\theta}). \end{aligned} \tag{3.91}$$

Note that in (3.91), the subscripts in v_1 and v_{n+1} indicate different $\mathbf{\Phi}$. A function of random observations $\mathbf{x}_1, \ldots, \mathbf{x}_n$ is called a *statistic*. The posterior density $f_k(\boldsymbol{\theta}|\mathbf{x}_1, \ldots, \mathbf{x}_n)$ in this case depends on $\mathbf{x}_1 \cdots, \mathbf{x}_n$ only indirectly through the statistic $\omega(n+1)$. At each stage, we need only to compute and store $\omega(n+1)$ and $\mathbf{\Phi}_{n+1}$. The advantage of (3.91) is thus obvious.

If $f_k(\mathbf{x}_1, \ldots, \mathbf{x}_n|\Theta)$ is a Gaussian density with known mean and unknown covariance Θ, and if the prior density $f_k(\Theta)$ is a Wishart density function, then the posterior density $f_k(\Theta|\mathbf{x}_1, \ldots, \mathbf{x}_n)$ is also a Wishart density function. Similarly, in learning both the mean vector and the covariance matrix of a Gaussian density, if the prior density is Gaussian–Wishart, the posterior density is again a Gaussian–Wishart density function (see Fu, 1968). Thus, by choosing the prior density properly, learning the parameters of a Gaussian distribution is very simple.

*3.3.3 Reproducing probability density functions**

The Gaussian, Wishart, and Gaussian–Wishart density functions discussed above are reproducing density functions. Let us drop the subscript k in the density functions. A probability density $f(\boldsymbol{\theta})$ is said to reproduce itself with respect to the conditional density $f(\mathbf{x}_1, \ldots, \mathbf{x}_n|\boldsymbol{\theta})$ if the posterior density $f(\boldsymbol{\theta}|\mathbf{x}_1, \ldots, \mathbf{x}_n)$ admits the same parametric description as $f(\boldsymbol{\theta})$. In other words, we may write

$$\begin{aligned} f(\boldsymbol{\theta}) &= v_1(\omega(1), \boldsymbol{\theta}), \\ f(\boldsymbol{\theta}|\mathbf{x}_1, \ldots, \mathbf{x}_n) &= v_{n+1}(\omega(n+1), \boldsymbol{\theta}), \quad n = 1, 2, \ldots, \end{aligned} \tag{3.92}$$

* Section may be omitted on first reading.

where v_1 and v_{n+1} are of the same functional form but may have different parameters in addition to different $\boldsymbol{\omega}$. The vector $\boldsymbol{\omega}(1)$ is a parameter vector of the prior density, while $\boldsymbol{\omega}(n+1) = \boldsymbol{\omega}(\mathbf{x}_1, \ldots, \mathbf{x}_n)$ is a statistic based on the observations $\mathbf{x}_1, \ldots, \mathbf{x}_n$. The vectors $\boldsymbol{\omega}(1), \boldsymbol{\omega}(2), \ldots, \boldsymbol{\omega}(n+1)$ are of the same fixed dimension. Probability density functions having this property are called reproducing densities.

We note that $f(\boldsymbol{\theta}|\mathbf{x}_1, \ldots, \mathbf{x}_{n-1})$ is the posterior density of $\boldsymbol{\theta}$ based on the observations $\mathbf{x}_1, \ldots, \mathbf{x}_{n-1}$; on the other hand, it may be regarded as a prior density for the evaluation of $f(\boldsymbol{\theta}|\mathbf{x}_1, \ldots, \mathbf{x}_n)$ in the Bayes learning scheme, as indicated by (3.80). Let us rewrite (3.80),

$$f(\boldsymbol{\theta}|\mathbf{x}_1, \ldots, \mathbf{x}_n) = \frac{f(\mathbf{x}_n|\boldsymbol{\theta}) f(\boldsymbol{\theta}|\mathbf{x}_1, \ldots, \mathbf{x}_{n-1})}{\int f(\mathbf{x}_n|\boldsymbol{\theta}) f(\boldsymbol{\theta}|\mathbf{x}_1, \ldots, \mathbf{x}_{n-1})\, d\boldsymbol{\theta}}.$$

It is important to note that the knowledge of the previous observations, $\mathbf{x}_1, \ldots, \mathbf{x}_{n-1}$, is summarized in $f(\boldsymbol{\theta}|\mathbf{x}_1, \ldots, \mathbf{x}_{n-1})$. For reproducing densities, this knowledge is contained in the statistic $\boldsymbol{\omega}(n) = \boldsymbol{\omega}(\mathbf{x}_1, \ldots, \mathbf{x}_{n-1})$. Indeed, in this case the parameter $\boldsymbol{\omega}(1)$ of the prior density could be regarded as a statistic obtained from previous observations, say $\mathbf{x}_{-n'}, \mathbf{x}_{-n'+1}, \ldots, \mathbf{x}_0$.

THEOREM 3.4

Let $\mathbf{x}_1, \ldots, \mathbf{x}_n$ be conditionally independent and identically distributed. The density functions $f(\boldsymbol{\theta})$ and $f(\boldsymbol{\theta}|\mathbf{x}_1, \ldots, \mathbf{x}_n)$ are reproducing densities if and only if

$$f(\mathbf{x}_1, \ldots, \mathbf{x}_n|\boldsymbol{\theta}) = u_{n+1}(\boldsymbol{\omega}(n+1), \boldsymbol{\theta}) h(\mathbf{x}_1, \ldots, \mathbf{x}_n), \tag{3.93}$$

where u_{n+1} is a function of the statistic $\boldsymbol{\omega}(n+1)$ and $\boldsymbol{\theta}$, and $h(\mathbf{x}_1, \ldots, \mathbf{x}_n)$ does not depend on $\boldsymbol{\theta}$.

Proof

If $f(\boldsymbol{\theta})$ and $f(\mathbf{x}_1, \ldots, \mathbf{x}_n|\boldsymbol{\theta})$ are reproducing densities, according to (3.92), we have,

$$\begin{aligned} f(\mathbf{x}_1, \ldots, \mathbf{x}_n|\boldsymbol{\theta}) &= \frac{f(\boldsymbol{\theta}|\mathbf{x}_1, \ldots, \mathbf{x}_n) f(\mathbf{x}_1, \ldots, \mathbf{x}_n)}{f(\boldsymbol{\theta})} \\ &= \frac{v_{n+1}(\boldsymbol{\omega}(n+1), \boldsymbol{\theta})}{v_1(\boldsymbol{\omega}(1), \boldsymbol{\theta})} f(\mathbf{x}_1, \ldots, \mathbf{x}_n). \end{aligned} \tag{3.94}$$

With $\omega(1)$ being a known parameter vector, (3.94) is obviously in the form of (3.93).

To prove the converse, we assume that (3.93) is true. Then

$$f(\boldsymbol{\theta}|\mathbf{x}_1, \ldots, \mathbf{x}_n) = \frac{f(\mathbf{x}_1, \ldots, \mathbf{x}_n|\boldsymbol{\theta})f(\boldsymbol{\theta})}{\int f(\mathbf{x}_1, \ldots, \mathbf{x}_n|\boldsymbol{\theta})f(\boldsymbol{\theta})\,d\boldsymbol{\theta}} = \frac{u_{n+1}(\omega(n+1), \boldsymbol{\theta})f(\boldsymbol{\theta})}{\int u_{n+1}(\omega(n+1), \boldsymbol{\theta})f(\boldsymbol{\theta})\,d\boldsymbol{\theta}}. \tag{3.95}$$

Therefore, for any $f(\boldsymbol{\theta})$, $f(\boldsymbol{\theta}|\mathbf{x}_1, \ldots, \mathbf{x}_n)$, $n = 1, 2, \ldots$, are of the same functional form, and we may write

$$f(\boldsymbol{\theta}|\mathbf{x}_1, \ldots, \mathbf{x}_n) = v_{n+1}(\omega(n+1), \boldsymbol{\theta}), \quad n = 1, 2, \ldots. \tag{3.96}$$

What remains to be shown is that $f(\boldsymbol{\theta})$ is of the same functional form as $f(\boldsymbol{\theta}|\mathbf{x}_1, \cdots, \mathbf{x}_n)$. We note that given $f(\mathbf{x}_1|\boldsymbol{\theta})$ and $f(\boldsymbol{\theta}|\mathbf{x}_1)$, the prior density $f(\boldsymbol{\theta})$ is unique. This can be seen from the following argument. Suppose there is a $f'(\boldsymbol{\theta})$, then

$$\frac{f(\boldsymbol{\theta}|\mathbf{x}_1)}{f(\mathbf{x}_1|\boldsymbol{\theta})} = \frac{f(\boldsymbol{\theta})}{f(\mathbf{x}_1)} = \frac{f'(\boldsymbol{\theta})}{f'(\mathbf{x}_1)}. \tag{3.97}$$

Since $f(\boldsymbol{\theta})$ and $f'(\boldsymbol{\theta})$ are functions of $\boldsymbol{\theta}$ only, and $f(\mathbf{x}_1)$ and $f'(\mathbf{x}_1)$ do not depend on $\boldsymbol{\theta}$, (3.97) implies $f(\boldsymbol{\theta}) = f'(\boldsymbol{\theta})$. Now $f(\boldsymbol{\theta})$ and $f(\boldsymbol{\theta}|\mathbf{x}_1)$ bear the same relationship to one another as do $f(\boldsymbol{\theta}|\mathbf{x}_1)$ and $f(\boldsymbol{\theta}|\mathbf{x}_1, \mathbf{x}_2)$, and we conclude from (3.96) that $f(\boldsymbol{\theta})$ has the same functional form as $f(\boldsymbol{\theta}|\mathbf{x}_1, \ldots, \mathbf{x}_n)$.

Condition (3.93) is the factorability condition of a sufficient statistic. A statistic $\omega(\mathbf{x}_1, \ldots, \mathbf{x}_n)$ is called a *sufficient statistic* if for any other statistic $\tilde{\omega}(\mathbf{x}_1, \ldots, \mathbf{x}_n)$,

$$f(\tilde{\omega}|\omega, \boldsymbol{\theta}) = f(\tilde{\omega}|\omega). \tag{3.98}$$

We note that

$$f(\boldsymbol{\theta}|\omega, \tilde{\omega}) = \frac{f(\tilde{\omega}|\omega, \boldsymbol{\theta})f(\omega, \boldsymbol{\theta})}{f(\tilde{\omega}|\omega)f(\omega)},$$

hence (3.98) implies

$$f(\boldsymbol{\theta}|\omega, \tilde{\omega}) = f(\boldsymbol{\theta}|\omega). \tag{3.99}$$

The converse is obviously also true. Thus, as far as the estimation of $\boldsymbol{\theta}$ is concerned, all relevant information obtainable from the observations $\mathbf{x}_1, \ldots, \mathbf{x}_n$ is contained in the sufficient statistic $\omega(\mathbf{x}_1, \ldots, \mathbf{x}_n)$, and the additional knowledge of $\tilde{\omega}$ will have no contribution.

When the factorability condition holds, (3.93) suggests that $\mathbf{x}_1, \ldots, \mathbf{x}_n$ depend indirectly on $\boldsymbol{\theta}$ through $\boldsymbol{\omega}$. Indeed $u(\boldsymbol{\omega}, \boldsymbol{\theta})$ in (3.93) may be interpreted as $f(\boldsymbol{\omega}|\boldsymbol{\theta})$, and since $\boldsymbol{\omega} = \boldsymbol{\omega}(\mathbf{x}_1, \ldots, \mathbf{x}_n)$, $h(\mathbf{x}_1, \ldots, \mathbf{x}_n)$ is essentially $f(\mathbf{x}_1, \ldots, \mathbf{x}_n|\boldsymbol{\omega})$, which does not depend on $\boldsymbol{\theta}$. Hence, for any statistic $\tilde{\boldsymbol{\omega}}$, its dependence on $\boldsymbol{\theta}$ is also indirectly through $\boldsymbol{\omega}$. In other words, (3.98) holds and $\boldsymbol{\omega}(\mathbf{x}_1, \ldots, \mathbf{x}_n)$ is a sufficient statistic. It can be shown that the converse is also true, and $\boldsymbol{\omega}$ is a sufficient statistic if and only if the factorability condition holds (Wilks, 1962). Thus we have reproducing densities if and only if there is a sufficient statistic.

In addition to Gaussian densities, other known conditional densities $f(\mathbf{x}_1, \ldots, \mathbf{x}_n|\boldsymbol{\theta})$ that admit sufficient statistics, hence reproducing densities, are binomial, multinomial, Poisson, Rayleigh, exponential, and zero-mean rectangular density functions (Spragins, 1965).

It can be seen from the proof of theorem 3.4 that if a sufficient statistic exists, we may choose an arbitrary $f(\boldsymbol{\theta})$ and obtain reproducing densities. The choice of $f(\boldsymbol{\theta})$ depends, of course, on our prior knowledge. From the computational point of view, however, there is usually a natural choice of $f(\boldsymbol{\theta})$. The following example illustrates this point.

EXAMPLE 3.4

Consider the estimation problem in example 3.1 where

$$f(\theta) = g(\theta; 0, \phi_1),$$

$$f(x_1, \ldots, x_n|\theta) = \prod_{i=1}^{n} g(x_i; \theta, r),$$

are Gaussian density functions. The variances ϕ_1 and r are known. We have shown in example 3.1 that the posterior densities are also Gaussian (figure 3.2),

$$f(\theta|x_1, \ldots, x_n) = g(\theta; \omega(n+1), \phi_{n+1}),$$

where $\phi_{n+1} = (\phi_1^{-1} + nr^{-1})^{-1}$, and

$$\omega(n+1) = \frac{\phi_{n+1}}{r} \sum_{i=1}^{n} x_i$$

is the Bayes estimate. The conditional density $f(x_1, \ldots, x_n|\theta)$ may be written as

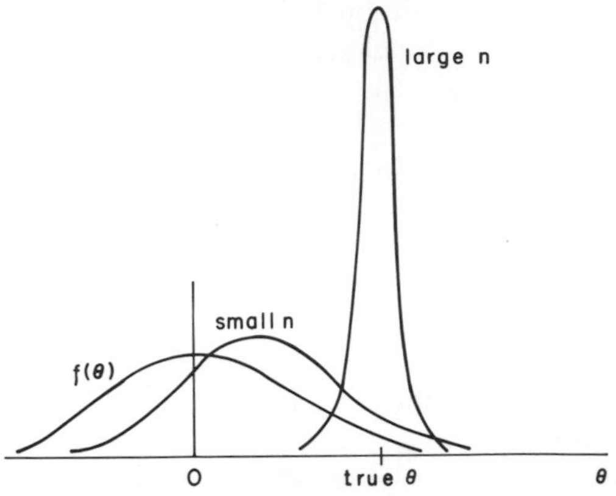

fig. 3.2 Gaussian prior density $f(\theta)$ and Gaussian posterior densities $f(\theta|x_1, \ldots x_n)$.

$$f(x_1, \ldots, x_n|\theta) = (2\pi r)^{-n/2} \exp\left[-\frac{1}{2r}\sum_{i=1}^{n}(x_i - \theta)^2\right]$$

$$= (2\pi r)^{-n/2} \exp\left[-\frac{1}{2r}\sum_{i=1}^{n} x_i^2\right] \exp\left[\theta\left(\frac{\omega(n+1)}{\phi_{n+1}} - \frac{n\theta}{2r}\right)\right],$$

which is in the form of (3.93), hence $\omega(n + 1)$ is a sufficient statistic. We note that the Gaussian prior density seems to be a natural choice for generating reproducing densities.

Suppose the prior density is two-sided exponential.

$$f(\theta) = \frac{1}{2} e^{-|\theta|}.$$

We may write

$$f(\theta) = \frac{1}{2} \frac{e^{-|\theta|}}{g(\theta; 0, \phi_1)} g(\theta; 0, \phi_1).$$

It should be obvious that in this case,

$$f(\theta|x_1, \ldots, x_n) = \frac{e^{-|\theta|} g(\theta; \omega(n+1), \phi_{n+1})}{2g(\theta; 0, \phi_1)} \left[\int \frac{e^{-|\theta|} g(\theta; \omega(n+1), \phi_{n+1})}{2g(\theta; 0, \phi_1)} d\theta\right]^{-1}, \quad (3.100)$$

where $\omega(n + 1)$ is the same sufficient statistic as before, but it is no longer the Bayes estimate. Note that we still have reproducing densities, and as n approaches infinity, $f(\theta|x_1, \ldots, x_n)$ will be concentrated about the true θ.

3.4 Unsupervised Parametric Learning

As in supervised parametric learning, we assume that there are K classes of pattern vectors, and the conditional density function for a given class C_k is known, except for a parameter $\boldsymbol{\theta}_k$. In unsupervised learning, the classification of each sample in the training sequence $\mathbf{x}_1, \mathbf{x}_2, \ldots$ is unknown, and we wish to learn the values of $\boldsymbol{\theta}_k$, $k = 1, 2 \cdots, K$, from observing the unclassified training sequence. Since the classifications of the samples are unknown, there is no way to learn separately the parameters of the density functions $f_k(\mathbf{x}|\boldsymbol{\theta}_k)$ as we did in supervised learning. Indeed, at first it was thought impossible to learn the parameters in an unsupervised manner. Considerable progress has been made since the early 1960s, and several approaches have been proposed for unsupervised learning. Some of the approaches are discussed in this and subsequent sections.

It is intuitively obvious that unsupervised learning is more difficult than supervised learning. In practice, it is reasonable that the machine learns at first with supervision, and that after a sufficient number of iterations, the machine may learn the parameter values without supervision, and perhaps at the same time classify the observed patterns.

Unsupervised parametric learning may be formulated in terms of a mixture model. Let us define a parameter vector $\boldsymbol{\theta}$,

$$\boldsymbol{\theta}^T = [\boldsymbol{\theta}_1^T, \ldots, \boldsymbol{\theta}_K^T]. \tag{3.101}$$

When a sample $\mathbf{x}$ is observed, we do not know to which class it belongs, but may assume that it has a probability p_k of belonging to C_k. Then we may write

$$f(\mathbf{x}|\boldsymbol{\theta}) = \sum_{k=1}^{K} p_k f_k(\mathbf{x}|\boldsymbol{\theta}_k), \tag{3.102}$$

where $f(\mathbf{x}|\boldsymbol{\theta})$ is the mixture density function for given $\boldsymbol{\theta}$, and the probabilities p_k are sometimes called mixing parameters. A typical mixture density is shown in figure 3.3. For a sequence of n samples, we assume that $\mathbf{x}_1, \ldots, \mathbf{x}_n$ are conditionally independent, i.e.,

$$f(\mathbf{x}_1, \ldots, \mathbf{x}_n|\boldsymbol{\theta}) = \prod_{i=1}^{n} f(\mathbf{x}_i|\boldsymbol{\theta}) = \prod_{i=1}^{n} [\sum_{k=1}^{K} p_k f_k(\mathbf{x}_i|\boldsymbol{\theta}_k)]. \tag{3.103}$$

Note that the independence is with respect to the mixture density rather than the density functions for each class.

We have assumed that the mixing parameters p_k are known. If they are unknown, we may let

$$\boldsymbol{\theta}^T = [\boldsymbol{\theta}_1^T, \ldots, \boldsymbol{\theta}_k^T, p_1, \ldots, p_k], \tag{3.104}$$

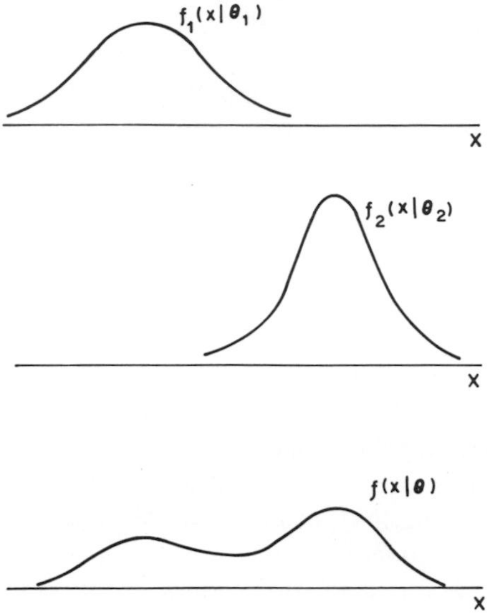

fig. 3.3 A typical mixture density function.

and (3.102) and (3.103) still hold. Sometimes even the number of classes K is unknown. In this case, we assume that the maximum possible number of classes is known, and some of the true p_k in (3.104) are zeros. The parameter $\boldsymbol{\theta}_k$ associated with zero p_k may be set to any convenient value.

3.4.1 Unsupervised Bayes learning

With the assumptions above, we can easily derive an unsupervised learning scheme similar to the supervised Bayes learning scheme. Equation (3.103), is mathematically equivalent to (3.71), although the physical interpretations of the two equations are different. Thus we obtain, in a fashion similar to the derivation of (3.80),

$$f(\boldsymbol{\theta}|\mathbf{x}_1, \ldots, \mathbf{x}_n) = \frac{f(\mathbf{x}_n|\boldsymbol{\theta}) f(\boldsymbol{\theta}|\mathbf{x}_1, \ldots, \mathbf{x}_{n-1})}{\int f(\mathbf{x}_n|\boldsymbol{\theta}) f(\boldsymbol{\theta}|\mathbf{x}_1, \ldots, \mathbf{x}_{n-1})\, d\boldsymbol{\theta}}. \tag{3.105}$$

The computations at different stages are similar. The total number of computations increases only linearly with n, and the storage space required remains fixed.

It is perhaps more instructive to substitute $f(\mathbf{x}_n|\boldsymbol{\theta})$ from (3.102) in (3.105).

We obtain

$$f(\boldsymbol{\theta}|\mathbf{x}_1, \ldots, \mathbf{x}_n) = \frac{f(\boldsymbol{\theta}|\mathbf{x}_1, \ldots, \mathbf{x}_{n-1}) \sum_{k=1}^{K} p_k f_k(\mathbf{x}_n|\boldsymbol{\theta}_k)}{\int f(\boldsymbol{\theta}|\mathbf{x}_1, \ldots, \mathbf{x}_{n-1}) \sum_{k=1}^{K} p_k f_k(\mathbf{x}_n|\boldsymbol{\theta}_k) d\boldsymbol{\theta}}. \quad (3.106)$$

The relationship between $\boldsymbol{\theta}$ and $\boldsymbol{\theta}_k$ is defined by (3.101) or (3.104). Equation (3.106) indicates more clearly the complexity of unsupervised learning compared with supervised learning. It is interesting to note that even when there is only one unknown parameter, vector $\boldsymbol{\theta}_1$, the posterior density $f(\boldsymbol{\theta}_1|\mathbf{x}_1, \ldots, \mathbf{x}_n)$ depends on the distributions of other classes. This is typical of unsupervised learning, and it is the reason for the complexity and difficulty in devising an optimal unsupervised learning scheme.

We note that the mixture density $f(\mathbf{x}|\boldsymbol{\theta})$ in (3.102) is a sum of $p_k f_k(\mathbf{x}|\boldsymbol{\theta}_k)$, hence $f(\mathbf{x}_1, \ldots, \mathbf{x}_n|\boldsymbol{\theta})$ cannot be factored in the form of (3.93). Thus, according to theorem 3.4, there exists no reproducing density for unsupervised learning, and the only way to compute $f(\boldsymbol{\theta}|\mathbf{x}_1, \ldots, \mathbf{x}_n)$ or the Bayes estimator for $\boldsymbol{\theta}$ is by numerical methods. Whenever the dimensionality of $\boldsymbol{\theta}$ is greater than 2 or 3, the computations, although similar at each stage, become excessive. For this reason, unsupervised Bayes learning is mostly of theoretical interest.

3.4.2 Decision-directed learning

The unsupervised Bayes estimator is difficult to implement, as is mentioned above. The maximum likelihood estimator is also impractical because the maximum likelihood equation for a mixture density is usually nonlinear, and we must solve the equation after every additional observation. One way to avoid these difficulties is to use decision-directed estimation.

Decision-directed learning was introduced in the early 1960s (Glaser, 1961; Jakowatz et al., 1961) for estimating signal waveforms. At the n-th time interval, the receiver receives either signal-plus-noise, $\mathbf{x}_n = \boldsymbol{\theta} + \mathbf{n}_n$, or noise only, $\mathbf{x}_n = \mathbf{n}_n$. The noise is Gaussian distributed, and the signal waveform $\boldsymbol{\theta}$ is to be estimated. It is easy to see that the problem can be formulated in terms of a mixture density as in (3.102) with $\boldsymbol{\theta}_1 = \mathbf{0}$ being known and $\boldsymbol{\theta}_2 = \boldsymbol{\theta}$.

The idea of decision-directed learning is rather simple. Let us consider a slightly more general case with $\boldsymbol{\theta}$ defined in (3.101) and $\boldsymbol{\omega}^T = [\boldsymbol{\omega}_1^T, \ldots, \boldsymbol{\omega}_K^T]$. Suppose we have at the n-th stage an estimator $\boldsymbol{\omega}(n) = \boldsymbol{\omega}(\mathbf{x}_1, \ldots, \mathbf{x}_{n-1})$ for $\boldsymbol{\theta}$, and an observation of $\mathbf{x}_n$ is made. If the classification of $\mathbf{x}_n$ were known,

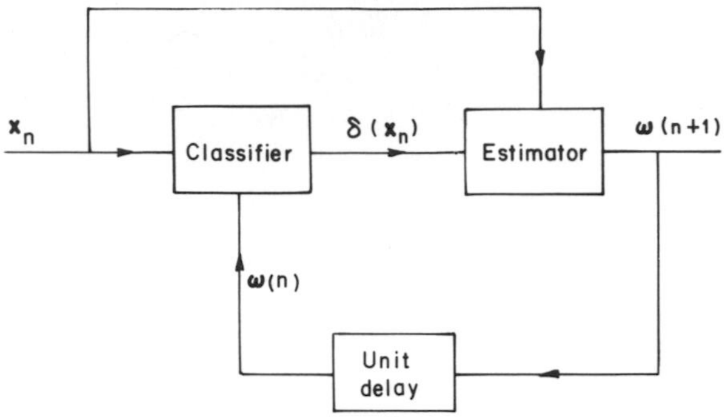

fig. 3.4 Block diagram for decision-directed learning.

say C_j, we would use $\mathbf{x}_n$ to update the estimation of $\boldsymbol{\theta}_j$ only. Since the classification of $\mathbf{x}_n$ is unknown, we let the machine classify $\mathbf{x}_n$, and if the machine decides that $\mathbf{x}_n$ belongs to C_j, $\mathbf{x}_n$ will be used to update the estimation of $\boldsymbol{\theta}_j$. As discussed in section 2.1, the Bayes classifier requires the knowledge of the likelihood functions $f_k(\mathbf{x}|\boldsymbol{\theta}_k)$. With $\boldsymbol{\theta}_k$ being unknown, we simply substitute $\boldsymbol{\theta}_k$ by its estimate $\omega_k(n)$, based on the first $(n-1)$ observations, and use $f_k(\mathbf{x}|\omega_k(n))$, $k = 1, 2, \ldots, K$, for the classification of $\mathbf{x}_n$.

A block diagram for decision-directed learning is shown in figure 3.4. The estimate $\omega(n+1)$ depends on $\mathbf{x}_n$ and $\delta(\mathbf{x}_n)$, the decision made by the machine. After the estimation, $\omega(n+1)$ is used to modify the structure of the classifier. The unit delay is necessary since at the n-th stage, we wish to calculate $\omega(n+1)$ while the classifier is based on $\omega(n)$. It is obvious that in such a scheme, the machine may perform classification and estimation at the same time. To be more specific, let us consider a simple example.

EXAMPLE 3.5

Let the mixture density be

$$f(x|m) = \frac{1}{2}g(x; 0, 1) + \frac{1}{2}g(x; m, 1). \tag{3.107}$$

If m of class C_2 were known, we could classify x_n using the following optimal decision rule

$$\delta(x_n) = \begin{cases} C_1 & \text{if } x_n < m/2, \\ C_2 & \text{if } x_n \geqslant m/2. \end{cases} \tag{3.108}$$

Now although m is unknown, we have at the n-th stage an estimate of m, $\omega(n)$, based on the observations $x_1, \ldots, x_{n-1}$. We substitute $\omega(n)$ for m in (3.108), and use x_n to update the estimation of m if and only if $\delta(x_n) = C_2$, i.e., if and only if $x_n \geqslant \omega(n)/2$. Thus, our decision-directed estimation scheme is

$$\omega(n+1) = \begin{cases} \omega(n) & \text{if } x_n < \omega(n)/2, \\ \omega(n) - \dfrac{2}{n}(\omega(n) - x_n) & \text{if } x_n \geqslant \omega(n)/2. \end{cases} \tag{3.109}$$

Note that when $x_n \geqslant \omega(n)/2$, the scheme is essentially the recursive form of the sample mean shown in (3.33), and the factor 2 is introduced because the prior probability of C_2 is 1/2.

Decision-directed learning is attractive because of its conceptual and computational simplicity. It is conceptually a natural extension of supervised Bayes learning. On the other hand, the analysis of a decision-directed scheme is relatively difficult because a decision must be made at each stage. Experience indicates that these schemes usually converge, but only to a value near $\boldsymbol{\theta}$ instead of to $\boldsymbol{\theta}$ itself. In other words, they are often inconsistent. Another problem in decision-directed learning is the possibility of a runaway. A runaway occurs when a sequence of misclassifications causes the degradation of parameter estimates, which in turn causes more misclassifications. Eventually the scheme converges to a value substantially different from the true value. Recent works (Davisson and Schwartz, 1970; Young and Farjo, 1972) indicate that some decision-directed schemes may be analyzed using stochastic approximation theory. The analysis will be discussed in section 5.1.2.

3.4.3 Other unsupervised learning schemes

There are many procedures for unsupervised learning, both parametric and nonparametric. In the following paragraphs we outline briefly three different approaches.

The first approach is a recursive algorithm for estimating $\boldsymbol{\theta}$. We have said that there is no reproducing density for unsupervised learning, i.e., $f(\boldsymbol{\theta}|\mathbf{x}_1, \ldots, \mathbf{x}_n)$ cannot reproduce itself, hence the Bayes estimator cannot be written recursively. Nevertheless, it is possible to have a recursive non-Bayes estimation scheme for $\boldsymbol{\theta}$. A convenient way to derive such a scheme is to use stochastic approximation. The theory of stochastic approximation is studied in detail in chapter 5. In addition to an analysis of the relationship between decision-directed learning and stochastic approximation, a gradient type algorithm for unsupervised learning is derived in section 5.5, which is asymptotically a maximum likelihood estimator.

The next approach is nonparametric estimation and clustering. We have been concerned with parametric schemes with the functional form of $f_k(\mathbf{x}|\boldsymbol{\theta}_k)$, known except for the parameters $\boldsymbol{\theta}_k$. Nonparametric schemes are needed when this knowledge is not available. In the next section, we discuss a nonparametric scheme that requires the storage of all samples $\mathbf{x}_1, \ldots, \mathbf{x}_n$, and uses these stored samples to approximate the mixture density function. There is a class of nonparametric schemes commonly known as clustering procedures. A clustering procedure divides the set of all samples into subsets or clusters, in the hope each cluster corresponds to one class. Clustering will be discussed in section 4.5.

The final approach considered here is unsupervised learning using moment estimators. The moments of the mixture density can be estimated recursively. For example, consider a one-dimensional mixture density $f(x|\boldsymbol{\theta})$. The mean value of x, $E[x]$, may be estimated by the sample mean, $(1/n)\sum_{i=1}^{n} x_i$, which can be written recursively as demonstrated by (3.32) and (3.33) in example 3.2. The higher-order moments, $E[x^2]$, $E[x^3], \ldots$, can also be estimated recursively. After estimating the moments, we may estimate the parameter $\boldsymbol{\theta}$ through the moment estimator. The following example illustrates this approach.

EXAMPLE 3.6

Consider a one-dimensional Gaussian mixture,

$$f(x|\theta) = pg(x; m_1, r_1) + (1-p)g(x; m_2, r_2).$$

Then the first three moments are

$$\begin{aligned} E[x] &= pm_1 + (1-p)m_2, \\ E[x^2] &= p(m_1^2 + r_1) + (1-p)(m_2^2 + r_2), \\ E[x^3] &= p(m_1^3 + 3m_1 r_1) + (1-p)(m_2^3 + 3m_2 r_2). \end{aligned} \tag{3.110}$$

(1) Assume that $r_1 = r_2 = r$ is known and $m_2 = 0$, and we wish to estimate $\boldsymbol{\theta}^T = [m_1, p]$. Using the first two equations in (3.110), we obtain

$$m_1 = \frac{E[x^2] - r}{E[x]},$$

$$p = \frac{E[x]}{m_1}.$$

In order to estimate the parameters m_1 and p, we simply substitute for $E[x]$ and $E[x^2]$ with their recursive estimates.

(2) Let $m_2 = 0$ and m_1, p and $r = r_1 = r_2$ be the parameters to be estimated. Then, (3.110) becomes

$$\begin{aligned} E[x] &= pm_1, \\ E[x^2] &= pm_1^2 + r, \\ E[x^3] &= p(m_1^3 + 3m_1 r). \end{aligned} \tag{3.111}$$

Solving the three equations simultaneously gives us

$$m_1^2 - 3m_1 E[x] + 3E[x^2] - E[x^3]/E[x] = 0.$$

This is a second-order equation in m_1, and it has a unique solution if and only if

$$9E^2[x] - 12E[x^2] + 4E[x^3]/E[x] = 0.$$

A substitution of (3.111) for the moments yields

$$m_1^2(3p - 2)^2 = 0.$$

The condition for unique solution is either $m_1 = 0$ or $p = 2/3$. When there are two solutions for (3.111), one way to resolve this difficulty is simply to estimate the fourth moment $E[x^4]$ and select the solution that is more consistent with the estimate of the fourth moment.

*3.4.4 Identifiability of finite mixtures**

In the mixture assumption for unsupervised learning, the densities $f_k(\mathbf{x}|\boldsymbol{\theta}_k)$ usually belong to the same family of density functions $\mathcal{G}$. For example, consider the family of one-dimensional Gaussian densities with nonzero variance, $\mathcal{G} = \{g(x; m, r), r > 0\}$. A Gaussian mixture may be written as

$$f(x|\boldsymbol{\theta}) = \sum_{k=1}^{K} f_k(x|\boldsymbol{\theta}_k)p_k, \qquad f_k(x|\boldsymbol{\theta}_k) \in \mathcal{G} \tag{3.112}$$

* Section may be omitted on first reading.

where

$$\begin{aligned} f_k(x|\boldsymbol{\theta}_k) &= g(x; m_k, r_k), \\ \boldsymbol{\theta}_k^T &= [m_k, r_k], \\ \boldsymbol{\theta}^T &= [\boldsymbol{\theta}_1^T, \ldots, \boldsymbol{\theta}_K^T, p_1, \ldots, p_K]. \end{aligned}$$

A major theoretical question is whether (3.112) is a unique representation of $f(x|\boldsymbol{\theta})$. In other words, we ask whether there exist θ_k', p_k', and K' such that K and K' are finite and

$$\begin{aligned} f(x|\boldsymbol{\theta}) = \sum_{k=1}^{K} f_k(x|\boldsymbol{\theta}_k)p_k &= \sum_{k=1}^{K'} f_k(x|\boldsymbol{\theta}_k')p_k', \\ f_k(x|\boldsymbol{\theta}_k), f_k(x|\boldsymbol{\theta}_k') &\in \mathcal{G}. \end{aligned} \tag{3.113}$$

A trivial cause for the lack of uniqueness is that by permutation the individual terms in (3.112) may be labeled in $K!$ ways. This difficulty may be resolved by establishing an *ordering* $<$ in $\mathcal{G}$ and arranging the terms in (3.112) in such a way that $f_1(x|\boldsymbol{\theta}_1) < f_2(x|\boldsymbol{\theta}_2) < \cdots$. For the family of Gaussian densities, we may define an ordering $g(x; m_j, r_j) < g(x; m_k, r_k)$ if $r_j > r_k$ or if $r_j = r_k$ and $m_j < m_k$. Note that, defined in this way, any subset of the Gaussian family has a unique ordering.*

Consider an arbitrary family $\mathcal{G}$. We assume that an ordering has been defined, and the densities $f_k(x|\boldsymbol{\theta}_k)$ in a mixture are arranged in this order. Under this assumption, the class of all finite mixtures of $\mathcal{G}$ is said to be *identifiable* if (3.113) implies $\boldsymbol{\theta}_k = \boldsymbol{\theta}_k'$, $p_k = p_k'$, and $K = K'$. The concept of identifiability was introduced by Teicher (1961, 1963). Its importance to unsupervised learning is fairly obvious, since the problem is defined in terms of finite mixtures and identifiability simply means that a unique solution to the problem is possible.

It is known that the class of finite mixtures of uniform densities is not identifiable. Let $\mathcal{G}$ be the family consisting of uniform density functions

$$f(x|u_1, u_2) = \begin{cases} \dfrac{1}{u_2 - u_1}, & u_1 \leqslant x < u_2, \\ 0, & \text{elsewhere}. \end{cases}$$

In order to show that, in this case, the class of all finite mixtures is not identifiable, it is necessary only to give an example that violates the uniqueness condition. A simple example is

* We have used the notation $<$ to denote both the ordering and the inequality. Its correct meaning is fairly obvious from the text.

$$f(x|0, u) = \frac{1}{2}f\left(x|0, \frac{u}{2}\right) + \frac{1}{2}f\left(x|\frac{u}{2}, u\right).$$

The following families are identifiable: Poisson distributions, gamma distributions, Cauchy distributions, N-dimensional Gaussian densities, and N-dimensional exponential densities. Let us prove identifiability for the case of one-dimensional Gaussian density functions.

THEOREM 3.5

The class of all finite mixtures of one-dimensional Gaussian density functions is identifiable.

Proof

We have $\mathcal{G} = \{g(x; m, r), r > 0\}$. To simplify the notation, let $g_k(x) = g(x; m_k, r_k)$ and $g'_k(x) = g(x; m'_k, r'_k)$. Assume that

$$\sum_{k=1}^{K} p_k g_k(x) = \sum_{k=1}^{K'} p'_k g'_k(x), \tag{3.114}$$

where $g_1(x) < \cdots < g_K(x)$, $g'_1(x) < \cdots < g'_{K'}(x)$, and

$$0 \lessdot p_k, p'_k \lessdot 1, \sum_{k=1}^{K} p_k = \sum_{k=1}^{K'} p'_k = 1. \tag{3.115}$$

We use the ordering that $g_j(x) < g_k(x)$ if $r_j > r_k$ or if $r_j = r_k$ and $m_j < m_k$.

Let $\tilde{g}(s; m, r)$ be the bilateral Laplace transform of $g(x; m, r)$, then

$$\tilde{g}(s; m, r) = \exp(rs^2 - ms). \tag{3.116}$$

With $\tilde{g}_k(s) = \tilde{g}(s; m_k, r_k)$ and $\tilde{g}'_k(s) = \tilde{g}(s, m'_k, r'_k)$, (3.114) may be written as

$$\sum_{k=1}^{K} p_k \tilde{g}_k(s) = \sum_{k=1}^{K'} p'_k \tilde{g}'_k(s). \tag{3.117}$$

Suppose $g_1(x) \neq g'_1(x)$, we may assume without loss of generality that $g_1(x) < g'_1(x)$. Dividing both sides of (3.117) by $\tilde{g}_1(s)$, we obtain

$$p_1 + \sum_{k=2}^{K} p_k \frac{\tilde{g}_k(s)}{\tilde{g}_1(s)} = \sum_{k=1}^{K'} p'_k \frac{\tilde{g}'_k(s)}{\tilde{g}_1(s)}. \tag{3.118}$$

Since

$$\frac{\tilde{g}_k(s)}{\tilde{g}_1(s)} = \exp[(r_k - r_1)s^2 - (m_k - m_1)s],$$

and with $k \geqslant 2$, $r_1 > r_k$ or $m_1 < m_k$ if $r_1 = r_k$, as $s \to \infty$,

$$\lim_{s\to\infty} \frac{\tilde{g}_k(s)}{\tilde{g}_1(s)} = 0,\ k = 2, 3, \ldots, K.$$

Similarly, since $g_1(x) < g'_1(x) < g'_2(x) < \cdots$, we have

$$\lim_{s\to\infty} \frac{\tilde{g}'_k(s)}{\tilde{g}'_2(s)} = 0,\ k = 1, 2, \ldots, K'.$$

Therefore, as $s \to \infty$, (3.118) implies $p_1 = 0$ which is contradictory to (3.115) that $p_1 > 0$. Hence, $g_1(x) = g'_1(x)$.

With $g_1(x) = g'_1(x)$, we have $\tilde{g}_1(s) = \tilde{g}'_1(s)$ for any value of s, and (3.118) becomes

$$(p_1 - p'_1) + \sum_{k=2}^{K} \frac{\tilde{g}_k(s)}{\tilde{g}_1(s)} = \sum_{k=2}^{K'} \frac{\tilde{g}'_k(s)}{\tilde{g}_1(s)}.$$

Again, by letting $s \to \infty$, we obtain $p_1 = p'_1$, and (3.114) reduces to

$$\sum_{k=2}^{K} p_k g_k(x) = \sum_{k=2}^{K'} p'_k g'_k(x).$$

By repeating the same arguments, we have $g_k(x) = g'_k(x)$ and $p_k = p'_k$, $k = 1, 2, \ldots, \min(K, K')$. Finally if $K \neq K'$, say $K > K'$, then

$$\sum_{k=K'+1}^{K} p_k g_k(x) = 0,$$

which implies $p_k = 0$, $K' + 1 \leqslant k \leqslant K$, in contradiction to $p_k > 0$. Therefore, $K = K'$, and since (3.114) is any finite Gaussian mixture, the class of all finite mixtures of Gaussian densities is identifiable.

3.5 Nonparametric Estimation and Classification

In parametric learning, we assume that the conditional density for class C_k, $f_k(\mathbf{x}|\boldsymbol{\theta})$, is known except for the parameter vector $\boldsymbol{\theta}$. In many pattern recognition problems we have no knowledge of the distributions, and must make estimations and classifications based on a sequence of samples $\mathbf{x}_1, \mathbf{x}_2, \ldots$, only. Since we do not even know the functional form of the density functions, the only ways to learn the density functions are nonparametric schemes.

A simple nonparametric method is illustrated in figure 3.5, where the one-dimensional pattern space is divided into K_i equally spaced intervals and two infinite intervals. When a sequence of samples $x_1, \ldots, x_n$ is observed, we simply count n_k, the number of samples falling into the k-th interval. Clearly n_k/n is an estimate of the probability that the random variable has a value within the k-th interval. In this way we have an estimation of the unknown density $f(x)$. The accuracy of the estimation depends on the size of the intervals and the number of samples n.

In the following paragraphs we discuss two important nonparametric approaches, empirical estimation of probability density functions, and the nearest-neighbor classification. Both methods have interesting theoretical properties.

3.5.1 Parzen's approximation of probability density functions

Consider the one-dimensional case. Let $x_1, x_2 \cdots$, be a sequence of statistically independent and identically distributed random variables with unknown density function $f(x)$. When n samples are observed, we use the following approximation for $f(x)$,

$$\hat{f}_n(x) = \frac{1}{n} \sum_{i=1}^{n} \frac{1}{\alpha_n} K\left(\frac{x - x_i}{\alpha_n}\right), \tag{3.119}$$

where α_n is a constant depending on the sample size n, and $K(x - x_i/\alpha_n)$ is a basis function for the approximation centered about x_i, the i-th sample. Typical choices for $K(v)$ are $K(v) = (1/2)e^{-|v|}$, $K(v) = (1/\sqrt{2\pi})e^{-v^2/2}$, and $K(v) = 1/2$ for $|v| \leqslant 1$, and zero elsewhere.

It is essential to note that while $f(x)$ is a deterministic function of x, $\hat{f}_n(x)$ is a random function of x due to the randomness of the samples $x_1, \ldots, x_n$.

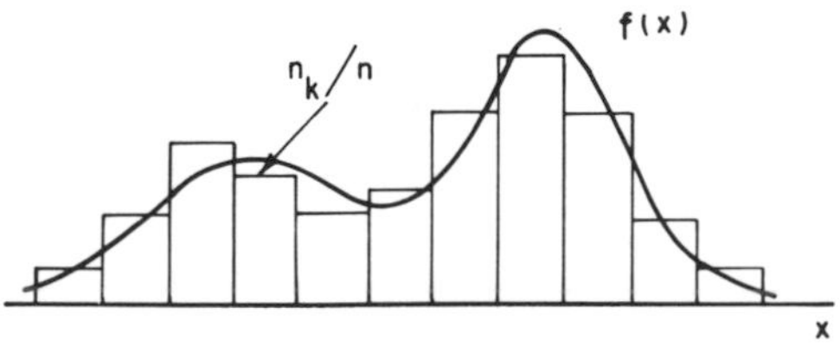

fig. 3.5 A nonparametric estimation scheme (adapted from Patrick and Hancock, 1966).

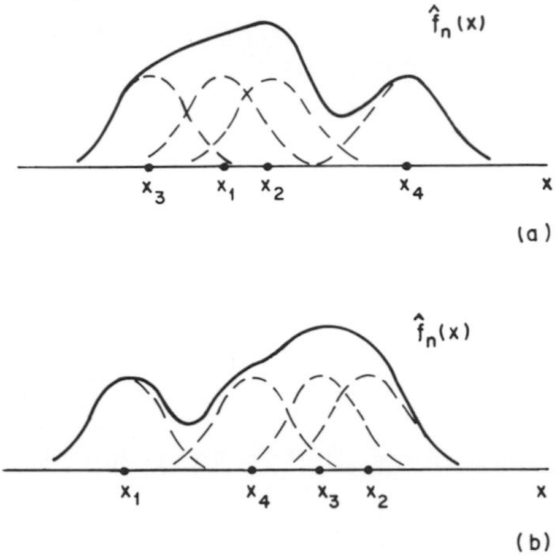

fig. 3.6 Sample functions of Parzen's approximation of $f(x)$ using Gaussian basis functions.

Parzen (1962) has shown that under some general conditions, the random function $\hat{f}_n(x)$ converges to the true density $f(x)$ as n approaches infinity.

A simple example is shown in figure 3.6, with $K(v)$ being a Gaussian density and $n = 4$. In (*a*) and (*b*) we show two sample functions of $\hat{f}_n(x)$, which are constructed from the observed values of the random sequence x_1, x_2, x_3, x_4.

THEOREM 3.6

Let $K(v)$ be a function satisfying the conditions

$$\begin{aligned} &0 \leqslant K(v) \leqslant M < \infty \qquad \text{for all } v, \\ &\int_{-\infty}^{\infty} K(v)\, dv = 1, \\ &\lim_{v\to\pm\infty} |vK(v)| = 0, \end{aligned} \tag{3.120}$$

and $\{\alpha_n\}$ be a sequence of positive numbers such that

$$\begin{aligned} \lim_{n\to\infty} \alpha_n &= 0, \\ \lim_{n\to\infty} n\alpha_n &= \infty. \end{aligned} \tag{3.121}$$

Then, at every point of continuity of $f(x)$,

$$\lim_{n\to\infty} E[\hat{f}_n(x)] = f(x),$$
$$\lim_{n\to\infty} \text{Var}\,[\hat{f}_n(x)] = 0, \tag{3.122}$$

where $\hat{f}_n(x)$ is defined in (3.119).

Proof

Let x_0 be a point of continuity of $f(x)$. Using (3.119) and taking expectation, we obtain

$$E[\hat{f}_n(x_0)] = \frac{1}{n}\sum_{i=1}^{n} E\left[\frac{1}{\alpha_n} K\left(\frac{x_0 - x_i}{\alpha_n}\right)\right]. \tag{3.123}$$

Note that the random variables, x_i, $i = 1, \ldots, n$, are identically distributed with density function $f(x)$. Hence

$$\begin{aligned} E[\hat{f}_n(x_0)] &= E_x\left[\frac{1}{\alpha_n} K\left(\frac{x_0 - x}{\alpha_n}\right)\right] \\ &= \int \frac{1}{\alpha_n} K\left(\frac{x_0 - x}{\alpha_n}\right) f(x)\, dx \\ &= \int \frac{1}{\alpha_n} K\left(\frac{x}{\alpha_n}\right) f(x_0 - x)\, dx. \end{aligned} \tag{3.124}$$

Let $u > 0$, and split the region of integration into two regions, $|x| \leqslant u$ and $|x| > u$. If we let $v = x/\alpha_n$, we have for $|x| > u$,

$$\begin{aligned} \int_{|x|>u} \frac{1}{\alpha_n} K\left(\frac{x}{\alpha_n}\right) f(x_0 - x)\, dx &= \int_{|x|>u} vK(v)\frac{1}{x} f(x_0 - x)\, dx \\ &\leqslant \frac{1}{u} \max_{|v|>u/\alpha_n} [|vK(v)|] \int f(x)\, dx. \end{aligned} \tag{3.125}$$

As $n \to \infty$, $\alpha_n \to 0$ and by the last equation of (3.120), (3.125) approaches zero. Hence,

$$\begin{aligned} \lim_{n\to\infty} E[\hat{f}_n(x_0)] &= \lim_{n\to\infty} \int_{|x|\leqslant u} \frac{1}{\alpha_n} K\left(\frac{x}{\alpha_n}\right) f(x_0 - x)\, dx \\ &= \lim_{n\to\infty} \int_{|v|\leqslant u/\alpha_n} K(v) f(x_0 - \alpha_n v)\, dv. \end{aligned}$$

Since $f(x)$ is continuous at x_0, as $\alpha_n \to 0$, $f(x_0 - \alpha_n v) \to f(x_0)$ and

$$\lim_{n\to\infty} E[\hat{f}_n(x_0)] = f(x_0)\int_{|v|\leqslant\infty} K(v)\,dv = f(x_0), \tag{3.126}$$

where we have used (3.120).

Next, let us consider the variance. Since $x_1, \ldots, x_n$ are independent and identically distributed, we have

$$\begin{aligned}\text{Var}\,[f_n(x_0)] &= \frac{1}{n^2}\sum_{i=1}^{n}\text{Var}\left[\frac{1}{\alpha_n}K\left(\frac{x_0-x_i}{\alpha_n}\right)\right] \\ &= \frac{1}{n}\text{Var}\left[\frac{1}{\alpha_n}K\left(\frac{x_0-x}{\alpha_n}\right)\right] \\ &= \frac{1}{n\alpha_n}\left\{\int\frac{1}{\alpha_n}K^2\left(\frac{x_0-x}{\alpha_n}\right)f(x)\,dx - \alpha_n E^2[\hat{f}_n(x_0)]\right\},\end{aligned} \tag{3.127}$$

where we have used (3.124). It is noted that (3.120) implies

$$0 \leqslant K^2(v) \leqslant M^2 < \infty,$$

$$\int K^2(v)\,dv < M\int K(v)\,dv = M,$$

$$\lim_{v\to\pm\infty}|vK^2(v)| \leqslant \lim_{v\to\pm\infty} M|vK(v)| = 0.$$

Hence, using an argument similar to the one that led us from (3.124) to (3.126), we obtain

$$\lim_{n\to\infty}\int\frac{1}{\alpha_n}K^2\left(\frac{x_0-x}{\alpha_n}\right)f(x)\,dx = f(x_0)\int K^2(v)\,dv, \tag{3.128}$$

which is finite. We note that as $\alpha_n \to 0$, $\alpha_n E^2[\hat{f}_n(x_0)] \to 0$, and from (3.127) and (3.128),

$$\lim_{n\to\infty} n\alpha_n\,\text{Var}\,[\hat{f}_n(x_0)] = f(x_0)\int K^2(v)\,dv. \tag{3.129}$$

The right-hand side of (3.129) is finite, and by (3.121) $n\alpha_n \to \infty$. Consequently,

$$\lim_{n\to\infty}\text{Var}\,[\hat{f}_n(x_0)] = 0.$$

It is noted that in applying the estimate (3.119), it is necessary to store all samples $x_1, \ldots, x_n$. Intuitively, if we have a very large number of samples, we should know the distribution. Theorem 3.6 gives us the conditions on $K(v)$ and α_n such that the estimator $\hat{f}_n(x)$ becomes a consistent estimator for $f(x)$.

The assumptions on $K(v)$ imply that $K(v)$ is a probability density function, which in turn implies that $\hat{f}_n(x)$ in (3.119) is a density function, i.e., $\hat{f}_n(x) \geqslant 0$, $\int \hat{f}_n(x)\,dx = 1$. As $\alpha_n \to 0$, $(1/\alpha_n)K(x/\alpha_n)$ approaches a delta function, and using this heuristic argument we may obtain immediately from (3.124) that $E[\hat{f}_n(x)] = f(x)$. Condition (3.121) suggests that we should use a relatively large α_n for small sample size n, and a small α_n when n becomes large. In practice, the selection of α_n is difficult.

Theorem 3.6 may be extended to multivariate densities. We have for the N-dimensional case

$$\hat{f}_n(\mathbf{x}) = \frac{1}{n}\sum_{i=1}^{n} (\alpha_n)^{-N} K\left(\frac{1}{\alpha_n}(\mathbf{x} - \mathbf{x}_i)\right). \tag{3.130}$$

It is convenient to use a $K(\mathbf{v})$ that is a product of $K(v)$ for the one-dimensional case. For example, we may use

$$K(\mathbf{v}) = g(\mathbf{v}; \mathbf{0}, \mathbf{I}) = \prod_{l=1}^{N} g(v_l; 0, 1),$$

where $\mathbf{I}$ is the identity matrix and v_l is the l-th component of $\mathbf{v}$. In this case, (3.130) becomes

$$\hat{f}_n(\mathbf{x}) = \frac{1}{n}\sum_{i=1}^{n} g(\mathbf{x}; \mathbf{x}_i, \alpha_n^2 \mathbf{I}). \tag{3.131}$$

3.5.2 Nearest-neighbor classification

The nearest-neighbor classification is a nonparametric method that does not assume the functional form of conditional density functions. Let $\mathcal{X}_n = \{\mathbf{x}_1, \mathbf{x}_2, \ldots, \mathbf{x}_n\}$ be a set of n independent samples. For simplicity, we consider the two-class problem, and assume that the classification of each sample in $\mathcal{X}_n$ is known. The set of samples and their classifications are stored in the machine. When a new pattern vector $\mathbf{x}$ is observed and is to be classified, we calculate the distances between $\mathbf{x}$ and $\mathbf{x}_i$, $i = 1, \ldots, n$, and call $\hat{\mathbf{x}}_n$ the nearest neighbor to $\mathbf{x}$ if

$$\min(\mathbf{x} - \mathbf{x}_i)^T(\mathbf{x} - \mathbf{x}_i) = (\mathbf{x} - \hat{\mathbf{x}}_n)^T(\mathbf{x} - \hat{\mathbf{x}}_n),\ \mathbf{x}_i, \hat{\mathbf{x}}_n \in \mathcal{X}_n, \tag{3.132}$$

where the subscript n in $\hat{\mathbf{x}}_n$ indicates that $\hat{\mathbf{x}}_n$ is the nearest neighbor to $\mathbf{x}$ among the set of n sample vectors. The vector $\mathbf{x}$ is classified according to the classification of its nearest neighbor $\hat{\mathbf{x}}_n$.

It is clear intuitively that as n becomes large, the nearest neighbor of $\mathbf{x}$ will be very close to $\mathbf{x}$. Let us assume that for the unknown mixture density

$f(\mathbf{x})$, and any two random samples $\mathbf{x}$ and $\mathbf{x}_i$,

$$P\{\|\mathbf{x} - \mathbf{x}_i\| < \varepsilon\} = p_\varepsilon > 0, \tag{3.133}$$

where $\varepsilon > 0$ and $\|\mathbf{x} - \mathbf{x}_i\|$ is the norm of $\mathbf{x} - \mathbf{x}_i$ defined by

$$\|\mathbf{x} - \mathbf{x}_i\|^2 = (\mathbf{x} - \mathbf{x}_i)^T(\mathbf{x} - \mathbf{x}_i). \tag{3.134}$$

Since $\mathbf{x}_1, \ldots, \mathbf{x}_n$ are independent and $\hat{\mathbf{x}}_n$ is the nearest neighbor of $\mathbf{x}$, we have

$$P\{\|\mathbf{x} - \hat{\mathbf{x}}_n\| \geqslant \varepsilon\} = \prod_{i=1}^{n} P\{\|\mathbf{x} - \mathbf{x}_i\| \geqslant \varepsilon\} = (1 - p_\varepsilon)^n,$$

hence, as $n \to \infty$,

$$\lim_{n\to\infty} P\{\|\mathbf{x} - \hat{\mathbf{x}}_n\| \geqslant \varepsilon\} = 0. \tag{3.135}$$

The nearest neighbor $\hat{\mathbf{x}}_n$ converges to $\mathbf{x}$ in probability.

We wish to investigate the asymptotic performance of the nearest-neighbor classification. More specifically, we shall show that its asymptotic error probability is less than twice thc Bayes error probability. This result is due to Cover and Hart (1967). We note that the Bayes classification is an optimal procedure based on the complete knowledge of the underlying probability distributions, while here the classification is based on the nearest neighbor only. That we are able to obtain this asymptotic error rate for any $f(\mathbf{x})$ is rather remarkable.

Let us return to Bayes classification. We have shown in (2.11) that the Bayes error rate is

$$\rho = \int_{\Omega_\mathbf{x}} \min[p_1 f_1(\mathbf{x}), p_2 f_2(\mathbf{x})]\, d\mathbf{x},$$

where $f_1(\mathbf{x})$ and $f_2(\mathbf{x})$ are conditional densities given C_1 and C_2, respectively, and p_1 and p_2 are prior probabilities. Let us define

$$q_1(\mathbf{x}) = \frac{p_1 f_1(\mathbf{x})}{f(\mathbf{x})}, \qquad q_2(\mathbf{x}) = \frac{p_2 f_2(\mathbf{x})}{f(\mathbf{x})}, \tag{3.136}$$

where $f(\mathbf{x}) = p_1 f_1(\mathbf{x}) + p_2 f_2(\mathbf{x})$ is the mixture density. It is essential to note that defined in this way

$$q_1(\mathbf{x}) = P\{\mathbf{x} \in C_1|\mathbf{x}\}, \quad q_2(\mathbf{x}) = P\{\mathbf{x} \in C_2|\mathbf{x}\} \tag{3.137}$$

are the posterior probabilities of C_1 and C_2 for given $\mathbf{x}$. Since in Bayes classification, $\mathbf{x}$ is classified into C_1 if $q_1(\mathbf{x}) > q_2(\mathbf{x})$, and into C_2 if

$q_1(\mathbf{x}) \leqslant q_2(\mathbf{x})$,

$$r(\mathbf{x}) = \min[q_1(\mathbf{x}), q_2(\mathbf{x})] \tag{3.138}$$

is the conditional Bayes error probability for given $\mathbf{x}$. It is obvious from these definitions that the Bayes error rate may be written as

$$\rho = \int f(\mathbf{x}) \min[q_1(\mathbf{x}), q_2(\mathbf{x})]\, d\mathbf{x} = E[r(\mathbf{x})], \tag{3.139}$$

where the expectation is over the mixture density.

For nearest-neighbor classification, the conditional error for given $\mathbf{x}$ is

$$\hat{r}(\mathbf{x}, \hat{\mathbf{x}}_n) = P\{\mathbf{x} \in C_1, \hat{\mathbf{x}}_n \in C_2 | \mathbf{x}\} + P\{\mathbf{x} \in C_2, \hat{\mathbf{x}}_n \in C_1 | \mathbf{x}\}, \tag{3.140}$$

and similarly to (3.139), the error rate is

$$\hat{\rho}_n = E[\hat{r}(\mathbf{x}, \hat{\mathbf{x}}_n)]. \tag{3.141}$$

Equation (3.140) should be obvious, since $\mathbf{x}$ is classified according to the classification of its nearest neighbor $\hat{\mathbf{x}}_n$. By (3.137) and the independence of $\mathbf{x}$ and $\hat{\mathbf{x}}_n$, we obtain

$$\hat{r}(\mathbf{x}, \hat{\mathbf{x}}_n) = q_1(\mathbf{x}) q_2(\hat{\mathbf{x}}_n) + q_2(\mathbf{x}) q_1(\hat{\mathbf{x}}_n). \tag{3.142}$$

We define as $n \to \infty$,

$$\begin{aligned} \hat{r}(\mathbf{x}) &= \lim_{n \to \infty} \hat{r}(\mathbf{x}, \hat{\mathbf{x}}_n), \\ \hat{\rho} &= \lim_{n \to \infty} \hat{\rho}_n . \end{aligned} \tag{3.143}$$

THEOREM 3.7

Let $f_1(\mathbf{x})$ and $f_2(\mathbf{x})$ be continuous probability density functions. The asymptotic nearest-neighbor error rate $\hat{\rho}$ is bounded by

$$\rho \leqslant \hat{\rho} \leqslant 2\rho(1 - \rho) \tag{3.144}$$

where ρ is the Bayes error rate.

Proof

Since $\hat{\mathbf{x}}_n$ converges to $\mathbf{x}$ in probability, we have for continuous $f_1(\mathbf{x})$ and $f_2(\mathbf{x})$,

$$\lim_{n \to \infty} q_k(\mathbf{x}_n) = q_k(\mathbf{x}), \quad k = 1, 2,$$

in probability. Hence, by (3.142) and (3.143),

$$\hat{r}(\mathbf{x}) = 2q_1(\mathbf{x})q_2(\mathbf{x}) = 2q_1(\mathbf{x})[1 - q_1(\mathbf{x})] = 2q_2(\mathbf{x})[1 - q_2(\mathbf{x})].$$

The conditional Bayes error rate $r(\mathbf{x})$ in (3.138) is either $q_1(\mathbf{x})$ or $q_2(\mathbf{x})$ depending on which one has a smaller value. Thus it is obvious that

$$\hat{r}(\mathbf{x}) = 2r(\mathbf{x})[1 - r(\mathbf{x})]. \tag{3.145}$$

The asymptotic nearest-neighbor error rate $\hat{\rho}$ is

$$\begin{aligned} \hat{\rho} &= \lim_{n\to\infty} E[\hat{r}(\mathbf{x}, \hat{\mathbf{x}}_n)] = E[\lim_{n\to\infty} \hat{r}(\mathbf{x}, \hat{\mathbf{x}}_n)] \\ &= E[\hat{r}(\mathbf{x})] = E[2r(\mathbf{x}) - 2r^2(\mathbf{x})]. \end{aligned} \tag{3.146}$$

Since $\rho = E[r(\mathbf{x})]$, we have

$$\hat{\rho} = 2\rho - 2\rho^2 - 2 \operatorname{Var}[r(\mathbf{x})],$$

hence,

$$\hat{\rho} \leqslant 2\rho(1 - \rho), \tag{3.147}$$

with equality if and only if $r(\mathbf{x}) = \rho$, i.e., $r(\mathbf{x})$ is independent of $\mathbf{x}$.

To show that $\rho \leqslant \hat{\rho}$, let us rewrite (3.146),

$$\hat{\rho} = E[r(\mathbf{x}) + r(\mathbf{x})(1 - 2r(\mathbf{x}))] = \rho + E[r(\mathbf{x})(1 - 2r(\mathbf{x}))]. \tag{3.148}$$

It is noted that

$$0 \leqslant r(\mathbf{x}) = \min[q_1(\mathbf{x}), q_2(\mathbf{x})] \leqslant \frac{1}{2},$$

and the term under the expectation sign of (3.148) is nonnegative for all $\mathbf{x}$. Hence,

$$\rho \leqslant \hat{\rho},$$

with equality if and only if $r(\mathbf{x})(1 - 2r(\mathbf{x})) = 0$.

The nearest-neighbor classification requires the storage of all samples $\mathbf{x}_1, \ldots, \mathbf{x}_n$, but uses only the nearest neighbor for classification. If we use Parzen's approximations for $f_1(\mathbf{x})$ and $f_2(\mathbf{x})$, as n approaches infinity, the approximations $\hat{f}_{n1}(\mathbf{x})$ and $\hat{f}_{n2}(\mathbf{x})$ converge to the true densities, hence it is possible to attain the Bayes error rate. The storage requirements for the two methods are the same, but using Parzen's approximations for classification requires more computation.

The bounds in theorem 3.7 are as tight as possible. That is, given any value of Bayes' error rate ρ, there exist density functions such that $\hat{\rho} = \rho$. There also exist density functions such that $\hat{\rho} = 2\rho(1 - \rho)$ for any given ρ.

For K-class classification problems, it can be shown that

$$\rho \leqslant \hat{\rho} \leqslant \rho\left(2 - \frac{K}{K-1}\rho\right)$$

where ρ is the Bayes error rate and $\hat{\rho}$ is the asymptotic error rate for nearest-neighbor classification in a K-class problem.

The idea of nearest-neighbor classification may be extended to several nearest neighbors, and a new vector $\mathbf{x}$ is classified according to the classification of the majority of its neighbors. This is commonly known as the k-nearest-neighbor classification.

3.6 Notes and Remarks

The first two sections are based on classical statistics. We have mentioned the names Bayes, Cramér, Fisher, and Rao. Interested readers are referred to standard textbooks on mathematical statistics by Cramér (1946), or Wilks (1962), or books written for engineers by Deutsch (1965), Papoulis (1965), or Van Trees (1968).

When the prior density of the unknown parameter $f(\theta)$ is known, we may use a Bayes estimator. We have shown that for a quadratic loss function $(\omega - \theta)^2$, the Bayes estimator is the conditional expectation $E_\theta[\theta|\mathbf{x}_1, \ldots, \mathbf{x}_n]$. We have also mentioned that if the loss function is symmetric and convex, and if the posterior density is symmetric about its mean, the same Bayes estimator results. Obviously when $f(\boldsymbol{\theta}|\mathbf{x}_1, \ldots, \mathbf{x}_n)$ is Gaussian, as in example 3.1, this condition is satisfied. For the Gaussian case, Sherman (1958) showed that the Bayes estimator is the conditional expectation if the loss function $l(\omega - \theta)$ is nonnegative, symmetric, and montonically increasing (decreasing) when $\omega - \theta \geqslant 0 (\leqslant 0)$, and Brown (1962) relaxed the condition further to asymmetric loss functions. DeGroot and Rao (1963) discussed the Bayes estimation using convex loss functions, without imposing the symmetric condition on the posterior density.

When the prior density $f(\theta)$ is unknown, the maximum likelihood estimator is often used, which, under some general conditions, is consistent, asymptotically efficient, and asymptotically Gaussian. The Cramér–Rao bound is important because when the conditions in theorem 3.2 or 3.3 are satisfied, no estimator can yield a smaller estimation error. The two extensions of Cramér–Rao bound to average mean-square error follow Van Trees (1968) and Young and Westerberg (1971).

Supervised Bayes learning was first formulated by Abramson and Braverman (1962) and Braverman (1962). Keehn (1965) discussed the reproducing property in estimating the covariance matrix or the mean and the covariance matrix of a Gaussian distribution. The important relationship between reproducing densities and sufficient statistics is due to Spragins (1965).

Early work on unsupervised Bayes learning (Daly, 1962) considers all possible ways of classifying the sequence of observations, $\mathbf{x}_1, \ldots, \mathbf{x}_n$. The idea is somewhat similar to the compound decision discussed briefly in the last chapter, and the complexity of the scheme increases exponentially with n. The Bayes scheme presented in section 3.4 is based on the work of Fralick (1967), and its complexity increases only linearly with n. Hilborn and Lainiotis (1968, 1969) and Patrick (1968) discussed unsupervised learning with dependent samples. Chen (1969) and Cooper and Freeman (1970) considered hybrid schemes using both supervised and unsupervised learning, and Agrawala (1970) proposed a scheme with probabilistic supervision.

The earliest works on unsupervised learning are decision-directed schemes for signal detection (Glaser, 1961; Jakowatz et al., 1961; Hinich, 1962). Various schemes were proposed, and the problems of error probability, convergence, consistency, and runaway were considered by Davisson and Schwartz (1970), Gregg and Hancock (1968), Lin and Yau (1967), Patrick and Costello (1968, 1969), Patterson and Womack (1966), Scudder (1965a, 1965b), Smith (1964), and Young and Farjo (1972).

Non-Bayesian, nondecision-directed, unsupervised learning schemes were investigated by Chien and Fu (1967), Cooper and Cooper (1964), Cooper (1967), Patrick and Hancock (1966), Sammon (1968), and Stanat (1968). A promising approach used stochastic approximation algorithms which maximized asymptotically a regression function $E[\log f(x|\theta)]$ (Patrick and Costello, 1969; Young and Coraluppi, 1970). Hence, asymptotically this is a maximum-likelihood estimator. Patrick and Costello (1970) discussed the relationship between this regression function and Bayes estimation. Stochastic approximation algorithms will be studied in detail in chapter 5.

The concept of identifiability was introduced and studied by Teicher (1961, 1963, 1967). Theorem 3.5 on the identifiability of Gaussian mixtures is a special case of Teicher's theorem (1963), and was known to Medgyessy (1961). Yakowitz and Spragins (1968) showed that the necessary and sufficient condition of identifiability is linear independence of the density functions of the family. The connection between unsupervised learning and the identifiability of a finite mixture was discussed by Patrick and Hancock (1966) and Yakowitz (1970).

Nearest-neighbor classification was investigated by Fix and Hodges (1951), and theorem 3.7 is due to Cover and Hart (1967). Cover (1968) investigated nearest neighbor estimation, and Hellman (1970) considered nearest-neighbor classification with a rejection option. A generalization of k-nearest-neighbor rule was discussed by Patrick and Fischer (1970). Parzen's approximation of probability density functions (1962) is an important nonparametric approach, and will be used in later chapters. The conditions of theorem 3.6 were relaxed and the method was generalized to multivariate densities by Murthy (1965, 1966).

Problems

3.1 Suppose $x_1, x_2, \ldots, x_n$ are samples from the Poisson distribution

$$P(x_1, \ldots, x_n|\lambda) = \prod_{i=1}^{n} P_0(x_i|\lambda),$$

$$P_0(x|\lambda) = \frac{\lambda^x e^{-\lambda}}{x!},$$

where x is limited to nonnegative integers only. Derive a maximum likelihood estimator for the unknown parameter λ and show that it is an efficient estimator.

3.2 Let $x_1, \ldots, x_n$ be independent samples with a Gaussian density function $g(x_i; m, r)$.

(a) Assume that the mean value m is known and derive a maximum likelihood estimator for the unknown variance r. Is the estimator an efficient estimator?

(b) Derive a maximum likelihood estimator when both m and r are unknown. Is the estimator biased?

3.3 Derive the lower bound on the average mean-square error shown in (3.65).

3.4 Let $x_1, \ldots, x_n$ be a sequence of independent and identically distributed samples with

$$f(x_1, \ldots x_n|\theta) = \prod_{i=1}^{n} g(x_i; \theta, r),$$

where the variance r is assumed known. The prior density for the unknown mean θ is also Gaussian,

$$f(\theta) = g(\theta; 0, \phi_1).$$

Find a lower bound on the average mean-square error. Compare the bound with the results in example 3.1.

3.5 Let θ be an unknown parameter with uniform prior density,

$$f(\theta) = \begin{cases} 1/2u, & -u \leqslant \theta \leqslant u, \\ 0, & \text{elsewhere.} \end{cases}$$

The Fisher information $\sigma_n^2(\theta) = n\sigma^2$ is a constant independent of θ. Show that for any estimator ω with continuously differentiable bias,

$$E_\theta E[(\omega - \theta)^2] \geqslant u^2 B(n\sigma^2 u^2),$$

where

$$B(\alpha) = \frac{1}{\alpha}(1 - \alpha^{-1/2} \tanh \alpha^{1/2}).$$

Sketch $(1/u^2) E_\theta[(\omega - \theta)^2]$ as a function of $n\sigma^2 u^2$ using a logarithmic scale.

3.6 Let $x_1, x_2, \ldots, x_n$ be a sequence of random samples and θ be an unknown parameter. We wish to use a linear estimator for the estimation of θ,

$$\omega = \alpha_1 x_1 + \alpha_2 x_2 + \cdots + \alpha_n x_n = \sum_{i=1}^{n} \alpha_i x_i .$$

Assume that

$$E[\theta] = E[x_i] = 0, \;\; E[x_i x_j] = r_{ij}, \;\; E[\theta x_j] = r_j .$$

A linear estimator that minimizes

$$E[(\omega - \theta)^2] = E[(\sum_j \alpha_i x_i - \theta)^2]$$

is called a linear mean-square estimator. Show that the linear mean-square estimator must satisfy

$$E[x_i(\sum_j \alpha_j x_j - \theta)] = 0, \quad i = 1, 2, \ldots, n,$$

hence

$$\mathbf{R}\boldsymbol{\alpha} = \mathbf{r},$$

where $\mathbf{R}$ is an $n \times n$ matrix with elements r_{ij} and $\mathbf{r}$ is an n-vector with elements r_j.

3.7 Let

$$f(x|\lambda) = \begin{cases} \lambda e^{-\lambda x}, & x \geqslant 0, \lambda > 0, \\ 0, & x < 0. \end{cases}$$

The observed random variable is x and we want to estimate λ. The prior density of λ depends on two parameters μ_1 and ν_1,

$$f(\lambda) = \begin{cases} \dfrac{(\mu_1)^{\nu_1}}{\Gamma(\nu_1)} e^{-\lambda\mu_1} \lambda^{\mu_1 - 1}, & \lambda \geqslant 0, \\ 0, & \lambda < 0, \end{cases}$$

where $\Gamma(\nu)$ is the gamma function.

(a) Assuming that one observation is made, find the posterior density $f(\lambda|x)$ and the Bayes estimator.

(b) Assuming that n conditionally independent observations are made,

$$f(x_1, \ldots, x_n|\lambda) = \sum_{i=1}^{n} f(x_i|\lambda),$$

what is the posterior probability $f(\lambda|x_1, \ldots, x_n)$?

3.8 Determine whether the class of all finite mixtures of each of the following families is identifiable:

(a) the family of binomial distributions;

(b) the family generated by translating a known density function, i.e., $\mathcal{G} = \{f(x; u) = f(x - u)\}$, where $f(x)$ is known.

If either is identifiable, give a proof; otherwise give an example to show that it is not identifiable.

3.9 The nearest-neighbor rule may be extended to K-class pattern classification problems. Show that in this case

$$\rho \leqslant \hat{\rho} \leqslant \rho\left(2 - \frac{K}{K-1}\rho\right)$$

where ρ is the Bayes error rate and $\hat{\rho}$ is the asymptotic nearest-neighbor error rate.

3.10 The bounds on the asymptotic nearest-neighbor error rate in theorem 3.9 are as tight as possible. Given a certain value of ρ,

(a) show that $\hat{\rho} = 2\rho(1 - \rho)$ if and only if

$$\frac{p_1 f_1(\mathbf{x})}{p_2 f_2(\mathbf{x})} = \frac{\rho}{(1-\rho)} \text{ or } \frac{(1-\rho)}{\rho}.$$

(b) show by an example that there exist $f_1(\mathbf{x})$ and $f_2(\mathbf{x})$ such that $\hat{\rho} = \rho$.

3.11 Consider the following mixture density function,

$$f(x) = 0.5g(x; \theta_1, 1) + 0.5g(x; \theta_2, 1), \quad \theta_1 < \theta_2.$$

(a) Devise a decision-directed scheme to estimate the two unknown means.

(b) Simulate the scheme on a digital computer. Use random number generators to generate the conditionally independent samples. The unknown true values are $\theta_1 = 0$ and $\theta_2 = 3$.

(c) Do the same as in (b) with $\theta_1 = 0$, $\theta_2 = 1$.

References

1. Abramson, N. and Braverman, D. 1962. Learning to recognize patterns in a random environment. *IRE Trans. Information Theory* IT-8: S58–63.

2. Agrawala, A. K. 1970. Learning with a probabilistic teacher. *IEEE Trans. Information Theory* IT-16:373–379.

3. Braverman, D. 1962. Learning filters for optimum pattern recognition. *IRE Trans. Information Theory* IT-8:280–285.

4. Brown, J. L. Jr. 1962. Asymmetric non mean-square error criteria. *IRE Trans. Automatic Control* AC-7:64–66.

5. Chen, C. H. 1969. A theory of Bayes learning systems. *IEEE Trans. Systems Science and Cybernetics* SSC-5:30–37.

6. Chien, Y. T. and Fu, K. S. 1967. On Bayesian learning and stochastic approximation. *IEEE Trans. Systems Science and Cybernetics* SSC-3:28–38.

7. Cooper, D. B. and Cooper, P. W. 1964. Nonsupervised adaptive signal detection and pattern recognition. *Information and Control*, 7:416–444.

8. Cooper, D. B. and Freeman, J. H. 1970. On the asymptotic improvement in the outcome of supervised learning provided by additional nonsupervised learning. *IEEE Trans. Computer*, C-19:1055–1063.

9. Cooper, P. W. 1967. Some topics on nonsupervised adaptive detection for multivariate normal distributions. In *Computer and Information Sciences II*, ed. J. T. Tou pp. 123–146. Academic Press, New York.

10. Cover, T. M. 1968. Estimation by the nearest neighbor rule. *IEEE Trans. Information Theory* IT-14:50–55.

11. Cover, T. M. and Hart, P. E. 1967. Nearest neighbor pattern classification. *IEEE Trans. Information Theory* IT-13:21–27.

12. Cramer, H. 1946. *Mathematical Methods of Statistics*. Princeton Univ. Press., Princeton, New Jersey.

13. Daly, R. F. 1962. The adaptive binary detection problem on the real line. Stanford University Technical Report 2003–3.

14. Davisson, L. D. and Schwartz, S. C. 1970. Analysis of a decision-directed receiver with unknown priors. *IEEE Trans. Information Theory* IT-16:270–276.

15. DeGroot, M. H. and Rao, M. M. 1963. Bayes estimation with convex loss, *Ann. Math. Stat.* 34:839–846.

16. Deutsch, R. 1965. *Estimation Theory*. Prentice-Hall, Englewood Cliffs, New Jersey.

17. Fix, E. and Hodges, J. L. Jr. 1951. Discriminatory analysis, nonparametric discrimination. USAF School of Aviation Medicine, Project 21-49-004. Randolph Field, Texas.

18. Fralick, S. C. 1967. Learning to recognize patterns without a teacher. *IEEE Trans. Information Theory* IT-13:57–64.

19. Fu, K. S. 1968. *Sequential Methods in Pattern Recognition and Machine Learning*. Academic Press, New York.

20. Gelfand, I. M. and Formin, S. V. 1963. *Calculus of Variations*. Prentice-Hall, Englewood Cliffs, New Jersey.

21. Glaser, E. M. 1961. Signal detection by adaptive filters. *IRE Trans. Information Theory* IT-7:87–98.

22. Gregg, W. D. and Hancock, J. C. 1968. An optimum decision-directed scheme for Gaussian mixtures. *IEEE Trans. Information Theory* IT-14:451–456.

23. Hellman, M. E. 1970. The nearest neighbor classification rule with a reject option. *IEEE Trans. Systems Science and Cybernetics* SSC-6:179–185.

24. Hilborn, C. G. Jr. and Lainiotis, D. G. 1968. Optimal unsupervised learning multicategory dependent hypotheses pattern recognition. *IEEE Trans. Information Theory* IT-14:468–470.

25. ———. 1969. Unsupervised learning minimum risk pattern classification for dependent hypotheses and dependent measurements. *IEEE Trans. Systems Science and Cybernetics* SSC-5:109–115.

26. Hinich, M. J. 1962. A model for a self-adapting filter. *Information and Control* 5:185–203.

27. Jakowatz, C. V., Shuey, R. L., and White, G. M. 1961. Adaptive waveform recognition. In *Proc. 4th London Symp. on Information Theory*, ed. C. Cherry. Butterworths, Washington, D.C.

28. Keehn, D. G. 1965. A note on learning for Gaussian properties. *IEEE Trans. Information Theory* IT-11:126–132.

29. Lin, T. T. and Yau, S. S. 1967. Bayesian approach to the optimization of adaptive systems. *IEEE Trans. Systems Science and Cybernetics* SSC-3:77–85.

30. Medgyessy, P. 1961. *Decomposition of Superpositions of Distribution Functions*. Plenum, New York.

31. Murthy, V. K. 1965. Estimation of probability density. *Ann. Math. Stat.* 36:1027–1031.

32. ———. 1966. Nonparametric estimation of multivariate densities with applications. In *Multivariate Analysis*. ed. P. R. Krishnaiah, pp.43–56. Academic Press, New York. 56.

33. Papoulis, A. 1965. *Probability, Random Variables and Stochastic Processes*. McGraw-Hill, New York.

34. Parzen, E. 1962. On estimation of a probability density function and Mode. *Ann. Math. Stat.* 33:1065–1076.

35. Patrick, E. A. 1968. On a class of unsupervised estimation systems. *IEEE Trans. Information Theory* IT-14:407–415.

36. Patrick, E. A. and Costello, J. P. 1968. Asymptotic probability of error using two decision-directed estimators for two unknown mean vectors. *IEEE Trans. Information Theory* IT-14:160–162.

37. ———. 1969. Unsupervised estimation and processing of unknown signals. Purdue Univ. Rept. TR-EE69-18.

38. ———. 1970. On unsupervised estimation algorithms. *IEEE Trans. Information Theory* IT-16:556–569.

39. Patrick, E. A. and Fischer, F. P. 1970. A generalization of the *k*-nearest neighbor rule. *Information and Control.* 16:128–152.

40. Patrick, E. A. and Hancock, J. C. 1966. Nonsupervised sequential classification and recognition of patterns. *IEEE Trans. Information Theory* IT-12:362–372.

41. Patterson, J. D. and Womack, B. F. 1966. An adaptive pattern classification system. *IEEE Trans. Systems Science and Cybernetics* SSC-2:62–67.

42. Sammon, J. W. 1968. An adaptive technique for multiple signal detection and identification. In *Pattern Recognition*, ed. L. Kanal, pp. 409–439. Thompson, Washington, D.C.

43. Scudder, H. J. III, 1965a. Adaptive communication receivers. *IEEE Trans. Information Theory* IT-11:167–174.

44. ———. 1965b. Probability of error of some adaptive pattern recognition machines. *IEEE Trans. Information Theory* IT-11:363–371.

45. Sherman, S. 1958. Non-mean-square error criteria. *IRE Trans. Information Theory* IT-4:125–126.

46. Smith, J. W. 1964. The analysis of multiple signal data. *IEEE Trans. Information Theory* IT-10:208–214.

47. Spragins, J. 1965. A note on the iterative application of Bayes rule. *IEEE Trans. Information Theory* IT-11:544–549.

48. Stanat, D. F. 1968. Unsupervised learning of mixtures of probability functions. In *Pattern Recognition*, ed. L. Kanal, pp. 357–389. Thompson, Washington, D.C.

49. Teicher, H. 1961. Identifiability of mixtures. *Ann. Math. Stat.* 32:244–248.

50. ———. 1963. Identifiability of finite mixtures. *Ann. Math. Stat.* 34:1265–1269.

51. ———. 1967. Identifiability of mixtures of product measures. *Ann. Math. Stat.* 38:1300–1302.

52. Van Trees, H. L. 1968. *Detection, Estimation, and Modulation Theory.* Wiley, New York.

53. Wilks, S. S. 1962. *Mathematical Statistics.* Wiley, New York.

54. Yakowitz, S. J. 1970. Unsupervised learning and the identification of finite mixtures. *IEEE Trans. Information Theory* IT-17:330–338.

55. Yakowitz, S. J. and Spragins, J. D. 1968. On the identifiability of finite mixtures. *Ann. Math. Stat.* 39:209–214.

56. Young, T. Y. and Coraluppi, G. 1970. Stochastic estimation of a mixture of normal density functions using an information criterion. *IEEE Trans. Information Theory* IT-16:258–263.

57. Young, T. Y. and Farjo, A. A. 1972. On decision-directed estimation and stochastic approximation. *IEEE Trans. Information Theory* IT-18:671–673.

58. Young, T. Y. and Westerberg, R. A. 1971. Error bounds for stochastic estimation of signal parameters. *IEEE Trans. Information Theory* IT-17:549–557.

4

Linear Discriminant Functions and Clustering

4.1 Discriminant Functions

In this chapter, we make no assumptions on the probability distributions of pattern vectors. The only knowledge we have is a sequence of training samples $\mathbf{x}_1, \ldots, \mathbf{x}_n$, with the classification of each sample being known or unknown. The sample size n is finite, and the dimensionality N of the pattern space $\Omega_{\mathbf{x}}$ is much less than n (sec. 4.6). The methods discussed in this chapter do not estimate the parameters of probability density functions, hence may be considered as nonparametric learning schemes. They differ from the nonparametric approaches described in section 3.5 in that no training samples are stored in the machine during the classification phase, although it may be necessary to store all training samples during the learning phase. For samples of known classifications, the learning experience of the machine is summarized in its discriminant functions.

We recall that in statistical pattern classification, the pattern space $\Omega_{\mathbf{x}}$ is divided into K disjoint decision regions, $\Omega_1, \ldots, \Omega_K$, each region corresponding to one class. The decision regions are determined by the likelihood ratio, and the decision surfaces separating these regions may be specified by discriminant functions. When the pattern vectors are Gaussian distributed, the form of discriminant functions is particularly simple. It is generally quadratic, and becomes linear when the covariance matrices of different classes are the same.

When the probability density functions are unknown, there is no way to find the likelihood ratio. We may, however, subjectively decide the general form of discriminant functions. The choice of this general form may be influenced by several factors: the allowable complexity of the machine, the desired classification accuracy, dimensionality and sample size, and perhaps some qualitative, nonprobabilistic prior knowledge of the pattern vectors. Once the general form is decided, the specific discriminant functions for a particular pattern recognition problem are determined by the machine through its learning experience using the training sequence.

4.1.1 Linear discriminant functions

The simplest form of discriminant function is linear. Linear discriminant functions are defined as

$$D_k(\mathbf{x}) = x_1\alpha_{1k} + x_2\alpha_{2k} +, \ldots, +x_N\alpha_{Nk} + \alpha_{N+1,k}, \qquad k = 1, 2, \ldots, K, \tag{4.1}$$

where K is the number of classes, $x_1, \ldots, x_N$ are the N components of the pattern vector $\mathbf{x}$, and $\alpha_{1k}, \ldots, \alpha_{N+1,k}$ are weighting coefficients. Using vector notation, we may write

$$D_k(\mathbf{x}) = \tilde{\mathbf{x}}^T\boldsymbol{\alpha}_k = \boldsymbol{\alpha}_k^T\tilde{\mathbf{x}}, \tag{4.2}$$

where

$$\tilde{\mathbf{x}}^T = [\mathbf{x}^T, 1],$$

is the transpose of $\tilde{\mathbf{x}}$ called *augmented pattern vector*, and $\boldsymbol{\alpha}_k$ is the k-th *weighting vector* consisting of the $N + 1$ weighting coefficients.

A machine that employs linear discriminant functions is called a *linear machine*. The K weighting vectors are usually estimated by the machine using the training samples. After the training or learning, the machine classifies the pattern vectors using the decision rule,

$$\delta(\mathbf{x}) = C_j \quad \text{if } D_j(\mathbf{x}) > D_k(\mathbf{x}) \quad \text{for all } k \neq j, \tag{4.3}$$

where $\delta(\mathbf{x})$ is the decision function. The decision surfaces are specified by the equation

$$D_j(\mathbf{x}) - D_k(\mathbf{x}) = 0. \tag{4.4}$$

A block diagram of a linear machine is shown in figure 4.1(*a*).

When there are only two classes, $K = 2$, it is more convenient to define a discriminant function,

$$D(\mathbf{x}) = D_1(\mathbf{x}) - D_2(\mathbf{x}) = \boldsymbol{\alpha}^T\tilde{\mathbf{x}}. \tag{4.5}$$

A threshold element is often used with its output $d(\mathbf{x})$ defined by

$$d(\mathbf{x}) = \begin{cases} 1 & \text{if } D(\mathbf{x}) > 0, \\ -1 & \text{if } D(\mathbf{x}) \leqslant 0. \end{cases} \tag{4.6}$$

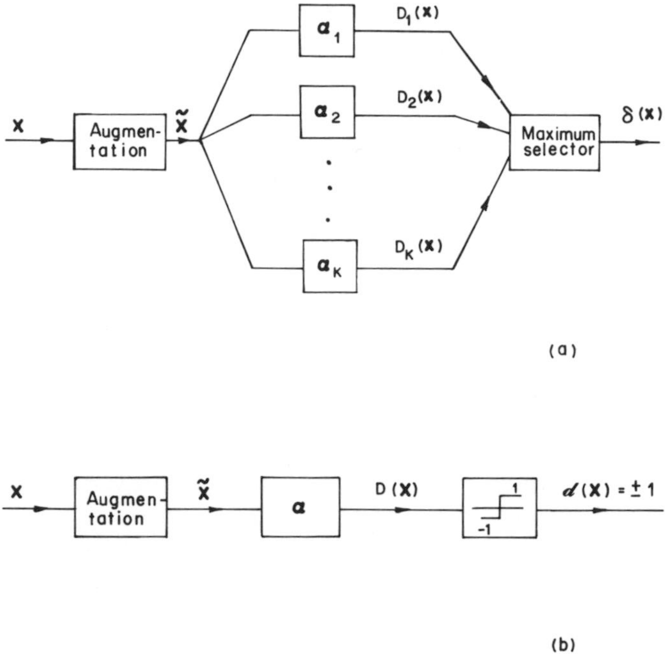

fig. 4.1 (a) A linear machine for multiple classes. (b) Threshold logic unit—a linear machine for two classes.

The values of $d(\mathbf{x})$, 1 and $-$ 1, correspond to $\mathbf{x}$ being classified to C_1 and C_2, respectively, and it is obvious that $d(\mathbf{x})$ is essentially a decision function similar to $\delta(\mathbf{x})$. A block diagram is shown in figure 4.1(*b*). Such a structure is often called a threshold logic unit (TLU).

4.1.2 Nonlinear discriminant functions

Let us consider the two-class problem. A quadratic discriminant function may be written as

$$D(\mathbf{x}) = \sum_{j=1}^{N} \sum_{l=1}^{j} x_l \alpha_{lj} x_j + \sum_{j=1}^{N} x_j \alpha_j + \alpha_{N+1}. \tag{4.7}$$

If we let

$$\begin{aligned} \boldsymbol{\phi}^T(\mathbf{x}) &= [x_1^2, \ldots, x_N^2, x_1 x_2, \ldots, x_{N-1} x_N, x_1, \ldots, x_N], \\ \tilde{\boldsymbol{\phi}}^T(\mathbf{x}) &= [\boldsymbol{\phi}^T(\mathbf{x}), 1], \end{aligned} \tag{4.8}$$

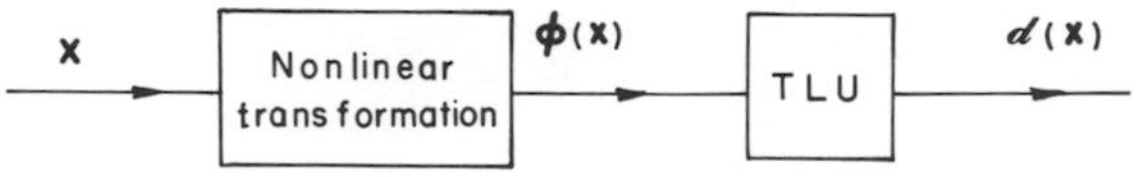

fig. 4.2 A nonlinear machine for two classes.

and

$$\boldsymbol{\alpha}^T = [\alpha_{11}, \ldots, \alpha_{NN}, \alpha_{12}, \ldots, \alpha_{N-1,N}, \alpha_1, \ldots, \alpha_N, \alpha_{N+1}], \tag{4.9}$$

then the quadratic discriminant function may be written as

$$D(\mathbf{x}) = \boldsymbol{\alpha}^T \tilde{\boldsymbol{\phi}}(\mathbf{x}). \tag{4.10}$$

Thus, if we decide to use a quadratic discriminant function, $\tilde{\boldsymbol{\phi}}(\mathbf{x})$ is known, and the machine will estimate the weighting vector $\boldsymbol{\alpha}$ using a sequence of training samples with known classifications.

In general, for any given set of nonlinear functions $\phi_1(\mathbf{x})$, $\phi_2(\mathbf{x}), \ldots,$ $\phi_M(\mathbf{x})$, and a nonlinear discriminant function,

$$D(\mathbf{x}) = \sum_{j=1}^{M} \alpha_j \phi_j(\mathbf{x}) + \alpha_{M+1} = \boldsymbol{\alpha}^T \tilde{\boldsymbol{\phi}}(\mathbf{x}), \tag{4.11}$$

a ϕ-machine will first transform the pattern vector $\mathbf{x}$ in $\Omega_{\mathbf{x}}$ into a vector $\boldsymbol{\phi}$ in an M-space $\Omega_{\boldsymbol{\phi}}$, and then use a linear scheme for classification. In other words, instead of a nonlinear discriminant function in $\Omega_{\mathbf{x}}$, we may think of a linear discriminant function in $\Omega_{\boldsymbol{\phi}}$. Therefore, a learning procedure developed for the linear machine is equally applicable to the ϕ-machine, with $\mathbf{x}$ replaced by $\boldsymbol{\phi}(\mathbf{x})$. Figure 4.2 represents a ϕ-machine for a two-class recognition problem.

In principle, a nonlinear function can be arbitrarily closely approximated by means of high-order polynominals. Thus, one might start out with a high-order polynomial discriminant function, and let the machine find the weighting vector automatically. We note that $\boldsymbol{\alpha}$ is an $(N + 1)$-dimensional vector for the linear machine, and becomes an $(N + 1)(N + 2)/2$-dimensional vector for the quadratic discriminant function. The dimensionality increases rapidly with the order of the polynominal. The machine becomes very complex, and the required sample size n for training is huge. For this reason, polynomials with an order higher than 2 are seldom used.

Another family of nonlinear discriminant functions is the family of piecewise linear discriminant functions, where more than one hyperplane is used to separate two classes of pattern vectors. The nearest-neighbor classification uses a piecewise linear discriminant function. This can easily be demonstrated by constructing a simple example with a small number of samples in a two-dimensional $\Omega_{\mathbf{x}}$.

4.1.3 Linear separability

Let $\mathcal{S}_{\mathbf{x}} = \{\mathbf{x}_i, i = 1, \ldots, n\}$ be the set of training samples with known classifications, and consider a two-class recognition problem. The set $\mathcal{S}_{\mathbf{x}}$ is *linearly separable* if there exists at least one linear discriminant function $D(\mathbf{x})$ such that

$$\begin{aligned} D(\mathbf{x}_i) &> 0 \quad \text{for every } \mathbf{x}_i \text{ in } C_1 \text{ and } \mathbf{x}_i \in \mathcal{S}_{\mathbf{x}}, \\ D(\mathbf{x}_i) &< 0 \quad \text{for every } \mathbf{x}_i \text{ in } C_2 \text{ and } \mathbf{x}_i \in \mathcal{S}_{\mathbf{x}}. \end{aligned} \tag{4.12}$$

The linear discriminant function $D(\mathbf{x}) = 0$ defines a separating hyperplane in $\Omega_{\mathbf{x}}$. Let $\Omega_{\tilde{\mathbf{x}}}$ be the augmented pattern space. We note that if $\mathcal{S}_{\mathbf{x}}$ is linearly separable in $\Omega_{\mathbf{x}}$, it is linearly separable in $\Omega_{\tilde{\mathbf{x}}}$ by a hyperplane passing through the origin since $\tilde{\mathbf{x}} = \mathbf{0}$ implies $D(\mathbf{x}) = \boldsymbol{\alpha}^T\tilde{\mathbf{x}} = 0$. This is illustrated in figure 4.3. Note that all pattern vectors lie in a hyperplane defined by $\tilde{x}_{N+1} = 1$, where $\tilde{x}_{N+1}$ is the $(N + 1)$-component of the augmented vector $\tilde{\mathbf{x}}$.

The pattern vectors, $\mathbf{x}_1, \ldots, \mathbf{x}_n$, are representative samples. That is, any $\mathbf{x}$ in C_k will be very close to an $\mathbf{x}_i$, which is a member of $\mathcal{S}_{\mathbf{x}}$ and belongs to C_k. In fact, we assume that $\mathbf{x}$ is so close to $\mathbf{x}_i$ that $\mathcal{S}_{\mathbf{x}}$ being linearly separable implies the linear separability of the two classes by the same hyperplane. This is fundamentally different from the assumptions in statistical classification, where a pattern vector $\mathbf{x}$ has probabilities $P(C_1|\mathbf{x})$ and $P(C_2|\mathbf{x})$ of belonging to C_1 and C_2, respectively. Here, we assume that $\mathbf{x}$ may belong to only one of the two classes, and the two classes occupy disjoint regions in $\Omega_{\mathbf{x}}$ separable by a hyperplane. Thus, there exists at least one linear discriminant function such that

$$\begin{aligned} D(\mathbf{x}) &> 0 \qquad \text{for every } \mathbf{x} \text{ in } C_1, \\ D(\mathbf{x}) &< 0 \qquad \text{for every } \mathbf{x} \text{ in } C_2. \end{aligned} \tag{4.13}$$

A linearly nonseparable set of pattern vectors $\mathcal{S}_{\mathbf{x}}$ often becomes linearly separable by increasing the number of linearly independent measurements, i.e., the dimensionality N. In addition to practical considerations of measurements, N is limited by the fact that it should be substantially less than n, the sample size. For instance, if N is greater than or equal to n, $\mathcal{S}_{\mathbf{x}}$ is definitely linearly separable, but generalization to the population of the two classes is often meaningless since in this case (4.12) can no longer imply

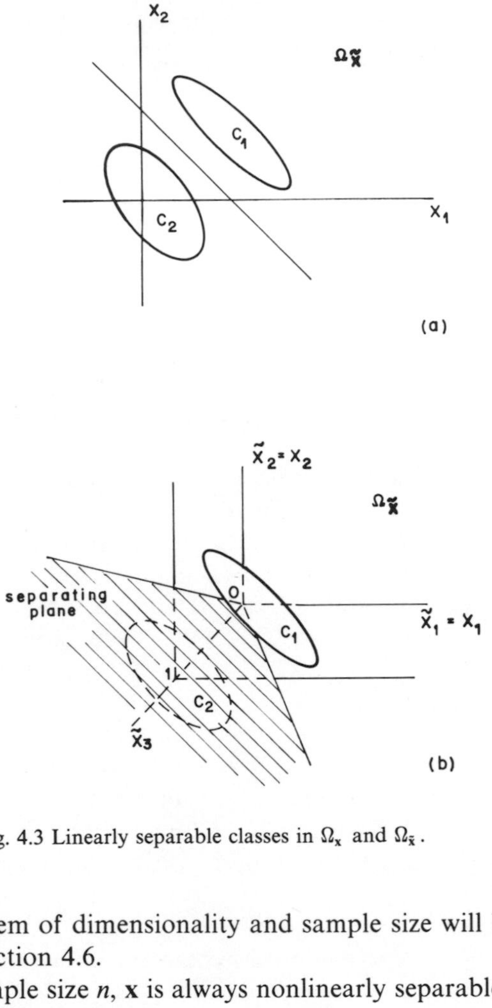

fig. 4.3 Linearly separable classes in $\Omega_{\mathbf{x}}$ and $\Omega_{\tilde{\mathbf{x}}}$.

(4.13). The problem of dimensionality and sample size will be discussed in some detail in section 4.6.

For a fixed sample size n, $\mathbf{x}$ is always nonlinearly separable, and one may use polynomials to approximate a nonlinear discriminant function. Using a high-order polynomial is equivalent to increasing the dimensionality, and the remarks in the last paragraph apply here.

For a multiclass problem with $K > 2$, the classes are said to be *linearly separable* if there exist linear discriminant functions $D_1(\mathbf{x}), \ldots, D_K(\mathbf{x})$ such that

$$D_j(\mathbf{x}) > D_k(\mathbf{x}) \quad \text{for every } \mathbf{x} \text{ in } C_j \text{ and all } k \neq j. \tag{4.14}$$

The classes are *pairwise linearly separable* if every pair of classes C_j and C_k

are linearly separable. In other words, there exists for every $j \neq k$ a linear discriminant function $D_{jk}(\mathbf{x})$ such that

$$\begin{aligned} D_{jk}(\mathbf{x}) &> 0 \quad \text{for every } \mathbf{x} \text{ in } C_j, \\ D_{jk}(\mathbf{x}) &< 0 \quad \text{for every } \mathbf{x} \text{ in } C_k. \end{aligned} \tag{4.15}$$

Clearly, if $C_1, \ldots, C_k$ are linearly separable, they are pairwise linearly separable, since (4.14) is a special case of (4.15) with $D_{jk}(\mathbf{x}) = D_j(\mathbf{x}) - D_k(\mathbf{x})$. The converse is not true.

In figure 4.4 (*a*) and (*b*), we show the separating hyperplanes for linearly separable classes and pairwise linearly separable classes, respectively. In both cases, there are $K(K-1)/2$ separating hyperplanes. We note that when the classes are separable, often 3 of the $(K-1)$-dimensional hyperplanes cross one another at a single $(K-2)$-dimensional hyperplane. This is obvious since, for example, $D_1(\mathbf{x}) - D_2(\mathbf{x}) = 0$ and $D_2(\mathbf{x}) - D_3(\mathbf{x}) = 0$ imply $D_1(\mathbf{x}) - D_3(\mathbf{x}) = 0$.

In order to use (4.15), it is necessary to compute the $K(K-1)/2$ discriminant functions, make the $K(K-1)/2$ comparisons, and then makes a decision based on the comparisons. For example, if an observed $\mathbf{x}$ is in Ω_2, we have $D_{21}(\mathbf{x})$, $D_{23}(\mathbf{x})$, and $D_{24}(\mathbf{x})$ all greater than zero, hence $\mathbf{x}$ is classified to C_2. This is essentially a two-stage decision rule. If $\mathbf{x}$ falls in the shaded region in figure 4.4(*b*), we note that $D_{21}(\mathbf{x}) > 0$, $D_{14}(\mathbf{x}) > 0$ and $D_{42}(\mathbf{x}) > 0$, and there is difficulty in classifying $\mathbf{x}$. Such difficulties do not arise when the classes are linearly separable, and the machine for classifying linearly separable patterns is simpler because only K discriminant functions need be evaluated. It is noted, however, that the assumption of linear separability is stronger than pairwise linear separability.

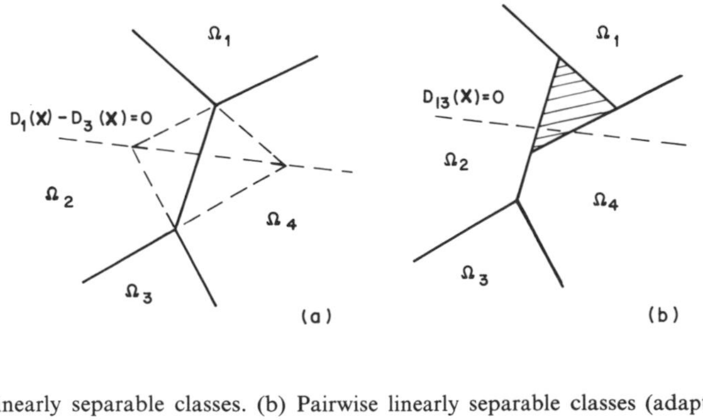

fig. 4.4 (a) Linearly separable classes. (b) Pairwise linearly separable classes (adapted from Nilsson, 1965).

4.2 The Perceptron—A Linear Machine

For the two-class pattern recognition problem, a linear machine is a threshold logic unit (TLU) shown in figure 4.1. The weighting vector of a TLU may be adjusted when training samples with known classifications are presented to the TLU. That a TLU can learn to classify patterns was proposed in the late 1950s by Rosenblatt, who called it an α-perceptron.

The perceptron was suggested by the McCulloch–Pitts (1943) model of a neuron. The nervous system proper may be viewed as a vast network of neurons interconnected in an extremely complex manner. It is estimated that there are 10^{11} neurons in the neural network of the human brain. There are many types of neurons, but for our purpose, the neuron is a cell that has a nucleus contained in the soma or body of the cell, and a long, thin axon carrying electrical impulses from the soma to other neurons. An impulse reaching a particular neuron may help to excite or inhibit the firing of an impulse along the axon of that neuron. With these impulses as input, the neuron will fire an electrical impulse if and only if, over a certain short period of time, the excitation exceeds the inhibition by a certain critical amount called the threshold of the neuron.

Thus, we have the following simplified model of a neuron. It has multiple inputs and a single output. The output of the neuron may assume one of two values, a $+1$ corresponding to firing, and a -1 corresponding to not firing. The inputs are weighted differently, with positive and negative weights representing excitation and inhibition, respectively, and the output equals $+1$ if and only if the linearly weighted sum of the inputs exceeds a certain threshold value. This is, of course, an extremely simplified model of a neuron, where many chemical and neurophysiological factors have not been taken into consideration (Arbib, 1964).

It is clear from the description above that a TLU is modeled after the neuron. The learning capability of a TLU in pattern classification is, for this reason, especially interesting.

4.2.1 Supervised learning of a perceptron

We now describe a procedure for the training of a TLU. Let $\mathcal{S}_{\mathbf{x}} = \{\mathbf{x}_1, \ldots, \mathbf{x}_n\}$ be a training set with known classification of each pattern vector in the set. Assume that there are two classes, and the pattern vectors in the set are linearly separable, i.e., there exists at least one unknown weighting vector $\boldsymbol{\alpha}$ such that

$$\begin{aligned} \boldsymbol{\alpha}^T\tilde{\mathbf{x}} &> 0 \quad \text{for every } \mathbf{x} \text{ in } C_1 \text{ and } \mathbf{x} \in \mathcal{S}_{\mathbf{x}}, \\ \boldsymbol{\alpha}^T\tilde{\mathbf{x}} &< 0 \quad \text{for every } \mathbf{x} \text{ in } C_2 \text{ and } \mathbf{x} \in \mathcal{S}_{\mathbf{x}}, \end{aligned} \tag{4.16}$$

where $\tilde{\mathbf{x}}$ is the vector augmented from $\mathbf{x}$.

It is more convenient to describe the training procedure using the augmented vectors. Let $\mathcal{S}_{\tilde{\mathbf{x}}} = \{\tilde{\mathbf{x}}_1, \ldots, \tilde{\mathbf{x}}_n\}$ be the set of augmented training vectors corresponding to $\mathcal{S}_{\mathbf{x}}$. We construct a training sequence $S_{\tilde{\mathbf{x}}}$ on the set $\mathcal{S}_{\tilde{\mathbf{x}}}$ in such a way that: (i) each $\tilde{\mathbf{x}}$ in $S_{\tilde{\mathbf{x}}}$ is a member of $\mathcal{S}_{\tilde{\mathbf{x}}}$; and (ii) every member of $\mathcal{S}_{\tilde{\mathbf{x}}}$ occurs with infinite frequency in $S_{\tilde{\mathbf{x}}}$. A typical example is

$$S_{\tilde{\mathbf{x}}} = \tilde{\mathbf{x}}_1, \tilde{\mathbf{x}}_2, \ldots, \tilde{\mathbf{x}}_n, \tilde{\mathbf{x}}_1, \tilde{\mathbf{x}}, \ldots, \tilde{\mathbf{x}}_n, \tilde{\mathbf{x}}_1, \tilde{\mathbf{x}}_2, \ldots, \tag{4.17}$$

where we simply use all samples in $\mathcal{S}_{\tilde{\mathbf{x}}}$ repeatedly.

Let $\tilde{\mathbf{x}}_i$ be the i-th member of the infinite sequence $S_{\tilde{\mathbf{x}}}$, and $\boldsymbol{\alpha}(i)$ be the i-th estimate of the weighting vector. The initial estimate $\boldsymbol{\alpha}(1)$ is chosen arbitrarily. The training algorithm is as follows.

(1) If $\tilde{\mathbf{x}}_i$ is correctly classified by the TLU with $\boldsymbol{\alpha}(i)$ as the weighting vector, then the weighting vector is unchanged. In other words,

$$\begin{aligned} \boldsymbol{\alpha}(i+1) = \boldsymbol{\alpha}(i) \qquad & \text{if } \boldsymbol{\alpha}^T(i)\tilde{\mathbf{x}}_i > 0 \quad \text{and } \tilde{\mathbf{x}}_i \text{ in } C_1, \\ & \text{or if } \boldsymbol{\alpha}^T(i)\tilde{\mathbf{x}} < 0 \quad \text{and } \tilde{\mathbf{x}}_i \text{ in } C_2. \end{aligned} \tag{4.18}$$

(2) If $\mathbf{x}_i$ is incorrectly classified by the TLU using $\boldsymbol{\alpha}(i)$, the weighting vector is adjusted by the rule,

$$\begin{aligned} \boldsymbol{\alpha}(i+1) &= \boldsymbol{\alpha}(i) + \tilde{\mathbf{x}}_i \qquad \text{if } \boldsymbol{\alpha}^T(i)\tilde{\mathbf{x}}_i \leqslant 0 \quad \text{and } \tilde{\mathbf{x}}_i \text{ in } C_1, \\ \boldsymbol{\alpha}(i+1) &= \boldsymbol{\alpha}(i) - \tilde{\mathbf{x}}_i \qquad \text{if } \boldsymbol{\alpha}^T(i)\tilde{\mathbf{x}}_i \geqslant 0 \quad \text{and } \tilde{\mathbf{x}}_i \text{ in } C_2. \end{aligned} \tag{4.19}$$

The training algorithm is an error-correction procedure that makes an adjustment of the weighting vector only when $\tilde{\mathbf{x}}_i$ is incorrectly classified. The adjustment is designed in such a way that it is less likely to classify incorrectly $\tilde{\mathbf{x}}_i$ if $\boldsymbol{\alpha}(i+1)$ is used instead of $\boldsymbol{\alpha}(i)$. This is because after the adjustment, $D(\mathbf{x}_i)$ is increased if $\mathbf{x}_i$ is in C_1, and decreased if $\mathbf{x}_i$ is in C_2. It will be shown later that the algorithm will converge in a finite number of steps to an $\boldsymbol{\alpha}$ that satisfies (4.16).

The training algorithm may be expressed in another form. Let us define a vector $\tilde{\mathbf{y}}$,

$$\tilde{\mathbf{y}} = \begin{cases} \tilde{\mathbf{x}} & \text{if } \tilde{\mathbf{x}} \text{ in } C_1, \\ -\tilde{\mathbf{x}} & \text{if } \tilde{\mathbf{x}} \text{ in } C_2. \end{cases} \tag{4.20}$$

Suppose the two classes are linearly separable. There is an $\boldsymbol{\alpha}$ such that

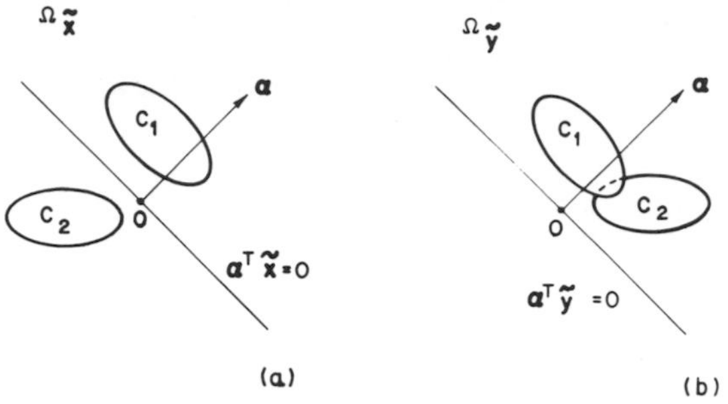

fig. 4.5 Separating hyperplanes for linearly separable classes.

$\boldsymbol{\alpha}^T\tilde{\mathbf{x}} = \boldsymbol{\alpha}^T\tilde{\mathbf{y}} > 0$ for every $\tilde{\mathbf{x}}$ in C_1, and $\boldsymbol{\alpha}^T\tilde{\mathbf{x}} = -\boldsymbol{\alpha}^T\tilde{\mathbf{y}} < 0$ for every $\tilde{\mathbf{x}}$ in C_2. Hence, we may say that two classes are linearly separable if there exists at least one $\boldsymbol{\alpha}$ such that

$$\boldsymbol{\alpha}^T\tilde{\mathbf{y}} > 0 \quad \text{for every } \tilde{\mathbf{y}}. \tag{4.21}$$

The linear hyperplanes $\boldsymbol{\alpha}^T\tilde{\mathbf{x}} = 0$ and $\boldsymbol{\alpha}^T\tilde{\mathbf{y}} = 0$ that separate the two classes in $\Omega_{\tilde{\mathbf{x}}}$ and $\Omega_{\tilde{\mathbf{y}}}$ are sketched in figure 4.5. It is recalled that since $\tilde{\mathbf{x}} = 0$ implies $\boldsymbol{\alpha}^T\tilde{\mathbf{x}} = 0$, the hyperplane passes through the origin in $\Omega_{\tilde{\mathbf{x}}}$. The vector $\boldsymbol{\alpha}$ is orthogonal to the hyperplane $\boldsymbol{\alpha}^T\tilde{\mathbf{x}} = 0$, and its direction is toward the pattern vectors in C_1 so that $\boldsymbol{\alpha}^T\tilde{\mathbf{x}} > 0$ if $\mathbf{x}$ is in C_1. In $\Omega_{\tilde{\mathbf{y}}}$, the vectors $\tilde{\mathbf{y}}$ in both C_1 and C_2 are on the same side of the hyperplane $\boldsymbol{\alpha}^T\tilde{\mathbf{y}} = 0$ that passes through the origin, and the vector $\boldsymbol{\alpha}$ is directed toward these vectors.

By means of (4.20) we may define a training set $\mathcal{S}_{\tilde{\mathbf{y}}}$ and a training sequence $S_{\tilde{\mathbf{y}}}$, that correspond to $\mathcal{S}_{\tilde{\mathbf{x}}}$ and $S_{\tilde{\mathbf{x}}}$, respectively. The training algorithm then becomes

$$\boldsymbol{\alpha}(i+1) = \begin{cases} \boldsymbol{\alpha}(i) & \text{if } \boldsymbol{\alpha}^T(i)\tilde{\mathbf{y}}_i > 0, \\ \boldsymbol{\alpha}(i) + \tilde{\mathbf{y}}_i & \text{if } \boldsymbol{\alpha}^T(i)\tilde{\mathbf{y}}_i \leqslant 0. \end{cases} \tag{4.22}$$

To illustrate the algorithm, we present a simple example.

EXAMPLE 4.1

Assume that $\Omega_{\tilde{\mathbf{y}}}$ is two dimensional, and the two classes are linearly separable so that the vectors $\tilde{\mathbf{y}}$ of C_1 and C_2 are on the same side of a certain hyperplane passing through the origin. Let the initial estimate be

$$\boldsymbol{\alpha}^T(1) = [-1, 1],$$

and $\tilde{\mathbf{x}}_1, \tilde{\mathbf{x}}_2, \ldots,$ be a training sequence with known classifications. Using (4.20), we may obtain easily a sequence $\tilde{\mathbf{y}}_1, \tilde{\mathbf{y}}_2, \ldots$. With $\tilde{\mathbf{y}}_1, \tilde{\mathbf{y}}_2, \ldots,$ given, we have, according to algorithm (4.22),

$$\tilde{\mathbf{y}}_1^T = [0.5, 0.4], \qquad \boldsymbol{\alpha}^T(1)\tilde{\mathbf{y}}_1 = -0.1 < 0, \qquad \boldsymbol{\alpha}^T(2) = [-0.5, 1.4];$$

$$\tilde{\mathbf{y}}_2^T = [0, 1], \qquad \boldsymbol{\alpha}^T(2)\tilde{\mathbf{y}}_2 = 1.4 > 0, \qquad \boldsymbol{\alpha}^T(3) = [-0.5, 1.4];$$

$$\tilde{\mathbf{y}}_3^T = [1.3, -0.2], \qquad \boldsymbol{\alpha}^T(3)\tilde{\mathbf{y}}_3^T = -0.93 < 0, \qquad \boldsymbol{\alpha}^T(4) = [0.8, 1.2].$$

The estimation of $\boldsymbol{\alpha}$ is illustrated by figure 4.6. It is noted that since $\tilde{\mathbf{y}}_2$ is on the same side of the hyperplane as $\boldsymbol{\alpha}(2)$, no adjustment is made at this step. Figure 4.6(*d*) shows that every vector $\tilde{\mathbf{y}}$ of C_1 and C_2 is on the positive side of thc hyperplane $\boldsymbol{\alpha}^T(4)\tilde{\mathbf{y}} = 0$. Hence, regardless of the values of the subsequent samples, $\tilde{\mathbf{y}}_4, \tilde{\mathbf{y}}_5, \ldots,$

$$\boldsymbol{\alpha}(4) = \boldsymbol{\alpha}(5) = \boldsymbol{\alpha}(6) = \cdots,$$

and the hyperplane $\boldsymbol{\alpha}^T(4)\tilde{\mathbf{x}} = 0$ will separate the two classes perfectly.

It should be mentioned that in a pattern classification problem $\tilde{\mathbf{x}}$, and hence $\tilde{\mathbf{y}}$, is an augmented vector, and $\tilde{\mathbf{y}}$ must lie in a hyperplane $\tilde{y}_{N+1} = 1$ or $\tilde{y}_{N+1} = -1$, depending on whether the vector $\tilde{\mathbf{y}}$ is in C_1 or in C_2. Thus, the example presented here is not a typical example of pattern classification, but represents a slightly more general case.

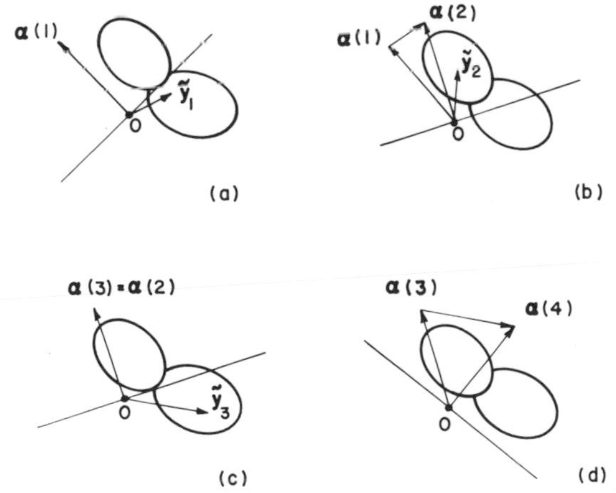

fig. 4.6 Estimation of the weighting vector and separating hyperplane.

4.2.2 Convergence theorem

We wish to show that the training algorithm converges after a finite number of steps. That is, for some finite index i_0,

$$\boldsymbol{\alpha}(i_0) = \boldsymbol{\alpha}(i_0 + 1) = \boldsymbol{\alpha}(i_0 + 2) = \cdots \tag{4.23}$$

defines a hyperplane that separates perfectly the pattern vectors in $\mathcal{S}_{\mathbf{x}}$.

We have introduced the set $\mathcal{S}_{\tilde{\mathbf{y}}}$ and the sequence $S_{\tilde{\mathbf{y}}}$. To facilitate the proof of convergence, we define a *reduced sequence*,

$$S_{\boldsymbol{\eta}} = \boldsymbol{\eta}_1, \boldsymbol{\eta}_2, \ldots, \tag{4.24}$$

which is a subsequence of $S_{\tilde{\mathbf{y}}}$ and consists of all $\tilde{\mathbf{y}}_i$ in $\mathcal{S}_{\tilde{\mathbf{y}}}$ such that $\boldsymbol{\alpha}^T(i)\tilde{\mathbf{y}}_i \leqslant 0$. In other words, all pattern vectors in $S_{\tilde{\mathbf{y}}}$ that are incorrectly classified by the training algorithm (4.22) are included in $S_{\boldsymbol{\eta}}$, and those correctly classified vectors are not included. In a similar manner, we construct a reduced sequence of weighting vectors, $\boldsymbol{\beta}(1), \boldsymbol{\beta}(2), \ldots$, from the sequence $\boldsymbol{\alpha}(1), \boldsymbol{\alpha}(2), \ldots$. Since adjustments of weighting vectors in a TLU are made only when $\boldsymbol{\alpha}^T(i)\tilde{\mathbf{y}}_i \leqslant 0$, it suffices to prove convergence using $S_{\boldsymbol{\eta}}$ and the reduced sequence of weighting vectors.

THEOREM 4.1

Let $\mathcal{S}_x = \{\mathbf{x}_1, \ldots, \mathbf{x}_n\}$ be a training set. Each pattern vector in $\mathcal{S}_{\mathbf{x}}$ belongs to either C_1 or C_2, and the classifications are known. If $\mathcal{S}_{\mathbf{x}}$ is linearly separable, the training algorithm (4.22) converges in a finite number of steps.

Proof

We construct from $\mathcal{S}_{\mathbf{x}}$ sets of vectors $\mathcal{S}_{\tilde{\mathbf{x}}}$, $\mathcal{S}_{\tilde{\mathbf{y}}}$ and sequences $S_{\tilde{\mathbf{x}}}$ and $S_{\tilde{\mathbf{y}}}$ as discussed in Section 4.2.1. A reduced sequence $S_{\boldsymbol{\eta}}$ may then be constructed using algorithm (4.22). Let us assume that the algorithm does not converge in a finite number of steps and show contradiction.

Let $\boldsymbol{\eta}_i$ and $\boldsymbol{\beta}(i)$ be the i-th members of the reduced sequences. We have,

$$\boldsymbol{\beta}^T(i)\boldsymbol{\eta}_i \leqslant 0 \quad \text{for all } i,$$

because of the way we construct $S_{\boldsymbol{\eta}}$. Therefore,

$$\boldsymbol{\beta}(i + 1) = \boldsymbol{\beta}(i) + \boldsymbol{\eta}_i, \quad i = 1, 2, \ldots, \tag{4.25}$$

according to (4.22), and with an arbitrarily chosen $\boldsymbol{\beta}(1)$,

$$\boldsymbol{\beta}(i + 1) = \boldsymbol{\beta}(1) + \boldsymbol{\eta}_1 + \boldsymbol{\eta}_2 + \cdots + \boldsymbol{\eta}_i. \tag{4.26}$$

Since $\mathcal{S}_{\mathbf{x}}$ is linearly separable, there exists a weighting vector $\boldsymbol{\alpha}$ such that $\boldsymbol{\alpha}^T\tilde{\mathbf{y}} > 0$ for all $\tilde{\mathbf{y}}$ in $\mathcal{S}_{\tilde{\mathbf{y}}}$. We define, for a fixed $\boldsymbol{\alpha}$,

$$\min_{\tilde{\mathbf{y}} \in \mathcal{S}_{\tilde{\mathbf{y}}}} \quad (\boldsymbol{\alpha}^T\tilde{\mathbf{y}}) = b_1 > 0. \tag{4.27}$$

If we premultiply (4.26) by $\boldsymbol{\alpha}^T$, we obtain,

$$\begin{aligned} \boldsymbol{\alpha}^T\boldsymbol{\beta}(i + 1) &= \boldsymbol{\alpha}^T\boldsymbol{\beta}(1) + \boldsymbol{\alpha}^T\boldsymbol{\eta}_1 + \cdots + \boldsymbol{\alpha}^T\boldsymbol{\eta}_i \\ &> \boldsymbol{\alpha}^T\boldsymbol{\beta}(1) + ib_1. \end{aligned} \tag{4.28}$$

The inequality in (4.28) is due to the fact that $\eta_i \in \mathcal{S}_{\tilde{\mathbf{y}}}$. By the Schwartz inequality,

$$(\boldsymbol{\alpha}^T\boldsymbol{\alpha})(\boldsymbol{\beta}^T(i + 1)\boldsymbol{\beta}(i + 1)) \geqslant (\boldsymbol{\alpha}^T\boldsymbol{\beta}(i + 1))^2,$$

hence (4.28) implies

$$\boldsymbol{\beta}^T(i + 1)\boldsymbol{\beta}(i + 1) \geqslant \frac{(\boldsymbol{\alpha}^T\boldsymbol{\beta}(1) + ib_1)^2}{(\boldsymbol{\alpha}^T\boldsymbol{\alpha})} \text{ for all } i. \tag{4.29}$$

Now, let us take another point of view and note from (4.25) that for all l,

$$\begin{aligned} \boldsymbol{\beta}^T(l + 1)\boldsymbol{\beta}(l + 1) &= (\boldsymbol{\beta}(l) + \boldsymbol{\eta}_l)^T(\boldsymbol{\beta}(l) + \boldsymbol{\eta}_l) \\ &= \boldsymbol{\beta}^T(l)\boldsymbol{\beta}(l) + 2\boldsymbol{\beta}^T(l)\boldsymbol{\eta}_l + \boldsymbol{\eta}_l^T\boldsymbol{\eta}_l. \end{aligned}$$

Since $\boldsymbol{\beta}^T(l)\boldsymbol{\eta}_l \leqslant 0$,

$$\boldsymbol{\beta}^T(l + 1)\boldsymbol{\beta}(l + 1) - \boldsymbol{\beta}^T(l)\boldsymbol{\beta}(l) \leqslant \boldsymbol{\eta}_l^T\boldsymbol{\eta}_l. \tag{4.30}$$

If we let $l = 1, 2, \ldots, i$, we obtain from the inequality (4.30),

$$\begin{aligned} \boldsymbol{\beta}^T(i + 1)\boldsymbol{\beta}(i + 1) &= \boldsymbol{\beta}^T(1)\boldsymbol{\beta}(1) + \sum_{l=1}^{i} [\boldsymbol{\beta}^T(l + 1)\boldsymbol{\beta}(l + 1) - \boldsymbol{\beta}^T(l)\boldsymbol{\beta}(l)] \\ &\leqslant \boldsymbol{\beta}^T(1)\boldsymbol{\beta}(1) + \sum_{l=1}^{i} \boldsymbol{\eta}_l^T\boldsymbol{\eta}_l \\ &\leqslant \boldsymbol{\beta}^T(1)\boldsymbol{\beta}(1) + ib_2 \quad \text{for all } i, \end{aligned} \tag{4.31}$$

where

$$b_2 = \max_{\tilde{\mathbf{y}} \in \mathcal{S}_{\tilde{\mathbf{y}}}} (\tilde{\mathbf{y}}^T\tilde{\mathbf{y}}) \tag{4.32}$$

A combination of (4.29) and (4.31) yields

$$\frac{(\boldsymbol{\alpha}^T\boldsymbol{\beta}(1) + ib_1)^2}{(\boldsymbol{\alpha}^T\boldsymbol{\alpha})} \leqslant \boldsymbol{\beta}^T(i+1)\boldsymbol{\beta}(i+1) \leqslant \boldsymbol{\beta}^T(1)\boldsymbol{\beta}(1) + ib_2. \tag{4.33}$$

We note that $\mathscr{S}_{\tilde{\mathbf{y}}}$ is a finite set and b_2 is a finite number. With b_1, b_2, $\boldsymbol{\alpha}^T\boldsymbol{\alpha}$, $\boldsymbol{\alpha}^T\boldsymbol{\beta}(1)$, and $\boldsymbol{\beta}^T(1)\boldsymbol{\beta}(1)$ being finite and fixed, the left-hand side of (4.33) increases faster with i than does the right-hand side. Hence, (4.33) cannot be true for an arbitrarily large i, and we arrive at a contradiction. The contradiction implies that $\boldsymbol{\beta}^T(i)\boldsymbol{\eta}_i \leqslant 0$ can be true only up to a certain finite i, say i_0. Thus, the reduced sequence is of finite length, and $\boldsymbol{\beta}(i_0)$ represents a hyperplane that separates perfectly the two classes in $\mathscr{S}_{\mathbf{x}}$.

The theorem above assumes that $\mathscr{S}_{\mathbf{x}}$ is linearly separable, and shows that algorithm (4.22) will converge in i_0 steps to an $\boldsymbol{\alpha}$, but it does not give any indication as to the magnitude of i_0. Sometimes it is unknown whether $\mathscr{S}_{\mathbf{x}}$ is linearly separable. With a training sequence constructed as in (4.17), we know that the algorithm terminates on a separating hyperplane if $\boldsymbol{\alpha}(i)$ is unchanged in n consecutive steps. On the other hand, with this algorithm we can never be sure that an $\mathscr{S}_{\mathbf{x}}$ is linearly nonseparable, since the algorithm may terminate at an extremely large i_0.

4.2.3 Extensions and generalizations

The idea of training a TLU can be extended or generalized in several directions. An obvious extension is to the training of a ϕ-machine. If we assume that the two classes are separable by a set of known nonlinear functions $\phi_1(\mathbf{x}), \phi_2(\mathbf{x}), \ldots, \phi_M(\mathbf{x})$, they are linearly separable in Ω_ϕ, i.e., there exists at least one $\boldsymbol{\alpha}$ such that

$$\begin{aligned} \boldsymbol{\alpha}^T\tilde{\boldsymbol{\phi}}(\mathbf{x}) &> 0 \qquad \text{for every } \mathbf{x} \text{ in } C_1, \\ \boldsymbol{\alpha}^T\tilde{\boldsymbol{\phi}}(\mathbf{x}) &< 0 \qquad \text{for every } \mathbf{x} \text{ in } C_2, \end{aligned} \tag{4.34}$$

where $\tilde{\boldsymbol{\phi}}(\mathbf{x})$ is the augmented ϕ-vector defined as

$$\tilde{\boldsymbol{\phi}}^T(\mathbf{x}) = [\boldsymbol{\phi}^T(\mathbf{x}), 1] = [\phi_1(\mathbf{x}), \ldots, \phi_M(\mathbf{x}), 1]. \tag{4.35}$$

Hence, the training algorithm for a linear machine is applicable to a ϕ-machine with slight modifications. Let us define

$$\tilde{\mathbf{y}} = \begin{cases} \tilde{\boldsymbol{\phi}}(\mathbf{x}) & \text{if } \mathbf{x} \text{ in } C_1, \\ -\tilde{\boldsymbol{\phi}}(\mathbf{x}) & \text{if } \mathbf{x} \text{ in } C_2. \end{cases} \tag{4.36}$$

Then, it is obvious that algorithm (4.22) may be used, and the algorithm converges in a finite number of steps according to theorem 4.1.

Another extension is to train a linear machine for multiple classes of pattern vectors. We assume that there are K classes, $K > 2$, and the K classes are linearly separable. In other words, there exist K weighting vectors, $\boldsymbol{\alpha}_1, \boldsymbol{\alpha}_2, \ldots, \boldsymbol{\alpha}_K$, such that

$$\boldsymbol{\alpha}_j^T \tilde{\mathbf{x}} > \boldsymbol{\alpha}_k^T \tilde{\mathbf{x}} \qquad \text{for every } \mathbf{x} \text{ in } C_j \text{ and every } k \neq j. \tag{4.37}$$

The training procedure is again based on the idea of error correction. Given a training set $\mathcal{S}_\mathbf{x} = \{\mathbf{x}_1, \ldots, \mathbf{x}_n\}$, a training sequence $S_{\tilde{\mathbf{x}}}$ is formed as in the two-class case. Let $\tilde{\mathbf{x}}_i$ be the i-th member of the training sequence $S_{\tilde{\mathbf{x}}}$, and $\boldsymbol{\alpha}_k(i)$ be the estimate of the k-th weighting vector at the i-th iteration. Suppose $\tilde{\mathbf{x}}_i$ belongs to C_j, then the training algorithm is as follows. If $\tilde{\mathbf{x}}_i$ is correctly classified to C_j, i.e., if

$$\boldsymbol{\alpha}_j^T(i)\tilde{\mathbf{x}}_i > \boldsymbol{\alpha}_k^T(i)\tilde{\mathbf{x}}_i \qquad \text{for every } k \neq j,$$

then no adjustment is made on the estimates of the weighting vectors,

$$\boldsymbol{\alpha}_k(i+1) = \boldsymbol{\alpha}_k(i), \qquad k = 1, 2, \ldots, K.$$

On the other hand, if

$$\boldsymbol{\alpha}_j^T(i)\tilde{\mathbf{x}}_i \leqslant \boldsymbol{\alpha}_l^T(i)\tilde{\mathbf{x}}_i \tag{4.38}$$

where

$$\boldsymbol{\alpha}_l^T(i)\tilde{\mathbf{x}}_i = \max\,[\boldsymbol{\alpha}_1(i)\tilde{\mathbf{x}}_i, \ldots, \boldsymbol{\alpha}_K^T(i)\tilde{\mathbf{x}}_i],\ l \neq j,$$

we then adjust $\boldsymbol{\alpha}_j(i)$ and $\boldsymbol{\alpha}_l(i)$ only,

$$\begin{aligned} &\boldsymbol{\alpha}_j(i+1) = \boldsymbol{\alpha}(i) + \mathbf{x}_i, \quad \boldsymbol{\alpha}_l(i+1) = \boldsymbol{\alpha}_l(i) - \tilde{\mathbf{x}}_i, \\ &\boldsymbol{\alpha}_k(i+1) = \boldsymbol{\alpha}_k(i),\ k \neq j,\ k \neq l. \end{aligned} \tag{4.39}$$

The inequality in (4.38) corresponds to classifying incorrectly $\tilde{\mathbf{x}}_i$ to C_l, and the equals sign is included there because of the definition of linear separability in (4.37). It can be shown that the training algorithm terminates in a finite number of steps to $\boldsymbol{\alpha}_1, \ldots, \boldsymbol{\alpha}_K$, which satisfy (4.37) for every $\mathbf{x}$ in $\mathcal{S}_\mathbf{x}$ (Nilsson, 1965).

If the K classes are pairwise linearly separable, we may find for each pair of classes a linear discriminant function $D_{jk}(\mathbf{x})$ by means of the training algorithm for the two-class case. As discussed in the last section, a second-stage decision rule must be devised to make the final classification.

Let us return to the two-class problem. It is tempting to use for classification a network of TLUs similar to the neuron network. One of the simplest TLU networks is the committee machine, which consists of two layers of TLUs. As shown in figure 4.7, the first layer consists of K_1 TLUs in parallel, where K_1 is odd. The second layer is a vote-taking TLU, which sums the binary outputs of the first-layer TLUs and compares the sum against a threshold of zero. Thus, if there are more +1's than −1's at the outputs of the first-layer TLUs, the vote-taking TLU will have as its output a +1, and the pattern vector is classified to C_1. The machine is trained by adjusting the K_1 weighting vectors of the first-layer TLUs.

Consider the two classes of augmented pattern vectors shown in figure 4.8. The vectors of C_1 cluster about the two vectors $\tilde{\mathbf{x}}_1$ and $\tilde{\mathbf{x}}_2$, and those of class C_2 cluster about $\tilde{\mathbf{x}}_3$. It is obvious from the figure that the two classes are not separable by a hyperplane; on the other hand, they are separable by two hyperplanes defined by $\boldsymbol{\alpha}_1^T \tilde{\mathbf{x}} = 0$ and $\boldsymbol{\alpha}_2^T \tilde{\mathbf{x}} = 0$. It is convenient in this case to introduce a third hyperplane, $\boldsymbol{\alpha}_3^T \tilde{\mathbf{x}}$, as shown in figure 4.8. We note that

$$
\begin{array}{llll}
\boldsymbol{\alpha}_1^T \tilde{\mathbf{x}}_1 > 0, & \boldsymbol{\alpha}_2^T \tilde{\mathbf{x}}_1 < 0, & \boldsymbol{\alpha}_3^T \tilde{\mathbf{x}}_1 > 0, & \sum_k \boldsymbol{\alpha}_k^T \tilde{\mathbf{x}}_1 = 1, \\
\boldsymbol{\alpha}_1^T \tilde{\mathbf{x}}_2 < 0, & \boldsymbol{\alpha}_2^T \tilde{\mathbf{x}}_2 > 0, & \boldsymbol{\alpha}_3^T \tilde{\mathbf{x}}_2 > 0, & \sum_k \boldsymbol{\alpha}_k^T \tilde{\mathbf{x}}_2 = 1, \\
\boldsymbol{\alpha}_1^T \tilde{\mathbf{x}}_3 < 0, & \boldsymbol{\alpha}_2^T \tilde{\mathbf{x}}_3 < 0, & \boldsymbol{\alpha}_3^T \tilde{\mathbf{x}}_3 > 0, & \sum_k \boldsymbol{\alpha}_k^T \tilde{\mathbf{x}}_3 = -1.
\end{array}
$$

Hence, a committee machine with $K_1 = 3$ and $\boldsymbol{\alpha}_1, \boldsymbol{\alpha}_2, \boldsymbol{\alpha}_3$ being the weighting vectors of its first-layer TLUs will be able to separate the two classes. It is clear from this discussion that a committee machine uses a piecewise linear discriminant function.

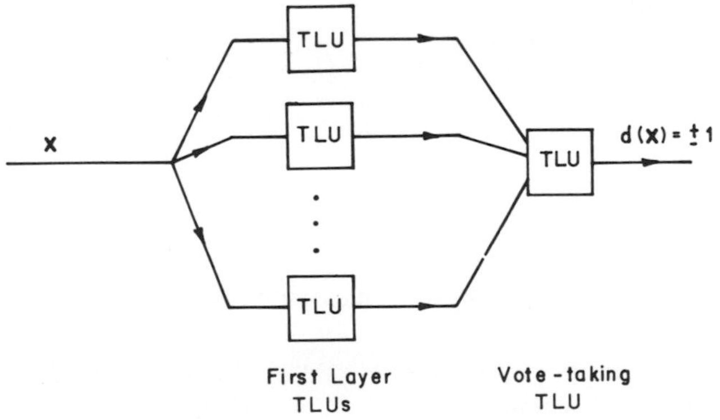

fig. 4.7 A committee machine.

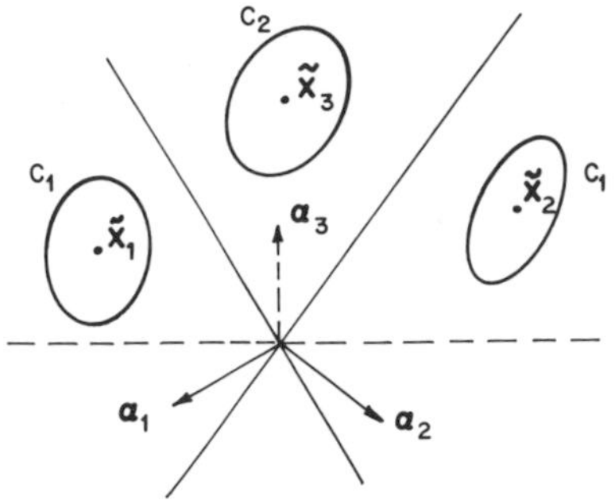

fig. 4.8 Pattern vectors separable by a committee machine (adapted from Nilsson, 1965).

The training of a committee machine may be illustrated by the case where $K_1 = 3$. The training is aimed at obtaining a minimum majority. Let $\tilde{\mathbf{x}}_i$, the i-th pattern vector in the training sequence, belong to class C_1. If the committee machine classifies $\tilde{\mathbf{x}}_i$ correctly, i.e., the responses of at least two of the three first-layer TLUs are positive, no adjustment of the weighting vectors is made. If the responses of two of them are negative, say $\boldsymbol{\alpha}_1^T(i)\tilde{\mathbf{x}}_i \leqslant \boldsymbol{\alpha}_2^T(i)\tilde{\mathbf{x}}_i \leqslant 0$ and $\boldsymbol{\alpha}_3^T(i)\tilde{\mathbf{x}}_i > 0$, the vector $\mathbf{x}_i$ is misclassified by the machine. In this case, we set $\boldsymbol{\alpha}_2(i+1) = \boldsymbol{\alpha}_2(i) + \tilde{\mathbf{x}}_i$ and keep $\boldsymbol{\alpha}_1(i)$ and $\boldsymbol{\alpha}_3(i)$ unchanged. The idea is to obtain a majority of one by making the most effective adjustment. Since $\boldsymbol{\alpha}_1^T(i)\tilde{\mathbf{x}}_i \leqslant \boldsymbol{\alpha}_2^T(i)\tilde{\mathbf{x}}_i$, it is more effective to adjust $\boldsymbol{\alpha}_2(i)$ than to adjust $\boldsymbol{\alpha}_1(i)$. If all three TLUs give negative responses, say $\boldsymbol{\alpha}_1^T(i)\tilde{\mathbf{x}}_i \leqslant \boldsymbol{\alpha}_2^T(i)\tilde{\mathbf{x}}_i \leqslant \boldsymbol{\alpha}_3^T(i)\tilde{\mathbf{x}}_i$, again the vector $\tilde{\mathbf{x}}_i$ is misclassified. To obtain a minimum majority, the adjustments are $\boldsymbol{\alpha}_3(i+1) = \boldsymbol{\alpha}_3(i) + \tilde{\mathbf{x}}_i$ and $\boldsymbol{\alpha}_2(i+1) = \boldsymbol{\alpha}_2(i) + \tilde{\mathbf{x}}_i$. A similar adjustment procedure is used when $\mathbf{x}_i$ belongs to C_2. The training algorithm can easily be generalized to the cases when $K_1 = 5, 7$, etc.

The training of a committee machine is based on the idea of error correction. Since the machine operates on the principle of majority rule, the training algorithm is designed accordingly. Experiments on the committee machine have shown that the training algorithm is satisfactory in many cases, but no convergence theorem has been proved.

4.3 Recursive Algorithms

The perceptron training procedure is a recursive algorithm. In this section we discuss recursive algorithms from a more general point of view.

Let us assume that the pattern vectors are linearly separable. As discussed in the previous section, supervised learning for two classes of linearly separable pattern vectors may be interpreted as searching for a weighting vector $\boldsymbol{\alpha}$ such that $\boldsymbol{\alpha}^T\tilde{\mathbf{y}} > 0$ for all $\tilde{\mathbf{y}}$ in the training set $\mathcal{S}_{\tilde{\mathbf{y}}}$. The vector $\tilde{\mathbf{y}}$ is defined in terms of the augmented pattern vector $\tilde{\mathbf{x}}$ as in (4.20). A training sequence $S_{\tilde{\mathbf{y}}}$ is constructed from the set $\mathcal{S}_{\tilde{\mathbf{y}}}$. Each $\tilde{\mathbf{y}}_i$ in the training sequence $S_{\tilde{\mathbf{y}}}$ is a member of $\mathcal{S}_{\tilde{\mathbf{y}}}$ and every member of $\mathcal{S}_{\tilde{\mathbf{y}}}$ occurs with infinite frequency in the sequence.

The algorithms in this section are viewed as gradient methods that seek the minimum of a certain criterion function. The criterion functions $J(\boldsymbol{\alpha}, \tilde{\mathbf{y}})$ are chosen in such a way that they are minimum when $\boldsymbol{\alpha}^T\tilde{\mathbf{y}} > 0$. The gradient descent procedure is then

$$\boldsymbol{\alpha}(i+1) = \boldsymbol{\alpha}(i) - a\nabla_{\boldsymbol{\alpha}} J\Big|_{\boldsymbol{\alpha}(i), \tilde{\mathbf{y}}_i}, \tag{4.40}$$

where $\boldsymbol{\alpha}(i)$ is the weighting vector at the i-th iteration, $\tilde{\mathbf{y}}_i$ is the i-th vector in the training sequence $S_{\tilde{\mathbf{y}}}$, and a is a predetermined positive gain constant. The gradient operator is defined by

$$\nabla_{\boldsymbol{\alpha}}^T = \left[\frac{\partial}{\partial \alpha_1}, \frac{\partial}{\partial \alpha_2}, \ldots, \frac{\partial}{\partial \alpha_{N+1}}\right], \tag{4.41}$$

where $\alpha_1, \alpha_2, \ldots, \alpha_{N+1}$ are elements of the $(N+1)$-vector $\boldsymbol{\alpha}$. A different choice of J results in a different recursive algorithm.

4.3.1 Criterion functions and recursive algorithms

There are several commonly used criterion functions. Let

$$J_1 = \tfrac{1}{2}[|\boldsymbol{\alpha}^T\tilde{\mathbf{y}}| - \boldsymbol{\alpha}^T\tilde{\mathbf{y}}]. \tag{4.42}$$

It is obvious that when $\boldsymbol{\alpha}^T\tilde{\mathbf{y}} \leqslant 0$, $J_1 = |\boldsymbol{\alpha}^T\tilde{\mathbf{y}}|$, and when $\boldsymbol{\alpha}^T\tilde{\mathbf{y}} > 0$, $J_1 = 0$ is a minimum. Taking the gradient of J_1, we obtain

$$\nabla_{\boldsymbol{\alpha}} J_1 = \tfrac{1}{2}[\tilde{\mathbf{y}} \operatorname{sgn}(\boldsymbol{\alpha}^T\tilde{\mathbf{y}}) - \tilde{\mathbf{y}}], \tag{4.43}$$

where the sgn function is defined by

$$\operatorname{sgn}(\boldsymbol{\alpha}^T\tilde{\mathbf{y}}) = \begin{cases} 1, & \text{if } \boldsymbol{\alpha}^T\tilde{\mathbf{y}} > 0, \\ -1, & \text{if } \boldsymbol{\alpha}^T\tilde{\mathbf{y}} \leqslant 0. \end{cases} \tag{4.44}$$

A substitution of (4.43) into the general algorithm (4.40) yields

$$\boldsymbol{\alpha}(i+1) = \boldsymbol{\alpha}(i) - \frac{a}{2}[\tilde{\mathbf{y}}_i \operatorname{sgn}(\boldsymbol{\alpha}^T(i)\tilde{\mathbf{y}}_i) - \tilde{\mathbf{y}}_i], \tag{4.45}$$

which is sometimes called the *fixed-increment algorithm*.

Algorithm (4.45) is an error correction procedure. If we substitute the sgn function in (4.45) by (4.44), we obtain

$$\boldsymbol{\alpha}(i+1) = \boldsymbol{\alpha}(i) + a\begin{cases} 0, & \text{if } \boldsymbol{\alpha}^T(i)\tilde{\mathbf{y}}_i > 0, \\ \tilde{\mathbf{y}}_i, & \text{if } \boldsymbol{\alpha}^T(i)\tilde{\mathbf{y}}_i \leqslant 0. \end{cases} \tag{4.46}$$

Thus an adjustment of $\boldsymbol{\alpha}(i)$ is made when and only when $\tilde{\mathbf{y}}_i$ is misclassified by the machine using $\boldsymbol{\alpha}(i)$ as the weighting vector. Note that in (4.45), sgn(0) has been assigned the value of -1 since it is desired to have a solution vector $\boldsymbol{\alpha}$ such that $\boldsymbol{\alpha}^T\tilde{\mathbf{y}} > 0$, not $\boldsymbol{\alpha}^T\tilde{\mathbf{y}} \geqslant 0$. Except for the gain constant a, algorithm (4.46) is the perceptron training algorithm. It can easily be seen that with a trivial modification, the proof of theorem 4.1 is applicable to the fixed-increment algorithm. Hence, if the two classes are linearly separable, algorithm (4.46) converges to a solution vector $\boldsymbol{\alpha}$ in a finite number of steps.

Let us consider another criterion function that is the square of J_1 in (4.42),

$$J_2 = \tfrac{1}{8}[\boldsymbol{\alpha}^T\tilde{\mathbf{y}} - |\boldsymbol{\alpha}^T\tilde{\mathbf{y}}|]^2. \tag{4.47}$$

Clearly, $J_2 \geqslant 0$, and when $\boldsymbol{\alpha}^T\tilde{\mathbf{y}} > 0$, $J_2 = 0$ is a minimum. Taking the gradient, we obtain the *relaxation algorithm*,

$$\boldsymbol{\alpha}(i+1) = \boldsymbol{\alpha}(i) - \frac{a}{4}[\tilde{\mathbf{y}}_i - \tilde{\mathbf{y}}_i \operatorname{sgn}(\boldsymbol{\alpha}^T(i)\tilde{\mathbf{y}}_i)][\boldsymbol{\alpha}^T(i)\tilde{\mathbf{y}}_i - |\boldsymbol{\alpha}^T(i)\tilde{\mathbf{y}}_i|]. \tag{4.48}$$

Algorithm (4.48) may be written as

$$\boldsymbol{\alpha}(i+1) = \boldsymbol{\alpha}(i) + a\begin{cases} 0, & \text{if } \boldsymbol{\alpha}^T(i)\tilde{\mathbf{y}}_i > 0, \\ \tilde{\mathbf{y}}_i|\boldsymbol{\alpha}^T(i)\tilde{\mathbf{y}}_i|, & \text{if } \boldsymbol{\alpha}^T(i)\tilde{\mathbf{y}}_i \leqslant 0. \end{cases} \tag{4.49}$$

Again the weighting vector $\boldsymbol{\alpha}(i)$ is adjusted only when $\mathbf{y}_i$ is misclassified. The magnitude of the adjustment depends on $|\boldsymbol{\alpha}^T(i)\tilde{\mathbf{y}}_i|$, which is the distance of $\mathbf{y}_i$ to the hyperplane defined by $\boldsymbol{\alpha}^T(i)\mathbf{y}_i = 0$. It can be shown that if the pattern vectors are linearly separable, the relaxation algorithm converges in a finite number of steps.

The algorithms above may result in a separating hyperplane that is very close to some of the pattern vectors. Assume that the two classes are reasonably far apart, and that there exists at lease one linear discriminant function $D(\mathbf{x}) = \boldsymbol{\alpha}^T\tilde{\mathbf{x}}$ such that

$$\begin{aligned} D(\mathbf{x}) &> b \qquad \text{for every } \mathbf{x} \text{ in } C_1, \\ D(\mathbf{x}) &< b \qquad \text{for every } \mathbf{x} \text{ in } C_2. \end{aligned} \tag{4.50}$$

The constant $b > 0$ defines a dead zone, $-b \leqslant D(\mathbf{x}) \leqslant b$, in $\Omega_{\tilde{\mathbf{x}}}$ as illustrated in figure 4.9, and there is no pattern vector in this zone. The two classes of pattern vectors satisfying (4.50) are called *b-separable* classes. In terms of $\tilde{\mathbf{y}}$, (4.51) becomes $\boldsymbol{\alpha}^T\tilde{\mathbf{y}} > b > 0$.

Let us define for b-separable classes a criterion function,

$$J_3 = \tfrac{1}{2}[|\boldsymbol{\alpha}^T\tilde{\mathbf{y}} - b| - (\boldsymbol{\alpha}^T\tilde{\mathbf{y}} - b)], \tag{4.51}$$

such that $J_3 = 0$ when $\boldsymbol{\alpha}^T\tilde{\mathbf{y}} > b$. Taking the gradient, we obtain a fixed increment algorithm,

$$\boldsymbol{\alpha}(i+1) = \boldsymbol{\alpha}(i) - \frac{a}{2}[\tilde{\mathbf{y}}_i \operatorname{sgn}(\boldsymbol{\alpha}^T(i)\tilde{\mathbf{y}}_i - b) - \tilde{\mathbf{y}}_i]. \tag{4.52}$$

The weighting vector $\boldsymbol{\alpha}(i)$ is adjusted when $\boldsymbol{\alpha}^T\tilde{\mathbf{y}}_i \leqslant b$, and algorithm (4.52) reduces to algorithm (4.45) if $b = 0$. If the two classes are b-separable, algorithm (4.52) converges to a solution vector $\boldsymbol{\alpha}$ in a finite number of steps, and the distance between the hyperplane $\boldsymbol{\alpha}^T\tilde{\mathbf{y}} = 0$ and any pattern vector is always greater than b. It is obvious that a similar modification can be made to the relaxation algorithm.

Finally, let us consider a square-error criterion defined by

$$J_4 = \tfrac{1}{2}(\boldsymbol{\alpha}^T\tilde{\mathbf{y}} - b)^2. \tag{4.53}$$

The algorithm based on the gradient of J_4 is

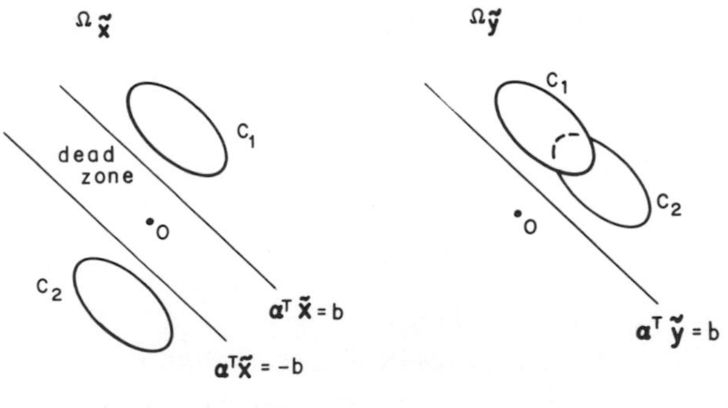

fig. 4.9 The b-separable classes.

$$\boldsymbol{\alpha}(i+1) = \boldsymbol{\alpha}(i) - a\tilde{\mathbf{y}}_i[\boldsymbol{\alpha}^T(i)\tilde{\mathbf{y}}_i - b]. \tag{4.54}$$

This is called the minimum square-error algorithm, and is conceptually quite different from the fixed-increment and thc relaxation algorithms. The idea here is to find a hyperplane $\boldsymbol{\alpha}^T\tilde{\mathbf{y}} = b$ with $b > 0$ such that all pattern vectors $\tilde{\mathbf{y}}$ are near the hyperplane. Since $b > 0$, it is likely that a vector $\tilde{\mathbf{y}}$ near the hyperplane will satisfy the condition $\boldsymbol{\alpha}^T\tilde{\mathbf{y}} > 0$.

It is noted that in algorithm (4.54), an adjustment of $\boldsymbol{\alpha}(i)$ is made even when $\boldsymbol{\alpha}^T(i)\tilde{\mathbf{y}}_i > b$. The only time that no adjustment is made is when $\boldsymbol{\alpha}^T(i)\tilde{\mathbf{y}}_i = b$. Therefore, the algorithm will continue to iterate indefinitely except for the trivial case that the equality, $\boldsymbol{\alpha}^T\tilde{\mathbf{y}} = b$, holds for all $\tilde{\mathbf{y}}$. For this reason, it is necessary to terminate the algorithm arbitrarily after a large number of iterations. As mentioned before, it is likely that the algorithm yields an $\boldsymbol{\alpha}$ such that $\boldsymbol{\alpha}^T\tilde{\mathbf{y}} > 0$ for all $\tilde{\mathbf{y}}$, but there is no guarantee that this is true.

4.3.2 The Ho-Kashyap Algorithm

Consider a training set $\mathcal{S}_{\tilde{\mathbf{y}}} = \{\tilde{\mathbf{y}}_1, \tilde{\mathbf{y}}_2, \ldots, \tilde{\mathbf{y}}_n\}$. The set is generated from a set $\mathcal{S}_{\tilde{\mathbf{x}}}$, which consists of two classes of linearly separable, augmented pattern vectors. In other words, there exists an $\boldsymbol{\alpha}$ such that $\boldsymbol{\alpha}^T\tilde{\mathbf{y}} > 0$ for all $\tilde{\mathbf{y}}$ in $\mathcal{S}_{\tilde{\mathbf{y}}}$. We define a criterion function,

$$J = \frac{1}{2}\sum_{l=1}^{n} (\boldsymbol{\alpha}^T\tilde{\mathbf{y}}_l - \beta_l)^2. \tag{4.55}$$

It differs from the criterion functions in 4.3.1 in two aspects. All n vectors in $\mathcal{S}_{\tilde{\mathbf{y}}}$ are included in defining J, and β_l is different for different $\tilde{\mathbf{y}}_l$ and will be estimated recursively.

The mean-square criterion J in (4.55) may be expressed in matrix notation. Let us define

$$\begin{aligned} \mathbf{Y}^T &= [\tilde{\mathbf{y}}_1, \tilde{\mathbf{y}}_2, \ldots, \tilde{\mathbf{y}}_n], \\ \boldsymbol{\beta}^T &= [\beta_1, \beta_2, \ldots, \beta_n]. \end{aligned} \tag{4.56}$$

Then, (4.55) may be written as

$$J = \tfrac{1}{2}(\mathbf{Y}\boldsymbol{\alpha} - \boldsymbol{\beta})^T(\mathbf{Y}\boldsymbol{\alpha} - \boldsymbol{\beta}). \tag{4.57}$$

The pattern space $\Omega_{\mathbf{x}}$ is N-dimensional, and the augmented spaces $\Omega_{\tilde{\mathbf{x}}}$ and $\Omega_{\tilde{\mathbf{y}}}$ are $(N+1)$-dimensional. Hence Y is an $n \times (N+1)$ matrix, and $\boldsymbol{\alpha}$ and

$\boldsymbol{\beta}$ are $(N+1)$- and n-vectors, respectively. We assume that the sample size is greater than the dimensionality of $\Omega_{\tilde{\mathbf{y}}}$, $n > N+1$, and that the matrix Y is of rank $(N+1)$.

Since we allow a different β_l for different $\tilde{\mathbf{y}}_l$ in $\mathcal{S}_{\tilde{\mathbf{y}}}$, and since $\tilde{\mathbf{y}}_l{}^T\boldsymbol{\alpha} > 0$ by assumption, there exists a $\boldsymbol{\beta}$ such that $\mathbf{Y}\boldsymbol{\alpha} = \boldsymbol{\beta}$ with every element of $\boldsymbol{\beta}$ greater than zero. The criterion function is minimum, $J = 0$, when $\mathbf{Y}\boldsymbol{\alpha} = \boldsymbol{\beta}$. and the Ho–Kashyap algorithm is a gradient descent procedure that minimizes J with respect to both $\boldsymbol{\alpha}$ and $\boldsymbol{\beta}$ subject to the constraint $\beta_l > 0$, $l = 1, 2, \ldots, n$ (Ho and Kashyap, 1965.) Note that $\mathbf{Y}\boldsymbol{\alpha} = \boldsymbol{\beta}$ implies $\tilde{\mathbf{y}}_l{}^T\boldsymbol{\alpha} = \beta_l$, which is possible since we allow different values of β_l for different l.

The gradients of J with respect to $\boldsymbol{\alpha}$ and $\boldsymbol{\beta}$ are

$$\begin{aligned} \nabla_{\boldsymbol{\alpha}} J &= \mathbf{Y}^T(\mathbf{Y}\boldsymbol{\alpha} - \boldsymbol{\beta}), \\ \nabla_{\boldsymbol{\beta}} J &= -(\mathbf{Y}\boldsymbol{\alpha} - \boldsymbol{\beta}). \end{aligned} \tag{4.58}$$

For a given $\boldsymbol{\beta}(i)$ at the i-th interation, J is minimized with respect to $\boldsymbol{\alpha}$ when $\boldsymbol{\alpha}(i)$ is the solution of the equation $\nabla_{\boldsymbol{\alpha}} J = \mathbf{0}$, i.e.,

$$\boldsymbol{\alpha}(i) = (\mathbf{Y}^T\mathbf{Y})^{-1}\mathbf{Y}^T\boldsymbol{\beta}(i) = \mathbf{Y}^{\dagger}\boldsymbol{\beta}(i), \tag{4.59}$$

where $(\mathbf{Y}^T\mathbf{Y})^{-1}$ exists, since $(\mathbf{Y}^T\mathbf{Y})$ is an $(N+1) \times (N+1)$ matrix and $\mathbf{Y}$ is of rank $(N+1)$, and

$$\mathbf{Y}^{\dagger} = (\mathbf{Y}^T\mathbf{Y})^{-1}\mathbf{Y}^T \tag{4.60}$$

is known as the *generalized inverse* of Y. Readers interested in the generalized inverse are referred to Deutsch (1965) and Greville (1959).

To simplify the notation, we denote the gradient with respect to $\boldsymbol{\beta}$ by

$$\gamma = -\nabla_{\boldsymbol{\beta}} J = \mathbf{Y}\boldsymbol{\alpha} - \boldsymbol{\beta}. \tag{4.61}$$

Since β_l is constrained to be greater than zero, we make an adjustment of $\beta_l(i)$ only when the l-th component of the gradient, $-\gamma_l(i) < 0$. Thus

$$\beta_l(i+1) = \beta_l(i) + \begin{cases} 2a\gamma_l(i) & \text{if } \gamma_l(i) > 0, \\ 0 & \text{if } \gamma_l(i) \leqslant 0, \end{cases} \tag{4.62}$$

where a is a gain constant. It is obvious that (4.62) and (4.59) may be rewritten as

$$\begin{aligned}\boldsymbol{\beta}(i+1) &= \boldsymbol{\beta}(i) + a[\boldsymbol{\gamma}(i) + |\boldsymbol{\gamma}(i)|],\\ \boldsymbol{\alpha}(i+1) &= \boldsymbol{\alpha}(i) + a\mathbf{Y}^{\dagger}[\boldsymbol{\gamma}(i) + |\boldsymbol{\gamma}(i)|].\end{aligned} \tag{4.63}$$

It may also be expressed as a recursive algorithm of $\boldsymbol{\gamma}$,

$$\boldsymbol{\gamma}(i+1) = \boldsymbol{\gamma}(i) + a(\mathbf{Y}\mathbf{Y}^{\dagger} - \mathbf{I})[\boldsymbol{\gamma}(i) + |\boldsymbol{\gamma}(i)|], \tag{4.64}$$

where $\mathbf{I}$ is an $n \times n$ identity matrix, and we have used the definition of $\boldsymbol{\gamma}$ in (4.61).

It is easy to see from (4.62) that $\beta_l(i) > 0$ for all l and all i if we choose $\beta_l(0) > 0$. In fact, $\beta_l(i)$ is a monotonically nondecreasing function of i. One might think that this nondecreasing property would cause difficulty in convergence since the true solution β_l could be small. Note that if $\boldsymbol{\alpha}$ and $\boldsymbol{\beta}$ are solutions of the equation $\mathbf{Y}\boldsymbol{\alpha} = \boldsymbol{\beta}$. multiplying $\boldsymbol{\alpha}$ and $\boldsymbol{\beta}$ by a large positive constant will not change the result. Hence, we may choose an arbitrary $\beta_l(0) > 0$, and the nondecreasing property of $\beta_l(i)$ will have no adverse effect on the convergence.

The algorithm for $\boldsymbol{\alpha}(i)$ is derived from (4.59), which minimizes at each iteration the criterion function J. The matrix $\mathbf{Y}$ consists of all n pattern vectors in $\mathcal{S}_{\tilde{\mathbf{y}}}$, and all of them are used at each iteration for the adjustment of $\boldsymbol{\alpha}(i)$ and $\boldsymbol{\beta}(i)$. For these reasons, the algorithm is expected to converge rapidly. The calculation of the generalized inverse $\mathbf{Y}^{\dagger}$ need only be performed once, and the dimension of the matrix to be inverted, $\mathbf{Y}^T\mathbf{Y}$, is $(N+1)$, which is usually not extremely large.

Let us introduce the expression $\boldsymbol{\gamma} < \mathbf{0}$ to mean that $\gamma_l < 0$ for all l, and the expression $\boldsymbol{\gamma} \leqslant \mathbf{0}$ to mean that $\gamma_l \leqslant 0$ for all l. The performance of the algorithm may be summarized as follows with the proofs presented later.

If the pattern vectors are linearly separable, then

$$\lim_{i\to\infty} \boldsymbol{\gamma}^T(i)\boldsymbol{\gamma}(i) = 0, \tag{4.65}$$

and there exists a finite positive integer i_0 such that $\mathbf{Y}\boldsymbol{\alpha}(i_0) > \mathbf{0}$. If the pattern vectors are not linearly separable, there exists a positive integer i_0 (finite or infinite) such that $\boldsymbol{\gamma}(i_0) \leqslant \mathbf{0}$ and $\boldsymbol{\gamma}(i_0) \neq \mathbf{0}$.

For linearly separable classes, a solution $\mathbf{Y}\boldsymbol{\alpha}(i_0) > \mathbf{0}$ is obtained, where i_0 is finite. Note that the only requirement on $\boldsymbol{\alpha}(i_0)$ is to satisfy $\mathbf{Y}\boldsymbol{\alpha}(i_0) = \boldsymbol{\beta}(i_0) + \boldsymbol{\gamma}(i_0) > \mathbf{0}$, and $\boldsymbol{\gamma}(i_0) = \mathbf{0}$ is a special case of this relationship. We note from algorithm (4.64) that $\boldsymbol{\gamma}(i_0) \leqslant \mathbf{0}$ implies $\boldsymbol{\gamma}(i_0) = \boldsymbol{\gamma}(i_0+1) = \boldsymbol{\gamma}(i_0+2) = \cdots$. It obviously implies that $\boldsymbol{\alpha}(i_0) = \boldsymbol{\alpha}(i_0+1) = \cdots$, and $\boldsymbol{\beta}(i_0) = \boldsymbol{\beta}(i_0+1) = \cdots$, and the algorithm terminates at the i_0-th iteration. Thus, if we find at a certain i_0 that $\boldsymbol{\gamma}(i_0) \leqslant \mathbf{0}$ and $\boldsymbol{\gamma}(i_0) \neq \mathbf{0}$, we immediately realize that the pattern vectors are not linearly separable. This is an additional advantage of the Ho–Kashyap algorithm.

4.3.3 A convergence theorem[*]

To prove the convergence of the Ho–Kashyap algorithm, we need two lemmas. Lemma 4.1 shows that when the pattern vectors are linearly separable, $\boldsymbol{\gamma}(i) \nleqslant \mathbf{0}$ for any i with the exception of $\boldsymbol{\gamma}(i) = \mathbf{0}$. Hence, whenever the algorithm terminates at the i_0-th iteration with $\boldsymbol{\gamma}(i_0) \leqslant 0$ and $\boldsymbol{\gamma}(i_0) \neq 0$, the vectors are not linearly separable. Let us define

$$\begin{aligned} V(\boldsymbol{\gamma}(i)) &= \boldsymbol{\gamma}^T(i)\boldsymbol{\gamma}(i) = \|\boldsymbol{\gamma}(i)\|^2, \\ \triangle V(\boldsymbol{\gamma}(i)) &= V(\boldsymbol{\gamma}(i+1)) - V(\boldsymbol{\gamma}(i)), \end{aligned} \tag{4.66}$$

where $\|\cdot\|$ is the norm of a vector. Lemma 4.2 shows that $\triangle V(\boldsymbol{\gamma}(i)) \leqslant 0$, hence $V(\boldsymbol{\gamma}(i))$ is a monotonically nonincreasing function of i. It then implies that in the linearly separable case, $V(\boldsymbol{\gamma}(i))$ converges to zero. Note that $V(\boldsymbol{\gamma}(i)) = 0$ if and only if $\boldsymbol{\gamma}(i) = \mathbf{Y}\boldsymbol{\alpha}(i) - \boldsymbol{\beta}(i) = \mathbf{0}$.

LEMMA 4.1

If there exist solution vectors $\boldsymbol{\alpha}$ to the inequality $\mathbf{Y}\boldsymbol{\alpha} > \mathbf{0}$, $\boldsymbol{\gamma}(i) \leqslant \mathbf{0}$ implies $\boldsymbol{\gamma}(i) = \mathbf{0}$.

Proof

We assume the existence of a $\boldsymbol{\gamma}(i)$ such that $\boldsymbol{\gamma}(i) \leqslant \mathbf{0}$ and $\boldsymbol{\gamma}(i) \neq \mathbf{0}$, and proceed to show the contradiction. Since for the solution vector $\boldsymbol{\alpha}$, $\mathbf{Y}\boldsymbol{\alpha} > \mathbf{0}$, there exists a $\boldsymbol{\beta}$ such that

$$\mathbf{Y}\boldsymbol{\alpha} = \boldsymbol{\beta} > \mathbf{0}. \tag{4.67}$$

Recalling the definitions of the inequalities, we obtain from (4.67) and the assumption on $\boldsymbol{\gamma}(i)$,

$$\boldsymbol{\beta}^T\boldsymbol{\gamma}(i) < 0. \tag{4.68}$$

Now for any $\boldsymbol{\gamma}(i)$,

[*] Section may be omitted on first reading.

$$\mathbf{Y}^T\gamma(i) = \mathbf{Y}^T[\mathbf{Y}\boldsymbol{\alpha}(i) - \boldsymbol{\beta}(i)] = \mathbf{Y}^T[\mathbf{Y}\mathbf{Y}^\dagger - \mathbf{I}]\boldsymbol{\beta}(i)$$
$$= [\mathbf{Y}^T\mathbf{Y}(\mathbf{Y}^T\mathbf{Y})^{-1}\mathbf{Y}^T - \mathbf{Y}^T]\boldsymbol{\beta}(i) = \mathbf{0}. \tag{4.69}$$

Hence by (4.67) and (4.69),

$$\boldsymbol{\beta}^T\gamma(i) = \boldsymbol{\alpha}^T\mathbf{Y}^T\gamma(i) = 0,$$

which is contradictory to (4.68).

LEMMA 4.2

If $0 < a < 1$,

$$\triangle V(\gamma(i)) \leqslant 0 \quad \text{for all } \gamma(i), \tag{4.70}$$

with equality if and only if $\gamma(i) \leqslant \mathbf{0}$.

Proof

Let us rewrite the recursive algorithm for $\gamma(i)$,

$$\gamma(i+1) = \gamma(i) + a(\mathbf{Y}\mathbf{Y}^\dagger - \mathbf{I})(\gamma(i) + |\gamma(i)|).$$

It is easy to see from the definition of $\mathbf{Y}^\dagger$ in (4.60) that $(\mathbf{Y}\mathbf{Y}^\dagger - \mathbf{I})$ is a symmetric matrix and that

$$(\mathbf{Y}\mathbf{Y}^\dagger - \mathbf{I})^T(\mathbf{Y}\mathbf{Y}^\dagger - \mathbf{I}) = -(\mathbf{Y}\mathbf{Y}^\dagger - \mathbf{I}).$$

Therefore, from the algorithm and the definition of $\triangle V(\gamma(i))$, we obtain

$$\triangle V(\gamma(i)) = 2a(\gamma(i) + |\gamma(i)|)^T(\mathbf{Y}\mathbf{Y}^\dagger - \mathbf{I})\gamma(i)$$
$$- a^2(\gamma(i) + |\gamma(i)|)^T(\mathbf{Y}\mathbf{Y}^\dagger - \mathbf{I})(\gamma(i) + |\gamma(i)|). \tag{4.71}$$

Since (4.69) holds for any $\gamma(i)$, and

$$\mathbf{Y}\mathbf{Y}^\dagger\gamma(i) = \mathbf{Y}(\mathbf{Y}^T\mathbf{Y})^{-1}\mathbf{Y}^T\gamma(i) = \mathbf{0},$$

the first term at the right-hand side of (4.71) reduces to

$$-2a(\gamma(i) + |\gamma(i)|)^T\gamma(i)$$
$$= -a(\gamma(i) + |\gamma(i)|)^T[(\gamma(i) + |\gamma(i)|) + (\gamma(i) - |\gamma(i)|)]$$
$$= -a(\gamma(i) + |\gamma(i)|)^T(\gamma(i) + |\gamma(i)|).$$

The last equality is due to the fact that either $\gamma_l(i) + |\gamma_l(i)| = 0$ or $\gamma_l(i) - |\gamma_l(i)| = 0$. Hence,

$$\triangle V(\boldsymbol{\gamma}(i)) = -(\boldsymbol{\gamma}(i) + |\boldsymbol{\gamma}(i)|)^T[a^2\mathbf{Y}\mathbf{Y}^\dagger + (a - a^2)\mathbf{I}](\boldsymbol{\gamma}(i) + |\boldsymbol{\gamma}(i)|).$$

For $0 < a < 1$, the matrix $[a^2\mathbf{Y}\mathbf{Y}^\dagger + (a - a^2)\mathbf{I}]$ is positive definite, and therefore,

$$\triangle V(\boldsymbol{\gamma}(i)) \leqslant 0 \qquad \text{for all } \boldsymbol{\gamma}(i).$$

The equality holds if and only if

$$\boldsymbol{\gamma}(i) + |\boldsymbol{\gamma}(i)| = \mathbf{0},$$

which is equivalent to $\boldsymbol{\gamma}(i) \leqslant \mathbf{0}$.

THEOREM 4.2

Let $0 < a < 1$. If there exist solution vectors $\boldsymbol{\alpha}$ to the inequality $\mathbf{Y}\boldsymbol{\alpha} > \mathbf{0}$, then

$$\lim_{i\to\infty} V(\boldsymbol{\gamma}(i)) = 0, \tag{4.72}$$

and a solution is obtained by algorithm (4.63) after a finite number of iterations. If there is no such solution, the algorithm will terminate at i_0 with $\boldsymbol{\gamma}(i_0) \leqslant \mathbf{0}$ and $\boldsymbol{\gamma}(i_0) \neq \mathbf{0}$.

Proof

Let us first consider the case that there exist solutions $\boldsymbol{\alpha}$ to the inequality $\mathbf{Y}\boldsymbol{\alpha} > \mathbf{0}$. Lemma 4.2 becomes

$$\begin{aligned} \triangle V(\boldsymbol{\gamma}(i)) &< 0 \qquad \text{if } \boldsymbol{\gamma}(i) \neq \mathbf{0}, \\ \triangle V(\boldsymbol{\gamma}(i)) &= 0 \qquad \text{if } \boldsymbol{\gamma}(i) = \mathbf{0}, \end{aligned} \tag{4.73}$$

since by lemma 4.1, $\boldsymbol{\gamma}(i) \leqslant \mathbf{0}$ implies $\boldsymbol{\gamma}(i) = \mathbf{0}$. With $V(\boldsymbol{\gamma}(i)) > 0$ and continuously decreasing except when $\boldsymbol{\gamma}(i) = \mathbf{0}$,

$$\lim_{i\to\infty} V(\boldsymbol{\gamma}(i)) = 0$$

Now, let us choose without loss of generality a vector $\boldsymbol{\beta}(1)$ such that $\beta_l(1) \geqslant b > 0$, $l = 1, 2, \ldots, n$, and note that according to (4.62), $\beta_l(i) \geqslant \beta_l(1) \geqslant b$ for all l and i. Since $V(\boldsymbol{\gamma})$ converges to zero in an infinite number of iterations, it must converge to a sphere $V(\boldsymbol{\gamma}) = (b - \varepsilon)^2$ in a finite number of iterations, say i_0. By the definition of $V(\boldsymbol{\gamma})$,

$$V(\boldsymbol{\gamma}(i_0)) = \sum_{l=1}^{n} |\gamma_l(i_0)|^2 < b^2$$

implies $|\gamma_l(i_0)| < b$ for all l. Since

$$\mathbf{Y}\boldsymbol{\alpha}(i_0) = \boldsymbol{\beta}(i_0) + \boldsymbol{\gamma}(i_0),$$

$|\gamma_l(i_0)| < b$ and $\beta_l(i_0) \geqslant b$ for all l imply $\mathbf{Y}\boldsymbol{\alpha}(i_0) > 0$.

To prove the second part, suppose there exists no solution to the inequality. Lemma 4.2 still holds except that in this case $\boldsymbol{\gamma}(i) \neq \mathbf{0}$ for all i, and thus

$$\begin{aligned} &\triangle V(\boldsymbol{\gamma}(i)) < 0 \qquad \text{if } \boldsymbol{\gamma}(i) \nleqslant \mathbf{0}, \\ &\triangle V(\boldsymbol{\gamma}(i)) = 0 \qquad \text{if } \boldsymbol{\gamma}(i) \leqslant \mathbf{0} \text{ and } \boldsymbol{\gamma}(i) \neq \mathbf{0}. \end{aligned} \tag{4.74}$$

Since $\boldsymbol{\gamma}(i) \neq \mathbf{0}$, $V(\boldsymbol{\gamma}(i)) > 0$ for all i, and (4.74) shows that $V(\boldsymbol{\gamma})$ converges to a certain positive constant. Hence, there exists a positive integer i_0 such that $\triangle\ V(\boldsymbol{\gamma}(i_0)) = 0$, and by (4.74) $\boldsymbol{\gamma}(i_0) \leqslant \mathbf{0}$ and $\boldsymbol{\gamma}(i_0) \neq \mathbf{0}$. The algorithm terminates at i_0.

4.4 Linear Transformation and Classification

The use of transformations for pattern classification is based on an intuitive notion. It is desirable to have a transformation such that the separation of different classes is improved after the transformation, and at the same time, pattern vectors of the same class remain close together. This is illustrated in figure 4.10. The precise meaning of separation depends on the definitions of interclass and intraclass distances.

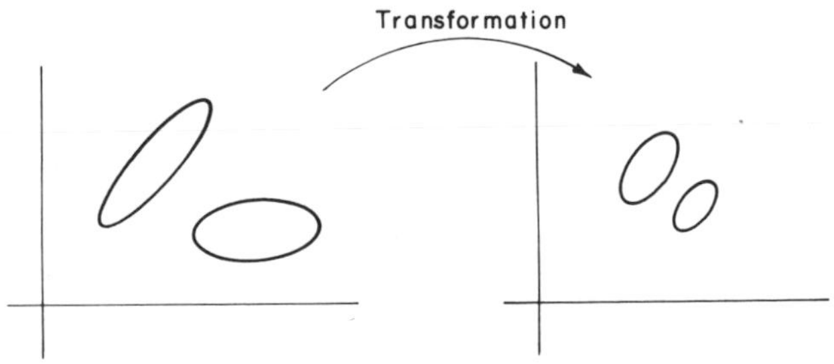

fig. 4.10 Transformation of pattern vectors.

Since the purpose is classification, the notion of separation of different classes should be somewhat related to thc classification method we use. Usually, the transformation and the classification method in the transformed space are both linear. Note that if we wish to find a quadratic transformation optimal in some sense, we may first make a transformation from $\Omega_{\mathbf{x}}$ to Ω_{ϕ} as in (4.8) of section 4.1, and then seek an optimal linear transformation from Ω_{ϕ}. Using a quadratic discriminant function in a linearly transformed space is equivalent to a linear discriminant function in a quadratically transformed space. Hence, the assumption of linear transformation and linear classification is not as restrictive as it appears to be.

Consider a two-class problem. With a linear transformation and a linear discriminant function, the classification of a pattern vector is based on its distance to a separating hyperplane in the transformed space, or equivalently, the classification is based on its projection on a one-dimensional space. The original idea is to find an $N \times N$ linear transformation so that it is easier to classify the pattern vectors in the new space, as illustrated in figure 4.10. For the two-class case, the end result is equivalent to finding an $1 \times N$ transformation $\boldsymbol{\alpha}^T$, which is obviously the same as finding a linear discriminant function in the original space.

The methods discussed in this section maximize or minimize some distance criteria that are related to the notion of separation. These are not recursive schemes, and computationally they are fairly simple. No assumption is made on the linear separability, and the methods are applicable to both separable and nonseparable cases.

4.4.1 Maximization of mean-square interclass distance

Consider a training set of n pattern vectors, $\mathcal{S}_{\mathbf{x}} = \{\mathbf{x}_1, \ldots, \mathbf{x}_n\}$. In the set $\mathcal{S}_{\mathbf{x}}$, n_1 vectors belong to C_1, $n_2 = (n - n_1)$ vectors belong to C_2, and the classification of each pattern vector is known. Let $\mathbf{T}$ be an $N \times N$ matrix representing the transformation. Sebestyen (1961) defines a mean-square interclass distance ν_T^2 in the transformed space by

$$\nu_T^2 = \frac{1}{n_1 n_2} \sum_{\mathbf{x}_i \in C_1} \sum_{\mathbf{x}_j \in C_2} \|\mathbf{T}\mathbf{x}_i - \mathbf{T}\mathbf{x}_j\|^2, \tag{4.75}$$

where $\mathbf{x}_i$ and $\mathbf{x}_j$ are members of $\mathcal{S}_{\mathbf{x}}$ and belong to C_1 and C_2, respectively.

As mentioned before, eventually we use a linear discriminant function in the transformed space. Hence, instead of the $N \times N$ transformation $\mathbf{T}$ in (4.75), we may use an $1 \times N$ transformation $\boldsymbol{\alpha}^T$, and define a mean-square interclass distance in the one-dimensional space,

$$\nu_1^2 = \frac{1}{n_1 n_2} \sum_{\mathbf{x}_i \in C_1} \sum_{\mathbf{x}_j \in C_2} [\boldsymbol{\alpha}^T(\mathbf{x}_i - \mathbf{x}_j)]^2, \tag{4.76}$$

The mean-square distance of all vectors in $\mathcal{S}_{\mathbf{x}}$ in the one-dimensional space is

$$\nu_0^2 = \frac{1}{n(n-1)} \sum_{\mathbf{x}_i} \sum_{\mathbf{x}_j} [\boldsymbol{\alpha}^T(\mathbf{x}_i - \mathbf{x}_j)]^2, \tag{4.77}$$

where the summations are over all vectors in $\mathcal{S}_{\mathbf{x}}$. Note that ν_0^2 may be regarded as an average of mean-square interclass and intraclass distance.

The mean-square interclass distance ν_1^2 is a measure of separation. We wish to choose an $\boldsymbol{\alpha}^T$ that maximizes ν_1^2 subject to the constraint that ν_0^2 is a constant. A constraint is necessary since otherwise ν_1^2 may increase indefinitely by simply changing the scale, i.e., by substituting $a\boldsymbol{\alpha}^T$ for $\boldsymbol{\alpha}^T$, where a is a large positive constant. The constraint on ν_0^2 imposes a limitation on the overall mean-square distance, hence $\boldsymbol{\alpha}^T$ also minimizes mean-square intraclass distance.

Let us define two $N \times N$ matrices

$$\begin{aligned} \mathbf{Q}_1 &= \frac{1}{n_1 n_2} \sum_{\mathbf{x}_i \in C_1} \sum_{\mathbf{x}_j \in C_2} (\mathbf{x}_i - \mathbf{x}_j)(\mathbf{x}_i - \mathbf{x}_j)^T, \\ \mathbf{Q}_0 &= \frac{1}{n(n-1)} \sum_{\mathbf{x}_i} \sum_{\mathbf{x}_j} (\mathbf{x}_i - \mathbf{x}_j)(\mathbf{x}_i - \mathbf{x}_j)^T. \end{aligned} \tag{4.78}$$

Clearly, (4.76) and (4.77) may be written as,

$$\nu_1^2 = \boldsymbol{\alpha}^T \mathbf{Q}_1 \boldsymbol{\alpha}, \qquad \nu_0^2 = \boldsymbol{\alpha}^T \mathbf{Q}_0 \boldsymbol{\alpha}. \tag{4.79}$$

Let λ be a Lagrange multiplier. We wish to maximize

$$\nu^2 \equiv \nu_1^2 - \lambda \nu_0^2 = \boldsymbol{\alpha}^T[\mathbf{Q}_1 - \lambda \mathbf{Q}_0]\boldsymbol{\alpha}. \tag{4.80}$$

Substituting $(\boldsymbol{\alpha} + d\boldsymbol{\alpha})$ for $\boldsymbol{\alpha}$, we obtain

$$\begin{aligned} \nu^2 + d\nu^2 &= (\boldsymbol{\alpha} + d\boldsymbol{\alpha})^T[\mathbf{Q}_1 - \lambda \mathbf{Q}_0](\boldsymbol{\alpha} + d\boldsymbol{\alpha}) \\ &= \nu^2 + 2(d\boldsymbol{\alpha})^T[\mathbf{Q}_1 - \lambda \mathbf{Q}_0]\boldsymbol{\alpha} + (d\boldsymbol{\alpha})^T[\mathbf{Q}_1 - \lambda \mathbf{Q}_1]d\boldsymbol{\alpha}. \end{aligned} \tag{4.81}$$

To maximize ν^2, the first-order term must equal zero,

$$(d\boldsymbol{\alpha})^T[\mathbf{Q}_1 - \lambda \mathbf{Q}_0]\boldsymbol{\alpha} = 0.$$

Since this must be true for an arbitrary variation $d\boldsymbol{\alpha}$, $\boldsymbol{\alpha}$ must satisfy the equation

$$\mathbf{Q}_1 \boldsymbol{\alpha} = \lambda \mathbf{Q}_0 \boldsymbol{\alpha}, \tag{4.82}$$

which is in the form of an eigenequation.

Thus, the $1 \times N$ transformation $\boldsymbol{\alpha}^T$ that maximizes ν_1^2 subject to the constraint of a constant ν_0^2 is an eigenvector satisfying (4.82), and the Lagrange multiplier λ is an eigenvalue. We assume that the sample size n is much greater than the dimension of $\Omega_{\mathbf{x}}$, N, and the matrices $\mathbf{Q}_1$ and $\mathbf{Q}_0$ are positive definite. There are N eigenvalues $\lambda_1 \geqslant \lambda_2 \geqslant \cdots \geqslant \lambda_N > 0$ and N associated eigenvectors. A substitution of (4.82) into (4.79) yields

$$\nu_1^2 = \boldsymbol{\alpha}^T \mathbf{Q}_1 \boldsymbol{\alpha} = \lambda \boldsymbol{\alpha}^T \mathbf{Q}_0 \boldsymbol{\alpha} = \lambda \nu_0^2. \tag{4.83}$$

Since ν_0^2 is a constant, a maximum ν_1^2 is obtained when $\lambda = \lambda_1$ is the largest eigenvalue and $\boldsymbol{\alpha}$ is the eigenvector associated with λ_1.

The $1 \times N$ transformation $\boldsymbol{\alpha}^T$ in fact defines a linear discriminant function except for a threshold value. The threshold value can be determined somewhat heuristically on the basis of the sample means and the sample variances of the two classes of pattern vectors after the transformation. When a new pattern vector $\mathbf{x}$ is observed and to be classified, we simply calculate $\boldsymbol{\alpha}^T\mathbf{x}$ and compare it with the threshold value.

It is interesting to note that in Sebestyen's original work, he was interested in finding an $N \times N$ transformation matrix $\mathbf{T}$, and the result was a singular matrix,

$$\mathbf{T}^T = [\boldsymbol{\alpha}, \boldsymbol{\alpha}, \ldots, \boldsymbol{\alpha}],$$

with every row vector of $\mathbf{T}$ being identical and equal to $\boldsymbol{\alpha}^T$ derived here.

When there are K classes, $K > 2$, one possibility is to find an $\boldsymbol{\alpha}^T$ for every pair of classes, and the transformation is $K(K-1)/2 \times N$.

4.4.2 The Fisher linear discriminant

Again, consider a two-class problem, and a training set $\mathcal{S}_{\mathbf{x}}$ of n pattern vectors with known classifications. We define sample mean vectors for the two classes

$$\begin{aligned} \mathbf{m}_1 &= \frac{1}{n_1} \sum_{\mathbf{x}_i \in C_1} \mathbf{x}_i, \\ \mathbf{m}_2 &= \frac{1}{n_2} \sum_{\mathbf{x}_i \in C_2} \mathbf{x}_i, \end{aligned} \tag{4.84}$$

and sample covariance matrices,

$$\begin{aligned}\mathbf{R}_1 &= \frac{1}{n_1} \sum_{\mathbf{x}_i \in C_1} (\mathbf{x}_i - \mathbf{m}_1)(\mathbf{x}_i - \mathbf{m}_1)^T, \\ \mathbf{R}_2 &= \frac{1}{n_2} \sum_{\mathbf{x}_i \in C_2} (\mathbf{x}_i - \mathbf{m}_2)(\mathbf{x}_i - \mathbf{m}_2)^T,\end{aligned} \tag{4.85}$$

where n_1 and n_2 are the numbers of vectors belonging to C_1 and C_2 respectively.

For a $1 \times N$ transformation $\boldsymbol{\alpha}^T$, the absolute value of

$$\nu_1 = \boldsymbol{\alpha}^T(\mathbf{m}_2 - \mathbf{m}_1), \tag{4.86}$$

$|\nu_1|$, is a measure of separation, and

$$\nu_0^2 = \tfrac{1}{2}\boldsymbol{\alpha}^T(\mathbf{R}_1 + \mathbf{R}_2)\boldsymbol{\alpha} = \boldsymbol{\alpha}^T\mathbf{R}\boldsymbol{\alpha}, \tag{4.87}$$

is the average sample variance of the two classes in the direction of $\boldsymbol{\alpha}$.

We wish to find an $\boldsymbol{\alpha}^T$ that minimizes the average variance ν_0^2 subject to the constraint of a constant ν_1. Let λ be the Lagrange multiplier.

$$\nu = \nu_0^2 - \lambda\nu_1 = \boldsymbol{\alpha}^T[\mathbf{R}\boldsymbol{\alpha} - \lambda(\mathbf{m}_2 - \mathbf{m}_1)] \tag{4.88}$$

is minimized when

$$(d\boldsymbol{\alpha})^T[2\mathbf{R}\boldsymbol{\alpha} - \lambda(\mathbf{m}_2 - \mathbf{m}_1)] = 0. \tag{4.89}$$

Since $d\boldsymbol{\alpha}$ is arbitrary, we obtain

$$\boldsymbol{\alpha} = \frac{\lambda}{2}\mathbf{R}^{-1}(\mathbf{m}_2 - \mathbf{m}_1), \tag{4.90}$$

where we have assumed that $\mathbf{R}^{-1}$ exists. The Lagrange multiplier λ may be evaluated by substituting (4.90) into the constraint equation (4.86),

$$\nu_1 = \boldsymbol{\alpha}^T(\mathbf{m}_2 - \mathbf{m}_1) = \frac{\lambda}{2}(\mathbf{m}_2 - \mathbf{m}_1)^T\mathbf{R}^{-1}(\mathbf{m}_2 - \mathbf{m}_1). \tag{4.91}$$

In (4.91), the value of ν_1 is considered as given, and we may assume without loss of generality that

$$\nu_1 = (\mathbf{m}_2 - \mathbf{m}_1)^T\mathbf{R}^{-1}(\mathbf{m}_2 - \mathbf{m}_1). \tag{4.92}$$

Then, $\lambda = 2$ and

$$\boldsymbol{\alpha} = \mathbf{R}^{-1}(\mathbf{m}_2 - \mathbf{m}_1). \tag{4.93}$$

When a new pattern vector $\mathbf{x}$ is observed and to be classified, we calculate

$$\boldsymbol{\alpha}^T\mathbf{x} = (\mathbf{m}_2 - \mathbf{m}_1)\mathbf{R}^{-1}\mathbf{x}, \tag{4.94}$$

which is called the *Fisher linear discriminant*. Its value is compared with a predetermined threshold, and $\mathbf{x}$ is classified as belonging to C_2 if $\boldsymbol{\alpha}^T\mathbf{x}$ is greater than the threshold value.

It is interesting to note that if $\mathbf{R}_1 = \mathbf{R}_2 = \mathbf{R}$ and we choose $\boldsymbol{\alpha}^T(\mathbf{m}_2 + \mathbf{m}_1)/2 = (\mathbf{m}_2 - \mathbf{m}_1)^T\mathbf{R}^{-1}(\mathbf{m}_2 + \mathbf{m}_1)/2$ as the threshold value, the result is identical to the optimal classification of Gaussian patterns discussed in section 2.2, with equal prior probabilities for the two classes. Thus, the same result is obtained if we approximate the probability densities of the two classes by Gaussian distributions with mean vectors $\mathbf{m}_1$ and $\mathbf{m}_2$ given by (4.84) and equal covariance matrix $\mathbf{R}$. This is not surprising in view of the fact that an optimal classifier for Gaussian distributions with equal covariance matrix is linear, and that the linear approach presented here utilizes the knowledge of the mean vectors and the covariance matrices only.

When $\mathbf{R}_1 \neq \mathbf{R}_2$, a possible choice of the threshold value is

$$\frac{1}{(\boldsymbol{\alpha}^T\mathbf{R}_1\boldsymbol{\alpha})^{1/2} + (\boldsymbol{\alpha}^T\mathbf{R}_2\boldsymbol{\alpha})^{1/2}}[(\boldsymbol{\alpha}^T\mathbf{R}_1\boldsymbol{\alpha})^{1/2}\boldsymbol{\alpha}^T\mathbf{m}_1 + (\boldsymbol{\alpha}^T\mathbf{R}_2\boldsymbol{\alpha})^{1/2}\boldsymbol{\alpha}^T\mathbf{m}_2], \tag{4.95}$$

where $\boldsymbol{\alpha}$ is given by (4.93). In other words, we select the threshold value in such a way that its distances to $(\boldsymbol{\alpha}^T\mathbf{m}_1)$ and $(\boldsymbol{\alpha}^T\mathbf{m}_2)$ are inversely proportional to the standard deviations of the two classes, $(\boldsymbol{\alpha}^T\mathbf{R}_1\boldsymbol{\alpha})^{1/2}$ and $(\boldsymbol{\alpha}^T\mathbf{R}_2\boldsymbol{\alpha})^{1/2}$.

4.4.3 Linear regression

We assume that the training set $\mathcal{S}_{\mathbf{x}}$ consists of pattern vectors from K classes, $K > 2$. Let us define for each class C_k a unit vector $\mathbf{u}_k$ with

$$\begin{aligned} \mathbf{u}_1^T &= [1, 0, 0, \ldots, 0], \\ \mathbf{u}_2^T &= [0, 1, 0, \ldots, 0], \\ &\cdots . \end{aligned} \tag{4.96}$$

These vectors are K-dimensional, and the distances between any pairs of them are identical. The classifications of the training vectors are known, and if $\mathbf{x}_i$ belongs to C_k, we set $\mathbf{v}_i = \mathbf{u}_k$. Thus the vector $\mathbf{v}_i$ denotes the classification of $\mathbf{x}_i$, and the vector pairs, $(\mathbf{x}_1, \mathbf{v}_1), (\mathbf{x}_2, \mathbf{v}_2), \ldots, (\mathbf{x}_n, \mathbf{v}_n)$, describe completely the information contained in the training set.

Let us consider a $K \times N$ matrix $\mathbf{T}$ and a K-vector $\mathbf{b}$. The equation,

$$\hat{\mathbf{v}} = \mathbf{T}\mathbf{x} + \mathbf{b}, \tag{4.97}$$

is a linear transformation from an N-space to a K-space. It is desirable that after the transformation, vectors of the same class will be close together. In the present case, we require that the vectors $\hat{\mathbf{v}}$ belonging to C_k are close to $\mathbf{u}_k$. Hence, we define a mean-square criterion,

$$\begin{aligned} \nu &= \sum_{i=1}^{n} (\mathbf{v}_i - \hat{\mathbf{v}}_i)^T(\mathbf{v}_i - \hat{\mathbf{v}}_i) \\ &= \sum_{i=1}^{n} (\mathbf{v}_i - \mathbf{b} - \mathbf{T}\mathbf{x}_i)^T(\mathbf{v}_i - \mathbf{b} - \mathbf{T}\mathbf{x}_i) \\ &= \sum_{i=1}^{n} tr(\mathbf{v}_i - \mathbf{b} - \mathbf{T}\mathbf{x}_i)(\mathbf{v}_i - \mathbf{b} - \mathbf{T}\mathbf{x}_i)^T, \end{aligned} \tag{4.98}$$

where $\mathbf{x}_i$, $i = 1, 2, \ldots, n$, are in $\mathscr{S}_{\mathbf{x}}$ and tr denotes the trace of a square matrix.

It is noted that in defining a $\mathbf{u}_k$ for each C_k, the separatons of the different classes are, in a sense, fixed, and the minimization of ν in (4.98) may be interpreted as minimizing the average intraclass distance. A translation vector $\mathbf{b}$ is needed in (4.98) because $\mathbf{u}_k$ are fixed, whereas in the previous cases, the constraints were on the distances only. The present approach has an advantage in that K classes, $K > 2$, are taken into consideration at the same time.

We wish to find a matrix $\mathbf{T}$ and a vector $\mathbf{b}$ that minimize ν in (4.98). Let us first vary $\mathbf{b}$ for a given $\mathbf{T}$. By setting the first-order term to zero, we obtain

$$2 \sum_{i=1}^{n} (d\mathbf{b})^T(\mathbf{v}_i - \mathbf{b} - \mathbf{T}\mathbf{x}_i) = 0.$$

Since this must be true for any $d\mathbf{b}$,

$$\mathbf{b} = \mathbf{m}_v - \mathbf{T}\mathbf{m}_x, \tag{4.99}$$

where

$$\mathbf{m}_v = \frac{1}{n} \sum_{i=1}^{n} \mathbf{v}_i, \quad \mathbf{m}_x = \frac{1}{n} \sum_{i=1}^{n} \mathbf{x}_i, \tag{4.100}$$

are the sample means of the vectors $\mathbf{v}$ and $\mathbf{x}$ respectively. Let us introduce the notation,

$$\begin{aligned} \mathbf{R}_v &= \frac{1}{n} \sum_{i=1}^{n} (\mathbf{v}_i - \mathbf{m}_v)(\mathbf{v}_i - \mathbf{m}_v)^T, \\ \mathbf{R}_x &= \frac{1}{n} \sum_{i=1}^{n} (\mathbf{x}_i - \mathbf{m}_x)(\mathbf{x}_i - \mathbf{m}_x)^T, \\ \mathbf{R}_{vx} &= \mathbf{R}_{xv}^T = \frac{1}{n} \sum_{i=1}^{n} (\mathbf{v}_i - \mathbf{m}_v)(\mathbf{x}_i - \mathbf{m}_x)^T. \end{aligned} \tag{4.101}$$

A substitution of (4.99) and (4.101) into (4.98) yields

$$\nu = tr(\mathbf{R}_\nu - \mathbf{T}\mathbf{R}_{x\nu} - \mathbf{R}_{\nu x}\mathbf{T}^T + \mathbf{T}\mathbf{R}_x\mathbf{T}^T). \tag{4.102}$$

Now let us vary the matrix $\mathbf{T}$. Substituting $\mathbf{T} + d\mathbf{T}$ for $\mathbf{T}$ in (4.102), we obtain

$$\nu + d\nu = \nu - tr[d\mathbf{T}(\mathbf{R}_{x\nu} - \mathbf{R}_x\mathbf{T}^T) + (\mathbf{R}_{\nu x} - \mathbf{T}\mathbf{R}_x)d\mathbf{T}^T - d\mathbf{T}\mathbf{R}_x d\mathbf{T}^T]. \tag{4.103}$$

The first-order term must be zero for any $d\mathbf{T}$. Taking advantage of the symmetry, we obtain

$$\mathbf{T} = \mathbf{R}_{\nu x}\mathbf{R}_x^{-1}. \tag{4.104}$$

A substitution of (4.99) and (4.104) into (4.97) gives us

$$\hat{\mathbf{v}} = \mathbf{R}_{\nu x}\mathbf{R}_x^{-1}(\mathbf{x} - \mathbf{m}_x) + \mathbf{m}_\nu. \tag{4.105}$$

Equation (4.105) is commonly called a linear regression function (Anderson, 1958). It may be considered as a linear estimation of $\mathbf{v}$.

When a new sample $\mathbf{x}$ is observed, it will first be transformed to $\hat{\mathbf{v}}$ by means of (4.105), and then classified according to the $\mathbf{u}_k$ nearest to $\hat{\mathbf{v}}$. This can easily be done by calculating $(\hat{\mathbf{v}} - \mathbf{u}_k)^T(\hat{\mathbf{v}} - \mathbf{u}_k)$, $k = 1, 2, \ldots, K$, and then selecting the one with the smallest value.

The vectors $\mathbf{u}_k$ in (4.96) are orthogonal vectors, which have the desirable property that the vectors have the same norm, and the distances between any pairs of vectors are the same. Another set of vectors having this property is a set of K simplex vectors, each vector being of $(K - 1)$ dimension. For example, with $K = 3$, the set of simplex vectors are $[1,0]$, $[-1/2, \sqrt{3}/2]$ and $[-1/2, -\sqrt{3}/2]$. We may use the simplex vectors instead of the orthogonal vectors; the matrix $\mathbf{T}$ in this case will have a dimension $(K - 1) \times N$.

4.5 Clustering

With the increasing availability of computers, there is a growing interest in the biological and the social sciences to identify clusters of "objects" based on empirical measurements. A cluster is loosely defined as a collection of vectors or points that are close together. Shown in figure 4.11 are three clusters, those points in the same cluster being close or similar in some sense, and those in different clusters being distant or dissimilar. An example of clustering in the biological sciences is numerical taxonomy (Sokal and Sneath, 1963).

Using pattern recognition terminology, we consider a set of pattern vectors $\mathcal{S}_{\mathbf{x}} = \{\mathbf{x}_1, \mathbf{x}_2 \cdots, \mathbf{x}_n\}$, and our problem is to partition the n pattern vectors into K_c subsets or clusters. Each cluster may or may not correspond to a class, depending on the particular problem and the clustering technique we use. Since we assume no prior knowledge as to the cluster to which a sample vector belongs, clustering is essentially unsupervised nonparametric learning. It is a difficult problem, especially when we have a large number of vectors in a high dimensional space.

Many clustering procedures have been proposed. These procedures are mostly ad hoc methods, and do not necessarily arrive at a mathematically meaningful solution. Roughly speaking, if the vectors form well structured clusters that are compact and well separated from one another, as in figure 4.11, a well designed clustering procedure will yield meaningful and unique clusters. On the other hand, if the distribution of the pattern vectors resembles a uniform distribution, the resulting clusters will be different with different clustering procedures or even with the same procedure in several attempts. Most practical cases perhaps lie somewhere between these two extremes. As pointed out by Ball (1965), one of the most useful aspects of clustering techniques is this ability to indicate whether the empirically measured data form reasonably well structured clusters. It may be advisable for this purpose to make several attempts or to use several clustering techniques on the same data. In the following paragraphs we discuss three general approaches to clustering.

4.5.1 Hierarchical clustering

A hierarchical clustering procedure groups the objects or vectors into small clusters and then, by steps, merges these into larger and larger clusters. At the l-th step, there are $K_c(l)$ clusters, and some of the clusters

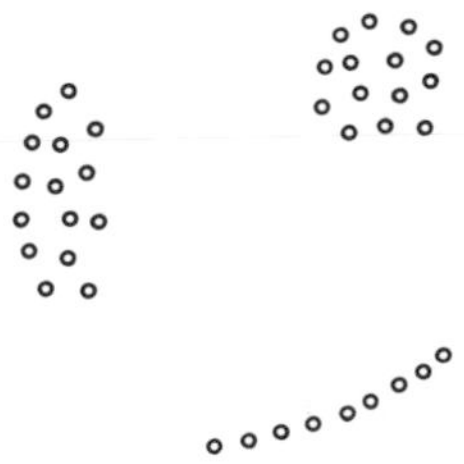

fig. 4.11 Three compact and well-separated clusters.

may be grouped together according to a certain criterion. Thus, at the $l+1$-st step, we have $K_c(l+1)$ clusters with $K_c(l+1) \leqslant K_c(l)$. When $l = 1$, each of the n pattern vectors is considered as a cluster, $K_c(1) = n$, and as l increases, $K_c(l)$ decreases until finally all of the vectors are considered to be in one cluster.

The clustering procedure depends on an $n \times n$ distance matrix $\mathbf{Z}$ or a similarity matrix $\mathbf{S}$. If we are concerned with the pattern vectors in Euclidean space, it is natural to use the distance matrix $\mathbf{Z}$ with its element z_{ij} being the Euclidean distance between $\mathbf{x}_i$ and $\mathbf{x}_j$. On the other hand, in some applications it is physically more meaningful to describe the relationship between two objects by a similarity measure. For example, one simple measure of similarity is the number of attributes common to the two objects.

The input to a hierarchical clustering procedure consists solely of the $n(n-1)/2$ similarity measures or the $n(n-1)/2$ distance measures among the n objects under study. We shall discuss the hierarchical clustering procedures in terms of distance measures. The modification to similarity measures is obvious if we recognize that distance is essentially a measure of dissimilarity.

A hierarchical procedure consists of a definition on the distance between clusters and a set of thresholds or levels, $A(l)$. A commonly used procedure is the *nearest-neighbor* procedure where the distance between two clusters is defined as the distance between their closest elements, one in each cluster. Let $z_{ij}(l)$ be the distance between two clusters $C_i(l)$ and $C_j(l)$ at the l-th step. The two clusters will be in the same cluster at the $l+1$-st step if $z_{ij}(l) \leqslant A(l)$. With $A(l)$ monotonically increasing, all pattern vectors will eventually form a single cluster.

Figure 4.12 illustrates the clustering procedure. Note that with $l = 3$, $A(3) = 4$, and since $z_{12}(3) = 3.4 < 4$ and $z_{23}(3) = 3.5 < 4$, the three clusters, $C_1(3)$, $C_2(3)$, and $C_3(3)$, are grouped together to form a single cluster $C_1(4)$, even though $z_{13}(3) = 7.3 > 4$. The calculation of cluster distance is as follows: suppose $C_1(l+1)$ consists of $C_1(l)$, $C_2(l)$, $C_3(l)$, and $C_2(l+1)$ consists of $C_4(l)$ and $C_5(l)$, then $z_{12}(l+1) = \min z_{ij}(l)$, $i = 1, 2, 3$, and $j = 4, 5$. That this rule yields nearest-neighbor distance should be obvious.

If we are primarily interested in classifying the vectors into several classes, we may choose a threshold value $A = A(2) = 3$, and decide that there are three classes as indicated in the figure. It should be emphasized that a hierarchical procedure provides additional information in its tree structure, which is very important in some applications.

There are other ways to define cluster distance. In the furthest-neighbor procedure, the distance between two clusters is defined as the distance

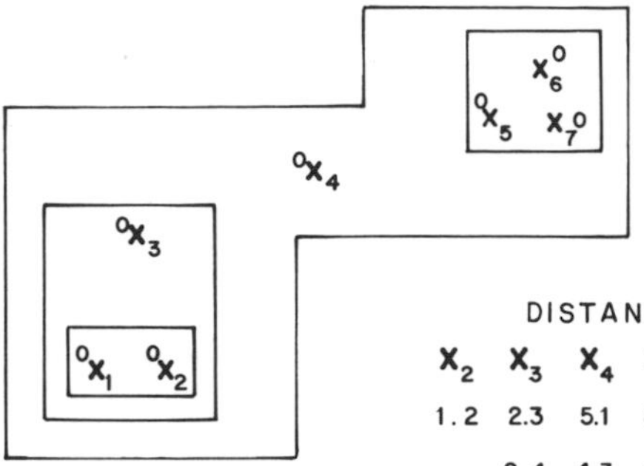

DISTANCE

	X_2	X_3	X_4	X_5	X_6	X_7
X_1	1.2	2.3	5.1	8.4	9.9	9.7
X_2		2.4	4.3	7.3	8.9	8.6
X_3			3.4	6.9	8.3	8.4
X_4				3.5	5.0	5.0
X_5					1.5	1.7
X_6						1.1

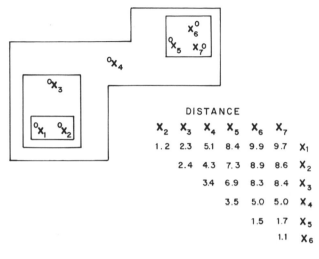

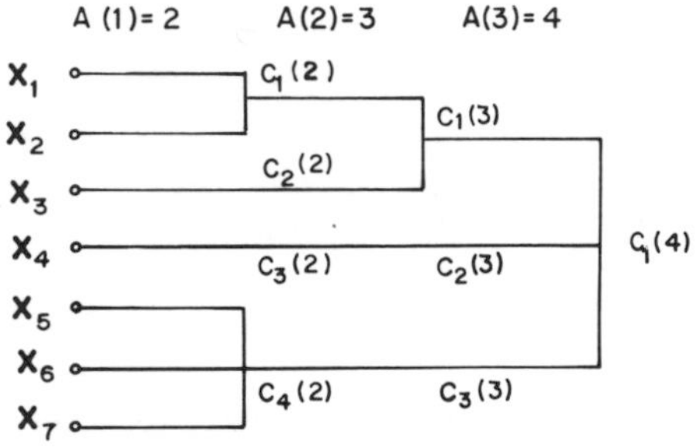

fig. 4.12 An example of hierarchical clustering by nearest neighbor (adapted from Hartigan, 1967).

between the two most remote elements, one in each cluster. Another distance measure is that between the two centroids. Note that these definitions on cluster distance are consistent when a single vector is considered as a cluster. Clearly, when we talk about clusters, the precise meaning of a cluster depends on how the cluster distance is defined.

4.5.2 Optimal clustering algorithm

Let us assume that there are K clusters or classes $C_1, C_2, \ldots, C_K$, and define a criterion

$$J_1 = \sum_{k=1}^{K} \sum_{\mathbf{x}_i \in C_k} \|\mathbf{x}_i - \mathbf{m}_k\|^2, \tag{4.106}$$

where $\mathbf{m}_k$ is the mean value of the k-th cluster or class and the number of clusters K is known. If we define n_k as the number of vectors in C_k, and the covariance matrix,

$$\mathbf{R}_k = \frac{1}{n_k} \sum_{\mathbf{x}_i \in C_k} (\mathbf{x}_i - \mathbf{m}_k)(\mathbf{x}_i - \mathbf{m}_k)^T, \tag{4.107}$$

clearly J_1 may be written as

$$J_1 = \mathrm{tr}(\sum_{k=1}^{K} n_k \mathbf{R}_k).$$

A *least-square clustering* procedure considers all possible K clusters obtainable from the n pattern vectors, evaluates J_1 for each combination, and selects the one with minimum J_1. This is obviously a global minimum, but it is not often used because it is computationally impractical for moderate or large n.

A commonly used, computationally feasible algorithm seeks the minimum iteratively. Suppose at the l-th step, the clusters are $C_1(l)$, $C_2(l), \ldots,$ $C_K(l)$, with mean vectors $\mathbf{m}_1(l)$, $\mathbf{m}_2(l), \ldots, \mathbf{m}_K(l)$, respectively. For each $\mathbf{x}_i$, we calculate the distance between $\mathbf{x}_i$, and $\mathbf{m}_k(l)$, and reclassify $\mathbf{x}_i$, $i = 1, 2, \ldots, n$, according to the following rule:

$$\mathbf{x}_i \in C_j(l+1) \text{ if } \|\mathbf{x}_i - \mathbf{m}_j(l)\| \leqslant \|\mathbf{x}_i - \mathbf{m}_k(l)\| \text{ for all } k \neq j. \tag{4.108}$$

The case of equal distance can be resolved arbitrarily. The mean vectors are then updated by

$$\mathbf{m}_k(l+1) = \frac{1}{n_k(l+1)} \sum_{\mathbf{x}_i \in C_k(l+1)} \mathbf{x}_i, \tag{4.109}$$

where $n_k(l+1)$ is the number of vectors in $C_k(l+1)$ according to (4.108). The algorithm stops when $C_k(l+1) = C_k(l)$ for all k. Note that all n vectors are taken into consideration at each iteration.

An examination of (4.106) and (4.108) indicates clearly that the algorithm tends to reduce J_1 after each iteration, hence it is essentially a *hill-climbing* technique. Like other hill-climbing approaches, the algorithm yields K clusters that minimize J_1, sometimes only locally. Experience indicates that the algorithm can be carried out in a reasonable length of time on a large computer with n in the order of 2000, provided that the dimensionality of the pattern space is moderate. The algorithm may also be interpreted as a decision-directed scheme; however, we feel that its hill-climbing optimization property is more important, and reserve the term decision-directed clustering for the procedure discussed in the next subsection.

To initiate the algorithm, we simply choose randomly $\mathbf{m}_1(1), \mathbf{m}_2(1), \ldots, \mathbf{m}_K(1)$. Another possibility is to select randomly a small subset of the n vectors, and use a hierarchical procedure or the globally optimal least-square procedure on the subset. The result may then be used to initiate the algorithm. In this way, the chance of converging to the global minimum of J_1 for the parent set may be improved.

The criterion J_1 is not invariant under nonsingular linear transformations of the vectors, i.e., by changing the coordinate system, the optimal clustering may be different. Friedman and Rubin (1967) introduced an invariant criterion,

$$J_2 = \mathrm{tr}\,(\sum_{k=1}^{K} n_k \mathbf{R}_k)^{-1}(\sum_{k=1}^{K} n_k \mathbf{m}_k \mathbf{m}_k^T), \tag{4.110}$$

where $\mathbf{R}_k$ is given by (4.107). Note that here an optimal clustering is the one that maximizes the criterion. It is difficult to derive an algorithm that seeks iteratively the maximum of J_2 in a manner similar to (4.108).

Fukunaga and Koontz (1970) proposed the application of a linear normalization transformation $\mathbf{T}$ before clustering defined by

$$\mathbf{T}(\sum_{i=1}^{n} \mathbf{x}_i \mathbf{x}_i^T)\mathbf{T}^T = \mathbf{I}, \tag{4.111}$$

the identity matrix. Clustering was performed in the transformed space with $\mathbf{x}_i$ replaced by $\mathbf{T}\mathbf{x}_i$. It was shown that when $K = 2$, maximizing J_2 is equivalent to minimizing J_1 in the transformed space.

The ISODATA program of Ball and Hall (1965) does not specify a criterion. It uses instead a mechanism for grouping and splitting clusters. Several pattern vectors are selected as cluster centers, and clusters are formed around these centers. A cluster is split in two if the maximum marginal standard deviation is too large, and clusters are grouped together if the clusters are too small. Cluster centers are modified after all n vectors have been examined. It is an iterative procedure, and the number of clusters or classes, K, need not be known.

4.5.3 Decision-directed clustering

In the subsection above, the number of clusters is assumed known, and each cluster corresponds to one class. Here we are concerned with the situation depicted by figure 4.13. In the figure, there are two classes of pattern vectors with a total of nine clusters. The distributions of the two classes are rather irregular, and it is more convenient to describe them by clusters. Each cluster is described by a mean vector $\mathbf{m}_k$, a covariance matrix

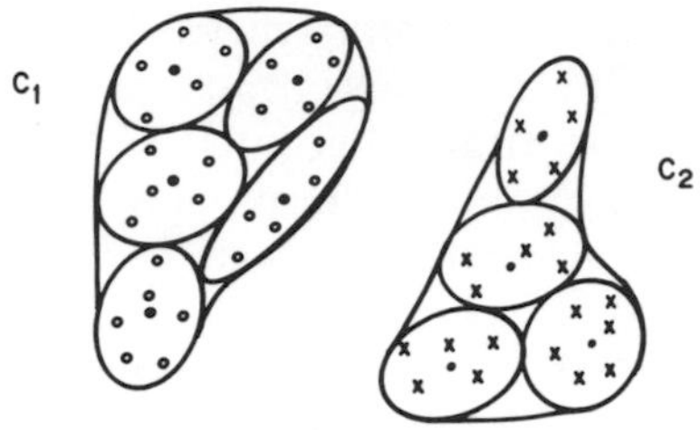

fig. 4.13 Two classes of pattern vectors with nine clusters.

$\mathbf{R}_k$, and the number of pattern vectors in the cluster n_k. The total number of clusters is denoted by K_c.

It is obvious from figure 4.13 that in this case the grouping into clusters is not unique. Nevertheless the clusters shown in the diagram give a good description of the distributions of the two classes. We regard the decision-directed clustering algorithm discussed in the following as a nonparametric approach to the estimation of probability density functions.

Consider a sequence of observations $\mathbf{x}_1, \mathbf{x}_2, \ldots$. Suppose that after observing $\mathbf{x}_1, \ldots, \mathbf{x}_{i-1}$, we have decided that there are $K_c(i)$ clusters with $\mathbf{m}_k(i)$, $\mathbf{R}_k(i)$, and $n_k(i)$ for the k-th cluster. When the vector $\mathbf{x}_i$ is observed, we calculate the quadratic form,

$$Q_k(\mathbf{x}_i) = (\mathbf{x}_i - \mathbf{m}_k(i))^T \mathbf{R}_k^{-1}(i)(\mathbf{x}_i - \mathbf{m}_k(i)), \tag{4.112}$$

which is essentially the square of the weighted distance between $\mathbf{x}_i$ and the mean of the k-th cluster, and find Q_j, the minimum value of Q, i.e.,

$$Q_j(\mathbf{x}_i) < Q_k(\mathbf{x}_i), \quad k = 1, 2, \ldots, K_c(i). \tag{4.113}$$

If, for a certain predetermined threshold A,

$$Q_j(\mathbf{x}_i) \leqslant A,$$

we decide that $\mathbf{x}_i$ belongs to the j-th cluster, and update the estimates,

$$n_j(i+1) = n_j(i) + 1.$$

$$\mathbf{m}_j(i+1) = \mathbf{m}_j(i) + \frac{1}{n_j(i)+1}[\mathbf{x}_i - \mathbf{m}_j(i)],$$

$$\mathbf{R}_j(i+1) = \mathbf{R}_j(i) + \frac{1}{n_j(i)+1}$$

$$\left[\frac{n_j(i)}{n_j(i)+1}(\mathbf{x}_i - \mathbf{m}_j(i))(\mathbf{x}_i - \mathbf{m}_j(i))^T - \mathbf{R}_j(i)\right],$$

where $\mathbf{m}_j(i+1)$ and $\mathbf{R}_j(i+1)$ are simply the sample mean and sample covariance of all the sample vectors in the j-th class. All other estimates are unchanged.

Now if for a certain $B > A$

$$Q_j(\mathbf{x}_i) \geqslant B,$$

where Q_j is the minimum Q, we decide that a new cluster is generated which consists of $\mathbf{x}_i$ only. The mean vector of the cluster is simply $\mathbf{x}_i$, and a predetermined covariance matrix is assigned to this new cluster. The number of clusters is increased by one, $K_c(i+1) = K_c(i) + 1$.

The hyperellipsoids defined by $Q_j(\mathbf{x}) = A$ and $Q_j(\mathbf{x}) = B$ are shown in figure 4.14. The region between the two hyperellipsoids is called the guard zone. If $\mathbf{x}_i$ falls into the guard zone,

$$A < Q_j(\mathbf{x}_i) < B,$$

it is temporarily stored and tagged for later processing. This will guard against generating unnecessary clusters.

It is noted that the algorithm is a heuristic procedure that requires updating the estimates, generating a new cluster, or storing $\mathbf{x}_i$ after every observation. The algorithm is not a hill-climbing type optimization procedure. It stops after a predetermined number of observations.

After finding the clusters, we may approximate each cluster by a Gaussian density, and the overall density function becomes

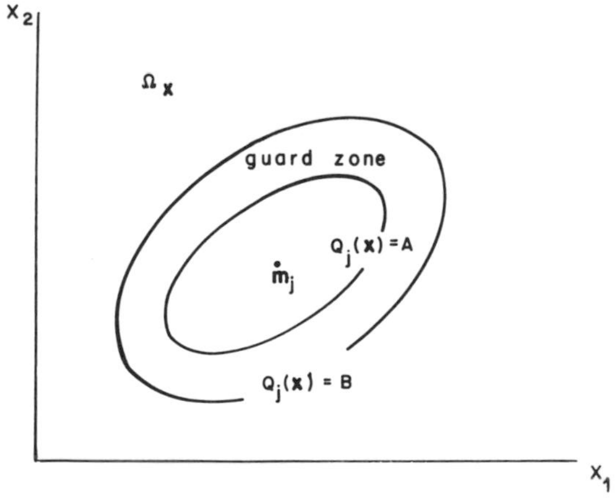

fig. 4.14 The decision regions and the guard zone for decision-directed clustering.

$$f(\mathbf{x}) = \sum_{k=1}^{K_c} \frac{n_k}{n} g(\mathbf{x}; \mathbf{m}_k, \mathbf{R}_k). \tag{4.114}$$

Other density functions with mean $\mathbf{m}_k$ and covariance $\mathbf{R}_k$ may also be used for the approximation.

Decision-directed clustering may be applied to both supervised and unsupervised learning. For supervised learning we simply find the clusters within the class. When the observed samples are unclassified, we may first find the clusters and then assign the clusters in a connected region to the same class. Clearly, unsupervised learning is possible in this case only if the classes are nonoverlapping.

The decision-directed clustering scheme was proposed and implemented successfully by Sebestyen and Edie (1966). It was applied to pattern recognition problems in spaces of as many as 80 dimensions by Mucciardi and Gose (1972). The covariance matrices, $\mathbf{R}_k$, were limited to diagonal matrices, and the thresholds A and B were determined empirically. It was found by geometrical arguments that A should increase linearly with N and the ratio B/A should be roughly a constant, 1.14, for large N, where N is the dimension of the pattern space.

4.6 Dimensionality and Sample Size

It is obvious that a large sample size is desirable for training purposes; however, the sample size must be finite and is limited by practical considerations. It also seems clear intuitively that the larger the number of useful measurements, N, the lower the classification errors. Since the measurements define the pattern space, N is the dimensionality of $\Omega_{\mathbf{x}}$.

Thus, it is desirable to have a large sample size, n, and a high dimensionality, N. For fixed N, increasing the number of samples will always yield better results. When n is fixed, however, it is not clear whether an arbitrarily high dimensionality is always desirable. An intuitive feeling is that high dimensionality will always give more "information" and better results whether n is finite or infinite. On the other hand, the machine must apply its experience gained during the learning phase to new pattern vectors, and it would not be able to do so if N were of the same order of magnitude as n or greater. The machine could perform very well in classifying the samples in the training sequence, but would generally have a very poor performance when used in classifying new samples. Hence, it is felt that for fixed n, the dimensionality N should not be arbitrarily increased, and should be much less than n.

The problem of dimensionality and sample size has been studied theoretically by Hughes (1968). He shows that for a given finite number of samples, n, there is an optimal dimensionality N above which average classification accuracy can decrease. This phenomenon has been observed experimentally, and in practice it is often required that the sample size be substantially larger than the dimensionality.

4.6.1 Dimensionality and the average classification accuracy

The probability of correct classification depends on the particular problem under study. In order to obtain general results, Hughes considers a class of pattern recognition problems, and investigates the relationship between dimensionality N and the average classification accuracy (which is simply the probability of correct classification averaged over that class).

Let us consider a pattern recognition problem where each component of a pattern vector x may assume one of only l discrete values. There is a total of N^l possible vectors or measurement states, $\mathbf{x} = \mathbf{s}_j$, $j = 1, 2, \ldots, N^l$. Assume that there are two classes C_1 and C_2 with prior probabilities

$$P(C_1) = P(C_2) = 1/2$$

and let

$$\begin{aligned} p_{j1} &= P(\mathbf{s}_j|C_1), \\ p_{j2} &= P(\mathbf{s}_j|C_2), j = 1, 2, \ldots, N^l \end{aligned} \tag{4.115}$$

be the probabilities that x equals the j-th measurement state conditioned on C_1 and C_2 respectively. The conditional probabilities, p_{j1} and p_{j2}, are unknown, and must be estimated or learned from a sequence of n training samples $\mathbf{x}_1, \mathbf{x}_2, \ldots, \mathbf{x}_n$ with known classifications. A simple estimation method is to use the relative frequencies. Let n_{j1} be the number of samples in the sequence such that $\mathbf{x} = \mathbf{s}_j$ and $\mathbf{x}$ belongs to C_1. Then n_{j1}/n is obviously an estimate of the joint probability $P(\mathbf{s}_j, C_1) = P(\mathbf{s}_j|C_1)P(C_1) = p_{j1}/2$. Similarly, n_{j2}/n is an estimate of $p_{j2}/2$.

As was discussed in section 2.1.1, a Bayes classifier that maximizes the probability of correct classification can easily be designed if p_{j1} and p_{j2} are known. Since they are unknown, we simply substitute $2n_{j1}/n$ and $2n_{j2}/n$ for p_{j1} and p_{j2}, respectively. It is noted that n_{j1} and n_{j2} are outcomes of an experiment, and depend on the unknown true values p_{j1} and p_{j2}. The detailed design of such a classifier and its performance will be discussed in the following subsection. It suffices for our discussion here to say that the probability of correct classification depends on N^l, n, p_{j1}, and p_{j2}, and is denoted by $P_{cr}(N^l, n; p_{j1}, p_{j2})$.

We are interested in the general effect of N and n on the probability of correct classification. In order to eliminate the effect of p_{j1} and p_{j2} on P_{cr}, we consider all possible pattern recognition problems with N^l states, n samples, and $P(C_1) = P(C_2) = 1/2$. Each set of $\{p_{j1}, p_{j2}\}$ satisfying the constraint

$$p_{j1} > 0, \quad p_{j2} > 0, \sum_{j=1}^{N^l} p_{j1} = \sum_{j=1}^{N^l} p_{j2} = 1, \tag{4.116}$$

represents a different pattern recognition problem. Assuming that each set of $\{p_{j1}, p_{j2}\}$ is equally likely, Hughes evaluated the average probability of correct classification,

$$\bar{P}_{cr}(N^l, n) = E[P_{cr}(N^l, n; p_{j1}, p_{j2})], \tag{4.117}$$

where the expectation is over all possible sets of $\{p_{j1}, p_{j2}\}$ satisfying the constraint (4.116). An expression for $\bar{P}_{cr}$ is derived for infinite and finite sample sizes in section 4.6.2.

The result is shown in figure 4.15 where the average probability $\bar{P}_{cr}$ is plotted versus the number of measurement states N^l for different sample sizes n. The case of $n = \infty$ corresponds to known p_{j1} and p_{j2}, and we note that in this case $\bar{P}_{cr}$ increases as N^l increases, but can never be over 0.75. It is important to note that for a given finite number of samples, n, there is an optimal value of N^l that maximizes the average probability of correct

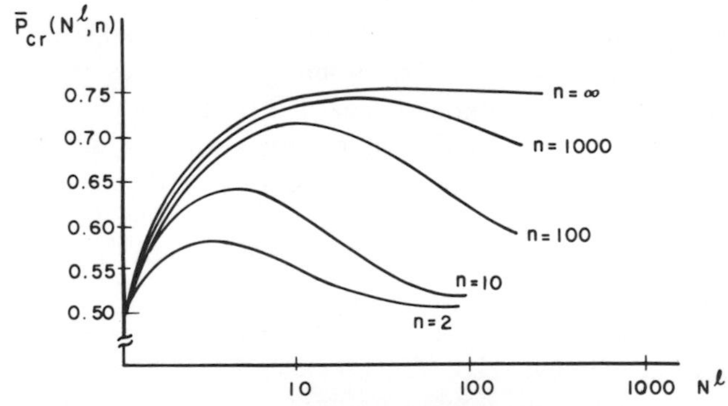

fig. 4.15 Average probability of correct classification versus number of measurement states (adapted from Hughes, 1968).

classification. Let the pattern vectors be binary, i.e., $l = 2$. From figure 4.15, we see that the optimal dimensionalities N for $n = 10$, 100, and 1000 are roughly 2, 3, and 5, respectively. If $l = 5$, the optimal dimensionalities for sample sizes 100 and 1000 are 1 and 2 respectively. Increasing the dimensionality or number of measurements over its optimal value will reduce the average probability of correct classification.

We recall that $\bar{P}_{cr}$ is averaged over a class of pattern recognition problems. There are problems in the class on which the machine can do much better than the average, and have, for fixed n, a probability of correct classification monotonically increasing with N. But there are also cases where the dimensionality N should not be arbitrarily increased, since above a certain value of N, the probability of correct classification starts to decrease. Hughes' remarkable result explains theoretically a long-standing phenomenon that has been observed experimentally.

Hughes' result should be viewed qualitatively rather than quantitatively. It helps to explain a phenomenon on dimensionality and sample size, but should not be used as a quantitative guide in designing a pattern recognition machine. Kanal and Chandrasekaran (1968) point out that his result is overly pessimistic. The reason is that Hughes uses a very general formulation. No assumption is made on the probability distribution, and the measurements may be statistically dependent or independent. Since his formulation includes those cases where the measurements are strongly correlated, it is felt that better performance can be obtained in most practical cases.

Chandrasekaran (1971) studied the same problem under the assumption of independent measurements. He showed that for the case of binary pattern vectors with infinite sample size, the average probability of correct classification approaches 1 as N approaches infinity, if the conditional probability of the i-th measurement satisifies

$$E[|P(x_i = 1|C_1) - P(x_i = 1|C_2)|] > 0 \text{ for all } i.$$

This assumption guarantees that each additional measurement provides additional information relevant to classification. A similar result was obtained by Chu and Chueh (1967). Chandrasekaran also evaluated the average probability of correct classification for finite sample size. His result suggests that for fixed n and statistically independent measurements, the average probability of correct classification is, at least in some cases, a monotonically increasing function of N. Hence, with the assumption of independent measurements, the results are more optimistic. It should be mentioned that in practical problems, arbitrarily large numbers of independent measurements are usually not available.

*4.6.2 Derivation of the average classification accuracy**

Let us consider first the case of infinite sample size. Since as n approaches infinity, $2n_{j1}/n$ and $2n_{j2}/n$ approach p_{j1} and p_{j2} respectively, this is equivalent to assuming known p_{j1} and p_{j2}. To simplify the notation, we let $M = N^l$, the number of measurement states.

With p_{j1} and p_{j2} known, we have a standard Bayes classification problem, i.e., when observing a $\mathbf{x} = \mathbf{s}_j$, we decide $\mathbf{x} \in C_2$ if $p_{j1} \leqslant p_{j2}$. Then, we obtain, as in the derivation of the Bayes error rate in (2.11),

$$P_{\text{cr}} = \frac{1}{2}\sum_{j=1}^{M} \max(p_{j1}, p_{j2}). \tag{4.118}$$

Recall that we are concerned with a class of pattern recognition problems and $\{p_{j1}, p_{j2}\}$ is regarded as a set of random variables uniformly distributed,

$$f(p_{11}, \ldots, p_{M1}, p_{12}, \ldots, p_{M2}) = h,$$

in a region specified by (4.116). The normalization constant h can be obtained from

$$\begin{aligned} 1 = h\Big[\int_0^1 dp_{11} \int_0^{1-p_{11}} dp_{21} \cdots \int_0^{1-p_{11}-\cdots-p_{M-2,1}} dp_{M-1,1}\Big] \\ \Big[\int_0^1 dp_{12} \int_0^{1-p_{12}} dp_{22} \cdots \int_0^{1-p_{12}-\cdots-p_{M-2,2}} dp_{M-1,2}\Big]. \end{aligned} \tag{4.119}$$

Only $2(M-1)$ integrals appear on the right on (4.119) because the two linear equations in (4.116) fix p_{M1} and p_{M2} in terms of the others, and the integrals represent the volume of the region given by (4.116). We note that

$$\begin{aligned} &\int_0^1 dp_{11} \cdots \int_0^{1-p_{11}-\cdots-p_{M-2,1}} dp_{M-1,1} \\ &\quad= \int_0^1 dp_{11} \cdots \int_0^{1-p_{11}-\cdots-p_{M-3,1}} \\ &\qquad (1 - p_{11} - \cdots - p_{M-2,1})\,dp_{M-2,1} \\ &\quad= \int_0^1 dp_{11} \cdots \int_0^{1-p_{11}-\cdots-p_{M-4,1}} \\ &\qquad [(1 - p_{11} - \cdots - p_{M-3,1})^2/2]\,dp_{M-3,1} \\ &\quad= \cdots\cdots\cdots \\ &\quad= \int_0^1 [(1-p_{11})^{M-2}/(M-2)!]\,dp_{11} \\ &\quad= 1/(M-1)!, \end{aligned} \tag{4.120}$$

* Section may be omitted on first reading.

and hence by (4.119),

$$h = [(M - 1)!]^2. \tag{4.121}$$

In order to evaluate the average probability of correct classification, it is necessary to take expectation of (4.118) over the probability density function of $\{p_{j1}, p_{j2}\}$. By symmetry, each of the M terms of (4.118) will have an identical expected value, and we may take the expected value of the first term and multiply it by M. Thus,

$$\begin{aligned}\overline{P}_{cr} = \frac{M[(M-1)!]^2}{2} \int_0^1 \int_0^1 \max(p_{11}, p_{12})\, dp_{11}\, dp_{12} \\ \left[\int_0^{1-p_{11}} dp_{21} \cdots \int_0^{1-p_{11}-\cdots-p_{M-2,1}} dp_{M-1,1}\right] \\ \left[\int_0^{1-p_{12}} dp_{22} \cdots \int_0^{1-p_{12}-\cdots-p_{M-2,2}} dp_{M-1,2}\right].\end{aligned} \tag{4.122}$$

Taking those integrations inside the brackets yields, according to (4.120), $(1 - p_{11})^{M-2}/(M-2)!$ and $(1 - p_{12})^{M-2}/(M-2)!$. Again, by symmetry we may consider only the case $p_{11} > p_{12}$ and multiply the integral by a factor of 2,

$$\begin{aligned}\overline{P}_{cr} &= M(M-1)^2 \int_0^1 dp_{11} \int_0^{p_{11}} p_{11}(1 - p_{11})^{M-2}(1 - p_{12})^{M-2}\, dp_{12} \\ &= M(M-1) \int_0^1 p_{11}(1 - p_{11})^{M-2}[1 - (1 - p_{11})^{M-1}]\, dp_{11},\end{aligned}$$

and obtain, by means of integration by parts.

$$\overline{P}_{cr} = \frac{3M - 2}{4M - 2} = \frac{3N^l - 2}{4N^l - 2}. \tag{4.123}$$

This is the curve plotted in figure 4.15 with $n = \infty$, and it approaches 0.75 as N^l approaches infinity.

For finite sample size n, we use the relative frequencies, $2n_{j1}/n$ and $2n_{j2}/n$, as estimates of p_{j1} and p_{j2}, respectively. Since $P(C_1) = P(C_2) = 1/2$, we assume that n is even, $n/2$ samples are drawn from C_1, and the other $n/2$ samples are from C_2. The conditional probability for n_{j1} and n_{j2} for given p_{j1} and p_{j2} is the product of two binomial distributions,

$$\begin{aligned}P(n_{j1}, n_{j2} \mid p_{j1}, p_{j2}) &= \frac{(n/2)!}{n_{j1}!\,(n/2 - n_{j1})!} (p_{j1})^{n_{j1}} (1 - p_{j1})^{n/2 - n_{ji}} \\ &\cdot \frac{(n/2)!}{n_{j2}!\,(n/2 - n_{j2})!} (p_{j2})^{n_{j2}} (1 - p_{j2})^{n/2 - n_{j2}},\end{aligned} \tag{4.124}$$

in which the probabilities of states other than $\mathbf{s}_j$ are lumped in the terms $(1 - p_{j1})$ and $(1 - p_{j2})$.

With $2n_{j1}/n$ and $2n_{j2}/n$ being the estimates of p_{j1} and p_{j2}, an observed pattern vector $\mathbf{x} = \mathbf{s}_j$ will be classified to C_1 if $n_{j1} > n_{j2}$ and to C_2 if $n_{j1} \leqslant n_{j2}$. Then, the probability of correct classification becomes

$$P_{cr} = \frac{1}{2}\sum_{j=1}^{M} [p_{j1}p(n_{j1} > n_{j2}|p_{j1}, p_{j2}) + p_{j2}p(n_{j1} \leqslant n_{j2}|p_{j1}, p_{j2})]. \quad (4.125)$$

We are interested in the average probability of correct classification which, by a symmetry argument, may be written as

$$\overline{P}_{cr}(M, n) = \frac{M}{2}E[p_{11}p(n_{11} > n_{12}|p_{11}, p_{12}) + p_{12}p(n_{11} \leqslant n_{12}|p_{11}, p_{12})], \quad (4.126)$$

where the expectation is over the uniform distribution of the set $\{p_{j1}, p_{j2}\}$ as in (4.122).

To evaluate $\overline{P}_{cr}$, we write (4.126) in the form of

$$\overline{P}_{cr}(M, n) = \frac{M}{2}E\Big[p_{11}\sum_{n_{11}=1}^{n/2}\sum_{n_{12}=0}^{n_{11}-1} P(n_{11}, n_{12}|p_{11}, p_{12}) + p_{12}\sum_{n_{12}=0}^{n/2}\sum_{n_{11}=0}^{n_{12}} P(n_{11}, n_{12}|p_{11}, p_{12})\Big], \quad (4.127)$$

and substitute $P(n_{11}, n_{12}|p_{11}, p_{12})$ by (4.124). The next steps are to interchange the expectation and the summations, and to take the expectation of each term in a manner that is similar to, but somewhat more tedious than, the derivation of (4.123) from (4.122). The result is

$$\overline{P}_{cr}(M, n) = \frac{M(M-1)^2}{(2M+n)}\sum_{n_{11}=0}^{n/2}\sum_{n_{12}=0}^{n/2} \psi(n_{11}; n, M)\,\psi(n_{12}; n, M)\max(n_{11}+1, n_{12}+1), \quad (4.128)$$

with the function ψ given by

$$\psi(n_{11}; n, M) = \frac{(n/2 - n_{11} + 1)(n/2 - n_{11} + 2)\cdots(n/2 - n_{11} + M - 2)}{(n/2 + 1)(n/2 + 2)\cdots(n/2 + M - 1)}.$$

Equation (4.128) was plotted in figure 4.15 with M replaced by N^l.

4.7 Notes and Remarks

The credit for the perceptron must go to Rosenblatt (1957, 1960, 1961). The convergence theorem was proven by Rosenblatt (1960) and many authors, including Block (1962), Charnes (1964), Novikoff (1963), Ridgway (1962), and Singleton (1962). Widrow (1962) studied TLU networks, which he called "Adalines." Other related works are Aizerman et al. (1964), Duda (1968), Farley and Clark (1954), Mays (1964), Sklansky (1965), and Winder (1962). The presentation of the first two sections of this chapter is strongly influenced by the authoritative book by Nilsson (1965).

The training algorithm may be interpreted as a recursive method for finding the solution of the linear inequality $\boldsymbol{\alpha}^T\tilde{\mathbf{y}} > 0$. The relaxation method for linear inequalities was studied by Agmon (1954) and Motzkin and Schoenberg (1954). The minimum-square algorithm was due to Widrow and Hoff (1960), and we have quoted Ho and Kashyap (1965) in presenting their algorithm. The formulation of recursive algorithms in terms of criterion functions is based on a report by Blaydon (1967).

Linear discriminant functions were studied by Highleyman (1962) and Wolff (1966), and polynomial discriminant functions were investigated by Cooper (1964) and Specht (1967). The linear transformation that maximizes the interclass distance was proposed by Sebestyen (1961, 1962). The linear regression method is a modification of a well known technique in statistics (Anderson, 1958), and was formulated by Young and Huggins (1964) for recognizing electrocardiograms. The Fisher discriminant approach is commonly used in signal detection, where it is known as the maximum signal-to-noise ratio filter.

The recursive algorithms discussed in this chapter are primarily for linearly separable classes. Highleyman (1962) derived an algorithm for classes that are not linearly separable, and which may even be overlapping, as described in chapter 3. The classifications of the n training samples are known. Let us define a criterion function

$$J(\boldsymbol{\alpha}) = \frac{1}{2}\sum_{l=1}^{n}[1 - \operatorname{sgn}(\boldsymbol{\alpha}^T\tilde{\mathbf{y}}_l)]. \tag{4.129}$$

Since

$$\frac{1}{2}[1 - \operatorname{sgn}(\boldsymbol{\alpha}^T\tilde{\mathbf{y}}_l)] = \begin{cases} 0 & \text{if } \boldsymbol{\alpha}^T\tilde{\mathbf{y}}_l > 0, \\ 1 & \text{if } \boldsymbol{\alpha}^T\tilde{\mathbf{y}}_l \leqslant 0, \end{cases} \tag{4.130}$$

minimization of $J(\boldsymbol{\alpha})$ is equivalent to minimizing the number of misclassified samples. Hence, we seek a hyperplane that minimizes $J(\boldsymbol{\alpha})$ as illustrated in figure 4.16(*a*). We note that the function $[1 - \operatorname{sgn}(\boldsymbol{\alpha}^T\tilde{\mathbf{y}})]$ in (4.130) has a

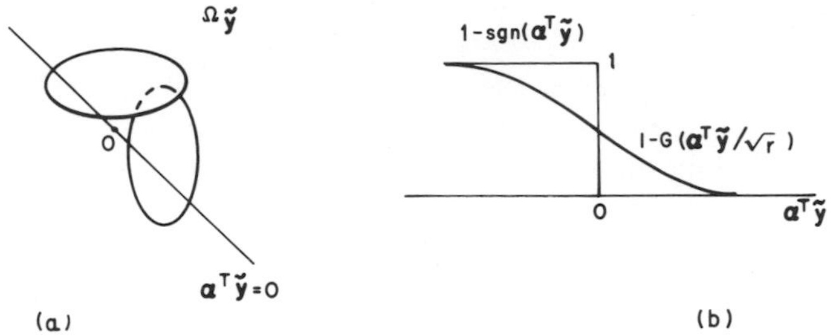

fig. 4.16 (a) Classes that are not linearly separable. (b) The function $1 - G(\alpha^T\tilde{y}/\sqrt{r})$.

discontinuity at $\alpha^T\tilde{y} = 0$, hence its gradient does not exist at that point. To avoid this difficulty, we approximate $J(\alpha)$ by

$$J(\alpha, r) = \sum_{l=1}^{n} [1 - G(\alpha^T\tilde{y}_l/r^{1/2})], \tag{4.131}$$

where $G(u)$ is a Gaussian distribution function,

$$G(u) = (2\pi)^{-1/2} \int_{-\infty}^{u} \exp\left(-\frac{v^2}{2}\right) dv. \tag{4.132}$$

It can easily be seen from figure 4.16(*b*) that

$$\lim_{r\to 0} J(\alpha, r) = J(\alpha). \tag{4.133}$$

Using (4.131), and taking gradient, we obtain a recursive algorithm

$$\alpha(i+1) = \alpha(i) + a(2\pi r)^{-1/2} \sum_{l=1}^{n} \tilde{y}_l \exp[-(\alpha^T(i)\tilde{y}_l)^2/2r]. \tag{4.134}$$

The Highleyman algorithm (4.134) may be used for overlapping classes. A more general theory for overlapping classes has been developed using stochastic approximation. This will be discussed in detail in the following chapter.

Hierarchical clustering has been considered by many authors, and we quote Hartigan (1967), Johnson (1967), Sokal and Sneath (1963), Wald (1963) and Wishart (1969). There have been efforts to compare and unify various hierarchical approaches (Gower, 1967; Jardine and Sibson, 1968; Lance and Williams, 1967). Recently, Fisher and Van Ness (1971) and Van Ness (1972) discussed the admissibility of both hierarchical and hill-climbing techniques.

Iterative hill-climbing algorithms have been considered by Ball (1965), Ball and Hall (1965), Casey and Nagy (1968), Friedman and Rubin (1967), and Fukunaga and Koontz (1970). The asymptotic properties of this type of algorithms have been investigated by Dorofeyuk (1966) and MacQueen (1967). The decision-directed clustering was proposed by Sebestyen and Edie (1966) and its properties in high-dimensional spaces were studied by Mucciardi and Gose (1972). The section on dimensionality and sample size is primarily based on Hughes (1968).

An interesting recent paper by Koontz and Fukunaga (1972) defines for clustering a criterion J as the total number of distinct pairs of vectors separated by a distance less than z_0 and assigned to different classes, where z_0 is predetermined. For a two-cluster problem, the criterion for clustering may be expressed as

$$J = \sum_{\mathbf{x}_i \in C_1} \sum_{\mathbf{x}_j \in C_2} \frac{1}{2}\{\operatorname{sgn}[z_0 - \|\mathbf{x}_i - \mathbf{x}_j\|] + 1\}. \tag{4.135}$$

Note that J may be evaluated by a counting procedure rather than by complex calculations. An iterative algorithm is derived that seeks the minimum of J in (4.135). Contributions to J come from pairs of vectors near the boundary separating the clusters, and a low value of this criterion corresponds to a boundary passing through a region of low vector concentration. Hence the algorithm is called by the authors a valley-seeking algorithm.

Problems

4.1 Consider the following vectors, $\tilde{\mathbf{y}}_i^T$, $i = 1, 2, \ldots, 8$,

$$[0, 1, 1, 1],\ [0, 0, 0, 1],\ [-1, 0, 0, -1],\ [-1, 0, -1, -1],$$
$$[0, 0, 1, 1],\ [1, 1, 1, 1],\ [-1, -1, 0, -1],\ [0, 1, 0, 1].$$

It is known that there exist solution vectors $\boldsymbol{\alpha}$ such that $\boldsymbol{\alpha}^T\tilde{\mathbf{y}}_i > 0$ for all i. Let the initial estimate be $\boldsymbol{\alpha}^T(1) = [1, 1, 1, 1]$. Find the solution vector recursively. It may be necessary to implement the solution on a digital computer.

4.2 The following are two classes of pattern vectors $\mathbf{x}^T$ with known classifications:

$$C_1\colon [0, 0, 0],\ [1, 0, 0],\ [0, 1, 1],\ [1, 1, 1],$$
$$C_2\colon [0, 1, 0],\ [1, 1, 0],\ [0, 0, 1],\ [1, 0, 1].$$

We wish to use a TLU or a TLU network to classify the vectors. Devise a training algorithm and find the solution.

4.3 Derive a recursive algorithm for the criterion function,

$$J(\alpha) = \frac{1}{2} \sum_{l=1}^{n} [|\boldsymbol{\alpha}^T \tilde{\mathbf{y}}_l| - \boldsymbol{\alpha}^T \tilde{\mathbf{y}}_l].$$

Show that if there exist solutions $\boldsymbol{\alpha}$ such that $\boldsymbol{\alpha}^T \tilde{\mathbf{y}}_l > 0$, $l = 1, 2, \ldots, n$, the algorithm converges after a finite number of iterations.

4.4 Let $\mathbf{y} = \mathbf{Tx}$ where $\mathbf{T}$ is an $N \times N$ matrix. We may define in the transformed space $\Omega_{\mathbf{y}}$ an interclass mean-square distance ν_1^2 and an overall mean-square distance ν_0^2 similar to (4.76) and (4.77). Find an optimal $\mathbf{T}$ such that ν_1^2 is maximized subject to the constraint that ν_0^2 is a constant.

4.5 Let the mean vectors and the covariance matrices of the two classes be

$$\mathbf{m}_1 = \begin{bmatrix} 0 \\ 1 \end{bmatrix}, \qquad \mathbf{R}_1 = \begin{bmatrix} 4 & 0 \\ 0 & 1 \end{bmatrix},$$

$$\mathbf{m}_1 = \begin{bmatrix} 1 \\ 0 \end{bmatrix}, \qquad \mathbf{R}_2 = \begin{bmatrix} 1/4 & 0 \\ 0 & 4 \end{bmatrix}.$$

Find a 1×2 linear transformation using the Fisher discriminant approach. Determine the threshold value and sketch the decision surface in the original space. Calculate the error probability for your classification scheme assuming that the two classes are Gaussian distributed with equal prior probabilities.

4.6 Use the linear regression method for problem 4.5 and compare the results.

4.7 Suppose we have 25 sample vectors for each class having mean vectors and covariance matrices as in problem 4.5. The sample vectors may be generated on a digital computer using a Gaussian random number generator. Find linear discriminant functions using the following approaches and compare the results in terms of error probabilities and computational difficulties.

(a) Sebestyen's maximization of interclass distance;

(b) Ho–Kashyap algorithm;

(c) Highleyman algorithm.

4.8 Consider the clustering criterion

$$J = \sum_{\mathbf{x}_i \in C_1} \sum_{\mathbf{x}_j \in C_2} \frac{1}{2}\{\text{sgn}[z_0 - \|\mathbf{x}_i - \mathbf{x}_j\|] + 1\},$$

that was discussed briefly at the end of section 4.7. Derive an iterative algorithm that seeks the minimum of J.

References

1. Abend, K., Harly, T. J. Jr., Chandrasekaran, B., and Hughes, G. F. 1969. Comments on "On the mean accuracy of statistical pattern recognizers." *IEEE Trans. Information Theory*. *IT-15*: *420–423*.

2. Agmon, S. 1954. The relaxation method for linear inequalities. *Canadian J. Math.* 6:383–392.

3. Aizerman, M. A., Braverman, E. N., and Rozonoer, L. I. 1964. Theoretical foundations of the potential function method in pattern recognition. *Automat. i. Telemech.* 25:917–936.

4. Anderson, T. W. 1958. *An Introduction to Multivariate Statistical Analysis*. Wiley, New York.

5. Arbib, M. A. 1964. *Brains, Machines, and Mathematics*. McGraw-Hill, New York.

6. Ball, G. H. 1965. Data analysis in the social sciences: what about the details? *AFIPS Proc. Fall Joint Computer Conf.* 27:pt. 1, 533–559.

7. Ball, G. H. and Hall, D. J. 1965. ISODATA, a novel method of data analysis and pattern classification. Tech. Report, Stanford Research Institute, Menlo Park, California.

8. Blaydon, C. C. 1967. Recursive algorithms for pattern classification. Tech. Report No. 520, Harvard Univ., Cambridge, Massachusetts.

9. Block, H. D. 1962. The perceptron: a model for brain functioning, I. *Rev. Modern Phys.* 34:123–135

10. Casey, R. G. and Nagy, G. 1968. An autonomous reading machine. *IEEE Trans. Computers* C-17: 492–503.

11. Chandrasekaran, B. 1971. Independence of measurements and the mean recognition accuracy. *IEEE Trans. Information Theory* IT-17: 452–456.

12. Charnes, A. 1964. On some fundamental theorems of perceptron theory and their geometry. In *Computer and Information Sciences*, eds. J. Tou and R. Wilcox. Spartan, Washington, D.C.

13. Chu, J. T. and Chueh, J. C. 1967. Error probabilities in decision functions for character recognition. *J. Assoc. Computing Machinery* 14: 273–280.

14. Cooper, P. W. 1964. Hyperplanes, hyperspheres, and hyperquadrics as decision boundaries. In *Computer and Information Sciences*, eds. J. Tou and R. Wilcox, pp. 111–138. Spartan, Washington, D.C.

15. Deutsch, R. 1965. *Estimation Theory*. Prentice-Hall, Englewood Cliffs, New Jersey.

16. Dorofeyuk, A. A. 1966. Teaching algorithm for a pattern recognition machine without a teacher, based on the method of potential functions. *Automat. I. Telemech.* 27:1728–1737.

17. Duda, R. O. 1968. Linear machines and Markov processes. In *Pattern Recognition*, ed. L. N. Kanal, pp. 251–282. Thompson, Washington, D.C.

18. Farley, B. and Clark, W. 1954. Simulation of self-organizing systems by digital computer. *IRE Trans. Information Theory* IT-4: 76–84.

19. Fisher, L. and Van Ness, J. 1971. Admissible clustering procedures. *Biometrika* 58:91–104.

20. Friedman, H.P. and Rubin, J. 1967. On some invariant criteria for grouping data. *J. Am. Stat. Assoc.* 62:1159–1178.

21. Fukunaga, K. and Koontz, W. L. G. 1970. A criterion and an algorithm for grouping data. *IEEE Trans. Computers* C-19:917–923.

22. Gower, J. C. 1967. A comparison of some methods of cluster analysis. *Biometrics* 23:523–637.

23. Greville, T. N. E. 1959. The pseudoinverse of a rectangular or singular matrix and its application to the solution of systems of linear equations. *SIAM Review*. 1:38–43.

24. Hartigan, J. A. 1967. Representation of similarity matrices by trees. *J. Am. Stat. Assoc., 62:1140–1158.*

25. Highleyman, W. H. 1962. Linear decision functions with application to pattern recognition. *Proc. IRE* 50: 1501–1514.

26. Ho, Y. C. and Kashyap, R. L. 1965. An algorithm for linear inequalities and its applications. *IEEE Trans. Electronic Computers* EC-14:683–688.

27. Hughes, G. F. 1968. On the mean accuracy of statistical pattern recognizers. *IEEE Trans. Information Theory*, IT-14:55–63.

28. Jardine, N. and Sibson, R. 1968. The construction of hierarchic and non-hierachic classifications. *Computer J.* 11:177–184.

29. Johnson, S. C. 1967. Hierarchical clustering schemes. *Psychometrika* 32:241–254.

30. Kanal, L. and Chandrasekaran, B. 1968. On dimensionality and sample size in statistical pattern classification. *Proc. Nat'l Electronics Conf.* 24:2–7.

31. Koontz, W. L. G. and Fukunaga, K. 1972. A nonparametric valley-seeking technique for cluster analysis. *IEEE Trans. Computers* C-21:171–178.

32. Lance, G. N. and Williams, W. T. 1966. A general theory of classificatory sorting strategies. 1. Hierarchical systems. *Computer J.* 9:373–380.

33. MacQueen, J. 1967. Some methods for classification and analysis of multivariate observations. *Proc. 5th. Berkeley Symp. Prob. and Stat.* 281–297.

34. Mays, C. H. 1964. Effect of adaptation parameters on convergence time and tolerance for adaptive threshold elements. *IEEE Trans. Electronic Computers* EC-13:465–468.

35. McCulloch, W. and Pitts, W. 1943. A logical calculus of the ideas immanent in nervous activity. *Bull. Math. Biophys.* 5:115–137.

36. Motzkin, T. S. and Schoenberg, I. J. 1954. The relaxation method for linear inequalities. *Canadian J. Math.* 6:393–404.

37. Mucciardi, A. N. and Gose, E. E. 1972. An automatic clustering algorithm and its properties in high-dimensional spaces. *IEEE Trans. Systems, Man and Cybernetics* SMC-2:247–254.

38. Nilsson, N. J. 1965. *Learning Machines*. McGraw-Hill, New York.

39. Novikoff, A. B. J. 1963. On convergence proofs for perceptrons. *Proc. Symp. Math. Theory of Automata*, 12:615–622. Polytech. Inst. of Brooklyn, New York.

40. Ridgway, W. C. 1962. An adaptive logic system with generalizing properties. Tech. Report. 1556-1, Stanford Electronic Laboratories, Stanford University, Stanford, California.

41. Rosenblatt, F. 1957. The perceptron: a perceiving and recognizing automaton. Report 85-460-1, Cornell Aeronautical Laboratory, Buffalo, New York.

42. ———. 1960. On the convergence of reinforcement procedures in simple perceptrons. Report VG-1196-G-4, Cornell Aeronautical Laboratory, Buffalo, New York.

43. ———. 1961. *Principle of Neurodynamics: Perceptrons and the Theory of Brain Mechanism.* Spartan, Washington, D.C.

44. Sebestyen, G.S. 1961. Recognition of membership in classes. *IRE Trans. Information Theory* IT-6:44–50.

45. ———. 1962. *Decision-Making Processes in Pattern Recognition.* Macmillan, New York.

46. Sebestyen, G. S. and Edie, J. 1966. An algorithm for nonparametric pattern recognition. *IEEE Trans. Electronic Computers* EC-15:908–915.

47. Singleton, R. C. 1962. A test for linear separability as applied to self-organizing machines. In *Self Organizing Systems 1962*, eds. M. C. Yovits, G. T. Jacobi, and G. D. Goldstein, pp. 503–524. Spartan, Washington, D.C.

48. Sklansky, J. 1965. Threshold training of two-mode signal detection. *IEEE Trans. Information Theory* IT-11:353–362.

49. Sokal, R. R. and Sneath, P. H. 1963. *Principles of Numerical Taxonomy.* Freeman, San Francisco, California.

50. Specht, D. F. 1967. Generation of polynomial discriminant functions for pattern recognition. *IEEE Trans. Electronic Computers* EC-16:308–319.

51. Van Ness, J. W. 1972. Admissible clustering procedures II. Tech. Report No. 61, Dept of Statistics, Carnegie-Mellon Univ., Pittsburgh, Pennsylvania.

52. Wald, H. J. 1963. Hierarchical grouping to optimize an objective function. *J. Am. Stat. Assoc.* 58:236–244.

53. Widrow, B. 1962. Generalization and information storage in networks of adaline neurons. In *Self Organizing Systems 1962*, Eds. M. C. Yovits, G. T. Jacobi, and G. D. Goldstein, pp. 435–461. Spartan, Washington, D.C.

54. Widrow, B. and Hoff, M.E. 1960. Adaptive switching circuits. *WESCON Convention Record*, Part 4: 96–104.

55. Winder, R. O. 1962. Threshold logic. Ph.D. Dissertation, Princeton Univ. Princeton, New Jersey.

56. Wishart, H. J. 1969. An algorithm for hierarchical classification. *Biometrices* 25:165–170.

57. Wolff, A. C. 1966. The estimation of optimum linear decision function with a sequential random method. *IEEE Trans. Information Theory* IT-12:312–315.

58. Young, T. Y. and Huggins, W. H. 1964. Computer analysis of electrocardiograms using a linear regression technique. *IEEE Trans. Biomedical Engineering* BME-11:60–67.

5

Stochastic Approximation and Pattern Recognition

5.1 Stochastic Approximation

Before we introduce stochastic approximation it will be helpful to consider a simple example of a deterministic algorithm.

Let $\mu(\omega)$ be a given function having a unique real root at θ, i.e.,

$$\mu(\omega)\Big|_{\omega=\theta} = 0. \tag{5.1}$$

For example, $\mu(\omega)$ may be a known polynomial function and it is assumed that in a certain interval of interest there is only one root that satisfies (5.1). One way to solve this equation is to use an iterative method such as the Newton–Raphson method in numerical analysis. An initial estimate $\omega(1)$ of θ is made, and at the i-th stage, if $\mu(\omega(i)) \neq 0$, a recursive algorithm,

$$\omega(i+1) = \omega(i) - a_i\,\mu(\omega(i)), \tag{5.2}$$

is used for updating the estimate. The gain coefficient a_i depends on the particular numerical method one chooses. In figure 5.1 we illustrate the Newton–Raphson method with

$$a_i = \left[\frac{d}{d\omega}\mu(\omega)\right]^{-1}\Bigg|_{\omega=\omega(i)}.$$

The recursive estimates in figure 5.1 converge to the root θ. A somewhat similar problem is to find numerically the maximum or minimum of a known function $\mu(\omega)$, and a gradient method,

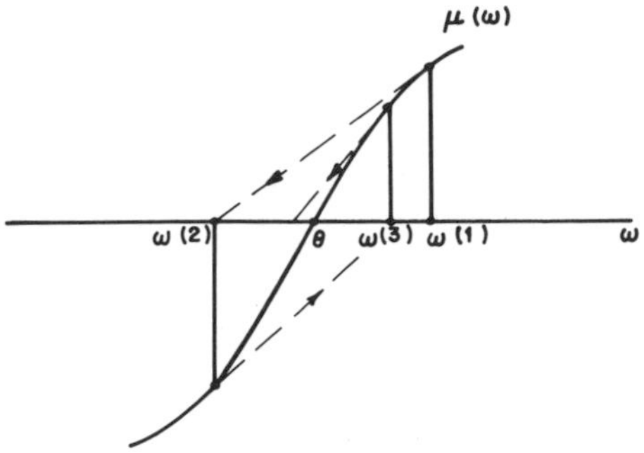

fig. 5.1 The Newton–Raphson iterative method.

$$\omega(i+1) = \omega(i) - a_i \frac{d}{d\omega}\mu(\omega)\bigg|_{\omega=\omega(i)}, \qquad (5.3)$$

may be used to solve this problem.

Consider the estimation of the mean discussed in chapter 3. Let x_1, x_2, . . . , be a set of statistically independent and identically distributed random samples. The true mean value θ is obviously the root of the equation

$$\mu(\omega) = \omega - E_x[x] = E_x[\omega - x] = 0, \qquad (5.4)$$

where $E_x[\cdot]$ indicates the expectation over the true distribution of x. It was shown in chapter 3 that the sample mean $\omega(i+1)$ based on the random samples may be written recursively as

$$\omega(i+1) = \omega(i) - a_i(\omega(i) - x_i), \quad a_i = \frac{1}{i}. \qquad (5.5)$$

It is well known from the law of large numbers that under some general conditions the sample mean converges to the true mean θ. Algorithm (5.5) may be interpreted as a stochastic approximation algorithm, and its resemblance to algorithm (5.2) is rather interesting. We want to find the root of the equation $\mu(\omega) = 0$. Since $\mu(\omega)$ is unknown and not observable, we use instead an observable random function whose expectation equals $\mu(\omega)$. For this reason, although we use a different function for each i, the overall effect is somewhat similar to observing $\mu(\omega)$ directly. The random function in algorithm (5.5) is $(\omega - x)$, which depends on the random sample x_i, and the function $\mu(\omega)$ is called the *regression function.* Figure 5.2 illustrates the random functions $(\omega - x)$ and the estimation scheme for an example where $\theta = 4.0$. Suppose the random observations x_i are 7, 3, 7, 2, 5, ... We choose as our initial estimate $\omega(1) = x_o = 7$, and the subsequent estimates become

$$\omega(2) = \omega(1) - 1(\omega(1) - x_1) = 7 - 1(7 - 3) = 3.0,$$

$$\omega(3) = \omega(2) - \frac{1}{2}(\omega(2) - x_2) = 3 - \frac{1}{2}(3 - 7) = 5.0,$$

$$\omega(4) = \omega(3) - \frac{1}{3}(\omega(3) - x_3) = 5 - \frac{1}{3}(5 - 2) = 4.0,$$

$$\omega(5) = \omega(4) - \frac{1}{4}(\omega(4) - x_4) = 4 - \frac{1}{4}(4 - 5) = 4.25,$$

$$\ldots .$$

Stochastic approximation is a recursive technique introduced by Robbins and Monro in 1951 for finding the root of a regression function. Robbins and Monro showed that under some general conditions the algorithm converges in the mean-square sense to the root. The original algorithm has been generalized and its convergence conditions have been relaxed by many authors. The basic theory is essentially a stochastic optimization theory, and has been applied to a variety of problems in the field of communication theory, control theory, and pattern recognition. In the following subsections we shall discuss in some detail the various versions of stochastic approximation and their convergence conditions.

5.1.1 The Robbins–Monro Algorithm

Let $\mu(\omega)$ be a fixed but unknown function having a unique root at θ. It is assumed that to each value ω corresponds a random variable $\xi(\omega)$ with probability density function $f(\xi|\omega)$ such that

$$\mu(\omega) = E_\xi[\xi(\omega)] = \int_{\Omega_\xi} \xi(\omega) f(\xi|\omega)\, d\xi \tag{5.6}$$

is the conditional expectation of ξ for given ω. The function $\mu(\omega)$ is called the regression function of ξ conditioned on ω. The regression function is unknown, and further $f(\xi|\omega)$ need not be known. The root θ of the equation $\mu(\omega) = 0$ may be found by observing a sequence of random variables $\xi_1(\omega(1)), \xi_2(\omega(2)), \ldots,$ and using the Robbins–Monro algorithm,

$$\omega(i+1) = \omega(i) - a_i \xi_i(\omega(i)). \tag{5.7}$$

In the previous example of estimating the mean, $\xi(\omega) = \xi(\omega; x) = \omega - x$ is a random function of ω due to the randomness of x, and for a given sample x_i, $\xi_i(\omega) = \xi(\omega; x_i) = \omega - x_i$.

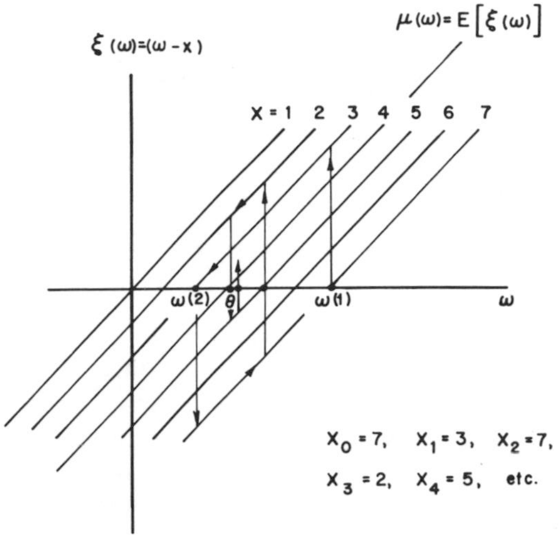

fig. 5.2 Stochastic approximation and regression function.

THEOREM 5.1

Let $\omega(1)$ be an arbitrary random variable, $E[\omega^2(1)] < \infty$, and $\{\omega(i)\}$ be the random sequence defined by algorithm (5.7) where $\xi_i(\omega) = \xi(\omega; x_i)$ and $x_1, x_2, \ldots,$ are statistically independent and identically distributed. The gain sequence $\{a_i\}$ is a sequence of positive numbers satisfying

$$\sum_{i=1}^{\infty} a_i = \infty, \qquad \sum_{i=1}^{\infty} a_i^2 < \infty, \tag{5.8}$$

and the regression function $\mu(\omega)$ satisfies the conditions

$$M_1(\omega - \theta)^2 \leqslant \mu(\omega)(\omega - \theta) \leqslant M_2(\omega - \theta)^2, \; 0 < M_1 \leqslant M_2 < \infty, \tag{5.9}$$

$$\operatorname{Var}[\xi(\omega)] = \int_{\Omega_\xi} [\xi - \mu(\omega)]^2 f(\xi|\omega)\, d\xi \leqslant \alpha^2 < \infty. \tag{5.10}$$

Then, the Robbins–Monro algorithm (5.7) converges in the mean-square sense.

$$\lim_{i\to\infty} E[(\omega(i) - \theta)^2] = 0. \tag{5.11}$$

Before proceeding to the proof of the theorem, let us explain briefly the meaning of the assumptions. Assumption (5.9) simply states that $\mu(\omega)$ must lie between two straight lines with positive slopes M_1 and M_2, respectively. The two lines cross each other at $\omega = \theta$, and this implies a unique root at

θ. Assumption (5.10) is a finite variance assumption that is often required in estimation theory. The assumption on the gain sequence $\{a_i\}$ has the following intuitive interpretation: because of the randomness of ξ, the gain coefficient a_i must approach zero as i approaches infinity; otherwise, the estimation algorithm would oscillate about θ and would never converge. In other words, a_i must approach zero so as to eliminate the oscillatory effect caused by using $\xi_i(\omega(i))$ in algorithm (5.7) instead of using $\mu(\omega(i))$ directly. On the other hand, since $\mu(\omega) = E[\xi(\omega)]$ is averaged over all possible samples $\xi_i(\omega)$, an infinite number of observations is needed in order to find the root of the equation $\mu(\omega) = 0$. As i approaches infinity, the observations ξ_i should still exert some influence on the outcome of the algorithm, suggesting that a_i should not be allowed to go to zero too quickly. The two somewhat conflicting requirements are reflected in assumption (5.8), and a typical choice of gain sequence is $a_i = a/i$, which is known to satisfy (5.8).

In defining the regression function $\mu(\omega)$ by (5.6), it is implied that the density functions $f(\xi_i|\omega(i))$ have the same functional form for all i. The assumption of statistical independence and identical distribution of x_1, x_2, ..., ensures that this is true. The independence assumption may be relaxed slightly. In most works, it is assumed that the conditional distribution of ξ_i for given $\omega(1), \ldots, \omega(i)$ is the same as its distribution for given $\omega(i)$ only. Because of the recursion, the relationship between $\omega(1), \ldots, \omega(i)$ and $x_1, \ldots, x_{i-1}$ is generally very complicated. Since statistical independence is satisfied in most problems of interest, and since it is easier to understand, we use it here instead of the weaker assumption.

Proof

From the Robbins–Monro algorithm (5.7), we have

$$[\omega(i+1) - \theta]^2 = [\omega(i) - \theta]^2 - 2a_i \xi_i(\omega(i))(\omega(i) - \theta) + a_i^2 \xi_i^2(\omega(i)). \tag{5.12}$$

Let us use the notation

$$V_i = E[(\omega(i) - \theta)^2]. \tag{5.13}$$

Taking expectation on both sides of (5.12) yields

$$V_{i+1} = V_i - 2a_i E[\xi_i(\omega(i))(\omega(i) - \theta)] + a_i^2 E[\xi_i^2(\omega(i))]. \tag{5.14}$$

If we first take expectation over the conditional density $f(\xi|\omega)$ and use (5.9), (5.10), and the independence assumption, we obtain

$$E[\xi_i(\omega(i))(\omega(i)-\theta)] = E[\mu(\omega(i))(\omega(i)-\theta)]$$
$$\geqslant E[M_1(\omega(i)-\theta)^2] = M_1 V_i,$$
$$E[\xi_i^2(\omega(i))] = E[\mu^2(\omega(i)) + \operatorname{Var} \xi_i(\omega(i))]$$
$$\leqslant E[M_2^2(\omega(i)-\theta)^2 + \alpha^2] = M_2^2 V_i + \alpha^2.$$

A substitution into (5.14) yields

$$V_{i+1} \leqslant (1 - 2M_1 a_i + M_2^2 a_i^2)V_i + a_i^2\alpha^2. \tag{5.15}$$

The assumption on the gain sequence implies $a_i \to 0$ as $i \to \infty$, and therefore, for an arbitrary ε, $0 \leqslant \varepsilon < 2$, there exists an $n(\varepsilon)$ such that

$$(1 - 2M_1 a_i + M_2^2 a_i^2) \leqslant [1 - (2-\varepsilon)M_1 a_i],$$
$$0 < [1 - (2-\varepsilon)M_1 a_i] < 1, \tag{5.16}$$

for all $i \geqslant n$. Inequality (5.15) becomes

$$V_{i+1} \leqslant V_i[1 - (2-\varepsilon)M_1 a_i] + a_i^2\alpha^2, \quad i \geqslant n. \tag{5.17}$$

Equation (5.17) may be expressed recursively,

$$V_{n+1} \leqslant V_n[1 - (2-\varepsilon)M_1 a_n] + a_n^2\alpha^2,$$
$$V_{n+2} \leqslant V_{n+1}[1 - (2-\varepsilon)M_1 a_{n+1}] + a_{n+1}^2\alpha^2$$
$$\leqslant V_n[1 - (2-\varepsilon)M_1 a_n][1 - (2-\varepsilon)M_1 a_{n+1}]$$
$$+ \alpha^2[a_n^2(1 - (2-\varepsilon)M_1 a_{n+1}) + a_{n+1}^2],$$
$$\ldots,$$

and

$$V_{i+1} \leqslant V_n\beta_{n-1,i} + \alpha^2 \sum_{j=n}^{i} a_j^2\beta_{ji}, \qquad i \geqslant n, \tag{5.18}$$

where β_{ji} is defined by

$$\beta_{ji} = \begin{cases} \prod_{l=j+1}^{i} [1 - (2-\varepsilon)M_1 a_l], & 0 \leqslant j < i, \\ 1, & j = i \\ 0, & j > i. \end{cases}$$

Using a known inequality of the logarithmic function, $\log u \leqslant u - 1$ if $u \geqslant 0$, we have

$$\log[1 - (2 - \varepsilon) M_1 a_j] \leqslant -(2 - \varepsilon) M_1 a_j, \quad j \geqslant n,$$

and as a result,

$$\beta_{n-1,i} \leqslant \exp[-(2 - \varepsilon) M_1 \sum_{j=n}^{i} a_j], \quad i \geqslant n.$$

Since by assumption (5.8), $\sum_{j=1}^{\infty} a_j$ diverges,

$$\lim_{i \to \infty} \beta_{n-1,i} = 0, \tag{5.19}$$

and the first term at the right-hand side of (5.18) becomes zero as $i \to \infty$.

Now consider the remaining term in (5.18). It is noted that

$$\alpha^2 \sum_{j=n}^{i} a_j^2 \beta_{ji} = \alpha^2 \sum_{j=n}^{\infty} a_j^2 \beta_{ji}$$

since by definition $\beta_{ji} = 0$ when $j > i$. With $0 \leqslant \beta_{ji} \leqslant 1$ bounded for all i and j, and $\sum_{j=1}^{\infty} a_j^2$ absolutely convergent according to assumption (5.8), we may interchange the limit and the summation, and obtain

$$\lim_{i \to \infty} \alpha^2 \sum_{j=n}^{i} a_j^2 \beta_{ji} = \lim_{i \to \infty} \alpha^2 \sum_{j=n}^{\infty} a_j^2 \beta_{ji}$$

$$= \alpha^2 \sum_{j=n}^{\infty} a_j^2 \lim_{i \to \infty} \beta_{ji} = 0, \tag{5.20}$$

where we have used (5.19) in the last step. Therefore, by combining (5.18), (5.19), and (5.20),

$$\lim_{i \to \infty} V_{i+1} = \lim_{i \to \infty} E[(\omega(i + 1) - \theta)^2] = 0.$$

Let us consider the problem of estimating the mean. With $\xi(\omega) = \xi(\omega; x) = \omega - x$ and its randomness due to the random variable x, clearly $\mu(\omega) = E[\xi(\omega)] = \omega - \theta$ and $M_1 = M_2 = 1$, where θ is the true mean value. The random samples $x_1, x_2, \ldots,$ are statistically independent and identically distributed. We choose a gain sequence $a_i = 1/i$ that satisfies (5.8). Therefore, if we make an additional assumption that

$$\mathrm{Var}[\xi(\omega)] = \mathrm{Var}[\omega - x] = \mathrm{Var}[x] = \alpha^2$$

is finite, all the conditions in theorem 5.1 are satisfied, and algorithm (5.5) converges in the mean-square sense. We emphasize that it is not necessary to know the density function $f(\xi|\omega)$ or $f(x)$. As mentioned earlier, algorithm (5.5) is essentially the sample mean, and its mean-square convergence is a special form of the law of large numbers.

In some problems, the regression function $\mu(\omega)$ is of the form shown in figure 5.3, and assumption (5.9) is not satisfied for all values of ω. However, if there is prior knowledge that the true value θ lies in a certain interval $[u_1, u_2]$, and (5.9) is satisfied for every $\omega \in [u_1, u_2]$, we may use a truncated Robbins–Monro algorithm,

$$\omega(i+1) = \text{trunc}_{u_1,u_2}[\omega(i) - a_i \xi_i(\omega(i))], \tag{5.21}$$

where the truncation is defined by

$$\text{trunc}_{u_1,u_2}(u) = \begin{cases} u_1, & u < u_1, \\ u, & u_1 \leqslant u \leqslant u_2, \\ u_2, & u > u_2. \end{cases}$$

The algorithm will converge if other conditions are satisfied. The argument goes as follows. Consider a new problem with a regression function $\mu'(\omega) = \mu(\omega)$ in the interval $[u_1, u_2]$ and $\mu'(\omega) = M_2(\omega - \theta)$ when $\omega < u_1$ or $\omega > u_2$. All other conditions being identical, the mean-square error will be the same for both problems if the truncated algorithm is used in both cases. Let V_{i+1} be the mean-square error associated with the truncated algorithm, V'_{i+1} be the mean-square error after i-th iteration that would occur for the case of $\mu'(\omega)$ if truncation were used up to the $(i-1)$-th interation but not used in the i-th iteration, and $V'_1 = V_1$. It is obvious from figure 5.3 that truncation always reduces $(\omega - \theta)^2$, hence

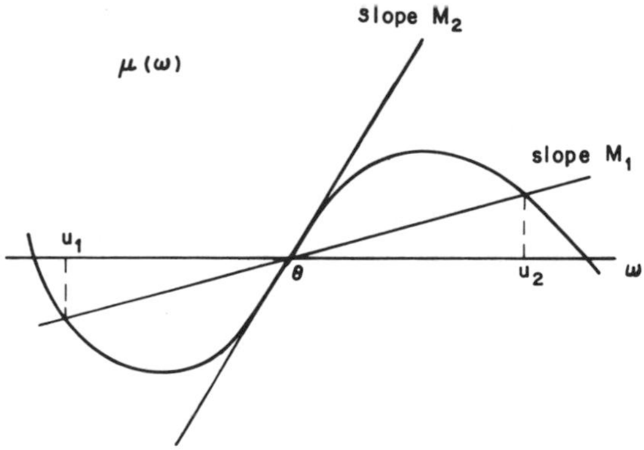

fig. 5.3 A regression function and truncation.

$$V_{i+1} \leqslant V'_{i+1}.$$

Since $\mu'(\omega)$ satisfies (5.9) and (5.10) for all ω, we obtain by the same arguments that lead to (5.15),

$$V'_{i+1} \leqslant (1 - 2M_1 a_i + M_2^2 a_i^2)V_i + a_i^2 \alpha^2.$$

A combination of these two equations shows that (5.15) holds for the truncated algorithm. Since i is chosen arbitrarily, the truncated algorithm (5.21) satisfies (5.15) for all i. It should be noted that V'_{i+1} was introduced artificially as an intermediary for showing this relationship. With the remaining part of the proof being identical to that of theorem 5.1, the truncated algorithm converges in the mean-square sense to θ.

The Robbins–Monro algorithm may be extended to the multidimensional case. Let us use matrix notation. The regression function is $\boldsymbol{\mu}(\boldsymbol{\omega}) = E[\boldsymbol{\xi}(\boldsymbol{\omega})]$, and $\boldsymbol{\mu}(\boldsymbol{\theta}) = \mathbf{0}$. The multidimensional Robbins–Monro algorithm,

$$\boldsymbol{\omega}(i+1) = \boldsymbol{\omega}(i) - a_i \boldsymbol{\xi}(\boldsymbol{\omega}(i); \mathbf{x}_i) \tag{5.22}$$

will converge in the mean-square sense,

$$\lim_{i\to\infty} E[\|\boldsymbol{\omega}(i) - \boldsymbol{\theta}\|^2] = 0,$$

if $\{a_i\}$ satisfies (5.8), the random vectors $\mathbf{x}_1, \mathbf{x}_2, \ldots,$ are statistically independent and identically distributed, and

$$M_1 \|\boldsymbol{\omega} - \boldsymbol{\theta}\|^2 < \mathbf{u}^T(\boldsymbol{\omega})(\boldsymbol{\omega} - \boldsymbol{\theta}) \leqslant M_2 \|\boldsymbol{\omega} - \boldsymbol{\theta}\|^2, \quad 0 < M_1 < M_2 < \infty,$$

$$\mathrm{Var}[\|\boldsymbol{\xi}(\boldsymbol{\omega})\|] \leqslant \alpha^2 < \infty.$$

5.1.2 Algorithms for decision-directed estimation

In section 3.4.2, we discussed briefly decision-directed estimation, and we pointed out problems of inconsistency and runaway. Experience indicates that a decision-directed scheme often converges to a value near θ instead of the true value θ itself, and becomes an inconsistent estimator. Sometimes a sequence of misclassifications in a decision-directed scheme causes additional misclassifications. Eventually the estimate becomes meaningless, and this phenomenon is called a runaway.

In this subsection we present two examples that express decision-directed estimation schemes as stochastic approximation algorithms. The purpose is twofold, namely, to explain in a mathematically meaningful way the phenomenon of inconsistency and runaway, and to illustrate the flexibility of applying stochastic approximation.

EXAMPLE 5.1

Consider the decision-directed estimation scheme in example 3.5. Let the probability density function $f(x)$ consist of two Gaussian densities,

$$f(x) = pg(x; 0, 1) + (1 - p)g(x; m, 1),$$

where $p = 1/2$ and the problem is to estimate the mean value m. A sequence of independent random samples $x_1, x_2, \ldots,$ with distribution $f(x)$ is available. Then a simple decision-directed scheme is

$$\omega(i + 1) = \begin{cases} \omega(i) + \dfrac{2}{i}(x_i - \omega(i)) & \text{if } x_i \geqslant \omega(i)/2, \\ \omega(i) & \text{if } x_i < \omega(i)/2, \end{cases}$$

which is the same equation as (3.109). In other words, the scheme considers x_i as belonging to C_2 and uses it for updating the estimation of m only if $x_i \geqslant \omega(i)/2$.

The scheme may be written in the form of a stochastic approximation algorithm. Let us use the notation $\theta = m$ for the true value and $a_i = 1/i$. Then the decision-directed scheme becomes

$$\omega(i + 1) = \omega(i) - a_i \xi(\omega(i); x_i),$$

with

$$\xi(\omega; x) = (\omega - x)[\operatorname{sgn}(x - \omega/2) + 1]. \tag{5.23}$$

Since $[\operatorname{sgn}(x - \omega/2) + 1] = 2$ if $x \geqslant \omega/2$ and $= 0$ if $x < \omega/2$, we have

$$\begin{aligned} \mu_\theta(\omega) &= E[\xi(\omega; x)] = \int_{\omega/2}^{\infty} (\omega - x)[g(x; 0, 1) + g(x; \theta, 1)]\, dx \\ &= \omega\left[1 - G\left(\frac{\omega}{2}\right)\right] + (\omega - \theta)\left[1 - G\left(\frac{\omega}{2} - \theta\right)\right] \\ &\quad - g\left(\frac{\omega}{2}; 0, 1\right) - g\left(\frac{\omega}{2}; \theta, 1\right), \end{aligned} \tag{5.24}$$

where the subscript θ indicates the dependence of the regression function on the true value θ, and $G(u)$ is the Gaussian distribution function

$$G(u) = \frac{1}{\sqrt{2\pi}} \int_{-\infty}^{u} e^{-x^2/2}\, dx.$$

The regression functions $\mu_\theta(\omega)$ for different values of θ are shown in figure 5.4(*b*).

It is noted that

$$\mu_\theta(\theta) < 0,\ \mu_\theta(\theta') = 0, \quad \theta < \theta'.$$

This can be explained by (5.24) and figure 5.4(*a*). Since

$$\int_{-\infty}^{\infty} (\theta - x) g(x; \theta, 1)\, dx = 0,$$

when $\omega = \theta$, (5.24) becomes

$$\mu_\theta(\theta) = -\int_{\theta/2}^{\infty} (x - \theta) g(x; 0, 1)\, dx + \int_{-\infty}^{\theta/2} (x - \theta) g(x; \theta, 1)\, dx.$$

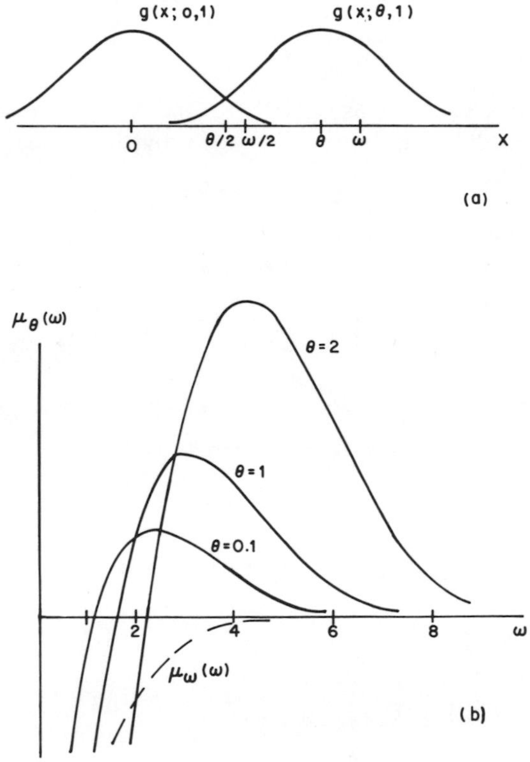

fig. 5.4 Decision-directed learning of the mean value θ (adapted from Young and Farjo, 1972).

Note that $x - \theta < 0$ when $-\infty < x \leqslant \theta/2$ and the second term is always negative, and further, it is obvious from figure 5.4(a) that the absolute value of the second term is greater than that of the first term. Hence, $\mu_\theta(\theta) < 0$. The variance of $\xi(\omega; x)$ in (5.23) for finite ω is obviously finite. Therefore, if we assume the prior knowledge that θ is greater than zero and less than a certain positive number, we may use a truncated algorithm, and all conditions of theorem 5.1 are satisfied. The algorithm converges in the mean-square sense not to the true mean θ, but to a certain $\theta' > \theta$. Thus, at least for this simple example, the decision-directed scheme converges to the wrong value θ', although when θ^2 is much greater than the variance, the difference between θ and θ' is small.

The algorithm may be modified so as to converge to θ. Let

$$\xi'(\omega, x) - \xi(\omega; x) \quad \mu_\omega(\omega), \tag{5.25}$$

where $\mu_\omega(\omega)$ is obtained from (5.24) by setting $\theta = \omega$, then

$$\mu_\theta'(\omega) = E[\xi'(\omega; x)] = \mu_\theta(\omega) - \mu_\omega(\omega),$$

and $\mu_\theta'(\theta) = 0$. The regression function $\mu_\theta'(\omega)$ can easily be obtained from the curves in figure 5.4(b), and it is easy to verify that the stochastic approximation algorithm,

$$\omega(i+1) = \omega(i) - a_i \xi'(\omega(i); x_i),$$

converges in the mean-square sense. The algorithm can still be interpreted as a decision-directed scheme with

$$\omega(i+1) = \begin{cases} \omega(i) + \dfrac{1}{i}\left(x_i - \omega + \mu_\omega(\omega)\right)\Big|_{\omega=\omega(i)} & \text{if } x_i \geqslant \omega(i)/2, \\ \omega(i) + \dfrac{1}{i}\mu_\omega(\omega)\Big|_{\omega=\omega(i)} & \text{if } x_i < \omega(i)/2. \end{cases}$$

It should be mentioned that for the simple example presented here, a simpler method is to estimate $\theta = m/2$. Noting that $m/2$ is the mean value of the mixture distribution function $f(x)$, we may use the algorithm

$$\omega(i+1) = \omega(i) + a_i(x_i - \omega(i)).$$

The regression function is linear, and the algorithm converges in the mean-square sense to $\theta = m/2$. This approach is not a decision-directed scheme, and is in fact the moment approach discussed in example 3.6. Recent investigation (Farjo, 1972) suggests that the convergence in this case is slower than that of the modified decision-directed scheme.

EXAMPLE 5.2

Let us assume that in the mixture density,

$$f(x) = pg(x; 0, 1) + (1 - p)g(x; m, 1),$$

where the mean value m is known and we wish to estimate the prior probability p. Suppose $\omega(i) = \omega(x_1, x_2, \ldots, x_{i-1})$ is the estimate for p based on the first $(i - 1)$ independent observations. When x_i is observed, we use the decision rule

$$d(x_i) = \begin{cases} 1 & \text{if } x_i < \dfrac{m}{2} + \dfrac{1}{m} \log \dfrac{\omega(i)}{1 - \omega(i)}, \\ 0 & \text{if } x_i \geqslant \dfrac{m}{2} + \dfrac{1}{m} \log \dfrac{\omega(i)}{1 - \omega(i)}, \end{cases}$$

which is essentially the Bayes decision discussed in chapter 2, except that we use $\omega(i)$ instead of p. Since $d(x_i) = 1$ corresponds to assigning x_i to the class with mean zero and prior probability p, the decision-directed estimator for p is

$$\omega(i + 1) = \frac{1}{i} \sum_{l=1}^{i} d(x_l) = \omega(i) - \frac{1}{i}\Big(\omega(i) - d(x_i)\Big). \tag{5.26}$$

This is in the form of a stochastic approximation algorithm with $\xi(\omega; x) = \omega - d(x)$ and $a_i = 1/i$. Let us use the notation $\theta = p$. The regression function is

$$\begin{aligned} \mu_\theta(\omega) &= E[\omega - d(x)] \\ &= \omega - \int_{-\infty}^{\infty} d(x)[\theta g(x; 0, 1) + (1 - \theta)g(x; m, 1)]\, dx \\ &= \omega - \theta G\left(\frac{m}{2} + \frac{1}{m} \log \frac{\omega}{1 - \omega}\right) - (1 - \theta)G\left(-\frac{m}{2} + \frac{1}{m} \log \frac{\omega}{1 - \omega}\right). \end{aligned} \tag{5.27}$$

The regression function $\mu_\theta(\omega)$ is plotted in figure 5.5. When $|m| > m_c$, a certain critical value, it has a form as shown in figure 5.5(a). There are five solutions to the equation $\mu_\theta(\omega) = 0$, and the regression function has positive slopes at three of them, θ'_1, θ'_3, and θ'_5. Since condition (5.9) of theorem 5.1 implies positive slope at the solution, θ'_1, θ'_3, and θ'_5 are called

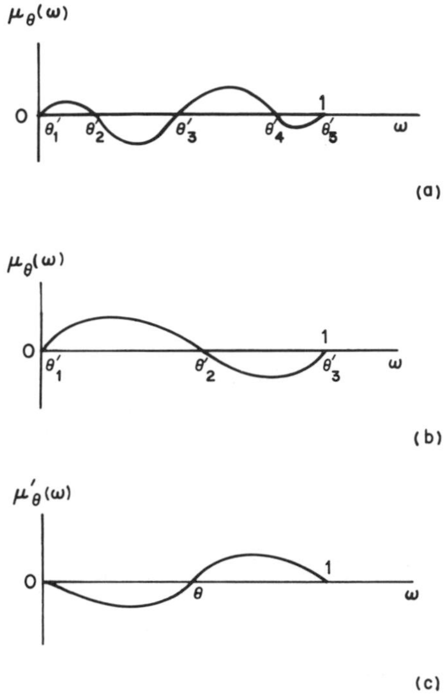

fig. 5.5 Regression functions and runaway.

stable solutions, and the algorithm will converge to one of them. The other two solutions are unstable because of the negative slope, and algorithm (5.26) will never converge to either of them. With the true θ being near θ_3', a runaway occurs when the algorithm converges to either $\theta_1' = 0$ or $\theta_5' = 1$. Davisson and Schwartz (1970) have shown that, roughly speaking, when $|m| > 2.5$, the probability of a runaway is very small. The consistency problem is also minor in this case.

When $|m| < m_c$, there are three solutions as shown in figure 5.5(*b*). The solution θ_2' in the figure is unstable, and the algorithm will converge to 0 or 1. Hence, the probability of a runaway is 1, and algorithm (5.26) should certainly not be used for this case.

Now, let us modify the algorithm as in example 5.1. Let

$$\xi'(\omega; x) = \xi(\omega; x) - \mu_\omega(\omega) = \omega - d(x) - \mu_\omega(\omega)$$

with $\mu_\omega(\omega)$ given by (5.27). The regression function $\mu_\theta'(\omega) = E[\xi'(\omega; x)]$ is shown in figure 5.5(*c*). The only stable solution in this case is θ, irrespective of the value of $|m|$. Thus, if we use $\xi'(\omega; x)$ instead of $\xi(\omega; x)$ in the algorithm, we are able to eliminate both the inconsistency and the runaway problem.

The examples above illustrate the problems of inconsistency and runaway. The modification improves the algorithm, and was conceived independently by Katopis and Schwartz (1972) and Young and Farjo (1972). Computationally it is more complex because of its requirement for computing $\mu_\omega(\omega)$ after each observation.

In both examples, the inconsistency and the runaway problem may be neglected when m^2 is large compared with the variance. The advantage of decision-directed estimation is its relative simplicity when estimating multiple parameters simultaneously. For example, in a Gaussian mixture, we may use $\mathbf{x}_i$ to update the estimation of p_k, $\mathbf{m}_k$, and $\mathbf{R}_k$ if we decide that $\mathbf{x}_i \in C_k$. The analysis of such cases is very difficult. Generally speaking, if we know that with the true parameter values used in the classification, the probability of a misclassification is small, and if we have reasonably accurate initial estimates, we may then use a decision-directed estimation scheme without considering the inconsistency or the runaway problem.

We have started by defining the runaway problem as the consequence of a sequence of misclassifications that degrades the estimates. It is clear from the discussion in example 5.2 that the runaway is a case of multiple solutions. The situation is, in a sense, very similar to the case of multiple maxima or minima in a deterministic gradient scheme.

5.1.3 The Kiefer–Wolfwitz algorithm

The Kiefer–Wolfwitz algorithm (1952) is a recursive method that searches for the value of θ that maximizes or minimizes a regression function $\mu(\omega) = E[\xi(\omega)]$. The algorithm is of the form,

$$\omega(i + 1) = \omega(i) - \frac{a_i}{b_i}\Big[\xi_i(\omega(i) + b_i) - \xi_i(\omega(i) - b_i)\Big], \tag{5.28}$$

where $\{a_i\}$ and $\{b_i\}$ are sequences of positive numbers satisfying

$$\sum_{i=1}^{\infty} a_i = \infty, \qquad \sum_{i=1}^{\infty} a_i b_i < \infty, \qquad \sum_{i=1}^{\infty} \left(\frac{a_i}{b_i}\right)^2 < \infty. \tag{5.29}$$

Typically, $a_i = ai^{-1}$ and $b_i = bi^{-1/4}$. It is interesting to note that the correction term in (5.28),

$$[\xi_i(\omega(i) + b_i) - \xi_i(\omega(i) - b_i)]/2b_i,$$

is essentially a two-sided approximation to $(d/d\omega)\xi(\omega)$. Generally speaking, the algorithm will converge to θ provided that $\{a_i\}$ and $\{b_i\}$ satisfy (5.29),

$$\mathrm{Var}[\xi(\omega)] \leqslant \alpha^2 < \infty, \tag{5.30}$$

and $\mu(\omega)$ satisfies a set of conditions similar to those required for the convergence of a deterministic gradient algorithm. The following is a set of conditions on $\mu(\omega)$ used by Venter (1967b).

(1) $\mu(\omega)$ and its second derivative are bounded.

(2) θ is a local minimum, i.e., for some $\varepsilon > 0$, $\mu(\theta) \leqslant \mu(\omega)$ if $|\omega - \theta| < \varepsilon$.

(3) θ is the only stationary point, i.e., $(d/d\omega)\mu(\omega) \neq 0$ if $\omega \neq \theta$.

In many problems of interest, $\xi(\omega) = \xi(\omega; x)$ and the randomness of $\xi(\omega)$ is due to the random variable x. In this case,

$$\mu(\omega) = \int_{\Omega_\xi} \xi(\omega) f(\xi|\omega)\, d\xi = \int_{\Omega_x} \xi(\omega; x) f(x)\, dx, \tag{5.31}$$

where $f(x)$ is the probability density function of the random variable x. Assume that $f(x)(d/d\omega)\xi(\omega; x)$ exists and is absolutely integrable. We may interchange the differentiation and the integration, and obtain

$$\frac{d}{d\omega}\mu(\omega) = \int_{\Omega_x} f(x)\frac{\partial}{\partial\omega}\xi(\omega; x)\, dx = E\left[\frac{\partial}{\partial\omega}\xi(\omega; x)\right], \tag{5.32}$$

with

$$\left.\frac{d}{d\omega}\mu(\omega)\right|_{\omega=\theta} = 0.$$

Thus, instead of searching for a minimum or a maximum of $\mu(\omega)$, we may use the Robbins–Monro algorithm to find the root of $(d/d\omega)\mu(\omega)$. By (5.32), the algorithm for finding the minimum is

$$\omega(i+1) = \omega(i) - a_i \left.\frac{\partial}{\partial\omega}\xi(\omega; x_i)\right|_{\omega=\omega(i)}, \tag{5.33}$$

which is very similar to (5.3), the gradient method for the deterministic case. The convergence conditions for algorithm (5.33) are, of course, the conditions in theorem 5.1 with $\mu(\omega)$ and $\xi(\omega)$ replaced by $(d/d\omega)\mu(\omega)$ and $(\partial/\partial\omega)\xi(\omega; x)$ respectlvely.

In this book, we are primarily interested in the Robbins–Monro approach. In fact, whenever it is possible to formulate the problem in the form of (5.33), it is the best approach in terms of convergence rate. However, there may be cases where (5.33) is not applicable. For example, $(\partial/\partial\omega)\xi(\omega; x)$ may not be well behaved, so that the interchange of differentiation and integration in (5.31) is not allowed. Under this circumstance, one may use the Kiefer–Wolfwitz algorithm.

5.1.4 The Dvoretzky algorithm

We have discussed the Robbins–Monro and the Kiefer–Wolfwitz algorithms. Dvoretzky (1956) takes a more general point of view and considers the algorithm,

$$\omega(i+1) = T_i(\omega(1), \ldots, \omega(i)) + \eta_i, \tag{5.34}$$

where T_i is a recursive transformation from an i-dimensional space into a one-dimensional space, and η_i is the random component with $E[\eta_i|\omega(1), \ldots, \omega(i)] = 0$. Both the Robbins–Monro and Kiefer–Wolfwitz algorithms may be interpreted as special cases of (5.34). For example, the Robbins–Monro algorithm,

$$\omega(i+1) = \omega(i) - a_i \xi_i(\omega(i)),$$

is equivalent to (5.34) with

$$\begin{aligned} T_i(\omega(1), \ldots, \omega(i)) &= \omega(i) - a_i \mu(\omega(i)), \\ \eta_i &= a_i[\mu(\omega(i)) - \xi_i(\omega(i))]. \end{aligned} \tag{5.35}$$

It is noted that $\mu(\omega)$ is unknown. By separating the algorithm into T_i and η_i as in (5.35), we are simply taking a somewhat different point of view.

Algorithm (5.34) converges under rather weak conditions. The following theorem is a special case. It is presented here because of the simplicity of the proof and because it is sufficient for most purposes.

THEOREM 5.2

Let the transformation T_i satisfy the condition

$$|T_i(\omega(1), \ldots, \omega(i)) - \theta| \leqslant F_i|\omega(1) - \theta|, \tag{5.36}$$

where F_i is a sequence of positive numbers satisfying

$$F_i \leqslant 1, \qquad \prod_{i=1}^{\infty} F_i = 0. \tag{5.37}$$

Then the conditions $E[\omega^2(1)] < \infty$,

$$\sum_{i=1}^{\infty} E[\eta_i^2] < \infty, \tag{5.38}$$

$$E[\eta_i|\omega(1), \omega(2), \ldots, \omega(i)] = 0, \tag{5.39}$$

imply that algorithm (5.34) converges in the mean-square sense.

Proof

Let us consider the term $E[\eta_i(T_i - \theta)]$, and note that since $\omega(1), \ldots, \omega(i)$ and η_i are random variables,

$$E[\eta_i(T_i - \theta)] = \int \cdots \int [\int \eta_i f(\eta_i|\omega(1), \ldots, \omega(i))\, d\eta_i](T_i - \theta)$$
$$f(\omega(1), \ldots, \omega(i))\, d\omega(1) \cdots d\omega(i).$$

But for given values of $\omega(1), \ldots, \omega(i)$,

$$\int \eta_i f(\eta_i|\omega(1), \ldots, \omega(i))\, d\eta_i = E[\eta_i|\omega(1), \ldots, \omega(i)] = 0,$$

according to (5.39) Hence,

$$E[\eta_i(T_i - \theta)] = 0, \tag{5.40}$$

and the mean-square error becomes

$$\begin{aligned} E(\omega(i+1) - \theta)^2 &= E[(T_i - \theta)^2] + E[\eta_i^2] \\ &\leqslant F_i^2 E[(\omega(i) - \theta)^2] + E[\eta_i^2], \end{aligned} \tag{5.41}$$

by (5.34), (5.36), and (5.40). Let $V_i = E[(\omega(i) - \theta)^2]$ and $\alpha_i^2 = E[\eta_i^2]$. We obtain by iteration

$$V_i \leqslant V_1 \beta_{0i} + \sum_{j=1}^{i} \alpha_j^2 \beta_{ji},$$

where

$$\beta_{ji} = \begin{cases} \prod_{l=j+1}^{i} F_l^2, & 0 \leqslant j < i, \\ 1, & j = i, \\ 0, & j > i. \end{cases}$$

With $n < i$, we may write

$$V_{i+1} \leqslant (V_1 + \sum_{j=1}^{n-1} \alpha_j^2) \max_{0 \leqslant j < n} \beta_{ji} + \sum_{j=n}^{i} \alpha_j^2 \beta_{ji}. \tag{5.42}$$

With n fixed, $\max_{0 \leqslant j < n} \beta_{ji}$ tends to zero as $i \to \infty$ according to the definition of β_{ji} and (5.37), and hence the first term at the right-hand side of (5.42) tends to zero. It is noted that by definition $\beta_{ji} = 0$ when $j > i$, and

$$\sum_{j=n}^{i} \alpha_j^2 \beta_{ji} = \sum_{j=n}^{\infty} \alpha_j^2 \beta_{ji}.$$

Since β_{ji} is uniformly bounded by 1, and $\sum_{j=n}^{\infty} \alpha_j^2$ is absolutely convergent, we obtain

$$\lim_{i\to\infty} \sum_{j=n}^{i} \alpha_j^2 \beta_{ji} = \lim_{i\to\infty} \sum_{j=n}^{\infty} \alpha_j^2 \beta_{ji} = \sum_{j=n}^{\infty} \alpha_j^2 \lim_{i\to\infty} \beta_{ji} = 0,$$

and $V_{i+1} \to 0$ as $i \to \infty$.

The proof above is very similar to the proof of theorem 5.1, although the former is much simpler. Indeed, theorem 5.1 is a special case of theorem 5.2, and the following example illustrates this point.

EXAMPLE 5.3

As discussed earlier, the Robbins–Monro algorithm may be written in the form of the Dvoretzky algorithm with

$$T_i(\omega(1), \ldots, \omega(i)) = \omega(i) - a_i \mu(\omega(i)),$$
$$\eta_i = a_i[\mu(\omega(i)) - \xi_i(\omega(i))].$$

Assume that all conditions in theorem 5.1 are satisfied. We shall show that all conditions in theorem 5.2 are satisfied.

Since $x_1, x_2, \ldots,$ are statistically independent and identically distributed, $\xi_i(\omega(i))$ depends on $\omega(i)$ only and $E[\xi_i(\omega(i))|\omega(1), \ldots, \omega(i)] = E[\xi_i(\omega(i))] = \mu(\omega(i))$. Obviously, condition (5.39) is satisfied. With $\text{Var}[\xi(\omega)] \leqslant \alpha^2 < \infty$ and $\sum_{i=1}^{\infty} a_i^2 < \infty$,

$$\sum_{i=1}^{\infty} E[\eta_i^2] = \sum_{i=1}^{\infty} a_i^2 \text{Var}[\xi_i(\omega(i))] \leqslant \alpha^2 \sum_{i=1}^{\infty} a_i^2 < \infty,$$

which is condition (5.38). Also, $\sum_{i=1}^{\infty} a_i^2 < \infty$ implies the existence of a finite n such that $M_1 a_i < 1$ for all $i \geqslant n$. Let $F_i = 1 - M_1 a_i$,

$$\log[\prod_{i=n}^{\infty} F_i] = \sum_{i=n}^{\infty} \log F_i \leqslant - \sum_{i=n}^{\infty} M_1 a_i,$$

and since $\sum_{i=n}^{\infty} a_i = \infty$, $\prod_{i=n}^{\infty} F_i = 0$. It is noted that

$$\begin{aligned} |T_i(\omega(1), \ldots, \omega(i)) - \theta| &= |\omega(i) - \theta - a_i \mu(\omega(i))| \\ &\leqslant |1 - M_1 a_i| \, |\omega(i) - \theta|, \; i \geqslant n, \end{aligned}$$

where we have used the condition $M_1(\omega - \theta)^2 \leqslant \mu(\omega)(\omega - \theta)$. Therefore, conditions (5.36)–(5.39) are all satisfied for $1 \geqslant n$, and the algorithm converges in the mean-square sense according to theorem 5.2.

Thus far we have been concerned for the most part with mean-square convergence, which implies convergence in probability. The Dvoretzky algorithm also converges with probability 1 (sec. 3.1.3).

THEOREM 5.2A

If all conditions in theorem 5.2 are satisfied, the Dvoretzky algorithm (5.34) converges with probability 1.

Proof

Given $\delta > 0$ and $\varepsilon > 0$, there exists an $n = n(\delta^2 \varepsilon)$ such that

$$V_i = E[(\omega(i) - \theta)^2] < \delta^2 \varepsilon, \quad i \geqslant n. \tag{5.43}$$

This is always possible because of the mean-square convergence of the algorithm. Let this n be fixed and define a new algorithm as follows:

$$\omega'(j + 1) = T'_j(\omega'(1), \ldots, \omega'(j)) + \eta'_j, \tag{5.44}$$

where

$$T'_j = T_j, \qquad \eta'_j = \eta_j, \qquad \text{if } j < n, \tag{5.45}$$

while for $j \geqslant n$,

$$T'_j(\omega'(1), \ldots, \omega'(j)) = \begin{cases} T_j(\omega'(1), \ldots, \omega'(j)) & \text{if } |\omega'(j) - \theta| < \delta, \\ \omega'(j) & \text{if } |\omega'(j) - \theta| \geqslant \delta, \end{cases}$$
$$\eta'_j = \begin{cases} \eta_j & \text{if } |\omega'(j) - \theta| < \delta, \\ 0 & \text{if } |\omega'(j) - \theta| \geqslant \delta. \end{cases} \tag{5.46}$$

We wish to show that (5.43) holds for algorithm (5.44), i.e.,

$$V'_i = E[(\omega'(i) - \theta)^2] < \delta^2 \varepsilon, \quad i \geqslant n. \tag{5.47}$$

Suppose there exists an l that is defined as the smallest integer such that $|\omega(l) - \theta| \geqslant \delta$ and $n \leqslant l \leqslant i$. Clearly, V'_j satisfies (5.47) when $n \leqslant j \leqslant l$. It is easy to verify from the definition of algorithm (5.44) that $\omega(l) = \omega'(l) = \omega'(l+1) = \cdots = \omega'(i)$ and $V_l = V'_l = V'_{l+1} = \cdots = V'_i$ satisfy (5.47). That it is satisfied when l does not exist is obvious.

We note that the existence of an l implies $|\omega'(i) - \theta| \geqslant \delta$, and that l exists if and only if $\max_j |\omega(j) - \theta| \geqslant \delta$, $n \leqslant j \leqslant i$. Hence,

$$P\{\max_{n \leqslant j \leqslant i} |\omega(j) - \theta| \geqslant \delta\} \leqslant P\{|\omega'(i) - \theta| \geqslant \delta\}. \tag{5.48}$$

Combining (5.47) and (5.48) and letting i approach ∞ yields

$$P\{\max_{j \geqslant n} |\omega(j) - \theta| \geqslant \delta\} < \frac{\delta^2 \varepsilon}{\delta^2} = \varepsilon,$$

or equivalently,

$$P\{|\omega(j) - \theta| < \delta, j = n, n+1, \ldots, \} > 1 - \varepsilon.$$

With δ and ε being arbitrary, the algorithm converges with probability 1.

The Dvoretzky algorithm may be extended to the multidimensional case. Let

$$\boldsymbol{\omega}(i+1) = \mathbf{T}_i(\boldsymbol{\omega}(1), \ldots, \boldsymbol{\omega}(i)) + \boldsymbol{\eta}_i, \tag{5.49}$$

where $\mathbf{T}_i$ is a transformation from a $K \times i$-dimensional Euclidean space into a K-dimensional Euclidean space. If the following conditions are satisfied,

$$\|\mathbf{T}_i(\boldsymbol{\omega}(1), \ldots, \boldsymbol{\omega}(i)) - \boldsymbol{\theta}\| \leqslant F_i \|\boldsymbol{\omega}(i) - \boldsymbol{\theta}\|,$$
$$E[\|\boldsymbol{\omega}(1)\|^2] = 0, \ \sum_{i=1}^{\infty} E[\|\boldsymbol{\eta}_i\|^2] < \infty, \tag{5.50}$$
$$E[\boldsymbol{\eta}_i | \boldsymbol{\omega}(1), \ldots, \boldsymbol{\omega}(i)] = \mathbf{0},$$

and the positive number F_i satisfy (5.37), algorithm (5.49) will converge to $\boldsymbol{\theta}$ in the mean-square sense and with probability 1.

5.2 The Performance of Stochastic Approximation Algorithms

We have presented various stochastic approximation algorithms and discussed their convergence conditions. In this section, we shall be primarily concerned with the performance of the Robbins–Monro algorithm. More specifically, we shall discuss the mean-square error at each stage, the convergence rate and the selection of the gain sequence. We shall also discuss briefly the estimation of parameters using stochastic approximation.

5.2.1 An upper bound on the Mean-square error

Consider the Robbins–Monro algorithm

$$\omega(i+1) = \omega(i) - a_i \xi_i(\omega(i))$$

with $E[\xi(\omega)] = \mu(\omega)$ and $\mu(\theta) = 0$. The mean-square error $V_i = E[(\omega(i) - \theta)^2]$ is difficult to obtain since the algorithm operates recursively, i.e., $\omega(2)$ depends on the distribution of $\omega(1)$, $\omega(3)$ depends on the distribution of $\omega(2)$, etc. The following upper bound is due to Dvoretzky (1956), and it is valid only for a particular choice of a gain sequence $\{a_i\}$.

THEOREM 5.3

If there exist positive numbers M_1, M_2, α^2, and V_1 such that

$$M_1(\omega - \theta)^2 \leqslant \mu(\omega)(\omega - \theta) \leqslant M_2(\omega - \theta)^2, \qquad 0 < M_1 \leqslant M_2 < \infty, \tag{5.51}$$

$$\mathrm{Var}[\xi(\omega)] \leqslant \alpha^2 < \infty, \tag{5.52}$$

$$E[\xi(\omega(i)) - \mu(\omega(i)) | \omega(1), \ldots, \omega(i)] = 0 \tag{5.53}$$

$$E[(\omega(1) - \theta)^2] = V_1 \leqslant \frac{2\alpha^2}{M_1(M_2 - M_1)}, \tag{5.54}$$

then with the gain sequence given by

$$a_i = \frac{M_1 V_1}{\alpha^2 + i M_1^2 V_1}, \tag{5.55}$$

the i-th estimate $\omega(i)$ of the Robbins–Monro algorithm satisfies

$$V_i = E[(\omega(i) - \theta)^2] \leqslant \frac{\alpha^2 V_1}{\alpha^2 + (i-1) M_1^2 V_1}. \tag{5.56}$$

Proof

The condition on the initial mean-square error V_1 implies that

$$a_i = \frac{M_1 V_1}{\alpha^2 + i M_1^2 V_1} \leqslant \frac{2 M_1}{M_1(M_2 - M_1) + 2i M_1^2} \leqslant \frac{2}{M_1 + M_2},$$

and hence $0 \leqslant a_i M_1 \leqslant 1$. Therefore, it is easy to see from conditions (5.51), (5.52), and (5.53) that

$$\begin{aligned} V_{i+1} &\leqslant E\{[\omega(i) - \theta - a_i \mu(\omega(i))]^2\} + a_i^2 \mathrm{Var}[\xi_i(\omega(i))] \\ &\leqslant (1 - a_i M_1)^2 V_i + a_i^2 \alpha^2. \end{aligned} \tag{5.57}$$

We now use mathematical induction to prove the theorem. For $i = 1$, the bound is obviously true since the right-hand side of (5.56) simply becomes V_1. Assume that (5.56) is true for i, then (5.57) becomes

$$V_{i+1} \leqslant (1 - a_i M_1)^2 \frac{\alpha^2 V_1}{\alpha^2 + (i-1) M_1^2 V_1} + a_i^2 \alpha^2.$$

A substitution of (5.55) into the above equation yields

$$V_{i+1} \leqslant \frac{[\alpha^2 + (i-1) M_1^2 V_1]\alpha^2 V_1}{(\alpha^2 + i M_1^2 V_1)^2} + \frac{M_1^2 V_1^2 \alpha^2}{(\alpha^2 + i M_1^2 V_1)^2} = \frac{\alpha^2 V_1}{\alpha^2 + i M_1^2 V_1}.$$

The conditions in theorem 5.3 are quite similar to those of theorem 5.1. The only additional requirements for the former are the particular choice of gain sequence (5.55) and that V_1 must be known and satisfies (5.54). It is noted that unlike a gain sequence $\{a/i\}$, the gain sequence in (5.55) takes into consideration the initial mean-square error V_1, and for this reason the sequence is expected to be a near-optimal choice for small i. As i becomes large, however, (5.55) is in general not an optimal choice. We shall elaborate on this point later.

5.2.2 *Multidimensional linear regression function*

Theorem 5.3 may be extended to the multidimensional case. Consider the multidimensional Robbins–Monro algorithm,

$$\omega(i+1) = \omega(i) - a_i \xi_i(\omega(i)).$$

If we assume that

$$M_1 \|\omega - \boldsymbol{\theta}\|^2 \leqslant \boldsymbol{\mu}^T(\omega)(\omega - \boldsymbol{\theta}) \leqslant M_2 \|\omega - \boldsymbol{\theta}\|^2, \quad 0 < M_1 \leqslant M_2 < \infty,$$

and modify the other conditions accordingly, it is obvious that with $V_i = E[\|\omega(i) - \boldsymbol{\theta}\|^2]$, the bound (5.56) holds for the multidimensional algorithm.

A more general approach to multidimensional stochastic approximation is to use a matrix-valued gain sequence $\{\mathbf{A}_i\}$,

$$\omega(i+1) = \omega(i) - \mathbf{A}_i \xi_i(\omega(i)). \tag{5.58}$$

This allows us the freedom to assign different weights to different directions, and with $\{\mathbf{A}_i\}$ properly chosen, the resultant mean-square error should be smaller. Unfortunately, a bound similar to (5.56) for a matrix-valued gain sequence has not been discovered. In the following paragraphs we consider the special case of linear regression functions.

Assume that

$$\begin{aligned} \boldsymbol{\mu}(\omega) &= E[\xi(\omega)] = \mathbf{M}(\omega - \boldsymbol{\theta}), \\ \mathrm{Cov}[\xi(\omega)] &= \mathbf{R}, \\ E[\xi(\omega(i)) - \boldsymbol{\mu}(\omega(i)) \,|\, \omega(1), \ldots, \omega(i)] &= \mathbf{0}. \end{aligned} \tag{5.59}$$

The first equation in (5.59) defines the linearity of the regression function, and the matrix $\mathbf{R}$ in the second equation is independent of ω. Let us define a matrix

$$\mathbf{V}_i = E[(\omega(i) - \boldsymbol{\theta})(\omega(i) - \boldsymbol{\theta})^T]. \tag{5.60}$$

Clearly the mean-square error V_i equals the trace of $\mathbf{V}_i$. With $\mathbf{V}_1$ assumed known, and the gain matrix given by

$$\mathbf{A}_i = (\mathbf{V}_1^{-1} + i\mathbf{M}^T\mathbf{R}^{-1}\mathbf{M})^{-1}\mathbf{M}^T\mathbf{R}^{-1}, \tag{5.61}$$

we proceed to show that

$$\mathbf{V}_i = (\mathbf{V}_1^{-1} + (i-1)\mathbf{M}^T\mathbf{R}^{-1}\mathbf{M})^{-1}. \tag{5.62}$$

The proof is almost identical to that of theorem 5.3. From (5.58) and (5.59) it is easy to see that

$$\mathbf{V}_{i+1} = (\mathbf{I} - \mathbf{A}_i\mathbf{M})\mathbf{V}_i(\mathbf{I} - \mathbf{A}_i\mathbf{M})^T + \mathbf{A}_i\mathbf{R}\mathbf{A}_i^T, \tag{5.63}$$

where $\mathbf{I}$ is the identity matrix. We now use mathematical induction and note that (5.62) is obviously true when $i = 1$. Assume that (5.62) is true for i. It is noted from (5.61) that

$$\begin{aligned} \mathbf{I} - \mathbf{A}_i\mathbf{M} &= (\mathbf{V}_1^{-1} + i\mathbf{M}^T\mathbf{R}^{-1}\mathbf{M})^{-1}(\mathbf{V}_1^{-1} + (i-1)\mathbf{M}^T\mathbf{R}^{-1}\mathbf{M}), \\ \mathbf{A}_i\mathbf{R}\mathbf{A}_i^T &= (\mathbf{V}_1^{-1} + i\mathbf{M}^T\mathbf{R}^{-1}\mathbf{M})^{-1}\mathbf{M}^T\mathbf{R}^{-1}\mathbf{M}(\mathbf{V}_1^{-1} + i\mathbf{M}^T\mathbf{R}^{-1}\mathbf{M})^{-1}. \end{aligned} \tag{5.64}$$

Since (5.62) holds for $\mathbf{V}_i$, a substitution of (5.62) and (5.64) into (5.63) yields

$$\mathbf{V}_{i+1} = (\mathbf{V}_1^{-1} + i\mathbf{M}^T\mathbf{R}^{-1}\mathbf{M})^{-1}.$$

The matrix $\mathbf{M}$ may be singular or asymmetric or both. On the other hand, $\mathbf{V}_1$ and $\mathbf{R}$ must be nonsingular. Since they are in fact covariance matrices, they are positive semidefinite, and will be singular only if some linear combination of the components of the vector under the expectation is known with certainty. If this occurred, the dimensionality of the estimation algorithm could be reduced, eliminating the known components. As long as $\mathbf{V}_1$ is nonsingular and finite, the matrix $(\mathbf{V}_1^{-1} + i\mathbf{M}^T\mathbf{R}^{-1}\mathbf{M})$ will be nonsingular since the sum of a positive definite matrix and a positive semidefinite matrix is positive definite.

If the true value $\boldsymbol{\theta}$ is known to lie in some bounded rectangular region of the parameter space, and the first two equations of (5.59) hold only for $\boldsymbol{\omega}$ in that region, a multidimensional truncated Robbins–Monro algorithm similar to (5.21) may be used. In this case, (5.62) holds with the equality replaced by an inequality, i.e.,

$$\mathbf{V}_i \leqslant (\mathbf{V}_1^{-1} + (i-1)\mathbf{M}^T\mathbf{R}^{-1}\mathbf{M})^{-1},$$

where we have used the convention that for two matrices $\mathbf{A}$ and $\mathbf{B}$, $\mathbf{A} \leqslant \mathbf{B}$ if the matrix $(\mathbf{B} - \mathbf{A})$ is positive definite or positive semidefinite. The bound on $\mathbf{V}_i$ is also true if $\text{Cov}[\xi(\omega)] \leqslant \mathbf{R}$.

It is instructive to note that the gain sequence (5.61) in fact minimizes the mean-square error $V_{i+1} = \text{tr}\, \mathbf{V}_{i+1}$ at each step. Let us assume for simplicity that $\mathbf{M}^{-1}$ exists, and note that (5.63) implies

$$V_{i+1} = \text{tr}[\mathbf{V}_i - \mathbf{A}_i\mathbf{M}\mathbf{V}_i - \mathbf{V}_i\mathbf{M}^T\mathbf{A}^T + \mathbf{A}_i(\mathbf{R} + \mathbf{M}\mathbf{V}_i\mathbf{M}^T)\mathbf{A}_i^T]. \tag{5.65}$$

If we vary the matrix $\mathbf{A}_i$ by the amount $d\mathbf{A}_i$, the first-order term is

$$-\mathrm{tr}\{d\mathbf{A}_i[\mathbf{M}\mathbf{V}_i - (\mathbf{R} + \mathbf{M}\mathbf{V}_i\mathbf{M}^T)\mathbf{A}_i^T] + [\mathbf{V}_i\mathbf{M}^T - \mathbf{A}_i(\mathbf{R} + \mathbf{M}\mathbf{V}_i\mathbf{M}^T)]d\mathbf{A}_i^T\}.$$

In order to have a minimum V_{i+1}, the first-order term must be zero for any $d\mathbf{A}_i$. Taking advantage of the symmetry, we obtain

$$\hat{\mathbf{A}}_i^T = (\mathbf{R} + \mathbf{M}\mathbf{V}_i\mathbf{M}^T)^{-1}\mathbf{M}\mathbf{V}_i = (\mathbf{V}_i^{-1}\mathbf{M}^{-1}\mathbf{R} + \mathbf{M}^T)^{-1}.$$

The resulting minimum V_{i+1} is a global minimum since (5.65) is essentially quadratic. It is noted that with $\mathbf{V}_1^{-1}$ substituted by (5.62), the gain matrix $\mathbf{A}_i$ in (5.61) becomes

$$\mathbf{A}_i^T = \mathbf{R}^{-1}\mathbf{M}(\mathbf{V}_i^{-1} + \mathbf{M}^T\mathbf{R}^{-1}\mathbf{M})^{-1} = (\mathbf{V}_i^{-1}\mathbf{M}^{-1}\mathbf{R} + \mathbf{M}^T)^{-1} = \hat{\mathbf{A}}_i^T.$$

Thus, the matrix-valued gain sequence $\{\mathbf{A}_i\}$ is optimum in this sense, and the mean-square error in this case should in general be less than (5.56).

EXAMPLE 5.4

Consider the estimation of the mean vector. Let $\boldsymbol{\theta}$ be the true mean vector, and $\boldsymbol{\xi}(\boldsymbol{\omega}) = \boldsymbol{\omega} - \mathbf{x}$ so that $\boldsymbol{\mu}(\boldsymbol{\theta}) = E[\boldsymbol{\xi}(\boldsymbol{\theta})] = \mathbf{0}$. The multidimensional stochastic approximation algorithm is

$$\boldsymbol{\omega}(i+1) = \boldsymbol{\omega}(i) - \mathbf{A}_i(\boldsymbol{\omega}(i) - \mathbf{x}_i).$$

The regression function $\boldsymbol{\mu}(\boldsymbol{\omega})$ is linear with $\mathbf{M} = \mathbf{I}$, and with the initial mean-square error $\mathbf{V}_1$ known, we have, according to (5.61) and (5.62),

$$\mathbf{A}_i = (\mathbf{V}_1^{-1} + i\mathbf{R}^{-1})^{-1}\mathbf{R}^{-1} = (\mathbf{V}_i^{-1} + \mathbf{R}^{-1})^{-1}\mathbf{R}^{-1},$$

$$\mathbf{V}_i = (\mathbf{V}_1^{-1} + (i-1)\mathbf{R}^{-1})^{-1} = \mathbf{R}\mathbf{A}_{i-1}^T.$$

Simple algebraic manipulation yields

$$\mathbf{A}_i = \mathbf{V}_i(\mathbf{V}_i + \mathbf{R})^{-1},$$

hence the algorithm becomes

$$\boldsymbol{\omega}(i+1) = \mathbf{R}(\mathbf{V}_i + \mathbf{R})^{-1}\boldsymbol{\omega}(i) + \mathbf{V}_i(\mathbf{V}_i + \mathbf{R})^{-1}\mathbf{x}_i,$$

$$\mathbf{V}_i = \mathbf{R}(\mathbf{V}_{i-1} + \mathbf{R})^{-1}\mathbf{V}_{i-1},$$

which is identical to (3.89). We note that the initial mean-square error matrix $\mathbf{V}_1$ reflects our prior knowledge about the unknown $\boldsymbol{\theta}$. If we take the point of view that $\boldsymbol{\theta}$ is a random vector and choose the initial estimate $\boldsymbol{\omega}(1) = E[\boldsymbol{\theta}]$, then $\mathbf{V}_1 = E[(\boldsymbol{\theta} - \boldsymbol{\omega}(1))(\boldsymbol{\theta} - \boldsymbol{\omega}(1))^T]$ is the covariance matrix of the random $\boldsymbol{\theta}$. Therefore, if the random samples $\mathbf{x}_1, \mathbf{x}_2, \ldots,$ are Gaussian distributed and $\boldsymbol{\theta}$ is also Gaussian distributed with covariance $\mathbf{V}_1$, the algorithm is the Bayes estimator.

5.2.3 Convergence rates

We have discussed the convergence conditions of the Robbins–Monro algorithm. One of the important practical questions is how fast the algorithm converges, and a convenient measure of the rate of convergence is the rate at which the mean square error V_i decreases as i approaches infinity. It is obvious that the convergence rate depends on the choice of the gain sequence.

Consider the one-dimensional case with the gain sequence specified by theorem 5.3. The gain sequence is a near optimal choice for small i; however, here we are primarily concerned with the asymptotic performance. As i approaches infinity, the gain sequence in (5.55) becomes $a_i = 1/iM_1$ and the convergence rate $iV_i \leqslant \alpha^2/M_1^2$ according to (5.56). Now consider the one-dimensional regression function shown in figure 5.6. Since we are only interested in an algorithm that converges, as i becomes very large the estimate $\omega(i)$ will have a high probability of being at the neighborhood of θ. But in the neighborhood of θ, the regression function is almost linear with the slope

$$M = M(\theta) = \frac{d}{d\omega}\mu(\omega)\bigg|_{\omega=\theta}, \tag{5.66}$$

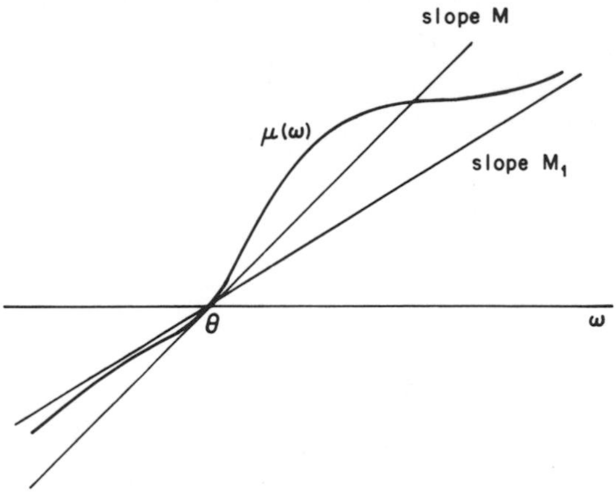

fig. 5.6 A regression function and its slope at $\omega = \theta$.

and $M \geqslant M_1$. As discussed previously ((5.61) and (5.62)), an optimum gain sequence for a linear regression function with slope M is simply $a_i = 1/iM$ for i sufficiently large, and $V_i = \alpha^2/iM^2$. This discussion suggests that for a nonlinear regression function, if we are interested in the asymptotic performance only, we should choose a gain sequence $a_i = 1/iM$ with M defined by (5.66), and the convergence rate will be

$$\lim_{i\to\infty} iV_i = \frac{\alpha^2}{M^2}. \tag{5.67}$$

The conclusion above can be made precise with a result due to Sacks (1958). The conditions used by Sacks are essentially the conditions of theorem 5.1 with $\mathrm{Var}[\xi(\omega)] = \alpha^2$, and in addition the slope of $\mu(\omega)$ at $\omega = \theta$ is M as defined in (5.66). Sacks then shows that for a gain sequence

$$a_i = a/i,$$

with $2aM > 1$, the random variable $i^{-1/2}(\omega(i) - \theta)$ is asymptotically Gaussian distributed with mean zero and variance

$$iV_i = iE[(\omega(i) - \theta)^2] = \frac{a^2\alpha^2}{2aM - 1}. \tag{5.68}$$

It is a simple matter to verify that (5.68) is minimum when $a = 1/M$ with the minimum value being α^2/M^2.

The result may be extended to the multidimensional case. Assume that

$$\mathbf{M} = \mathbf{M}(\boldsymbol{\theta}) = [\nabla_\omega \boldsymbol{\mu}^T(\omega)]^T_{\omega=\boldsymbol{\theta}},$$

$$\mathrm{Cov}[\xi(\omega)] = \mathbf{R},$$

and that all other conditions of the multidimensional Robbins–Monro algorithm (5.27) are satisfied. If we assume that $\mathbf{M}^{-1}$ exists and use a gain sequence

$$\mathbf{A}_i = \frac{1}{i}\mathbf{M}^{-1},$$

asymptotically the mean-square error is

$$\mathbf{V}_i = \frac{1}{i}\left(\mathbf{M}^T\mathbf{R}^{-1}\mathbf{M}\right)^{-1},$$

and the convergence rate

$$\lim_{i\to\infty} iV_i = \lim_{i\to\infty} i \operatorname{tr} \mathbf{V}_i = \operatorname{tr}(\mathbf{M}^T\mathbf{R}^{-1}\mathbf{M})^{-1},$$

is optimum.

In some problems, such as the estimation of the mean vector discussed in example 5.4, the matrix $\mathbf{M} = \mathbf{M}(\boldsymbol{\theta})$ is known. In other cases, the regression function $\boldsymbol{\mu}(\omega)$ is known only qualitatively, and $\mathbf{M}(\boldsymbol{\theta})$ is unknown. In order to obtain a good convergence rate, a possible approach is to estimate, along with $\boldsymbol{\theta}$, the matrix $\mathbf{M}(\boldsymbol{\theta})$. In other words, we use a gain sequence $\mathbf{A}_i = i^{-1}\mathbf{M}^{-1}(i)$ where $\mathbf{M}(i)$ is the i-th estimate of $\mathbf{M}(\boldsymbol{\theta})$ and $\mathbf{M}(i) \rightarrow M(\boldsymbol{\theta})$ as $i \rightarrow \infty$. This approach was used by Sakrison (1965) and Kashyap and Blaydon (1966).

EXAMPLE 5.5

Consider the problem of linear approximation of a known function $h(\mathbf{x})$ by a set of linearly independent basis functions $\phi_1(\mathbf{x}), \phi_2(\mathbf{x}), \ldots, \phi_K(\mathbf{x})$. We assume that the scalar function $h(\mathbf{x})$ is a nonlinear transformation of the random vector $\mathbf{x}$ with unknown probability density $f(\mathbf{x})$, and hence a reasonable criterion for the approximation is the mean-square criterion,

$$E[(h(\mathbf{x}) - \omega^T\boldsymbol{\phi}(\mathbf{x}))^2] = \int f(\mathbf{x})[h(\mathbf{x}) - \omega^T\boldsymbol{\phi}(\mathbf{x})]^2\, d\mathbf{x}, \tag{5.69}$$

where we have used matrix notation with $\boldsymbol{\phi}^T(\mathbf{x}) = [\phi_1(\mathbf{x}), \phi_2(\mathbf{x}), \ldots, \phi_K(\mathbf{x})]$. Thus, the problem is to find a K-vector $\boldsymbol{\theta}$ such that (5.69) is minimum when $\omega = \boldsymbol{\theta}$. Obviously the solution is

$$\boldsymbol{\theta} = \{E[\boldsymbol{\phi}(\mathbf{x})\boldsymbol{\phi}^T(\mathbf{x})]\}^{-1} E[\boldsymbol{\phi}(\mathbf{x})h(\mathbf{x})], \tag{5.70}$$

but this equation cannot be evaluated directly since $f(\mathbf{x})$ is assumed unknown. We assume, as in many pattern recognition problems, that a sequence of statistically independent random samples $\mathbf{x}_1, \mathbf{x}_2 \cdots$, with identical distribution $f(\mathbf{x})$ is available. Then, a Robbins–Monro algorithm,

$$\omega(i + 1) = \omega(i) + a_i\boldsymbol{\phi}(\mathbf{x}_i)[h(\mathbf{x}_i) - \boldsymbol{\phi}^T(\mathbf{x}_i)\omega(i)], \tag{5.71}$$

may be used for this purpose. Note that the correction term in (5.71) is the gradient of the term $(h - \omega^T\boldsymbol{\phi})^2$ in (5.69), hence the algorithm minimizes the mean-square criterion. The regression function,

$$\boldsymbol{\mu}(\omega) = -E[\boldsymbol{\phi}(\mathbf{x})h(\mathbf{x}) - \boldsymbol{\phi}(\mathbf{x})\boldsymbol{\phi}^T(\mathbf{x})\omega],$$

is linear in ω, and it is obvious that with $\boldsymbol{\theta}$ of (5.70), $\boldsymbol{\mu}(\boldsymbol{\theta}) = \mathbf{0}$.

For a fast convergence rate, one would like to use a matrix-valued gain sequence $\mathbf{A}_i = i^{-1}\mathbf{M}^{-1}$ with

$$\mathbf{M} = [\nabla_\omega \boldsymbol{\mu}^T(\omega)]^T = E[\boldsymbol{\phi}(\mathbf{x})\boldsymbol{\phi}^T(\mathbf{x})].$$

Since **M** is unknown, we use as an approximation

$$\mathbf{M}(i+1) = \frac{1}{i}\sum_{j=1}^{i} \boldsymbol{\phi}(\mathbf{x}_j)\boldsymbol{\phi}^T(\mathbf{x}_j),$$

which may be written recursively

$$\mathbf{M}(i+1) = \mathbf{M}(i) + \frac{1}{i}(\boldsymbol{\phi}(\mathbf{x}_i)\boldsymbol{\phi}^T(\mathbf{x}_i) - \mathbf{M}(i)). \tag{5.72}$$

It is more convenient to have a recursive relationship for $\mathbf{M}^{-1}$, and the algorithm becomes

$$\begin{aligned} \omega(i+1) &= \omega(i) + \frac{1}{i}\mathbf{M}^{-1}(i)\boldsymbol{\phi}(\mathbf{x}_i)[h(\mathbf{x}_i) - \boldsymbol{\phi}^T(\mathbf{x}_i)\omega(i)], \\ \mathbf{M}^{-1}(i+1) &= \frac{i}{i-1}\left[\mathbf{M}^{-1}(i) - \frac{\mathbf{M}^{-1}(i)\boldsymbol{\phi}(\mathbf{x}_i)\boldsymbol{\phi}^T(\mathbf{x}_i)\mathbf{M}^{-1}(i)}{(i-1) + \boldsymbol{\phi}^T(\mathbf{x}_i)\mathbf{M}^{-1}(i)\boldsymbol{\phi}(\mathbf{x}_i)}\right]. \end{aligned} \tag{5.73}$$

It is a simple matter to verify that the recursive algorithm for $\mathbf{M}^{-1}$ is equivalent to (5.72). Algorithms (5.71) and (5.73) are sometimes called the first-order and the second-order algorithms respectively.

5.2.4 Stochastic estimation of parameters

The theory of parameter estimation was presented in chapter 3. We discuss here some of the relationships between estimation theory and stochastic approximation. Let $x_1, x_2, \ldots,$ be a sequence of statistically independent and identically distributed random samples. The likelihood function

$$f(x_1, x_2, \ldots, x_n|\omega) = \prod_{i=1}^{n} f(x_i|\omega),$$

is assumed known, and the unknown true parameter is denoted by θ. A maximum likelihood estimate is a root of the equation

$$-\frac{1}{n}\frac{\partial}{\partial\omega}[\sum_{i=1}^{n} \log f(x_i|\omega)] = 0. \tag{5.74}$$

As n approaches infinity, (5.74) becomes

$$\begin{aligned} \lim_{n\to\infty}\frac{1}{n}\sum_{i=1}^{n}\left[-\frac{\partial}{\partial\omega}\log f(x_i|\omega)\right] &= E\left[-\frac{\partial}{\partial\omega}\log f(x|\omega)\right] \\ &= -\int f(x|\theta)\frac{\partial}{\partial\omega}\log f(x|\omega)\,dx, \end{aligned} \tag{5.75}$$

since the random samples are distributed according to $f(x|\theta)$.

Assume that both $(\partial/\partial\omega)f(x|\omega)$ and $(\partial^2/\partial\omega^2)f(x|\omega)$ exist and are absolutely integrable, and let

$$\mu(\omega) = E\left[-\frac{\partial}{\partial\omega}\log f(x|\omega)\right]. \tag{5.76}$$

It is obvious from (5.75) and (5.76) that

$$\mu(\theta) = -\int_{\Omega_x}\frac{\partial}{\partial\theta}f(x|\theta)\,dx = -\frac{\partial}{\partial\theta}\int_{\Omega_x}f(x|\theta)\,dx = 0.$$

The interchange of integration and differentiation is allowed as discussed in section 3.2. Therefore, asymptotically the maximum likelihood estimator is equivalent to finding the root of the regression function $\mu(\omega)$. The Robbins–Monro algorithm,

$$\omega(i+1) = \omega(i) + a_i\frac{\partial}{\partial\omega}\log f(x_i|\omega)\bigg|_{\omega=\omega(i)}, \tag{5.77}$$

may be used. The algorithm searches for the θ that maximizes the regression function $E[\log f(x|\omega)]$, and may be regarded as a special case of algorithm (5.33). It is emphasized that in many cases, the maximum likelihood equation is difficult to solve. Algorithm (5.77) offers us an alternative approach that is relatively simple in computation and behaves asymptotically like a maximum likelihood estimator.

A maximum likelihood estimate is, under some general conditions, asymptotically Gaussian distributed and asymptotically efficient. Let us choose for algorithm (5.77) a gain sequence $a_i = 1/iM$ where

$$M = \frac{d}{d\omega}\mu(\omega)\bigg|_{\omega=\theta} = \frac{\partial}{\partial\omega}E\left[-\frac{\partial}{\partial\omega}\log f(x|\omega)\right]\bigg|_{\omega=\theta}.$$

By interchanging the partial differentiation and expectation, we obtain

$$M = -E\left[\frac{\partial^2}{\partial\omega^2}\log f(x|\omega)\right]\bigg|_{\omega=\theta} = \sigma^2(\theta), \tag{5.78}$$

which is the familiar Fisher information. We also note that

$$\alpha^2 \geqslant \operatorname{Var}\left[-\frac{\partial}{\partial\omega}\log f(x|\omega)\right],$$

including the case that $\omega = \theta$. Since $\mu(\theta) = 0$,

$$\alpha^2 \geqslant E\left[\left(\frac{\partial}{\partial\omega}\log f(x|\omega)\right)^2\right]\bigg|_{\omega=\theta} = \sigma^2(\theta), \tag{5.79}$$

according to (3.52). In the case that $\alpha^2 = \sigma^2(\theta)$, Sack's result may be applied,

$$\lim_{i\to\infty} iV_i = \frac{\alpha^2}{M^2} = \frac{1}{\sigma^2(\theta)}.$$

Asymptotically, the algorithm is efficient and Gaussian.

The algorithm may also be used for small i. In this case, we use the gain sequence given in (5.55) so as to take into consideration the initial mean-square error. Since

$$M_1 \leqslant M = \sigma^2(\theta) \leqslant \alpha^2,$$

the bound on mean-square error may be written as

$$V_{i+1} \leqslant (V_1^{-1} + iM_1^2\alpha^{-2})^{-1} \leqslant V_1(1 + i\rho^2\sigma^2 V_1)^{-1} \tag{5.80}$$

where $\rho = M_1/\alpha^2$. In figure 5.7 we plot the dimensionless V_{i+1}/V_1 versus $i\sigma^2 V_1$ as given by (5.80). The curves correspond to the upper bounds on V_{i+1}. For comparison purpose, we also plot $(i\sigma^2 V_1)^{-1}$, which corresponds to an asymptotically efficient estimator.

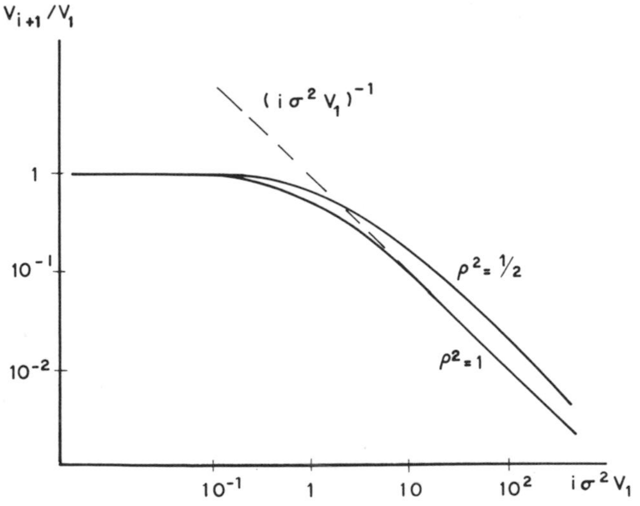

fig. 5.7 Performance curves of the stochastic approximation algorithm for estimating parameters (adapted from Young and Westerberg, 1971).

5.3 Stochastic Estimation of Discriminant Functions

We return to the two-class pattern recognition problem. As discussed in chapter 4, an important approach to pattern recognition is to find a discriminant function,

$$D(\mathbf{x}) = \sum_{j=1}^{K} \theta_j \phi_j(\mathbf{x}) = \boldsymbol{\phi}^T(\mathbf{x})\boldsymbol{\theta}. \tag{5.81}$$

The basis functions in the set, $\phi_1(\mathbf{x}), \ldots, \phi_K(\mathbf{x})$, are linearly independent and known. If the basis functions are components of the vector $\mathbf{x}$, $D(\mathbf{x})$ is a linear discriminant function. The selection of basis functions depends on practical considerations and the allowable complexity of the discriminant function. The probability density functions of the two classes of pattern vectors are unknown. We have instead a sequence of training samples whose classifications are known. This is a supervised learning problem, and in this section we shall develop stochastic approximation algorithms for estimating the discriminant function.

Let $\mathbf{x}_1, \mathbf{x}_2, \ldots,$ be a sequence of training samples with known classifications, and define

$$d(\mathbf{x}) = \begin{cases} 1 & \text{If } \mathbf{x} \in C_1 \\ 0 & \text{if } \mathbf{x} \in C_2. \end{cases} \tag{5.82}$$

We use a mean-square criterion

$$J(\omega) = E[(d(\mathbf{x}) - \boldsymbol{\phi}^T(\mathbf{x})\omega)^2], \tag{5.83}$$

and seek a vector $\boldsymbol{\theta}$ that minimizes $J(\omega)$. The discriminant function is $D(\mathbf{x}) = \boldsymbol{\phi}^T(\mathbf{x})\omega$, and when a new pattern $\mathbf{x}$ is observed, $D(\mathbf{x})$ is evaluated and compared with the threshold value 1/2. If $d(\mathbf{x}) \geqslant 1/2$, the new pattern is classified as belonging to C_1; otherwise, it belongs to C_2. Therefore, it is reasonable to use the mean-square criterion $J(\omega)$ with $d(\mathbf{x})$ defined in (5.82).

The solution vector $\boldsymbol{\theta}$ that minimizes $J(\omega)$ is

$$\boldsymbol{\theta} = \mathbf{M}^{-1} E[\boldsymbol{\phi}(\mathbf{x}) d(\mathbf{x})] \tag{5.84}$$

with

$$\mathbf{M} = E[\boldsymbol{\phi}(\mathbf{x})\boldsymbol{\phi}^T(\mathbf{x})], \tag{5.85}$$

where we have assumed that $\mathbf{M}^{-1}$ exists. The vector $\boldsymbol{\theta}$ in (5.84) cannot be evaluated directly since the distributions of the two classes of pattern vectors are unknown. The function $J(\omega)$ may be regarded as a regression function to be minimized, hence a Robbins–Monro algorithm

$$\omega(i+1) = \omega(i) + a_i \boldsymbol{\phi}(\mathbf{x}_i)[d(\mathbf{x}_i) - \boldsymbol{\phi}^T(x_i)\omega(i)], \tag{5.86}$$

may be used, where the correction term is the gradient with respect to ω of the term under the expectation of (5.83). Another possibility, as discussed in the previous section, is to use a second-order algorithm

$$\begin{aligned} \omega(i+1) &= \omega(i) + \frac{1}{i}\mathbf{M}^{-1}(i)\boldsymbol{\phi}(\mathbf{x}_i)[d(\mathbf{x}_i) - \boldsymbol{\phi}^T(\mathbf{x}_i)\omega(i)], \\ \mathbf{M}^{-1}(i+1) &= \frac{i}{i-1}\left[\mathbf{M}^{-1}(i) - \frac{\mathbf{M}^{-1}(i)\boldsymbol{\phi}(\mathbf{x}_i)\boldsymbol{\phi}^T(\mathbf{x}_i)\mathbf{M}^{-1}(i)}{(i-1) + \boldsymbol{\phi}^T(\mathbf{x}_i)\mathbf{M}(i)\boldsymbol{\phi}(\mathbf{x}_i)}\right]. \end{aligned} \tag{5.87}$$

Mathematically, algorithms (5.86) and (5.87) are identical to algorithms (5.71) and (5.73), respectively, in example 5.5. There is, however, a subtle difference; while $h(\mathbf{x})$ in the example is a deterministic function, $d(\mathbf{x})$ is a random function of $\mathbf{x}$. We note that $d(\mathbf{x})$ specifies the classification of $\mathbf{x}$, and, for a given value of $\mathbf{x}$, there is a probability $P(C_1|\mathbf{x})$ that $d(\mathbf{x}) = 1$ and a probability $P(C_2|\mathbf{x}) = 1 - P(C_1|\mathbf{x})$ that $d(\mathbf{x}) = 0$. Let us take the expectation of the random function $d(\mathbf{x})$,

$$E_d[d(\mathbf{x})] = 1 \times P(C_1|\mathbf{x}) + 0 \times P(C_2|\mathbf{x}) = P(C_1|\mathbf{x}), \tag{5.88}$$

where the subscript d denotes that the expectation is over the distribution of d for given $\mathbf{x}$. Hence, $d(\mathbf{x})$ may be regarded as being a deterministic component $P(C_1|\mathbf{x})$ plus a zero-mean random component $\zeta(\mathbf{x})$

$$d(\mathbf{x}) = P(C_1|\mathbf{x}) + \zeta(\mathbf{x}) \tag{5.89}$$

with

$$\begin{aligned} E_\zeta[\zeta(\mathbf{x})] &= E_d[d(\mathbf{x})] - P(C_1|\mathbf{x}) = 0, \\ E_\zeta[\zeta^2(\mathbf{x})] &= E_d[d^2(\mathbf{x}) - 2d(\mathbf{x})P(C_1|\mathbf{x}) + P^2(C_1|\mathbf{x})] \\ &= P(C_1|\mathbf{x}) - P^2(C_1|\mathbf{x}), \end{aligned} \tag{5.90}$$

since by (5.82) $d^2(\mathbf{x}) = d(\mathbf{x})$. Therefore, the mean-square criterion becomes

$$\begin{aligned} J(\omega) &= E[(d(\mathbf{x}) - \boldsymbol{\phi}^T(\mathbf{x})\omega)^2] = E_\mathbf{x} E_d[(d(\mathbf{x}) - \boldsymbol{\phi}^T(\mathbf{x})\omega)^2] \\ &= E_\mathbf{x} E_\zeta[(P(C_1|\mathbf{x}) - \boldsymbol{\phi}^T(\mathbf{x})\omega + \zeta(\mathbf{x}))^2] \\ &= E_\mathbf{x}[(P(C_1|\mathbf{x}) - \boldsymbol{\phi}^T(\mathbf{x})\omega)^2] + E_\mathbf{x}[P(C_1|\mathbf{x}) - P^2(C_1|\mathbf{x})]. \end{aligned}$$

The second term is independent of ω, and the discriminant function $D(\mathbf{x}) = \boldsymbol{\phi}^T(\mathbf{x})\boldsymbol{\theta}$ that minimizes $J(\omega)$ is in fact a mean-square approximation of the conditional probability $P(C_1|\mathbf{x})$. Since $P(C_1|\mathbf{x})$ is unknown and not observable, we use instead the known $d(\mathbf{x})$ in the stochastic approximation algorithm.

The discussion above is important for two reasons. First, it demonstrates clearly the relationship between the discriminant function and the approximation of a probability function. Second, and more generally, it is a major advantage of stochastic approximation. When it is desirable to estimate a function that is unknown and not observable, it is sometimes possible to use in its stead a known function whose expectation equals the function to be estimated. This approach will be used later on in some other situations.

We now return to algorithm (5.86) and consider its convergence conditions.

THEOREM 5.4

Algorithm (5.86) converges in the mean-square sense and with probability 1 if the following conditions are satisfied.

(1) The training samples $\mathbf{x}_1, \mathbf{x}_2, \ldots,$ are statistically independent with known classifications.

(2) $\sum_{i=1}^{\infty} a_i = \infty, \quad \sum_{i=1}^{\infty} a_i^2 < \infty.$

(3) $E[\boldsymbol{\phi}(\mathbf{x})\boldsymbol{\phi}^T(\mathbf{x})]$ and $E[\boldsymbol{\phi}(\mathbf{x})\boldsymbol{\phi}^T(\mathbf{x})\boldsymbol{\phi}(\mathbf{x})\boldsymbol{\phi}^T(x)]$ exist and are positive definite.

(4) $E[\boldsymbol{\phi}(\mathbf{x})P(C_1|\mathbf{x})]$ and $E[\boldsymbol{\phi}(\mathbf{x})\boldsymbol{\phi}^T(\mathbf{x})\boldsymbol{\phi}(\mathbf{x})P(C_1|\mathbf{x})]$ exist.

Proof

We use the multidimensional version of theorems 5.2 and 5.2*a* to show the convergence. Algorithm (5.86) may be rewritten as

$$\omega(i + 1) = \mathbf{T}_i(\omega(1), \ldots, \omega(i)) + \boldsymbol{\eta}_i, \tag{5.91}$$

with

$$\begin{aligned} \mathbf{T}_i(\omega(1), \ldots, \omega(i)) &= \omega(i) - a_i\boldsymbol{\phi}(\mathbf{x}_i)\boldsymbol{\phi}^T(\mathbf{x}_i)[\omega(i) - \boldsymbol{\theta}], \\ \boldsymbol{\eta}_i &= a_i\boldsymbol{\phi}(\mathbf{x}_i)[d(\mathbf{x}_i) - \boldsymbol{\phi}^T(\mathbf{x}_i)\boldsymbol{\theta}]. \end{aligned} \tag{5.92}$$

It is easy to verify from the assumptions that

$$E[\boldsymbol{\eta}_i|\omega(1), \ldots, \omega(i)] = \mathbf{0},$$

$$\sum_{i=1}^{\infty} E[\|\boldsymbol{\eta}_i\|^2] < \infty.$$

The verification of the first equation in (5.50),

$$\|\mathbf{T}_i(\omega(1), \ldots, \omega(i)) - \boldsymbol{\theta}\| \leqslant F_i \|\omega(i) - \boldsymbol{\theta}\|, \tag{5.93}$$

is rather difficult, and we shall show instead that

$$E[\|\mathbf{T}_i(\omega(1), \ldots, \omega(i)) - \boldsymbol{\theta}\|^2] \leqslant F_i E[\|\omega(i) - \boldsymbol{\theta}\|^2], \tag{5.94}$$

which is weaker than (5.93). It is clear from the proofs of theorems 5.2 and 5.2*a* that the weaker condition (5.94), together with the other conditions, is sufficient for the proof of the convergence (see (5.41)).

We have from (5.92) that

$$E[\|\mathbf{T}_i(\omega(1), \ldots, \omega(i)) - \boldsymbol{\theta}\|^2] = E[\|(\mathbf{I} - a_i \boldsymbol{\phi}(\mathbf{x}_i)\boldsymbol{\phi}^T(\mathbf{x}_i))(\omega(i) - \boldsymbol{\theta})\|^2].$$

Since $\mathbf{x}_i$ and $\omega(i)$ are statistically independent, we may perform the expectation of $\mathbf{x}_i$ first and obtain

$$E[\|\mathbf{T}_i(\omega(1), \ldots, \omega(i)) - \boldsymbol{\theta}\|^2] = E[\|(\mathbf{I} - a_i \mathbf{M})(\omega(i) - \boldsymbol{\theta})\|^2], \tag{5.95}$$

where

$$\mathbf{M} = E[\boldsymbol{\phi}(\mathbf{x}_i)\boldsymbol{\phi}^T(\mathbf{x}_i)] = E[\boldsymbol{\phi}(\mathbf{x})\boldsymbol{\phi}^T(\mathbf{x})].$$

Let λ_0 be the smallest eigenvalue of the matrix $\mathbf{M}$ and note that $0 < \lambda_0 < \infty$ due to condition (3). Therefore, there exists a finite integer n such that for all $i \geqslant n$, $a_i \lambda_0 < 1$ and

$$E[\|\mathbf{T}_i(\omega(1), \ldots, \omega(i)) - \boldsymbol{\theta}\|^2] \leqslant (1 - a_i \lambda_0)^2 E[\|\omega(i) - \boldsymbol{\theta}\|^2]. \tag{5.96}$$

Let $F_i = (1 - a_i \lambda_0)$ and note that $\sum_{i=n}^{\infty} a_i = \infty$ implies $\Pi_{i=n}^{\infty} F_i = 0$. Therefore, (5.96) is equivalent to (5.94) for $i > n$ where n is finite, and this completes the proof.

5.4 The Method of Potential Functions

The method of potential functions was introduced and studied extensively by Aizerman et al. in a series of papers in 1964. The method is used to find recursively a discriminant function for pattern recognition. Let $\mathbf{x}_1$, $\mathbf{x}_2$, ..., be a sequence of training samples with known classifications. For each sample function $\mathbf{x}_i$, a potential function $K(\mathbf{x}, \mathbf{x}_i)$ is defined over the space $\Omega_{\mathbf{x}}$ with $\mathbf{x}_i$ considered as a vector-valued parameter. The learning or the estimation of the discriminant function depends on the samples $\mathbf{x}_i$, and the potential function expresses the dependence explicitly. For a sequence of training samples $\mathbf{x}_1, \mathbf{x}_2, \ldots$, a sequence of potential functions $K(\mathbf{x}, \mathbf{x}_1)$, $K(\mathbf{x}, \mathbf{x}_2), \ldots$, is used to construct the discriminant function recursively,

$$D_{i+1}(\mathbf{x}) = D_i(\mathbf{x}) + b_i K(\mathbf{x}, \mathbf{x}_i), \tag{5.97}$$

where $D_i(\mathbf{x})$ is the i-th estimate of the discriminant function.

It is natural to ask how the potential functions are selected. There are two ways to accomplish this. The first method assumes that $D(\mathbf{x})$ may be expressed as a linear combination of K known basis functions $\phi_1(\mathbf{x})$, $\phi_2(\mathbf{x})$, $\ldots$, $\phi_K(\mathbf{x})$, as in (5.81), and uses a potential function

$$K(\mathbf{x}, \mathbf{x}_i) = \sum_{k=1}^{K} \phi_k(\mathbf{x})\phi_k(\mathbf{x}_i) = \boldsymbol{\phi}^T(\mathbf{x})\boldsymbol{\phi}(\mathbf{x}_i). \tag{5.98}$$

The gain sequence $\{b_i\}$ may be chosen in such a way that a correction is made only when $\mathbf{x}_i$ is misclassified by $D(\mathbf{x}_i)$. Assuming a threshold value of 1/2, we use a gain sequence

$$b_i = \begin{cases} 0 & \text{if } D(\mathbf{x}_i) \geqslant 1/2 \text{ and } \mathbf{x}_i \in C_1, \\ a_i & \text{if } D(\mathbf{x}_i) < 1/2 \text{ and } \mathbf{x}_i \in C_1, \\ -a_i & \text{if } D(\mathbf{x}_i) \geqslant 1/2 \text{ and } \mathbf{x}_i \in C_2, \\ 0 & \text{if } D(\mathbf{x}_i) < 1/2 \text{ and } \mathbf{x}_i \in C_2. \end{cases} \tag{5.99}$$

Aizerman et al. (1964c) showed that with $\sum_{i=1}^{\infty} a_i = \infty$ and $\sum_{i=1}^{\infty} a_i^2 < \infty$, algorithm (5.97) converges to $D(\mathbf{x}) = \boldsymbol{\phi}^T(\mathbf{x})\boldsymbol{\theta}$ in the mean-square sense.

There may be other choices of the gain sequence $\{b_i\}$. For example, since we choose 1/2 as the threshold value, it seems reasonable to use a correction term that is proportional to $1 - D(\mathbf{x}_i)$ when $x_i \in C_1$ and proportional to $-D(\mathbf{x}_i)$ when $\mathbf{x}_i \in C_2$. Thus,

$$b_i = a_i[d(\mathbf{x}_i) - D(\mathbf{x}_i)], \tag{5.100}$$

where $d(\mathbf{x}_i)$ has been defined in (5.82). A substitution of (5.98) and (5.100) into (5.97) yields

$$D_{i+1}(\mathbf{x}) = D_i(\mathbf{x}) + a_i[d(\mathbf{x}_i) - D(\mathbf{x}_i)]\boldsymbol{\phi}^T(\mathbf{x})\boldsymbol{\phi}(\mathbf{x}_i). \tag{5.101}$$

If we let

$$D_i(\mathbf{x}) = \boldsymbol{\phi}^T(\mathbf{x})\omega(i),$$

(5.101) becomes

$$\boldsymbol{\phi}^T(\mathbf{x})\omega(i+1) = \boldsymbol{\phi}^T(\mathbf{x})\{\omega(i) + a_i\boldsymbol{\phi}(\mathbf{x}_i)[d(\mathbf{x}_i) - \boldsymbol{\phi}^T(\mathbf{x}_i)\omega(i)]\},$$

which is equivalent to the stochastic approximation algorithm (5.86). Therefore, algorithm (5.101) converges in the mean-square sense and with probability 1. Also, $D(\mathbf{x})$ is in fact an approximation of the conditional probability $P(C_1|\mathbf{x})$.

The discussion above suggests that the method of potential function may be regarded as a stochastic approximation algorithm. It should be mentioned, however, that historically the potential function method precedes the application of stochastic approximation to pattern recognition, and the original idea is closer to the perceptron than to stochastic approximation. The following potential function approach is somewhat different from stochastic approximation.

Let us consider more generally a set of complete orthonormal functions $\{\phi_k(\mathbf{x}), k = 1, 2, \ldots\}$. In other words,

$$\int_{\Omega_\mathbf{x}} \phi_k(\mathbf{x})\phi_j(\mathbf{x})\,d\mathbf{x} = \delta_{kj}, \tag{5.102}$$

where

$$\delta_{kj} = \begin{cases} 1 & \text{when } k = j, \\ 0 & \text{when } k \neq j, \end{cases}$$

and any function $h(\mathbf{x})$ which is square integrable on $\Omega_\mathbf{x}$ can be arbitrarily closely approximated in the integral-square sense by a linear combination of $\phi_k(\mathbf{x})$. We define a potential function

$$K(\mathbf{x}, \mathbf{x}') = \sum_{k=1}^{\infty} \lambda_k \phi_k(\mathbf{x})\phi_k(\mathbf{x}'), \qquad \lambda_k > 0. \tag{5.103}$$

In order to represent $P(C_1|\mathbf{x})$ by this set of functions, i.e.,

$$P(C_1|\mathbf{x}) = D(\mathbf{x}) = \sum_{k=1}^{\infty} \theta_k \phi_k(\mathbf{x}), \tag{5.104}$$

the function $P(C_1|\mathbf{x})$ or $D(\mathbf{x})$ is assumed to satisfy the condition

$$\sum_{k=1}^{\infty} \theta_k^2 < \infty. \tag{5.105}$$

Note that here we are using a complete set of basis functions, and the representation of $P(C_1|\mathbf{x})$ is exact, not just an approximation.

In practice, of course, it is impossible to use an infinite number of basis functions. There is, however, a possible alternative, namely, (5.103) may converge to a symmetric function $K(\mathbf{x}, \mathbf{x}')$ in closed form. For example, a commonly used potential function is

$$K(\mathbf{x}, \mathbf{x}') = K(\mathbf{x} - \mathbf{x}') = \exp\left[-\frac{1}{\alpha^2}\|\mathbf{x} - \mathbf{x}'\|^2\right], \tag{5.106}$$

and it is known that (5.106) may be expanded into the form

$$K(\mathbf{x}, \mathbf{x}') = \sum_{k=1}^{\infty} \lambda_k \phi_k(\mathbf{x})\phi_k(\mathbf{x}'),$$

where $\phi_k(\mathbf{x})$ is the solution to the eigenequation,

$$\int_{\Omega_{\mathbf{x}'}} K(\mathbf{x}, \mathbf{x}')\phi(\mathbf{x}')\, d\mathbf{x}' = \lambda\phi(\mathbf{x}),$$

and the set of eigenfunctions $\{\phi_k(\mathbf{x})\}$ is complete. Then algorithm (5.97) becomes

$$\begin{aligned} D_{i+1}(\mathbf{x}) &= D_i(\mathbf{x}) + b_i \exp\left[-\frac{1}{\alpha^2}\|\mathbf{x} - \mathbf{x}_i\|^2\right] \\ &= \sum_{l=1}^{i} b_l \exp\left[-\frac{1}{\alpha^2}\|\mathbf{x} - \mathbf{x}_l\|^2\right] \end{aligned} \tag{5.107}$$

where b_i is specified by (5.99) or (5.100). We note that in this approach it is necessary to store in the computer all previous potential functions $K(\mathbf{x}, \mathbf{x}_1)$, $K(\mathbf{x}, \mathbf{x}_2), \ldots, K(\mathbf{x}, \mathbf{x}_i)$. The storage requirement is the same as that of the nearest-neighbor classification or Parzen's empirical estimation of density functions as discussed in chapter 3. Indeed, the potential function $K(\mathbf{x}, \mathbf{x}_i)$ in (5.106) is essentially a Gaussian distribution with mean $\mathbf{x}_i$ and covariance $\alpha^2\mathbf{I}$, and the approach is closely related to Parzen's estimation. Thus, algorithm (5.107) requires a large number of storage spaces, but has the advantage of converging to the unknown conditional probability $P(C_1|\mathbf{x})$. Algorithm (5.101), on the other hand, is essentially a stochastic approximation algorithm that estimates a vector $\boldsymbol{\theta}$ of relatively low dimensionality, but has the disadvantage that $D(\mathbf{x}) = \boldsymbol{\phi}^T(\mathbf{x})\boldsymbol{\theta}$ is usually only an approximation of $P(C_1|\mathbf{x})$.

Only general principles can be given for the choice of potential functions. A potential function $K(\mathbf{x}, \mathbf{x}_i)$ represents the effect of the sample vector $\mathbf{x}_i$ on the function to be estimated, which in our case is $D(\mathbf{x})$ or $P(C_1|\mathbf{x})$. Hence, intuitively, it should be maximum when $\mathbf{x} = \mathbf{x}_i$ and should decrease with the distance between $\mathbf{x}$ and $\mathbf{x}_i$. It is also desirable that

$K(\mathbf{x}, \mathbf{x}_i)$ be symmetric and reasonably smooth. Further, it is preferable to have a potential function whose eigenfunctions are complete, and the following theorem is useful in this regard.

THEOREM 5.5

Let Ω be a bounded region of a N-dimensional Euclidean space, and let $K(\boldsymbol{v})$ be a continuous function in this space whose N-dimensional Fourier transform

$$\tilde{K}(\boldsymbol{\kappa}) = \int_\Omega K(\boldsymbol{v}) \exp(-j\boldsymbol{\kappa}^T \boldsymbol{v})\, d\boldsymbol{v}$$

is positive for almost all $\boldsymbol{\kappa}$. Then $K(\mathbf{x} - \mathbf{x}')$ can be expanded into an infinitive series of the form (5.103) in this region, where $\{\phi_k(\mathbf{x})\}$ is a complete set of functions.

Proof

It is known from the theory of integral equations that if $K(\mathbf{x}, \mathbf{x}')$ is positive definite, i.e.,

$$\int_\Omega \int_\Omega K(\mathbf{x}, \mathbf{x}') h(\mathbf{x}) h(\mathbf{x}')\, d\mathbf{x}\, d\mathbf{x}' > 0$$

for any $h(\mathbf{x})$ such that $\int_\Omega h^2(\mathbf{x})\, d\mathbf{x} > 0$, then the eigenfunctions of $K(\mathbf{x}, \mathbf{x}')$ form a complete set, and by Mercer's theorem

$$K(\mathbf{x}, \mathbf{x}') = \sum_{k=1}^{\infty} \lambda_k \phi_k(\mathbf{x}) \phi_k(\mathbf{x}'),$$

where λ_k and $\phi_k(\mathbf{x})$ are the eigenvalues and eigenfunctions respectively. Now

$$\begin{aligned} &\iint K(\mathbf{x} - \mathbf{x}') h(\mathbf{x}) h(\mathbf{x}')\, d\mathbf{x}\, d\mathbf{x}' \\ &\qquad = \frac{1}{(2\pi)^N} \iiint \tilde{K}(\boldsymbol{\kappa}) e^{j\boldsymbol{\kappa}^T(\mathbf{x}-\mathbf{x}')} h(\mathbf{x}) h(\mathbf{x}')\, d\mathbf{x}\, d\mathbf{x}'\, d\boldsymbol{\kappa} \\ &\qquad = \frac{1}{(2\pi)^N} \int \tilde{K}(\boldsymbol{\kappa}) |\tilde{h}(\boldsymbol{\kappa})|^2 d\boldsymbol{\kappa}, \end{aligned} \tag{5.108}$$

where $\tilde{h}(\boldsymbol{\kappa})$ is the Fourier transform of $h(\mathbf{x})$. Therefore, if $\tilde{K}(\boldsymbol{\kappa}) > 0$ for almost all $\boldsymbol{\kappa}$, (5.108) is greater than zero, and $K(\mathbf{x} - \mathbf{x}')$ is representable by (5.103) with $\{\phi_k(\mathbf{x})\}$ constituting a complete set of functions.

We can now demonstrate easily that the eigenfunctions of $K(\mathbf{x}, \mathbf{x}')$ in (5.106) form a complete set. The Fourier transform of (5.106) is

$$\tilde{K}(\boldsymbol{\kappa}) = (2\pi\alpha^2)^{N/2} \exp(-\alpha^2 \|\boldsymbol{\kappa}\|^2)$$

which is greater than zero for all finite $\boldsymbol{\kappa}$. Hence, according to theorem 5.5, $K(\mathbf{x}, \mathbf{x}')$ of (5.106) is a proper potential function with a complete set of eigenfunctions.

The method of potential functions may also be applied to the perceptron-type pattern recognition problem in which a finite sequence of training patterns with known classifications is used repeatedly for the estimation of the discriminant function. An error correction procedure is used. Assume a threshold value of zero, then after observing $\mathbf{x}_i$, $D_{i+1}(\mathbf{x}) = D_i(\mathbf{x}) + K(\mathbf{x}, \mathbf{x}_i)$ if $x_i \in C_1$ and $D_i(\mathbf{x}) < 0$, and $D_{i+1}(\mathbf{x}) = D_i(\mathbf{x}) - K(\mathbf{x}, \mathbf{x}_i)$ if $\mathbf{x}_i \in C_2$ and $D_i(\mathbf{x}) \geqslant 0$; otherwise no correction will be made. Thus, if we use the convention that $d(\mathbf{x}) = 1$ if $\mathbf{x} \in C_1$ and $d(\mathbf{x}) = -1$ if $\mathbf{x} \in C_2$, the error correction algorithm may be written as

$$D_{i+1}(\mathbf{x}) = D_i(\mathbf{x}) + \frac{1}{2}[d(\mathbf{x}_i) - \operatorname{sgn} D_i(\mathbf{x}_i)] K(\mathbf{x}, \mathbf{x}_i), \tag{5.109}$$

or equivalently

$$\omega(i + 1) = \omega(i) + \frac{1}{2}[d(\mathbf{x}_i) - \operatorname{sgn} D_i(\mathbf{x}_i)] \boldsymbol{\phi}(\mathbf{x}_i), \tag{5.110}$$

where we have assumed that $K(\mathbf{x}, \mathbf{x}_i)$ may be represented by (5.98) with a finite number of basis functions. If the training patterns are separable by a hypersurface defined by $D(\mathbf{x}) = \boldsymbol{\phi}^T(\mathbf{x})\boldsymbol{\theta} = 0$, algorithm (5.110) will converge to a $\boldsymbol{\theta}$ after a finite number of steps. Note that since we are dealing with perceptron-type problems, we assume that the vector $\boldsymbol{\phi}(\mathbf{x})$ is augmented by a constant component.

It is interesting to note that when the number of available training patterns is finite, it is not physically meaningful to use an infinite number of basis functions as in (5.103). Figure 5.8 shows the training samples and the separating hypersurface that would result if we used a large number of basis functions. While the hypersurface separates the two classes of training samples perfectly, it is doubtful that the hypersurface represents a good decision rule for classifying new patterns. This is due to the fact that the sample size is smaller than the dimensionality of $\Omega_{\boldsymbol{\phi}}$, as discussed in chapter 4. A better decision rule is illustrated by the dashed line in figure 5.8.

5.5 Stochastic Estimation of Probability Density Functions

Many pattern recognition problems may be interpreted as density estimation problems. In supervised parametric learning, the form of the probability density functions of each class is known, and the problem is to estimate the unknown parameters of the density functions. In unsupervised learning, a mixture approach is often used, and the learning is again the estimation of parameters—the parameters of the mixture density function. And as discussed in the previous section, the estimation of discriminant functions is essentially an approximation of the conditional probability $P(C_1|\mathbf{x})$. Hence, the estimation of a probability density function is a fundamental problem of pattern recognition, and deserves further attention.

In section 3.5 we studied Parzen's empirical estimation of probability density functions, which requires that a computer store every sample observed. The requirement of a large number of storage spaces is a major drawback. In this section, we study in some detail stochastic approximation algorithms for the estimation or approximation of an unknown probability density function. A sequence of independent samples $x_1, x_2, \ldots,$ is available, and the estimate is updated after each observation. To simplify the discussion, we shall be concerned mostly with the estimation of one-dimensional probability density functions.

5.5.1 Linear approximation

Consider the approximation of an unknown density function $f(x)$ by a linear combination of linearly independent basis functions, $\phi_1(x)$, $\phi_2(x)$, $\ldots$, $\phi_K(x)$. We use for approximation an integral-square criterion,

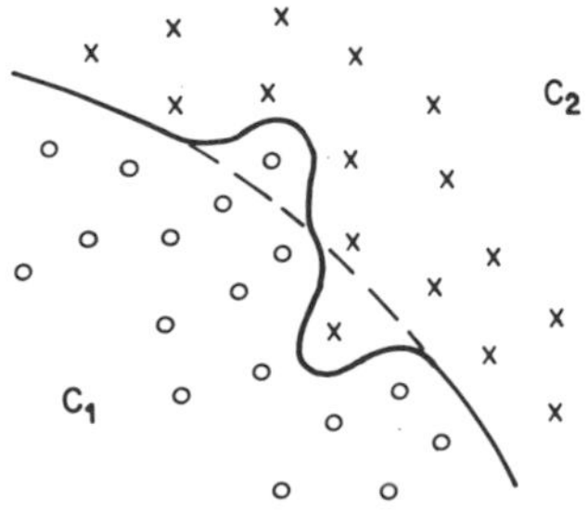

fig. 5.8 The separation of two classes using a finite number of training samples and a large number of basis functions.

$$I(\omega) = \int [f(x) - \omega^T \phi(x)]^2 \, dx. \tag{5.111}$$

Taking the gradient with respect to ω, we obtain

$$\begin{aligned} \nabla_\omega I(\omega) &= -2 \int \phi(x)[f(x) - \phi^T(x)\omega] \, dx \\ &= -2\{E[\phi(x)] - \mathbf{M}\omega\}, \end{aligned} \tag{5.112}$$

where $\mathbf{M}$ is defined as

$$\mathbf{M} = \int \phi(x)\phi^T(x) \, dx. \tag{5.113}$$

The minimum integral-square approximation is

$$\hat{f}(x) = \boldsymbol{\theta}^T \phi(x), \tag{5.114}$$

with

$$\boldsymbol{\theta} = \mathbf{M}^{-1} E[\phi(x)] \tag{5.115}$$

being the solution of the equation $\nabla_\omega I(\omega)|_{\omega=\boldsymbol{\theta}} = \mathbf{0}$.

The solution $\boldsymbol{\theta}$ cannot be evaluated directly since $E[\phi(x)]$ cannot be evaluated without knowing $f(x)$. We have assumed that a sequence of random samples $x_1, x_2, \ldots,$ with identical distribution $f(x)$ is available, and we wish to use a stochastic approximation algorithm,

$$\omega(i+1) = \omega(i) - a_i \xi(\omega(i); x_i), \tag{5.116}$$

to estimate the unknown $\boldsymbol{\theta}$. Since $\nabla I(\omega)$ is the gradient, we would have used (5.112) for $\xi(\omega; x)$ if it were possible. As it is, $\nabla I(\omega)$ cannot be evaluated directly, and we must choose a $\xi(\omega; x)$ such that

$$\xi(\omega; x) = \frac{1}{2} \nabla_\omega I(\omega) + \zeta(x) \tag{5.117}$$

with

$$E[\zeta(x)] = \mathbf{0}. \tag{5.118}$$

An obvious choice is

$$\begin{aligned} \xi(\omega; x) &= -[\phi(x) - \mathbf{M}\omega], \\ \zeta(x) &= \phi(x) - E[\phi(x)], \end{aligned} \tag{5.119}$$

which satisfies (5.118). The situation is very similar to the stochastic estimation of discriminant functions.

The overall algorithm is

$$\omega(i+1) = \omega(i) + a_i[\boldsymbol{\phi}(x_i) - \mathbf{M}\omega(i)]. \tag{5.120}$$

It may be written in Dvoretzky's form

$$\omega(i+1) = \mathbf{T}_i(\omega(1), \ldots, \omega(i)) + \boldsymbol{\eta}_i$$

with

$$\mathbf{T}_i(\omega(1), \ldots, \omega(i)) - \boldsymbol{\theta} = (\mathbf{I} - a_i\mathbf{M})(\omega(i) - \boldsymbol{\theta}),$$

$$\boldsymbol{\eta}_i = a_i\boldsymbol{\zeta}_i = a_i\{\boldsymbol{\phi}(x_i) - E[\boldsymbol{\phi}(x_i)]\},$$

where we have used (5.115). Therefore, it should be easy to show that algorithm (5.120) converges to $\boldsymbol{\theta}$ both in the mean-square sense and with probability 1 if:

(1) the matrix $\mathbf{M}$ is finite and positive definite;

(2) $E[\|\boldsymbol{\zeta}(x)\|^2] = \mathrm{Var}[\|\boldsymbol{\phi}(x) - E[\boldsymbol{\phi}(x)]\|]$ is finite;

(3) $\sum_{i=1}^{\infty} a_i = \infty$, $\sum_{i=1}^{\infty} a_i^2 < \infty$.

The second-order algorithm is

$$\omega(i+1) = \omega(i) + \frac{1}{i}\mathbf{M}^{-1}[\boldsymbol{\phi}(x_i) - \mathbf{M}\omega(i)]. \tag{5.121}$$

Note that in this problem $\mathbf{M}$ is defined by (5.113) and hence both $\mathbf{M}$ and $\mathbf{M}^{-1}$ may be evaluated before making any observations. This is in contrast to the second-order algorithm (5.87) for estimating the discriminant functions. If the basis functions $\phi_1(x), \ldots, \phi_K(x)$ are orthonormal, $\mathbf{M} = \mathbf{I}$ and algorithm (5.120) and (5.121) are essentially the same.

A stochastic approximation algorithm using a mean square criterion,

$$J(\omega) = E[(f(x) - \omega^T\boldsymbol{\phi}(x))^2] = \int f(x)[f(x) - \omega^T\boldsymbol{\phi}(x)]^2\,dx, \tag{5.122}$$

for the estimation of the probability density function $f(x)$ has also been developed (Kashyap and Blaydon, 1968). The algorithm is more complex than (5.120) mainly in the fact that at each iteration, n samples, $x_{i-n+1}, \ldots, x_i$ are used for the recursive estimation. Similar algorithms can be developed for estimating the probability distribution function. Kashap and Blaydon presented an experimental example where a probability distribution function

$$F(x) = 1 - \exp(-x), \qquad x \geqslant 0,$$

was approximated by the first three terms of the Laguerre polynomials,

$$\begin{aligned}\phi_1(x) &= 1,\\ \phi_2(x) &= -x + 1,\\ \phi_3(x) &= \frac{x^2}{2} - 2x + 1.\end{aligned} \tag{5.123}$$

The approximation was intended for the region $0 \leqslant x \leqslant 4$ only, using the mean-square criterion, and at each iteration, $n = 400$, i.e., the last 400 samples were stored and used for the estimation. The algorithm converged to the correct values after several hundred iterations. As predicted by theory, the second-order algorithm converges faster than the first-order algorithm.

5.5.2 Gaussian mixture estimation and approximation

Let us assume that the unknown one-dimensional probability density function $f(x)$ may be approximated with sufficient accuracy by a set of K Gaussian density functions

$$\hat{f}(x) = \sum_{k=1}^{K} c_k g(x; m_k, r_k), \tag{5.124}$$

where $\hat{f}(x)$ is the estimate of $f(x)$ and $g(x; m_k, r_k)$ is a Gaussian density function with mean m_k and variance r_k. The set of coefficients $\{c_k\}$ satisfy the constraints,

$$c_k \geqslant 0, \qquad \sum_{k=1}^{K} c_k = 1, \tag{5.125}$$

and it is noted that under these constraints, the estimate $\hat{f}(x)$ is indeed a probability density function, i.e.,

$$\hat{f}(x) \geqslant 0, \qquad \int \hat{f}(x)\, dx = 1. \tag{5.126}$$

This is an advantage over the linear approximation, where the estimate may not be a legitimate density function. The problem is to estimate from the sequence of independent samples $x_1, x_2, \ldots,$ the values of c_k, m_k, and r_k, and a stochastic approximation algorithm will be developed for this nonlinear estimation problem. The algorithm will seek the set of parameter values that maximizes the regression function

$$J_0 = E[\log \hat{f}(x)] = \int f(x) \log \hat{f}(x)\, dx. \tag{5.127}$$

The estimation criterion (5.127) may be discussed from two slightly different points of view. If there is prior knowledge to indicate that the true density function is indeed a linear combination of K Gaussian densities, J_0 is simply interpreted as the expected value of the log-likelihood function, and the stochastic approximation algorithm that maximizes J_0 is asymptotically a maximum likelihood estimator. In unsupervised learning, the unclassified patterns are assumed drawn from a mixture of density functions, and the mixture is often assumed to be a Gaussian mixture.

When we have no knowledge as to the functional form of the true density function $f(x)$, it is desirable to have an error criterion. Let

$$J_1 = E\left[\log \frac{f(x)}{\hat{f}(x)}\right] = \int f(x) \log \frac{f(x)}{\hat{f}(x)} dx. \tag{5.128}$$

It will be shown in lemma 6.2 that

$$J_1 \geqslant 0,$$

with equality if and only if $f(x) = \hat{f}(x)$ for almost all x, and hence J_1 is a proper error criterion. Since $\int f(x) \log f(x)\, dx$ is independent of c_k, m_k, and r_k, it is obvious that maximizing J_0 is equivalent to minimizing the error criterion J_1.

A major question that arises in an approximation problem is that of the completeness of the basis functions. Normally, completeness is defined in terms of integral-square error and the class of square integrable functions. Since we are primarily interested in the approximation of density functions using J_1 as an error criterion, the completeness should be discussed in terms of J_1. Let us first consider the empirical estimation of the density function from a set of independent observations $x_1, x_2, \ldots, x_n$:

$$\hat{f}_n(x) = \frac{1}{n} \sum_{k=1}^{n} g(x; x_k, \alpha_n^2), \tag{5.129}$$

where the variance α_n^2 depends on the number of observations n. We remark that (5.129) is a special case of (5.124) with $c_k = 1/n$, $m_k = x_k$ and $r_k = \alpha_n^2$.

The estimate $\hat{f}_n(x)$ is a random function because of its dependence on the random observations. It has been shown in chapter 3 that if $\alpha_n \to 0$ and $n\alpha_n \to \infty$ as $n \to \infty$, then $\hat{f}_n(x)$ will have mean $f(x)$ and zero variance at all points x of continuity of $f(x)$. Therefore, for the class of continuous probability density functions,

$$\lim_{n\to\infty} \int f(x) \log \frac{f(x)}{\hat{f}_n(x)} dx = 0 \tag{5.130}$$

for almost all $\hat{f}_n(x)$. The estimate $\hat{f}_n(x)$ is a Gaussian mixture as shown in (5.129), and (5.130) indicates that there exist $\hat{f}_n(x)$ such that J_1 approaches zero as n approaches infinity. Therefore, any continuous density function $f(x)$ can be approximated by a Gaussian mixture with J_1 arbitrarily close to zero, and the set of Gaussian density functions is "complete" in this sense.

We remark that (5.124) is used instead of (5.129), since the empirical estimation will require an extremely large number of storage spaces, and since we expect that in many practical cases a small number of Gaussian densities will provide a reasonably good approximation.

Let us denote $r_k^{-1/2}$ by q_k, $g(x; m_k, r_k)$ by g_k and the i-th estimate of $f(x)$ by $\hat{f}(i)$. The Robbins–Monro algorithm for estimating the Gaussian mixture is

$$m_k(i+1) = m_k(i) + a_i \frac{\partial}{\partial m_k} \log \hat{f}(i)\Big|_{x=x_i}, k = 1, 2, \ldots, K,$$

$$q_k(i+1) = q_k(i) + a_i \frac{\partial}{\partial q_k} \log \hat{f}(i)\Big|_{x=x_i}, k = 1, 2, \ldots, K, \tag{5.131}$$

$$c_k(i+1) = c_k(i) + a_i \frac{\partial}{\partial c_k} \log \hat{f}(i)\Big|_{x=x_i}, k = 1, 2, \ldots, K-1,$$

with

$$\frac{\partial}{\partial m_k} \log \hat{f} = \frac{1}{\hat{f}} c_k q_k^2 (x - m_k) g_k,$$

$$\frac{\partial}{\partial q_k} \log \hat{f} = \frac{1}{\hat{f}} c_k \left[\frac{1}{q_k} - q_k (x - m_k)^2 \right] g_k, \tag{5.132}$$

$$\frac{\partial}{\partial c_k} \log \hat{f} = \frac{1}{\hat{f}} [g_k - g_K].$$

In algorithm (5.131), $\hat{f}(i)$ is evaluated at $x = x_i$, and the constraint that $\sum_{k=1}^K c_k = 1$ has been taken into account.

It is noted that by letting

$$d_k = \sum_{j=1}^{k-1} c_j, \qquad d_1 = 0,$$

the constraints on c_k may be rewritten as

$$0 \leqslant c_k \leqslant 1 - d_k = 1 - \sum_{j=1}^{k-1} c_j, \qquad k = 1, 2, \ldots, K-1,$$

$$c_K = 1 - d_K = 1 - \sum_{j=1}^{K-1} c_j.$$

We also note that (5.132) does not behave well at some points of the parameter space. For instance, $(\partial/\partial q_k)\log \hat{f}$ approaches infinity as q_k approaches zero. Likewise, when c_k is close to zero,

$$\frac{\partial}{\partial c_k} \log \hat{f}(i)\bigg|_{x=x_i} = [\sum_{j=1}^{K} c_j g_j(x_i)]^{-1}[g_k(x_i) - g_K(x_i)]$$

may become very large if at $x = x_i$, $g_k(x_i) \gg g_j(x_i), j \neq k$. This will happen when the true c_k is small and the true m_k is far apart from other mean values. To avoid this difficulty and to satisfy the constraints, we introduce two new variables,

$$\begin{aligned} \rho_k &= q_k - \frac{1}{q_k}, \qquad 0 < q_k < \infty, \\ q_k &= \frac{1}{2}\left(\rho_k + \sqrt{\rho_k^2 + 4}\right), \end{aligned} \tag{5.133}$$

and

$$\begin{aligned} \gamma_k &= \frac{2c_k - (1 - d_k)}{c_k(1 - d_k - c_k)}, \qquad 0 \leqslant c_k \leqslant 1 - d_k, \\ c_k &= \frac{1}{2\gamma_k}\left[(1 - d_k)\gamma_k - 2 + \sqrt{(1 - d_k)^2\gamma_k^2 + 4}\right]. \end{aligned} \tag{5.134}$$

The variables ρ_k and γ_k are monotonically increasing functions of q_k and c_k, respectively. Equation (5.133) maps the open interval $(0, \infty)$ into the interval $(-\infty, \infty)$, while (5.134) maps the closed interval $[0, 1 - d_k]$ into the interval $[-\infty, \infty]$ for each c_k. Therefore, with the algorithm expressed in terms of the new variables,

$$\begin{aligned} m_k(i + 1) &= m_k(i) + a_i \frac{\partial}{\partial \mu_k} \log \hat{f}(i)\bigg|_{x=x_i}, \\ \rho_k(i + 1) &= \rho_k(i) + a_i\left[\frac{\partial q_k(i)}{\partial \rho_k} \frac{\partial}{\partial q_k} \log \hat{f}(i)\right]\bigg|_{x=x_i}, \\ \gamma_k(i + 1) &= \gamma_k(i) + a_i\left[\sum_{l=k}^{K-1} \frac{\partial c_l(i)}{\partial \gamma_k} \frac{\partial}{\partial c_l} \log \hat{f}(i)\right]\bigg|_{x=x_i}, \end{aligned} \tag{5.135}$$

the constraints on q_k and c_k are automatically satisfied. Algorithm (5.135) is evaluated by means of (5.132), (5.133), (5.134) and the relationships

$$\frac{\partial q_k}{\partial \rho_k} = \frac{1}{2}\left[1 + \frac{\rho_k}{\sqrt{\rho_k^2 + 4}}\right],$$

$$\frac{\partial c_k}{\partial \gamma_k} = \frac{1}{\gamma_k^2}\left[1 - \frac{2}{\sqrt{(1 - d_k)^2 \gamma_k^2 + 4}}\right], \tag{5.136}$$

$$\frac{\partial c_l}{\partial l_k} = -\frac{1}{2}\sum_{j=k}^{l-1} \frac{\partial c_j}{\partial \delta_k}\left[1 + \frac{(1 - d_l)\gamma_l}{\sqrt{(1 - d_l)^2 \gamma_l^2 + 4}}\right], \qquad k < l < k,$$

which exist for all values of ρ_k and γ_k.

The algorithm will converge, but possibly to a local maximum of J_o, because of the nonlinearity of the problem (Young and Coraluppi, 1970). One possible way to avoid the difficulty of local maxima is to assume that the global maximum is located in a known convex region of the parameter space, and that it is the only stationary point in this region. Whenever the estimation moves out of this region, it is simply brought back to the nearest boundary, similar to the truncated algorithm in the one-dimensional case. With this modification, the algorithm (5.135) will converge to the global maximum. When such prior knowledge is lacking, one must resort to the parallel application of the algorithm to a set of different initial estimates, and then make the choice by comparing the values of J_o for the different initial estimates. The regression function J_o may be evaluated from the recursive algorithm

$$J_0(i + 1) = J_0(i) + a_i[\log \hat{f}(i) - J_0(i)]\Big|_{x=x_i}. \tag{5.137}$$

A computer simulation was performed by Young and Coraluppi for the estimation of a mixture of three Gaussian density functions while the true density function consisted of two Gaussian densities only. An algorithm that was slightly different from algorithm (5.135) was used, and the sequence of samples was generated by a Gaussian random-number generator. The true density function was

$$f(x) = 0.5g(x; 0, 1) + 0.5g(x; 3, 1),$$

and the initial estimate was

$$\hat{f}(1) = 0.33g(x; -0.29, 0.74) + 0.33g(x; 1.59, 1.56) + 0.34g(x; 3.31, 0.85).$$

The estimates at 1000, 5000, and 10000 iterations were

$$\hat{f}(1000) = 0.35g(x; -0.23, 0.88) + 0.40g(x; 1.90, 2.75) + 0.25g(x; 2.93, 1.41),$$

$$\hat{f}(5000) = 0.45g(x; 0.04, 1.10) + 0.53g(x; 2.74, 1.34) + 0.02g(x; 3.57, 0.50),$$

$$\hat{f}(10000) = 0.49g(x; 0.01, 0.98) + 0.51g(x; 2.98, 1.12) + 0.$$

The following results were also obtained

$$f(x) = 0.50g(x; 0, 1) + 0.50g(x; 1, 1),$$

$$\hat{f}(1) = 0.33g(x; 1, 1) + 0.33g(x; 2, 0.25) + 0.34g(x; 4, 16),$$

$$\hat{f}(1000) = 0.59g(x; 0.10, 1.66) + 0.33g(x; 1.25, 0.64) + 0.08g(x; 2.35, 3.56),$$

$$\hat{f}(5000) = 0.52g(x; 0.11, 0.90) + 0.48g(x; 1.08, 0.85) + 0,$$

$$\hat{f}(10000) = 0.50g(x; -0.11, 0.92) + 0.50g(x; 1.12, 0.92) + 0.$$

The experimental results are interesting because they represent a general mixture approach for unsupervised learning with all parameters unknown. They also demonstrate the application of stochastic approximation to a complicated nonlinear problem. The convergence rate is more than ten times slower then the rate obtained in the linear approximation. This is partially explained by the large number of unknowns in this example and by the nonlinearity of the problem.

The assumption of a Gaussian mixture is quite natural, and a multimode distribution can be approximated very well by a Gaussian mixture. An important property of a multidimensional Gaussian mixture is that its marginal densities are also Gaussian mixtures with lower dimensionality. Hence, algorithm (5.135) may be used to estimate the one-dimensional marginal densities, and the correlation coefficients may be estimated afterward based on the parameters of the marginal densities. In this way, the problem is divided into two stages, and the computational advantages should be obvious.

5.6 Notes and Remarks

Stochastic approximation was introduced by Robbins and Monro (1951) for finding the roots of a regression function. Robbins and Monro showed that the algorithm converges in the mean-square sense. Wolfwitz (1952) showed that under weaker conditions the algorithm converges in probability, and Blum (1954a) proved convergence with probability 1. Kiefer and Wolfwitz (1952) developed algorithms for finding the value of θ that corresponds to the maximum or minimum of a regression function. Both the Robbins–Monro and Kiefer–Wolfwitz algorithms were generalized to the multidimensional case by Blum (1954b). Dvoretzky (1956) formulated his algorithm in a very general manner and showed that the Robbins–Monro and Kiefer–Wolfwitz algorithms may be considered as special cases. The choice of gain sequences, the convergence conditions and convergence rates, and the asymptotic distributions of stochastic approximation algorithms were studied by many authors, including Albert and Gardner (1967), Burkholder (1956), Chung (1954), Dupac (1965), Fabian (1967), Gladyshev (1965), Hodges and Lehmann (1956), Kesten (1958), Sacks (1958), Schmetterer (1961), and Venter (1967a,b).

Stochastic approximation is attractive for engineering applications for several reasons. It is a recursive algorithm that processes the incoming samples one at a time without requiring storage spaces. The algorithm can easily be applied to nonlinear problems as well as to linear problems, and the computations are usually fairly simple. Although in some of the applications treated in this chapter we have assumed considerable prior knowledge, stochastic approximation can be applied in the absence of detailed prior knowledge. For example, in estimating the discriminant function, the probability distributions of the pattern classes are unknown, and essentially the only requirements are mild conditions on the basis functions. Furthermore, as discussed somewhat heuristically in section 5.2, the convergence rate of stochastic approximation is in fact optimum if we choose a proper gain sequence. On the other hand, for a small number of iterations, we may use the gain sequence specified by theorem 5.3, which was discussed by Dvoretzky (1956) and Block (1957).

In presenting the proofs of the convergence theorems, we were not concerned with the most general proof or the most elegant. Instead we selected those that are relatively simple to comprehend. The proof of theorem 5.1 is based on a paper by Sakrison (1966a), and theorem 5.2 is a much simplified version of Dvoretzky's theorem. The relationship between Bayes estimation and stochastic approximation is an extension of the work of Chien and Fu (1967). The estimation of parameters using $E[\log f]$ is based on the work of Sakrison (1966a) and Young and Westerberg (1971). The algorithm is asymptotically a maximum-likelihood estimator, and it is also asymptotically related to a Bayes estimator as discussed by Patrick and Costello (1970).

The method of potential function was proposed and investigated extensively by Aizerman et al. (1964-a,b,c), and theorem 5.5 follows Braverman (1965). Tsypkin (1965) pointed out the close relationship between the potential function method and stochastic approximation. In this country, stochastic approximation algorithms for pattern recognition were studied by Blaydon (1967), Cooper (1964), Kashyap and Blaydon (1966), Yau and Schumpert (1968), and others, and our presentation follows the report by Blaydon (1967). The section on stochastic estimation of probability density functions follows Kashyap and Blaydon (1968) and Young and Coraluppi (1970). Other works on the estimation of probability density functions and stochastic approximation algorithms for unsupervised learning include Chien and Fu (1967), Patrick and Costello (1969), Saridis et al. (1967), and Tyspkin (1966). Stochastic approximation is also applied to other areas, and some of the papers are listed in the references.

Problems

5.1 Show that the multidimensional Robbins–Monro algorithm (5.27) converges in the mean-square sense.

5.2 Express the Kiefer–Wolfwitz algorithm,

$$\omega(i+1) = \omega(i) - \frac{a_i}{b_i}[\xi_i(\omega(i) + b_i) - \xi_i(\omega(i) - b_i)]$$

as a special case of the Dvoretzky algorithm. Discuss the required conditions for convergence.

5.3 Let $\mathbf{x}_1, \mathbf{x}_2, \ldots,$ be a sequence of independent random vectors. The vectors are Gaussian distributed with zero mean and unknown covariance $\mathbf{R}$. Consider the algorithm

$$\mathbf{R}(i+1) = \mathbf{R}(i) + a_i[\mathbf{x}_i\mathbf{x}_i^T - \mathbf{R}(i)],$$

where $\mathbf{R}(i)$ is the i-th estimate of $\mathbf{R}$. Show that the algorithm converges to the true $\mathbf{R}$ in the mean-square sense and with probability 1.

5.4 Let $\mathbf{x}_1, \mathbf{x}_2, \ldots,$ be a sequence of independent random vectors, and

$$z_i = h(\mathbf{x}_i) + \eta_i.$$

At each stage i we can observe $\mathbf{x}_i$ and z_i, and the problem is to obtain a suitable approximation for the unknown function $h(\mathbf{x}_i)$. In other words, we wish an approximation based on the noisy observations z_i and the sample vector $\mathbf{x}_i$. The noise component η_i has zero mean, and $h(\mathbf{x})$ is to be approximated by a set of known basis functions $\phi_1(\mathbf{x}), \phi_2(\mathbf{x}), \ldots, \phi_K(\mathbf{x})$. Derive a stochastic approximation algorithm and determine the convergence conditions.

5.5 Consider the approximation of $h(x) = x^3$ by a linear form θx. Let x be a uniformly distributed random variable in the interval $[-1, 1]$, Using a sequence of independent samples $x_1, x_2, \ldots$, we construct the following algorithms:

$$\omega(i+1) = \omega(i) - a_i x_i[\omega(i)x_i - h(x_i)],$$

$$\omega(i+1) = \omega(i) - a_i x_i \operatorname{sgn}[\omega(i)x_i - h(x_i)],$$

$$\omega(i+1) = \omega(i) - a_i \operatorname{sgn}[x_i(\omega(i)x_i - h(x_i))].$$

Verify that all three algorithms converge and find the limiting value of $\omega(i)$ in all three cases.

5.6 Let x be a random variable with an exponential density function,

$$f(x) = \begin{cases} \theta e^{-\theta x}, & x \geqslant 0, \\ 0, & x < 0, \end{cases}$$

where the parameter θ is unknown. Let $x_1, x_2, \ldots, x_n$ be a sequence of independent samples. Find a maximum likelihood estimator for θ, and derive a stochastic approximation algorithm that is asymptotically a maximum likelihood estimator. Determine the convergence rate of the algorithm.

5.7 The upper bound on mean-square error (theorem 5.3) may be extended to time-varying regresssion functions. Let $\mu_i(\omega)$ be a regression function at the i-th iteration, and,

$$M_{1i}(\omega - \theta)^2 \leqslant \mu_i(\omega)(\omega - \theta) \leqslant M_{2i}(\omega - \theta)^2.$$

The other conditions are essentially the same as that of theorem 5.3. Determine a gain sequence for this case and derive the upper bound on the mean-square error.

5.8 Derive a stochastic approximation algorithm for the linear approximation of a distribution function $F(x)$. The algorithm uses a sequence of independent samples, and minimizes an integral error criterion

$$I(\omega) = \int_{u_1}^{u_2} [F(x) - \omega^T \phi(x)]^2 \, dx.$$

The basis functions $\phi_1(x), \phi_2(x), \ldots, \phi_K(x)$ are known, and the integral limits u_1 and u_2 are finite.

5.9 Consider an ensemble of stochastic signals $\{x(t), t_1 \leqslant t \leqslant t_2\}$. It is desired to approximate the ensemble by a set of basis functions $\phi(t; \theta_1)$,

$\phi(t; \theta_2), \ldots, \phi(t; \theta_K)$. The functional form of $\phi(t; \theta_k)$ is known but the parameter θ_k is not (for example, $\phi_k(t) = \phi(t; \theta_k) = e^{-\theta_k t}, 0 \leqslant t < \infty$). For a given signal $x(t)$, the set of coefficients $\{\alpha_k\}$ is obtained in such a way that the integral-square error

$$\begin{aligned}\varepsilon^2 &= \int_{t_1}^{t_2} [x(t) - \sum_{k=1}^{K} \alpha_k \phi(t; \theta_k)]^2 \, dt \\ &= \int_{t_1}^{t_2} [x(t) - \boldsymbol{\alpha}^T \boldsymbol{\phi}(t; \boldsymbol{\theta})]^2 \, dt,\end{aligned}$$

is minimized. Note that both $\boldsymbol{\alpha}$ and ε^2 are random, due to the randomness of $x(t)$. Since we wish to approximate the ensemble, we should find a $\boldsymbol{\theta}$ that minimizes $E[\min_{\boldsymbol{\alpha}} \varepsilon^2]$, where the expectation is over the ensemble of stochastic signals. Given a sequence of independent sample signals $x_1(t)$, $x_2(t), \ldots,$ derive a stochastic approximation algorithm for finding the optimal parameter vector $\boldsymbol{\theta}$.

5.10 Simulate the stochastic approximation algorithm for finding the discriminant function on a digitial computer. Let the probability density functions for the two classes of patterns be Gaussian with

$$\mathbf{m}_1 = \begin{bmatrix} 0 \\ 1 \end{bmatrix}, \quad \mathbf{R}_1 = \begin{bmatrix} 4 & 0 \\ 0 & 1 \end{bmatrix},$$

$$\mathbf{m}_2 = \begin{bmatrix} 1 \\ 0 \end{bmatrix}, \quad \mathbf{R}_2 = \begin{bmatrix} 1/4 & 0 \\ 0 & 4 \end{bmatrix}.$$

The prior probabilities of the two classes are the same, and the samples can be generated by means of random number generators with the classification of each sample assumed known. Find the quadratic discriminant function by simulation. Compare your result with the theoretical result obtained by hypothesis testing, and discuss the reasons for any discrepancies.

References

1. Aizerman, M. A., Braverman, E. M., and Rozonoer, L. I. 1964a. Theoretical foundations of the potential function method in pattern recognition learning. *Automat. i Telemech.* 25:917–936.

2. ———. 1964b. The probability problem of pattern recognition learning and the method of potential functions. *Automat i Telemech.* 25:1307–1323.

3. ———. 1964c. The method of potential functions for the problem of restoring the characteristic of a function converter from randomly observed points. *Automat. i Telemech.*, 26:1951–1954.

4. Albert, A. and Gardner, L. A. Jr. 1967. *Stochastic Approximation and Nonlinear Regression*. MIT Press, Cambridge, Massachusetts.

5. Blaydon, C. C. 1967. Recursive Algorithms for Pattern Classifications. Rept. No. 520, Harvard Univ., Cambridge, Massachusetts.

6. Block, H. D. 1957. Estimates of error for two modification of the Robbins–Monro stochastic approximation process. *Ann. Math. Stat.* 28:1003–1010.

7. Blum, J. R. 1954a. Approximation method which converges with probability one. *Ann. Math. Stat.* 25:382–386.

8. ———. 1954b. Multidimensional stochastic approximation procedure. *Ann. Math. Stat.* 25:737–744.

9. Braverman, E. M. 1965. On the method of potential functions. *Automat. i. Telemech.* 26:2205–2213.

10. Burkholder, D. 1956. On a class of stochastic approximation processes. *Ann. Math. Stat.* 27:1044–1059.

11. Chien, Y. T. and Fu, K. S. 1967. On Bayesian Learning and Stochastic Approximation. *IEEE Trans. Systems Science and Cybernetics* SSC-3:28–38.

12. ———. 1969. Stochastic Learning of Time Varying Parameters in Random Environment. *IEEE Trans. Systems Science and Cybernetics* SSC-5:237–246.

13. Chung, K. L. 1954. On a stochastic approximation method. *Ann. Math. Stat.* 25:463–483.

14. Cooper, D. B. 1964. Adaptive pattern recognition and signal detection using stochastic approximation. *IEEE Trans. Electronic Computers*, EC-13:306–307.

15. Coraluppi, G. and Young, T. Y. 1969. Stochastic signal representation. *IEEE Trans. Circuit Theory*, CT-16:155–161.

16. Davisson, L. D. and Schwartz, S. C. 1970. Analysis of a decision-directed receiver with unknown priors. *IEEE Trans. Information Theory* IT-16:270–276.

17. Dupac, V. 1965. A dynamic stochastic approximation method. *Ann. Math. Stat.* 36:1695–1701.

18. Dvoretzky, A. 1956. On stochastic approximation. *Proc. 3rd Berkeley Symp. Math. Stat. and Prob.* pp. 39–55. Univ. of Calif. Press, Berkeley, California.

19. Fabian, V. 1967. Stochastic approximation of minima with improved asymptotic speed. *Ann. Math. Stat.* 38:191–200.

20. Farjo, A. A. 1972. Analysis and design of decision-directed estimation schemes using stochastic approximation. Ph. D. Dissertation, Carnegie-Mellon Univ., Pittsburgh, Pennsylvania.

21. Gladyshev, E. G. 1965. On stochastic approximation. *Theory Prob. and Its Applic.* 10:275–278.

22. Hodges, J. L. Jr. and Lehmann, E. L. 1956. Two approximations to the Robbins–Monro process. *Proc. 3rd Berkeley Symp. Math. Stat. and Prob.*, pp 95–104. Univ. of Calif. Press, Berkeley, California.

23. Kashyap, R. L. and Blaydon, C. C. 1966. Recovery of functions from noisy measurements taken at randomly selected points and its application to pattern classification. *Proc. IEEE*, 54:1127–1129.

24. ———. 1968. Estimation of probability density and distribution functions. *IEEE Trans. Information Theory*, IT-14:549–556.

25. Kashyap, R. L., Blaydon, C. C., and Fu, K. S. 1970. Stochastic approximation. *Adaptive, Learning and Pattern Recognition Systems.* eds. J. M. Mendel and K. S. Fu, pp. 329–355 Academic Press, New York.

26. Katopis, A. and Schwartz, S. C. 1972. Decision-directed learning using stochastic approximation. *Proc. Modeling and Simulation Conf.* 473–481.

27. Kesten, H. 1958. Accelerated stochastic approximation method. *Ann. Math. Stat.* 29:41–59.

28. Kiefer J. and Wolfwitz, J. 1952. Stochastic estimation of the maximum of a regression function, *Ann. Math. Stat.* 23:462–466.

29. Nikolic, Z. J. and Fu, K. S. 1966. Algorithm for learning without external supervision and its applications to learning control systems. *IEEE Trans. Automatic Control* AC-11:414–422.

30. Parzen, E. 1962. On estimation of a probability density function and mode. *Ann. Math. Stat.* 33:1065–1076.

31. Patrick, E. A. and Costello, J. P. 1969. Unsupervised estimation and processing of unknown signals. Rept. TR-EE69-18, Purdue Univ., Lafayette, Indiana.

32. ———. 1970. On unsupervised estimation algorithms. *IEEE Trans. Information Theory*, IT-16:556–569.

33. Robbins, H. and Monro, S. 1951. A stochastic approximation method. *Ann. Math. Stat.*, 22:400–407.

34. Sacks J. 1958. Asymptotic distribution of stochastic approximation procedures. *Ann. Math. Stat.* 29:373–386.

35. Sakrison, D. J. 1964. A continuous Kiefer–Wolfwitz procedure for random processes. *Ann. Math. Stat.* 35:590–599.

36. ———. 1965. Efficient recursive estimation: application to estimating the parameters of a covariance function. *Intern. J. Engr. Sci.* 3:461–483.

37. ———. 1966a. Stochastic approximation: a recursive method for solving regression functions. *Advances in Communication Systems*, Vol. 2, ed., A. V. Balakrishnan, pp. 51–106. Academic Press, New York.

38. ———. 1966b. Efficient recursive estimation of the parameters of a radar or radio astronomy target. *IEEE Trans. Information Theory*, IT-12:35–41.

39. Saridis, G. N., Nikolic, Z. J., and Fu, K. S. 1967. Stochastic approximation algorithms for system identification, estimation and decomposition of mixtures. *Proc. 5th Symp. Circuit and System Theory*, Allerton, Illinois.

40. Schalkwijk, J. P. M. and Kailath, T. 1966. A coding scheme for additive noise channels with feedback—Part I: no bandwidth constraint. *IEEE Trans. Information Theory*, IT-12:172–182.

41. Schmetterer, L. 1961. Stochastic Approximation. *Proc. 4th Berkeley Symp. Math. Stat. and Prob.*. Univ. of Calif. Press, Berkeley, California.

42. Tsypkin, Ya. Z. 1965. Establishing characteristics of a function transformer from randomly observed points. *Automat. i Telemech.* 26:1947–1950.

43. ———. 1966. Use of the stochastic approximation method in estimating unknown distribution densities from observations. *Automat. i Telemech.* 27:432–434.

44. Venter, J. H. 1967a. An extension of the Robbins–Monro procedure. *Ann. Math. Stat.* 38:181–190.

45. ———. 1967b. On the convergence of the Kiefer–Wolfwitz approximation procedure. *Ann. Math. Stat.* 38:1031–1036.

46. Wagner, T. J. 1968. The Rate of convergence of an algorithm for recovering functions from noisy measurement taken at randomly selected points. *IEEE Trans. Systems Science and Cybernetic* SSC-4:151–154.

47. Wolfwitz, J. 1952. On the stochastic approximation method of Robbins and Monro. *Ann. Math. Stat.* 23:457–461.

48. Wolverton, C. T. and Rawgen, J. T. 1968. A Counterexample to Dvoretzky's stochastic approximation theorem. *IEEE Trans. Information Theory*, 14:157–158.

49. Yau, S. S. and Schumpert, J. M. 1968. Design of pattern classifiers with the updating property using stochastic approximation techniques. *IEEE Trans. Computers* C-17:861–872.

50. Young, T. Y. and Coraluppi, G. 1970. Stochastic estimation of a mixture of normal density functions using an information criterion *IEEE Trans. Information Theory* IT-16:258–263.

51. Young, T. Y. and Farjo, A. A. 1972. On decision-directed estimation and stochastic approximation. *IEEE Trans. Information Theory* IT-18:671–673.

52. Young, T. Y. and Westerberg, R. A. 1971. Error bounds for stochastic estimation of signal parameters. *IEEE Trans. Information Theory* IT-17:549–557.

53. ———. 1972. Stochastic approximation with a nonstationary regression function. *IEEE Trans. Information Theory* IT-18:518–519.

54. ———. 1973. Stochastic estimation of signal parameters with a nonstationary regression function. *Intern. J. Electronics* 34:369–380.

6

Feature Extraction Theory

6.1 Feature Extraction and Feature Selection

As shown in figure 6.1, the problem of pattern recognition may be divided into two stages, feature extraction and classification. Let $\Omega_{\mathbf{x}}$ be an N-dimensional pattern space and $\Omega_{\mathbf{y}}$ be an M-dimensional feature space, typically with $M < N$. A *feature extractor* is a linear or nonlinear transformation that maps an N-vector $\mathbf{x}$ in $\Omega_{\mathbf{x}}$ into an M-vector $\mathbf{y}$ in $\Omega_{\mathbf{y}}$,

$$\mathbf{y} = \mathcal{T}(\mathbf{x}), \quad \mathbf{x} \text{ in } \Omega_{\mathbf{x}}, \quad \mathbf{y} \text{ in } \Omega_{\mathbf{y}}. \tag{6.1}$$

It should be noted that since typically $M < N$, the mapping is not one-to-one, and the inverse $\mathcal{T}^{-1}(\mathbf{y})$ is not unique. *Feature selection* is a special case of feature extraction, where the M components of $\mathbf{y}$ are a subset of the N components of $\mathbf{x}$.

The terms "feature" and "measurement" are sometimes used indistinguishably in the literature. In this chapter we associate measurements with the pattern space. The *selection of measurements* is based on our prior knowledge or experience on the particular pattern recognition problem, and the pattern space $\Omega_{\mathbf{x}}$ is defined by the measurements we select. Feature extraction or selection is, on the other hand, essentially a scheme that reduces the dimensionality from N to M. The measurements are usually selected by an individual prior to processing, while feature extraction is implemented automatically by the machine.

This chapter deals with the theory of feature extraction. It is assumed that the question of what to measure has been settled, or equivalently, the pattern space $\Omega_{\mathbf{x}}$ has been defined. Pattern vectors and/or their properties are available, and the problem is to select a suitable transformation $\mathcal{T}$. It is desirable to have a transformation that maximizes or minimizes a certain criterion, and a major theoretical question is which criteria are reasonable and physically meaningful for feature extraction.

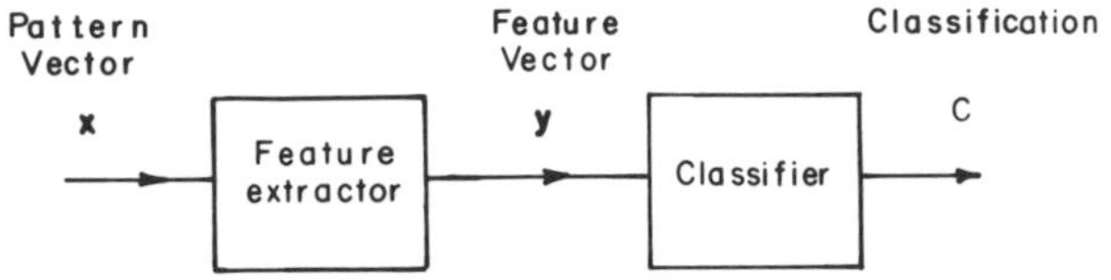

fig. 6.1 Block diagram of a pattern recognition system.

It should be emphasized that the discussion above does not mean that measurement selection is unimportant. On the contrary, the success or failure of a pattern recognition project depends largely on the selection of which measurements to make. The difficulty in systematically discussing the measurement selection is that it is inseparable from the particular pattern recognition problem under consideration. Consider the electrocardiogram classification problem and character recognition. The two kinds of measurements for the two problems are certainly different, and their selection is based on different physical reasons. Yet, once the measurements have been selected, the same feature extraction and classification techniques could be used for both cases. In the next two chapters we discuss the electrocardiogram classification problem and the character recognition problem in some detail, and an important part of the material deals with specific ways for measurement selection and feature extraction.

6.1.1 Linear feature extraction

A linear feature extractor is defined as an $M \times N$ matrix $\mathbf{T}$,

$$\mathbf{y} = \mathbf{T}\mathbf{x} \tag{6.2}$$

where the row vectors of $\mathbf{T}$ are linearly independent. Note that in (6.2) we neglect a constant term that represents linear translation. Except in the last section, we shall be concerned mostly with linear feature extraction simply because nonlinear transformations are difficult to handle.

A commonly used method in character recognition is the mask or template matching, which is essentially linear feature extraction. If a two-dimensional image is considered to be made up of N discrete points, it can then be represented as an N-dimensional vector $\mathbf{x}$, where the value of the i-th component is the density of the i-th point on the image. Then a mask for this image can also be written as an N-dimensional vector, say $\mathbf{v}$, and the operation of matching the pattern to the mask is $\mathbf{v}^T\mathbf{x}$. If there are M masks, $\mathbf{v}_1, \mathbf{v}_2, \ldots, \mathbf{v}_M$, we have (6.2) with

$$\mathbf{T}^T = [\mathbf{v}_1, \mathbf{v}_2, \ldots, \mathbf{v}_M].$$

Thus the linear feature extractor $\mathbf{T}$ is just the collection of M masks. The advantage of masks is that they can be applied optically to the images.

In other applications, linear feature extraction in the form of (6.2) is simply a computation scheme separated from the classification. One might ask in this case why it is necessary to use linear feature extraction. If a linear classifier is used in cascade to the feature extractor, the discriminant function becomes

$$D(\mathbf{y}) = \boldsymbol{\theta}^T\mathbf{y} = \boldsymbol{\theta}^T\mathbf{T}\mathbf{x}. \tag{6.3}$$

Thus, instead of finding the $M \times N$ matrix $\mathbf{T}$ and the M-vector $\boldsymbol{\theta}^T$ separately, why not find the N-vector $\boldsymbol{\theta}^T\mathbf{T}$ directly, which seems computationally simpler? We first note that the relative simplicity of calculating $\boldsymbol{\theta}^T\mathbf{T}$ is deceptive. If we use stochastic approximation algorithms or perceptron-type algorithms to find the linear discriminant function, the convergence is usually slower in an N-space than in an M-space, especially if N is much larger than M. If, on the other hand, we choose a linear transformation method, as discussed in section 4.4, it is necessary to take the inverse of a $N \times N$ matrix, and the computational complexity is about the same as calculating $\mathbf{T}$ and $\boldsymbol{\theta}$ separately.

Since feature extraction reduces the dimensionality, obviously some of the information contained in the pattern space $\Omega_{\mathbf{x}}$ is lost. But one may be willing to use feature extraction for one of the following reasons.

(1) The feature space $\Omega_{\mathbf{y}}$ is physically more meaningful than $\Omega_{\mathbf{x}}$. For example, it is well known that in speech analysis, the frequency spectrum is more meaningful than the speech waveform. A Fourier transform may be taken, and the frequency components are better features for classification than are the features in time domain. The dimensionality may be reduced by combining some of the frequency components and neglecting the phase information.

(2) There may be prior knowledge that the measurements are redundant and the data are highly correlated. Then, the dimensionality may be reduced with very little loss of information.

(3) The measurements and the classification are performed at different locations, and it is necessary to transmit the data over a communication channel.

(4) There is very little prior knowledge of the pattern vectors, and it is desirable to use complicated learning techniques such as the estimation of probability density functions. Such techniques are

often difficult to apply to the data in a high-dimensional space, and it becomes imperative to reduce the dimensionality first. After learning in an M-space, one may then increase the dimensionality and estimate the additional parameters.

In linear feature extraction, the *feature space* $\Omega_{\mathbf{y}}$ is a subspace of $\Omega_{\mathbf{x}}$, and it is sometimes convenient to define a *complementary space* $\Omega_{\mathbf{z}}$ as the subspace of $\Omega_{\mathbf{x}}$ that is complementary to $\Omega_{\mathbf{y}}$. For any pattern vector $\mathbf{x}$ in $\Omega_{\mathbf{x}}$, we may write

$$\mathbf{y} = \mathbf{T}\mathbf{x}, \quad \mathbf{z} = \mathbf{S}\mathbf{x}, \quad \mathbf{y}^T\mathbf{z} = 0. \tag{6.4}$$

The matrices $\mathbf{T}$ and $\mathbf{S}$ are $M \times N$ and $(N - M) \times N$ singular matrices, but the $N \times N$ matrix $[\mathbf{T}^T, \mathbf{S}^T]$ is nonsingular. It is convenient to assume that the matrix $[\mathbf{T}^T, \mathbf{S}^T]$ represents an *orthogonal transformation*, i.e., each row vector of $\mathbf{T}$ and $\mathbf{S}$ is normalized and orthogonal to the remaining $(n - 1)$ row vectors, and $\mathbf{T}$ and $\mathbf{S}$ are projection operators. This assumption is made throughout the chapter unless it is stated otherwise.

The problem of linear feature extraction is to find a $\mathbf{T}$ such that much of the "information" contained in $\Omega_{\mathbf{x}}$ is preserved in $\Omega_{\mathbf{y}}$. The term "information" is used rather vaguely here.

6.1.2 Feature selection

Feature selection may be regarded as a special case of linear feature extraction. We wish to select as the M components of $\mathbf{y}$ a subset of the N components of $\mathbf{x}$. In other words, the M features selected are a subset of the N measurements. Thus, (6.2) holds for this case with each of the M row vectors of $\mathbf{T}$ consisting of a one-element and $(N - 1)$ zero-elements. Note that the procedure is regarded as feature selection rather than measurement selection, the latter being a selection procedure that defines the N measurements.

The features are selected by finding which M of the N measurements minimize the error probability or some other reasonable selection criteria. The calculation of the criterion is usually based on the available pattern vectors or the known probability densities of the pattern classes. Except in a few very special cases, the optimal selection can only be done by testing all possible sets of M features chosen from the N measurements, i.e., by applying the criterion $\binom{N}{M} = N!/M!(N - M)!$ times. The difficulty is that this often results in excessive computation. Consider the case where 10 features are to be selected from 60 measurements. Then the selection criterion must be calculated $60!/10!\,50! > 7.5 \times 10^{10}$ times. Even if the criterion could be calculated 1000 times per second, we should still require 7.5×10^7 seconds of machine time, i.e., more than 20,800 hours. Since even this modest problem is infeasible, it is obvious that heuristic approaches must be employed. We shall not go into the details of various heuristic approaches.

It is interesting to note that in many cases, feature extraction is easier to calculate than feature selection. This is because of the additional constraint imposed on $\mathbf{T}$ for feature selection.

6.2 The Karhunen–Loève Expansion

The best known and most useful feature extraction scheme is the Karhunen–Loève expansion. It minimizes a mean-square criterion.

Consider a set of pattern vectors $\mathbf{x}$ with probability density function

$$f(\mathbf{x}) = \sum_{k=1}^{K} p_k f_k(\mathbf{x}), \tag{6.5}$$

where p_k is the prior probability of the class C_k, $f_k(\mathbf{x})$ is the conditional density of $\mathbf{x}$ for given C_k, and the number of classes K is usually greater than 2. We assume without loss of generality that $E[\mathbf{x}] = \mathbf{0}$, since a random vector with nonzero mean can be transformed into one with zero mean by translation, which is a linear operation. Then the covariance matrix $\mathbf{R}$ is

$$\mathbf{R} = E[\mathbf{x}\mathbf{x}^T] = \sum_{k=1}^{K} p_k E_k[\mathbf{x}\mathbf{x}^T], \tag{6.6}$$

where $E_k[\cdot]$ denotes the expectation over the pattern vectors of class C_k. The Karhunen–Loève expansion is an expansion of the random vector $\mathbf{x}$ in terms of the eigenvectors of $\mathbf{R}$.

6.2.1 The eigenvalue problem

The eigenvalue problem is well known. Given an $N \times N$ matrix $\mathbf{R}$, we wish to determine the scalars λ and the nonzero vectors $\mathbf{u}$, which simultaneously satisfy the equation

$$\mathbf{R}\mathbf{u} = \lambda\mathbf{u}. \tag{6.7}$$

The solutions, λ and $\mathbf{u}$, are called eigenvalues and eigenvectors, respectively. The following lemma on the properties of eigenvectors is useful.

LEMMA 6.1

Let λ_j and $\mathbf{u}_j$ be the j-th eigenvalue and eigenvector of $\mathbf{R}$ satisfying the eigenequation (6.7). If $\mathbf{R}$ is symmetric and positive semidefinite, then

$$\lambda_j \geqslant 0, \tag{6.8}$$

$$\mathbf{u}_j^T \mathbf{u}_l = 0 \text{ if } \lambda_j \neq \lambda_l. \tag{6.9}$$

Proof

Since $\mathbf{u}_j$ satisfies (6.7),

$$\mathbf{u}_j^T \mathbf{R} \mathbf{u}_j = \lambda_j \mathbf{u}_j^T \mathbf{u}_j \geqslant 0$$

due to the positive semidefiniteness of $\mathbf{R}$. We are not interested in the case that $\mathbf{u}_j$ is a zero vector, and hence $\mathbf{u}_j^T \mathbf{u}_j > 0$ and $\lambda_j \geqslant 0$. For two eigenvalues λ_j and λ_l,

$$\mathbf{u}_l^T \mathbf{R} \mathbf{u}_j = \lambda_j \mathbf{u}_l^T \mathbf{u}_j,$$

$$\mathbf{u}_j^T \mathbf{R} \mathbf{u}_l = \lambda_l \mathbf{u}_j^T \mathbf{u}_l.$$

Since $\mathbf{R}$ is symmetric,

$$(\mathbf{u}_l^T \mathbf{R} \mathbf{u}_j)^T = \mathbf{u}_j^T \mathbf{R} \mathbf{u}_l = \lambda_l \mathbf{u}_j^T \mathbf{u}_l.$$

Hence

$$(\lambda_j - \lambda_l)\mathbf{u}_j^T \mathbf{u}_l = 0, \tag{6.10}$$

and $\lambda_j \neq \lambda_l$ implies $\mathbf{u}_j^T \mathbf{u}_l = 0$.

It is easy to verify that the covariance matrix $\mathbf{R}$ defined by (6.6) is symmetric and positive semidefinite, and its eigenvalues and eigenvectors have the properties in lemma 6.1. We are not interested in the case that $\mathbf{R}$ has a rank less than N, and simply assume that $\mathbf{R}$ is positive definite. It is noted that if $\mathbf{u}$ is a solution of the eigenequation (6.7) $c\mathbf{u}$ is also a solution for an arbitrary constant c, hence $\mathbf{u}_j$ can be normalized, $\mathbf{u}_j^T \mathbf{u}_j = 1$. If $\lambda_j = \lambda_l$, any linear combination of $\mathbf{u}_j$ and $\mathbf{u}_l$ also satisfies (6.7), and we can always select two orthogonal vectors from the linear combinations. Thus, we have for the covariance matrix $\mathbf{R}$ a set of N orthonormal eigenvectors $\mathbf{u}_1, \mathbf{u}_2, \ldots, \mathbf{u}_N$ with eigenvalues $\lambda_1 \geqslant \lambda_2 \geqslant \cdots \geqslant \lambda_N > 0$.

6.2.2 Optimality of the Karhunen–Loève expansion

Let us consider feature extraction and use the notation

$$\mathbf{T}^T = [\mathbf{v}_1, \mathbf{v}_2, \ldots, \mathbf{v}_M],$$
$$\mathbf{S}^T = [\mathbf{v}_{M+1}, \mathbf{v}_{M+2}, \ldots, \mathbf{v}_N], \tag{6.11}$$

where $\{\mathbf{v}_j\}$ is a set of orthonormal vectors. If we expand $\mathbf{x}$ in terms of $\{\mathbf{v}_j\}$, we have

$$\mathbf{x} = \sum_{j=1}^{N} c_j \mathbf{v}_j, \tag{6.12}$$

with the coefficients

$$c_j = \mathbf{x}^T \mathbf{v}_j. \tag{6.13}$$

Note that c_j is a random variable due to the randomness of $\mathbf{x}$. The feature vector $\mathbf{y}$ becomes

$$\mathbf{y}^T = \mathbf{x}^T \mathbf{T}^T = \sum_{j=1}^{N} c_j \mathbf{v}_j^T [\mathbf{v}_1, \ldots, \mathbf{v}_M] = [c_1, c_2, \ldots, c_M]. \tag{6.14}$$

The last step is due to the orthonormality of $\mathbf{v}_j$. Thus, the feature vector $\mathbf{y}$ consists of the first M coefficient, and the vector $\mathbf{z} = \mathbf{Sx}$ consists of the remaining $(N - M)$ coefficients. It is reasonable to expect that a properly chosen $\mathbf{T}$ will generally give us a large $\|\mathbf{y}\|^2$ and a small $\|\mathbf{z}\|^2$. $E[\|\mathbf{z}\|^2]$ is the mean-square error in approximating $\mathbf{x}$ by $\mathbf{v}_1, \ldots, \mathbf{v}_M$.

THEOREM 6.1

An optimal $M \times N$ linear feature extractor that maximizes $E[\|\mathbf{y}\|^2]$ or equivalently minimizes $E[\|\mathbf{z}\|^2]$ is

$$\hat{\mathbf{T}}^T = [\mathbf{u}_1, \mathbf{u}_2, \ldots, \mathbf{u}_M], \tag{6.15}$$

where $\mathbf{u}_1, \ldots, \mathbf{u}_M$ are the eigenvectors associated with the M largest eigenvalue of $\mathbf{R}$.

Proof

Let $\mathbf{T}^T = [\mathbf{v}_1, \mathbf{v}_2, \ldots, \mathbf{v}_M]$, where $\{\mathbf{v}_j\}$ are orthonormal. From (6.14), we have,

$$E[\|\mathbf{y}\|^2] = E[\mathbf{y}^T\mathbf{y}] = \sum_{j=1}^{M} E[c_j^2].$$

Substituting (6.13) for c_j, we obtain

$$E[\|\mathbf{y}\|^2] = \sum_{j=1}^{M} E[\mathbf{v}_j^T\mathbf{x}\mathbf{x}^T\mathbf{v}_j] = \sum_{j=1}^{M} \mathbf{v}_j^T\mathbf{R}\mathbf{v}_j. \tag{6.16}$$

We note that with $E[\|\mathbf{y}\|^2]$ expressed in this form, its value increases with the magnitudes of $\mathbf{v}_j$. Hence, the constraint that $\mathbf{v}_j^T\mathbf{v}_j = 1$ must be imposed, and

$$E[\|\mathbf{y}\|^2] - \sum_{j=1}^{M} \gamma_j\mathbf{v}_j^T\mathbf{v}_j = \sum_{j=1}^{M} (\mathbf{v}_j^T\mathbf{R}\mathbf{v}_j - \gamma_j\mathbf{v}_j^T\mathbf{v}_j) \tag{6.17}$$

will be maximized with γ_j being the Lagrange multipliers. Replacing $\mathbf{v}_j$ by $\mathbf{v}_j + d\mathbf{v}_j$ and setting the first-order term to zero, we obtain

$$\mathbf{R}\mathbf{v}_j = \gamma_j\mathbf{v}_j, \tag{6.18}$$

an eigenequation. Substituting (6.18) into (6.16) yields

$$E[\|\mathbf{y}\|^2] = \sum_{j=1}^{M} \gamma_j. \tag{6.19}$$

Lemma 6.1 shows that there are N orthonormal eigenvectors $\mathbf{u}_1, \mathbf{u}_2, \ldots, \mathbf{u}_N$ with eigenvalues $\lambda_1 \geqslant \lambda_2 \geqslant \cdots \geqslant \lambda_N \geqslant 0$. Hence, $\gamma_j = \lambda_j$, $\mathbf{v}_j = \mathbf{u}_j$, and we must choose the M eigenvectors associated with the M largest eigenvalues. Note that the requirement of $\{\mathbf{v}_j\}$ being orthogonal is used in substituting c_j by (6.13), and is verified by the orthogonality of the eigenvectors.

The expansion in terms of eigenvectors,

$$\mathbf{x} = \sum_{j=1}^{N} c_j\mathbf{u}_j, \quad c_j = \mathbf{x}^T\mathbf{u}_j, \tag{6.20}$$

is called the Karhunen–Loève expansion. Since we assume $E[\mathbf{x}] = \mathbf{0}$, $E[c_j] = 0$, and by (6.6), (6.7), and the orthonormality of $\mathbf{u}_j$,

$$E[c_jc_l] = E[\mathbf{u}_j^T\mathbf{x}\mathbf{x}^T\mathbf{u}_l] = \mathbf{u}_j^T\mathbf{R}\mathbf{u}_l = \lambda_j\delta_{jl}. \tag{6.21}$$

In other words, the random variables c_j and c_l are uncorrelated if $j \neq l$, and $E[c_j^2]$ equals the eigenvalue λ_j. This property of zero correlation is an important and unique property of the Karhunen–Loève expansion. Finally, a substitution of (6.20) and (6.21) into (6.6) yields

$$\mathbf{R} = E[\sum_{j=1}^{N} \sum_{l=1}^{N} c_j c_l \mathbf{u}_j \mathbf{u}_l^T] = \sum_{j=l}^{N} \lambda_j \mathbf{u}_j \mathbf{u}_j^T . \qquad (6.22)$$

The use of Karhunen–Loève expansion for feature extraction is illustrated in figure 6.2. The ellipses in figure 6.2(a) are defined by the equation $\mathbf{x}^T\mathbf{R}\mathbf{x} = c$, where c is a constant and $\mathbf{R}$ is the covariance matrix of the mixture density $f(\mathbf{x})$. The eigenvectors, $\mathbf{u}_1$ and $\mathbf{u}_2$, are the major and minor axes, and the eigenvalues λ_1 and λ_2 represent the variances in these directions. If we are allowed to choose one feature vector only, we should choose $\mathbf{u}_1$ according to theorem 6.1.

A disadvantage of the Karhunen–Loève expansion is that it does not take discrimination of classes into consideration. For example, the two ellipses in figure 6.2(b) represent the covariances of the conditional densities of the two classes C_1 and C_2. The mixture of the two classes has a covariance depicted by figure 6.2(a). It should be obvious from the figure that for discrimination purposes one should choose $\mathbf{u}_2$ instead of $\mathbf{u}_1$. Thus, the Karhunen–Loève method is inadequate for this case. We remark that the example is a pathological case and does not occur very often.

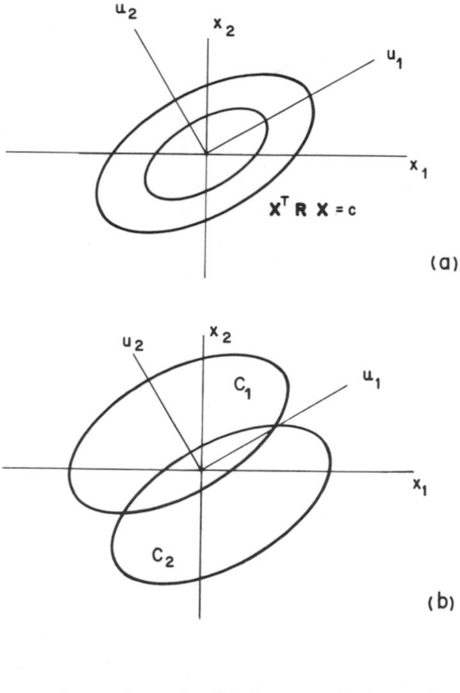

fig. 6.2 Feature extraction using Karhunen–Loève expansion.

The Karhunen–Loève expansion has been successfully applied to many practical pattern recognition problems. When the number of classes K is large, it is perhaps the only available method for feature extraction. In any case, the Karhunen–Loève expansion always makes it possible to project into the M-space in which $E[\|\mathbf{y}\|^2]$ is maximized. Thus if $\varepsilon > \lambda_{M+1} \geqslant \lambda_{M+2} \cdots \geqslant \lambda_N$ where ε is some measure of the square of interclass distances, it would be appropriate to choose $\mathbf{T}$ and M so that the inequality is satisfied.

6.3 Feature Extraction Using an Entropy Criterion

Entropy has been commonly associated with information content since Shannon published his celebrated paper on information theory in 1948. In this section we discuss the application of entropy as a criterion for feature extraction. We shall first introduce the idea of entropy and discuss very briefly its physical meaning. It is impossible to do justice to the subtle meaning of entropy and all of its ramifications in a book of this nature. The interested reader is referred to the books on information theory by Abramson (1963), Ash (1965), and Gallager (1968).

6.3.1 The entropy criterion

Consider a finite set $\mathscr{X} = \{x_1, x_2, \ldots, x_n\}$, where the set may be a set of patterns, a set of symbols, etc. The set is often called an *information source.* Let the probability of each member of the source be $p_1, p_2, \ldots, p_n$, then the entropy of the source is defined as

$$H(x) = E_x[-\log_2 p(x)] = -\sum_{i=1}^{n} p_i \log_2 p_i, \tag{6.23}$$

where the logarithmic function has 2 as its base and the unit of $H(x)$ is in bits.

Entropy is commonly interpreted as the *average uncertainty* of the information source. Information is gained when we observe an x drawn from the source. The average amount of *information gained* by making an observation equals the average uncertainty we had before the observation.

The entropy function has many interesting properties. It is continuous in p_i for all $0 \leqslant p_i \leqslant 1$. It is symmetric, i.e., the value of the entropy is unchanged if we interchange a pair of probabilities, p_i and p_j. Its value is greater than or equal to zero, and for a source of size n, is maximum when

$p_i = 1/n$, $i = 1, 2, \ldots, n$. The last property is especially satisfying since it is in agreement with the intuition that uncertainty should always be positive or zero, and it should be maximum when the n symbols are equally likely.

To derive the maximum, let us take partial derivative of H with respect to p_i. Noting that $p_n = 1 - (p_1 + \cdots + p_{n-1})$, we have

$$\frac{\partial H}{\partial p_i} = -(\log_2 e + \log_2 p_i) + (\log_2 e + \log_2 p_n)$$
$$= -\log_2(p_i/p_n).$$

Setting it to zero yields $p_i = p_n$. Since p_i was chosen arbitrarily, we must have $p_1 = p_2 = \cdots = p_n = 1/n$. The maximum entropy is

$$H_{\max} = -\sum_{i=1}^{n} \frac{1}{n} \log_2(1/n) = \log_2 n.$$

Entropy as a function of p_1 is sketched in figure 6.3 for the case $n = 2$. It is maximum, $H = 1$ bit, when $p_1 = 1/2$, and $H = 0$ when $p_1 = 0$ or 1. With $p_1 = 1$, we are certain that the outcome of drawing a symbol from the source is x_1, hence the uncertainty or the information is zero.

Information theory has its most important applications in communication problems. In communication, an information source is often coded into binary codes for ease of transmission, using 0 and 1 as code symbols. The average length of a code, L, is defined as the average number of code

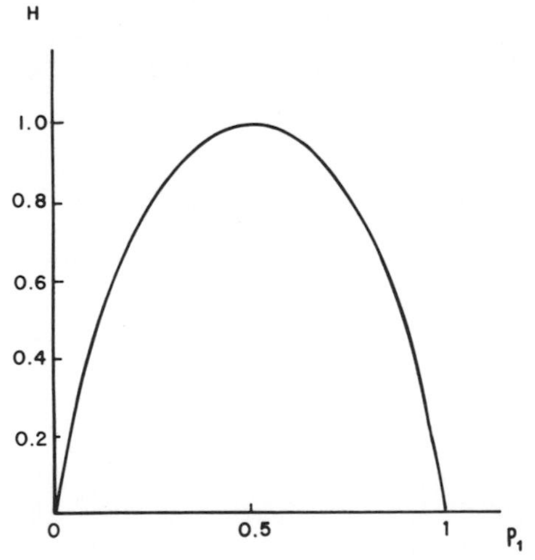

fig. 6.3 The entropy function.

symbols required to encode a source symbol. We assume that the transmission channel is perfect, i.e., it introduces no error during transmission. In order to utilize the channel efficiently it is desirable to have a small L. It can be shown that (Shannon, 1948)

$$H(x) \leqslant L. \tag{6.24}$$

Further, the average length L can be made arbitrarily close to H by a complicated coding method. Intuitively, the more uncertainty or information contained in the source, the larger the number of code symbols required to transmit the information. Equation (6.24) suggests that entropy is a reasonable measure of the information content in this sense. The following simple example illustrates the relationship between H and L.

Example 6.1

Consider an information source $\{A, B\}$ with $P(A) = 0.7$, $P(B) = 0.3$, and the entropy

$$H = -0.7 \log_2 0.7 - 0.3 \log_2 0.3 = 0.881.$$

A typical message sequence generated from the source is AAB $AAAABBAA \cdots$. If we encode A by 0 and B by 1, obviously $L = 1$ and $H < L$.

Let us consider pairs of source symbols AA, AB, BA, and BB, and construct a code

Message	*Probability*	*Code*
AA	0.49	0
AB	0.21	10
BA	0.21	110
BB	0.09	111.

The code is uniquely decodable since the zeros in the code act in a way similar to the commas in a sentence, and when we receive three ones following a zero, we know that it corresponds to BB. The average length, in this case, is

$$\begin{aligned} L &= 1 \times 0.49 + 2 \times 0.21 + 3 \times 0.21 + 3 \times 0.09 \\ &= 1.81 \text{ code symbol/pair of source symbols} \\ &= 0.905 \text{ code symbol/source symbol.} \end{aligned}$$

This is closer to $H = 0.881$ than the previous case where $L = 1$, and the reason is simply that we have assigned a code word with a single code symbol to the pair AA, which has a probability of 0.49. More complicated codes may be constructed by assigning a code word to every block of l source symbols. In this way, the average length can be made arbitrarily close to H, but it can never be less than H.

We are primarily interested in using entropy as a criterion for feature extraction. Let $\Omega_{\mathbf{x}}$ be the N-dimensional pattern space, and the feature space $\Omega_{\mathbf{y}}$ be an M-dimensional subspace of $\Omega_{\mathbf{x}}$. The relationship between $\mathbf{x}$ and $\mathbf{y}$ may be expressed by $\mathbf{y} = \mathbf{Tx}$ where $\mathbf{T}$, an $M \times N$ matrix, is the linear feature extractor. The pattern vector $\mathbf{x}$ is distributed according to a continuous probability density function $f(\mathbf{x})$. Then the density function for $\mathbf{y}$, $h(\mathbf{y})$, is a marginal density of $f(\mathbf{x})$, and depends also on $\mathbf{T}$. We define two entropies

$$
\begin{aligned}
H(\mathbf{x}) &= E_{\mathbf{x}}[-\log f(\mathbf{x})] = -\int f(\mathbf{x}) \log f(\mathbf{x})\, d\mathbf{x}, \\
H(\mathbf{y}) &= E_{\mathbf{y}}[-\log h(\mathbf{y})] = -\int h(\mathbf{y}) \log h(\mathbf{y})\, d\mathbf{y},
\end{aligned}
\tag{6.25}
$$

where we use the natural logarithm and the units are in nats.

We wish to find for feature extraction a matrix $\mathbf{T}$ that reduces the dimensionality to M and at the same time preserves as much information content as possible. It is known that the entropy defined in (6.23) for the information source with discrete probability is nonnegative and finite. Unfortunately, this is not true for the entropies defined in (6.25), which may be positive or negative, finite or infinite. For this reason, the values of $H(\mathbf{x})$ and $H(\mathbf{y})$ cannot be interpreted directly as information content. For two spaces of the same dimension, however, the relative values of two entropies are still meaningful, and our criterion is to find the M-space $\Omega_{\mathbf{y}}$ that preserves the maximum entropy compared with other M-spaces.

6.3.2 *Gaussian patterns*

We shall show that when the pattern vectors are Gaussian distributed, the linear feature extractor that maximizes the entropy has as its row vectors eigenvectors of $\mathbf{R}$. Let $f(\mathbf{x})$ be a Gaussian density function with zero mean and covariance matrix $\mathbf{R}$,

$$
f(\mathbf{x}) = g(\mathbf{x}; \mathbf{0}, \mathbf{R}). \tag{6.26}
$$

The entropy then becomes

$$H(\mathbf{x}) = -\int f(\mathbf{x}) \log f(\mathbf{x})\, d\mathbf{x}$$
$$= \int g(\mathbf{x}; \mathbf{0}, \mathbf{R}) \left[\frac{N}{2} \log 2\pi + \frac{1}{2} \log|\mathbf{R}| + \frac{1}{2} \mathbf{x}^T \mathbf{R}^{-1} \mathbf{x} \right] d\mathbf{x}, \tag{6.27}$$

where $|\mathbf{R}|$ is the determinant of $\mathbf{R}$. Noting that

$$E[\mathbf{x}^T \mathbf{R}^{-1} \mathbf{x}] = E[\text{tr } \mathbf{R}^{-1} \mathbf{x}\mathbf{x}^T] = \text{tr } \mathbf{I} = \frac{N}{2}, \tag{6.28}$$

we obtain

$$H(\mathbf{x}) = \frac{1}{2} \log|\mathbf{R}| + \frac{N}{2} \log 2\pi e. \tag{6.29}$$

Let $\mathbf{y} = \mathbf{T}\mathbf{x}$ and $\mathbf{T}$ be an $M \times N$ matrix with orthonormal row vectors. Since the marginal density of a Gaussian distribution is Gaussian, we have

$$H(\mathbf{y}) = \frac{1}{2} \log|\mathbf{R}_y| + \frac{M}{2} \log 2\pi e, \tag{6.30}$$

where

$$\mathbf{R}_y = \mathbf{T}\mathbf{R}\mathbf{T}^T \tag{6.31}$$

is the covariance matrix of $h(\mathbf{y})$. Since the determinant of a matrix is equivalent to the product of its eigenvalues, (6.30) may be rewritten as

$$H(\mathbf{y}) = \frac{1}{2} \sum_{j=1}^{M} \log \rho_j + \frac{M}{2} \log 2\pi e, \tag{6.32}$$

with ρ_j being the eigenvalues of the covariance matrix $\mathbf{R}_y$.

THEOREM 6.2

Let $f(\mathbf{x})$ be a Gaussian density function with zero-mean and covariance matrix $\mathbf{R}$. The optimum $M \times N$ linear feature extractor that maximizes $H(\mathbf{y})$ is

$$\hat{\mathbf{T}}^T = [\mathbf{u}_1, \mathbf{u}_2, \ldots, \mathbf{u}_M], \tag{6.33}$$

where $\mathbf{u}_1, \mathbf{u}_2, \ldots, \mathbf{u}_M$ are the eigenvectors associated with the M largest eigenvalues $\lambda_1, \lambda_2, \ldots, \lambda_M$ in the Karhunen–Loève expansion. The maximum entropy is

$$H(\mathbf{y}) = \frac{1}{2} \sum_{j=1}^{M} \log \lambda_j + \frac{M}{2} \log 2\pi e. \tag{6.34}$$

Proof

Let $\mathbf{T}^T = [\mathbf{v}_1, \mathbf{v}_2, \ldots, \mathbf{v}_M]$ be a linear feature extractor. We wish to maximize $H(\mathbf{y})$ subject to the constraint

$$\mathbf{T}\mathbf{T}^T = \mathbf{I}. \tag{6.35}$$

In proving the theorem, we shall use the constraint,

$$\mathbf{v}_j^T \mathbf{v}_j = 1, \qquad j = 1, 2, \ldots, M,$$

explicitly in the maximization of $H(\mathbf{y})$ in (6.32), and show that the solution satisfies the requirement of orthogonality.

Let γ_j be the Lagrange multiplier. We shall maximize

$$H(\mathbf{y}) - \sum_{j=1}^{M} \gamma_j \mathbf{v}_j^T \mathbf{v}_j = \frac{1}{2}\sum_{j=1}^{M} \log \rho_j + \frac{M}{2} \log 2\pi e - \sum_{j=1}^{M} \gamma_j \mathbf{v}_j^T \mathbf{v}_j. \tag{6.36}$$

By differentiating with respect to ρ_j and $\mathbf{v}_j$ and setting the result to zero, we obtain

$$\frac{1}{2}\sum_{j=1}^{M} \rho_j^{-1}\, d\rho_j - 2\sum_{j=1}^{M} \gamma_j\, d\,\mathbf{v}_j^T \mathbf{v}_j = 0. \tag{6.37}$$

It is noted that the second term in (6.37) may be written as

$$2\sum_{j=1}^{M} \gamma_j\, d\,\mathbf{v}_j^T \mathbf{v}_j = 2\,\mathrm{tr}[(d\mathbf{T})\mathbf{T}^T\mathbf{\Gamma}], \tag{6.38}$$

where $\mathbf{\Gamma}$ is a diagonal matrix with the diagonal elements being γ_j.

Now ρ_j are the eigenvalues of the covariance matrix $\mathbf{R}_y = \mathbf{TRT}^T$,

$$\mathbf{TRT}^T \mathbf{w}_j = \rho_j \mathbf{w}_j, \tag{6.39}$$

where $\mathbf{w}_j$ are the orthonormal eigenvectors. If we differentiate (6.39) and take advantage of the symmetry, we obtain,

$$2(d\mathbf{T})\mathbf{RT}^T\mathbf{w}_j = -(\mathbf{TRT}^T - \rho_j)\, d\,\mathbf{w}_j + \mathbf{w}_j\, d\rho_j. \tag{6.40}$$

The set of eigenvectors, $\{\mathbf{w}_j\}$, may be considered as an orthonormal basis of the M-space. Hence, $d\,\mathbf{w}_j$ may be expanded in terms of $\mathbf{w}_j$,

$$d\,\mathbf{w}_j = \sum_{l=1}^{M} \mathbf{w}_l \mathbf{w}_l^T\, d\,\mathbf{w}_j. \tag{6.41}$$

where $\mathbf{w}_l^T\, d\,\mathbf{w}_j$ are the coefficients of the expansion. Substituting (6.41) into (6.40) yields,

$$
\begin{aligned}
2(d\mathbf{T})\mathbf{RT}^T\mathbf{w}_j &= -(\mathbf{TRT}^T - \rho_j)\sum_{l=1}^{M} \mathbf{w}_l\mathbf{w}_l^T d\mathbf{w}_j + \mathbf{w}_j d\rho_j \\
&= -\sum_{l=1}^{M} (\rho_l - \rho_j)\mathbf{w}_l\mathbf{w}_l^T d\mathbf{w}_j + \mathbf{w}_j d\rho_j,
\end{aligned}
\tag{6.42}
$$

where we have used the eigenequation (6.39). If we premultiply (6.42) by $\mathbf{w}_j^T$ and make use of the orthonormal condition of the eigenvectors $\mathbf{w}_j$, the first term at the right-hand side becomes zero, hence,

$$
d\rho_j = 2\mathbf{w}_j^T[(d\mathbf{T})\mathbf{RT}^T]\mathbf{w}_j = 2\ \mathrm{tr}[(d\mathbf{T})\mathbf{RT}^T\mathbf{w}_j\mathbf{w}_j^T]. \tag{6.43}
$$

A substitution of (6.43) and (6.38) into (6.37) yields

$$
\mathrm{tr}[d\mathbf{T}(\mathbf{RT}^T \sum_{j=1}^{M} \mathbf{w}_j\mathbf{w}_j^T \rho_j^{-1} - 2\mathbf{T}^T\mathbf{\Gamma})] = 0. \tag{6.44}
$$

Since $d\mathbf{T}$ is arbitrary, (6.44) implies the solution

$$
\mathbf{RT}^T \sum_{j=1}^{M} \mathbf{w}_j\mathbf{w}_j^T \rho_j^{-1} - 2\mathbf{T}^T\mathbf{\Gamma} = \mathbf{0}. \tag{6.45}
$$

Premultiplying (6.45) by $\mathbf{T}$ and using (6.39) and the constraint equation (6.35), we obtain

$$
\mathbf{\Gamma} = \frac{1}{2}\sum_{j=1}^{M} \mathbf{w}_j\mathbf{w}_j^T = \frac{1}{2}\mathbf{I}. \tag{6.46}
$$

The last step follows from the fact that any M-vectors may be expanded in terms of the eigenvectors $\mathbf{w}_j$ as in (6.41), hence the summation must equal $\mathbf{I}$. Now if we postmultiply (6.45) by $\mathbf{w}_k\rho_k$ and make use of (6.46) and the orthonormality of $\mathbf{w}_k$, we have

$$
\mathbf{RT}^T\mathbf{w}_k - \rho_k\mathbf{T}^T\mathbf{w}_k = (\mathbf{R} - \rho_k)\mathbf{T}^T\mathbf{w}_k = \mathbf{0}. \tag{6.47}
$$

This is the eigenequation for the matrix $\mathbf{R}$, hence

$$
\rho_j = \lambda_j, \qquad \mathbf{T}^T\mathbf{w}_j = \mathbf{u}_j. \tag{6.48}
$$

Since both $\{\mathbf{w}_j\}$ and $\{\mathbf{u}_j\}$ are sets of orthonormal vectors, (6.48) implies that the matrix $\mathbf{T}^T = [\mathbf{v}_1, \mathbf{v}_2, \ldots \mathbf{v}_M]$ defines the same M-space as $\mathbf{u}_1, \mathbf{u}_2, \ldots, \mathbf{u}_M$. A convenient choice is simply $\mathbf{v}_j = \mathbf{u}_j$ with $\mathbf{w}_j$ becoming unit vectors, and this completes the proof.

6.3.3 Minimax feature extraction

In theorem 6.2, we have shown that if $f(\mathbf{x})$ is a Gaussian density function, the optimum feature extractor that maximizes $H(\mathbf{y})$ is the Karhunen–Loève expansion. In pattern recognition, $f(\mathbf{x})$ is a mixture of probability density functions of several classes, and the Gaussian assumption is not realistic. In fact, the probability distributions of the patterns are often not completely known. To reflect the lack of complete knowledge, let us assume a family of density functions and consider the true density function as a member of that family. For example, if the only knowledge of $f(\mathbf{x})$ is its zero mean and covariance matrix $\mathbf{R}$, we may define a family

$$\mathcal{G} = \{f(\mathbf{x}): E[\mathbf{x}] = \mathbf{0},\ E[\mathbf{x}\mathbf{x}^T] = \mathbf{R}\}, \tag{6.49}$$

and the true density is certainly a member of this family.

Given an $M \times N$ linear feature extractor $\mathbf{T}$ and a family of density functions $\mathcal{G}$, there is a $f(\mathbf{x})$ belonging to $\mathcal{G}$ that has maximum entropy in $\Omega_{\mathbf{y}}$. Let us define

$$C(\mathcal{G}, \mathbf{T}) = \max_{f(\mathbf{x}) \in \mathcal{G}} H(\mathbf{y}), \tag{6.50}$$

which is simply the maximum entropy obtainable in the M-space $\Omega_{\mathbf{y}}$. Since it is desirable to have a large $H(\mathbf{y})$, we shall call $C(\mathcal{G}, \mathbf{T})$ the *capacity*, and the concept is somewhat related to the idea of channel capacity in information theory. The channel capacity is a very important concept partly because in designing a communication system we have some control over the input probabilities by signal design or coding. This is contrary to the situation in pattern recognition where the probability distributions of the pattern vectors are beyond our control. Thus it is perhaps more meaningful to consider a least-favorable distribution that has the smallest $H(\mathbf{y})$ in $\Omega_{\mathbf{y}}$, and the minimum $H(\mathbf{y})$ could be used as a standard for comparing different linear feature extractors. Unfortunately, in many cases $\min H(\mathbf{y}) = -\infty$ with the density function being linear combinations of delta functions. As an alternative, let us define for a given $\mathbf{T}$ a *least-favorable distribution* as the one that has the maximum entropy in the complementary space $\Omega_{\mathbf{z}}$, and

$$Q(\mathcal{G}, \mathbf{T}) = \alpha - \max_{f(\mathbf{x}) \in \mathcal{G}} H(\mathbf{z}), \tag{6.51}$$

where α is an arbitrary constant independent of the feature extractor $\mathbf{T}$. A convenient choice is

$$\alpha = \max_{f(\mathbf{x}) \in \mathcal{G}} H(\mathbf{x}), \tag{6.52}$$

so that $Q = 0$ if $\Omega_{\mathbf{z}} = \Omega_{\mathbf{x}}$, i.e., if no feature is extracted.

We note that $\Omega_{\mathbf{z}}$ is the complementary space, and it would be desirable to have a small $H(\mathbf{z})$ or a large $\alpha - H(\mathbf{z})$ if $f(\mathbf{x})$ were completely known. But sincc this is not the case, we define $Q(\mathcal{F}, \mathbf{T})$ so that no matter what the true density function $f(\mathbf{x})$ is, $f(\mathbf{x}) \in \mathcal{F}$ and $\alpha - H(\mathbf{z})$ will be greater than or equal to $Q(\mathcal{F}, \mathbf{T})$. Thus, $Q(\mathcal{F}, \mathbf{T})$ serves as a lower bound to $\alpha - H(\mathbf{z})$, a measure of robustness of the feature extractor $\mathbf{T}$ for given $\mathcal{F}$, and we should select a feature extractor that maximizes $Q(\mathcal{F}, \mathbf{T})$. Thus, we define a $\hat{\mathbf{T}}$ by the relationship

$$Q(\mathcal{F}, \hat{\mathbf{T}}) = \max_{\mathbf{T}} Q(\mathcal{F}, \mathbf{T}) = \alpha - \min_{\mathbf{T}} \max_{f(\mathbf{x}) \in \mathcal{F}} H(\mathbf{z}), \tag{6.53}$$

and shall call $\hat{\mathbf{T}}$ a *minimax feature extractor*. A common property of a minimax approach is that the performance is usually relatively insensitive to the variations of the true parameters, in this case the true density function $f(\mathbf{x})$.

In pattern recognition, the only available knowledge is often the mean value and the covariances, especially when the dimension of $\Omega_{\mathbf{x}}$ is high. Thus, we are interested in the family of density functions defined by the mean and the covariances. We may assume without loss of generality that the mean is zero, and have a family $\mathcal{F} = \{f(\mathbf{x}): E[\mathbf{x}] = \mathbf{0},\ E[\mathbf{x}\mathbf{x}^T] = \mathbf{R}\}$. We shall find C, Q, and the minimax feature extractor $\hat{\mathbf{T}}$ for this family of density functions. Before doing that, we consider first a lemma that was in fact used in the last chapter in connection with the error criterion for density approximations and is presented here formally because of its importance to the materials in this chapter.

LEMMA 6.2

Let $f(\mathbf{x})$ and $\hat{f}(\mathbf{x})$ be arbitrary probability density functions. Then

$$-\int f(\mathbf{x}) \log f(\mathbf{x})\, d\mathbf{x} \leqslant -\int f(\mathbf{x}) \log \hat{f}(\mathbf{x})\, d\mathbf{x}, \tag{6.54}$$

with equality if and only if $f(\mathbf{x}) = \hat{f}(\mathbf{x})$ for almost all $\mathbf{x}$.

Proof

Since $\log \alpha \leqslant \alpha - 1$ for any $\alpha \geqslant 0$ with equality if and only if $\alpha = 1$, we have

$$f(\mathbf{x}) \log \frac{\hat{f}(\mathbf{x})}{f(\mathbf{x})} \leqslant f(\mathbf{x}) \left[\frac{\hat{f}(\mathbf{x})}{f(\mathbf{x})} - 1\right] = \hat{f}(\mathbf{x}) - f(\mathbf{x}), \tag{6.55}$$

with equality if and only if $f(\mathbf{x}) = \hat{f}(\mathbf{x})$. In (6.55), we use the convention that $\hat{f}(\mathbf{x})/f(\mathbf{x}) = 0$ when $f(\mathbf{x}) = \hat{f}(\mathbf{x}) = 0$ and $0 \log 0 = 0 \log \infty = 0$. Thus, by integration,

$$\int f(\mathbf{x}) \log \frac{\hat{f}(\mathbf{x})}{f(\mathbf{x})} d\mathbf{x} \leqslant \int \hat{f}(\mathbf{x})\, d\mathbf{x} - \int f(\mathbf{x})\, d\mathbf{x} = 0, \tag{6.56}$$

with equality if and only if $f(\mathbf{x}) = \hat{f}(\mathbf{x})$ for almost all $\mathbf{x}$.

THEOREM 6.3

For the family of probability density functions, $\mathcal{G} = \{f(\mathbf{x}): E[\mathbf{x}] = 0, E[\mathbf{x}\mathbf{x}^T] = \mathbf{R}\}$ and an $M \times N$ linear feature extractor $\mathbf{T}$,

$$C(\mathcal{G}, \mathbf{T}) = \frac{1}{2} \log |\mathbf{R}_y| + \frac{M}{2} \log 2\pi e, \tag{6.57}$$

$$Q(\mathcal{G}, \mathbf{T}) = \frac{1}{2} \log |\mathbf{R}| - \frac{1}{2} \log |\mathbf{R}_z| + \frac{M}{2} \log 2\pi e, \tag{6.58}$$

where $\mathbf{R}_y = \mathbf{TRT}^T$ and $\mathbf{R}_z = \mathbf{SRS}^T$. The minimax feature extractor $\hat{\mathbf{T}}$ is the Karhunen–Loève expansion, i.e.,

$$\begin{aligned} \hat{\mathbf{T}}^T &= [\mathbf{u}_1, \mathbf{u}_2, \ldots, \mathbf{u}_M], \\ Q(\mathcal{G}, \hat{\mathbf{T}}) &= \frac{1}{2} \sum_{j=1}^{M} \log \lambda_j + \frac{M}{2} \log 2\pi e, \end{aligned} \tag{6.59}$$

where $\lambda_1 \geqslant \lambda_2 \cdots$ and $\mathbf{u}_1, \mathbf{u}_2, \ldots$, are the eigenvalues and eigenvectors of $\mathbf{R}$.

Proof

Let $\mathcal{H} = \{h(\mathbf{y}): E[\mathbf{y}] = \mathbf{0},\ E[\mathbf{y}\mathbf{y}^T] = \mathbf{R}_y\}$. Consider an arbitrary $h(\mathbf{y}) \in \mathcal{H}$ and a Gaussian density function,

$$g(\mathbf{y}; \mathbf{0}, \mathbf{R}_y) = (2\pi)^{-M/2} |\mathbf{R}_y|^{-1/2} \exp\left(-\frac{1}{2} \mathbf{y}^T \mathbf{R}_y^{-1} \mathbf{y}\right), \tag{6.60}$$

$g(\mathbf{y}; \mathbf{0}, \mathbf{R}_y) \in \mathcal{H}$. According to lemma 6.2,

$$H(\mathbf{y}) = -\int h(\mathbf{y}) \log h(\mathbf{y})\, d\mathbf{y} \leqslant -\int h(\mathbf{y}) \log g(\mathbf{y}; \mathbf{0}, \mathbf{R}_y)\, d\mathbf{y}. \tag{6.61}$$

Now, substituting (6.60) into the right-hand side of (6.61) yields

$$-\int h(\mathbf{y}) \log g(\mathbf{y}; \mathbf{0}, \mathbf{R}_y)\, d\mathbf{y} = \frac{1}{2} \log|\mathbf{R}_y| + \frac{M}{2} \log 2\pi e,$$

where we have used the relationship

$$\int \mathbf{y}^T \mathbf{R}_y^{-1} \mathbf{y} h(\mathbf{y})\, dy = \int \operatorname{tr}(\mathbf{R}_y^{-1} \mathbf{y}\mathbf{y}^T) h(\mathbf{y})\, d\mathbf{y} = E[\operatorname{tr} \mathbf{R}_y^{-1} \mathbf{y}\mathbf{y}^T]$$

$$= \operatorname{tr} \mathbf{R}_y^{-1} \mathbf{R}_y = M.$$

Thus, for any $h(\mathbf{y}) \in \mathcal{H}$ the entropy

$$H(\mathbf{y}) \leqslant \frac{1}{2} \log|\mathbf{R}_y| + \frac{M}{2} \log 2\pi e. \tag{6.62}$$

The equality holds when $h(\mathbf{y}) = g(\mathbf{y}; \mathbf{0}, \mathbf{R}_y)$, hence

$$\max_{h(\mathbf{y}) \in \mathcal{H}} H(\mathbf{y}) = \frac{1}{2} \log|\mathbf{R}_y| + \frac{M}{2} \log 2\pi e, \tag{6.63}$$

where the maximization is over the family $\mathcal{H}$. Since $f(\mathbf{x}) \in \mathcal{G}$ implies $h(\mathbf{y}) \in \mathcal{H}$,

$$C(\mathcal{G}, \mathbf{T}) = \max_{f(\mathbf{x}) \in \mathcal{G}} H(\mathbf{y}) \leqslant \max_{h(\mathbf{y}) \in \mathcal{H}} H(\mathbf{y}). \tag{6.64}$$

The inequality in (6.64) reduces to equality since if we let $f(\mathbf{x}) = g(\mathbf{x}; \mathbf{0}, \mathbf{R}) \in \mathcal{G}$, the marginal density $h(\mathbf{y}) = g(\mathbf{y}; \mathbf{0}, \mathbf{R}_y)$ and its entropy equals (6.63). Thus, we have proved (6.57), and using similar arguments we can prove (6.58).

It is obvious from the expression of $Q(\mathcal{G}, \mathbf{T})$ in (6.58) that to find the minimax $\hat{\mathbf{T}}$ is equivalent to minimizing $\log|\mathbf{R}_z|$. An examination of (6.30) and theorem 6.2 shows that the minimization of $\log|\mathbf{R}_z|$ can be obtained by a method identical to the proof of theorem 6.2. Thus,

$$\min_{\mathbf{S}} \log|\mathbf{R}_z| = \frac{1}{2} \sum_{j=M+1}^{N} \log \lambda_j,$$

and the matrix corresponding to the minimum is

$$\hat{\mathbf{S}}^T = [\mathbf{u}_{M+1}, \ldots, \mathbf{u}_N]$$

which is obviously equivalent to (6.59).

The theorem above is interesting since it shows that the Karhunen–Loève expansion is optimum in the minimax sense when our knowledge of the pattern distribution is limited to its mean value and its covariance matrix. The idea of minimax feature extraction may be applied to other families of density functions and to other feature extraction criteria.

6.4 The Divergence and the Bhattacharyya Coefficient

Thus far we have been concerned with feature extraction without considering discrimination between different classes. Since pattern recognition is concerned with classification of patterns, an obvious criterion for feature extraction is the error probability. We would like to find an M-dimensional subspace of $\Omega_{\mathbf{x}}$ such that the probability of classification errors is minimum compared with other M-subspaces. Unfortunately, the error probability is generally very difficult to calculate, and it is practically impossible to use as a criterion for feature extraction. We consider in the following subsections two alternative criteria.

6.4.1 The Divergence

Consider two classes of patterns C_1 and C_2 with probability density functions $f_1(\mathbf{x})$ and $f_2(\mathbf{x})$. As discussed in chapter 2, the classification of a pattern $\mathbf{x}$ is based on the log-likelihood ratio,

$$\log \Lambda(\mathbf{x}) = \log \frac{f_2(\mathbf{x})}{f_1(\mathbf{x})}. \tag{6.65}$$

If $\log \Lambda(\mathbf{x})$ is greater than a certain threshold value, $\mathbf{x}$ is classified as belonging to C_2; otherwise it belongs to C_1.

Since the classification is based on $\log \Lambda(\mathbf{x})$, intuitively the error probability will be small if on the average $\log \Lambda(\mathbf{x})$ is large for the patterns belonging to C_2 and small for those belonging to C_1. Therefore, we define

$$\begin{aligned} J_1(\mathbf{x}) &= E_1\left[\log \frac{f_1(\mathbf{x})}{f_2(\mathbf{x})}\right] = \int f_1(\mathbf{x}) \log \frac{f_1(\mathbf{x})}{f_2(\mathbf{x})}\, d\mathbf{x}, \\ J_2(\mathbf{x}) &= E_2\left[\log \frac{f_2(\mathbf{x})}{f_1(\mathbf{x})}\right] = \int f_2(\mathbf{x}) \log \frac{f_2(\mathbf{x})}{f_1(\mathbf{x})}\, d\mathbf{x}, \end{aligned} \tag{6.66}$$

where $E_1[\cdot]$ and $E_2[\cdot]$ indicate the expectation over the densities $f_1(\mathbf{x})$ and $f_2(\mathbf{x})$ respectively. $J_1(\mathbf{x})$ may be interpreted as the average information for discrimination in favor of C_1 against C_2, and $J_2(\mathbf{x})$ may be interpreted in a similar manner. The divergence is defined as

$$J(\mathbf{x}) = J_1(\mathbf{x}) + J_2(\mathbf{x}), \tag{6.67}$$

and is therefore a measure of information for discrimination of the two classes.

In defining (6.66), we have used the convention that $f_1(\mathbf{x})/f_2(\mathbf{x}) = 0$ if $f_1(\mathbf{x}) = f_2(\mathbf{x}) = 0$ and $0 \log 0 = 0 \log \infty = 0$. It is interesting to note that when the two classes are separable, i.e., $f_2(\mathbf{x}) = 0$ if $f_1(\mathbf{x}) > 0$ and vice versa, the patterns may be classified without error and $J(\mathbf{x}) = \infty$. On the other hand, when $f_1(\mathbf{x}) = f_2(\mathbf{x})$ for almost all $\mathbf{x}$, the two classes are indistinguishable and $J(\mathbf{x}) = 0$.

Now, let $\mathbf{y} = \mathbf{T}\mathbf{x}$, $\mathbf{z} = \mathbf{S}\mathbf{x}$ and $\Omega_{\mathbf{y}}$ and $\Omega_{\mathbf{z}}$ be complementary subspaces of $\Omega_{\mathbf{x}}$. As in (6.66) and (6.67) we may define $J_1(\mathbf{y})$, $J_2(\mathbf{y})$ and the divergence $J(\mathbf{y})$, and it is desirable to select a linear feature extractor $\mathbf{T}$ such that the divergence $J(\mathbf{y})$ is large. Let $l_1(\mathbf{z}|\mathbf{y})$ and $l_2(\mathbf{z}|\mathbf{y})$ be the conditional densities of $\mathbf{z}$ for given $\mathbf{y}$ for classes C_1 and C_2 respectively, and $h_1(\mathbf{y})$ and $h_2(\mathbf{y})$ be the marginal densities. We may define

$$J_1(\mathbf{z}|\mathbf{y}) = E_1\left[\log \frac{l_1(\mathbf{z}|\mathbf{y})}{l_2(\mathbf{z}|\mathbf{y})}\right] = \iint h_1(\mathbf{y}) l_1(\mathbf{z}|\mathbf{y}) \log \frac{l_1(\mathbf{z}|\mathbf{y})}{l_2(\mathbf{z}|\mathbf{y})} d\mathbf{z}\, d\mathbf{y},$$

$$J(\mathbf{z}|\mathbf{y}) = J_1(\mathbf{z}|\mathbf{y}) + J_2(\mathbf{z}|\mathbf{y}).$$

THEOREM 6.4

Let $\mathbf{y} = \mathbf{T}\mathbf{x}$ and $\mathbf{z} = \mathbf{S}\mathbf{x}$ where the matrix $[\mathbf{T}^T, \mathbf{S}^T]$ is an orthogonal matrix. Then, the divergences $J(\mathbf{x})$, $J(\mathbf{y})$, and $J(\mathbf{z}|\mathbf{y})$ have the following properties:

$$J(\mathbf{x}) \geqslant 0, \tag{6.68}$$

with equality if and only if $f_1(\mathbf{x}) = f_2(\mathbf{x})$ for almost all $\mathbf{x}$.

$$J(\mathbf{x}) = J(\mathbf{y}) + J(\mathbf{z}|\mathbf{y}), \tag{6.69}$$

and

$$J(\mathbf{x}) = J(\mathbf{y}) + J(\mathbf{z}) \tag{6.70}$$

if $\mathbf{y}$ and $\mathbf{z}$ are statistically independent.

$$J(\mathbf{x}) \geqslant J(\mathbf{y}), \tag{6.71}$$

and $J(\mathbf{x}) = J(\mathbf{y})$ if $\mathbf{T}$ is nonsingular.

Proof

It suffices to prove the properties for $J_1(\mathbf{x})$, $J_1(\mathbf{y})$, and $J_1(\mathbf{z}|\mathbf{y})$. According to lemma 6.2,

$$J_1(\mathbf{x}) = \int f_1(\mathbf{x}) \log \frac{f_1(\mathbf{x})}{f_2(\mathbf{x})} d\mathbf{x} \geqslant 0,$$

and hence (6.68). By the definition of $J_1(\mathbf{y})$ and $J_1(\mathbf{z}|\mathbf{y})$,

$$\begin{aligned} J_1(\mathbf{y}) + J_1(\mathbf{z}|\mathbf{y}) &= \iint h_1(\mathbf{y}) l_1(\mathbf{z}|\mathbf{y}) \log \frac{h_1(\mathbf{y}) l_1(\mathbf{z}|\mathbf{y})}{h_2(\mathbf{y}) l_2(\mathbf{z}|\mathbf{y})} d\mathbf{z}\, d\mathbf{y} \\ &= \int f_1(\mathbf{x}) \log \frac{f_1(\mathbf{x})}{f_2(\mathbf{x})} d\mathbf{x} \\ &= J_1(\mathbf{x}). \end{aligned} \tag{6.72}$$

The last step is valid since the matrix $[\mathbf{T}^T, \mathbf{S}^T]$ is nonsingular, and we have $f_1(\mathbf{x})\, d\mathbf{x} = h_1(\mathbf{y}) l_1(\mathbf{z}|\mathbf{y})\, d\mathbf{z}\, d\mathbf{y}$ and $f_2(\mathbf{x})\, d\mathbf{x} = h_2(\mathbf{y}) l_2(\mathbf{z}|\mathbf{y})\, d\mathbf{z}\, d\mathbf{y}$. It is obvious from (6.72) that when $\mathbf{y}$ and $\mathbf{z}$ are statistically independent, $J_1(\mathbf{x}) = J_1(\mathbf{y}) + J_1(\mathbf{z})$.

Next we note that

$$J_1(\mathbf{z}|\mathbf{y}) = \int h_1(\mathbf{y}) \left[\int l_1(\mathbf{z}|\mathbf{y}) \log \frac{l_1(\mathbf{z}|\mathbf{y})}{l_2(\mathbf{z}|\mathbf{y})} d\mathbf{z} \right] d\mathbf{y}. \tag{6.73}$$

The term inside the bracket is greater than or equal to zero according to lemma 6.2. Hence, $J_1(\mathbf{z}|\mathbf{y}) \geqslant 0$, which implies that $J_1(\mathbf{x}) \geqslant J_1(\mathbf{y})$ because of (6.72). When $\mathbf{T}$ is nonsingular, $\Omega_\mathbf{y} = \Omega_\mathbf{x}$ and $J_1(\mathbf{x}) = J_1(\mathbf{y})$.

Kullback and Leibler (1951) showed that $J(\mathbf{x}) \geqslant J(\mathbf{y})$ for any transformation $\mathbf{y} = \mathcal{T}(\mathbf{x})$, linear or nonlinear, and $J(\mathbf{x}) = J(\mathbf{y})$ if the transformation $\mathcal{T}$ is nonsingular. This property is of considerable theoretical importance, and $J_1(\mathbf{x})$ and $J_2(\mathbf{x})$ are often called the Kullback–Leibler numbers.

The idea of divergence may be extended to the case where there are more than two classes. Let $f_k(\mathbf{x})$ be the probability density function for the pattern vectors of C_k, $k = 1, 2, \ldots, K$. We may define

$$J(\mathbf{x}) = \sum_{j=1}^{K} \sum_{k=1}^{K} \left\{ E_j \left[\log \frac{f_j(\mathbf{x})}{f_k(\mathbf{x})} \right] + E_k \left[\log \frac{f_k(\mathbf{x})}{f_j(\mathbf{x})} \right] \right\}. \tag{6.74}$$

When the prior probabilities, p_k, are known, each term in (6.74) may be weighted by p_k.

There is another extension that is rather interesting. Let

$$f(\mathbf{x}) = \sum_{k=1}^{K} p_k f_k(\mathbf{x}) \tag{6.75}$$

be the mixture density. We define

$$I(\mathbf{x}) = \sum_{k=1}^{K} p_k E_k\left[\log \frac{f_k(\mathbf{x})}{f(\mathbf{x})}\right], \tag{6.76}$$

where each term represents the information for discrimination in favor of C_k against the overall mixture. Equation (6.76) may be written as

$$\begin{aligned} I(\mathbf{x}) &= \sum_{k=1}^{K} \int p_k f_k(\mathbf{x}) \log \frac{f_k(\mathbf{x})}{f(\mathbf{x})} d\mathbf{x} \\ &= -\int f(\mathbf{x}) \log f(\mathbf{x})\, d\mathbf{x} + \sum_{k=1}^{K} p_k \int f_k(\mathbf{x}) \log f_k(\mathbf{x})\, d\mathbf{x}. \end{aligned}$$

Noting that $f_k(\mathbf{x})$ is the conditional density for given C_k, we have,

$$I(\mathbf{x}) = H(\mathbf{x}) - \sum_{k=1}^{K} p_k H(\mathbf{x}|C_k), \tag{6.77}$$

where $H(\mathbf{x})$ is the entropy and $H(\mathbf{x}|C_k)$ is the conditional entropy for given C_k defined by the conditional densities. This is in the form of *mutual information*, a well known concept in information theory. Thus, $I(\mathbf{x})$ is the mutual information between $\mathbf{x}$ and the set $\{C_k\}$, and may be interpreted as the information about C_k obtained by observing the random patterns $\mathbf{x}$.

6.4.2 The Bhattacharyya coefficient

The Bhattacharyya coefficient is defined as

$$\beta(\mathbf{x}) = \int \sqrt{f_1(\mathbf{x}) f_2(\mathbf{x})}\, d\mathbf{x}, \tag{6.78}$$

where $f_1(\mathbf{x})$ and $f_2(\mathbf{x})$ are the probability density functions for pattern vectors of C_1 and C_2 respectively. It is noted that the integral in (6.78) may be interpreted as the inner product of two vectors $\sqrt{f_1(\mathbf{x})}$ and $\sqrt{f_2(\mathbf{x})}$. Since $\int f_k(\mathbf{x})\, dx = 1$, i.e., $\sqrt{f_1(\mathbf{x})}$ and $\sqrt{f_2(\mathbf{x})}$ have unit norm, $\beta(\mathbf{x})$ may be regarded as the cosine of the angle between the two vectors. We note that

$$0 \leqslant \beta(\mathbf{x}) \leqslant 1, \tag{6.79}$$

since the direction-cosine is always less than 1, and since both $\sqrt{f_1(\mathbf{x})}$ and $\sqrt{f_2(\mathbf{x})}$ are greater than or equal to zero for all $\mathbf{x}$.

When $f_1(\mathbf{x}) = f_2(\mathbf{x})$ for almost all $\mathbf{x}$, the pattern vectors are practically indistinguishable, and in this case we have $\beta(\mathbf{x}) = 1$. On the other hand, if $f_1(\mathbf{x}) > 0$ implies $f_2(\mathbf{x}) = 0$ and vice versa, the patterns may be classified without error, and we have $\beta(\mathbf{x}) = 0$. An important property of the Bhattacharyya coefficient is that $\frac{1}{2}\beta(\mathbf{x})$ is an upper bound on the Bayes error probability, and in the two extreme cases we mentioned, it is indeed the error probability.

THEOREM 6.5

For any α such that $0 \leqslant \alpha \leqslant 1$, the Bayes error probability, i.e., the Bayes risk when the costs for the two kinds of errors are one, satisfies the inequality

$$P_e \leqslant p_1^\alpha p_2^{1-\alpha} \int [f_1(\mathbf{x})]^\alpha [f_2(\mathbf{x})]^{1-\alpha}\, d\mathbf{x}. \tag{6.80}$$

Proof

It was shown in chapter 2 that

$$P_e = \int \min(p_1 f_1(\mathbf{x}), p_2 f_2(\mathbf{x}))\, d\mathbf{x}. \tag{6.81}$$

Since for $0 \leqslant \alpha \leqslant 1$, $\alpha_1 \geqslant 0$ and $\alpha_2 \geqslant 0$

$$\min(\alpha_1, \alpha_2) \leqslant \alpha_1^\alpha \alpha_2^{1-\alpha},$$

it follows that

$$P_e \leqslant \int [p_1 f_1(\mathbf{x})]^\alpha [p_2 f_2(\mathbf{x})]^{1-\alpha}\, d\mathbf{x}.$$

COROLLARY

$$P_e \leqslant \frac{1}{2}\beta(\mathbf{x}). \tag{6.82}$$

Proof

Let $\alpha = \frac{1}{2}$, we have

$$P_e \leqslant \sqrt{p_1 p_2} \int \sqrt{f_1(\mathbf{x}) f_2(\mathbf{x})}\, d\mathbf{x} \leqslant \frac{1}{2}\beta(\mathbf{x}).$$

The last inequality follows from the fact that $\sqrt{p_1 p_2} \leqslant 1/2$.

The theorem is known as the *Chernoff bound*, and in some problems it is possible to find an optimum α that minimizes the upper bound in (6.80). In pattern recognition problems, we usually use the bound in the corollary because ot its relative simplicity.

Sometimes it is more convenient to use the Bhattacharyya distance

$$B(\mathbf{x}) = -\log \beta(\mathbf{x}), \tag{6.83}$$

so that $B(\mathbf{x}) = 0$ when $f_1(\mathbf{x}) = f_2(\mathbf{x})$ and $B(\mathbf{x}) = \infty$ when the two classes are perfectly separable. This is consistent with the behavior of the divergence $J(\mathbf{x})$. We remark that although $B(\mathbf{x})$ is called a distance, it does not obey the triangle inequality.

For feature extraction, let $\mathbf{y} = \mathbf{Tx}$ and we may define $\beta(\mathbf{y})$ and $B(\mathbf{y})$ similarly to (6.78) and (6.83). Since $\beta(\mathbf{y})/2$ is the upper bound on error probability when classifying in $\Omega_{\mathbf{y}}$, it is desirable to have a small $\beta(\mathbf{y})$ or equivalently a large $B(\mathbf{y})$. It is easy to show from the definitions that $\beta(\mathbf{y}) \geqslant \beta(\mathbf{x})$ and $B(\mathbf{y}) \leqslant B(\mathbf{x})$. Hence, the bound on error probability becomes larger when we reduce the dimensionality. Also, β remains the same under nonsingular transformations.

6.4.3 Feature extraction

We discussed in some detail the divergence and the Bhattacharyya coefficients. We now illustrate the application of these criteria in feature extraction with the following simple examples.

EXAMPLE 6.2

Assume that

$$\begin{aligned} f_1(\mathbf{x}) &= g(\mathbf{x}; \mathbf{0}, \mathbf{R}_1), \\ f_2(\mathbf{x}) &= g(\mathbf{x}; \mathbf{m}, \mathbf{R}_2), \end{aligned} \tag{6.84}$$

are two Gaussian densities. For a linear feature extractor $\mathbf{T}$, the marginal densities, $h_1(\mathbf{y})$ and $h_2(\mathbf{y})$, are Gaussian with

$$h_1(\mathbf{y}) = g(\mathbf{y}; \mathbf{0}, \mathbf{R}_{y1}),$$
$$h_2(\mathbf{y}) = g(\mathbf{y}; \mathbf{m}_y, \mathbf{R}_{y2}),$$

where

$$\mathbf{m}_y = \mathbf{T}\mathbf{m}, \quad \mathbf{R}_{y1} = \mathbf{T}\mathbf{R}_1\mathbf{T}^T, \quad \mathbf{R}_{y2} = \mathbf{T}\mathbf{R}_2\mathbf{T}^T. \tag{6.85}$$

We obtain, by straightforward calculation, the divergence and the Bhattacharyya distance,

$$\begin{aligned} J(\mathbf{y}) &= \frac{1}{2}\mathbf{m}_y^T(\mathbf{R}_{y1}^{-1} + \mathbf{R}_{y2}^{-1})\mathbf{m}_y + \frac{1}{2}\operatorname{tr}(\mathbf{R}_{y1} - \mathbf{R}_{y2})(\mathbf{R}_{y2}^{-1} - \mathbf{R}_{y1}^{-1}), \\ B(\mathbf{y}) &= \frac{1}{4}\mathbf{m}_y^T(\mathbf{R}_{y1} + \mathbf{R}_{y2})^{-1}\mathbf{m}_y + \frac{1}{2}\log\frac{|(\mathbf{R}_{y1} + \mathbf{R}_{y2})/2|}{|\mathbf{R}_{y1}|^{1/2}|\mathbf{R}_{y2}|^{1/2}} \end{aligned} \tag{6.86}$$

$J(\mathbf{x})$ and $B(\mathbf{x})$ are similar to $J(\mathbf{y})$ and $B(\mathbf{y})$ in (6.86) with $\mathbf{m}_y$, $\mathbf{R}_{y1}$, and $\mathbf{R}_{y2}$ substituted by $\mathbf{m}$, $\mathbf{R}_1$, and $\mathbf{R}_2$. Let us consider two special cases.

(1) *Equal covariance case* In this case

$$\mathbf{R}_1 = \mathbf{R}_2 = \mathbf{R}, \qquad \mathbf{R}_{y1} = \mathbf{R}_{y2} = \mathbf{R}_y,$$

and obviously,

$$J(\mathbf{x}) = \mathbf{m}^T\mathbf{R}^{-1}\mathbf{m}, \qquad B(\mathbf{x}) = \frac{1}{8}\mathbf{m}^T\mathbf{R}^{-1}\mathbf{m}.$$

If we select a $1 \times N$ linear feature extractor,

$$\hat{\mathbf{T}} = \mathbf{m}^T\mathbf{R}^{-1}, \tag{6.87}$$

and substitute (6.85) and (6.87) into (6.86), we obtain

$$\begin{aligned} J(\mathbf{y}) &= \mathbf{m}^T\mathbf{R}^{-1}\mathbf{m}(\mathbf{m}^T\mathbf{R}^{-1}\mathbf{m})^{-1}\mathbf{m}^T\mathbf{R}^{-1}\mathbf{m} = \mathbf{m}^T\mathbf{R}^{-1}\mathbf{m} = J(\mathbf{x}), \\ B(\mathbf{y}) &= \frac{1}{8}\mathbf{m}^T\mathbf{R}^{-1}\mathbf{m} = B(\mathbf{x}). \end{aligned} \tag{6.88}$$

The results suggest that the other directions do not contribute to the discrimination of the two classes. This is expected, since, as discussed in section 2.2, the optimum classification is based on the statistic $\mathbf{m}^T\mathbf{R}^{-1}\mathbf{x} = \hat{\mathbf{T}}\mathbf{x}$.

(2) *Equal mean case* In this case, the mean of the second class is also zero, $\mathbf{m} = \mathbf{0}$. We assume that both $\mathbf{R}_1$ and $\mathbf{R}_2$ are positive definite.

Then, there exists a real and nonsingular matrix $\mathbf{U}$, $\mathbf{U}^T = [\mathbf{u}_1, \ldots, \mathbf{u}_N]$ (e.g., Anderson, 1958, pp. 337–341)

$$\mathbf{U}\mathbf{R}_1\mathbf{U}^T = \mathbf{\Lambda}, \qquad \mathbf{U}\mathbf{R}_2\mathbf{U}^T = \mathbf{I}, \tag{6.89}$$

where $\mathbf{\Lambda}$ is a diagonal matrix with real and positive elements $\lambda_1, \lambda_2, \ldots, \lambda_N$ and $\mathbf{I}$ is the identity matrix. In fact, the row vectors of $\mathbf{U}$ are the solutions of the equation,

$$\mathbf{R}_1\mathbf{u} = \lambda\mathbf{R}_2\mathbf{u}. \tag{6.90}$$

It is noted that (6.89) implies a weighted orthonormality condition,

$$\mathbf{u}_j^T\mathbf{R}_2\mathbf{u}_j = 1, \qquad \mathbf{u}_j^T\mathbf{R}_2\mathbf{u}_l = 0, \qquad j \neq l. \tag{6.91}$$

Since $\mathbf{U}$ is nonsingular, and $J(\mathbf{x})$ and $B(\mathbf{x})$ are invariant under nonsingular transformations, we may use (6.86) to calculate $J(\mathbf{x})$ and $B(\mathbf{x})$ with $\mathbf{R}_{y1}$ and $\mathbf{R}_{y2}$ substituted by $\mathbf{\Lambda}$ and $\mathbf{I}$. Thus

$$\begin{aligned} J(\mathbf{x}) &= \frac{1}{2}\operatorname{tr}(\mathbf{\Lambda} - \mathbf{I})(\mathbf{I} - \mathbf{\Lambda}^{-1}) = \frac{1}{2}\sum_{j=1}^{N}\left(\lambda_j + \frac{1}{\lambda_j} - 2\right), \\ B(\mathbf{x}) &= \frac{1}{2}\log\frac{|(\mathbf{\Lambda} + \mathbf{I})/2|}{|\mathbf{\Lambda}|^{1/2}|\mathbf{I}|^{1/2}} = \frac{1}{4}\sum_{j=1}^{N}\log\frac{1}{4}\left(\lambda_j + \frac{1}{\lambda_j} + 2\right). \end{aligned} \tag{6.92}$$

Equation (6.92) suggest that we should choose a feature extractor

$$\tilde{\mathbf{T}}^T = [\mathbf{u}_1, \mathbf{u}_2, \ldots, \mathbf{u}_M] \tag{6.93}$$

where $\mathbf{u}_j$ is associated with λ_j which is ordered according to

$$\lambda_1 + \frac{1}{\lambda_1} \geqslant \lambda_2 + \frac{1}{\lambda_2} \geqslant \cdots \geqslant \lambda_N + \frac{1}{\lambda_N}. \tag{6.94}$$

The resulting values of $J(\mathbf{y})$ and $B(\mathbf{y})$ are

$$\begin{aligned} J(\mathbf{y}) &= \frac{1}{2}\sum_{j=1}^{M}\left(\lambda_j + \frac{1}{\lambda_j} - 2\right), \\ B(\mathbf{y}) &= \frac{1}{4}\sum_{j=1}^{M}\log\frac{1}{4}\left(\lambda_j + \frac{1}{\lambda_j} + 2\right). \end{aligned} \tag{6.95}$$

The proof of (6.93) and (6.95) is omitted, and interested readers may consult Kadota and Shepp (1967) or Henderson and Lainiotis (1970). It is noted that the row vectors of $\tilde{\mathbf{T}}$ are orthonormal in the sense of (6.91) instead of $\mathbf{u}_j^T\mathbf{u}_l = 0$, which is a property of the optimal $\mathbf{T}$ considered in the previous sections.

EXAMPLE 6.3

As the second example for feature extraction, we discuss a minimax approach to feature extraction using the Bhattacharyya coefficient. Assume that the two classes have mean values $\mathbf{m}_1$ and $\mathbf{m}_2$ and equal covariance matrix $\mathbf{R}$, and that this is the only knowledge we have. Let us first consider the case that $\mathbf{R} = \mathbf{I}$. We define two families of density functions,

$$\begin{aligned} \mathcal{G}_1 &= \{f_1(\mathbf{x}): E[\mathbf{x}] = \mathbf{m}_1, \quad E[(\mathbf{x} - \mathbf{m}_1)(\mathbf{x} - \mathbf{m}_1)^T] = \mathbf{I}\} \\ \mathcal{G}_2 &= \{f_2(\mathbf{x}): E[\mathbf{x}] = \mathbf{m}_2, \quad E[(\mathbf{x} - \mathbf{m}_2)(\mathbf{x} - \mathbf{m}_2)^T] = \mathbf{I}\}. \end{aligned} \tag{6.96}$$

We may define, similarly to (6.51), a robustness measure,

$$Q_B(\mathcal{G}_1, \mathcal{G}_2, \mathbf{T}) = \min_{\mathcal{G}_1, \mathcal{G}_2} B(\mathbf{y}) \tag{6.97}$$

and note that as long as $f_1 \in \mathcal{G}_1$ and $f_2 \in \mathcal{G}_2$, $B(\mathbf{y})$ is guaranteed to be greater than Q_B when we use $\mathbf{T}$. Let $\hat{\mathbf{T}}$ be defined by the relationship

$$Q_B(\mathcal{G}_1, \mathcal{G}_2, \hat{\mathbf{T}}) = \max_{\mathbf{T}} Q_B(\mathcal{G}_1, \mathcal{G}_2, \mathbf{T}). \tag{6.98}$$

We have used the Bhattacharyya distance $B(\mathbf{y})$ in defining Q_B and $\hat{\mathbf{T}}$, and note that $\hat{\mathbf{T}}$ is a minimax feature extractor in terms of the Bhattacharyya coefficient $\beta(\mathbf{y})$. We wish to show that for this example, if the row space of a matrix $\mathbf{T}_0$ contains the vector $\mathbf{m}_2 - \mathbf{m}_1$, $\mathbf{T}_0$ is a minimax feature extractor.

Let us define similarly to (6.96) two families of density functions $\mathcal{H}_1$ and $\mathcal{H}_2$ with mean vectors $\mathbf{T}_0\mathbf{m}_1$ and $\mathbf{T}_0\mathbf{m}_2$, respecively, and covariance matrix $\mathbf{R}_y = \mathbf{T}_0\mathbf{R}\mathbf{T}_0^T = \mathbf{I}$, since the row vectors of $\mathbf{T}_0$ are assumed orthonormal. Using $\beta(\mathbf{y})$ instead of $B(\mathbf{y})$, we have

$$\begin{aligned} \max_{\mathcal{G}_1, \mathcal{G}_2} \int \sqrt{f_1(\mathbf{x}) f_2(\mathbf{x})}\, d\mathbf{x} &\leqslant \max_{\mathcal{G}_1, \mathcal{G}_2} \int \sqrt{h_1(\mathbf{y}) h_2(\mathbf{y})}\, d\mathbf{y} \\ &\leqslant \max_{\mathcal{H}_1, \mathcal{H}_2} \int \sqrt{h_1(\mathbf{y}) h_2(\mathbf{y})}\, d\mathbf{y}. \end{aligned} \tag{6.99}$$

The first inequality is due to the known fact that $\beta(\mathbf{x}) \leqslant \beta(\mathbf{y})$, and the second inequality holds since $f_1(\mathbf{x}) \in \mathcal{G}_1$ and $f_2(\mathbf{x}) \in \mathcal{G}_2$ imply $h_1(\mathbf{y}) \in \mathcal{H}_1$ and $h_2(\mathbf{y}) \in \mathcal{H}_2$. Note that the middle term in (6.99) is the maximum $\beta(\mathbf{y})$ corresponding to Q_B.

Now consider a linear feature extractor $\mathbf{T}_0$ and assume that its row space contains $\mathbf{m}_2 - \mathbf{m}_1$. Since under this assumption, the marginal densities in the complementary space, $l_1(\mathbf{z})$ and $l_2(\mathbf{z})$, will both have zero mean and covariance $\mathbf{I}$, it is possible to have $l_1(\mathbf{z}) = l_2(\mathbf{z})$ and the distribution in $\Omega_\mathbf{z}$ will have no contribution to $\beta(\mathbf{x})$. Let us consider the case that $l_1(\mathbf{z}) = l_2(\mathbf{z}) = l(\mathbf{z})$ and that with $\mathbf{y} = \mathbf{T}_0\mathbf{x}$ and $\mathbf{z} = \mathbf{S}_0\mathbf{x}$,

$$\hat{f}_1(\mathbf{x}) = \hat{h}_1(\mathbf{T}_0\mathbf{x})l(\mathbf{S}_0\mathbf{x}), \quad \hat{f}_2(\mathbf{x}) = \hat{h}_2(\mathbf{T}_0\mathbf{x})l(\mathbf{S}_0\mathbf{x}),$$

where $\hat{h}_1$ and $\hat{h}_2$ are the density functions that maximize $\beta(\mathbf{y})$ over the families $\mathscr{H}_1$ and $\mathscr{H}_2$. Clearly, in this case,

$$\int \sqrt{\hat{f}_1(\mathbf{x})\hat{f}_2(\mathbf{x})}\, d\mathbf{x} = \max_{\mathscr{H}_1,\mathscr{H}_2} \int \sqrt{h_1(\mathbf{y})h_2(\mathbf{y})}\, d\mathbf{y}. \tag{6.100}$$

A comparison of (6.99) and (6.100) shows immediately that for our $\mathbf{T}_0$,

$$\max_{\mathscr{F}_1,\mathscr{F}_2} \int \sqrt{f_1(\mathbf{x})f_2(\mathbf{x})}\, d\mathbf{x} = \max_{\mathscr{H}_1,\mathscr{H}_2} \int \sqrt{h_1(\mathbf{y})h_2(\mathbf{y})}\, d\mathbf{y}. \tag{6.101}$$

This is the minimax $\beta(\mathbf{y})$ since according to (6.99) no other feature extractor can yield a smaller maximum of $\beta(\mathbf{y})$. Hence, the matrix $\mathbf{T}_0$ is a minimax feature extractor defined by (6.98). It is interesting to note that the minimax feature extractor is not unique, and according to the minimax strategy, the remaining $(M - 1)$ dimensions may be chosen arbitrarily.

We now consider the case that $\mathbf{R}_1 = \mathbf{R}_2 = \mathbf{R} \neq \mathbf{I}$. Let $\infty > \lambda_1 \geqslant \lambda_2 \cdots \geqslant \lambda_N > 0$ be the eigenvalues and $\mathbf{u}_1, \mathbf{u}_2, \ldots, \mathbf{u}_N$ be the orthonormal eigenvectors of $\mathbf{R}$. We have shown in section 6.2 that

$$\mathbf{R} = \sum_{j=1}^{N} \lambda_j \mathbf{u}_j \mathbf{u}_j^T.$$

It is easy to verify that the inverse of $\mathbf{R}$, $\mathbf{R}^{-1}$, may be written as

$$\mathbf{R}^{-1} = \sum_{j=1}^{N} \lambda_j^{-1} \mathbf{u}_j \mathbf{u}_j^T.$$

Let us define a symmetric, nonsingular matrix,

$$\mathbf{R}^{-1/2} = \sum_{j=1}^{N} \lambda_j^{-1/2} \mathbf{u}_j \mathbf{u}_j^T,$$

and a transformation

$$\mathbf{x}' = \mathbf{R}^{-1/2}\mathbf{x}.$$

The mean vectors and the covariance matrix are

$$\mathbf{m}_1' = \mathbf{R}^{-1/2}\mathbf{m}_1, \qquad \mathbf{m}_2' = \mathbf{R}^{-1/2}\mathbf{m}_2$$

$$\mathbf{R}' = \mathbf{R}^{-1/2}\mathbf{R}\mathbf{R}^{-1/2} = \mathbf{I}.$$

Since β is invariant under nonsingular transformations, finding a minimax feature extractor for the random vector $\mathbf{x}$ in $\Omega_{\mathbf{x}}$ is equivalent to finding a minimax feature extractor for $\mathbf{x}'$ in $\Omega_{\mathbf{x}'}$. Noting that $\mathbf{R}' = \mathbf{I}$, we conclude that the row space of the minimax feature extractor of $\mathbf{x}'$ must contain the vector $\mathbf{m}_2' - \mathbf{m}_1' = \mathbf{R}^{-1/2}(\mathbf{m}_2 - \mathbf{m}_1)$. Since $\mathbf{x}' = \mathbf{R}^{-1/2}\mathbf{x}$, a minimax feature extractor for $\mathbf{x}$ must first perform this transformation and will have a row space containing $\mathbf{R}^{-1/2}(\mathbf{m}_2' - \mathbf{m}_1') = \mathbf{R}^{-1}(\mathbf{m}_2 - \mathbf{m}_1)$.

In some pattern recognition problems, the probability density functions are unknown, but a sequence of samples $\mathbf{x}_1, \mathbf{x}_2, \ldots,$ with known classifications is available. A possible approach for this case is to use the multidimensional version of Parzen's empirical approximation. Thus, the two probability densities are approximated by

$$\begin{aligned} \hat{f}_1(\mathbf{x}) &= \frac{1}{n_1} \sum_{\mathbf{x}_i \in C_1} g(\mathbf{x}; \mathbf{x}_i, \alpha^2 \mathbf{I}), \\ \hat{f}_2(\mathbf{x}) &= \frac{1}{n_2} \sum_{\mathbf{x}_i \in C_2} g(\mathbf{x}; \mathbf{x}_i, \alpha^2 \mathbf{I}), \end{aligned} \tag{6.102}$$

where n_1 and n_2 are numbers of samples belonging to C_1 and C_2 respectively. The divergence or the Bhattacharyya coefficient may be calculated numerically using this approximation. For a given $\mathbf{T}$, $J(\mathbf{y})$ and $\beta(\mathbf{y})$ may be calculated in a similar way since the marginal densities of $\hat{f}_1(\mathbf{x})$ and $\hat{f}_2(\mathbf{x})$ are also mixtures of Gaussian densities. Thus, we may compare $J(\mathbf{y})$ or $\beta(\mathbf{y})$ for different feature extractors and select the best one. For example, in feature selection we may consider all possible combinations of M features selected from the set of N measurements, calculate numerically $\beta(\mathbf{y})$ for each combination, and select the set of M features that has the smallest $\beta(\mathbf{y})$. It should be cautioned that the numerical computation of $\beta(\mathbf{y})$ using (6.102) is rather difficult, and it is sometimes advisable to use mixtures of uniform distributions instead of the Gaussian mixtures in (6.102). The computation time required is usually rather long even when using uniform mixtures; on the other hand, the results are generally superior to those obtained using mean values and covariance matrices only.

6.5 Nonlinear Feature Extraction

When the feature extractor is nonlinear, it can be written as

$$\mathbf{y} = \mathcal{T}(\mathbf{x}), \qquad \mathbf{x} \text{ in } \Omega_{\mathbf{x}}, \qquad \mathbf{y} \text{ in } \Omega_{\mathbf{y}} \tag{6.103}$$

where the N-vector $\mathbf{x}$ is transformed into the M-vector $\mathbf{y}$ and where M may be greater or less than N. This expression, which is just (6.1), is not very helpful since $\mathcal{T}(\cdot)$ is now the set of all transformations mapping an N-space into an M-space so that discrimination is easier in the M-space. The two major approaches to finding $\mathcal{T}(\cdot)$ involve either forming a complete series expansion of the original space and hoping that only a small number of terms is needed or having some prior knowledge of the way the classes are distributed based on the physical origin of the patterns. Although it is quite difficult to find nonlinear transformations, the simplification can be so great that considerable effort is justified. This can be well illustrated with two examples.

EXAMPLE 6.4

Consider a two-dimensional two-class problem where the classes are distributed according to:

$$\begin{aligned} f_1(\mathbf{x}) &= \frac{1}{\pi\alpha_0^2} \qquad 0 \leqslant \|\mathbf{x}\| \leqslant \alpha_0 \\ &= 0 \qquad \text{elsewhere} \end{aligned} \tag{6.104}$$

$$\begin{aligned} f_2(\mathbf{x}) &= \frac{1}{\pi(\alpha_2^2 - \alpha_1^2)} \qquad \alpha_1 \leqslant \|\mathbf{x}\| \leqslant \alpha_2 \\ &= 0 \qquad \text{elsewhere.} \end{aligned} \tag{6.105}$$

This is illustrated in figure 6.4. The obvious feature extractor $\mathcal{T}(\cdot)$ is now

$$y = (\mathbf{x}^T\mathbf{x})^{1/2} \tag{6.106}$$

The optimal discriminant function will now be linear in the y-space and dimensionality has been reduced from two to one.

This is a very simple example when the distributions for the classes are known. It is interesting to question how we could have arrived at it if we had no prior knowledge. A power series expansion up to M terms is:

$$\begin{aligned} y_1 &= x_1 \\ y_2 &= x_2 \\ y_3 &= x_1^2 \\ y_4 &= x_2^2 \\ y_5 &= x_1 x_2 \\ y_6 &= x_1^3 \\ &\text{etc.} \end{aligned}$$

Then a linear discriminant function on $\mathbf{y}$ could be found by an appropriate

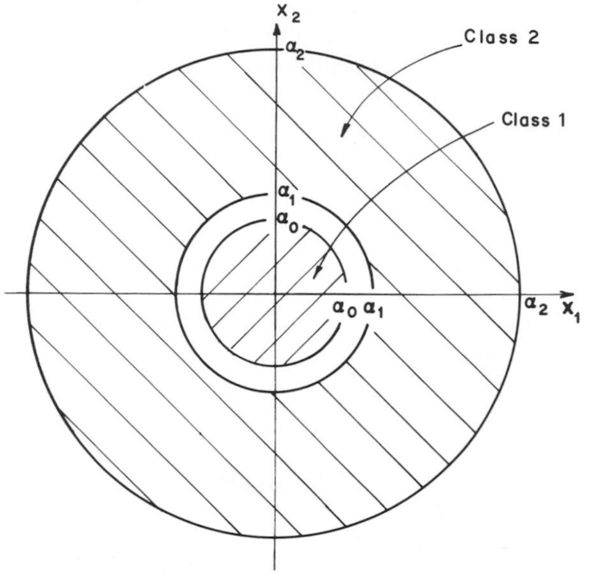

fig. 6.4 An example of two classes which are separable with a nonlinear function in two dimensions.

algorithm. Provided there were sufficient training samples, it would presumably be found that

$$\theta_3 = \theta_4 = \alpha$$

$$\theta_i < \varepsilon \qquad \text{for } i = 1, 2, 5, \ldots, M$$

where $D(\mathbf{y}) = \boldsymbol{\theta}^T\mathbf{y}$ and ε is a constant $\ll \alpha$. This shows that only two terms are important and that the required nonlinear transformation is that of (6.106).

EXAMPLE 6.5

Consider another two-dimensional two-class problem where the classes are distributed according to:

$$f_1(\mathbf{x}) = \frac{1}{16}\sum_{i=0}^{3}\sum_{j=0}^{3} g\left(\mathbf{x}; \left[2\pi i + \frac{\pi}{2}, 2\pi j\right]^T, \sigma^2\mathbf{I}\right)$$
$$f_2(\mathbf{x}) = \frac{1}{16}\sum_{i=0}^{3}\sum_{j=0}^{3} g\left(\mathbf{x}; \left[2\pi i + \frac{3\pi}{2}, 2\pi j + \pi\right]^T, \sigma^2\mathbf{I}\right). \tag{6.107}$$

This is illustrated in figure 6.5(*a*), which shows that each class consists of 16 Gaussian clusters. Obviously no simple linear or low-order polynomial discriminant function will give good results although a nearest-neighbor scheme would be helpful.

If the features are chosen to be

$$\begin{aligned} y_1 &= \sin x_1 \\ y_2 &= \cos x_2 \end{aligned} \tag{6.108}$$

then in the new space the classes are distributed as shown in figure 6.5(*b*).

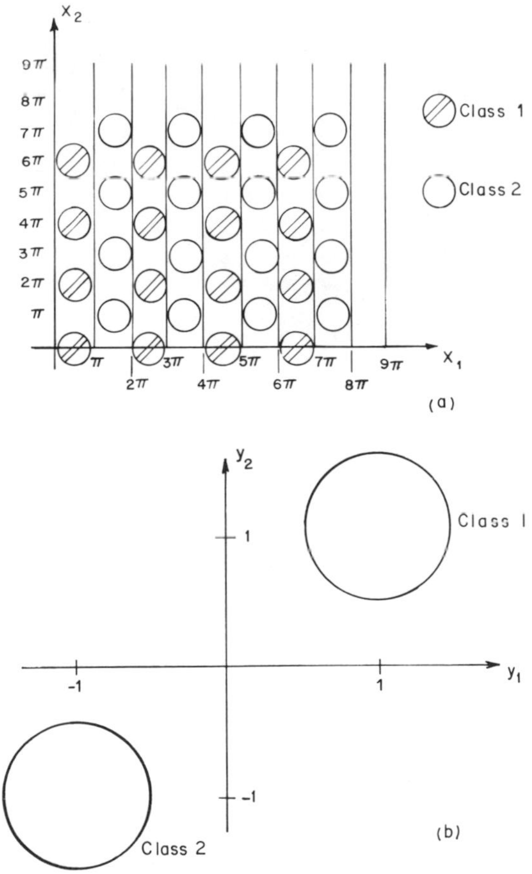

fig. 6.5 This example shows how two classes which are quite difficult to separate in the original space (a), can become linearly separable in a new space (b) if an appropriate nonlinear transformation is applied.

Obviously this nonlinear transformation provides a very useful simplification. A polynomial series expansion of **x** would certainly not indicate those functions. However, a Fourier series expansion could indicate the features if it were applied intelligently.

These two examples have shown that a well chosen nonlinear transformation can greatly simplify the problem. The difficulty is to choose the appropriate transformation where the data are of more than two dimensions (two-dimensional data can be examined graphically) and where the required functions are not as simple as those in our contrived examples.

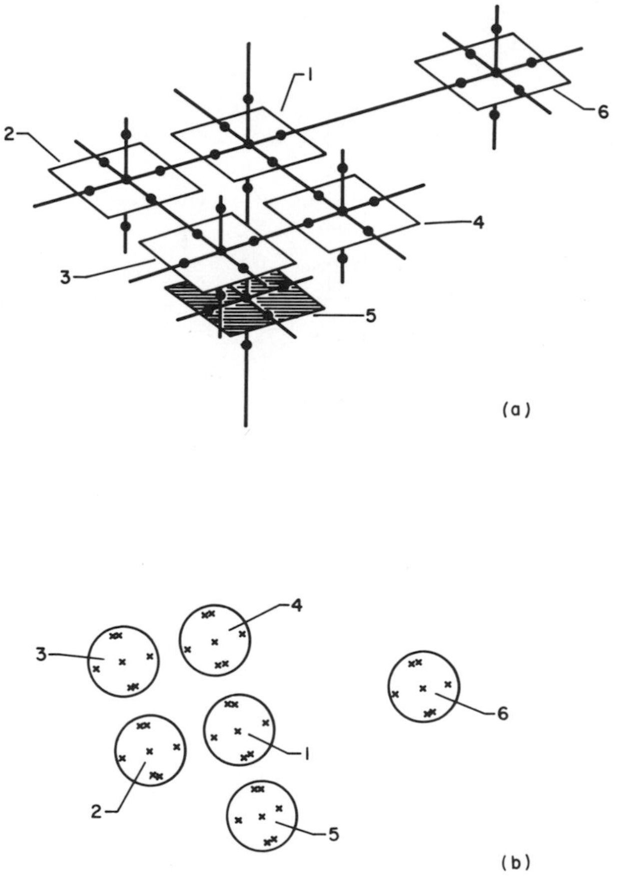

fig. 6.6 (a) An example of six classes with seven points each, in three dimensions. (b) The six classes have been projected non-orthogonally into two dimensions. (Calvert, 1970)

Although there is no substitute for a priori knowledge of the class distributions, we will discuss two approaches that can sometimes be helpful.

6.5.1 Dimensionality reduction of arbitrary data structures

As an illustrative example, consider the six linearly separable classes in three dimensions sketched in figure 6.6(*a*). It will be seen that there is no way to guarantee a feature space of dimensionality lower than three, i.e., it is impossible to project these classes orthogonally to two dimensions without causing the classes to overlap. Nevertheless, it would be desirable to find a transformation to a configuration in, say, two dimensions, such as that in figure 6.6(*b*). In the new configuration, some of the interrelationships between the classes have been lost but the classes are still linearly discriminable. It would be ideal if a criterion could be found that determined a transformation to a lower dimensional space while maintaining classification accuracy. Unfortunately, except for cases where the classes are normally distributed, it is difficult to develop such a criterion.

Some interesting heuristic approaches to reducing the dimensionality of arbitrarily distributed data have been developed by Shepard and Carroll (1966). The aim is to project N-dimensional data to a space of lower dimensionality M, while preserving the local structure of the data. This means that in the new space of lower dimensionality, each point bears approximately the same relationship to its neighbors that it did in the original space, but its relationship to points relatively distant in the original space may be quite different in the new space. The technique used by Shepard and Carroll to achieve this involves the use of a "continuity" criterion J, given by

$$J = \frac{\sum_{i,j} \dfrac{d_{ij}^2}{D_{ij}^4}}{\left[\sum_{i,j} \dfrac{1}{D_{ij}^2}\right]^2}, \tag{6.109}$$

where

d_{ij} = distance from point i to point j in the original space;

D_{ij} = distance from point i to point j in the new space.

This criterion is independent of the scale of D_{ij} and is minimum when d_{ij}/D_{ij} is constant for all i, j. If the new space (for D_{ij}) is constrained to be of lower dimensionality than the original space (for d_{ij}), generally, the absolute minimum will not be attainable. Since the terms in the numerator are of the form $(d_{ij}^2/D_{ij}^2) \times (1/D_{ij}^2)$, i.e., d_{ij}^2/D_{ij}^2 weighted by $1/D_{ij}^2$, it is clear that at any constrained minimum the largest distances will have least effect. The result is a new configuration where the smallest distances are nearly equal to the corresponding distances in the original space, but the largest can vary considerably.

To implement the procedure, the d_{ij}'s are obtained using the points in the original space, and an equal number of points in the new space are chosen arbitrarily. Points in the new space are then iteratively moved (by steepest-descent methods, for example) so as to minimize the criterion J. If the original data configuration is of a dimensionality no greater than that of the new space, then the configuration will be completely recovered (within a scaling constant). If, on the other hand, the original data configuration is of greater dimensionality than the new space, then, as discussed above, the interrrelationships of neighboring points will be approximately the same as in the original space, but more widely separated points may lose their original interrelationships. The new structure for widely separated points is certainly not unique and may depend on the order in which the points are processed.

The use of this technique is well illustrated by one of Shepard and Carroll's examples reproduced in figure 6.7. This shows how points distributed on the surface of a sphere are projected into two dimensions with what is essentially a conformal transformation. This is very similar to azimuthal equidistant projections used to map the surface of the world onto a plane. The original data in figure 6.7(a) consists of 62 points at the intersections of 5 equally spaced parallels and 12 equally spaced meridians on the surface of the sphere. The new two-dimensional configuration in figure 6.7(b) shows that the sphere has been punctured and opened out around the hole. It will be noted that the local distance relationships between points are maintained except that those points that have been separated by the puncture are now on opposite sides of the diagram. The nonuniqueness of the solution is illustrated by the arbitrary position of the puncture.

6.5.2 Structure preserving nonlinear transformations for dimensionality reduction

Nonlinear mapping can be applied to multiclass pattern recognition data in a number of ways. In principle, all training patterns could be mapped to a space of a lower dimensionality. This would have the advantage that either supervised or unsupervised training sequences could be handled equally well since no knowledge of the classes would be necessary.

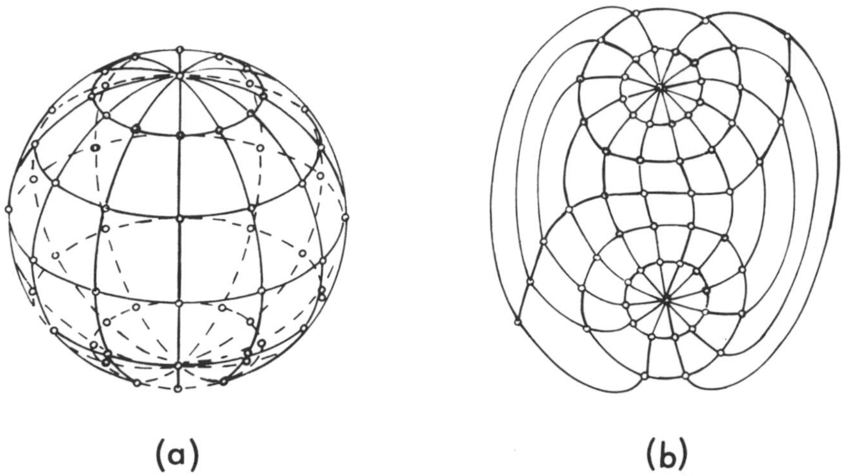

fig. 6.7 An example from Shepard and Carroll (1966). The original configuration (a) consists of 62 points distributed on the surface of a sphere. Minimizing the continuity criterion results in conformal "unfolding" into two dimensions as shown in (b).

However, if there were P training patterns, Shepard and Carroll's technique would require the use of $P(P-1)/2$ distances, so that even for simple problems the storage would be formidable. A more efficient approach is to replace the original pattern data with some representative samples. For unsupervised training sets this can be done by finding the modes or clusters in the data and by representing each mode by its mean. With classified training sets each class can be represented either by its mean or if necessary by the means of each of its modes.

Assume that the K classes have been appropriately represented in the original N dimensions by the n points

$$\mathbf{x}_i \qquad i = 1, 2, \ldots, n \qquad \text{where } n \geqslant K.$$

Then we apply the information-preserving constraint iteratively to find a new configuration of n points in the new space of reduced dimensionality M. The result is

$$\mathbf{y}_i \ \text{ for } i = 1, 2, \ldots, n.$$

The only remaining problem is to find a transformation such that $\hat{\mathbf{y}}_i = \mathcal{T}(\mathbf{x}_i)$. Generally this will be nonlinear.

If a polynomial is used to describe the transformation, the first three terms will be

$$\hat{\mathbf{y}}_i = \beta_{N+1} + \boldsymbol{\beta}^T \mathbf{x}_i + \mathbf{x}_i^T \mathbf{A} \mathbf{x}_i + \cdots . \tag{6.110}$$

The higher-order terms follow in an obvious manner but the notation becomes rather tedious. The coefficients of the polynomial are found by applying linear regression, which minimizes the mean square error, i.e.,

$$\sum_{i=1}^{n} (\hat{\mathbf{y}}_i - \mathbf{y}_i)^T (\hat{\mathbf{y}}_i - \mathbf{y}_i).$$

EXAMPLE 6.6

If this approach is applied to the admittedly contrived data of figure 6.6(*a*), the results are as shown in figure 6.6(*b*). The six classes were represented with their means, i.e., $K = n = 6$, and the dimensionality was

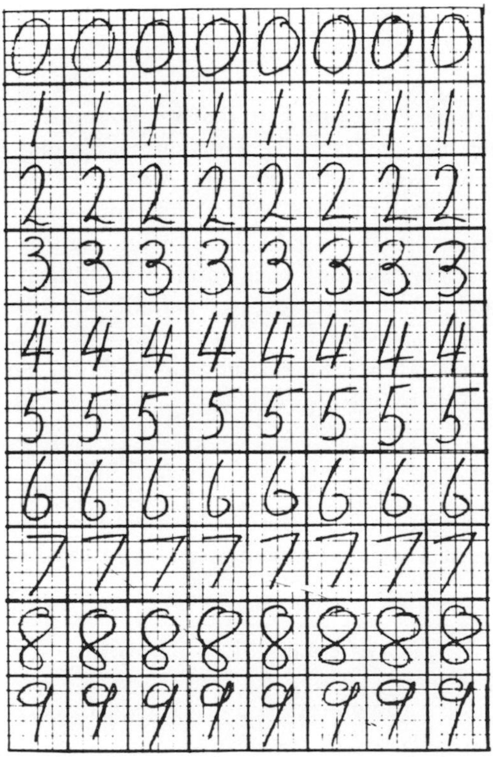

fig. 6.8 Eight examples of each of ten hand-drawn digits. (Calvert, 1970).

TABLE 6.1

	Original Measurement Dimensionality	Minimum Dimensionality M for Linear Separation
Scheme 1	20	3
Scheme 2	18	4

reduced from $N = 3$ to $M = 2$. The transformation that resulted was linear. Obviously the distribution of points within each class has been changed and although classes 1, 2, 3, 4, and 6 bear their original relationship to each other, class 5 does not. However the transformation is a useful feature extractor since classification accuracy is maintained.

EXAMPLE 6.7

A more significant example of this approach is based on the handwritten digits shown in figure 6.8. There are eight examples of each of 10 handwritten characters. To test the generality of the approach two deliberately naive digitizing schemes are used.

Scheme 1 A 10×8 mesh of 80 cells was used for each numerical character; this mesh was simplified into a 5×4 mesh of 20 main cells. Each main cell was scored 0–4 according to the number of original cells crossed by the character. The result was 20 numbers, each having an integer value 0, 1, 2, 3, or 4 for each character. Thus the resultant measurement dimensionality was $N = 20$.

Scheme 2 The 10×8 fine mesh of 80 cells was as in scheme 1. For each of the ten horizontal rows, the number of times a character crossed any of the eight vertical lines was scored, and for each of the eight vertical rows the number of times a character crossed one of the ten horizontal lines was scored. The resultant measurement dimensionality was $N = 18$.

Each class was represented by its mean, the classes were fitted into spaces of increasing dimensionality (starting with two), described with a transformation (which was linear), and tested for linear separability. The results in Table 6.1 show that a large reduction in the number of features was possible with both schemes, but that (not surprisingly) the encoding of scheme 1 was more effective. For illustrative purposes the two-dimensional configuration

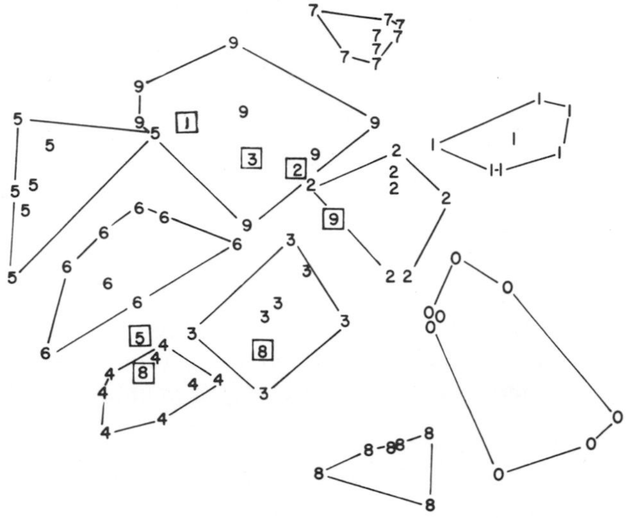

fig. 6.9 A non-orthogonal projection of the data for ten hand-drawn digits into two dimensions. Points which overlap with another class are surrounded by a square and class boundaries are added for clarity. (Calvert, 1970).

for scheme 1 is shown in figure 6.9. This is interesting in itself and indicates the advantage of representing data with two features since the graphic representation gives some insight into the interclass relationships. It appears that better results could be obtained for this example if each class were represented by two or more points.

To summarize, it is possible to use heuristic techniques for the nonlinear manipulation of data structures to reduce the dimensionality of a feature space. The nonlinear mapping results in a data configuration in a space of reduced dimensionality where the local structure of the data is preserved, i.e., the transformation is conformal. This tends to maintain classification accuracy. The procedure will only be useful if the work involved in applying the nonlinear transformation is outweighed by the savings due to representation of the patterns in a feature space of lower dimensionality.

6.5.3. Randomly generated nonlinear transformations

The transformation found with the method described in section 6.5.2 will simplify the classification process by reducing the dimensionality. These transformations will not generally change a class configuration from nonlinearly separable to linearly separable. There would be obvious advantages in transforming the classes as shown in figure 6.10, where classes that are separable with nonlinear discriminant functions become linearly separable. This can take place with or without a decrease in dimensionality.

To be useful the transformation should have the following properties.

(1) *Simple form of classes* The cluster of points for each class should unfold to a simple form (approximately hyperellipsoidal) as in figure 6.10. This facilitates an economic description in the transformed space and may lead to a decrease in dimensionality.

(2) *Local information preservation* The relative position of each point to its nearest neighbors should be approximately the same in the new space as in the old space (i.e., the transformation should be essentially conformal). This is necessary for a reasonable description of the transformation.

(3) *Linear separation* To be useful for pattern recognition each class must be linearly separable from all others in the transformed space.

Perhaps the ideal way to find a suitable configuration of points for the transformed space would be to build the described requirements above into a criterion function, the minima of which correspond to acceptable final configurations. Then each point could be moved from its original position in a direction that would tend to decrease the criterion, and the final configuration could be found iteratively. Unfortunately, such criteria are difficult to find. Another method is to apply random perturbations within constraints until a suitable configuration results. This is a very general approach suitable for a wide class of data, but does not yield a unique solution.

Consider n points in N dimensions, i.e., $\mathbf{x}_i$ for $i = 1, 2, \ldots, n$, each belonging to one of K classes. Denote a point of the original configuration by $\mathbf{x}_i(0)$ and after j iterations of random perturbations by $\mathbf{x}_i(j)$. On each iteration every point is perturbed by a different random vector $\mathbf{r}$ such that

$$\mathbf{x}_i(j+1) = (\mathbf{x}_i(j) + \mathbf{r}_i)\Big|_C \tag{6.111}$$

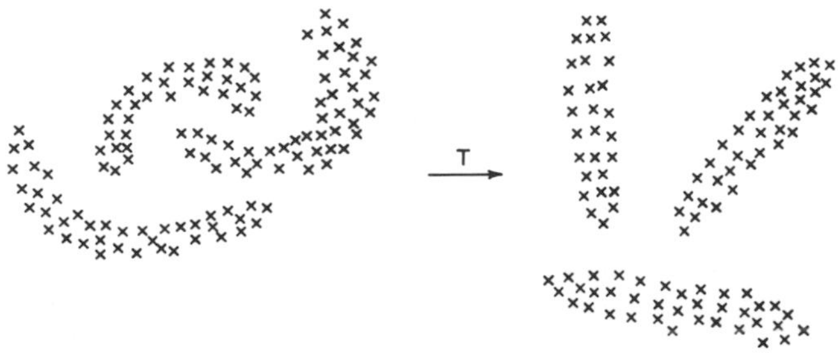

fig. 6.10 A nonlinear transformation which gives a simpler configuration. (Calvert and Young, 1969).

where C denotes the constraints to be checked. If the constraints are not satisfied then the perturbation is not acceptable and it is either modified or rejected completely. The magnitude and direction of $\mathbf{r}$ are both random, and it is convenient to choose $\mathbf{r}$ from an n-dimensional Gaussian distribution with each component independent and of identical variance. The variance σ^2 is adjusted at each step of the iteration to ensure that it is large enough to give appreciable change, but not so large that every perturbation is rejected. Although ideally the final configuration should depend only on the constraints, in practice, since there is no unique solution, it also depends on σ^2.

Constraints can be implemented without difficulty to ensure that the random perturbations tend to make the classes become linearly separable and to unfold. The separation constraint is simply that after a point has been perturbed its Euclidean distance from the nearest point in another class should not have decreased.

The unfolding of contorted classes (as in figure 6.10) can be obtained with the constraint that after a perturbation there must be an increase in the normalized variance of the distances among all points of the class to which the perturbed point belongs. The effect of this constraint is that interpoint distances less than average tend to get smaller whereas those greater than average tend to get larger.

A local information- or structure-preserving constraint can be obtained from the continuity criterion of Shepard and Carroll shown above in equation (6.109). This criterion J is a measure of the smoothness or continuity of the transformation, $\mathbf{x}(j) = \mathcal{T}(\mathbf{x}(0))$. At each iteration of the procedure, after a random perturbation as in (6.111) has been checked against separation and unfolding constraints, a correction is applied such that

$$\mathbf{x}_i'(j) = (\mathbf{x}_i(j) - a\nabla_{\mathbf{x}_i} J)\Big|_D . \tag{6.112}$$

This has the effect of moving each point $\mathbf{x}_i(j)$ a small distance determined by a in the direction of the negative gradient of J. However, this in turn is subject to the constraint D, that interclass separation not be reduced.

The procedure is best summarized by the flowchart in figure 6.11. The random perturbations (equation (6.111)) terminate when the data become linearly separable but after that the continuity correction (equation (6.112)) is applied iteratively until no further improvement is possible. A heuristic procedure such as that described here can only be justified on the basis of its performance. Calvert and Young (1969) have shown that useful results can be obtained with 36-dimensional character recognition data. Two simple examples in two dimensions are shown in figure 6.12.

After the linearly separable configuration $\mathbf{x}(j)$ is found, it must be described explicitly, i.e., we must find $\mathcal{T}(\cdot)$ such that

$$\mathbf{y} = \mathcal{T}(\mathbf{x}(0)) \tag{6.113}$$

where $\mathbf{y}$ is the estimate of $\mathbf{x}(j)$. If a mean-square error criterion is used to determine $\mathcal{T}(\cdot)$, then we should minimize

$$\epsilon^2 = \sum_{i=1}^{n} (\mathbf{y} - \mathbf{x}(j))^T(\mathbf{y} - \mathbf{x}(j)). \tag{6.114}$$

$\mathcal{T}(\cdot)$ can be a polynomial as in (6.110) above or any other series expansion of $\mathbf{x}(0)$.

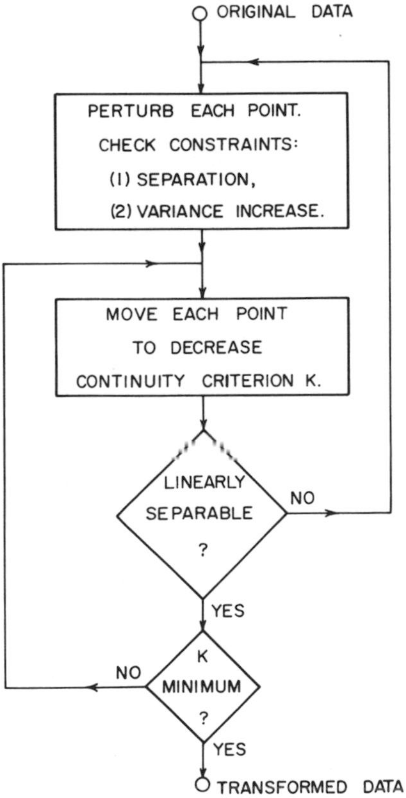

fig. 6.11 The implementation of minimization of the continuity criterion as a means of maintaining structure. (Calvert and Young, 1969).

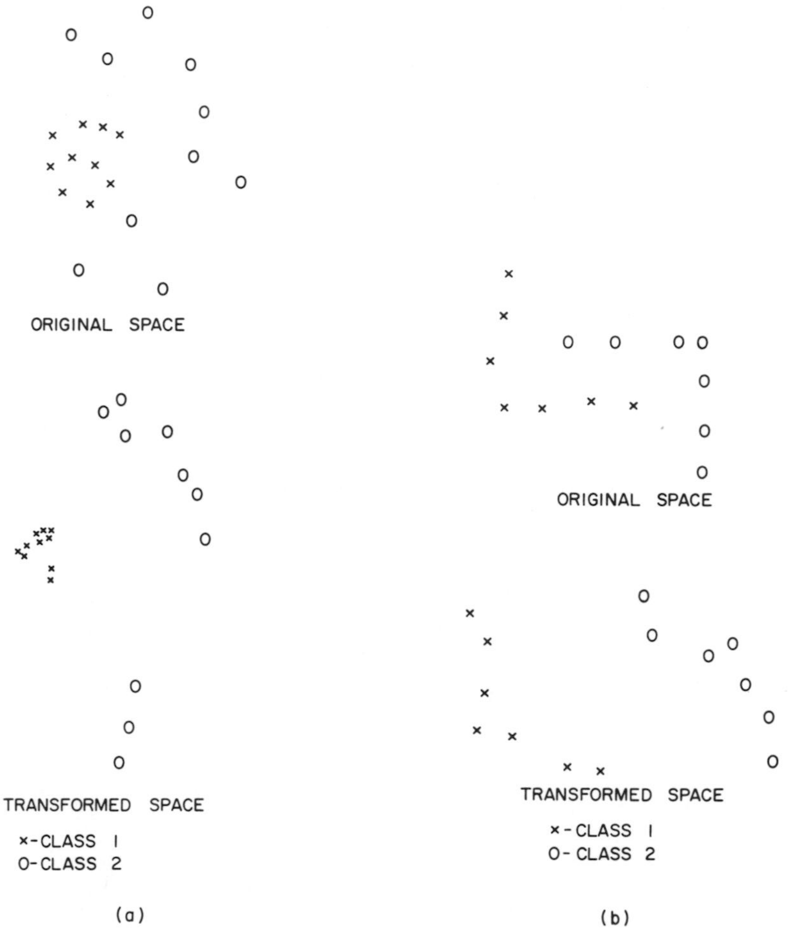

fig. 6.12 Simple examples of the transformation. (Calvert and Young, 1969).

6.6 Notes and Remarks

We have been concerned with the theory and general principles of feature extraction without considering the selection of measurements for pattern recognition. In a broad sense, measurement selection may be regarded as feature extraction, but depends heavily on the particular pattern recognition problem under consideration. In the following chapters, we shall deal with two specific problems, namely the computer analysis of electrocardiograms and character recognition. Readers will note that a major concern is, in fact, measurement selection and feature extraction. The *IEEE Transac-*

tions on Computers published in 1971 a special issue on feature extraction and selection in pattern recognition, which includes both theory and practice. Reviews of feature extraction schemes may be found in Levine (1969) and Nagy (1968).

The Karhunen–Loève expansion was derived originally for random processes. A random process $x(t)$, $-T/2 \leqslant t \leqslant T/2$, may be expanded into the form

$$x(t) = \sum_{j=1}^{\infty} c_j u_j(t), \tag{6.115}$$

$$c_j = \int_{-T/2}^{T/2} x(t) u_j(t)\, dt, \tag{6.116}$$

where $\{u_j(t)\}$ is a set of orthonormal eigenfunctions satisfying the eigene-quations

$$\int_{-T/2}^{T/2} R(t_1, t_2) u(t_2)\, dt_2 = \lambda u(t_1), \quad -T/2 \leqslant t_1 \leqslant T/2. \tag{6.117}$$

The covariance $R(t_1, t_2)$ is defined as $E[x(t_1)x(t_2)]$ with the mean $E[x(t)]$ assumed zero. The coefficients are uncorrelated,

$$E[c_j c_l] = 0, \qquad j \neq l. \tag{6.118}$$

It can be shown that if in the expansion (6.115), the coefficients c_j given by (6.116) satisfy (6.118), then the functions $u_j(t)$ must be the eigenfunctions satisfying (6.117). Conversely, if $u_j(t)$ are eigenfunctions and

$$\hat{x}(t) = \sum_{j=1}^{\infty} c_j u_j(t), \tag{6.119}$$

with c_j as in (6.116), then $\hat{x}(t)$ equals $x(t)$ in the mean-square sense, i.e.,

$$E[|x(t) - \hat{x}(t)|^2] = 0. \tag{6.120}$$

These results may be extended to random vectors considered in this chapter. In fact, there will be only a finite number of eigenvectors for the random vector case, and the results are simpler. For more detail, see Papoulis (1965).

The application of the Karhunen–Loève expansion to feature extraction is due to Chien and Fu (1968) and Watanabe (1965). They proved, in addition to theorem 6.1, that the expansion minimizes the entropy function defined over the variances of the coefficients c_j in the expansion. Let

$$\rho_j = E[c_j^2] \Big/ \sum_{l=1}^{N} E[c_l^2], \tag{6.121}$$

the entropy

$$H(\rho) = -\sum_{j=1}^{N} \rho_j \log \rho_j, \tag{6.122}$$

associated with the Karhunen–Loève expansion is minimal compared with any other coordinate system. It is noted that $H(\rho)$ is different from $H(\mathbf{y})$ defined in section 6.3, and the minimization of the former does not contradict the maximization of the latter. In fact, generally speaking, the two criteria yield similar results. Watanabe et al. (1967) extended and applied the idea of the entropy-minimizing coordinate system separately to a set of samples of each class. Fukunaga and Koontz (1970) modified the Karhunen–Loève expansion to take into consideration the discrimination of two classes. It should be mentioned that the Karhunen–Loève expansion was applied successfully by these authors to character recognition and by Young and Huggins (1963) to the representation of electrocardiograms.

The entropy criterion has been attractive to investigators in various disciplines since Shannon published his classical paper, *A Mathematical Theory of Communication*, in 1948. Theorem 6.2 on feature extraction using Gaussian patterns is due to Tou and Heydorn (1967), and the minimax feature extraction is based on the work of Young (1971). The mutual information was used as a feature extraction criterion by Lewis (1962). In addition to the authors mentioned so far, the entropy criterion was used in pattern recognition in one way or another by Bledsoe (1966), Brown (1959), Chow and Liu (1968), Christensen (1968), and others.

The divergence was proposed and investigated by Kullback (1968) and Kullback and Leibler (1951), and the Bhattacharyya coefficient was introduced in 1943. The relationship between the Bhattacharyya coefficient and the error probability is due to Kailath (1967) and Lainiotis (1969), and related works include Chernoff (1952), Chu and Chueh (1967), Hellman and Raviv (1970), and Heydorn (1968). The divergence and the Bhattacharyya coefficient were applied to signal detection and pattern recognition by many authors including Fu et al. (1970), Grettenberg (1963), Henderson and Lainiotis (1969, 1970), Kadota and Shepp (1967), Marill and Green (1963), Schweppe (1967), and Tou and Heydorn (1967).

The use of Parzen's empirical approximation for feature extraction was considered by Fu et al. (1970), Heydorn (1968), Lainiotis (1969), and Patrick and Fischer (1969). Patrick and Fischer derived algorithms for finding optimal linear feature extractors that minimized the criterion,

$$\int [\hat{h}_1(\mathbf{y}) - \hat{h}_2(\mathbf{y})]^2 \, d\mathbf{y},$$

where $\hat{h}_1(\mathbf{y})$ and $\hat{h}_2(\mathbf{y})$ are marginal densities of the Parzen's approximation defined in (6.102). Wee (1970) discussed the design of feature extractor and classifier under a single, rather than separate, performance criterion.

Heuristic approaches to nonlinear data structures were originally developed for nonmetric psychological data by Shepard (1962 *a*, *b*) and Kruskal (1964). The techniques were elaborated and generalized by Shepard and Carroll (1966). This general approach was applied by Bennett (1969) and Fukunaga and Olsen (1971) to determine the intrinsic dimensionality of a data set. Sammon (1969) and Calvert (1970) used similar approaches to obtain dimensionality reduction for feature extraction and to display pattern recognition data on computer graphics.

The nonlinear transformation of a feature space is equivalent to finding nonlinear discriminant functions. (A typical approach to the determination of nonlinear discriminant functions is due to Specht (1967) and is described in chapter 7.) The use of random perturbations to find nonlinear transformations was developed by Calvert and Young (1969), and recently a noniterative approach to this problem was developed by Koontz and Fukunaga (1972).

Problems

6.1 Let $\mathbf{y} = \mathbf{T}\mathbf{x}$ and $\mathbf{T}$ is an arbitrary $M \times N$ matrix. Show that $\beta(\mathbf{y}) \geqslant \beta(\mathbf{x})$ and $\beta(\mathbf{y}) = \beta(\mathbf{x})$ if $\mathbf{T}$ is nonsingular.

6.2 Consider the mutual information $I(\mathbf{x})$ defined in (6.77). Show that $I(\mathbf{x}) \geqslant 0$ with equality if and only if the random observation $\mathbf{x}$ and the classification $\{C_k\}$ are statistically independent.

6.3 Let $\hat{f}(\mathbf{x})$ be an arbitrary probability density function and $f(\mathbf{x})$ be a mixture of density functions,

$$f(\mathbf{x}) = \sum_{k=1}^{K} p_k f_k(\mathbf{x}).$$

Show that

$$\sum_{k=1}^{K} p_k \int f_k(\mathbf{x}) \log \frac{f_k(\mathbf{x})}{\hat{f}(\mathbf{x})} d\mathbf{x} \geqslant \int f(\mathbf{x}) \log \frac{f(\mathbf{x})}{\hat{f}(\mathbf{x})} d\mathbf{x},$$

and give a physical interpretation to this result.

6.4 Let the prior probability $p_1 = p_2 = 1/2$ and $f_1(\mathbf{x}) = g(\mathbf{x}; \mathbf{m}_1, \mathbf{R}_1)$ and $f_2(\mathbf{x}) = g(\mathbf{x}; \mathbf{m}_2, \mathbf{R}_2)$ be Gaussian densities with

$$\mathbf{m}_1 = \begin{bmatrix} 0 \\ 1 \end{bmatrix}, \qquad \mathbf{R}_1 = \begin{bmatrix} 4 & 0 \\ 0 & 1 \end{bmatrix},$$

$$\mathbf{m}_2 = \begin{bmatrix} 1 \\ 0 \end{bmatrix}, \qquad \mathbf{R}_2 = \begin{bmatrix} 1/4 & 0 \\ 0 & 4 \end{bmatrix}.$$

Find a 1×2 feature extractor by (a) Karhunen–Loève expansion, (b) maximizing the divergence, and (c) minimizing the Bhattacharyya coefficient. Compare the results in terms of error probability.

6.5 Assume that for each of the two classes, the components of the random vector $\mathbf{x}$ are statistically independent. In other words, both $f_1(\mathbf{x})$ and $f_2(\mathbf{x})$ are the products of their own marginal densities. Let the mean values $\mathbf{m}_1 = \mathbf{m}_2 = \mathbf{0}$, and the covariance matrices $\mathbf{R}_1 = \mathbf{I}$ and $\mathbf{R}_2 = \mathbf{R}$ where $\mathbf{R}$ is a diagonal matrix with the diagonal elements $r_1, r_2, \ldots, r_n$. Consider the following cases where the marginal densities for both classes are:

(a) uniform density functions;
(b) two-sided exponential densities of the form $\alpha e^{-\gamma|x|}$;
(c) Gaussian density functions.

Find a feature selection scheme for each case using the Bhattacharyya coefficient.

6.6 Given two families of one-dimensional probability density functions

$$\mathcal{F}_1 = \{f_1(x): -\alpha \leqslant x \leqslant \alpha, E[x] = 0, E[x^2] = 1\},$$

$$\mathcal{F}_2 = \{f_2(x): -\alpha \leqslant x \leqslant \alpha, E[x] = 0, E[x^2] = r\},$$

find

$$\max_{\mathcal{F}_1,\mathcal{F}_2} \beta(x) = \max_{\mathcal{F}_1,\mathcal{F}_2} \int \sqrt{f_1(x) f_2(x)}\, dx,$$

and the associated least-favorable densities. Note that since $\beta(x)/2$ is an upper bound on error probability, max $\beta(x)/2$ is the upper bound for any $f_1(x) \in \mathcal{F}_1$ and any $f_2(x) \in \mathcal{F}_2$.

6.7 Let $x(t)$, $-T/2 \leqslant t \leqslant T/2$ be a random process with $E[x(t)] = 0$ and $E[x(t_1)x(t_2)] = R(t_1, t_2)$. Given a set of orthonormal basis functions $\{u_j(t)\}$, show that if in the expansion,

$$x(t) = \sum_{j=1}^{\infty} c_j u_j(t),$$

$$c_j = \int_{-T/2}^{T/2} x(t) u_j(t)\, dt,$$

the coefficients c_j are uncorrelated, $E[c_j c_l] = 0, j \neq l$, then $u_j(t)$ must be the eigenfunctions satisfying

$$\int_{-T/2}^{T/2} R(t_1, t_2)u(t_2)dt_2 = \lambda u(t_1), \quad -T/2 \leqslant t \leqslant T/2,$$

and $E[c_j^2] = \lambda_j$ are the eigenvalues.

References

1. Abramson, N. 1963. *Information Theory and Coding*. McGraw-Hill, New York.
2. Anderson, T. W. 1958. *An Introduction to Multivariate Statistical Analysis*. Wiley, New York.
3. Ash, R. A. 1965. *Information Theory*. Wiley, New York.
4. Bennett, R. S. 1969. The intrinsic dimensionality of signal collections. *IEEE Trans. Information Theory* IT-15:517–525.
5. Bhattacharyya, A. 1943. On a measure of divergence between two statistical populations defined by their probability distributions. *Bull. Calcutta Math. Soc.* 35:99–109.
6. Bledsoe, W. W. 1966. Some results on multicategory pattern recognition. *J. Assoc. Computing Machinery* 13:304–316.
7. Brown, D. T. 1959. A note to approximations to discrete probability distributions. *Information and Control* 2:386–392.
8. Calvert, T. W. 1968. Projections of multidimensional data for use in man computer graphics. *1968 Fall Joint Computer Conf., AFIPS Proc.*, vol. 33. Thompson, Washington, D. C.
9. ———. 1970. Nonorthogonal projections for feature extraction in pattern recognition. *IEEE Trans. Computers* C-19:447–452.
10. Calvert, T. W. and Young, T. Y. 1969. Randomly generated nonlinear transformations for pattern recognition. *IEEE Trans. Systems Science and Cybernetics* SSC-5:266–273.
11. Chernoff, H. 1952. A Measure of asymptotic efficiency for tests of hypothesis based on the sum of observations. *Ann. Math. Stat.* 23:493–507.
12. Chien, Y. T. and Fu, K. S. 1968. Selection and ordering of feature observations in a pattern recognition system. *Information and Control* 12:395–414.

13. Chow, C. K. and Liu, C. N. 1968. Approximating discrete probability distributions with dependence trees. *IEEE Trans. Information Theory* IT-14:462–467.

14. Christensen, R. A. 1968. A general approach to pattern discovery. Technical Rept. No. 20, Univ. of California Computer Center.

15. Chu, J. T. and Chueh, J. C. 1967. Error probability in decision functions for character recognition. *J. Assoc. Computing Machinery* 14:273–280.

16. Fu, K. S. ed. 1971. Special issue on feature extraction and selection in pattern recognition. *IEEE Trans. Computers*, C-20.

17. Fu, K. S., Min, P. J., and Li, T. J. 1970. Feature selection in pattern recognition. *IEEE Trans. System Science and Cybernetics* SSC-6:33–39.

18. Fukunaga, K. and Koontz, W. L. G. 1970. Application of the Karhunen–Loève expansion to feature selection and ordering. *IEEE Trans. Computers* C-19:311–318.

19. Fukunaga, K. and Krile, T. F. 1968. A minimum distance feature effectiveness criterion. *IEEE Trans. Information Theory* IT-14:780–782.

20. Fukunaga, K. and Olsen, D. R. 1971. An algorithm for finding intrinsic dimenionality of data. *IEEE Trans. Computers* C-20:176–183.

21. Gallager, R. G. 1968. *Information Theory and Reliable Communication.* Wiley, New York.

22. Grettenberg, T. L. 1963. Signal selection in communication and radar systems. *IEEE Trans. Information Theory* IT-9:265–275.

23. Hellman, M. E. and Raviv, J. 1970. Probability of error, equivocation and the Chernov bound. *IEEE Trans. Information Theory* IT-16:368–372.

24. Henderson, T. L. and Lainiotis, D. G. 1969. Comments on linear feature extraction. *IEEE Trans. Information Theory* IT-15:728–730.

25. ———. 1970. Application of state variable technique to optimal feature extraction—multichannel analog data. *IEEE Trans. Information Theory* IT-16:396–406.

26. Heydorn, R. P. 1968. An upper bound estimate on classification error. *IEEE Trans. Information Theory* IT-15:783–784.

27. Huber, P. J. 1964. Robust estimation of a local parameter. *Ann. Math Stat.* 35:73–101.

28. Kadota, T. T. and Shepp, L. A. 1967. On the best finite set of linear observables for discriminating two Gaussian signals. *IEEE Trans. Information Theory* IT-13:278–284.

29. Kailath, T. 1967. The divergence and Bhattacharyya distance measures in signal selection. *IEEE Trans. Communications Technology* COM-15:52–60.

30. Koontz, W. L. G. and Fukunaga, K. 1972. A nonlinear feature extraction algorithm using distance transformations. *IEEE Trans. Computers* C-21:56–63.

31. Kruskal, J. B. 1964. Nonmetric multidimensional scaling: a numerical method. *Psychometrika* 29:187–195.

32. Kullback, S. 1968. *Information Theory and Statistics.* Dover, New York.

33. Kullback, S. and Leibler, R. A. 1951. On information and sufficiency. *Ann. Math. Stat.* 22:79–96.

34. Lainiotis, D. G. 1969. A class of upper bounds on probability of error for multihypothesis pattern recognition. *IEEE Trans. Information Theory* IT-15:730–731.

35. Levine, M. D. 1969. Feature extraction: a survey. *Proc. IEEE,* 57:1391–1407.

36. Lewis, P. M. 1962. The characteristic selection problem in recognition systems. *IRE Trans. Information Theory* IT-8:171–178.

37. Marill, T. and Green, D. M. 1963. On the effectiveness of receptors in recognition systems. *IEEE Trans. Information Theory* IT-9:11–17.

38. Nagy, G. 1968. State of the art on pattern recognition. *Proc. IEEE* 56:2101–2114.

39. Papoulis, A. 1965. *Probability, Random Variables and Stochastic Processes.* McGraw-Hill, New York.

40. Patrick, E. A. Anderson, D. R., and Bechtel, F. K. 1968. Mapping multidimensional space to one dimension for computer output display. *Proc. 23rd Natl. Conf. ACM* pp. 511–515. Braden/ Systems press, Princeton, New Jersey.

41. Patrick, E. A. and Fischer, F. P. II 1969. Nonparametric feature selections. *IEEE Trans. Information Theory* IT-15:577–584.

42. Sammon, J. W. 1968. On-line pattern analysis and recognition systems (OLPARS). Tech. Rept. RADC-TR-68-263. Rome Air Development Center, Rome, New York.

43. ———. 1969. A nonlinear mapping for data structure analysis. *IEEE Trans. Computers* C-18:401–409.

44. Schweppe, F. 1967. On the Bhattacharyya distance and the divergence between Gaussian processes. *Information and Control* 11:373–395.

45. Shannon, C. E. 1948. A mathematical theory of communication. *Bell Syst. Tech. J.* 27:379–423; 623–656.

46. Shepard, R. N. 1962a. The analysis of proximities: multi-dimensional scaling with an unknown function, pt. I. *Psychometrika* 27:125–140.

47. ———. 1962b. The analysis of proximities: multi-dimensional scaling with an unknown function, pt. II. *Psychometrika* 27:219–246.

48. Shepard, R. N. and Carroll, J. D. 1966. Parametric representation of nonlinear data structures. In *Proc. Intern. Symp. Multivariate Analysis* ed. P. R. Krishnaiah. Academic Press, New York.

49. Specht, D. F. 1967. Generation of polynomial discriminant functions for pattern recognition. *IEEE Trans. Electronic Computers* EC-16:309–319.

50. Tou, J. T. and Heydorn, R. P. 1967. Some approaches to optimum feature extraction. *Computer and Information Sciences II*, ed. J. T. Tou, pp. 57–89. Academic Press, New York.

51. Watanabe, S. 1965, Karhunen–Loève expansion and factor analysis—theoretical remarks and application. *Proc. 4th Conf. Information Theory*, Prague. pp. 635–660.

52. Watanabe, S., Lambert, P. F., Kulikowski, C. A., Buxton, J. L., and Walker, R. 1967. Evaluation and selection of variables in pattern recognition. In *Computer and Information Sciences II*, ed. J. T. Tou, pp. 91–122. Academlc Press, New York.

53. Wee, W. G. 1970. On feature selection in a class of distribution-free pattern classifiers. *IEEE Trans. Information Theory* IT-16:47–55.

54. Young, T. Y. 1971. The reliability of linear feature extractors. *IEEE Trans. Computers* C-20:967–971.

55. Young, T. Y. and Huggins, W. H. 1963. On the representation of electrocardiograms. *IEEE Trans. Biomedical Electronics* BME-10:86–95.

7

Pattern Recognition of Electrocardiograms and Vectorcardiograms

7.1 Electrocardiograms and Vectorcardiograms

The classification of electrocardiograms (ECGs) and vectorcardiograms (VCGs) has been chosen for detailed discussion for several reasons. This is a problem to which pattern recognition theory has been applied and been implemented in practice with useful results. However, it is typical of many practical problems in that, although the theoretical basis is well established, the features used in practical pattern recognition schemes are those developed over the years by physicians. There are good reasons for this situation to occur. The ECG/VCG problem is an example of how pattern recognition theory can be usefully applied to practical problems only to the extent that it meets with user acceptability.

The ECG and its variant the VCG are easily measured electrical signals that give useful diagnostic information about the state of the heart. From an engineer's point of view, the ECG/VCG is an obvious candidate for machine processing since the electrical signal is relatively large (50 mV), of moderate bandwidth (0–100 Hz), can be measured with low electrical and physiological noise, and is quite consistent from heartbeat to heartbeat. The medical criteria for classifications of ECGs and VCGs are well established and it is quite easy to implement a computer pattern recognition system that will perform well for a large proportion (say 70%) of the normal and diseased populations. Accurate classification of difficult cases has, however, proved to be elusive (say for 5–10% of the population), and since human life can be at stake, the system cannot be judged satisfactory until error rates are very low indeed. Although the best machine classifiers of ECG/VCGs are probably better than many human classifiers, this is not of much consolation to a patient (Caceres and Dreifus, 1970).

As with many measurements used in medicine, the ECG/VCG can be used in a number of rather different ways, which can radically alter the machine pattern recognition scheme that is devised. These different applications can be described as screening, disease diagnosis, and monitoring.

In *screening*, a large population of known characteristics is tested quickly and cheaply. This may consist of one test or may be one stage in a multiphasic health screening system. In this application, the population is large and contains a small proportion of abnormals. Thus, it is usually satisfactory merely to decide between normal and abnormal and to set the decision criteria to give a small probability of false negatives (diagnosed normal when in fact diseased, i.e., errors of the second kind) and a much larger probability of false positives (errors of the first kind), i.e., to minimize the risk in a Bayes sense. All cases classified as abnormal can be reprocessed with a more comprehensive scheme and examined in detail by a physician.

Diagnosis of disease from ECG/VCGs differs only in degree from screening. Typically, the patient is being tested either because he is known to be ill or because a careful health check is required. Thus, it is necessary to discriminate among many possible abnormalities, and the proportion of abnormals in the population will be much higher. Also, high speed and low cost are less important. This test will always be under the supervision of a physician. We can still make a minimum-risk Bayes decision between the K possible classes ($K = 8$–13 depending on how finely the classes are subdivided). However, since the results must be reviewed by a physician and correlated with other data, it is probably preferable to print out the most likely classifications together with their probabilities, i.e.,

Class C_i with probability $P(C_i|\mathbf{x})$
Class C_j with probability $P(C_j|\mathbf{x})$
etc.,

where $P(C_i|\mathbf{x})$, is estimated parametrically or nonparametrically (chapter 3).

Monitoring of ECG/VCGs is a quite different application. The patient is generally quite ill and is in an intensive care or coronary care unit. His condition is known in detail and he may have undergone surgery or may be recovering from a heart attack. The purpose of machine monitoring is to detect automatically any change in the ECG/VCG. In particular, it is necessary to check for arrhythmias that can be precursors of a heart attack. Generally the output is in the form of an alarm to alert a nurse or physician. The situation is similar to that discussed above for screening, i.e., the signal is either normal or abnormal. The result of a false positive is that a physician and/or nurse is called unnecessarily. Clearly, the cost of this can be estimated. A false negative could result in the death of a patient within a few minutes. Typically, the designer is unwilling to assign a cost to this but he must do so, unless he can afford to have sufficient medical staff to deal with the unlikely situation of all patients having heart attacks simultaneously.

In the future the interpretation of many other medical tests will be automated in ways similar to those applied to the ECG/VCG. Pattern recognition will certainly be applied to the combined results of all tests and machine diagnosis will improve. Although it seems that for the foreseeable future the entire system will be monitored by a physician, eventually we can expect routine medical examinations to be completely automated (Crichton, 1969).

In this chapter we shall discuss the machine interpretation of ECG/VCGs from several points of view. In this section (7.1) we describe the electrical characteristics of the signal, and discuss the most popular lead systems for ECGs and VCGs. In section 7.2 we develop the theoretical basis for electrocardiography in terms of both multipole expansions and intrinsic

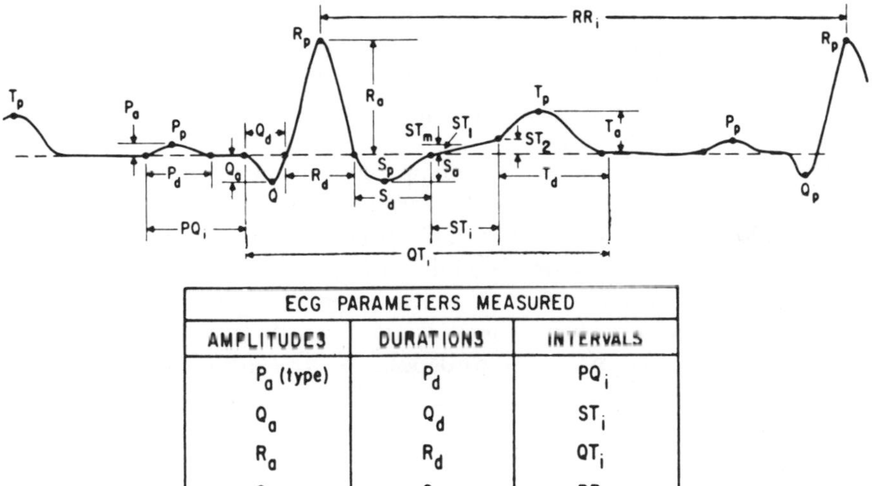

ECG PARAMETERS MEASURED		
AMPLITUDES	DURATIONS	INTERVALS
P_a (type)	P_d	PQ_i
Q_a	Q_d	ST_i
R_a	R_d	QT_i
S_a	S_d	RR_i
T_a	T_d	
ST_1		
ST_m		
ST_2		

fig. 7.1 The ECG waveform and typical parameters which are measured. (Caceres and Dreifus, 1970).

components. These are seen to parallel some approaches to feature extraction. The enhancement of interclass separation is described in section 7.3. It is shown that, based on physiological insight, a linear normalization technique can be developed that minimizes the effects of body differences. Feature selection is discussed in 7.4, and in 7.5 we describe two of the most interesting applications of pattern recognition theory to research on ECG/VCG classification. The schemes that have been implemented in clinical practice are described in 7.6 and some practical constraints are pointed out. The reader interested in applications of pattern recognition theory should pay most attention to sections 7.3, 7.4, and 7.5. The theoretical basis for the signal is developed in section 7.2, and the state of the art of clinical classification is found in 7.6.

7.1.1 The electrical signal

The waveform shown in figure 7.1 is a stylized version of an ECG; a variant of this can be recorded from almost any two different points on the torso. The letters P, Q, R, S, and T are standard notation for the prominent characteristics of the waveform. In fact, there are standard positions on the body for recording different forms of the ECG or VCG, the most popular combinations being the scalar "12-lead system" of Einthoven and the 3-lead vector system of Frank.

The function of the heart is to pump blood throughout the circulatory system of the body. Venous blood enters the right atrium, shown in figure 7.2. Rhythmic electrical activity in the SA node causes the atrial muscle to depolarize and weakly pump blood down into the right ventricle. Simultaneously the left atrium is receiving blood from the lungs and pumping it into the left ventricle. Atrial depolarization results in the P wave of the ECG and causes the AV node to depolarize. The electrical activity then spreads down a bunch of fibers and causes the ventricles to depolarize. This is observed in the ECG as the QRS complex. The depolarization causes contraction of the ventricles and blood is pumped into the lungs from the right ventricle and into the arterial system from the left ventricle. The ventricles eventually repolarize and this activity is seen as the T wave on the ECG. The maximum voltage between the electrodes is about 70 mV. The recording amplifiers typically have a bandwidth from 0.05 to 100 Hz or sometimes rather less. For processing by a digital computer, the signal is usually sampled 200–500 times per second. The signal can be contaminated by muscle noise if the subject is moving or by 60-Hz noise if care is not taken to avoid pickup from the power system. The 60-Hz noise can be removed with analog or digital filters. In digitizing the signal, a precision of

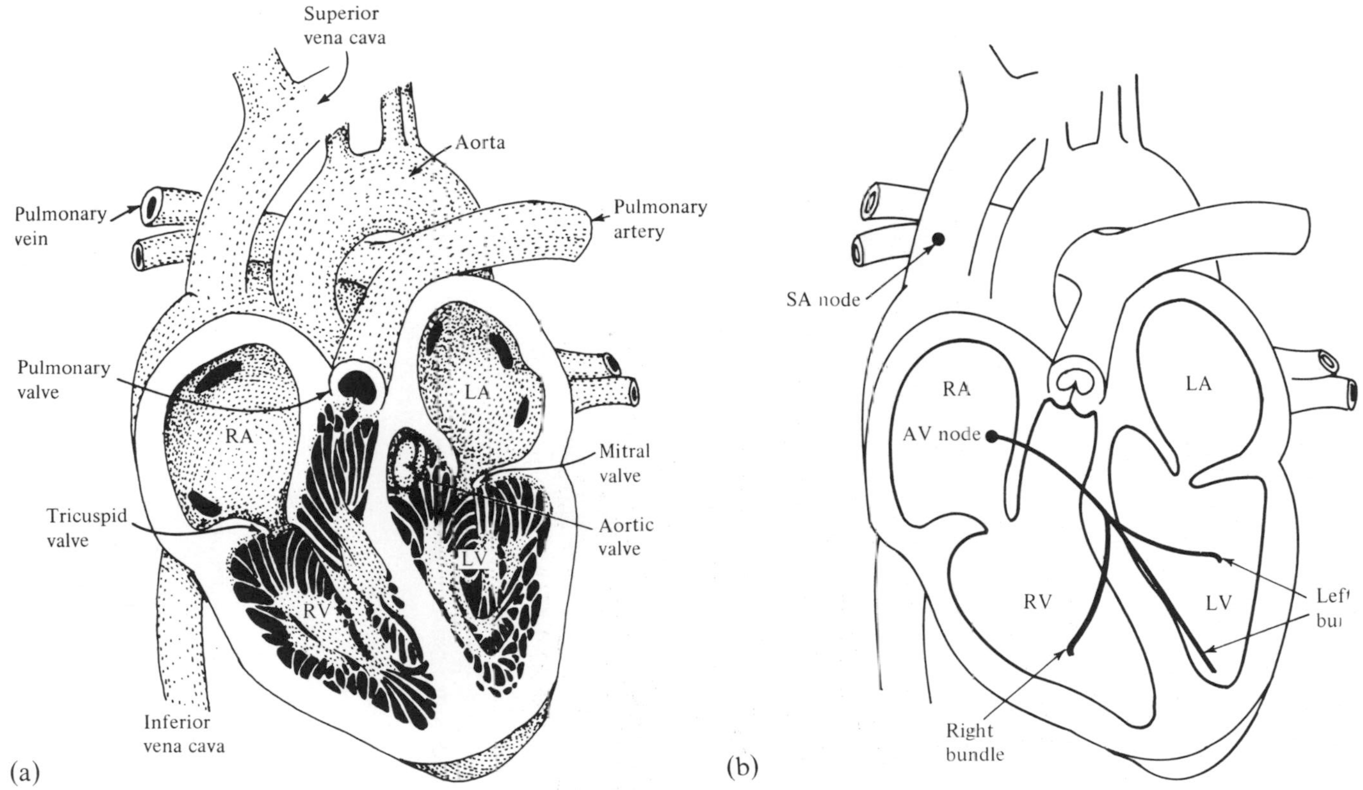

fig. 7.2 (a) The chambers of the heart. (b) The depolarizing wavefront spreads non-uniformly because of specialized conduction fibers. (from *Bioelectric Phenomena* by R. Plonsey, © 1969, McGraw-Hill Book Company. Used with permission of McGraw-Hill Book Company).

one part in 100 or 200 is probably sufficient (i.e., no more than seven or eight bits), but to give some immunity to dc shifts (baseline drift) an analog-to-digital converter with an output of 10 or 12 bits is usually used.

7.1.2 Scalar (12-lead) electrocardiograms

As the cardiac muscle depolarizes, a time-varying charge distribution is set up over the surface of the heart. It is oftcn convenient to describe this as a collection of dipoles distributed throughout the heart. In any case, the result is current flow in the body and a time-varying potential distribution on the body surface. The potential distribution can be sampled by leads attached to the body surface. The most popular arrangement is the scalar 12-lead system of Einthoven. This is a scalar system since the 12 measurements are made serially from different electrode positions. A typical set of recordings from the 12 leads is shown in figure 7.3, which also shows the electrode positions—*a* (left arm), *b* (right arm), *c* (left leg), and 1, 2, . . . , 6, which are on the chest. The first three of the 12 leads consist of:

$$V_I = V_{ab},\ V_{II} = V_{cb},\ V_{III} = V_{ca}.$$

The next three, the augmented unipolar leads, are obtained by connecting between one of the limbs and a neutral point formed at the junction between two 5000-ohm resistors connected to the other two limbs, i.e.,

aV_R = right arm - reference between left arm and left leg,
aV_L = left arm - reference between right arm and left leg,
aV_F = left leg - reference between left arm and right arm.

The six precordial leads ($V_1, V_2, \ldots, V_6$) are obtained by connecting in turn between points 1–6 on the chest and a neutral formed at the junction of three 5000-ohm resistors, each connected to a limb. As will be discussed below, the information in these 12 leads is highly redundant (clearly V_I, V_{II}, V_{III}, aV_R, aV_L, and aV_F contain at most three linearly independent time functions). The presentation shown in figure 7.3 is similar to that typically used for diagnosis.

7.1.3 The vectorcardiogram and the dipole component of the heart

The vectorcardiogram consists of three simultaneously recorded surface potentials obtained in such a way that the three-lead pairs are roughly spatially orthogonal. These electrode systems have been chosen to minimize all but the dipole component of the heart. This is possible since the distributed current sources in the cardiac muscle are approximated by a dipole if the recording electrodes are some distance away. Since the precordial leads ($V_1, \ldots, V_6$) of the scalar electrocardiogram are recorded on the chest close to the heart they might not be accounted for by a dipole model of the heart. In fact it has been shown by Pipberger et al. (1961), for example, that all 12 of the leads can usually be synthesized by a linear combination of the three vector leads. Several electrode arrangments are used, but the most popular is the Frank system shown in figure 7.4(*a*). Since the three leads (X, Y, and Z) are recorded simultaneously (figure 7.4(*b*)), they can also be plotted against each other to show the rotation of a vector in the XY (or frontal), YZ (or left sagital), and XZ (or tranverse) planes (figure 7.4(*c*, *d* and *e*)). The vector presentation can give new insight for diagnosis and the simultaneous recording of three signals makes machine analysis easier.

7.2 Theory of Electrocardiography

In chapter 6 there is a general discussion of feature extraction. For many pattern recognition problems, however, efficient ways of extracting features are suggested by studying the physical origin of the patterns. We will present here two such ways of efficiently describing surface potentials due to the heart. Interestingly, these methods, based on electromagnetic field theory, turn out to be closely related to methods developed in feature extraction theory.

The difficulties in developing a theory that relates body surface potentials to heart activity are twofold. In the first place, the heart is not a simple electrical source. It consists of a time-varying charge distribution that can be described by a time-varying current dipole moment distributed throughout the volume of the heart. It can be approximated by a distributed collection of discrete dipoles—in a way that is comparable to the approximation of a probability density function. One way to describe this mathematically is to expand the source as a series of dipoles, quadrupoles, and higher-order multipoles—similar to the description of a p.d.f. by its moments. The second difficulty is that even if the heart is completely described as an electrical source, we must also characterize the body through which the current flows to produce the surface potentials. The body is a linear, inhomogeneous, anisotropic, and time-varying volume conductor. There are also wide variations between individuals. Since it is almost impossible to characterize in detail the conduction paths in the body, most analysis is based on finding the electrical source that would produce the observed surface potentials if the body were homogeneous, isotropic, and non-time-varying.

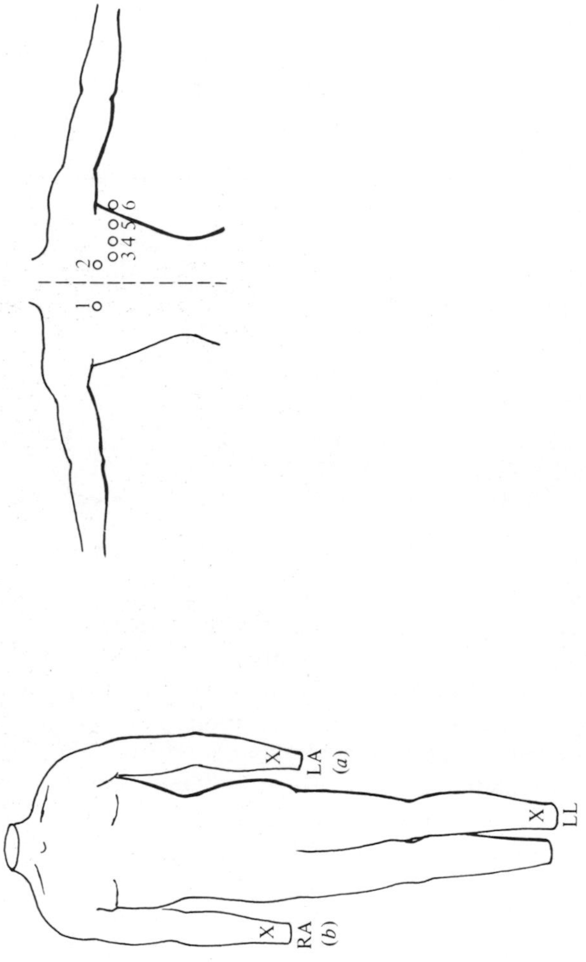

fig. 7.3 (a) The electrode positions used for the 12 lead scalar ECG (from *Bioelectric Phenomena* by R. Plonsey, © 1969, McGraw-Hill Book Company. Used with permission of McGraw-Hill Book Company).

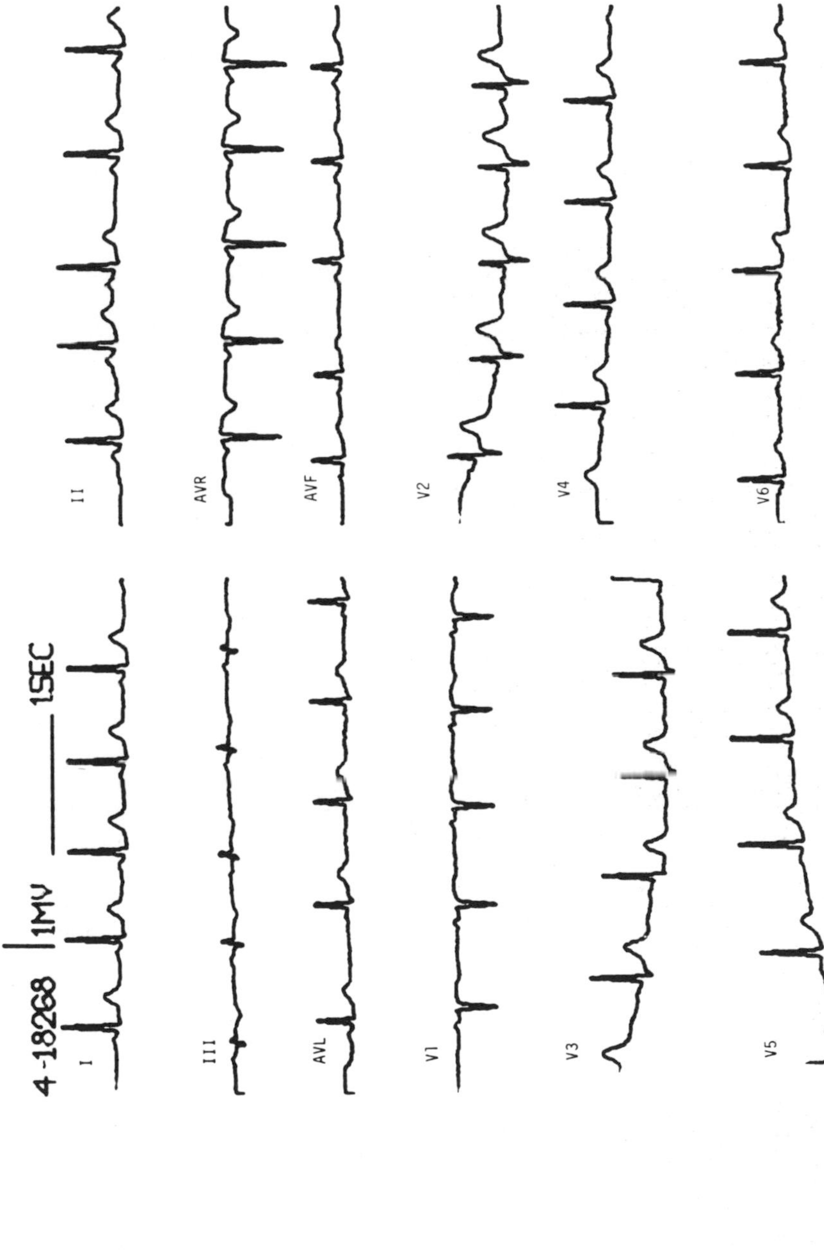

fig 7.3 (b) typical examples of the resulting tracings.

7.2.1 Multipole expansion (Geselowitz, 1960)

Although the body is inhomogeneous, anisotropic, and time-varying, it is a linear conductor and at the frequencies concerned it is purely resistive. Thus, the problem is quasistatic since the body surface potentials at any instant are linearly related to the sources at that instant and do not depend on their previous history.

For $\mathbf{p}(r, \theta, \phi, t)$, the current moment/unit volume at a point (r, θ, ϕ) at time t in an unbounded homogeneous conductor of conductivity g, the potential V' at a point outside the source region may be expanded in an infinite multipole series as:

$$V'(r, \theta, \phi) = \frac{1}{4\pi g} \sum_{n=0}^{\infty} \sum_{m=0}^{n} \frac{1}{r^{n+1}} (a_{nm} \cos(m\phi) + b_{nm} \sin(m\phi)) p_n^m(\cos\theta), \quad (7.1)$$

where (r, θ, ϕ) are the spherical coordinates of a point in the volume, and p_n^m is an associated Legendre polynomial. The multipole coefficients a_{nm} and b_{nm} are related to the source distribution by

$$a_{nm} + jb_{nm} = \int_{\text{Volume}} \mathbf{p} \cdot \nabla \psi_{nm} dv, \quad (7.2)$$

where

$$\psi_{nm} = (2 - \delta_{mo}) \frac{(n-m)!}{(n+m)!} r^n p_n^m(\cos\theta) e^{jm\phi}, \quad (7.3)$$

and

$$\begin{aligned} \delta_{mo} &= 1 \text{ if } m = 0, \\ &= 0 \text{ if } m \neq 0. \end{aligned}$$

There are three dipole coefficients a_{10}, a_{11}, and b_{11} that are obtained with $n = 1$. With $n = 2$, we obtain the five quadrupole coefficients: a_{20}, a_{21}, b_{21}, a_{22}, b_{22}.

These results do not, of course, apply to the body since it is not an unbounded, homogeneous conductor. It is possible, however, to define the *equivalent source distribution* in an isomorphic homogeneous conductor that would give rise to an identical surface potential distribution. This source distribution, the "equivalent cardiac generator," is a useful way to characterize the heart signal.

At a point (r, θ, ϕ) on the body surface and at time t, the potential V can now be obtained by applying superposition

$$V(r, \theta, \phi, t) = \sum_{n=1}^{\infty} \sum_{m=0}^{n} [T_{nm}^a(r, \theta, \phi) a_{nm}(t) + T_{nm}^b(r, \theta, \phi) b_{nm}(t)], \quad (7.4)$$

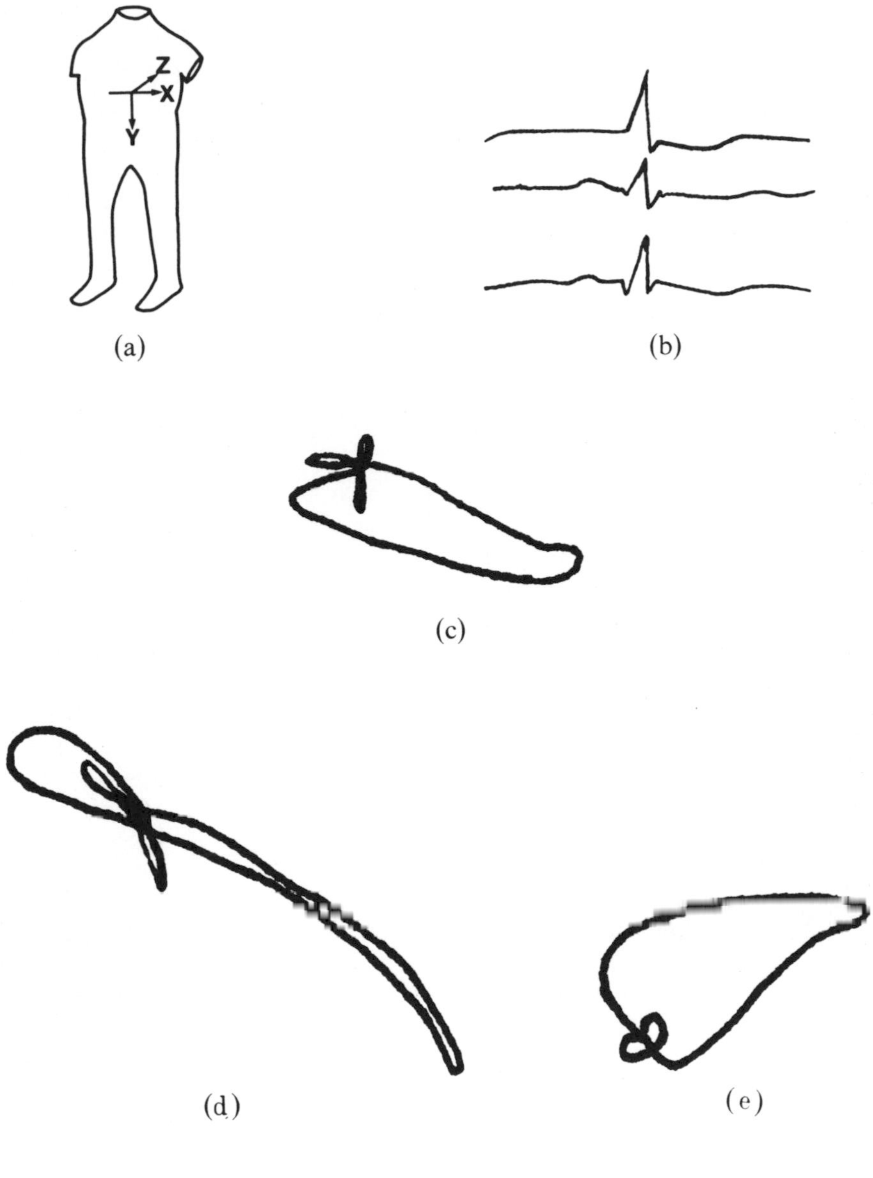

fig. 7.4 The Frank lead system. (a) The axes relative to the body, (b) the three time functions $x(t)$, $y(t)$ and $z(t)$, (c) the frontal or x-y plane, (d) the saggital or y-z plane, (e) the horizontal or x-z plane.

where T is a "transfer function" that relates the potential at a particular point (r, θ, ϕ) to a unit multipole coefficient. Note that the T's characterize the body and that the a's and b's characterize the time-varying signal from various multipole components of a source equivalent to the heart.

In theory, $a_{nm}(t)$ and $b_{nm}(t)$ may be obtained by integration over the body surface. In practice, if measurements are taken at N points on the body surface, then N equations result, which can be solved for the coefficients. When this is done it is found that only the three dipole and five quadrupole terms need be considered. In fact, approximately 97% of the signal energy can often be represented on the dipole terms, and almost all of the energy can be represented if two quadrupole terms are included.

7.2.2 Intrinsic component theory (Young and Huggins, 1962)

An alternative description of the heart may be obtained with intrinsic component analysis. In equation (7.4) above, the multipole coefficients $a_{nm}(t)$ and $b_{nm}(t)$ were time functions related to the physical properties of an equivalent multipole source. Since it is difficult to ascribe physiological significance to a fictitious equivalent source, little is lost by expanding $V(r, \theta, \phi, t)$ as a linear combination of orthonormal time functions or intrinsic components, $u_1(t)$, $u_2(t)$, $\ldots$, $u_m(t)$ such that

$$V(r, \theta, \phi, t) = \sum_{k=1}^{m} c_k(r, \theta, \phi) u_k(t), \tag{7.5}$$

where

$$\int u_i(t) u_j(t)\, dt = 0 \quad \text{for} \quad i \neq j.$$

If N simultaneous measurements of one heart beat of duration T are made on the surface of the body, we have $x_1(t)$, $x_2(t)$, $\ldots$, $x_N(t)$. In order to find the orthonormal time functions, we can find the eigenvalues and eigenvectors of a cross-correlation matrix $\mathbf{H}$ of the measurements. Thus

$$\mathbf{H} = [h_{ij}] \tag{7.6}$$

is an $N \times N$ matrix where

$$h_{ij} = \int_0^T x_i(t) x_j(t)\, dt. \tag{7.7}$$

Then

$$\mathbf{H}\mathbf{e}_k = \lambda_k \mathbf{e}_k, \tag{7.8}$$

where

$$\lambda_k = k\text{-th eigenvalue of } \mathbf{H} \text{ for } k = 1, \ldots, N,$$
$$\mathbf{e}_k = k\text{-th eigenvector of } \mathbf{H} \text{ for } k = 1, \ldots, N.$$

It is convenient to rank the eigenvalues and eigenvectors according to $\lambda_1 \geqslant \lambda_2 \geqslant \cdots \geqslant \lambda_N$. The intrinsic components are then given by

$$u_k(t) = \sum_{i=1}^{N} e_{ik}\, x_i(t) = \mathbf{e}_k^T \mathbf{x}(t). \tag{7.9}$$

This is, of course, closely related to the Karhunen–Loève expansion described in chapter 6.

It is easy to show that the intrinsic components are orthogonal and that the eigenvalue λ_k is a measure of the magnitude of its corresponding intrinsic component $u_k(t)$. To prove this, we note that

$$\begin{aligned}\int_0^T u_l(t)u_k(t)\,dt &= \int_0^T \sum_i \sum_j e_{il}\, x_i(t) e_{jk}\, x_j(t)\,dt \\ &= \sum_{i,j} e_{il} \int_0^T x_i(t)\, x_j(t)\,dt\, e_{jk} \\ &= \sum_{i,j} e_{il}\, h_{ij}\, e_{jk}. \end{aligned} \tag{7.10}$$

By rewriting the eigenequation (7.8) we obtain

$$\sum_j h_{ij}\, e_{jk} = \lambda_k\, e_{ik}. \tag{7.11}$$

By multiplying (7.11) by e_{il} and summing over the index i, we obtain the result from (7.10) that

$$\begin{aligned}\int_0^T u_l(t)u_k(t)\,dt &= \lambda_k \sum_i e_{il}\, e_{ik} \\ &= \lambda_k\, \delta_{lk}\end{aligned} \tag{7.12}$$

since the eigenvectors $\mathbf{e}_l$ and $\mathbf{e}_k$ are orthonormal.

Since the N measurements are usually not linearly independent, there will only be $m \leqslant N$ nonzero eigenvalues (i.e., $\lambda_{m+1} = \lambda_{m+2} = \cdots = \lambda_N = 0$). Since the square root of the eigenvalue λ_k has been shown to be proportional to the magnitude of the corresponding intrinsic component $u_k(t)$, obviously there will only be m significant intrinsic components.

The coefficients $c_k(r, \theta, \phi)$ in (7.5) depend only on the physical properties of the body and not on time. They are easily calculated from

$$c_k(r, \theta, \phi) = \int_0^T V(r, \theta, \phi, t) u_k(t)\, dt. \tag{7.13}$$

It should be noted that if the heart were a dipole and if the body were a homogeneous isotropic sphere with the heart at its center, then the first three (and only) intrinsic components would be related by an orthogonal transformation to the dipole components of equation (7.4). In the general case, the relation between intrinsic and multipole components is not simple. The first three intrinsic components will not, generally, correspond to the dipole components of the heart.

Both multipole and intrinsic component expansions describe the heart with seven or eight terms. Since the intrinsic components are time-orthogonal, they will often result in fewer (and never in more) significant terms than the multipoles. It does not follow that they will necessarily be more effective features for pattern recognition.

The VCG is a special case where only three measurements are made. When the intrinsic components of a VCG are calculated, it is often found that normal patients have almost all signal energy in the first two components, i.e., in the $u_1(t)$, $u_2(t)$ plane. A typical plot is shown in figure 7.5.

7.3 The Enhancement of Interclass Separation by Linear Normalization

In a general pattern recognition problem it is difficult to find linear methods that will decrease intraclass distances and increase interclass separation. The obvious approach is to look at the physical processes producing the patterns and then try to eliminate any sources of irrelevant

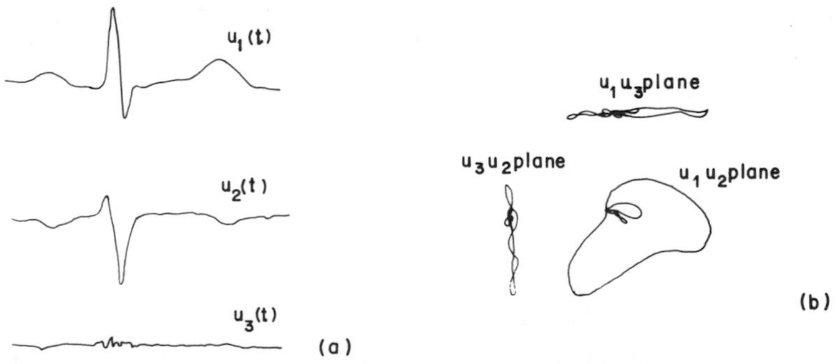

fig. 7.5 (a) The intrinsic components u_1, u_2 and u_3 of a dipole. (b) The essential loop of the vectorcardiogram. (Young and Huggins, 1962).

variation between patterns of the same class. We will describe here an attempt to remove the effect of body differences from vectorcardiograms (Kelly et al., 1971).

The linear transformation which the body applies to the heart signal (equations (7.4) or (7.5)) depends in a complicated way on the body shape and structure. However, the heart position and orientation, the venous and arterial branching and location, the quantity and location of fat and muscle, and the size of bones and bone structures, as well as the volume of the lungs, vary considerably from one individual to the next. The result is that identical hearts in different bodies will result in different VCGs.

It is interesting to consider how the cardiologist interprets the VCG after it has been through the linear transformation caused by the thorax. The cardiologist tries to take thoracic differences into account, but he can only judge the outward appearance of the thorax, and is normally unable to make more than a crude guess at the transformation that the heart signal has undergone. In practice the cardiologist has one set of criteria for judging heavy people, and another set for judging thin people, but as previously shown, there are many variables in the body that determine the thoracic transformation, so that there are many different transformations for heavy people and many different transformations for thin people.

7.3.1 The principle of normalization

It is clear that if the transformation applied by the body could be removed or canceled, the intraclass differences between VCGs would become much smaller and clustering would take place. Suppose patient #1 has an observed VCG $\mathbf{x}_1(t)$, (the vector $\mathbf{x}_1(t)$ represents three simultaneously recorded time functions), and a "true" heart signal $\mathbf{h}_1(t)$. If the heart can be approximated by its equivalent dipole then these should be related by a 3×3 matrix $\mathbf{A}_1$ (cf. (7.4) and (7.5)) such that:

$$\mathbf{x}_1(t) = \mathbf{A}_1 \mathbf{h}_1(t). \tag{7.14}$$

Then for other patients we observe $\mathbf{x}_2(t)$. $\mathbf{x}_3(t)$, $\mathbf{x}_4(t)$, ..., and at least in principle obtain $\mathbf{A}_2$, $\mathbf{A}_3$, $\mathbf{A}_4$, ..., and $\mathbf{h}_2(t)$, $\mathbf{h}_3(t)$, $\mathbf{h}_4(t)$, ... If our hypothesis is correct, we should find that the intraclass differences between the **h**'s are much smaller than between the **x**'s, and that the interclass differences are much larger. Before considering how this can be implemented, we must consider whether the linear transformation matrices, $\mathbf{A}_1$, $\mathbf{A}_2$, ..., contain any diagnostic information. Examination of various heart diseases shows that their effects on the VCG are generally nonlinear, i.e., they consist of changes in the time or duration of parts of the cycle or of changes in the magnitude of the voltage output at one time point relative to another. Some of the differences between two VCGs that can be removed by a general linear transformation are due not to thoracic differences, but to the heart. However, any linear differences could be caused by the thorax, and, particularly if they are small, a physician cannot possibly distinguish between linear thoracic and cardiac effects. If the linear differences can be removed, the nonlinear differences that are definitely related to the heart function will be emphasized.

Because of the complexity of the thoracic structure, and our inability to take any internal measurements on the patient whose VCG we are recording, it is impossible to calculate directly the transformation matrix **A** caused by a given person's thorax. Other methods must be found to remove this thoracic transformation. One approach is to remove the linear transformation between the individual and a "standard." Consider an arbitrarily chosen standard VCG, $\mathbf{s}(t)$, which could be from an individual typical of the class of normals. Then

$$\mathbf{s}(t) = \mathbf{A}_s \mathbf{h}_s(t), \tag{7.15}$$

where

$\mathbf{A}_s$ is the standard's thoracic transformation,

$\mathbf{h}_s(t)$ is the standard's "true" heart signal.

Normalization consists of finding a 3×3 transformation matrix $\mathbf{T}_1$ for the patient VCG $\mathbf{x}_1(t)$ such that a normalized version $\mathbf{y}_1(t)$ of $\mathbf{x}_1(t)$ is found to match $\mathbf{s}(t)$ as closely as possible. Thus

$$\mathbf{y}_1(t) = \mathbf{T}_1 \mathbf{x}_1(t), \tag{7.16}$$

where $\mathbf{T}_1$ is chosen to minimize in some sense the error

$$\boldsymbol{\varepsilon}(t) = \mathbf{s}(t) - \mathbf{y}_1(t). \tag{7.17}$$

If $\mathbf{s}(t)$ and $\mathbf{x}_1(t)$ were produced by identical hearts (true signal $\mathbf{h}(t)$) then the error would be zero and we would have

$$\mathbf{s}(t) = \mathbf{T}_1 \mathbf{x}_1(t),$$

or from (7.14) and (7.15),

$$\begin{aligned} \mathbf{A}_s \mathbf{h}(t) &= \mathbf{T}_1 \mathbf{A}_1 \mathbf{h}(t), \\ \mathbf{T}_1 &= \mathbf{A}_s \mathbf{A}_1^{-1}. \end{aligned} \tag{7.18}$$

Thus, rather than finding the true thoracic transformation produced by a patient's body $\mathbf{A}_1$, we find the transformation $\mathbf{T}_1$ to match his body to a "standard body." Clearly, as far as removing variations due to body differences is concerned, the two are equivalent. Logically a different standard $\mathbf{s}_j(t)$ should be used for each of the K disease classes. Then an unknown VCG $\mathbf{x}(t)$ can be normalized to the standard that results in lowest error $\boldsymbol{\varepsilon}(t)$. In fact, it has been found that useful results can be obtained by matching all VCGs to a standard chosen from the class of normals.

In implementing this procedure, the error can be minimized in a number of ways. Where the transformation is performed with analog hardware, "eyeball" matching of two VCGs is possible. Brown (1968) has developed a manual one-pass procedure in which nine knobs corresponding to the matrix elements of $\mathbf{T}$ can be adjusted by paramedical personnel in less than a minute. For most purposes, a more quantitative technique is desirable, and on a digital computer it is convenient to minimize the mean-square error, i.e.,

$$\int_0^T \boldsymbol{\varepsilon}^T(t)\boldsymbol{\varepsilon}(t)\,dt, \tag{7.19}$$

where T = period of the VCG.

If the mean-square error is to be minimized it is well known (e.g. Papoulis, 1965) that

$$\mathbf{T}_1 = \int_0^T \mathbf{s}(t)\mathbf{x}_1^T(t)\,dt \quad \left[\int_0^T \mathbf{x}_1(t)\mathbf{x}_1^T(t)\,dt\right]^{-1}. \tag{7.20}$$

7.3.2 *Results of applying normalization*

Brown (1968) applied normalization to clinical data. He implemented the approach with analog hardware that was manually adjusted. He reported that when a cardiologist diagnosed a number of transformed VCGs, the results were either the same or clearer than with the untransformed data.

An automated procedure has been applied to a library of digitized Frank lead VCGs supplied by Hubert V. Pipberger, M.D., of the Veterans' Administration Research Center for Cardiovascular Data Processing (Pipeberger, 1966). This library consists of examples of normal VCGs and of 13 disease categories. Twenty randomly selected examples of each of these classes have been normalized, using a typical normal as a standard. A typical result is shown in figure 7.6. The upper histogram shows the distribution of normals (above the line) and cases of posterior myocardial infarction before normalization using the peak of the P-wave as a feature.

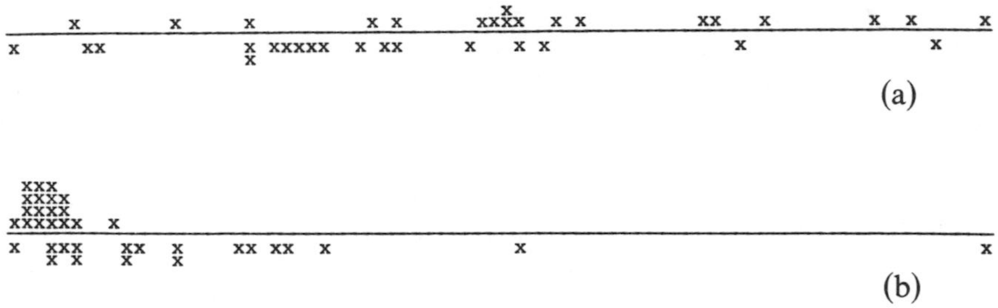

fig. 7.6 (a) A histogram showing the value of one VCG measurement on 20 normal (above the line) and 20 posterior myocardial infarct (below the line) patients. (b) The same patients after normalization. The normals are tightly clustered relative to the PMI's. (Kelly et al., 1971).

The lower histogram shows corresponding results after normalization. Clearly normalization has enhanced class separation, at least on this feature.

The results suggest that normalization will improve the classification accuracy of both human and machine pattern recognition of VCGs. If these results are borne out by more extensive clinical tests, it will be economically and technologically feasible to provide an automatic normalizer, containing either a special purpose digital or analog computer for use in clinical vectorcardiography. No hardware would be required to implement normalization in existing schemes for computer classification of VCGs (see below). The problem in applying normalization either to human- or machine-interpreted VCGs is that new features must be developed that are appropriate to the normalized data. In comparing "VCG normalization" with other approaches for clustering data, it should be remembered that this approach is motivated by insight into the physiology of the body. This is probably typical of all practical pattern recognition problems, i.e., general clustering and feature extraction approaches cannot replace a thorough understanding of the physical process that produced the data.

7.4 Feature Selection

In this pattern recognition problem the measurements are well defined. For both the ECG and the VCG a signal of four or five heart beats (approximately 4 seconds) is recorded. If this is then digitized at 500 samples per second, the 12-lead ECG gives 12 serial records of about 2000 time samples each (a total of 24,000 samples) and the VCG gives three simultaneous records of 2000 time samples each (a total of 6000 samples).

Editing can then reduce this to one selected heartbeat in each lead. Then we will need about 4800 time samples to describe a 12-lead ECG and 1200 samples for a VCG. These samples completely describe the waveform and could, in principle, be used as features for the input to a pattern recognition system. This would obviously be quite wasteful since the sampling rate is not minimal and some segments of the waveform (e.g., the baseline between the T and the P waves) carry very little information.

The engineer is tempted to represent these signals by expanding them on a set of basis functions, i.e.,

$$x_j(t) = \sum_{i=1}^{N} c_{ij}\,\phi_i(t) \tag{7.21}$$

where $x_j(t)$ is the j-th lead of the ECG or VCG and $\phi_i(t)$ is one of a family of N suitable basis functions. An obvious choice for $\phi_i(t)$ would be a family of sinusoids (giving a Fourier series expansion), but it has been shown that a smaller number of significant terms will result if a series of orthogonalized real exponentials is used (Young and Huggins, 1963). Another possible choice is based on the intrinsic components developed above.

All of the systems that have been applied clinically (some typical examples are described below) have used features that can be measured directly from the waveform. This is the result of the unwillingness of many physicians to accept automatic classification based on criteria that they cannot (at least in principle) check by hand. Thus, since all of the large-scale tests of ECG/VCG pattern recognition have been based on features that are measurements from the waveform, we have no comprehensive comparisons with more theoretically based features. All of the indications are that they would perform with about the same error rate but that an orthogonal expansion might be more efficient and might result in fewer features.

The simplest practical choice for a set of features is to measure the magnitude of the waveform at selected times in the heartbeat. A typical choice is that of Specht (1967a), who used 15 equally spaced points in the QRS complex of each of the three VCG leads plus the duration of the QRS complex, so that he had 46 features. Pipberger (1970), in studying discrimination between normal VCGs and those found in pulmonary emphysema, initially used 333 scalar and vectorial measurements but by a crude selection process reduced this to 30. He then used discriminant analysis to find the best 14 of these 30. This was done by finding a linear discriminant function, i.e.,

$$D(\mathbf{x}) = \boldsymbol{\alpha}^T \mathbf{x}. \tag{7.22}$$

Then the 14 largest elements of $\boldsymbol{\alpha}$ were used to identify the 14 most important components of the feature vector **x** (the elements of **x** were the 30 measurements).

In addition to raw amplitude measurements at selected time points, features can also be obtained from the ratios of selected amplitude measurements, and from the time duration of the complete heartbeat and of various complexes (P, Q, R, S, and T) in the heartbeat. A typical set of features is that used by the scalar ECG program developed by the U. S. Public Health Service (this is described in more detail below, and by Weihrer et al. (1970)). The 18 features are the amplitudes and durations of the P-wave, Q-wave, R-wave, S-wave, S-T segment, and T-wave and, in addition, the Q/S ratios and the heart rate. Since there are 12 leads, a total of 216 features results. These are available to the user together with the results of the classification (a typical print-out is shown in figure 7.7). Similar measurements are made on VCGs, but although there are fewer leads, there are now vectorial as well as scalar measurements. Also, such things as the area of the QRS loop are used.

Mucciardi and Gose (1970) have made a comprehensive study of methods that can be used to select a small number of VCG features from the large group available. They used the 147 features developed by Pipberger's group plus 10 of their own to give a total of 157 (Pipberger, 1966). Using data supplied by Pipberger with a training set of 247 and a test set of 240 distributed among nine classes, they showed that training set error rates of the order of 20% and testing set error rates of the order of 40% could be obtained with 15 features and that the error rates decreased very slowly as more features were added. The specific error rates obtained are not very significant because of the small size of the training and test sets (Pipberger (1970) has found empirically that the number of examples in each class should exceed the square of the number of features), but the indication that there is little improvement with more than 15 features is probably significant.

7.5 Classification Schemes

Almost every conceivable method of classification has been applied to ECGs or VCGs at one time or another. All of the systems that have been implemented on a large scale essentially use medical criteria for each of the features or parameters and the decision process is implemented by table look-up, decision tables, or a decision tree. These methods give identical results but while a decision tree can be implemented more efficiently, decision tables allow the criteria to be changed more easily. Other schemes have been implemented on a smaller scale but so far have only been applied in a research environment. Some of the more important approaches are the multivariate analysis of Pipberger et al. (1965), the nonlinear decision function of Specht (1967a and 1967b), the linear regression of Young and Huggins (1964), the approximation of classes by multimodal mixtures of Gaussian distributions of Mucciardi and Gose (1970), the Fourier expansion of Cady et al. (1961), the matched-filter approach of Stark et al. (1962), and the cross-correlation approach of Balm (1967). Since Pipberger's group has made a comprehensive application of pattern recognition theory to the ECG/VCG problem, and since Specht has used innovative pattern recognition theory with good results, these two approaches will be discussed in some detail.

INSTRUMENTATION FIELD STATION --- HEART DISEASE CONTROL PROGRAM
COMPUTER PROCESSED ELECTROCARDIOGRAM

G.W. HEART STATION

NAME NUMBER 046853 DATE 2- 4-76 TIME 15--05--50

DIAGNOSIS MEDS NONE

HEIGHT 67 WEIGHT 140 AGE 58 MALE TAPE 627

B.P. NORMAL-SYSTOLIC 139 OR LESS AND DIASTOLIC 89 OR LESS OPTION 154

	I	II	III	AVR	AVL	AVF	V1	V2	V3	V4	V5	V6	
PA	.05	.14	.14	-.09	-.06	.14	.09	.06	.05	.09	.06	.07	PA
PD	.05	.10	.08	.09	.06	.08	.03	.03	.06	.05	.04	.04	PD
P'A	.00	.00	.00	.00	.00	.00	-.05	.00	.00	.00	.00	.00	P'A
P'D	.00	.00	.00	.00	.00	.00	.05	.00	.00	.00	.00	.00	P'D
QA	.00	-.31	.00	.00	-.08	.00	.00	.00	-.11	-.08	-.03	.00	QA
QD	.00	.02	.00	.00	.02	.00	.00	.00	.02	.02	.02	.00	QD
RA	.45	.05	.12	.05	.52	.10	.00	.00	.41	.79	.58	.64	RA
RD	.08	.00	.02	.01	.06	.03	.00	.00	.02	.03	.04	.06	RD
SA	.00	-.50	-.75	-.25	.00	-.63	-1.35	-1.78	-.64	-.12	.00	.00	SA
SD	.00	.03	.06	.02	.00	.06	.05	.11	.06	.02	.00	.00	SD
R'A	.00	.00	.00	.10	.00	.00	.00	.00	.00	.00	.00	.00	R'A
R'D	.00	.00	.00	.00	.00	.00	.00	.00	[illegible]	.00	.00	.00	R'D
ST	.12	.12	.12	.12	.12	.12	[illegible]	[illegible]	[illegible]	[illegible]	.12	.12	ST
STO	[illegible]	[illegible]	.02	.02	.03	-.05	.06	.23	.16	.02	-.05	-.03	STO
STM	-.03	-.01	.00	.02	-.01	-.02	.16	.31	.18	-.01	-.03	-.05	STM
STE	-.02	-.01	.00	.01	.00	-.01	.20	.58	.33	-.03	-.05	-.05	STE
TA	-.09	.00	.10	.06	-.09	.00	.56	1.06	.57	-.24	-.22	-.21	TA
PR	.10	.16	.14	.15	.14	.13	.16	.13	.14	.11	.10	.11	PR
QRS	.08	.05	.08	.05	.08	.09	.05	.11	.10	.07	.06	.06	QRS
QT	.34	.00	.35	.31	.35	.00	.34	.39	.36	.36	.36	.35	QT
RATE	78	79	78	78	76	71	77	78	77	72	76	76	RATE
CODE	2	2	2	2	2	3	3	3	3	2	4	2	
CAL	84	84	84	84	84	84	84	84	84	84	84	84	CAL

	P	QRS	T	Q	R	S	STO	ST-T	QRS-T	
AXIS IN DEGREES	90	260			41	-70	-84			ANGLE IN DEGREES

5122 SMALL OR ABSENT R AND NEGATIVE T 2 LEADS V2-5 . CONSISTENT WITH AGE UNDETERMINED . INFARCT - ANTERIOR

8311 QRS AXIS RANGE 240 TO -80 . SUPERIORLY DIRECTED AXIS

fig. 7.7 A typical printout for the USPHS system.

7.5.1 Multivariate analysis (*Pipberger, 1965, 1970*)

The Research Center for Cardiovascular Data Processing of the V. A. Hospital in Washington, D.C., headed by Hubert V. Pipberger, M.D., has the advantage of an unrivaled data base of corrected Frank-lead VCGs. Not only do they have in excess of 30,000 different examples in their library, but all of these have been diagnosed independently of the VCG and many of the diagnoses have been verified by autopsy. The Pipberger group has investigated many aspects of the application of pattern recognition theory to differential diagnoses of VCGs. An important part of their work has been a study of the use of multivariate analysis to select features for VCGs described by scalar or vector time samples from the QRS complex and ST segment.

It is assumed that each class (typically, normal plus eight diseases) has a multidimensional Gaussian distribution, i.e.,

$$f_i(\mathbf{x}) = g(\mathbf{x}; \mathbf{m}_i, \mathbf{R}_i), \tag{7.23}$$

where $\mathbf{x}$ is an M-dimensional feature vector. The means and covariance matrices are estimated from

$$\hat{\mathbf{m}}_i = \frac{1}{N_j} \sum_{i=1}^{N_i} \mathbf{x}_j, \tag{7.24}$$

$$\hat{\mathbf{R}}_i = \frac{1}{N_i - 1} \sum_{j=1}^{N_i} (\mathbf{x}_j - \hat{\mathbf{m}}_i)(\mathbf{x}_j - \hat{\mathbf{m}}_i)^T, \tag{7.25}$$

where there are N_i examples of class i. Then differential diagnosis is based on

$$D_i(\mathbf{x}) = (\mathbf{x} - \mathbf{m}_i)^T \mathbf{R}_i^{-1} (\mathbf{x} - \mathbf{m}_i) + D_{0i}, \tag{7.26}$$

where we decide class i if

$$D_i(\mathbf{x}) \leqslant D_j(\mathbf{x}) \text{ for } j = 1, 2, \ldots, K \text{ where there are } K \text{ classes}.$$

These distance measures $D_i(\mathbf{x})$ are directly related to the probabilities

$$P(\mathbf{x} \in C_i) = (2\pi)^{-M/2} |\mathbf{R}_i|^{-1} \exp[-D_i(\mathbf{x})/2]. \tag{7.27}$$

Thus, since the distances $D_i(\mathbf{x})$ and the probabilities of class membership $P(\mathbf{x} \in C_i)$ are inversely monotonically related for a given $\mathbf{R}_i$, the lower the distance $D_i(\mathbf{x})$, the higher the probability $P(\mathbf{x} \in C_i)$ that $\mathbf{x}$ belongs to class C_i. The constants D_{0i} in equation (7.26) are determined by linear programming to minimize the number of classification errors for the training set samples.

Pipberger and his colleagues have applied this approach to a wide variety of problems and have investigated many combinations of features. Some typical results are shown in table 7.1 below.

The assumption of a Gaussian distribution for the classes is not unduly restrictive provided the classes are unimodal. Mucciardi and Gose (1970) have used the less restrictive assumption that the classes can be approximated with two Gaussian distributions. Although this was also done with Pipberger's data, it is impossible to compare results because of differences in sample size. In any case the main interest of Pipberger's group and Mucciardi and Gose was in selecting the most useful features rather than in validating the error rates achievable with these features on a given population.

7.5.2 Nonlinear discriminant functions

Specht (1967a and b) has developed a method for generating polynomial discriminant functions and has applied this to pattern recognition of VCGs. A polynomial discriminant function applied to an N-dimensional feature vector **x** can be written as:

$$D_k(\mathbf{x}) = \beta_{n+1} + \boldsymbol{\beta}^T\mathbf{x} + \mathbf{x}^T\mathbf{A}\mathbf{x} + \cdots, \tag{7.28}$$

TABLE 7.1 (Pipberger, 1965)

Computer Printout of the Differential Diagnosis of Four ECG Records, Based on Analysis of $ST - T$*

Record 1		Record 2		Record 3		Record 4	
PDI	29.2	N	23.1	RVCD	18.6	LVH	23.0
N	33.6	PDI	33.7	N	29.8	N	23.9
LVH	47.3	LVH	41.9	LVH	37.5	RVH	24.8
RVCD	73.2	RVH	52.4	PDI	58.1	PDI	26.4
LVCD	87.7	RVCD	56.3	RVH	63.0	LVCD	34.8

* Out of nine possible diagnoses only the first five with the highest probabilities are listed. Figures following each diagnosis indicate the vector difference between the mean of the diagnostic group and the record under study. The most likely diagnoses are characterized by small vector differences, the less likely ones by large ones. Note the similarities of vector differences in record 4. In this case the *ST-T* vectors did not lead to a clear-cut separation of various diagnostic entities and several possibilities need to be considered.

N = normal record; LVH = left ventricular hypertrophy; RVH = right ventricular hypertrophy; BVH = biventricular hypertrophy; LVCD = left ventricular conduction defect; RVCD = right ventricular conduction defect; PDI = posterodiaphragmatic infarct; AI = anterior infarct; ApI = apical infarct.

where for convenience cubic and higher terms are not written explicitly. If the order of the polynomial is decided in advance, then any of the linear algorithms discussed above can be used to find the coefficients. The problem is linear in the new set of features that are powers and cross-products of the original features. The difficulty is to minimize the number of terms in the polynomial so that a reasonable computation will result.

Specht has developed a method based on the Parzen approximation of a class probability density function to find the polynomial coefficients. It was shown in chapter 3 that if n training patterns are available for class C_k, then its density function can be approximated by

$$f_k(\mathbf{x}) = \frac{1}{n} \sum_{\mathbf{x}_j \in C_k} g(\mathbf{x}; \mathbf{x}_j, \mathbf{R}_j) \tag{7.29}$$

where $\mathbf{x}_j$ are the n training patterns and $\mathbf{R}_j = \sigma^2 \mathbf{I}$ with σ^2 a "smoothing parameter." Clearly (7.29) can be written as

$$\begin{aligned} f_k(\mathbf{x}) &= \frac{1}{\sigma^N (2\pi)^{N/2}} \frac{1}{n} \sum_{\mathbf{x}_j \in C_k} \exp\left(-\frac{(\mathbf{x}-\mathbf{x}_j)^T(\mathbf{x}-\mathbf{x}_j)}{2\sigma^2}\right) \\ &= \frac{1}{\sigma^N (2\pi)^{N/2}} \frac{1}{n} \sum_{\mathbf{x}_j \in C_k} \exp\left(-\frac{\mathbf{x}^T\mathbf{x} - 2\mathbf{x}^T\mathbf{x}_j + \mathbf{x}_j^T\mathbf{x}_j}{2\sigma^2}\right) \\ &= \frac{1}{\sigma^N (2\pi)^{N/2}} \frac{1}{n} \sum_{x_j \in C_k} \exp\left(-\frac{\mathbf{x}^T\mathbf{x}}{2\sigma^2}\right) \exp\left(\frac{2\mathbf{x}^T\mathbf{x}_j - \mathbf{x}_j^T\mathbf{x}_j}{2\sigma^2}\right) \\ &= \frac{1}{\sigma^N (2\pi)^{N/2}} \exp\left(-\frac{\mathbf{x}^T\mathbf{x}}{2\sigma^2}\right) \frac{1}{n} \sum_{x_j \in C_k} \exp\left(-\frac{\mathbf{x}_j^T\mathbf{x}_j}{2\sigma^2}\right) \exp\left(\frac{\mathbf{x}^T\mathbf{x}_j}{\sigma^2}\right). \end{aligned} \tag{7.30}$$

By taking a Taylor series expansion of the term $\exp(\mathbf{x}^T\mathbf{x}_j/\sigma^2)$ we obtain from (7.30)

$$\begin{aligned} f_k(\mathbf{x}) &= \frac{1}{\sigma^N (2\pi)^{N/2}} \exp\left(-\frac{\mathbf{x}^T\mathbf{x}}{2\sigma^2}\right) \\ &\quad \frac{1}{n} \sum_{x_j \in C_k} \exp\left(-\frac{\mathbf{x}_j^T\mathbf{x}_j}{2\sigma^2}\right)\left(1 + \frac{\mathbf{x}^T\mathbf{x}_j}{\sigma^2} + \frac{(\mathbf{x}^T\mathbf{x}_j)^2}{2!\,\sigma^4} + \cdots\right) \\ &= \frac{1}{\sigma^N (2\pi)^{N/2}} \exp\left(-\frac{\mathbf{x}^T\mathbf{x}}{2\sigma^2}\right) D_k(\mathbf{x}), \end{aligned} \tag{7.31}$$

where $D_k(\mathbf{x})$ is of the same form as in (7.28). The coefficients of the general polynomial from (7.28) can now be calculated by comparison with (7.31). Thus:

TABLE 7.2 (Specht, 1967 a and b)

Comparison of Machine Classification with Clinical Diagnosis

	Normal		Abnormal	
	No. of cases	Percent correct	No. of cases	Percent correct
Training Set - Machine Classification	192	95%	57	86%
Test Set - Machine Classification	32	97%	31	90%
Test Set - Clinical Diagnosis	—	95%	30	53%

$$\beta_{n+1} = \frac{1}{n} \sum_{\mathbf{x}_j \in C_k} \exp\left(-\frac{\mathbf{x}_j^T \mathbf{x}_j}{2\sigma^2}\right), \tag{7.32}$$

$$\boldsymbol{\beta} = \frac{1}{n} \sum_{\mathbf{x}_j \in C_k} \exp\left(-\frac{\mathbf{x}_j^T \mathbf{x}_j}{2\sigma^2}\right)\left(\frac{1}{\sigma^2}\mathbf{x}_j\right), \tag{7.33}$$

and

$$\mathbf{A} = \frac{1}{n} \sum_{\mathbf{x}_j \in C_k} \exp\left(-\frac{\mathbf{x}_j^T \mathbf{x}_j}{2\sigma^2}\right)\left(\frac{1}{2\sigma^4}\mathbf{x}_j \mathbf{x}_j^T\right). \tag{7.34}$$

Higher-order terms are calculated in a similar way but the notation becomes very tedious. Details can be found in Specht (1967b).

To classify an unknown pattern $\mathbf{x}$ among K classes, the simplest procedure is to find C_i such that

$$D_i(\mathbf{x}) \geqslant D_k(\mathbf{x}) \quad \text{for } k = 1, \ldots, K.$$

Clearly, for any given $\mathbf{x}$, $D_i(\mathbf{x})$ differs only by a constant from $f_i(\mathbf{x})$ and a Bayes decision, as discussed in chapter 2, could be implemented if desired. It is also clear that for a two-class problem only one discriminant function $D(\mathbf{x}) = D_1(\mathbf{x}) - D_2(\mathbf{x})$ is necessary.

Specht has applied this approach to VCGs recorded with the Helm lead system. It might be expected that a nonlinear discriminant function would be useful since Mucciardi and Gose (1970) have found it advantageous to approximate VCG classes with two Gaussian distributions. The features consisted of 15 equally spaced time points from the QRS complex of each of the three VCG leads plus the time duration of the QRS complex giving 46 features in all. The data consisted of 224 normal and 88 abnormal female subjects. The data were split into a training set of 249 cases (192 normal and 57 abnormal) and a test set of 63 cases (32 normal and 31 abnormal). The results obtained with $\sigma = 4.0$ are given in table 7.2, where they are compared with the results of clinical diagnosis. It was found that the polynomial to achieve this only had 30 significant coefficients (27 linear, two squared terms, and a constant) although it potentially contained terms up to the eighth order (a total of 369 coefficients if cross terms are not considered).

It is interesting to consider the effect of the smoothing term σ. If this is very small, the polynomial will have many significant terms and the decision process will approach the nearest-neighbor procedure described in chapter 3. If $\sigma \rightarrow \infty$, then the higher-order terms become very small relative to the linear terms and the decision function is effectively linear. Specht showed that the lowest classification errors for his data occurred when $3 < \sigma < 10$ with an optimum of $\sigma = 4$. The percentage correct for abnormals tended to 74% as $\sigma \rightarrow 0$ and 81% as $\sigma \rightarrow \infty$ compared to 90% for $\sigma = 4$.

7.6 The Implementation of Automatic Classification for ECG/VCGs

While numerous groups have conducted research into the application of pattern recognition to ECGs and VCGs, only a very few schemes have been implemented as complete systems, and even fewer have had any impact on clinical medicine. Every scheme that has been applied clinically has used as features only those measurements that could be made from a graphic plot of the ECG or VCG. It is important to realize that the physician (at least so far) has insisted on knowing on exactly what basis a machine classifier makes it decision. Thus, it is acceptable to use as features all of the graphic measurements on the waveform, but it is *not acceptable*, for example, to perform a Fourier series expansion of the waveform and use the components as features.

Most of the systems that have been developed perform all operations with software after the ECG or VCG has been edited and digitized. The software is generally in two parts. The first performs waveform analysis (unfortunately referred to as "pattern recognition" in the ECG literature) that consists of identifying the complexes of the waveform (P, Q, R, S, and T) and of making time duration and amplitude measurements on the complexes. This is equivalent to measurement and feature extraction in standard terminology. The second part of the software performs classification based on the features from the first part. The classification is usually carried out by comparing the features with criteria built up over the years by clinical cardiographers. Since many cardiographers disagree on diagnostic criteria, a computer program will require adjustment for the needs of individual users. Often the physician is given a print-out of the numerical values of the features, in addition to the results of the classification, so that he can check the results against his own experience.

The systems that have currently been implemented on a large scale are (1) the scalar ECG program of the U.S. Public Health Service, and (2) the VCG program developed jointly by Mayo Clinic and IBM. We shall describe briefly the characteristics of these systems.

7.6.1 The USPHS program (Caceres and Dreifus, 1970)

The Medical Systems Development Laboratory of the U.S. Public Health Service, under the leadership of Cesar Caceres, over a number of years developed a highly successful system for computer interpretation of ECGs. This is truly a complete system since Cacere's group has stimulated the development of all elements from the hardware at the bedside to dedicated computers sold specifically for this purpose. This program has now been implemented in a number of different situations and is available in FORTRAN IV from the USPHS "Data Pool." It is possible to purchase a complete dedicated computer system with all peripherals and software tailored for this operation for approximately $70,000, or to obtain remote use of this program on a commercial basis from a time-shared system. Apart from the USPHS, the major installations using this program include the Missouri Regional Medical Program, Queens University of Kingston in Ontario, the TVA, Hartford Hospital in Connecticut, and St. Lukes Hospital in Denver, Colorado. Approximately 20 commercial organizations either offer or plan to offer this program on a time-shared system to any customer who cares to send his data by telephone.

The ECG is transmitted from the bedside to the computer by telephone, analog magnetic tape, digital magnetic tape, or a combination of these. Each of the 12 ECG leads is digitized for 3.72 seconds at 500 samples per

TABLE 7.3 (Weihrer et al, 1970)

Computer Classification Compared with Cardiologist Classification.

	Abnormal (n=598)		Normal (n=146)	
Complete Agreement	436	(73%)	107	(72%)
Agreement of abnormality but disagreement on nature of abnormality	157	(26%)		
Disagreement	5	(0.8%)	41	(28%)

second. The complexes in each lead are then identified and measured giving a table of 216 features as shown in the top half of the sample print-out in figure 7.7. The decision logic then analyzes the features to arrive at some classification and/or comments. Since there is considerable redundancy in the 12 leads, one or more can be missing or noisy without voiding the classification. A typical diagnostic print-out is shown in the lower portion of figure 7.7. The results of comparing this program with diagnoses made by physicians in a hospital environment are shown in table 7.3. Although the overall error rates are quite high (~ 27%), it should be noted that the decision criteria are chosen to minimize the rate of clinically dangerous false negatives and these are quite low (0.8%).

7.6.2 The Mayo Clinic–IBM program (*Alexander, 1970*)

In 1968 Dr. Ralph Smith of the Mayo Clinic in Rochester, Minnesota, released a FORTRAN program developed jointly with IBM for the computer classification of Frank VCGs (see Alexander, 1970). This has since been updated and variants of it have been implemented by Hahneman Medical School in Philadelphia, the Nebraska Regional Medical Program, and others. This program includes arrythmia-detection proce-

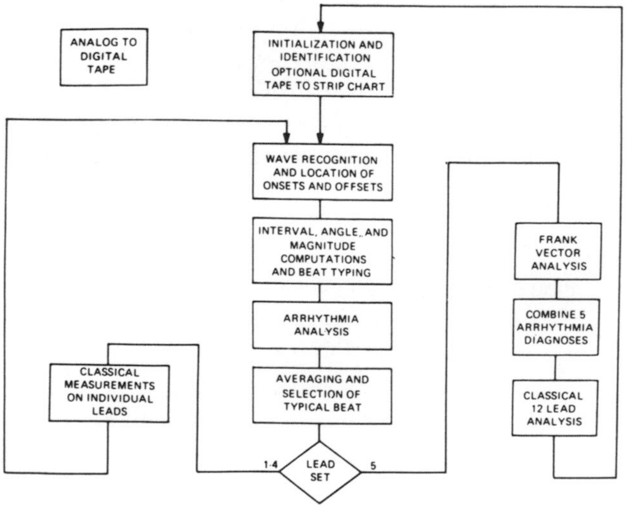

fig. 7.8 The flow-chart for the ECG/VCG analysis system developed at Mayo Clinic. (Alexander, 1970).

dures based on the 12-lead system developed by IBM in conjunction with Mount Sinai Hospital in New York (Pordy et al., 1970).

This program gives the physician the best of both worlds (ECG and VCG). The standard 12 leads are recorded in four sets of three in addition to the three Frank leads. The system can give the physician a classification based on the 12-lead scalar and/or on the three-lead Frank system. This is convenient to the user and builds more redundancy into the system. The weakest link in any waveform analysis system is invariably the recognition of the various complexes (P,Q,R,S, and T) and the determination of their onset and termination. This is much easier when three leads are recorded simultaneously. The features used in this program are generally similar to those investigated by Pipberger for VCGs and used by the USPHS program for ECGs. A flowchart of how the system operates is shown in figure 7.8.

It is quite difficult to evaluate the performance of a system for medical diagnosis since this depends not only on the population to which it is applied but also on the motivation for its use, i.e., screening or diagnosis. A comparison of some applications of the USPHS, Mayo Clinic, and some other programs is given in table 7.4, which is reproduced from Cox, et al. (1972).

7.7 Notes and Remarks

Engineers and physical scientists had a keen interest in the ECG/VCG long before computers made automatic classification feasible. The vector nature of the signal lent itself to the application of simple, but elegant mathematics that gave the quantitative physical scientist reason to feel superior to his medical colleague who wondered at the triangle of Einthoven (Einthoven et al., 1913). Thus the theory of electrocardiography developed early and this led to lead-system design (Frank, 1954), and even to analog hardware to perform signal rotations (Schmitt, 1947; McFee and Baule, 1966). The major theoretical developments then stemmed from electromagnetic field theory, which yielded the multipole expansions of the source (Geselowitz, 1960), and from signal and statistical theory, which led to factor analysis (Scher et al., 1960); and the elegant intrinsic component theory (Young and Huggins, 1962). Current research in electrocardiography was recently surveyed by McFee and Baule (1972).

After character recognition, the ECG has probably received more attention than any other pattern recognition application. A variety of approaches in the late 1950s and early 1960s (Cady et al., 1961; Stark et al., 1962; Steinberg et al., 1962; Pipberger et al., 1965) resulted in a very few long-term efforts. The best known and most widely implemented was the very

TABLE 7.4 (Cox, Nolle and Arthur, 1972)

Screening Results of Selected Heart-Station Evaluations

Source of Program	Source of Records	Date of Test	Leads	Agreement (%)	Normals (Negative) Number of Records	True Negative (%)	False Positive (%)	Abnormals (Positive) Number of Records	True Positive (%)	False Negative (%)
USPHS	George Washington University Hospital	1966	ECG	73	148	72	28	598	99.2	0.8
USPHS	Hartford Hospital	1967	ECG	87	113	100	0	253	81	19
USPHS	Hartford Hospital	1967	ECG	78	276	80	20	52	67	33
USPHS	George Washington University Hospital	1968	ECG	81	178	97.3	2.2	469	96.6	3.4
USPHS and Queen's University	Queen's University Teaching Hospital	1969	ECG	82	112	86	14	88		
USPHS and Queen's University	Hotel Diev Hospital and Kingston General Hospital	1970	ECG	85	762	90	10	1257	96	4
Mt. Sinai Hospital	Mt. Sinai Hospital	1967	ECG	91	996	91	9	1064	94	6
Mayo Clinic	University of Washington and Group Health Hospitals	1970	VCG	74	289	75	25	84	76	24
Latter-day Saints Hospital	Latter-day Saints Hospital	1969	VCG	95	195	99	1	92	91	9
Osaka Center for Adult Diseases	Osaka Center for Adult Diseases	1966	VCG	82	100	80	20	105	84	16
Iowa Methodist Hospital	Iowa Methodist Hospital	1967	I, II, V2		1708	99.7	0.3	3090	91	9
Mt. Sinai Hospital and Mayo Clinic	l'Hospital Brugmann		VCG	81	105	83	17			
		1970	ECG	85	432	91.5	8.5	1303		
Mt. Sinai Hospital and Mayo Clinic	l'Hospital Brugmann		VCG	67	2589	78	22	603	95.6	4.4
		1971	ECG	89	1487	95	5	5334		
Mt. Sinai Hospital and Mayo Clinic	CHU Bretonneau à Tours		ECG	85	73	93	7	427	83	17
		1971	ECG+VCG	87	73			427		
Royal Infirmary Glasgow	Royal Infirmary Glasgow		VCG	81	205	73	27	419	85	15
		1971	ECG	82	205	73	27	419	86	14
VA Research Center	VA Hospitals	1971	VCG	74	597	90	10	2005	89	11

straightforward and effective approach of Caceres and his colleagues while they were at the U. S. Public Health Service (Steinberg, 1962). This resulted in the only system in wide clinical use today. Two groups at IBM developed working systems for the ECG (Pordy et al., 1970) and the VCG(Alexander, 1970). The VCG system developed at the Mayo Clinic has been used in a number of locations and has served as the basis for a number of rather different implementations. The current effort with the USPHS and IBM/ Mayo Clinic programs seems to be to extend them (e.g., for exercise ECGs) and to improve their accuracy by building in patches to handle more and more of the rare cases. In parallel with the effort to implement practical systems, several research groups have been investigating a number of aspects of ECG/VCG classification. The most spectacular effort is that of Pipberger and his colleagues who have unrivaled experience in applying the computer to the VCG (Pipberger, 1965, 1966, 1970; Steinberg et al. 1962). This subject was recently reviewed by Cox et al. (1972).

It appears that while the classification of ECG/VCGs still presents many unsolved problems, it has lost its excitement (at least in medical circles), and further spectacular advances are more likely to occur in other problem areas. Perhaps the biggest challenge is to design comprehensive automated multiphasic health screening systems (Berkley, 1971).

References

1. Alexander, D. C. 1970. Multichannel simultaneous analysis of the electocardiogram using simultaneously recorded 3-lead sets. In *Clinical Electrocardiography and Computers*, eds. C. A. Caceres and L. S. Dreifus, pp. 149–156. Academic Press, New York.

2. Balm, G. J. 1967. Cross-correlation techniques applied to the electrocardiogram interpretation problem. *IEEE Trans. Biomedical Engineering* BME-14:258–262.

3. Berkley, C. ed. 1971. *Automated Multiphasic Health Testing*. Engineering Foundation, New York.

4. Brown, J. P. 1968. Compensating the normal and abnormal vectorcardiogram for individual anatomic variations. Unpublished Ph.D. Thesis, Carnegie-Mellon University.

5. Caceres, C. A. and Dreifus, L. S., eds. 1970. *Clinical Electrocardiography and Computers*. Academic Press, New York.

6. Cady, L. D., Woodbury, M. A., Tich, L. J., and Gertler, N. N. 1961. A method for electrocardiogram wave pattern estimation. *Circulation Research* 9:1078–1082.

7. Cox, J. R., Nolle, F. M., and Arthur, R. M. 1972. Digital analysis of the electroencephalogram, blood pressure wave and the electrocardiogram. *Proc. IEEE* 60:1137–1164.

8. Crichton, M. 1969. *The Andromeda Strain*. Dell, New York.

9. Einthoven, W., Fahr, G., and deWaart, A. 1913. Uber die Richtung und die Manifeste Grosse der Potential Schwankungen im Menschlichen Herzen und uber den Einfluss der Herzlage auf die Form des Electrokardiogramms. *Arch. ges Physiol.* 150:275. *Translation*. Hoff, H. E. and Sekelj, P. 1950. On the direction and manifest size of the variations of potential in the human heart and on the influence of the position of the heart on the form of the electrocardiogram. *Am. Heart J.* 40:163.

10. Frank, E. 1954. A direct experimental study of three systems of spatial vectorcardiography. *Circulation* 10:101–113.

11. Geselowitz, D. B. 1960. Multipole representation of an equivalent cardiac generator. *Proc. IRE* 48:75–79.

12. Geselowitz, D. B. and Schmitt, O. H. 1969. Electrocardiography. In *Biological Engineering*. ed. H. P. Schwann. McGraw Hill, New York.

13. Kelly, K. K., Calvert, T. W., Longini, R. L., and Brown, J. P. 1971. Feature enhancement of vectorcardiograms by linear normalization. *IEEE Trans. Computers* C-20:1109–1111.

14. McFee, R. and Baule, G. M. 1966. A Compact rotater integrator for rapidly obtaining spatial parameters of the electrocardiogram, In *Proc. Long Island Jewish Hosp. Symposium Vectorcardiography*, eds. I. Hoffman and R. C. Taymor. J. B. Lippincott, Philadelphia and Montreal.

15. ———. 1972. Research in electrocardiography and magnetocardiography. *Proc. IEEE*, 60:290–321.

16. Mucciardi, A. N. and Gose, E. E. 1970. A comparison of seven techniques for choosing subsets of pattern recognition properties. *IEEE Trans. Computers* C-20:1023–1031.

17. Papoulis, A. 1965. *Probability, Random Variables and Stochastic Processes*. McGraw-Hill, New York.

18. Pipberger, H. V. 1965. Computer analysis of the electrocardiogram. In *Computers in Biomedical Research*, eds. R. W. Stacy and B. D. Waxman, pp. 377–407. Academic Press, New York.

19. ———. 1966. Users' guide to electrocardiographic data analysis computer programs. Tech. Rept. Veterans' Administration Research Center for Cardiovascular Data Processing, Washington, D. C.

20. ———. 1970. Computer analysis of electrocardiograms. In *Clinical Electrocardiography and Computers*, eds. C. A. Caceres and L. S. Drėifus, pp. 109–119. Academic Press, New York.

21. Pipberger, H. V., Bialek, S. M., Perloff, J. K., and Schnaper, H. W. 1961. Correlation of clinical information in the standard 12-lead ECG and in a corrected orthogonal 3-lead ECG. *Am. Heart J.* 61:34–43.

22. Pipberger, H. V., Stallmann, F. W., Yano, K. and Draper, H. W. 1965. Digital computer analysis of the normal and abnormal electrocardiogram. *Progress Cardiovascular Disease* 5:378–392.

23. Plonsey, R. 1969. *Bioelectric Phenomena.* McGraw-Hill, New York.

24. Pordy, L., Jaffe, H., Chesky, K., Friedberg, C. K. Bonner, R. E., Schwetman, H. D. and Alexander, D. C., Computer analysis of the electrocardiogram: a joint project. In *Clinical Electrocardiography and Computers*, eds. C. A. Caceres and L. S. Dreifus, pp. 133–147. Academic Press, New York

25. Scher, A. M., Young, A. C. and Meredith, W. M. 1960. Factor analysis of the electrocardiogram. A test of electrocardiography theory: Normal leads. *Circulation Research* 8:519–526.

26. Schmitt, O. H. 1947. Cathode ray presentation of three dimensional data. *J. Appl. Phys.* 18:819–829.

27. Specht, D. F. 1967a. Generation of polynomial discriminant functions for pattern recognition. *IEEE Trans. Electronic Computers* EC-16:309–319.

28. ———. 1967b. Vectorcardiographic diagnosis using the polynomial discriminant method of pattern recognition. *IEEE Trans. Biomedical Engineering* BME-14:90–95.

29. Stark, L., Okajima, M., and Whipple, G. H. 1962. Computer pattern recognition techniques:electrocardiographic diagnosis. *Communications ACM* 5:527–532.

30. Steinberg, C. A., Abraham, S., and Caceres, C. A. 1962. Pattern recognition in the clinical electrocardiogram. *IRE Trans. Biomedical Electronics* BME-9:23–30.

31. Weihrer, A. L., Whitman, J. R., Zimmerman, A., and Caceres, C. A. 1970. Computer programs for an automated electrocardiograph-

ic system. In *Clinical Electrocardiography and Computers*, eds. C. A. Caceres and L. S. Dreifus, pp. 81–108. Academic Press, New York.

32. Young, T. Y. and Huggins, W. H. 1962. The intrinsic component theory of electrocardiography. *IRE Trans. Biomedical Electronics* BME-9:214–221.

33. ———. 1963. On the representation of electrocardiograms. *IEEE Trans. Biomedical Electronics* BME-10:89–95.

34. ———. 1964. Computer analysis of electrocardiograms using a linear regression technique, *IEEE Trans. Biomedical Engineering* BME-11:60–67.

8

Image Analysis and Character Recognition

8.1 The Representation of Images

Animals have developed a very effective system for the analysis of scenes and two-dimensional images. This varies from a primitive and highly specific system in the frog to the human system that can quickly analyze complicated scenes. It is not surprising that by far the greatest application for pattern recognition has been in trying to develop machines for image analysis in general, and character recognition in particular. Many of these applications have been highly successful—we will describe commercially available machines that can read many thousands of printed characters per second. On the other hand, there are many unsolved problems—for example, many millions of dollars have been poured into efforts to read handwriting, analyze aerial photographs, and classify chromosomes, with very limited success. This chapter will describe some general techniques for analyzing images, discuss some approaches to character recognition, and give some examples of the state of the art in commercially available systems.

An image is generally a two-dimensional representation of a three-dimensional scene. It may be stored as an opaque image (e.g., a photograph), a transparency, or an array of numbers. Whatever the source representation, we will assume that it is represented as an $M \times N$ dimensional array $[x(i,j)]$, although most of the numerical operation that will be discussed can also be performed optically. The discrete representation does not represent a loss of generality since the original image is limited in definition by its source. If the maximum spatial frequency that can be represented is f_m cycles/mm, then, according to the sampling theorem, it will not be necessary to have more than $2f_m$ samples/mm. If the image has up to K gray levels, then it will be necessary to represent each sample with an equivalent precision, i.e., $\log_2 K$ bits. Thus, the maximum possible "information content" or storage requirement of such an image would be $MN \log_2 K$ bits. Obviously, most images will have much less information than this, and much of what there is may be irrelevant to a particular pattern recognition task. Thus, it is not surprising that there is considerable interest in transforms that efficiently represent the meaningful information both for storage and for classification.

There are two rather different approaches to image analysis. In the first, various spatial filtering procedures are applied to enhance the relevent details (e.g., edges and lines) of the image, but the original spatial representation is maintained. A number of heuristic techniques are then applied to break the image into its constituent parts, e.g., straight lines, curves, intersections, areas of constant density, etc. It is then usually convenient to recognize the objects in the image by applying the syntactic approach. The main point of this approach is that the objects are described by their geometric components that could, at least in principle, be extracted by the human observer. In the second approach transformations are applied to the original image to give a more effective representation, but not necessarily to maintain the original image geometry (an example would be a spatial Fourier transformation). The objects in the image are then categorized by applying pattern recognition techniques to the transformed image or some subset of it. While the philosophy of these two approaches is somewhat different, the practical realizations can be almost indistinguishable for simple problems (e.g., machine-printed characters). Both approaches can make use of a variety of spatial transformations and these will be discussed in the next section.

8.2 Spatial Transformations

An image may be transformed for one or more of the following reasons:

(1) to allow more efficient storage and representation;

(2) to emphasize features for classification;

(3) to permit certain filtering that can be accomplished more conveniently in a transformed space. The image is transformed, filtered, and then transformed back to the original space.

In selecting an appropriate transform, it is important to balance how well it represents the data against the computation time required.

A general transformation of the $M \times N$ image can be written as

$$y(k,l) = \frac{1}{\sqrt{MN}} \sum_{i=0}^{M-1} \sum_{j=0}^{N-1} x(i,j)w(i,j,k,l), \tag{8.1}$$

where $w(i,j,k,l)$ is some weighting function. In the special case where the weighting function is separable on the two axes, this can be written in as

$$\begin{aligned} y(k,l) &= \frac{1}{\sqrt{MN}} \sum_{i=0}^{M-1} \sum_{j=0}^{N-1} b(k,i)x(i,j)a(j,l), \\ \mathbf{Y} &= \frac{1}{\sqrt{MN}} \mathbf{B}^T \mathbf{X} \mathbf{A}, \end{aligned} \tag{8.2}$$

where the $M \times N$ matrix $\mathbf{X} = [x(i,j)]$,

the $M \times N$ matrix $\mathbf{Y} = [y(k,l)]$,

the $M \times M$ matrix $\mathbf{B} = [\mathbf{b}_1, \mathbf{b}_2, \ldots, \mathbf{b}_M]$,

the $N \times N$ matrix $\mathbf{A} = [\mathbf{a}_1, \mathbf{a}_2, \ldots, \mathbf{a}_N]$.

The columns of **A** and **B** are the basis vectors for the two axes of the image. If the image is square ($M = N$) and the same basis vectors are used on each axis, then $\mathbf{A} = \mathbf{B}$ and

$$\mathbf{Y} = \frac{1}{N} \mathbf{A}^T \mathbf{X} \mathbf{A}. \tag{8.3}$$

Earlier in this work we considered in some detail the representation of functions of one variable with a Karhunen–Loève expansion (sections 6.2 and 7.2). Thus we formed

$$\mathbf{x} = \sum_{i=0}^{N-1} c_i \boldsymbol{\phi}_i, \tag{8.4}$$

where $\boldsymbol{\phi}_i$ are a family of basis vectors and c_i are coefficients. The basis vectors are the eigenvectors of the covariance matrix of the ensemble of functions to be represented. The expansion is generally very effective (i.e., most of the image energy can be represented on a very few basis vectors) since the basis vectors are calculated from the data to be represented. However, this implies the disadvantage that the basis functions must be recalculated for each application. Also, there is no straight forward generalization that allows representation of functions of two variables, i.e., how are $\boldsymbol{A}$ or $\boldsymbol{B}$ of equation (8.2) to be calculated? Images have been treated by converting them to vectors, i.e., the $M \times N$ image $[x(i,j)]$ becomes the $M \times N$ vector $[x(i)]$. However, since this is one-dimensional it does not take direct account of the contiguity of points on one of the axes. Thus, although this gives efficient representation of the image (in the mean-square error sense), it does not necessarily result in meaningful features for pattern recognition.

8.2.1 The Fourier transformation

An obvious special case of (8.1) is:

$$y(k,l) = \frac{1}{\sqrt{MN}} \sum_{i=0}^{M-1} \sum_{j=0}^{N-1} x(i,j) \exp\left\{-2\pi j\left(\frac{ik}{M} + \frac{jl}{N}\right)\right\}, \tag{8.5}$$

where the meaning of the two j's should be obvious. The Fourier expansion represents the images as a sum of sinusoids and the coefficients k and l identify the spatial frequencies (e.g., $k = 1$ and $l = 1$ refer to sinusoids that have periods of the dimensions of the image). In matrix notation this becomes

$$\mathbf{Y} = \mathbf{B}^T\mathbf{X}\mathbf{A}, \tag{8.6}$$

where

$$b(i,k) = \frac{1}{\sqrt{M}} \exp\left\{-2\pi j\left(\frac{ik}{M}\right)\right\},$$

$$a(j,l) = \frac{1}{\sqrt{N}} \exp\left\{-2\pi j\left(\frac{jl}{N}\right)\right\}.$$

Since $[y(k,l)]$ is generally complex, it appears that $2NM$ components are needed to describe the transformed image. However, since $[x(i,j)]$ is real and positive $[y(k,l)]$ has redundant elements. To illustrate this, rewrite (8.5) as

$$\begin{aligned} y(k,l) &= \mathrm{Re}(y(k,l)) + j\,\mathrm{Im}(y(k,l)) \\ &= \frac{1}{\sqrt{MN}} \sum_{i=0}^{M-1} \sum_{j=0}^{N-1} x(i,j)\left\{\cos 2\pi\left(\frac{ik}{M} + \frac{jl}{N}\right) - j \sin 2\pi\left(\frac{ik}{M} + \frac{jl}{N}\right)\right\}. \end{aligned} \tag{8.7}$$

Since $x(i,j)$ is real, the real part of $y(k,l)$ is given by

$$\mathrm{Re}(y(k,l)) = \frac{1}{\sqrt{MN}} \sum_{i=0}^{M-1} \sum_{j=0}^{N-1} x(i,j) \cos 2\pi\left(\frac{ik}{M} + \frac{jl}{N}\right),$$

and the imaginary part by

$$\mathrm{Im}(y(k,l)) = \frac{-1}{\sqrt{MN}} \sum_{i=0}^{M-1} \sum_{j=0}^{N-1} x(i,j) \sin 2\pi\left(\frac{ik}{M} + \frac{jl}{N}\right).$$

Since $\mathrm{Re}(y(k,l))$ is even and $\mathrm{Im}(y(k,l))$ is odd in k and l we have

$$\begin{aligned} \mathrm{Re}(y(k,l)) &= \mathrm{Re}(y(-k,-l)), \\ \mathrm{Im}(y(k,l)) &= -\mathrm{Im}(y(-k,-l)), \\ y(k,l) &= y^*(-k,-l), \end{aligned} \tag{8.8}$$

so that the transformed image exhibits conjugate symmetry. Thus, as in the original image, there are MN independent components.

The transformation can be implemented directly from Equation (8.5) or (8.7), but this will require of the order of $M^2 \times N^2$ complex operations (i.e., complex addition and complex multiplication). The well known "fast Fourier" transform (see Cooley and Tukey (1965), for example) requires only of the order of $M(\log_2 M)\ N(\log_2 N)$ complex operations although M and N must both be powers of two.

The advantage of this transformed representation of the image is that it is often possible to represent most of the energy in the image on a relatively small number of Fourier components. The application to characters will be discussed in some detail below.

8.2.2 The Walsh/Hadamard transform

It is possible to develop a tranformation based on binary functions that is analogous to the Fourier transform based on sinusoidal functions. This is known as the Walsh/Hadamard transform and the binary functions on which it is based are known as Walsh functions (Walsh, 1923).

In figure 8.1 some Walsh functions and their sinusoidal analogs are shown as functions of normalized time $\theta = t/T$ on the half open interval $[-1/2, 1/2)$. The notation $\mathrm{sal}(i,\theta)$ and $\mathrm{cal}(i,\theta)$ is used for the Walsh functions to emphasize the relationship to sine and cosine functions. Walsh functions form a complete basis and are defined by

$$\left.\begin{aligned} \mathrm{cal}(i,\theta) &= \mathrm{wal}(2i,\theta) \\ \mathrm{sal}(i,\theta) &= \mathrm{wal}(2i-1,\theta) \end{aligned}\right\} \quad -1/2 \leqslant \theta < 1/2,$$
$$\mathrm{wal}(2i,\,\theta) = \mathrm{wal}(2i-1,\,\theta) = 0 \qquad \theta < -1/2, \text{ or } \theta \geqslant 1/2, \tag{8.9}$$

where $\mathrm{wal}(k,\theta)$ can be obtained from the difference equation

$$\begin{aligned} \mathrm{wal}(2k+q,\theta) = (-1)^{2k+q}[&\mathrm{wal}(k,2\theta+1/2) \\ &+ (-1)^{k+q}\mathrm{wal}(k,2\theta-1/2)] \end{aligned} \tag{8.10}$$

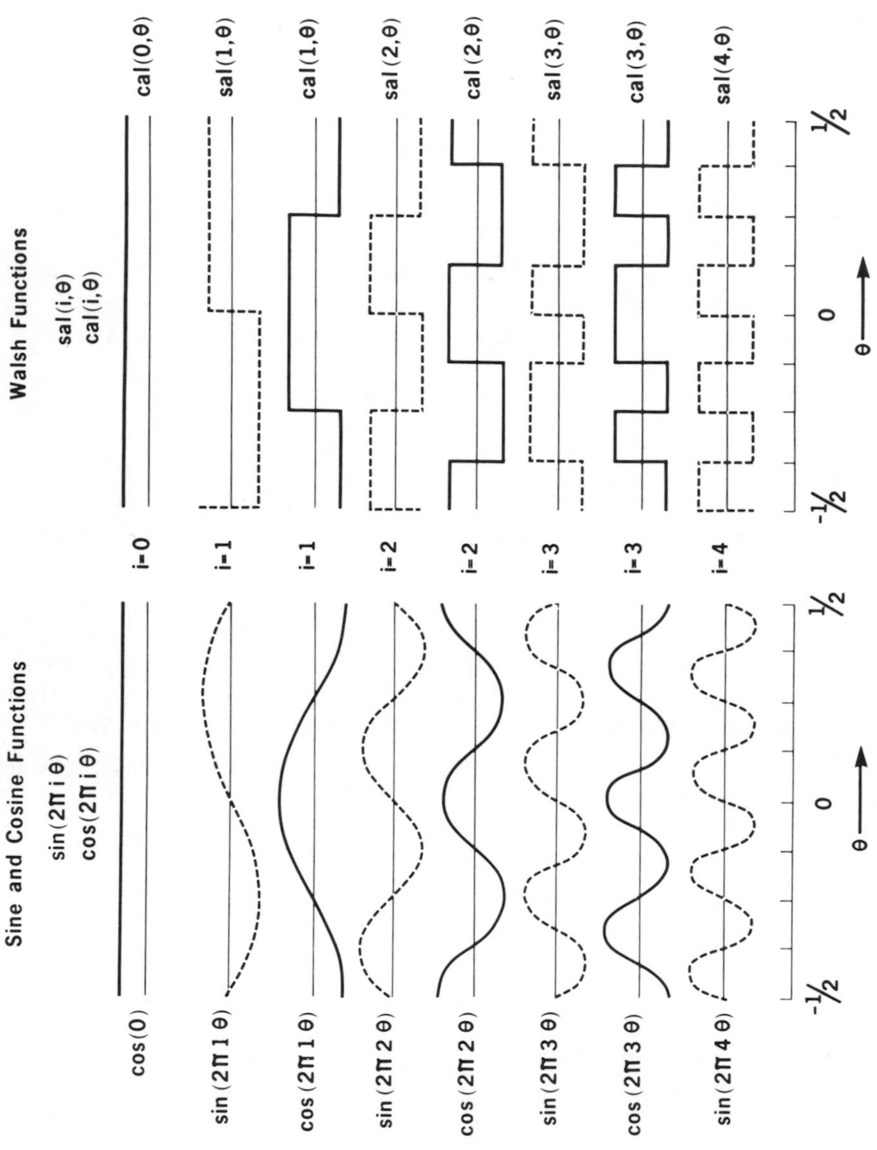

fig. 8.1 A comparison of sinusoidal and Walsh functions (adapted from Harmuth, 1969a).

with

$$\text{wal}(0, \theta) = 1, \; -1/2 \leqslant \theta < 1/2$$
$$= 0, \; \theta < -1/2, \; \theta \geqslant 1/2,$$

and

$$q = 0 \text{ or } 1; \; k = 0, 1, 2, \ldots .$$

It is easy to check that this gives the functions shown in figure 8.1. Note that while the first functions look like squared-off sinusoids or cosinusoids, this is not generally true.

A Walsh–Fourier series expansion of a function $f(\theta)$ defined in the interval $-1/2 \leqslant \theta < 1/2$ is given by

$$f(\theta) = a(0)\,\text{wal}(0, \theta) + \sum_{i=1}^{\infty} [a_c(i)\,\text{cal}(i, \theta) + a_s(i)\,\text{sal}(i, \theta)], \tag{8.11}$$

where

$$a(0) = \int_{-1/2}^{1/2} f(\theta)\,\text{wal}(0, \theta)\, d\theta = \int_{-1/2}^{1/2} f(\theta)\, d\theta,$$

$$a_c(i) = \int_{-1/2}^{1/2} f(\theta)\,\text{cal}(i, \theta)\, d\theta,$$

$$a_s(i) = \int_{-1/2}^{1/2} f(\theta)\,\text{sal}(i, \theta)\, d\theta.$$

For sinusoidal functions we usually define frequency as the number of cycles in a unit of time, but it would be just as appropriate to use half the number of zero crossings. The latter interpretation is applied to Walsh functions, but the rate of oscillation is called sequency. The unit of sequency is zps in analogy to cps (Hz) for sinusoidals. A Walsh–Fourier transform wal (s, θ) is related to the Walsh series in the same way that the Fourier transform is related to the Fourier series (see Harmuth (1968), for example).

Example 8.1

Find the Walsh–Fourier expansion coefficients ($a_c(i)$ and $a_s(i)$) and magnitude spectra $(a_c^2(i) + a_s^2(i))^{1/2}$ for the two examples shown in figure 8.2. Compare these with the corresponding results for a sinusoidal–Fourier expansion.

(1) By comparison with figure 8.1, it can be seen that

$$f(\theta) = 1/2 \text{ wal}(0,\theta) + 1/2 \text{ cal}(1,\theta)$$
$$= 1/2[\text{wal}(0,\theta) + \text{wal}(2,\theta)].$$

The magnitude spectra are shown in figure 8.3(*a*) and compared with the corresponding sinusoidal–Fourier results.

(2) Again, by comparison with figure 8.1, it can be seen that

$$f(\theta) = 5 \text{ sal}(2,\theta) + 5 \text{ sal}(3,\theta)$$
$$= 5[\text{wal}(3,\theta) + \text{wal}(5,\theta)].$$

The magnitude spectra are shown in figure 8.3(*b*), and compared with the Fourier results. Note that the Walsh expansion is sequency limited, but the sinusoidal expansion is not frequency limited.

The application of Walsh–Fourier series to represent images that are discrete functions of two variables is straightforward. However, in practice, it is convenient to generate the basis functions from a Hadamard matrix (Hadamard, 1893) and for this reason the transformation is often known as Walsh/Hadamard. The Hadamard matrix is a square array of plus and minus ones whose rows (and columns) are orthogonal to one another and, in fact, are Walsh functions.

If **H** is an $N \times N$ Hadamard matrix then

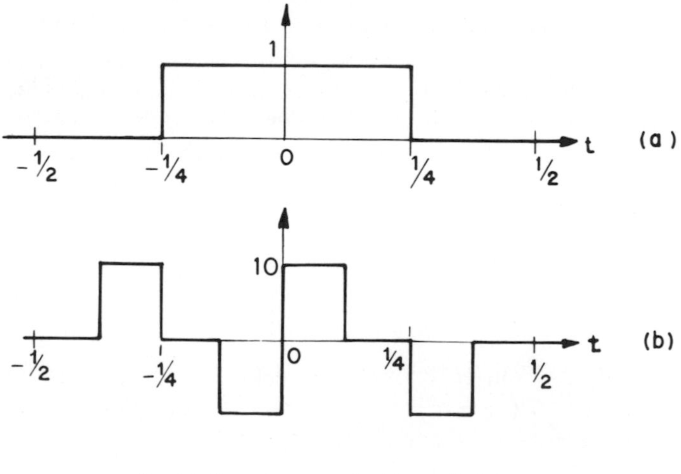

fig. 8.2 Time functions for Example 8.1.

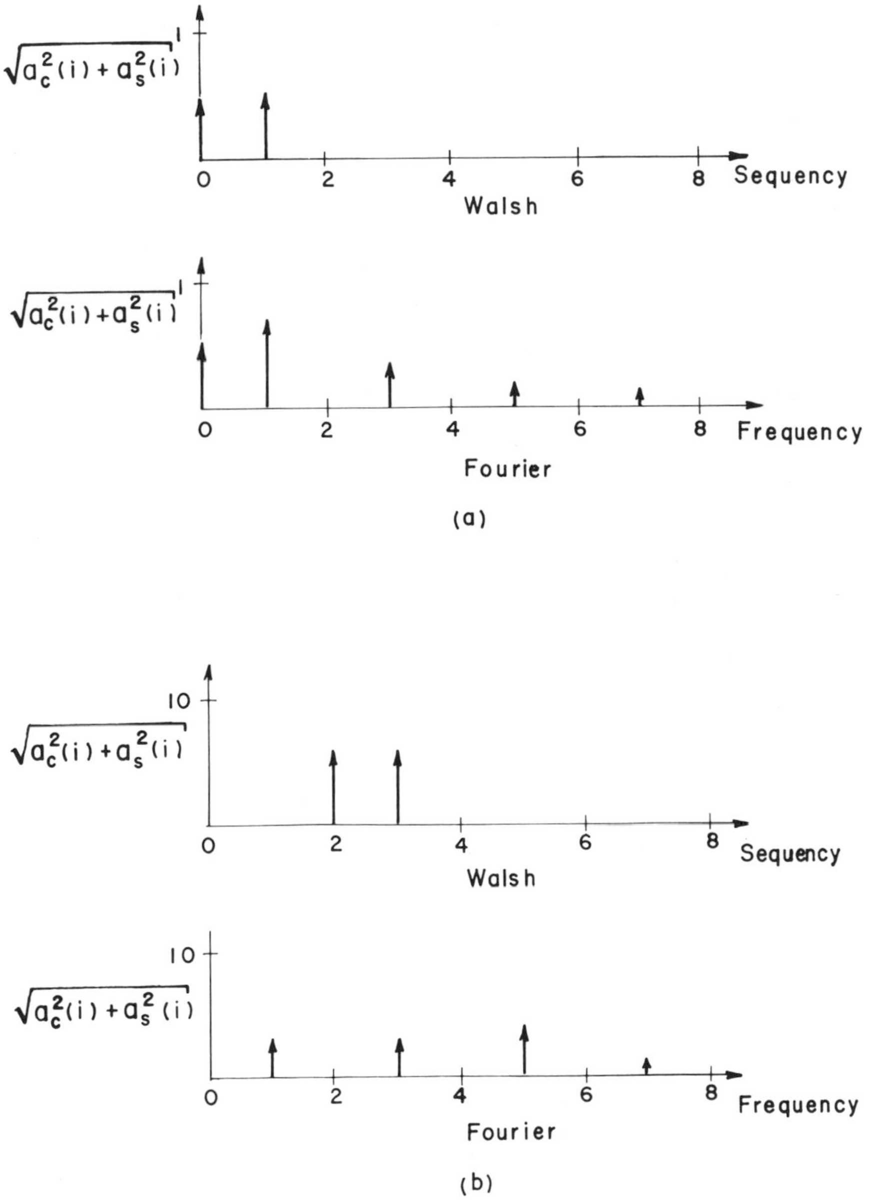

fig. 8.3 Sinusoidal and Walsh magnitude spectra for Example 8.1.

$$\mathbf{HH}^T = N\mathbf{I}, \tag{8.12}$$

and if **H** is symmetric

$$\mathbf{HH} = N\mathbf{I}. \tag{8.13}$$

The simplest Hadamard matrix is for $N = 2$:

$$\mathbf{H} = \begin{bmatrix} 1 & 1 \\ 1 & -1 \end{bmatrix}. \tag{8.14}$$

The efficient construction of higher-order matrices has been studied in some detail and a number of methods exist. A Hadamard matrix $\boldsymbol{G}$ of order $2N$ can always be constructed from a Hadamard matrix $\boldsymbol{H}$ of order N by using the relation

$$\mathbf{G} = \begin{bmatrix} \mathbf{H} & \mathbf{H} \\ \mathbf{H} & -\mathbf{H} \end{bmatrix}. \tag{8.15}$$

EXAMPLE 8.2

Construct a Hadamard matrix of order 8 and label the sequency of each row.

Using the 2×2 matrix given in (8.14) and the relation in (8.15) we obtain the matrix $\mathbf{G}_4$ of order 4 to be

$$\mathbf{G}_4 = \begin{bmatrix} 1 & 1 & 1 & 1 \\ 1 & -1 & 1 & -1 \\ 1 & 1 & -1 & -1 \\ 1 & -1 & -1 & 1 \end{bmatrix}.$$

Similarly the Hadamard matrix $\mathbf{G}_8$ of order 8 is

$$\mathbf{G}_8 = \begin{bmatrix} 1 & 1 & 1 & 1 & 1 & 1 & 1 & 1 \\ 1 & -1 & 1 & -1 & 1 & -1 & 1 & -1 \\ 1 & 1 & -1 & -1 & 1 & 1 & -1 & -1 \\ 1 & -1 & -1 & 1 & 1 & -1 & -1 & 1 \\ 1 & 1 & 1 & 1 & -1 & -1 & -1 & -1 \\ 1 & -1 & 1 & -1 & -1 & 1 & -1 & 1 \\ 1 & 1 & -1 & -1 & -1 & -1 & 1 & 1 \\ 1 & -1 & -1 & 1 & -1 & 1 & 1 & -1 \end{bmatrix} \quad \begin{matrix} \textit{Sequency} \\ 0 \\ 7 \\ 3 \\ 4 \\ 1 \\ 6 \\ 2 \\ 5. \end{matrix}$$

Note that the rows (or columns) are not in order of increasing sequency.

To obtain the Walsh/Hadamard transform of an $N \times N$ image $[x(i,j)]$, it is necessary to pre- and postmultiply by an N-th order symmetric Hadamard matrix. Then the transformed image $[y(k,l)]$ is given by

$$[y(k,l)] = \frac{1}{N}[h(k,i)][x(i,j)][h(j,l)], \tag{8.16}$$

or

$$\mathbf{Y} = \frac{1}{N}\mathbf{HXH}.$$

It is easily shown that the inverse transform is

$$[x(i,j)] = \frac{1}{N}[h(i,k)][y(k,l)][h(l,j)], \tag{8.17}$$

or

$$\mathbf{X} = \frac{1}{N}\mathbf{HYH}.$$

For symmetric Hadamard matrices of order $N = 2^n$ the transform may be written in series form as

$$[y(k,l)] = \frac{1}{N}\sum_{i=0}^{N-1}\sum_{j=0}^{N-1} x_{ij}(-1)^{p(i,j,k,l)}, \tag{8.18}$$

where

$$p(i,j,k,l) = \sum_{s=0}^{n-1}(k_s i_s + l_s j_s).$$

The notation k_s, i_s, l_s, and j_s denotes the s-th bit in the binary representations of k, i, l, and j respectively. Thus,

$$k = \text{a decimal integer} = (k_{n-1}k_{n-2}k_{n-3}\cdots k_1 k_0)$$

$$[\text{note } k_s = 0 \text{ or } 1].$$

This will result in the "natural" Walsh/Hadamard transformation, which is quite satisfactory in theory, but may be difficult to interpret visually since the elements are not ordered in increasing sequency (recall example 8.2). The "ordered" form of the transformation in which the sequency of each row is larger than the preceding row is given by:

$$[y(k,l)] = \sum_{i=0}^{N-1}\sum_{j=0}^{N-1} x(i,j)(-1)^{q(i,j,k,l)}, \tag{8.19}$$

where

$$q(i,j,k,l) = \sum_{s=0}^{N-1}[g_s(k)i_s + g_s(l)j_s],$$

and

$$g_0(k) = k_{n-1}$$
$$g_1(k) = k_{n-1} + k_{n-2}$$
$$g_2(k) = k_{n-2} + k_{n-3}$$
$$\dots$$
$$g_{n-1}(k) = k_1 + k_0 .$$

Examination of (8.18) or (8.19) indicates that the transformation can be implemented without multiplications. In fact, fast Hadamard algorithms have been developed (Whelchel and Guinn, 1968) that require of the order of $(N \log_2 N)^2$ operations. This is the same as for the fast Fourier transform, but here "operation" means addition or subtraction whereas for the Fourier transform it means addition plus multiplication. Clearly, the Walsh/Hadamard transform can be very efficient computationally.

Because of its binary nature, the Walsh/Hadamard transform can also be efficiently implemented optically. The image is cross-correlated with a

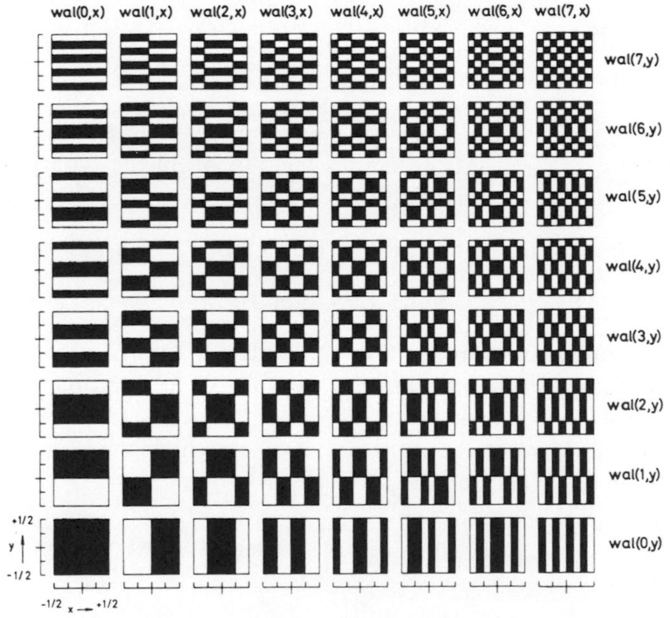

fig. 8.4 The first 64 Walsh masks. (Andrews, 1971).

Walsh mask by placing the image transparency and the mask between a light source and a detector. The first 64 Walsh masks are illustrated in figure 8.4.

8.2.3 The Haar transform

A set of orthogonal functions having both local and global sensitivity has been defined by Haar (1910). The orthogonal, but not orthonormal, Haar functions consist of ones, minus ones, and zeros. The orthonormal functions require nonbinary normalization constants. These functions sample the input images at progressively finer intervals starting with the lowest resolution and increasing in powers of two. Haar functions differ from Walsh functions in that, except for the first two, they emphasize a region of the image. An example of an eighth order Haar matrix **H** is

$$\mathbf{H} = \begin{bmatrix} 1 & 1 & 1 & 1 & 1 & 1 & 1 & 1 \\ 1 & 1 & 1 & 1 & -1 & -1 & -1 & -1 \\ \sqrt{2} & \sqrt{2} & -\sqrt{2} & -\sqrt{2} & 0 & 0 & 0 & 0 \\ 0 & 0 & 0 & 0 & \sqrt{2} & \sqrt{2} & -\sqrt{2} & -\sqrt{2} \\ 2 & -2 & 0 & 0 & 0 & 0 & 0 & 0 \\ 0 & 0 & 2 & -2 & 0 & 0 & 0 & 0 \\ 0 & 0 & 0 & 0 & 2 & -2 & 0 & 0 \\ 0 & 0 & 0 & 0 & 0 & 0 & 2 & -2 \end{bmatrix}.$$

The discrete Haar transform (Andrews, 1971) is obtained from the matrix in the same way as the Walsh/Hadamard transform. In analogy to equation (8.16) we have:

$$[y(k,l)] = \frac{1}{N}[h(k,i)][x(i,j)][h(j,l)], \tag{8.20}$$

or

$$\mathbf{Y} = \frac{1}{N}\mathbf{HXH}^T.$$

In addition to possibly valuable spatial properties, the Haar transform can be efficiently implemented. The "fast Haar" algorithm requires of the order of an $(2(N-1))^2$ additions for an $N \times N$ image.

It should be pointed out that many other transformations are possible. They need not have the properties of completeness or orthogonality. The only requirements are that they should represent the image efficiently and be computationally efficient. We have chosen to discuss these techniques as transformations since they have some nice theoretical properties. We could equally well have discussed them as examples of feature extraction, but we prefer to reserve that term for approaches that aim to keep only the information that is pertinent to classification.

8.2.4 A comparison of spatial transforms

The utility of a transformed image depends on how well it represents the important features of the image and how efficiently it can be calculated. The Fourier, Walsh/Hadamard, and Haar transforms have been compared by Andrews (1971) using 10 classes of handwritten digits. The images were on a 12×16 grid with eight levels of gray. To compare the different transformed images, features were selected on the basis of decreasing variance. Thus, the first feature (or element of the transformed image) was chosen as that which had maximum variance over 500 training patterns, the second feature had the next highest variance, and so on.

As shown in figure 8.5, the classification errors decreased consistently as the number of features increased for each transformation. It can be seen that the Fourier and Walsh/Hadamard transformations were comparable and considerably better than the Haar transform, which was itself rather better than raw features from the pattern space. The Haar transform emphasizes pattern space location and thus its similarity to the pattern space is not surprising.

Andrews has drawn on the same graph his conjecture for the performance of the Karhunen–Loève expansion, which is optimal in that it minimizes the mean-square error. If he is correct, then both the Fourier and Walsh/Hadamard transformations are very nearly optimal. In terms of implementation, the Walsh/Hadamard transform is much more efficient since it requires $M(\log_2 M)N(\log_2 N)$ additions in contrast to a similar number of multiplications required for the Fourier transform. The reader may be interested in comparing these results with those obtained by Mucciardi and Gose (1971) for vectorcardiograms, which are discussed in chapter 7. They were comparing different heuristics for feature selection. It is interesting to speculate whether the efficient Walsh/Hadamard expansion would also be useful for vectorcardiograms.

8.3 Image Analysis

As we discuss it here, image analysis is a very general problem. The input is some two-dimensional representation of the physical world. From this

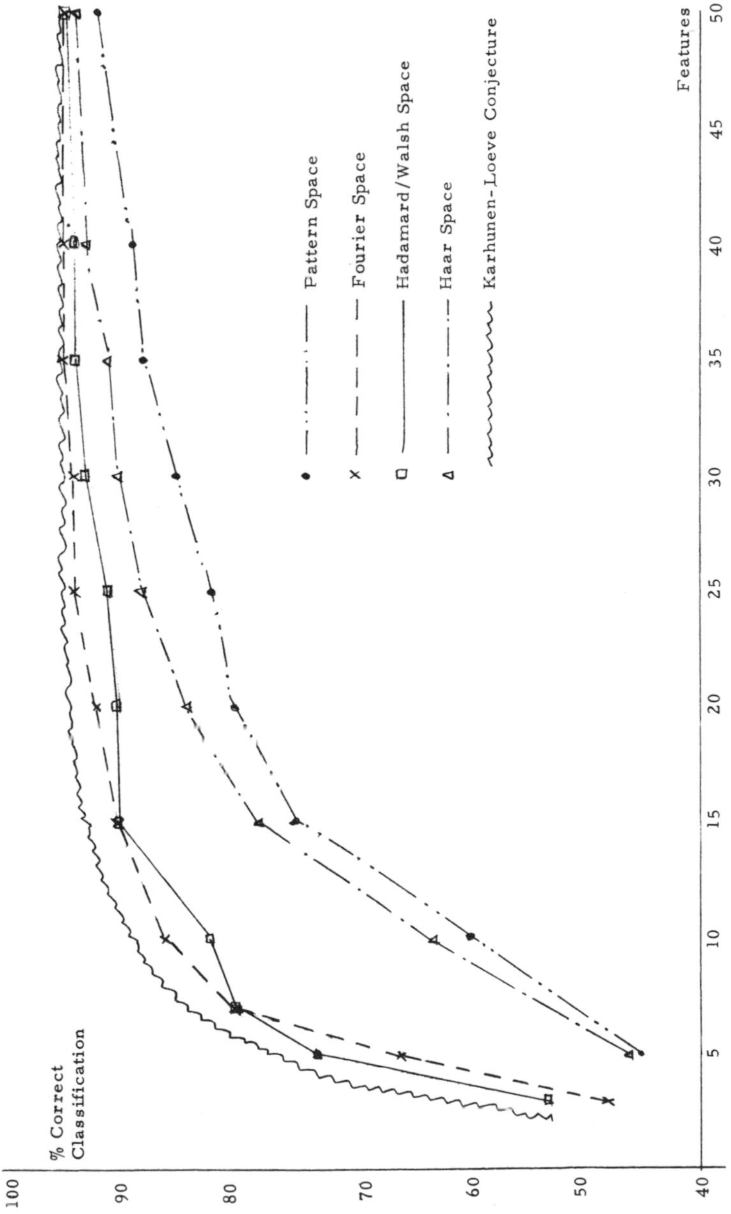

fig. 8.5 The percentage of correct classification versus the number of features retained. (Andrews, 1971).

image certain information is to be extracted. If the image is to be used to classify chromosomes, the clusters of chromosomes from a cell must be found, the chromosomes in the cluster must be identified, and a decision must be made if an abnormality exists. If the image represents a scene from a room in which a robot is to operate, it will be necessary to locate objects that form obstructions. Elements of the scene must be synthesized into objects and the objects must be identified.

Thus, the problem is not simply to recognize objects. First, the image must be *analyzed* into its component parts and these must be *synthesized* into configurations for recognition as meaningful objects. Significant success has only been achieved in cases where there is significant a priori knowledge about the structure of the scene. The recognition of machine-printed characters where there is a known set of objects of uniform size and orientation is a very trivial problem compared with the recognition of randomly oriented cubes on a plane surface.

In considering image analyzers we will first discuss the preprocessing that can enhance the details in the image. We will then describe analysis techniques for extracting the geometrical features of the image. The synthesis of objects for recognition will be described in the context of the so-called linguistic approach.

8.3.1 Preprocessing

The geometric features of an image can be made more prominent with spatial filtering. This can take the form of correction for distortion in the data collection system, such as that produced in radioisotope scanners used in nuclear medicine, or of the deblurring of photographs from a camera that was vibrating or was not in perfect focus. Alternatively, the filter may be designed to emphasize low frequencies to minimize the effects of noise or to emphasize high frequencies to enhance edges.

If the original image is $[x(i,j)]$ and the filtered image is $[z(i,j)]$, then the filter can be represented as two-dimensional convolution

$$z(i,j) = h(i,j) ** x(i,j), \tag{8.21}$$

where $[h(i,j)]$ is the impulse response of the filter. Note that there is no necessity for the filtering to be isotropic. While the convolution can be implemented directly on a digital computer, it is often more efficient to Fourier transform the image and filter in the spatial frequency domain since the filtering will then only involve multiplication. A low-pass frequency function leads to a spatial point-spread function that represents the blur produced by a point input. A high-pass or high-emphasis frequency domain filter will emphasize edges and reduce blurring. It is interesting that the human sensory systems impose high-emphasis spatial filtering. (Von Bekesy, 1967). This is known as lateral inhibition and produces the phenomenon on Mach bands in vision (Ratliff, 1972).

Other techniques can be applied to images to enhance their contrast and give a more uniform distribution of intensity over the dynamic range. The details of those useful techniques will not be discussed here, but it is important to realize that they generally involve a nonlinear position invariant function (Rosenfeld, 1969).

8.3.2 Analysis by feature extraction

Although most geometric feature extraction techniques are heuristic, they draw upon signal detection theory and knowledge of biological systems. We shall list some of the common approaches. A recent survey by Levine (1969) is more detailed, and useful descriptions of approaches to particular problems have been described by Hall et al. (1971) and Lendaris and Stanley (1970).

(1) *Contour tracing* The shape of objects or parts of objects can often be outlined by tracing contours of equal gray level. Obviously, for an image made up of thin lines this will amount to following the lines. A simple algorithm consists of finding a point $x(i,j)$ in the desired range of gray levels, and surrounding it by a 3×3 window centered on the point. The next point on the contour is chosen as that point (out of seven possibilities) not already on the contour for which the gray level is maximum and within the chosen limits. The contour point is labeled and other points not already on the contour or not connected to the new point are set to zero. Obviously many variants of this and other schemes are possible.

(2) *Edge detection* This is a special case of contour tracing, where the contour is very sharp. Spatial filtering has been used to detect edges throughout the image in one pass. Consider the spatial impulse response for a filter shown in figure 8.6(*a*). If this is convolved with the edge shown in figure 8.6(*b*), then the output of the filter will be as shown in figure 8.6(*c*). This edge detector will be sensitive to direction. A two-dimensional edge detector that is approximately rotationally invariant can consist of the sum of the absolute values of the outputs of two orthogonal edge detectors such as were described above.

(3) *Regional identification* A corollary to contouring and edge tracing is the identification of regions on the basis of some common property.

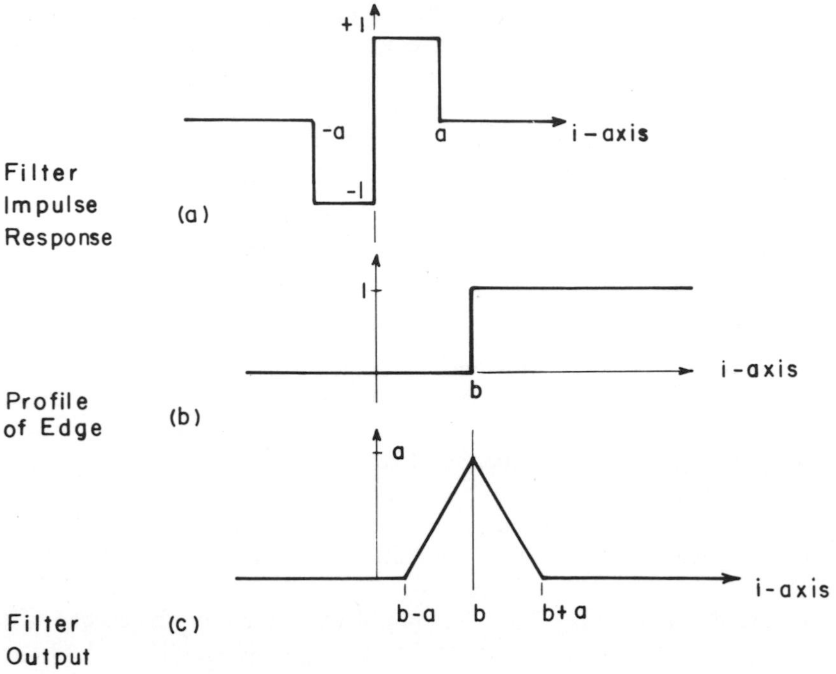

fig. 8.6 A spatial edge detector. (a) Filter impulse response. (b) Profile of edge. (c) Filter output.

An obvious tactic is to identify as a region those contiguous points for which the gray level is within some preset limits.

(4) *Local topological features—shape and curvature* When a contour or edge has been determined, it can then be described in terms of its topological components, such as straight lines, curves, intersections, etc. For larger objects this may directly yield the shape.

(5) *Frequency signatures* Another approach that can be very helpful for certain features involves searching for their signature in a Fourier or Walsh/Hadamard transform of the image. The frequency signature is the transform of the spatial representation of the object being sought. This will obviously be efficient for regular patterns of lines in the original image. It should also be clear that a frequency domain window that is on annular ring will be sensitive to objects with circular symmetry. This is, of course, very close to the well known matched filter (see sections 2.2.2 and 4.4.2).

(6) *Miscellaneous* Many other approaches are possible. These include the use of masks, moments, directional signatures, Golay logic,

texture, etc. These and other techniques are receiving particular attention from those artificial intelligence groups that are developing a visual input for a robot.

8.3.3 Object synthesis—the linguistic approach (*Miller and Shaw, 1968*)

If the task is to recognize objects in an image, it is reasonable to expect that there is some prior knowledge of the structural properties of the objects of interest. Then it should be possible to use the features that are being identified to synthesize one of these objects. While it might be possible to do this by fitting them together in turn in the same way that a child approaches a jig-saw puzzle, it would be much more satisfying to find a mathematical formalism that could be used. Such a formalism has been developed in mathematical linguistics to perform a similar synthesis of sentences and paragraphs from component words and phrases (Chomsky, 1965). When applied to pattern recognition this is variously known as the linguistic, syntactic, contextual, descriptive, or articular approach.

Although this class of methods has been applied in a number of other ways, most can be described by the following hierarchy.

- Level 1 A property detector or feature extractor makes measurements of the image. These were described above.
- Level 2 A name is assigned to certain classes of property lists. The property lists will usually consist of quantitative measures of the various properties.
- Level 3 Statements are made about ordered relationships among objects, classes, and properties.
- Level 4 An object is identified (or synthesized) by examining the hierarchial syntactical definitions, including parts and their relationships.

These concepts are best illustrated with a simple example taken from the work of Ledley et al. (1965) on the classification of chromosomes.

For this purpose we assume that the chromosome is described by a closed curve representing its edges. Ledley then breaks the edge contour into a number of primitive components identified as $A - E$ in figure 8.7(*a*). This results in a linear string of letters that is an ordered list of the components. An attempt is then made to parse the string with the syntactic descriptions of the various types of chromosomes. It is necessary to develop some formalism to describe the syntax and Ledley uses Backus–Naur form grammar notation, which is widely used to define computer and natural

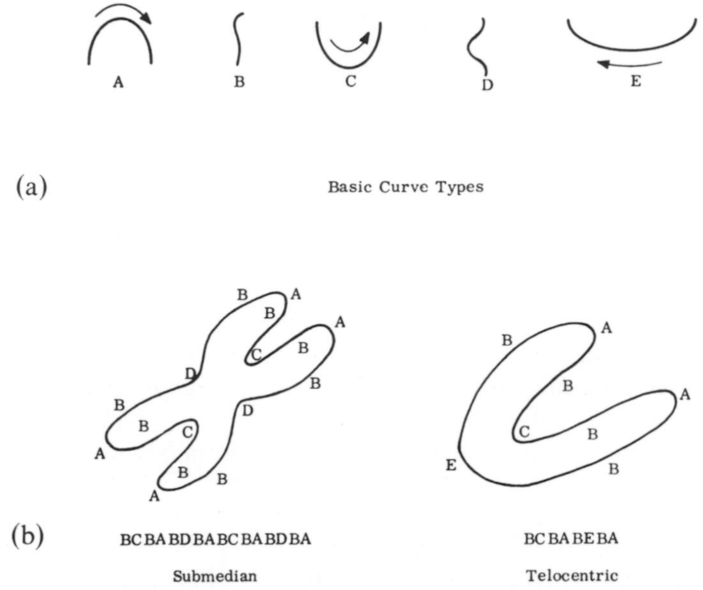

fig. 8.7 Ledley's chromosome description. (a) Basic curve types. (b) Chromosome examples. (Miller and Shaw, 1968).

languages. The notation used means:

⟨component⟩ is to be defined or is already defined;
A⟨component⟩ is a string of *A* and the component;
⟨component⟩*A* is a string of the component and *A*;
A|*B* is either *A* or *B*.

Thus ⟨arm⟩ : : = *B*⟨arm⟩|⟨arm⟩*B*|*A*

means that an "arm" consists of a string of *B* and an "arm," a string of an "arm" and *B*, or *A* alone. Clearly, an "arm" could be *BAB*, *BA*, *AB*, *BBA*, etc.

In applying this to chromosomes consider three simple definitions:

⟨arm⟩ : : = *B*⟨arm⟩|⟨arm⟩*B*|*A*
⟨side⟩ : : = *B*⟨side⟩|⟨side⟩*B*|*B*|*D*
⟨right part⟩ : : = *C*⟨arm⟩
⟨left part⟩ : : = ⟨arm⟩*C*
⟨armpair⟩ : : = ⟨side⟩⟨armpair⟩|⟨armpair⟩⟨side⟩|⟨arm⟩
⟨right part⟩|⟨left part⟩⟨arm⟩
⟨submedian chromosome⟩ : : = ⟨armpair⟩⟨armpair⟩.

Thus, of the two chromosomes shown in figure 8.7(*b*) one is identified as a submedian type and the other is rejected.

The linguistic–syntactic approach has been applied to a wide variety of problems. These include characters, bubble chamber images, and many types of line drawings and half-tone scenes. A recent development has been the work on stochastic grammars by Swain and Fu (1972). In this work the tools of statistical decision theory are combined with the formalism of mathematical linguistics to yield a potentially very powerful methodology.

8.3.4 An example of image analysis—radiographic images

To illustrate some of the techniques described above , we have chosen to describe an approach to the analysis of radiographic images in general, and chest X-rays in particular. This draws heavily on the work of the Bioengineering Group at the University of Missouri, Columbia (Hall et al. 1971 and Harlow and Eisenbeis, 1973).

The analysis of chest X-ray images by machine is a reasonable goal. The images are always taken in one of a small number of standard views and all subjects have essentially the same components in their body. Thus the task is to enhance the image if necessary, to identify the main components (heart, lungs, ribs, etc.), and to detect any abnormalities. Since some millions of these X-rays are performed each year, often for screening, it is clear than an efficient solution could be very useful.

A schematic representation of the X-ray image is shown in figure 8.8 and it can be seen that there are several regions of different density. Harlow and

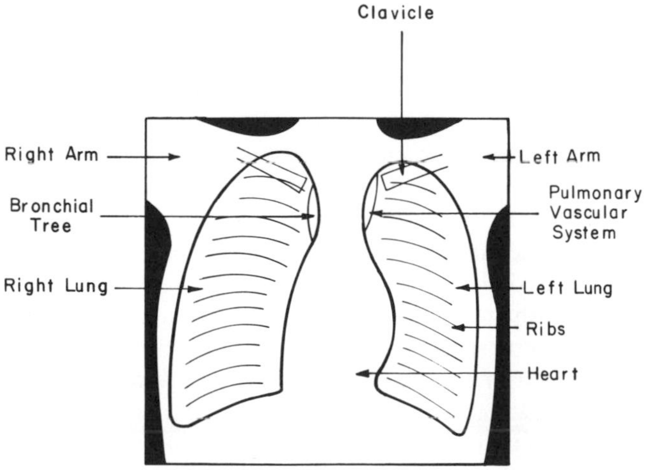

fig. 8.8 Posteroanterior view of the chest. (Harlow and Eisenbeis, 1973).

Eisenbeis (1973) identify different regions on the basis of their density. They then analyze the image by the top-down application of a tree graph. Figure 8.9 shows the tree that contains the structural information about this class of images—different classes (e.g., knee X-rays) will require quite different structural descriptions. First, at a low resolution (16 × 16), gross regions are identified. Each node on the tree has associated with it a descriptor list of each of the nodes of level one on the tree. If a node cannot fit any region to its descriptor list, then the parameters are adjusted. In this way the system can adapt to variations in the image. After each region is identified with a node, the analysis switches to a higher resolution (128 × 128) and the boundaries of the regions are refined.

The system then moves to level two of the tree and refines the "left lung area" and "right lung area" into two subregions each. These are then matched to the level-two nodes. The object of this procedure was to identify on the image regions representing anatomical structures in the body. When this has been done, these regions can be further compared with a set of parameters to determine if any abnormality exists. For example, if a region identified as the heart was of unusual size, this might indicate a coronary aneurysm, or if in a region identified as the lungs there was a portion with high absorption (i.e., high image density) then this might indicate edema.

8.4 Character Recognition

8.4.1 The problem

Optical character recognition (OCR) is a very special case of image analysis. For rather obvious reasons it has received more attention than any other pattern recognition problem and has yielded more success than any other. It is claimed that many businesses could not operate economically today without OCR. In spite of the many successful applications to high quality machine printed input there are still many very difficult problems in handling hand-printed characters.

The only real problem is the design of a system to efficiently extract features that reliably describe the characters. Thus, most of our attention will be devoted to feature extraction and relatively little to classification—with good features almost any classification scheme will work. In reading the pattern recognition literature it should be realized that many approaches and techniques are tested with character data although the final goal may not be to design a character recognition system. Thus, many apparently

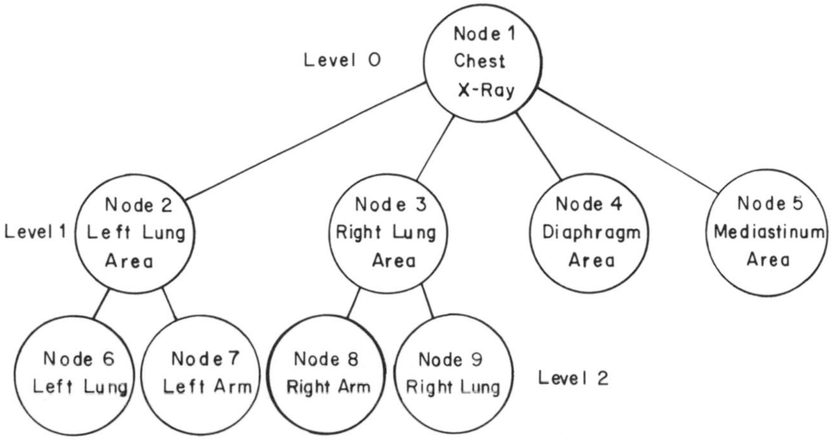

fig. 8.9 Partial vertical ordering of a PA chest X-ray picture. (Harlow and Eisenbeis, 1973).

esoteric and complex schemes are applied to characters that can be handled effectively in simpler and more direct ways. This is done because character data are easily available with a wide range of variability, and it is relatively simple to compare the results of different approaches. In fact, a data bank has been set up by the IEEE Computer Society to distribute:

(1) machine-imprinted alphanumeric characters (Ryan, 1969);

(2) hand-printed numeric characters (Knoll. 1969);

(3) hand-printed FORTRAN alphanumeric characters (Munson, 1968);

(4) hand-printed alphanumeric and machine-printed numeric characters (Highleyman, 1963);

(5) hand-printed numeric characters (Genchi et al., 1968).

Details of this bank can be found in the IEEE publication *COMPUTER*.

8.4.2 *Feature extraction*

It will be assumed that the characters to be classified can be easily normalized for size and position on a $M \times N$ grid. If the image is of high quality and the characters are all of one font, then effective feature extraction can be achieved by using masks (or a matched filter as was described in section 2.2.2). There is one mask $[h_k(i,j)]$ for each of the K

characters in the alphabet and the characters to be classified $[x(i,j)]$ are cross-correlated with each mask. Then

$$y(k) = \sum_{i=0}^{M-1} \sum_{j=0}^{N-1} x(i,j).h_k(i,j). \tag{8.22}$$

The decision is class l where

$$y(l) \geqslant y(k) \text{ for } k = 1, \ldots, K.$$

Obviously this can easily be implemented optically.

Most of the simple commercially available machines use masks. Performance can be improved by using stylized fonts, which are fairly easy to read by eye, but emphasize the differences between characters. These can be found on bank checks, credit cards, and many cash register receipts. Several stylized alphabets are available—one of the most popular for general applications is the USASC OCR-A, which is illustrated in figure 8.10.

Normal text (as opposed to that prepared specifically for character recognition) contains a wide variety of sizes and styles. (It is estimated that over 300,000 symbols are in common use by the US printing industry.) It then becomes necessary to store a mask for each character that could be encountered. (Some commercially available machines claim to be able to handle 800 distinct characters simultaneously.) There is no real evidence that multifont character recognition machines with high quality input can profit from features more complicated than character masks, except possi-

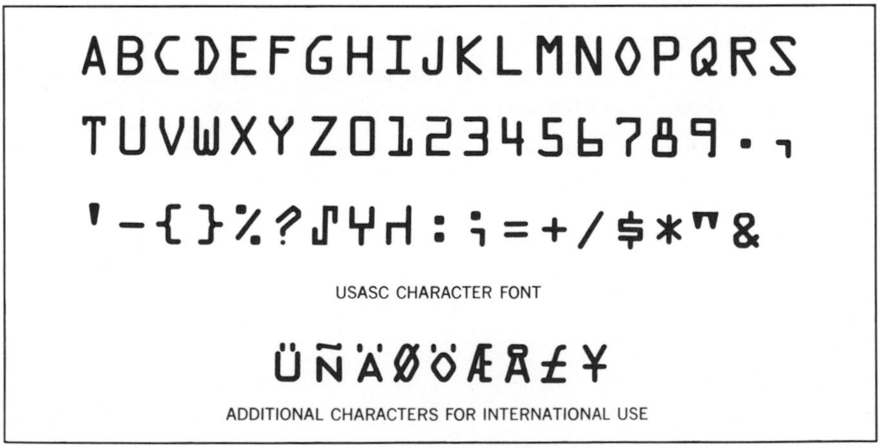

fig. 8.10 A stylized font.

bly by building in special tests for characters that are frequently confused. An attempt to solve the multifont problem will be described in section 8.5.

The real interest for pattern recognition theory lies in the recognition of handwritten characters. In this problem, there is a relatively small number of prototypes, but a large variability for the same subject and a larger variability between subjects. (This contrasts with the multifont machine-printed character problem, which has low variability and a very large number of prototypes.) A multitude of schemes for feature extraction from characters have been suggested and many have been tried. Only the simplest have been implemented commercially. We shall discuss *geometric features* that are obtained from the original image and *transform features* that are obtained from a transformation of the image. In each case, we shall indicate a number of approaches of practical importance and theoretical interest. In section 8.6 the SRI approach to hand-printed FORTRAN characters (Munson, 1968; Duda and Hart, 1968) will be discussed in some detail.

Geometric features are obtained by making measurements on the original image. A simple technique is to cross-correlate the image with masks representing various shapes. A typical set of masks is that developed at SRI (Nagy, 1968) and shown in figure 8.11. These can be applied digitally or optically to each pattern, yielding as many features as there are masks, i.e.,

$$y(k) = \sum_{i=0}^{M-1} \sum_{j=0}^{N-1} x(i,j) g_k(i,j) \tag{8.23}$$

where $y(k)$ is the k-th component of the feature vector y, and $[x(i,j)]$ is the unknown character. This is easily implemented optically.

Other geometric features can be obtained by edge tracing as described above for images. When the character topology has been traced it is possible to search for line segments of various orientations, bays, enclosures, indentations, symmetry, etc. In attempting to summarize the geometric information efficiently, the use of moments has been proposed (Alt, 1962 and Hu, 1962). Define

$$M_{st} = \frac{1}{MN} \sum_{i=0}^{M-1} \sum_{j=0}^{N-1} i^s j^t x(i,j). \tag{8.24}$$

Then the zero order moment M_{00} is the "mass," and the "center of gravity" or "centroid" $(\bar{i},\bar{j})$ is given by

$$(\bar{i},\bar{j}) = \left(\frac{M_{10}}{M_{00}}, \frac{M_{01}}{M_{00}}\right). \tag{8.25}$$

The higher-order moments can then be normalized for translation by

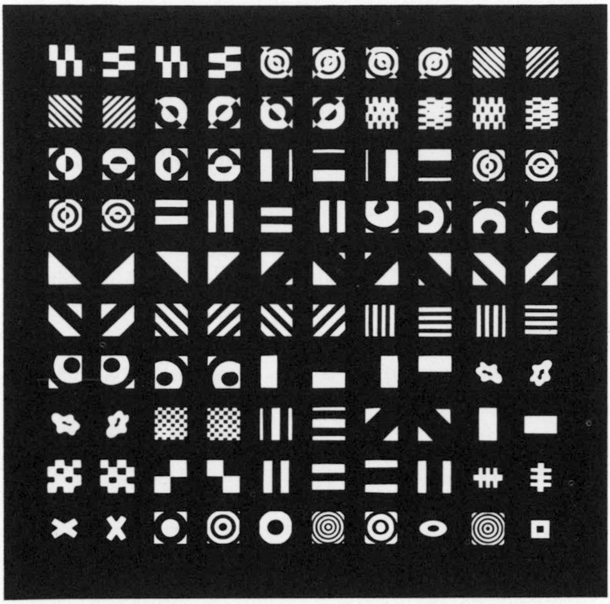

fig. 8.11 A set of 100 optical masks developed at SRI. (Nagy, 1968).

moving the origin of the coordinate system to the centroid, i.e.,

$$\overline{M}_{20} = M_{20} - \frac{M_{10}^2}{M_{00}}. \tag{8.26}$$

Size normalization can be accomplished with the variances σ_i^2 and σ_j^2 where

$$\sigma_i^2 = \frac{\overline{M}_{20}}{M_{00}} \text{ and } \sigma_j^2 = \frac{\overline{M}_{02}}{M_{00}}. \tag{8.27}$$

Then the normalized coordinates become

$$\begin{aligned} i' &= \frac{i - \bar{i}}{\sigma_i}, \\ j' &= \frac{j - \bar{j}}{\sigma_j}. \end{aligned} \tag{8.28}$$

These normalizing constants themselves constitute features and the normalized higher-order moments should be sensitive to shape, but not to size or position. Alt (1962) found that he could distinguish 35 machine-printed characters and digits using moments up to the fifth order. While this is not very spectacular, the moments are useful for normalization before applying other schemes.

An interesting approach to geometrical features has been proposed by Granlund (1972) and Zahn and Roskies (1972) based on earlier work by Brill (1968). Consider initially the contour C shown in figure 8.12. For convenience this is shown on a complex plane $z = x + jy$. A point moving around C at constant velocity v generates a complex valued function of time $u = u(t)$. This function has a period T such that

$$u(t) = u(nT + t), \tag{8.29}$$

where $n = 1, 2, 3, \ldots$. For simplicity we shall choose v such that $T = 2\pi$. A Fourier series expansion of u can be formed with

$$a_n = \frac{1}{2\pi}\int_0^{2\pi} u(t)\exp(-jnt)\,dt, \tag{8.30}$$

and

$$u(t) = \sum_{n=-\infty}^{\infty} a_n \exp(jnt). \tag{8.31}$$

Since the Fourier coefficients depend on the starting point on the contour, we assume that an arbitrary starting point gives $u_0(t)$ and any other starting

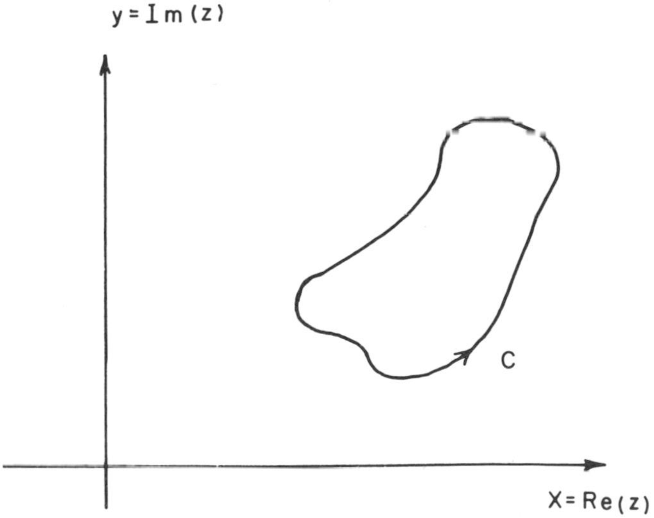

fig. 8.12 A closed contour C.

point represents a "time" shift relative to this so that $u(t) = u_0(t + \tau)$. Then the Fourier coefficents are

$$a_n = \frac{1}{2}\int_0^{2\pi} u(t + \tau)\exp(-jnt)\,dt = a_{n,0}\exp(jn\tau). \tag{8.32}$$

We now consider how the coefficients depend on translation and dilation.

Translation by a constant complex vector z gives

$$u(t) = u_0(t) + z = \sum_{n=-\infty}^{\infty} a_{n,0}\exp(jnt) + z, \tag{8.33}$$

so that

$$a_n = \begin{cases} a_{n,0} \text{ for } n \neq 0 \\ a_{0,0} + z \text{ for } n = 0 \end{cases}$$

i.e., all coefficients for $n \neq 0$ are invariant to translation and a_0 is the "center of gravity" of the contour.

Rotation is considered to take place about the center of gravity, which will now be considered the origin. Then a positive rotation ϕ gives a function

$$u(t) = \exp(j\phi)u_0(t). \tag{8.34}$$

Clearly, $a_n = \exp(j\phi)a_{n,0}$.

Dilation by a factor R with the center of gravity as the origin gives

$$a_n = Ra_{n,0}. \tag{8.35}$$

Thus, with translation, rotation, and dilation we have

$$a_n = \exp(jn\tau)R\exp(j\phi)a_{n,0}. \tag{8.36}$$

To obtain invariant coefficients, Granlund (1972) has suggested

$$b_n = \frac{a_{1+n}\,a_{1-n}}{a_1^2}. \tag{8.37}$$

By substituting (8.36) and canceling they reduce to

$$b_n = \frac{a_{1+n,0}\,a_{1-n,0}}{(a_{1,0})^2} = b_{n,0}. \tag{8.38}$$

The coefficient b_n is completely invariant to translation, rotation, or dilation, but does depend on the form of the contour. Granlund has also defined

$$d_{mn} = \frac{(a_{1+m})^n (a_{1-n})^m}{(a_1)^{m+n}}$$

$$\text{for } m = 1, 2, 3, \ldots, n = 1, 2, 3, \ldots. \qquad (8.39)$$

This easily reduces to

$$d_{mn} = \frac{(a_{1+m,0})^n (a_{1-n,0})^m}{(a_{1,0})^{m+n}}. \qquad (8.40)$$

This coefficient is also invariant and has proven more sensitive to shape.

Granlund tested the set of coefficients d_{11}, d_{12}, d_{21}, d_{13}, d_{31}, and d_{44} with seven hand-printed samples of 25 different letters digitized on a 35×35 binary matrix. This training set was used to estimate a multidimensional Gaussian distribution for each class. Then maximum-likelihood classification with a test set of 175 gave only six errors. Such a result is not particularly conclusive, but does suggest that these rather elegant features may prove valuable in problems where there is insufficient a priori knowledge to design masks. Zahn and Roskies (1972) have developed a similar approach and have investigated, in some detail, the relationships between the coefficients and the shapes of the contour.

Transform features are considered in the following paragraphs. We described in section 8.2 the application of the Karhunen–Loève, Fourier, Walsh/Hadamard, and Haar transforms to two-dimensional images. While these transformations can be justified if they allow more efficient representation of the image, it is possible (but not necessarily the case) that the components may form useful features for pattern recognition. We describe the comparison of these transformations performed by Andrews (1971) in which he showed that merely by selecting the components on the basis of decreasing variance he could achieve satisfactory character recognition (figure 8.5). Thus it is reasonable to select a subset of the components of the transformations and use them as features. However, it should be recalled that the transformations are linear, and that if all of the components are used this is equivalent to using the data points of the original image and nothing is gained.

Kabrisky (1970) has argued that the visual cortex of the brain can perform linear image transformations similar to the Fourier or Walsh/Hadamard, and there is some physiological and psychophysical evidence for this (Pollen et al., 1971). In particular, it is argued that the brain computes only the low-frequency components and that these are sufficient features for character recognition. As evidence for this, Kabrisky and his group claim that if a character is normalized for size and translation (using first- and second-order moments, for example) then it can be classified using the first 36 components of the complex Fourier transform with an error no greater than that achieved by a human. Their classification technique involves finding the minimum Euclidean distance to a prototype in the 36-dimensional feature space. It is claimed that this is equally valid for Russian and Chinese characters. Kabrisky has speculated that if the brain does, in fact, use these features, then it may be that our characters have evolved to be recognizable in this feature space. His group at Wright Patterson Air Force Base is implementing a special-purpose computer to perform the Fourier transform of a character in 10 msec. This will be used in conjunction with a high-speed program for the translation of technical Russian.

8.5 An Example of a System for Recognizing Machine-printed Characters

As typical of the state of the art in 1972, we have chosen to discuss the system being developed by Ascher et al. (1971) at IBM. This is an interactive system for reading unformatted printed text from a variety of documents. They believe that because of the extreme variability encountered in even a modest range of publications, a completely automatic system is not feasible at this time, and suggest that it is both practical and economic to incorporate an operator into the system. It is envisaged that this system could be used, for example, to convert U. S. patents (more than three million) to machine storage, to code legal statutes, to store newspaper files, to serve as an input for technical translation, and to index technical journals.

It is considered impractical for a machine to have available a complete set of reference characters (recall that up to 300,000 are in common use). However, in a given publication about 400 characters will include the bulk of the material. Mathematical equations will probably not be read, but will be reproduced in digital video form. Photographs must be recognized and discarded or saved in facsimile. Because of the way books and journals are composed, the major difficulty is not to find and recognize the alphanumeric information on a page, but to scan it and store it in an acceptable sequence.

The overall scheme consists of three steps.

(1) The operator specifies the areas of the page to be processed with a stylus. The text is read with computer control of line-finding, centering, normalization, registration, and segmentation.

(2) Using cross-correlation, the machine decides whether each character that is read is new. If so, it is stored as a prototype of that

character. At the end of a batch the prototypes are displayed and identified by the operator on his keyboard.

(3) The identified and labeled prototypes are now used to characterize the text as it is read. The text is postedited by displaying an entire page. Characters recognized with an insufficient margin of certainty are intensified to attract the operator's attention.

This scheme was implemented on an IBM 1800 computer and 2250 display. The scanners could handle 8-1/2 × 11-inch paper or 35 mm film. Each character was represented on a binary matrix 32 elements high and of variable width. Classification was achieved by cross-correlating (or masking) the bit patterns of ones and zeros of the incoming characters with the bit patterns of the prototypes. This was done in every shift position of a 5 × 7 matrix and the maximum cross-correlation was used as follows:

$$\text{score (\%)} = 100 \times \frac{(\text{maximum number of matching ones in prototype and character})^2}{(\text{number of ones in character})(\text{number of ones in prototype})}.$$

Efficiency and accuracy depend on the search strategy. This could be either "exhaustive," in which each prototype is tested, "sequential in order of occurrence," in which search is stopped when a correlation above a threshold is found or "sequential ordered by usage," which is similar to the second category, but the most commonly used prototypes are checked first. Obviously, with a nonexhaustive search the thresholds must be carefully chosen.

Typical results obtained by Ascher et al. (1971) are shown in table 8.1. The first column shows the total number of characters, the second shows the average length of search before a prototype was found to match, the third has the fraction of the total number of characters used as prototypes (note that this is 300–600 actual characters) and the last column shows the

TABLE 8.1 (Ascher et al., 1971)

Typical classification results in recognizing machine-printed characters

Material	Number of Characters	Average Length of Search	Fraction Saved as Prototype	Substitution Errors (%)
SPECTRUM,				
February, 1970. p. 114	2819	54.3	0.14	0.31
ALR, Vol. 91, p. 43	2374	58.6	0.17	0.17
Patent 2802067	2000	48.7	0.14	0.25

percentage of substitution errors. These were obtained without any editing by the operator and are probably typical of what should be expected.

An important engineering problem in designing this system is to arrange the processing so that the computer and/or scanner is not idle while the operator is identifying the prototypes or editing.

8.6 Reading Hand-printed FORTRAN Coding Sheets

8.6.1 The problem

A group at Stanford Research Institute (SRI) has developed a number of systems for pattern recognition and artificial intelligence. We will describe here their system for reading hand-printed FORTRAN coding sheets (Munson, 1968) and the use of context to improve the performance (Duda and Hart, 1968). The reading of FORTRAN coding sheets is a realistic problem to tackle since a restricted set of characters and symbols is used and they are written in a constrained manner. Also, it is possible to evaluate the success of the machine objectively since this task is normally performed by a human keypuncher whose error rates and cost are easily determined. The system is particularly interesting since it was extended to utilize contextual information in the FORTRAN to improve the performance.

The characters to be classified consisted of 26 upper-case letters, 10 numerals, and the 10 symbols [, =, *, /, +, -, ·, ·, $,] to give a total of 46. These were obtained in two ways: *the multiple-coder* set consisted of three alphabets from each of 49 people and the *single-coder* set consisted of 1727 training characters and 1042 test characters from one person. The human error rates for single-character recognition by five subjects on the multiple-coder data averaged 4.5% and for 10 subjects on the single-coder data averaged 0.7%. The characters were scanned from the source documents with a vidicon TV camera under the control of an XDS 910 computer. This resulted in single characters being isolated on a 24 × 24 matrix with no corrections for magnification or rotation. (Those data are currently available to other users—see section 8.4.1.)

8.6.2 Feature extraction

Two different methods were used to make measurements on the characters and to construct feature vectors. The first, PREP, relied solely on edge detection in different locations while the second, TOPO, measured a variety of geometric and topological features.

PREP utilized edge-detection masks which consisted of two 2×8 rectangular arrays adjacent to each other. One mask was given a positive weight and the other a negative weight, and the threshold was set so that an edge was indicated if the positive mask encountered six more figure points than did the negative one. The basic edge detector was applied to different regions of the 24×24 field. When the image was split into nine regions, the edge detector was applied in the orientation of each of the four major compass directions and for the image split into six regions, the detector was applied at eight orientations (every 30°). This resulted in 84 binary components. To give some translation invariance, each mask application at a given orientation in a given region consisted of the output of a logical OR from five such masks within the region. To give further invariance, each quantitized image was presented nine different times, first in the center of the 24×24 field, and then in eight positions formed by translating it up to two units vertically and/or horizontally. Thus, for each pattern a set was formed of nine feature vectors each with 84 binary elements.

TOPO was a collection of routines to measure the presence, size, location, and orientation of such topographic features as enclosures, concavities, and stroke tips on the character. In outline, these detailed procedures performed the following:

(1) Characters that were not connected were made so by growing bridges. (The = sign was sought out and treated as a special case).

(2) The perimeter consisting of all points on the periphery was found.

(3) The convex hull boundary (like stretching a rubber band around the perimeter) was found.

(4) Enclosures and concavities were found by subtracting the character from the convex hull boundary. These were sorted for size.

(5) Spurs, i.e., strokes that end in isolated tips, were found.

From these and other measurements 68 features scaled to be in the range 0–100 were found. These were broken down as follows:

16 from spurs
16 from concavities
8 from enclosures
6 from overall size and shape
22 from special calculations involving the width of the character at various points.

This feature extraction technique was arrived at by a "cut and try" approach, and is typical of that used in a number of successful schemes.

8.6.3 Classification

The 46 classes were in either an 86-dimensional (PREP) or 68-dimensional (TOPO) feature space. Classification was performed nonparametically with linear decision functions. The decision functions were obtained by using a training set of patterns with a fixed increment error correction as in equation (4.46).

The training set was presented iteratively until there was no further improvement in performance. The multicoder-data had a training set of 96 alphabets or 4416 characters and a test set of 51 alphabets or 2346 characters. The single-coder data had a training set of 15 alphabets or 690 characters plus 1037 characters from FORTRAN text on coding sheets while the test set consisted of 1042 characters from coding sheets.

The experimental results are summarized in table 8.2. The PREP 1-view results were obtained by only using the PREP features for the character in its central location. In contrast, the PREP-9 view results used the nine different views to train the machine and for classification used the nine different views to obtain nine classifications that were combined to give a compound result.

It can be seen that the results for the single-coder data become quite good for a combination of PREP-9 and TOPO features, i.e., 97% correct compared to a 99.3% average for humans. However, for the multicoder-data the machine could do no better than 85% correct compared to 95.5% for an average over several humans. For comparison purposes, results are shown

TABLE 8.2 (Munson, 1968)

Results of Classification

Data	Feature Extraction	No. of Iterations for Learning	Final Score% Training	Test
Single Coder	PREP - 1 view	10	99	88
	PREP - 9 view	27	89	96
	TOPO	10	94	91
	PREP - 9 + TOPO			97
	HUMAN			99.3
Multiple Coder	PREP - 9	18	65	78
	TOPO	4	86	77
	PREP - 9 + TOPO			85
	HUMAN			95.5
Highleyman 36 classes	PREP - 9			68
	HUMAN			89

as obtained for PREP-9 features and for human classification with the data of Highleyman (1963).

8.6.4. The use of contextual information

It is quite obvious that a human keypuncher does not recognize characters one at a time. Even if the keypuncher does not know FORTRAN he will soon learn that certain character combinations occur frequently. If he knows the programming language he can often make very accurate decisions as to what a character should be only on the basis of context. Most programmers know that a compiler, which must translate the source language into machine code, can point out many errors in keypunching and can often make an appropriate correction. It seems very reasonable that in a language with such a simple syntax as FORTRAN it should be possible for a character recognition scheme to improve its performance by using context.

Since the contextual information is to be used to improve on the results of the character classification scheme, it is necessary to have some ranking of the most likely choices. Then the contextual analysis can choose between them. Since the character recognition scheme is nonparametric, no explicit estimates are available of the probabilities for each character. However, a good heuristic approach is to use the linear decision functions. By computing the dot products of the weight and feature vectors we get $S_i = \mathbf{w}_i^T \mathbf{y}$ for all 46 classes. Then a confidence C_i is defined as

$$C_i = \frac{S_i - S_{\max}}{S_{\max}} \tag{8.41}$$

where $i = 1, \ldots, 46$ and $S_{\max}$ is the largest S_i.

In practice it is found that almost invariably the correct character has a confidence of at least 50% of the maximum—this reduces the number of possible choices to five or six. As an illustration consider the following characters with confidence figures shown in parentheses

$$\begin{array}{lllll} 6(-60) & 0(-20) & T(-30) & D(-50) & S(-30) \\ G(-70) & & & 0(-60) & 5(-40) \\ & & & = (-70). & \end{array}$$

Of the 12 possible strings that can be formed, eight are illegal in FORTRAN (e.g., 60TDS) and the six legal combinations with their combined confidences are

```
GO TO S        -210
GO TO 5        -220
GOT = S        -220
GOT = 5        -230.
```

It is clear that to choose between these alternatives one needs to know more about the program.

Ideally, it is possible to compute the confidence of every string of characters of a given length and to bias it by adding the logarithm of the prior probability of that string. Then the choice should be the string with the highest biased confidence. In the example above, if there is a label "5" then the solution is probably "GO TO 5." In practice this is difficult to implement because of the large number of possible strings—up to 46^n for 46 characters in string length n and $4^{10} (> 10^6)$ for a string of 10 characters with four alternatives for each. In addition, it is difficult to determine the a priori string probabilities for a short program.

TABLE 8.3 (Duda and Hart, 1968)

Raw Classifier Output, Context-Directed Analysis *

```
        CØMMØN AGC, WESGHT, AGEMEAN, WTMCAN, CØV
        DIMENSIØN AGE[100], UEIGHT[100]
1       READ 1001 IFLAG, MØK[
100     FØRM/T[218]
        IF [MER =] 60,5,5
5       RKAD 101,AGE,WEIGHT
101     FQRMATCF10.2]
        GØ TØ [IN, = 0130], IFLAG
10      D7 11 I=1,100
1/      WEIGHT = [I]=AGECS]
        G3 TØ 10
20      DØ 21 I=1,100
21      AGE[I]=WEIGHT[I]
70      CALL AVE[AGE,100,AGEMEAN]
        [ALL AVE[WEIGHT,100,WTMEAN]
        [ØV=0.
        GD 5Q I=1,100
50      CØV = CØV + [AGE[I]-AG [HCAN]*[WEIGHT[I]-UTMEAN]
        CØV=CØV/100.
        TYPE 102,IFLDG,CØV
1Q2     FØRMAT[18,F10.5]
        GØ TQ 1
60      =TØF
        END
```

* Errors underlined.

Duda and Hart (1968) implemented a context-directed analysis that retains the flavor of the decision-theoretic solution, but minimizes the combinatorial problems. This was implemented in LISP on an XDS-940 computer for XDS FORTRAN II, which is restricted only in that the I/0 lists in input–output statements are simple lists of identifiers. The analyzer is a two-pass program that first accepts the most likely characters, identifies each statement by type, and constructs a table of identifier names. During the second pass each statement is resolved and the final classification of FORTRAN text is made.

Statement identification is greatly simplified by the existance of a limited set of FORTRAN control words (e.g., IF, DO, DIMENSION, GOTO, etc.). Once a statement is identified, the string can be analyzed with the syntax of that type of statement. The arithmetic statement is most difficult to analyze.

Considerable simplification is possible if an identifier table is compiled.

TABLE 8.4 (Duda and Hart, 1968)

Final output of analyzer, Context-Directed Analysis *

```
        CØMMØN AGE, WEIGHT, AGEMEAN, WTMCAN, CØV
        DIMENSIØN AGE[100], WEIGHT[100]
1       READ 100, IFLAG,MØKE
100     FØRMAT[218]
        IF[MERE]60,5,5
5       READ 101,AGE,WEIGHT
101     FØRMAT CF10.2]
        GØ TØ [10,20130],IFLAG
10      D7 11 I=1,100
11      WEIGHT[I]=AGE[S]
        GØ TØ 30
20      DØ 21 I=1,100
21      AGE[I]=WEIGHT[I]
70      CALL AVE[AGE,100,AGEMEAN]
        CALL AVE[WEIGHT,100,WTMCAN]
        CØV=0
        DØ 50 I=1,100
50      CØV=CØV+[AGE[I]-AGEMEAN]*[WEIGHT[I]-WTMCAN]
        CØV=CØV/100.
        TYPE 102,IFLAG,CØV
102     FØRMAT[18,F10.5]
        GØ TØ 1
60      STØP
        END
```

* Errors underlined.

Every DIMENSION and COMMON and INPUT/OUTPUT statement is a source of identifiers. After the table is compiled it is clustered—i.e., identifiers differing by only one or two characters may be resolved into one if this seems appropriate. The identifier list is then used in the analysis of arithmetic and control statements on the second pass of the program.

The operation of this scheme is best illustrated with an example from Duda and Hart. Table 8.3 shows the raw output of the classifier with the errors underlined (38 out of 610 characters or 9.3%). Table 8.4 shows the result of context analysis. Twenty eight of the 38 errors have been corrected to leave an error rate of 2.4%. Three of these errors were due to the appearance of WTMCAN instead of WTMEAN in the identifier table and three more were due to problems with the identifiers MOKE, MERE, and S. The other errors were in FORMAT and DO statements and in labels and could be fairly easily corrected.

The potential difficulties in applying this approach to the English language, for example, are obvious. However, it is clear that if machines are to read hand-printed or handwritten input of less than the highest quality this will be essential unless high error rates are to be tolerated.

8.7 Commercially Available Machines

Between 1969 and 1971 the number of manufacturers of character recognition equipment increased from 10 to 26 and the number of machines installed from about 1000 to over 3000 (Andersson, 1971). The commercial impact has been greatest in the businesses that use credit cards. Several organizations have multiple machine installations with each machine costing between $750,000 and $1,000,000. The economics of machine character recognition are such that in 1972 there was argument as to whether a $100,000 installation could replace 30 or 25 keypunch operators. Presumably the decreasing costs of digital hardware can only make these installations more economic in the future.

In comparing machines, it is useful to keep two different classes of capabilities in mind. Generally, the range of input a machine can handle falls into one of four categories:

(1) mark-sense readers—i.e., marks must be made in preformatted locations;

(2) stylized-font readers (e.g., for OCR-A—see figure 8.10);

(3) multifont readers;

(4) hand-printed character readers.

Mark-sense readers are of no great engineering interest, but are quite important commercially. Stylized-font readers may be able to handle more than one character set and possibly a few hand-printed characters. The multifont machines can generally handle several standard type sets and possibly some hand-printed characters. Hand-printed characters can only be read successfully if they are carefully written. Apparently this is most successful if the writer is well motivated (e.g., by profit).

Machines can also be classified by the form of the material they read. Three general categories are:

(1) *document readers* with the capability to read a few lines from a preformatted location on a card or stub (e.g., credit card receipts);

(2) *journal tape readers* read rolls of cash register tapes from stores, etc.;

(3) *page readers* read text from 8-1/2 × 11-inch or 8-1/2 × 14-inch pages.

It is interesting that the speed of many machines is limited by how fast they can manipulate the paper and not by the speed of character recognition.

The majority of machines use masks to classify the characters (this is usually referred to as matrix matching). Others determine the positions of the strokes and use these as features. Still others hide their techniques under the description "feature analysis."

The characteristics of some typical machines are shown in table 8.5. This list is far from complete and for more complete and up-to-date information, the reader should consult the state of the art surveys published every one to two years in DATAMATION, MODERN DATA, and other trade journals (Rabinow, 1969; Andersson, 1969, 1971; Poitevent, 1969; Gray, 1971).

8.8 Notes and Remarks

The processing of images by computer has been the subject of many contributions to journals and conferences for almost two decades. A text on the subject has been written by Andrews (1970). The use of Walsh functions in communications and image processing has generated considerable interest in the last five years. Expository papers and a book by Harmuth (1968, 1969a, 1969b) have helped to popularize the technique and the Association for the Advancement of Sequency Theory has held annual conferences since 1970. Further background on a variety of approaches to image processing can be found in special issues of the journal, PATTERN RECOGNITION (Huang, 1970; Ledley, 1970), the PROCEEDINGS OF

TABLE 8.5

SOME TYPICAL COMMERCIALLY AVAILABLE EQUIPMENT

MANUFACTURER AND MODEL	FONT STYLES READ	CHARACTER SET	SCANNING METHOD	USUAL IMPRESSING METHOD	READING SPEED	DOCUMENT SIZE	MISC. COMMENTS	PRICE RANGE	APPLICATIONS (TYPICAL)
Cognitronics, System 70	All machine generated numbers OCR-A	OCR-A plus special symbols	Laser	Typewriters, high speed printers, cash registers, etc., handprinting	25-50 char/sec.	2" × 3 1/4 " to 8 1/2" × 14"	Uses topological feature analysis	\$30 - 50 K	Banking, Inventory, Updating Files, Sales, Transportation
Compuscan, 370	Can be programmed for any common font.	Alphanuanumeric, punctuation, special symbols.	Flying spot	Typewriter, Highspeed printer	Up to 2000 char/sec	16 or 35 mm microfilm	Uses "matrix matching and feature pattern learning"	\$900 K	Text Conversion
Control Data, 961 Document reader	OCR-A OCR-B Handprint	Numeric and symbols	Laser Mechanical Scan	Typewriter, Highspeed printer Pencil.	Up to 2000 char/sec. 1200 documents/minute	2.6" × 4.5" to 4.5" × 9"	Uses "matrix matching" 1200 documents per minute	\$40 - 50 K	Turn around documents, Credit charging etc.
Farrington 3040 Tape Reader	OCR-A Selfchek 12F, 12L IBM 1428 NCR NOF	Numeric plus alphabetic control symbols	Flying spot	Cash registers Adding machines	Up to 1000 char/sec	Standard journal tapes 1.31" to 3 1/4"			Register Sales, Inventory
IBM, 1288 Page Reader	OCR-A, Hand printed numerals plus special symbols	Machine alphanumeric Handprinted numeric	Flying spot	Typewriter, Highspeed printer Hand printing	100 char/sec 444 documents/minute	3" × 6.5" to 9" × 14"	Uses "curve tracing" and "matrix matching"	\$220 K	Sales and inventory reporting, updating files
Recognition Equipment Inc., Input 80 Optical Reader	Multifont Handprinting	Alphanumeric	Integrated retina	Typewriter, Highspeed printer, Pencil	Machine - 3600 char/sec Handprint - 1200 char/sec	5 3/4" × 4" to 9" × 16"	Reads intermixed fonts and selective fields	\$450 K	Status charges Premium statements, updating files
Scan Data 300 Page Reader	Multifont Handprinting	Alphanumeric plus symbols	Flying spot	Typewriter, Highspeed printer Pencil	Up to 800 char/sec.	6 1/2" × 8" to 11" × 14" to Journal tapes	Uses "feature analysis"	\$400 K	Insurance claims order entries Inventory, updating files.

IEEE (Andrews and Enloe, 1972), and the IEEE TRANSACTIONS ON COMPUTERS (Hall, 1972). Image and scene analysis is treated extensively in the recent book by Duda and Hart (1972). Syntactic pattern recognition is the topic of two special issues of PATTERN RECOGNITION edited by Fu (1971, 1972); and is surveyed by Miller and Shaw (1968). Much of this work was stimulated by Narasimhan (1964).

Character recognition has been the subject of innumerable papers and conferences for over two decades. The very real progress that has been made can be gauged by comparing recent state of the art reviews (Gray, 1971; Andersson, 1969, 1971; Rabinow, 1969) with the proceedings of a conference held in 1962 (Fisher et al.), or with the papers of Bledsoe and Browning (1959) or Grimsdale et al. (1959). Some of the current interest in theoretical approaches to character recognition can be found in a special issue of PATTERN RECOGNITION (Stevens, 1970). The use of complex Fourier components has been investigated by Kabrisky (1970) and his students at the Air Force Institute of Technology. Much of it is only reported in unpublished M.S. Theses.

References

1. Alt, F. L. 1962. Digital pattern recognition by moments. In *Optical Character Recognition*, eds. G. L. Fisher et al, 153–179. Spartan Books, Washington, D.C.
2. Andersson, P. L. 1969. Optical character recognition—A Survey. *Datamation* July:43–48.
3. ———. 1971. OCR enters the practical stage. *Datamation* December: 22–27.
4. Andrews, H. C. 1970. *Computer Techniques in Image Processing*. Academic Press, New York.
5. ———. 1971. Multidimensional rotations in feature selection. *IEEE Trans. Computers* C-20:1045–1051.
6. Andrews, H. C. and Enloe, L. H. eds. 1972. Special Issue on Digital Picture Processing. *Proc. IEEE* 60.
7. Ascher, R. N., Koppelman, G. M., Miller, M. J., Nagy, G., and Shelton, G. L. 1971. An interactive system for coding unformatted printed text. *IEEE Trans. Computers* C-20:1527–1543.
8. Bledsoe, W. W. and Browning, I. 1959. Pattern recognition and reading by machine. *Proc. Eastern Joint Computer Conf.* 225–237. Also in Uhr, 1966.

9. Brill, E. L. 1968. Character recognition via Fourier descriptors. *WESCON Tech. Papers*, Session 25, Los Angeles, California.

10. Chomsky, N. 1965. *Aspects of the Theory of Syntax*. MIT Press, Cambridge, Massachusetts.

11. Cooley, J. W. and Tukey, J. W. 1965. An algorithm for the machine calculation of complex Fourier series. *Math. Computation* 19:297–301.

12. Duda, R. O. and Hart, P. E. 1968. Experiments in the recognition of hand-printed text: Part II—context analysis. *Proc. FJCC* 33:1139–1149.

13. ———. 1973. *Pattern Recognition and Scene Analysis*. Wiley, New York.

14. Fisher, G. L., Pollock, D. K., Raddock, B., and Stevens, M. E. 1962. *Optical Character Recognition*. Spartan Books, Washington, D.C.

15. Fu, K. S., ed. 1971. Special issue on syntactic pattern recognition. *Pattern Recognition* 3:No. 4.

16. ———. 1972 Special issue on syntactic pattern recognition. *Pattern Recognition* 6:No. 1.

17. Genchi, H., Mari, K., Watanabe, S., and Katsuragi, S. 1968. Recognition of handwritten numerical characters for automatic letter sorting. *Proc. IEEE* 56:1292–1301.

18. Granlund, G. H. 1972. Fourier preprocessing for handprint character recognition. *IEEE Trans. Computers* C-21:195–201.

19. Gray, P. J. 1971. Optical readers and OCR. *Modern Data* January, 66–82.

20. Grimsdale, R. L., Sumner, F. H., Tunis, C. J., and Kilburn, T. 1959. A system for the automatic recognition of patterns. *Proc. IEE* 106: Part B:210–221. Also in Uhr, 1966.

21. Haar, A. 1910. Zur theorie der orthogonalen funktionen systeme. *Math. Ann.* 69:331–371.

22. Hadamard, J. 1893. Resolution d'une question relative aux determinants. *Bull. Sci. Math.* 2:17, pt. 1:240–246.

23. Hall, E. L. ed. 1972. Special issue on two-dimensional digital signal processing. *IEEE Trans. Computers* C-21:No. 7.

24. Hall, E. L., Kruger, R. P., Dwyer, S. J., Hall, D. L., McLaren, R. W., and Lodwick, G. S. 1971. A survey of preprocessing and feature extraction techniques for radiographic images. *IEEE Trans. Computers* C-20:1032–1044.

25. Harlow, C. A. and Eisenbeis, S. A. 1973. The analysis of radiographic images. *IEEE Trans. Computers* C-22:678–689.

26. Harmuth, H. F. 1968. A generalized concept of frequency and some applications. *IEEE Trans. Information Theory* IT-14:375–382.

27. ———. 1969a. Applications of Walsh functions in communications. *IEEE Spectrum* 6:82–91.

28. ———. 1969b. *Transmission of Information by Orthogonal Functions*. Springer, New York.

29. Highleyman, W. H. 1963. Data for character recognition studies. *IEEE Trans. Electronic Computers* EC-12:135–136.

30. Hu, M. K. 1962. Visual pattern recognition by moment invariants. *IEEE Trans. Information Theory* IT-8:179–187.

31. Huang, T. S. ed. 1970. Special issue on image enhancement. *Pattern Recognition* 2:No. 2.

32. Kabrisky, M. et al. 1970. A theory of pattern perception based upon human physiology. In *Contemporary Problems in Perception* eds. A. T. Welford and E. H. Houssiadas. Francis and Taylor, London .

33. Knoll, A. L. 1969. Experiments with "characteristic loci" for recognition of handprinted characters. *IEEE Trans. Computers* C-18:366–372.

34. Ledley, R. S., ed. 1970. Special issue on conceptual aspects of two-dimensional picture processing. *Pattern Recognition* 2:No. 1.

35. Ledley, R. S., Rotolo, L. S., Golab, T. J., Jacobsen, J. D., Ginsberg, M. D., and Wilson, J. B. 1965. FIDAC: film input to digital automatic computers and associated syntax-directed pattern recognition programming system. In *Optical and Electro-optical Information Processing* eds. J. Tippett, et al., chapter 33. MIT Press, Cambridge, Massachusetts 591–613.

36. Lendaris, G. G. and Stanley, G. L. 1970. Diffraction-pattern sampling for automatic pattern recognition. *Proc. IEEE* 58:198–216.

37. Levine, M. D. 1969. Feature extraction: a survey. *Proc. IEEE* 57:1408–1418.

38. Miller, W. F. and Shaw, A. C. 1968. Linguistic methods in picture processing—a survey. *Proc. FJCC* 33:279–289.

39. Mucciardi, A. N. and Gose, E. E. 1971. A comparison of seven techniques for choosing subsets of pattern recognition properties. *IEEE Trans. Computers* C-20:1023–1031.

40. Munson, J. H. 1968. Experiments in the recognition of hand-printed text: Part I—character recognition. *Proc. FJCC* 33:1125–1138.

41. Nagy, G. 1968. State of the art in pattern recognition. *Proc. IEEE* 56:836–862.

42. Narasimhan, R. 1964. Labeling schemata and syntactic description of pictures. *Information and Control* 7:151–179

43. Poitevent, J. L. 1969. OCR for credit card processing. *Datamation* July: 49–56.

44. Pollen, D. A., Lee, J. R., and Taylor, J. H. 1971. How does the striate cortex begin the reconstruction of the visual world. *Science* 173:74–77.

45. Rabinow, J. C. 1969. Whither OCR and whence. *Datamation* July: 38–42.

46. Ratliff, F. 1965. *Mach Bands: Quantitative Studies of Neural Networks in the Retina*. Holden–Day, San Francisco.

47. ———1972. Contour and contrast. *Scientific American* 226:90–103.

48. Rosenfeld, A. 1969. *Picture Processing by Computer*. Academic Press, New York.

49. Ryan, H. F. 1969. Automatic property generation techniques. Tech. Rep. XM-2260-X-2, Cornell Aeronautical Lab., Inc., Buffalo, New York.

50. Stevens, M. E., ed. 1970. Special issue on optical character recognition. *Pattern recognition* 2: September.

51. Swain, P. H. and Fu, K. S. 1972. Stochastic programmed grammars for syntactic pattern recognition. *Pattern Recognition* 4:83–100.

52. Uhr, L. 1966. *Pattern Recognition*. Wiley, New York.

53. Von Bekesy, G. 1967. *Sensory Inhibition*. Princeton Univ. Press, Princeton, New Jersey.

54. Walsh, J. L. 1923. A closed set of orthogonal functions. *Am. J. Math.* 55:5–24.

55. Whelchel, J. E. and Guinn, D. F. 1968. The fast Fourier-Hadamard transform and its use in signal representation and classification. *EASCON 1968 Record* 561–573.

56. Zahn, C. T. and Roskies, R. Z. 1972. Fourier descriptors for plane closed curves. *IEEE Trans. Computers* C-21:269–281.

Author Index

Subject Index